MULTI-AGENT SYSTEMS - MODELING, INTERACTIONS, SIMULATIONS AND CASE STUDIES

Edited by **Faisal Alkhateeb, Eslam Al Maghayreh** and **Iyad Abu Doush**

Multi-Agent Systems - Modeling, Interactions, Simulations and Case Studies
Edited by Faisal Alkhateeb, Eslam Al Maghayreh and Iyad Abu Doush

Published by InTech

Janeza Trdine 9, 51000 Rijeka, Croatia

Publishing Process Manager Katarina Lovrecic

Technical Editor Teodora Smiljanic

Cover Designer InTech Design Team

Additional hard copies can be obtained from orders@intechopen.com

Multi-Agent Systems - Modeling, Interactions, Simulations and Case Studies
Edited by Faisal Alkhateeb, Eslam Al Maghayreh and Iyad Abu Doush
p. cm.
ISBN 978-953-307-176-3

For EU product safety concerns:
IN TECH d.o.o., Prolaz Marije Krucifikse Kozulić 3, 51000 Rijeka, Croatia,
info@intechopen.com or visit our website at intechopen.com.

Meet the editors

Faisal Alkhateeb is an assistant professor at the department of computer science at Yarmouk University. He holds a Ph.D. from Grenoble 1 university (2008), M.Sc from Grenoble 1 university (2004), M.Sc from Yarmouk University (2003), and a B.Sc. from Yarmouk University (1999). He published several journal articles and conference papers. He became the chairman of computer science department at Yarmouk University in September 2010.

Dr. Eslam Al Maghayreh is currently an assistant professor at the Computer Science department at Yarmouk University. Dr. Al Maghayreh received a PhD degree in Computer Science from Concordia University (Canada) in 2008, a Master degree in Computer Science from Yarmouk University (Jordan) in 2003, and a Bachelor degree in Computer Science from Yarmouk University in 2001.

Iyad Abu Doush is an assistant professor at the department of computer science at Yarmouk University (YU) in Jordan. He obtained his Ph.D degree in Artificial Intilligence from NMSU (USA). His master degree is in Computer Science from YU. He had B.sc degree in computer science from YU. Dr. Abu Doush has published several journal articles and conference papers and he is a reviewer for several international conferences and journals.

Contents

Preface

A multi-agent system (MAS) is a system composed of multiple interacting intelligent agents. Multi-agent systems can be used to solve problems which are difficult or impossible for an individual agent or monolithic system to solve. Agent systems are open and extensible systems that allow for the deployment of autonomous and proactive software components. Multi-agent systems have been brought up and used in several application domains. This book is a collection of 22 excellent works on multi-agent systems divided into four sections: Multi-Agent Systems Modeling, Interaction and Decision Making on Agent Environments, Multi-Agent Systems Simulation and Case Studies.

Faisal Alkhateeb, Eslam Al Maghayreh and Iyad Abu Doush,
Yarmouk University,
Jordan

Part 1

Multi-Agent Systems Modeling

1

Agent-Based Modeling and Simulation of Species Formation Processes

Rafal Drezewski
Department of Computer Science, AGH University of Science and Technology
Poland

1. Introduction

Agent-based modeling and simulation becomes increasingly popular in social and biological sciences. It is due to the fact that agent-based models allow to elegant and explicitly represent entities, environment, and relations between them Gilbert (2008). Scientist can develop agent-based-model (agents, environment, and relations between them), directly observe interactions and emergent phenomena resulting from them, and experiment with the model. Agent-based approach also allows for very intuitive modeling—entities from the real world can be directly represented in the model. It is also possible to represent heterogeneous entities and environment in the model, as well as model intelligent behavior of entities. Also, the very important mechanism is environment with potentially spatial/geographical structure—agents can be located within such environment, migrate from one place to another, and one can model obstacles, barriers, and geographical elements Gilbert (2008).

The notions *agent* and *multi-agent system* have many different meanings in the literature of the field—in this chapter the following meaning of these terms will be used. *Agent* is considered physical of virtual entity capable of acting within environment, capable of communicating with other agents, its activities are driven by individual goals, it possesses some resources, it may observe the environment (but only local part of it), it possesses only partial knowledge about the environment (or no knowledge about it at all), it has some abilities and may offer some services, and it may be able to reproduce Ferber (1999).

Multi-agent system is a system composed of environment, objects (passive elements of the system), agents (active elements of the system), relations between different elements, set of operations which allow agents to observe and interact with other elements of the system (including other agents), and operators which aim is to represent agent's actions and reactions of the other elements of the system Ferber (1999).

Agent systems become popular in different areas, such as distributed problem solving, collective robotics, construction of distributed computer systems which easily adapt to changing conditions. The applications in the area of modeling and simulation include models of complex biological, social, and economical systems Epstein (2006); Epstein & Axtell (1996); Gilbert (2008); Gilbert & Troitzsch (2005); Uhrmacher & Weyns (2009).

Evolutionary algorithms are heuristic techniques which can be used for finding approximate solutions of global optimization problems Bäck, Fogel & Michalewicz (1997). Co-evolutionary algorithms are particular branch of the evolutionary algorithms Paredis (1998). Co-evolutionary algorithms allow for solving problems for which it is impossible to formulate explicit fitness function because of their specific property—the fitness of the given individual is estimated on the basis of its interactions with other individuals existing in the population. The form of these interactions serves as the basic way of classifying co-evolutionary algorithms. There are two types of co-evolutionary algorithms: co-operative and competitive.

Agent-based evolutionary algorithms are the result of merging evolutionary computations and multi-agent systems paradigms Cetnarowicz et al. (1996). In fact two approaches to constructing agent-based evolutionary algorithms are possible. In the first one the multi-agent layer of the system serves as a "manager" for decentralized evolutionary computations. In the second approach individuals are agents, which "live" within the environment, posses the ability to reproduce, compete for limited resources, die when they run out of resources, and make independently all their decisions concerning reproduction, migration, etc., taking into consideration conditions of the environment, other agents present within the neighborhood, and resources possessed. Hybrid systems, which mix these two approaches are also possible.

The example of the second approach is the model of co-evolutionary multi-agent system (CoEMAS) Dreżewski (2003), which results from the realization of co-evolutionary processes in multi-agent system. Agent-based co-evolutionary systems have some interesting features, among which the most interesting seems to be the possibility of constructing hybrid systems, in which many different computational intelligence techniques are used together within one coherent agent-based computational model, and the possibility of introducing new evolutionary operators and social relations, which were hard or impossible to introduce in the case of "classical" evolutionary computations.

Co-evolutionary multi-agent systems (CoEMAS) utilizing mentioned above second kind of approach to merging evolutionary computations and multi-agent systems have already been applied with good results to multi-modal optimization Dreżewski (2006), multi-objective optimization Dreżewski & Siwik (2008), generating investment strategies Dreżewski, Sepielak & Siwik (2009), and solving Traveling Salesman Problem Dreżewski, Woźniak & Siwik (2009).

Agent-based systems with evolutionary mechanisms can also be used in the area of modeling and simulation. Agent-based modeling and simulation is particularly suited for exploring biological, social, economic, and emergent phenomena. Agent-based systems with evolutionary mechanisms give us the possibility of constructing agent-based models with integrated mechanisms of biological evolution and social interactions. This approach can be especially suitable for modeling biological ecosystems and socio-economical systems. With the use of mentioned approach we have all necessary tools to create models and of such systems: environment, agents, agent-agent and agent-environment relations, resources, evolution mechanisms (competing for limited resources, reproduction), possibility of defining species, sexes, co-evolutionary interactions between species and sexes, social relations, formation of social structures, organizations, teams, etc.

In this chapter we will mainly focus on processes of species formation and agent-based modeling and simulation of such phenomena. The understanding of species formation processes (*speciation*) still remains the greatest challenge for evolutionary biology. The biological models of speciation include *allopatric models* (which require geographical separation of sub-populations) and *sympatric models* (where speciation takes place within one population without physical barriers) Gavrilets (2003). Sympatric speciation may be caused by different kinds of co-evolutionary interactions between species and sexes (*sexual selection*). Allopatric speciation can take place when sub-populations of original species become geographically separated. They live and evolve in different conditions (adapt to conditions of different environments), and eventually become reproductively isolated even after the disappearance of physical barriers. Reproductive isolation causes that natural selection works on each sub-population independently and there is no exchange of gene sequences what can lead to formation of new species. The separation of sub-populations can result not only from the existence of geographical barriers but also from different habits, preferences concerning particular part of the nest, low mobility of individuals, etc.

Sexual selection is the result of co-evolution of interacting sexes. Usually one of the sexes evolves to attract the second one to mating and the second one tries to keep the rate of reproduction (and costs associated with it) on optimal level (what leads to *sexual conflict*) Gavrilets (2003). The proportion of two sexes (females and males) in population is almost always 1 : 1. This fact combined with higher females' reproduction costs causes, that in the majority of cases, females choose males in the reproduction process according to some males' features. In fact, different variants of sexual conflict are possible. For example there can be higher females' reproduction costs, equal reproduction costs (no sexual conflict), equal number of females and males in population, higher number of males in population (when the costs of producing a female are higher than producing a male), higher number of females in population (when the costs of producing a male are higher than producing a female) Krebs & Davies (1993).

The main goal of this chapter is to introduce new coherent model of multi-agent system with biological and social layers and to demonstrate that systems based on such model can be used as agent-based modeling and simulation tools.

It will be demonstrated that using proposed approach it is possible to model complex biological phenomena—species formation caused by different mechanisms. Spatial separation of sub-populations (based on geographical barriers and resulting from forming flocks) and sexual selection mechanisms will be modeled.

In the first part of the chapter we will describe formally bio-social multi-agent system (BSMAS) model. Then using introduced notions we will show that it is possible to define three models of species formation: two based on isolation of sub-populations, and one based on co-evolutionary interactions between sexes (sexual selection). In the experimental part of the chapter selected results of experiments showing that speciation takes place in all constructed models, however the course of evolution of sub-populations is different will be presented.

2. General model of multi-agent system with biological and social mechanisms

In this section the general model of multi-agent system with two layers: biological and social is presented. On the basis of such abstract model concrete simulation and computational systems can be constructed. In the following sections I will present examples of such systems. The model presented in this section includes all elements required in agent-based modeling of biological and social mechanisms: environment, objects, agents, relations between environment, objects, and agents, actions and attributes.

2.1 Bio-Social Multi-Agent System (BSMAS)

The *BSMAS* in time t is described as 8-tuple:

$$\begin{aligned} BSMAS(t) = \langle & EnvT(t), Env(t), ElT(t) = VertT(t) \cup ObjT(t) \cup AgT(t), \\ & ResT(t), InfT(t), Rel(t), Attr(t), Act(t) \rangle \end{aligned} \tag{1}$$

where:

- $EnvT(t)$ is the set of environment types in the time t;
- $Env(t)$ is the set of environments of the $BSMAS$ in the time t;
- $ElT(t)$ is the set of types of elements that can exist within the system in time t;
- $VertT(t)$ is the set of vertice types that can exist within the system in time t;
- $ObjT(t)$ is the set of object (not an object in the sense of object-oriented programming but object as an element of the simulation model) types that may exist within the system in time t;
- $AgT(t)$ is the set of agent types that may exist within the system in time t;
- $ResT(t)$ is the set of resource types that exist in the system in time t, the amount of resource of type $rest(t) \in ResT(t)$ will be denoted by $res^{rest}(t)$;
- $InfT(t)$ is the set of information types that exist in the system, the information of type $inft(t) \in InfT(t)$ will be denoted by $inf^{inft}(t)$;
- $Rel(t)$ is the set of relations between sets of agents, objects, and vertices;
- $Attr(t)$ is the set of attributes of agents, objects, and vertices;
- $Act(t)$ is the set of actions that can be performed by agents, objects, and vertices.

In the rest of this chapter, for the sake of notation clarity, all symbols related to time will be omitted until it is necessary to indicate time relations between elements.

2.2 Environment

The environment type $envt \in EnvT$ of $BSMAS$ may be described as 4-tuple:

$$envt = \langle EnvT^{envt}, VertT^{envt}, ResT^{envt}, InfT^{envt} \rangle \tag{2}$$

$EnvT^{envt} \subseteq EnvT$ is the set of environment types that may be connected with the $envt$ environment at the beginning of its existence. $VertT^{envt} \subseteq VerT$ is the set of vertice types that may exist within the environment of type $envt$. $ResT^{envt} \subseteq ResT$ is the set of resource types that may exist within the environment of type $envt$. $InfT^{envt} \subseteq InfT$ is the set of information types that may exist within the environment of type $envt$.
The environment $env \in Env$ of type $envt$ is defined as 2-tuple:

$$env = \langle gr^{env}, Env^{env} \rangle \tag{3}$$

where gr^{env} is directed graph with the $cost$ function defined: $gr^{env} = \langle Vert, Arch, cost \rangle$, $Vert$ is the set of vertices, $Arch$ is the set of arches. The distance between two nodes is defined as the length of the shortest path between them in graph gr^{env}. $Env^{env} \subseteq Env$ is the set of environments of types from $EnvT$ connected with the environment env.
Vertice type $vertt \in VertT^{env}$ is defined as follows:

$$vertt = \langle Attr^{vertt}, Act^{vertt}, ResT^{vertt}, InfT^{vertt}, VertT^{vertt}, ObjT^{vertt}, AgT^{vertt} \rangle \tag{4}$$

where:

- $Attr^{vertt} \subseteq Attr$ is the set of attributes of $vertt$ vertice at the beginning of its existence;
- $Act^{vertt} \subseteq Act$ is the set of actions, which $vertt$ vertice can perform at the beginning of its existence, when asked for it;

- $ResT^{vertt} \subseteq ResT$ is the set of resource types, which can exist within *vertt* vertice at the beginning of its existence;
- $InfT^{vertt} \subseteq InfT$ is the set of information, which can exist within *vertt* vertice at the beginning of its existence;
- $VertT^{vertt}$ is the set of types of vertices that can be connected with the *vertt* vertice at the beginning of its existence;
- $ObjT^{vertt} \subseteq ObjT$ is the set of types of objects that can be located within the *vertt* vertice at the beginning of its existence;
- $AgT^{vertt} \subseteq AgT$ is the set of types of agents that can be located within the *vertt* vertice at the beginning of its existence.

Element of the structure of system's environment (vertice) $vert \in Vert$ of type $vertt \in VertT^{env}$ is given by:

$$vert = \langle Attr^{vert}, Act^{vert}, Res^{vert}, Inf^{vert}, Vert^{vert}, Obj^{vert}, Ag^{vert} \rangle \quad (5)$$

where:

- $Attr^{vert} \subseteq Attr$ is the set of attributes of vertice *vert*—it can change during its lifetime;
- $Act^{vert} \subseteq Act$ is the set of actions, which vertice *vert* can perform when asked for it—it can change during its lifetime;
- Res^{vert} is the set of resources of types from $ResT$ that exist within the *vert*;
- Inf^{vert} is the set of information of types from $InfT$ that exist within the *vert*;
- $Vert^{vert}$ is the set of vertices of types from $VertT$ connected with the vertice *vert*;
- Obj^{vert} is the set of objects of types from $ObjT$ that are located in the vertice *vert*;
- Ag^{vert} is the set of agents of types from AgT that are located in the vertice *vert*.

Each object and agent is located within one of the vertices. The set of all objects that exist within the system $Obj = \bigcup_{vert \in Vert} Obj^{vert}$, and the set of all agents that exist within the system $Ag = \bigcup_{vert \in Vert} Ag^{vert}$. $El = Vert \cup Obj \cup Ag$ is the set of all elements (vertices, objects, and agents) that exist within the system.

2.3 Objects

Object type $ot \in ObjT$ is defined as follows:

$$objt = \langle Attr^{objt}, Act^{objt}, ResT^{objt}, InfT^{objt}, ObjT^{objt}, AgT^{objt} \rangle \quad (6)$$

where:

- $Attr^{objt} \subseteq Attr$ is the set of attributes of *objt* object at the beginning of its existence;
- $Act^{objt} \subseteq Act$ is the set of actions, which *objt* object can perform when asked for it at the beginning of its existence;
- $ResT^{objt} \subseteq ResT$ is the set of resource types, which can be used by *objt* object at the beginning of its existence;
- $InfT^{objt} \subseteq InfT$ is the set of information, which can be used by *objt* object at the beginning of its existence;

- $ObjT^{objt} \subseteq ObjT$ is the set of types of objects that can be located within the $objt$ object at the beginning of its existence;
- $AgT^{objt} \subseteq AgT$ is the set of types of agents that can be located within the $objt$ object at the beginning of its existence.

Passive element of the system (object) $obj \in Obj$ of type $objt \in ObjT$ is defined in the following way:

$$obj = \langle Attr^{obj}, Act^{obj}, Res^{obj}, Inf^{obj}, Obj^{obj}, Ag^{obj} \rangle \tag{7}$$

where:

- $Attr^{obj} \subseteq Attr$ is the set of attributes of object obj—it can change during its lifetime;
- $Act^{obj} \subseteq Act$ is the set of actions, which object obj can perform when asked for it—it can change during its lifetime;
- Res^{obj} is the set of resources of types from $ResT$, which exist within object obj;
- Inf^{obj} is the set of information of types from $InfT$, which exist within object obj;
- Obj^{obj} is the set of objects of types from $ObjT$ that are located within the object obj;
- Ag^{obj} is the set of agents of types from AgT that are located within the object obj.

2.4 Agents

Agent type $agt \in AgT$ is defined as follows:

$$agt = \langle Gl^{agt}, Attr^{agt}, Act^{agt}, ResT^{agt}, InfT^{agt}, ObjT^{agt}, AgT^{agt} \rangle \tag{8}$$

where:

- Gl^{agt} is the set of goals of agt agent at the beginning of its existence;
- $Attr^{agt} \subseteq Attr$ is the set of attributes of agt agent at the beginning of its existence;
- $Act^{agt} \subseteq Act$ is the set of actions, which agt agent can perform at the beginning of its existence;
- $ResT^{agt} \subseteq ResT$ is the set of resource types, which can be used by agt agent at the beginning of its existence;
- $InfT^{agt} \subseteq InfT$ is the set of information, which can be used by agt agent at the beginning of its existence;
- $ObjT^{agt} \subseteq ObjT$ is the set of types of objects that can be located within the agt agent at the beginning of its existence;
- $AgT^{agt} \subseteq AgT$ is the set of types of agents that can be located within the agt agent at the beginning of its existence.

Active element of the system (agent) ag of type $agt \in AgT$ is defined as follows:

$$ag = \langle Gl^{ag}, Attr^{ag}, Act^{ag}, Res^{ag}, Inf^{ag}, Obj^{ag}, Ag^{ag} \rangle \tag{9}$$

where:

- Gl^{ag} is the set of goals, which agent ag tries to realize—it can change during its lifetime;
- $Attr^{ag} \subseteq Attr$ is the set of attributes of agent ag—it can change during its lifetime;

- $Act^{ag} \subseteq Act$ is the set of actions, which agent ag can perform in order to realize its goals—it can change during its lifetime;
- Res^{ag} is the set of resources of types from $ResT$, which are used by agent ag;
- Inf^{ag} is the set of information of types from $InfT$, which agent ag can possess and use;
- Obj^{ag} is the set of objects of types from $ObjT$ that are located within the agent ag;
- Ag^{ag} is the set of agents of types from AgT that are located within the agent ag.

2.5 Relations

The set of relations contains all types of relations between sets of elements of the system that can perform particular actions. The set of all relations that exist in the system is defined as follows:

$$Rel = \left\{ \xrightarrow[Act2]{Act1} : Act1, Act2 \subseteq \bigcup_{el \in El} Act^{el} \right\} \tag{10}$$

where el is an element (vertice, object, or agent) of the system, El is the set of all elements of the system, and Act^{el} is the set of actions that el can perform.
Relation $\xrightarrow[Act2]{Act1}$ is defined as follows:

$$\xrightarrow[Act2]{Act1} = \left\{ \left\langle El^{Act1}, El^{Act2} \right\rangle \in 2^{El} \times 2^{El} \right\} \tag{11}$$

El^{Act1} is the set of elements of the system (vertices, objects, and agents) that can perform all actions from the set $Act1 \subseteq Act$, and El^{Act2} is the set of elements of the system (vertices, objects, and agents) that can perform all actions from the set $Act2 \subseteq Act$.

3. Multi-agent systems for species formation simulation

In this part of the chapter three systems used during simulation experiments we will be formally described with the use of notation introduced in section 2. First of the presented systems uses mechanism of allopatric speciation in which species formation is a result of existing geographical barriers between sub-populations. The second one uses flock forming mechanisms. The third one uses sexual selection mechanism. In all systems competition for limited resources takes place.

3.1 Multi-agent system with geographical barriers

Multi-agent system with geographical barriers (aBSMAS) is the model of allopatric speciation. In allopatric speciation the eventual new species is born as a result of splitting the origin species into sub-populations, which are separated with some kind of physical (geographical) barrier. In the case of aBSMAS there exist environment composed of vertices which are connected with paths (see fig. 1). Agents can migrate between vertices but the cost of migration is very high and in fact such a migration takes place very rarely. Within each vertice agents compete for limited resources—there is no competition for resources between sub-populations located within different vertices.
Agents reproduce when they have enough resource. Agent which is ready for reproduction tries to find another agent that can reproduce and that is located within the same vertice of the environment. Reproduction takes place with the use of recombination and mutation operators—operators from evolution strategies were used: intermediate

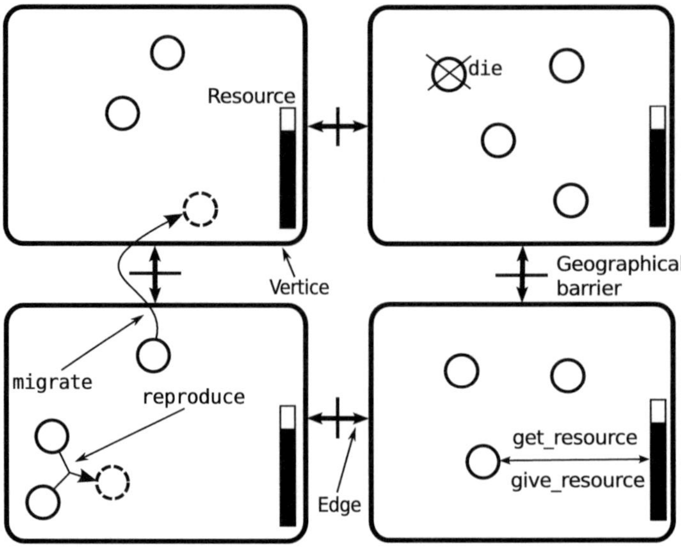

Fig. 1. Multi-Agent System with Geographical Barriers

recombination Booker et al. (1997), and mutation with self-adaptation Bäck, Fogel, Whitley & Angeline (1997). The offspring receives some resource from parents.
The multi-agent system with geographical barriers is defined as follows (compare eq. (1)):

$$\begin{aligned} aBSMAS(t) = \langle & EnvT(t) = \{et\}, Env(t) = \{env\}, ElT(t) = VertT(t) \cup ObjT(t) \cup \\ & AgT(t), ResT(t) = \{rt\}, InfT(t) = \emptyset, \\ & Rel(t), Attr(t) = \{genotype\}, Act(t) \rangle \end{aligned} \tag{12}$$

where $VertT = \{vt\}$, $ObjT = \emptyset$, and $AgT = \{ind\}$.
The set of actions is defined as follows:

$$Act = \{die, reproduce, get\_resource, give\_resource, migrate, \} \tag{13}$$

Environment type *et*:

$$et = \langle EnvT^{et} = \emptyset, VertT^{et} = VertT, ResT^{et} = ResT, InfT^{et} = \emptyset \rangle \tag{14}$$

Environment *env* of type *et* is defined as follows:

$$env = \langle gr^{env}, Env^{env} = \emptyset \rangle \tag{15}$$

Vertice type *vt* is defined in the following way:

$$\begin{aligned} vt = \langle & Attr^{vt} = \emptyset, Act^{vt} = \{give\_resource\}, ResT^{vt} = ResT, \\ & InfT^{vt} = \emptyset, VertT^{vt} = VertT, ObjT^{vt} = \emptyset, AgT^{vt} = AgT \rangle \end{aligned} \tag{16}$$

where *give_resource* is the action of giving resource to agent of type *ind*.
Each $vert \in Vert$ is defined as follows:

$$\begin{aligned} vert = \langle & Attr^{vert} = \emptyset, Act^{vert} = Act^{vt}, Res^{vert} = \{res^{vert}\}, Inf^{vert} = \emptyset, \\ & Vert^{vert}, Obj^{vert} = \emptyset, Ag^{vert} \rangle \end{aligned} \tag{17}$$

res^{vert} is the amount of resource of type rt that is possessed by the $vert$. $Vert^{vert}$ is the set of nine (for Michalewicz fitness landscape—see sec. 4.1), thirty (for Rastrigin fitness landscape), sixty three (for Schwefel fitness landscape), or sixteen (for Waves fitness landscape) vertices connected with the vertice $vert$. Ag^{vert} is the set of agents located within the vertice $vert$.
There is one type of agents in the system (ind):

$$\begin{aligned} ind = \langle Gl^{ind} &= \{gl_1, gl_2, gl_3\}, Attr^{ind} = \{genotype\}, Act^{ind} = \{die, reproduce, \\ &get\_resource, migrate\}, ResT^{ind} = ResT, InfT^{ind} = \emptyset, \\ &ObjT^{ind} = \emptyset, AgT^{ind} = \emptyset \rangle \end{aligned} \tag{18}$$

where gl_1 is the goal "get resource from environment", gl_2 is the goal "reproduce", and gl_3 is the goal "migrate to other vertice". die is the action of death—agent dies when it runs out of resources, $reproduce$ is the action of reproducing (with the use of recombination and mutation operators), $get\_resource$ is the action of getting resource from environment, and $migrate$ is the action of migrating to other vertice.
Agent ag^{ind} (of type ind) is defined as follows:

$$\begin{aligned} ag^{ind} = \langle Gl^{ag,ind} &= Gl^{ind}, Attr^{ag,ind} = Attr^{ind}, Act^{ag,ind} = Act^{ind}, Res^{ag,ind} = \{r^{ag,ind}\}, \\ &Inf^{ag,ind} = \emptyset, Obj^{ag,ind} = \emptyset, Ag^{ag,ind} = \emptyset \rangle \end{aligned} \tag{19}$$

Notation $Gl^{ag,ind}$ means "the set of goals of agent ag of type ind". $r^{ag,ind}$ is the amount of resource of type rt that is possessed by the agent ag^{ind}.
The set of relations is defined as follows:

$$Rel = \left\{ \xrightarrow[\{get\_resource\}]{\{get\_resource\}} \right\} \tag{20}$$

The relation is defined as follows:

$$\xrightarrow[\{get\_resource\}]{\{get\_resource\}} = \left\{ \left\langle Ag^{ind,\{get\_resource\}}, Ag^{ind,\{get\_resource\}} \right\rangle \right\} \tag{21}$$

$Ag^{ind,\{get\_resource\}}$ is the set of agents of type ind capable of performing action $get\_resource$. This relation represents competition for limited resources between ind agents.

3.2 Multi-agent system with flock formation mechanisms

In multi-agent system with flock formation mechanisms (fBSMAS) speciation takes place as a result of flock formation (see fig. 2). Each agent (individual) can reproduce, die and migrate between flocks—it searches for flock that occupies the same ecological niche. Agents can mate only with agents from the same flock. Reproduction is initiated by the agent that has enough resources to reproduce. Such agent searches for ready for reproduction partner from the same flock. When the partner is chosen then the reproduction takes place. Offspring is generated with the use of intermediate recombination Booker et al. (1997), and mutation with self-adaptation Bäck, Fogel, Whitley & Angeline (1997).
Flocks can merge and split. Merging takes place when two flocks are located within the same ecological niche (basin of attraction of some local minima in the multi-modal fitness landscape—see section 4). Flock splits into two flocks when there exists an agent within the flock which in fact occupies different ecological niche than other agents in the flock and there is

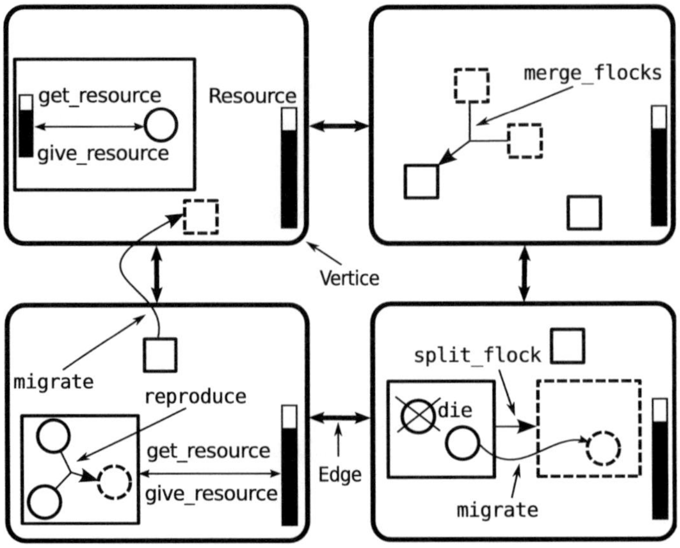

Fig. 2. Multi-Agent System with Flock Formation Mechanisms

no existing flock that such agent can migrate to. Flocks compete for limited resources located within the environment, and agents compete for limited resources located within their flocks. Flocks can migrate within environment.
The multi-agent system with flocks is defined as follows (compare eq. (2)):

$$fBSMAS(t) = \langle EnvT(t) = \{et\}, Env(t) = \{env\}, ElT(t) = VertT(t) \cup ObjT(t) \cup AgT(t), ResT(t) = \{rt\}, InfT(t) = \emptyset, Rel(t), Attr(t) = \{genotype\}, Act(t) \rangle \tag{22}$$

where $VertT = \{vt\}, ObjT = \emptyset$, and $AgT = \{flock, ind\}$.
The set of actions is defined as follows:

$$Act = \{die, reproduce, get\_resource, give\_resource, migrate, search\_flock, merge\_flocks, split\_flock\} \tag{23}$$

Environment type *et*:

$$et = \langle EnvT^{et} = \emptyset, VertT^{et} = VertT, ResT^{et} = ResT, InfT^{et} = \emptyset \rangle \tag{24}$$

Environment *env* of type *et* is defined as follows:

$$env = \langle gr^{env}, Env^{env} = \emptyset \rangle \tag{25}$$

Vertice type *vt* is defined in the following way:

$$vt = \langle Attr^{vt} = \emptyset, Act^{vt} = \{give\_resource\}, ResT^{vt} = ResT, InfT^{vt} = \emptyset, VertT^{vt} = VertT, ObjT^{vt} = \emptyset, AgT^{vt} = \{flock\} \rangle \tag{26}$$

where *give_resource* is the action of giving resource to flock.

Each $vert \in Vert$ is defined as follows:

$$vert = \langle Attr^{vert} = \emptyset, Act^{vert} = Act^{vt}, Res^{vert} = \{res^{vert}\}, \\ Inf^{vert} = \emptyset, Vert^{vert}, Obj^{vert} = \emptyset, Ag^{vert} \rangle \tag{27}$$

res^{vert} is the amount of resource that is possessed by the $vert$. $Vert^{vert}$ is the set of four vertices connected with the vertice $vert$ (see fig. 2). Ag^{vert} is the set of agents of type $flock$ located within the vertice $vert$.

There are two types of agents in the system: $flock$ and ind. $flock$ type of agent is defined in the following way:

$$flock = \langle Gl^{flock} = \{gl_1, gl_2, gl_3\}, Attr^{flock} = \emptyset, Act^{flock} = \{get\_resource, give\_resource, \\ migrate, merge\_flocks\}, ResT^{flock} = ResT, InfT^{flock} = \emptyset, \\ ObjT^{flock} = \emptyset, AgT^{flock} = \{ind\} \rangle \tag{28}$$

where gl_1 is the goal "get resource from environment", gl_2 is the goal "merge with other flock", and gl_3 is the goal "migrate to other vertice". *get_resource* is the action of getting resource from environment, *give_resource* is the action of giving resource to *ind* type agent, *migrate* is the action of migrating to other vertice, and *merge_flocks* is the action of merging with other flock.

ind type of agent is defined in the following way:

$$ind = \langle Gl^{ind} = \{gl_4, gl_5, gl_6, gl_7\}, Attr^{ind} = \{genotype\}, Act^{ind} = \{die, reproduce, \\ get\_resource, migrate, search\_flock, split\_flock\}, ResT^{ind} = ResT, \\ InfT^{ind} = \emptyset, ObjT^{ind} = \emptyset, AgT^{ind} = \emptyset \rangle \tag{29}$$

where gl_4 is the goal "get resource from flock agent", gl_5 is the goal "reproduce", gl_6 is the goal "migrate to other flock", and gl_7 is the goal "split flock". *die* is the action of death—agent dies when it runs out of resources, *reproduce* is the action of reproducing (with the use of recombination and mutation operators), *get_resource* is the action of getting resource from $flock$ type agent, *migrate* is the action of migrating to other flock, *search_flock* is the action of searching for another flock—located within the same ecological niche, and *split_flock* is the action of creating a new flock.

Agent ag^{flock} (of type $flock$) is defined as follows:

$$ag^{flock} = \langle Gl^{ag,flock} = Gl^{flock}, Attr^{ag,flock} = \emptyset, Act^{ag,flock} = Act^{flock}, \\ Res^{ag,flock} = \{r^{ag,flock}\}, Inf^{ag,flock} = \emptyset, Obj^{ag,flock} = \emptyset, Ag^{ag,flock} \rangle \tag{30}$$

Notation $Gl^{ag,flock}$ means "the set of goals of agent ag of type $flock$". $r^{ag,flock}$ is the amount of resource of type rt that is possessed by the agent ag^{flock}. $Ag^{ag,flock}$ is the set of agents of type ind that currently belong to the flock agent.

Agent ag^{ind} (of type ind) is defined as follows:

$$ag^{ind} = \langle Gl^{ag,ind} = Gl^{ind}, Attr^{ag,ind} = Attr^{ind}, Act^{ag,ind} = Act^{ind}, Res^{ag,ind} = \{r^{ag,ind}\}, \\ Inf^{ag,ind} = \emptyset, Obj^{ag,ind} = \emptyset, Ag^{ag,ind} = \emptyset \rangle \tag{31}$$

$r^{ag,ind}$ is the amount of resource of type rt that is possessed by the agent ag^{ind}.

The set of relations is defined as follows:

$$Rel = \left\{ \xrightarrow[\{get\_resource\}]{\{get\_resource\}} \right\} \tag{32}$$

The relation is defined as follows:

$$\xrightarrow[\{get\_resource\}]{\{get\_resource\}} = \left\{ \left\langle Ag^{flock,\{get\_resource\}}, Ag^{flock,\{get\_resource\}} \right\rangle, \left\langle Ag^{ind,\{get\_resource\}}, Ag^{ind,\{get\_resource\}} \right\rangle \right\} \tag{33}$$

$Ag^{flock,\{get\_resource\}}$ is the set of agents of type $flock$ capable of performing action $get\_resource$. $Ag^{ind,\{get\_resource\}}$ is the set of agents of type ind capable of performing action $get\_resource$. This relation represents competition for limited resources between agents of the same type.

3.3 Multi-agent system with sexual selection

In multi-agent system with sexual selection (sBSMAS) speciation takes place as a result of sexual selection. There exist two sexes (see fig. 3). Agents compete for limited resources, can reproduce and die. Reproduction takes place when pair is formed composed of agents from opposite sexes. Reproduction process is initiated by a female agent (when it has enough resources to reproduce). Then it searches for the partner in such a way that it chooses one male agent from all male agents that are ready for reproduction in the given vertice. The partner is chosen on the basis of genotype similarity—the more similar are two agents from opposite sexes the more probable is that female agent will choose that male agent. The offspring is generated with the use of mutation and recombination operators (intermediate recombination Booker et al. (1997), and mutation with self-adaptation Bäck, Fogel, Whitley & Angeline (1997)). The offspring receives some of the resources from parents.

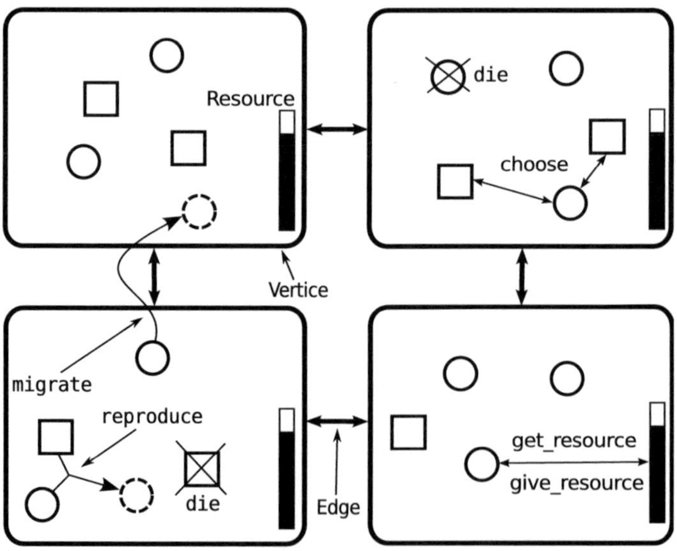

Fig. 3. Multi-Agent System with Sexual Selection

The multi-agent system with sexual selection is defined as follows (compare eq. (2)):

$$\begin{aligned} BSMAS(t) = & \langle EnvT(t) = \{et\}, Env(t) = \{env\}, ElT(t) = VertT(t) \cup ObjT(t) \cup \\ & AgT(t), ResT(t) = \{rt\}, InfT(t) = \emptyset, Rel(t), \\ & Attr(t) = \{genotype\}, Act(t) \rangle \end{aligned} \quad (34)$$

where $VertT = \{vt\}, ObjT = \emptyset$, and $AgT = \{female, male\}$.
The set of actions is defined as follows:

$$Act = \{die, reproduce, get\_resource, give\_resource, migrate, choose\} \quad (35)$$

Environment type et is defined in the following way:

$$et = \langle EnvT^{et} = \emptyset, VertT^{et} = VertT, ResT^{et} = ResT, InfT^{et} = \emptyset \rangle \quad (36)$$

Environment env of type et is defined as follows:

$$env = \langle gr^{env}, Env^{env} = \emptyset \rangle \quad (37)$$

Vertice type vt is defined in the following way:

$$\begin{aligned} vt = & \langle Attr^{vt} = \emptyset, Act^{vt} = \{give\_resource\}, ResT^{vt} = ResT, \\ & InfT^{vt} = \emptyset, VertT^{vt} = VertT, ObjT^{vt} = \emptyset, AgT^{vt} = AgT \rangle \end{aligned} \quad (38)$$

where $give\_resource$ is the action of giving resource to agents.
Each $vert \in Vert$ is defined as follows:

$$\begin{aligned} vert = & \langle Attr^{vert} = \emptyset, Act^{vert} = Act^{vt}, Res^{vert} = \{res^{vert}\}, Inf^{vert} = \emptyset, \\ & Vert^{vert}, Obj^{vert} = \emptyset, Ag^{vert} \rangle \end{aligned} \quad (39)$$

res^{vert} is the amount of resource of type rt that is possessed by the $vert$. $Vert^{vert}$ is the set of four vertices connected with the vertice $vert$ (see fig. 3). Ag^{vert} is the set of agents located within the vertice $vert$.
There are two types of agents in the system: $female$ and $male$. $female$ agent type is defined in the following way:

$$\begin{aligned} female = & \langle Gl^{female} = \{gl_1, gl_2, gl_3\}, Attr^{female} = \{genotype\}, \\ & Act^{female} = \{die, reproduce, choose, get\_resource, migrate, \}, \\ & ResT^{female} = ResT, InfT^{female} = \emptyset, ObjT^{female} = \emptyset, AgT^{female} = \emptyset \rangle \end{aligned} \quad (40)$$

where gl_1 is the goal "get resource from environment", gl_2 is the goal "reproduce", and gl_3 is the goal "migrate to other vertice". *die* is the action of death—agent dies when it runs out of resources, *reproduce* is the action of reproducing (with the use of recombination and mutation operators), *choose* is the action of choosing partner for reproduction from the set of *male* agents that are located within the same vertice and are ready for reproduction, *get_resource* is the action of getting resource from environment, and *migrate* is the action of migrating to other vertice.

male agent type is defined in the following way:

$$\begin{aligned} male = \langle Gl^{male} = \{gl_1, gl_2, gl_3\}, Attr^{male} = \{genotype\}, \\ Act^{male} = \{die, reproduce, get\_resource, migrate, \}, \\ ResT^{male} = ResT, InfT^{male} = \emptyset, ObjT^{male} = \emptyset, AgT^{male} = \emptyset\rangle \end{aligned} \tag{41}$$

where gl_1 is the goal "get resource from environment", gl_2 is the goal "reproduce", and gl_3 is the goal "migrate to other vertice". *die* is the action of death—agent dies when it runs out of resources, *reproduce* is the action of reproducing (with the use of recombination and mutation operators), *get_resource* is the action of getting resource from environment, and *migrate* is the action of migrating to other vertice.
Agent ag^{female} (of type *female*) is defined in the following way:

$$\begin{aligned} ag^{female} = \langle Gl^{ag,female} = Gl^{female}, Attr^{ag,female} = Attr^{female}, Act^{ag,female} = Act^{female}, \\ Res^{ag,female} = \left\{r^{ag,female}\right\}, Inf^{ag,female} = \emptyset, \\ Obj^{ag,female} = \emptyset, Ag^{ag,female} = \emptyset\rangle \end{aligned} \tag{42}$$

Notation $Gl^{ag,female}$ means "the set of goals of agent ag of type $female$". $r^{ag,female}$ is the amount of resource of type rt that is possessed by the agent ag^{female}.
Agent ag^{male} (of type *male*) is defined in the following way:

$$\begin{aligned} ag^{male} = \langle Gl^{ag,male} = Gl^{male}, Attr^{ag,male} = Attr^{male}, Act^{ag,male} = Act^{male}, \\ Res^{ag,male} = \left\{r^{ag,male}\right\}, Inf^{ag,male} = \emptyset, Obj^{ag,male} = \emptyset, Ag^{ag,male} = \emptyset\rangle \end{aligned} \tag{43}$$

Notation $Gl^{ag,male}$ means "the set of goals of agent ag of type $male$". $r^{ag,male}$ is the amount of resource of type rt that is possessed by the agent ag^{male}.
The set of relations is defined as follows:

$$Rel = \left\{ \xrightarrow[\{get\_resource\}]{\{get\_resource\}}, \xrightarrow[\{reproduce\}]{\{choose,reproduce\}} \right\} \tag{44}$$

The relation $\xrightarrow[\{get\_resource\}]{\{get\_resource\}}$ is defined as follows:

$$\xrightarrow[\{get\_resource\}]{\{get\_resource\}} = \left\{ \left\langle Ag^{\{get\_resource\}}, Ag^{\{get\_resource\}} \right\rangle \right\} \tag{45}$$

$Ag^{\{get\_resource\}}$ is the set of agents capable of performing action *get_resource*. This relation represents competition for limited resources between agents.
The relation $\xrightarrow[\{reproduce\}]{\{choose,reproduce\}}$ is defined as follows:

$$\xrightarrow[\{reproduce\}]{\{choose,reproduce\}} = \left\{ \left\langle Ag^{female,\{choose,reproduce\}}, Ag^{male,\{reproduce\}} \right\rangle \right\} \tag{46}$$

$Ag^{female,\{choose,reproduce\}}$ is the set of agents of type $female$ capable of performing actions *choose* and *reproduce*. $Ag^{male,\{reproduce\}}$ is the set of agents of type *male* capable of performing action *reproduce*. This relation represents sexual selection mechanism—*female* agents choose partners for reproduction form *male* agents and then reproduction takes place.

4. Experimental results

The main goal of experiments was to investigate whether the speciation takes place in the case of all three simulation models: aBSMAS (allopatric speciation), fBSMAS (sub-populations isolation resulting from flock formation behavior), and sBSMAS (speciation resulting from the existence of sexual selection). Four multimodal fitness landscapes were used—Michalewicz, Rastrigin, Schwefel, and Waves. Presented results include illustration of species formation processes, as well as changes of the population size during speciation processes.

4.1 Fitness landscapes

As it was said, four multimodal fitness landscapes were used during experiments. Each minima of the fitness function is considered as "ecological niche" which should be populated by distinct species during experiments.

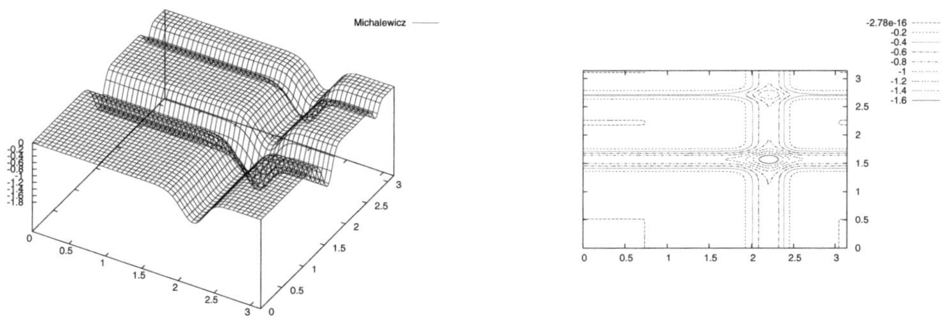

(a) (b)

Fig. 4. Michalewicz fitness landscape

Michalewicz fitness landscape is given by (Michalewicz (1996)):

$$f_1(\vec{x}) = -\sum_{i=1}^{n} \left(\sin(x_i) * \left(\sin(i * x_i^2/\pi) \right)^{2*m} \right) \quad x_i \in [0;\pi] \text{ for } i = 1,\ldots,n \tag{47}$$

This function has $n!$ local minima, where n is the number of dimensions. m parameter regulates the steepness of "valleys". During experiments the values of parameters were $m = 10$ and $n = 2$ (see fig. 4).

Rastrigin multimodal fitness landscape is defined as follows (Potter (1997)):

$$f_2(\vec{x}) = 10 * n + \sum_{i=1}^{n} \left(x_i^2 - 10 * \cos(2 * \pi * x_i) \right) \quad x_i \in [-2.5;2.5] \text{ for } i = 1,\ldots,n \tag{48}$$

This function has many regularly placed local minima. During experiments $n = 2$ was assumed (see fig. 5).

Schwefel fitness landscape is defined as follows (Potter (1997)):

$$f_3(\vec{x}) = \sum_{i=1}^{n} \left(-x_i * \sin\left(\sqrt{|x_i|} \right) \right) \quad x_i \in [-500.0;500.0] \text{ for } i = 1,\ldots,n \tag{49}$$

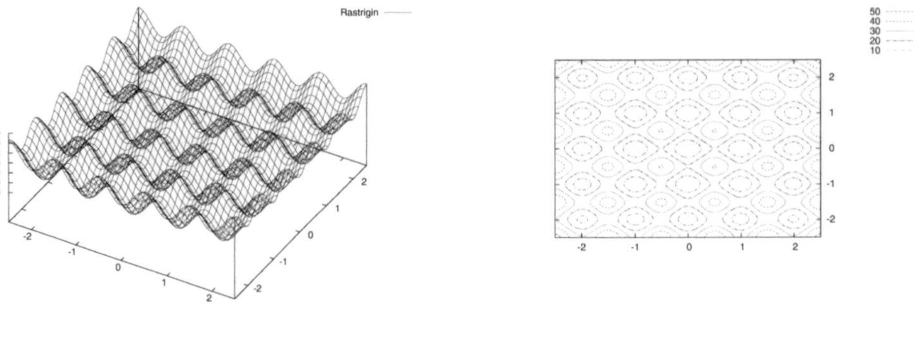

(a) (b)

Fig. 5. Rastrigin fitness landscape

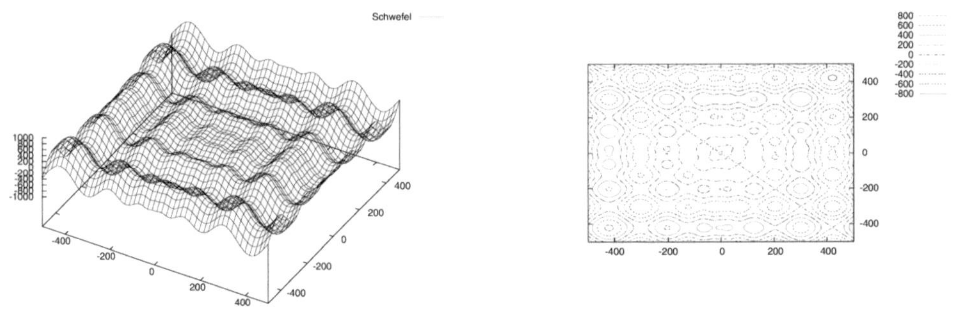

(a) (b)

Fig. 6. Schwefel fitness landscape

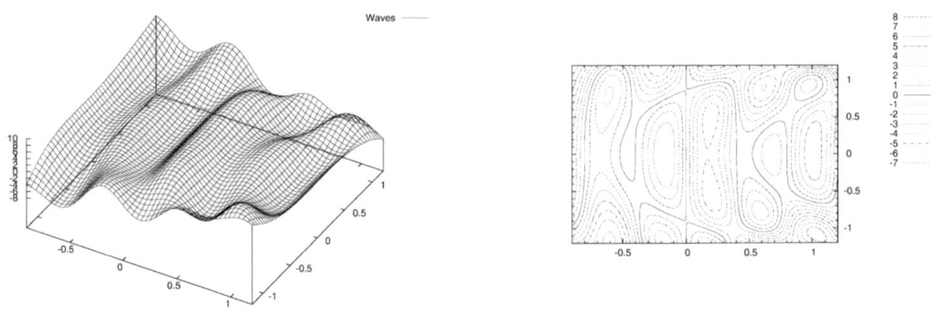

(a) (b)

Fig. 7. Waves fitness landscape

This function has many irregularly placed local minima. During experiments $n = 2$ was assumed (see fig. 6).

Waves fitness landscape is defined as follows (Ursem (1999)):

$$\begin{aligned} f_4(\vec{x}) = &-\big(\,(0.3 * x_1)^3 - \left(x_2^2 - 4.5 * x_2^2\right) * x_1 * x_2 - \\ &4.7 * \cos\left(3 * x_1 - x_2^2 * (2 + x_1)\right) * \sin(2.5 * \pi * x_1)\big) \\ &x_1 \in [-0.9; 1.2],\ x_2 \in [-1.2; 1.2] \end{aligned} \tag{50}$$

This function has many irregularly placed local minima (see fig. 7).

4.2 Species formation processes

In this section species formation processes are illustrated. Fig. 8– 19 show the course of evolution and speciation processes for all three models of speciation and for four mentioned above fitness landscapes. Experiments' results show location of agents after 0, 50, 500, and 5000 simulation steps.

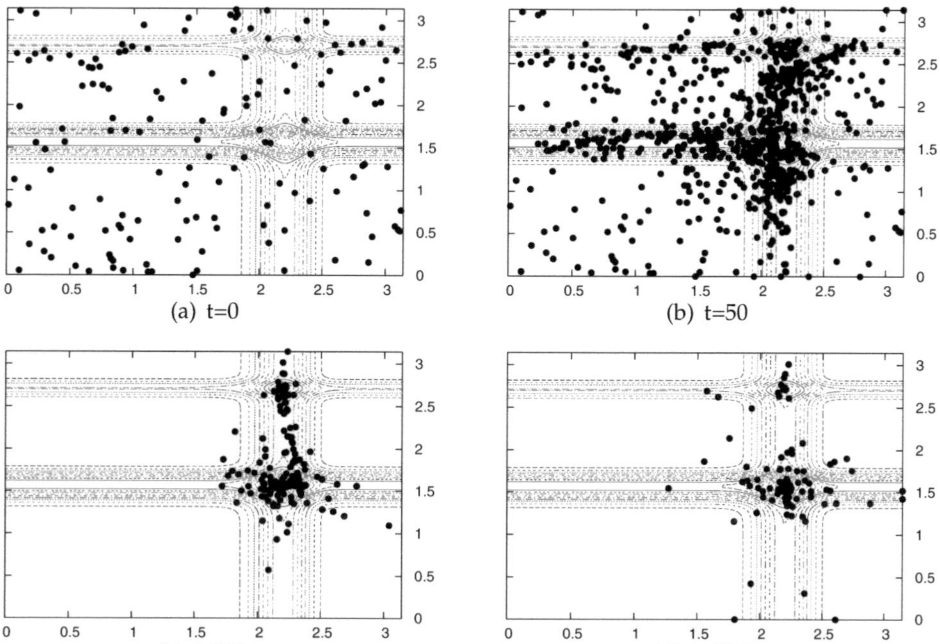

(a) t=0 (b) t=50

(c) t=500 (d) t=5000

Fig. 8. Species formation processes in aBSMAS with Michalewicz fitness landscape

Fig. 8–11 show the course of speciation in model with geographical barriers. In the case of all fitness landscapes speciation takes place—it can be seen that distinct species are formed. Species are located within the basins of attraction of local minima which are "ecological niches" for species. However not in all of the niches there exist some species, for example see fig. 9, 10, and 11. Also, it can be seen that rather high level of population diversity within species is maintained—agents are spread over rather large areas of fitness landscape.

Fig. 12– 15 show speciation processes taking place under second model—multi-agent system with flocks. As it can be seen in the figures, the speciation takes place and the diversity within the species is rather low, as compared to aBSMAS model, and especially sBSMAS model. Also,

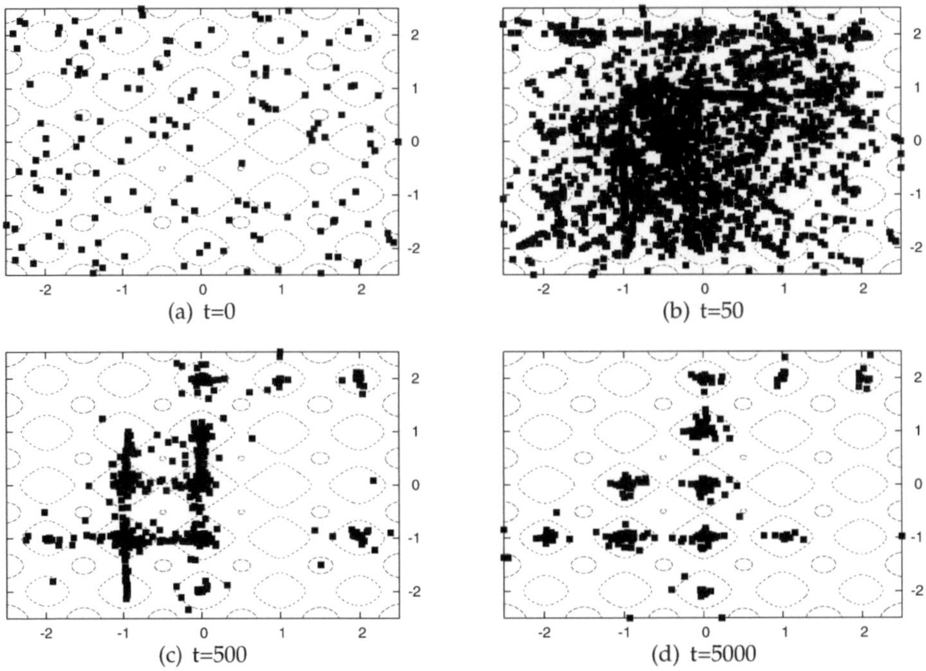

Fig. 9. Species formation processes in aBSMAS with Rastrigin fitness landscape

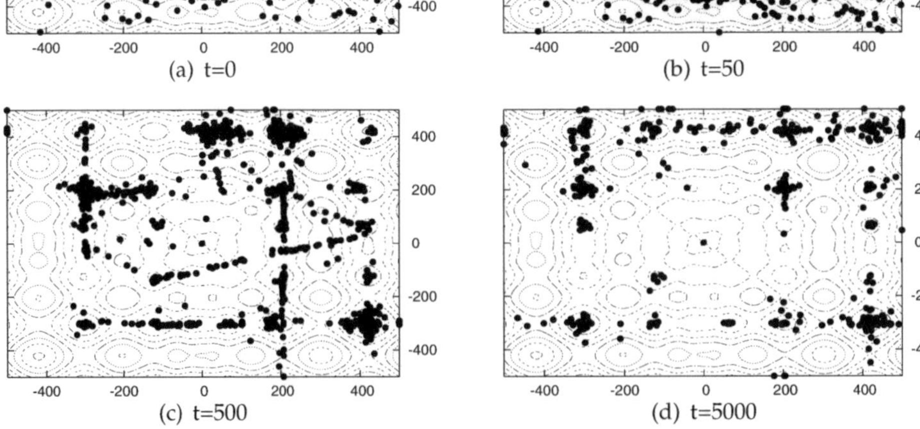

Fig. 10. Species formation processes in aBSMAS with Schwefel fitness landscape

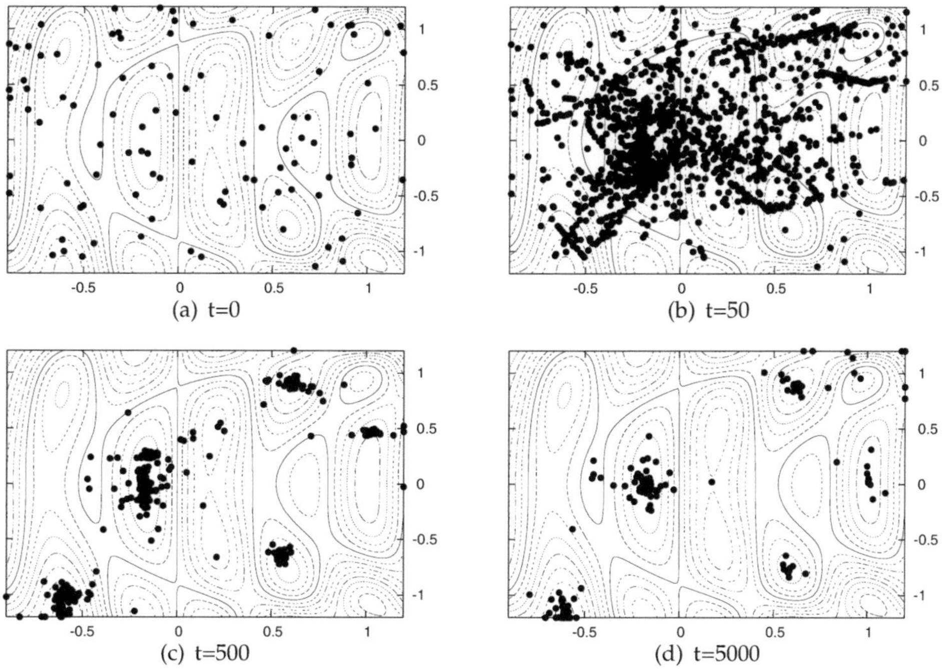

Fig. 11. Species formation processes in aBSMAS with Waves fitness landscape

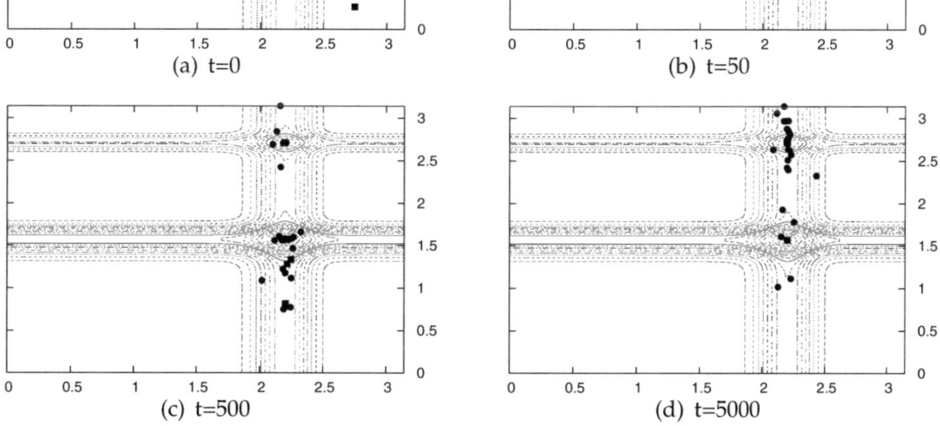

Fig. 12. Species formation processes in fBSMAS with Michalewicz fitness landscape

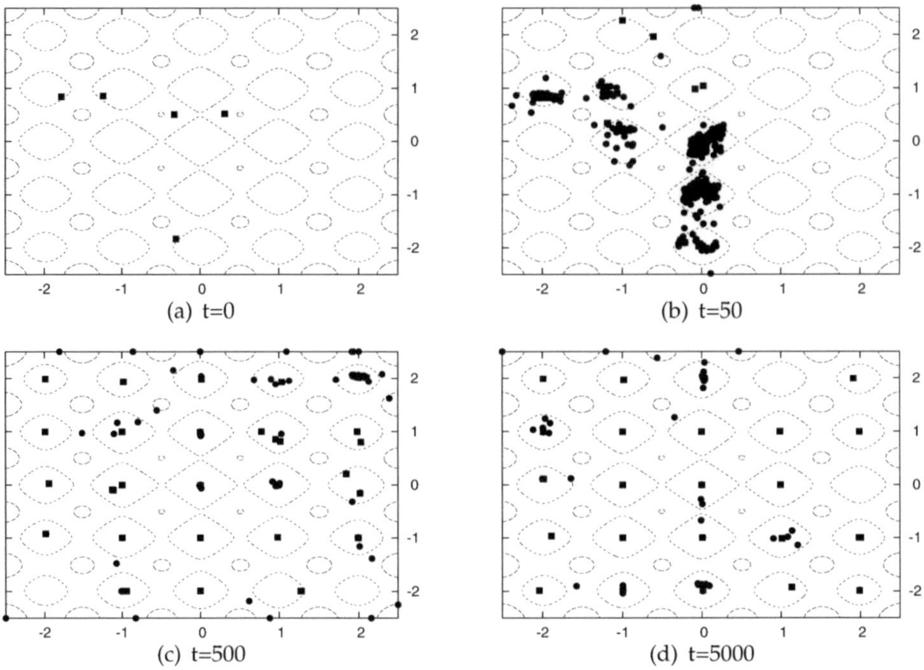

Fig. 13. Species formation processes in fBSMAS with Rastrigin fitness landscape

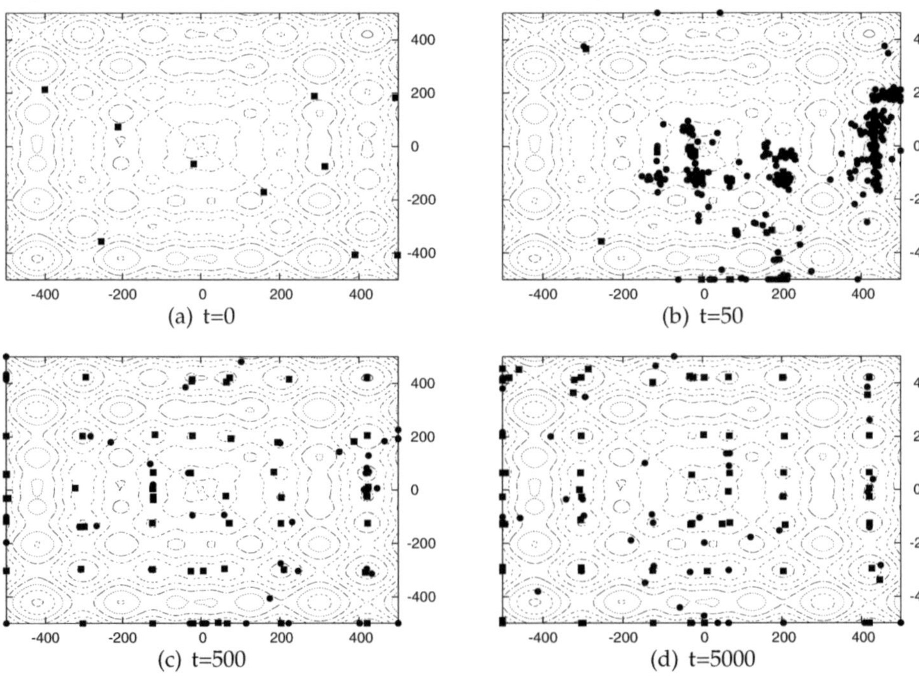

Fig. 14. Species formation processes in fBSMAS with Schwefel fitness landscape

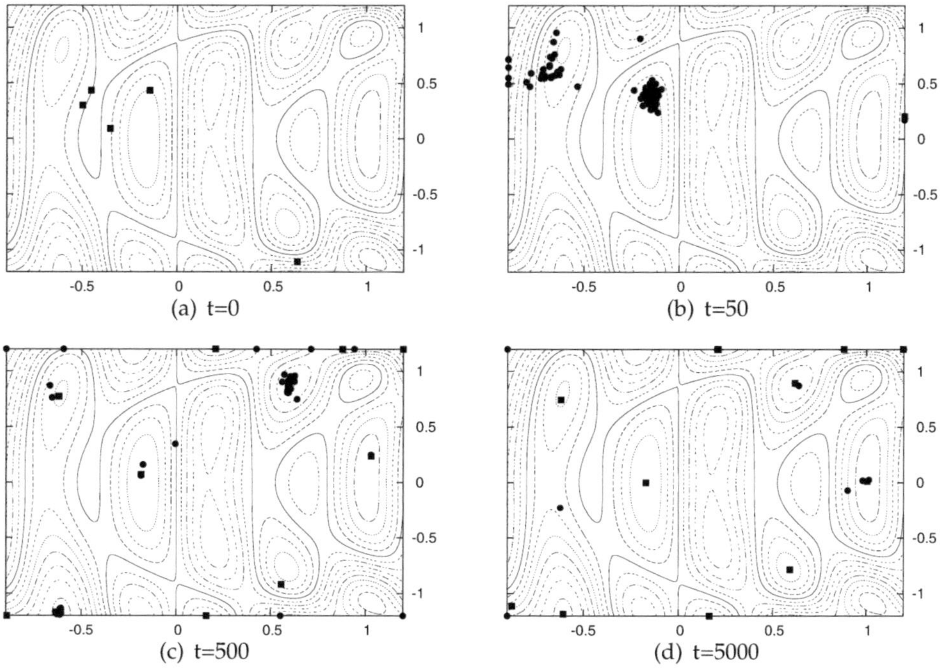

Fig. 15. Species formation processes in fBSMAS with Waves fitness landscape

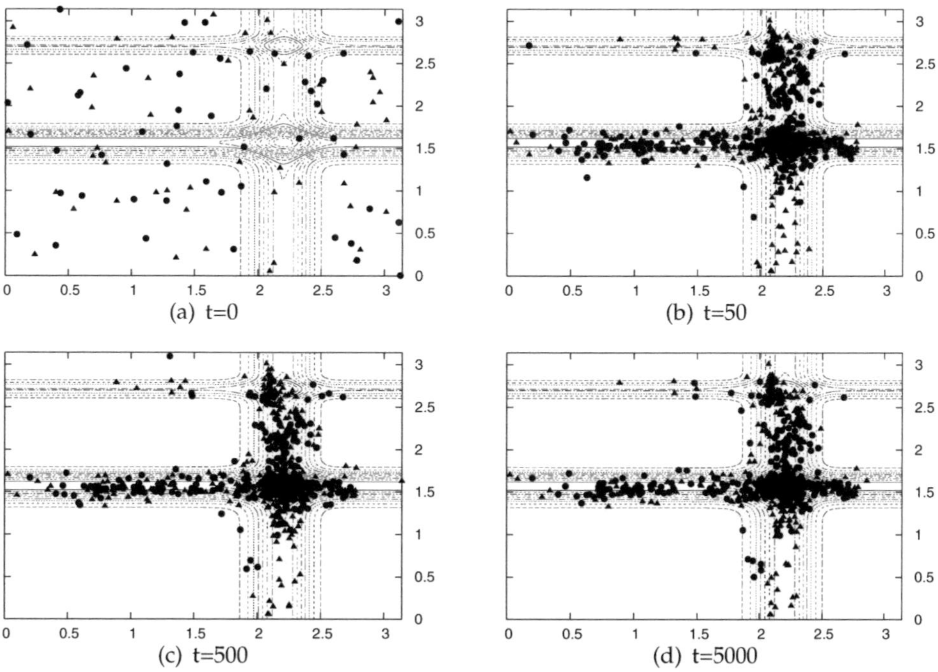

Fig. 16. Species formation processes in sBSMAS with Michalewicz fitness landscape

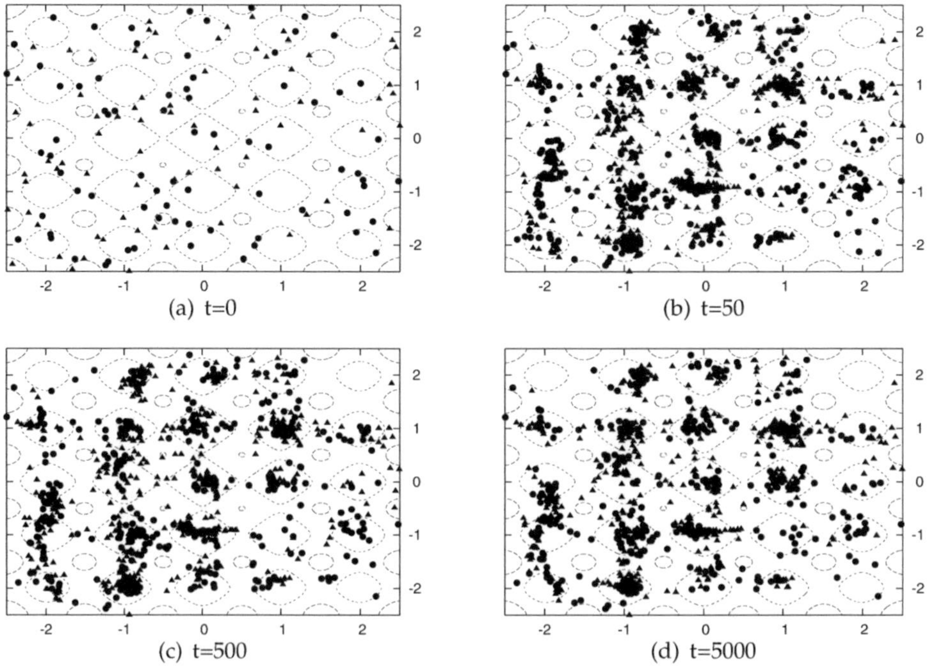

Fig. 17. Species formation processes in sBSMAS with Rastrigin fitness landscape

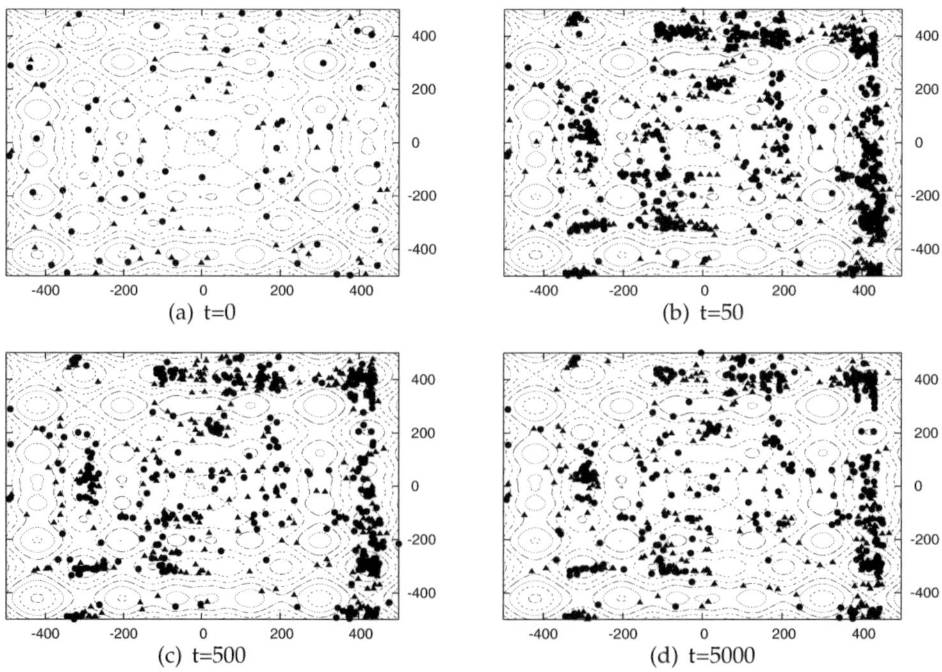

Fig. 18. Species formation processes in sBSMAS with Schwefel fitness landscape

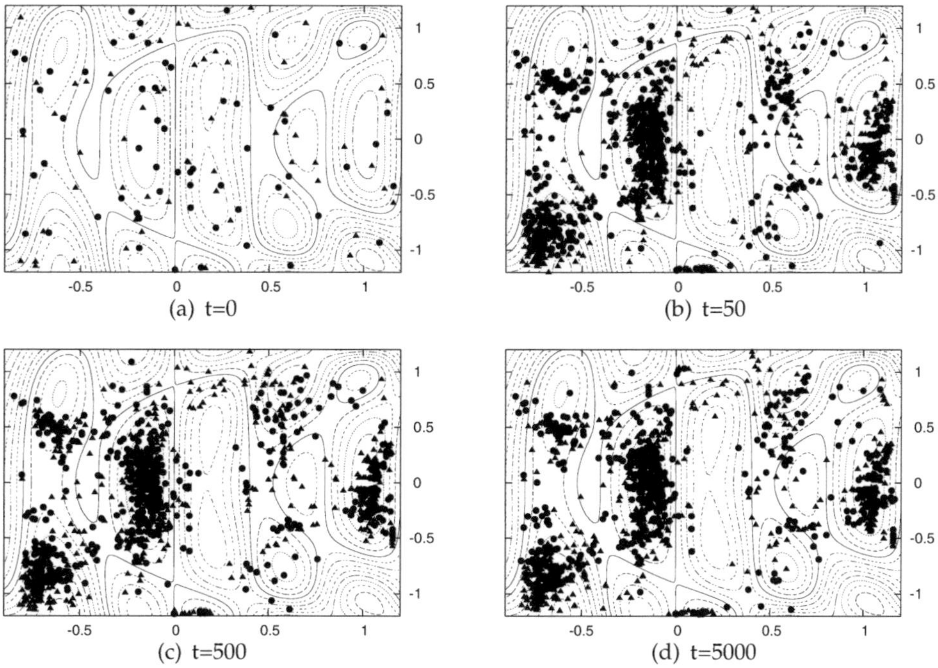

Fig. 19. Species formation processes in sBSMAS with Waves fitness landscape

there are generally more species formed—in most cases, in 5000 step almost in all niches there exist some species.
In the case of third model—multi-agent system with sexual selection—the population diversity within species is very high (see fig. 16– 19). Species are formed, but the boundaries between them are not clear in most cases (see fig. 16 and 18).

4.3 Population size during experiments

In fig. 20 and 21 changes of the population size during experiments in the three systems are shown. In all cases the number of agents changes rapidly during initial steps of the simulation but stabilizes after some time.
In the case of fBSMAS model after the rapid increase in the number of agents, there can be observed the tendency to slightly decrease the population size—it appears after the intensive epoch of species formation and populating environmental niches and it results from the existence of mechanism of merging flocks located within the same ecological niche.
In aBSMAS model the population is much more numerous than in the case of other two models. This is caused by the fact that aBSMAS model uses much more vertices in the environment and also more agents are needed to populate these vertices and maintain evolutionary processes.

5. Summary and conclusions

In this paper the model of bio-social multi-agent system (BSMAS) was introduced. Presented model is based on CoEMAS approach Dreżewski (2003), which has already been applied in several computational systems. The BSMAS approach allows for agent-based modeling of biological and social phenomena due to the possibility of defining in a very natural way of all

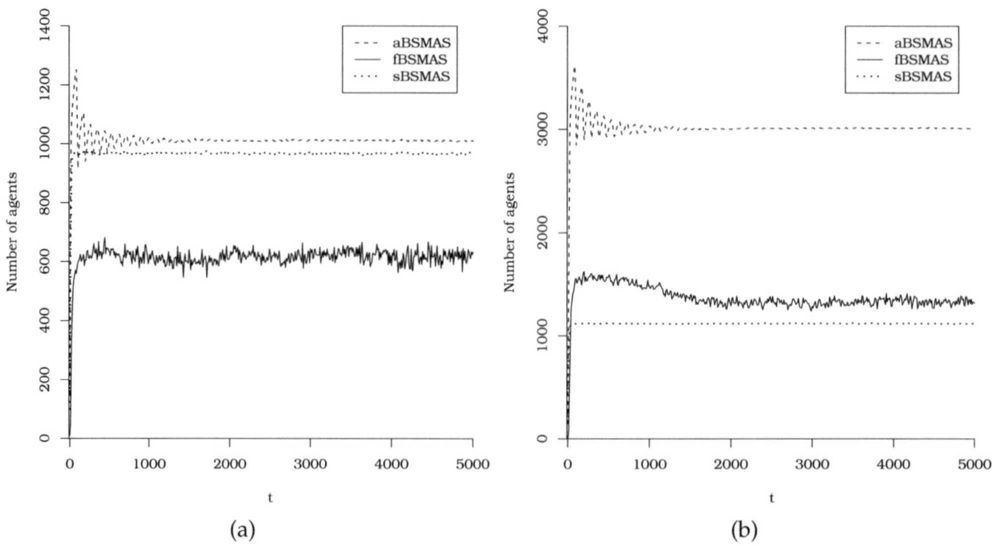

Fig. 20. Number of agents in the aBSMAS, fBSMAS, and sBSMAS during experiments with Michalewicz (a) and Rastrigin (b) landscapes

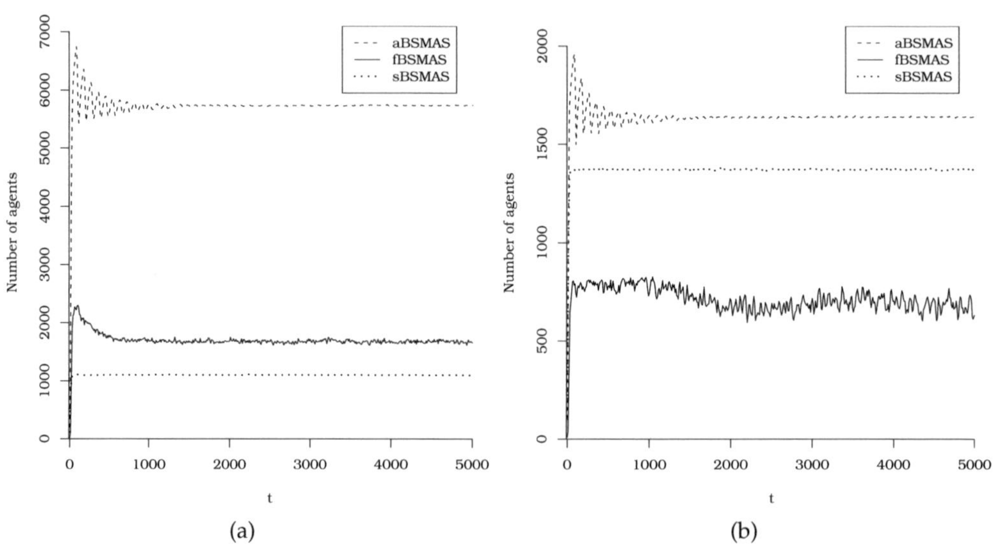

Fig. 21. Number of agents in the aBSMAS, fBSMAS, and sBSMAS during experiments with Schwefel (a) and Waves (b) landscapes

elements of multi-agent simulation: heterogeneous environment, passive elements (objects), active elements (agents), relations between them, resources, actions and attributes.

With the use of BSMAS model three systems with speciation were defined: system with allopatric speciation, system with speciation resulting from flock formation, and system with sexual selection. Presented results show that in all three cases speciation takes place, however the course of the evolution is in each case different, there are differences in the number of

formed species and population diversity within species. Also, in each model the population size changes in a different way during experiments.
Future work will include the application of BSMAS model to different areas—mainly social and economical simulations. Also the implementation of dedicated simulation system is included in future plans.

6. References

Bäck, T., Fogel, D. B., Whitley, D. & Angeline, P. J. (1997). Mutation, *in* Bäck, Fogel & Michalewicz (1997).

Bäck, T., Fogel, D. & Michalewicz, Z. (eds) (1997). *Handbook of Evolutionary Computation*, IOP Publishing and Oxford University Press.

Booker, L. B., Fogel, D. B., Whitley, D. & Angeline, P. J. (1997). Recombination, *in* Bäck, Fogel & Michalewicz (1997).

Cetnarowicz, K., Kisiel-Dorohinicki, M. & Nawarecki, E. (1996). The application of evolution process in multi-agent world to the prediction system, *in* M. Tokoro (ed.), *Proceedings of the 2nd International Conference on Multi-Agent Systems (ICMAS 1996)*, AAAI Press, Menlo Park, CA.

Dreżewski, R. (2003). A model of co-evolution in multi-agent system, *in* V. Mařík, J. Müller & M. Pěchouček (eds), *Multi-Agent Systems and Applications III*, Vol. 2691 of *LNCS*, Springer-Verlag, Berlin, Heidelberg, pp. 314–323.

Dreżewski, R. (2006). Co-evolutionary multi-agent system with speciation and resource sharing mechanisms, *Computing and Informatics* 25(4): 305–331.

Dreżewski, R., Sepielak, J. & Siwik, L. (2009). Classical and agent-based evolutionary algorithms for investment strategies generation, *in* A. Brabazon & M. O'Neill (eds), *Natural Computation in Computational Finance*, Vol. 2, Springer-Verlag, Berlin, Heidelberg.

Dreżewski, R. & Siwik, L. (2008). Agent-based multi-objective evolutionary algorithm with sexual selection, *Proceedings of the IEEE Congress on Evolutionary Computation, CEC 2008, June 1-6, 2008, Hong Kong, China*, IEEE.

Dreżewski, R., Woźniak, P. & Siwik, L. (2009). Agent-based evolutionary system for traveling salesman problem, *in* E. Corchado, X. Wu, E. Oja, Á. Herrero & B. Baruque (eds), *HAIS*, Vol. 5572 of *LNAI*, Springer-Verlag, pp. 34–41.

Epstein, J. M. (2006). *Generative social science. Studies in agent-based computational modeling*, Princeton University Press.

Epstein, J. M. & Axtell, R. (1996). *Growing artificial societes. Social science from bottom up*, Brookings Institution Press, The MIT Press.

Ferber, J. (1999). *Multi-Agent Systems: An Introduction to Distributed Artificial Intelligence*, Addison-Wesley.

Gavrilets, S. (2003). Models of speciation: what have we learned in 40 years?, *Evolution* 57(10): 2197–2215.

Gilbert, N. (2008). *Agent-based models*, SAGE Publications.

Gilbert, N. & Troitzsch, K. G. (2005). *Simulation for the social scientist*, Open University Press.

Krebs, J. & Davies, N. (1993). *An Introduction to Behavioural Ecology*, Blackwell Science Ltd.

Michalewicz, Z. (1996). *Genetic Algorithms + Data Structures = Evolution Programs*, Springer -Verlag.

Paredis, J. (1998). Coevolutionary algorithms, *in* T. Bäck, D. Fogel & Z. Michalewicz (eds), *Handbook of Evolutionary Computation, 1st supplement*, IOP Publishing and Oxford University Press.

Potter, M. A. (1997). *The Design and Analysis of a Computational Model of Cooperative Coevolution*, PhD thesis, George Mason University, Fairfax, Virginia.

Uhrmacher, A. M. & Weyns, D. (eds) (2009). *Multi-agent systems. Simulation and applications*, CRC Press.

Ursem, R. K. (1999). Multinational evolutionary algorithms, *in* P. J. Angeline, Z. Michalewicz, M. Schoenauer, X. Yao & A. Zalzala (eds), *Proceedings of the 1999 Congress on Evolutionary Computation (CEC-1999)*, IEEE Press, Piscataway, NJ, USA, pp. 1633–1640.

2

A Multi-Agent based Multimodal System Adaptive to the User's Interaction Context

Manolo Dulva Hina[1,2], Chakib Tadj[1],
Amar Ramdane-Cherif[2] and Nicole Levy[2]
[1]*Université du Québec, École de technologie supérieure,*
[2]*Université de Versailles-Saint-Quentin-en-Yvelines,*
[1]*Canada*
[2]*France*

1. Introduction

Communication is an important aspect of human life; it is with communication that helps human beings connect with each other as individuals and as independent groups. In informatics, the very purpose of the existence of computer is *information dissemination* - to be able to send and receive information. Humans are quite successful in conveying ideas with one another and reacting appropriately because we share the richness of our language, have a common understanding of how things work and have an implicit understanding of everyday situations. When human communicate with human, they comprehend the information that is apparent to the current situation, or *context*, hence increasing the conversational bandwidth. This ability to convey ideas, however, does not transfer when human interacts with computer. On its own, computers do not understand our language, do not understand how the world works and cannot sense information about the current situation. In a typical impoverished computing set-up where providing computer with information is through the use of mouse, keyboard and screen, the result is we explicitly provide information to computers, producing an effect that is contrary to the promise of *transparency* and *calm technology* in Marc Weiser's vision of *ubiquitous computing* (Weiser 1991; Weiser 1993; Weiser and Brown 1996). To reverse this, it is imperative that methodologies are developed that will enable computers to have access to context. It is through *context-awareness* that we can increase the richness of communication in human-computer interaction, through which we can reap the most likely benefit of more useful computational services.
Context (Dey and Abowd 1999; Gwizdka 2000; Dey 2001; Coutaz, Crowley et al. 2005) is a subjective idea and its interpretation is personal. Context evolves and the acquisition of contextual information is essential. However, we believe that the one with the final word on whether the envisioned context is correctly captured/acquired or not is the *end user*. Current research works indicate that some contextual information are already predefined by their systems from the very beginning - this is correct if the application domain is fixed but is incorrect if we infer that a typical user does different computing tasks in different occasions. With the aim of coming up with more conclusive and inclusive design, we conjure that the contextual information that is important to the user should be left to the judgment of the end

user. This leads us to the *incremental* acquisition of context where context parameters are added, modified or deleted one context parameter at a time.

In conjunction with the idea of inclusive context, we enlarge the notion of context that it has become interaction context. *Interaction context* refers to the collective context of the user (i.e. user context), of his working environment (i.e. environmental context) and of his computing system (i.e. system context). Each of these interaction context elements - *user context*, *environmental context* and *system context* - is composed of various parameters that describe the state of the user, of his workplace and his computing resources as he undertakes an activity in accomplishing his computing task, and each of these parameters may evolve over time. For example, user location is a user context parameter and its value will evolve as the user moves from one place to another. The same can be said about noise level as an environment context parameter; its value evolves over time. This also applies to the available bandwidth, which continuously evolves, which we consider as a system context parameter.

The evolution of the interaction context, from the time the user starts working on his computing task up to its completion, informs us that the contextual information changes instantaneously, and as such the computing system needs to adapt appropriately. Too often, a regular computing system remains static - it does nothing - even in the eventuality that a certain interaction context parameter changes that the user has no option but to intervene. For instance, when the bandwidth becomes too limited, downloading data becomes too slow that the user needs to intervene to stop the software application. This is the challenge of our time - **how can we design a computing system that adapts appropriately to the constantly evolving interaction context?** Our review of the state-of-the-art indicates that in the existing context-sensitive applications, very large efforts were expended by researchers in defining how to capture context and then disseminate it to the system. And yet, precise answer is still missing as to how the application itself will adapt to the given context. It is in this last direction that this chapter work registers.

The remaining contents of this chapter are as follows. Section 2 focuses on the review of the state-of-the-art; it tells us what has been done by other researchers in this domain and what is missing or lacking in the current endeavors. Section 3 introduces us to agents and the multi-agent system that will attempt to provide solutions to the cited problem. Section 4 is concentrated on modalities and the multimodal computing system. The multi-agent system's adaptation to interaction context is the main focus of Chapter 5. This work is concluded in Chapter 6.

2. Review of the state-of-the-art

The term "*context*" comes in many flavours, depending on which researcher is talking. In Shilit's early research, (Schilit and Theimer 1994), context means the answers to the questions "*Where are you?*", "*With whom are you?*", and "*Which resources are in proximity with you?*" He defined context as the changes in the physical, user and computational environments. This idea is taken later by Pascoe (Pascoe 1998) and Dey (Dey, Salber et al. 1999). Brown considered context as "*the user's location, the identity of the people surrounding the user, as well as the time, the season, the temperature, etc.*" (Brown, Bovey et al. 1997). Ryan defined context as the environment, the identity and location of the user as well as the time involved (Ryan, Pascoe et al. 1997). Ward viewed context as the possible environment states of an application (Ward, Jones et al. 1997). In Pascoe's definition, he added the pertinence of the notion of state: "*Context is a subset of physical and conceptual states having an interest to a particular entity*". Dey specified the notion of an entity: "*Context is any information that can be used to characterize the situation of an entity. An entity is a person, place or object that is considered relevant to the interaction between a user and an application, including the user and application themselves*" (Dey 2001). This definition became the basis for Rey and Coutaz to coin the term interaction context: "*Interaction context is a combination of situations. Given a user U engaged in an activity A, then the interaction context at time t is the composition of situations between time t_0 and t in the conduct of A by U*" (Rey and Coutaz 2004).

The efforts made in defining context within the domain of context awareness were in fact attempts in formalism, as in the case of definition proposed in (Abowd and Mynatt 2000). Other researchers, not satisfied with general definitions, attempted to define context formally (Chen and Kotz 2000; Dey 2001; Prekop and Burnett 2003). Pascoe (Pascoe 1998) and Dey (Dey and Abowd 1999) brought more precision in context definition by specifying that context is a set of information that describes an entity.

In other works related to sensitivity to context, various researchers started resolving the issue concerning the user's mobility. Then, research deepens within their emphasis on the whereabouts of the user. For example, *Teleporting* (Bennett, Richardson et al. 1994) and *Active Map* (Schilit and Theimer 1994) are few works on applications that are sensitive to the geographic location of a user. Dey (Dey 2001) and Chen and Kotz (Chen and Kotz 2000) made constraints on context research by putting emphasis on applications, the contextual information that is being used and their use. Gwizdka (Gwizdka 2000) identified two categories of context: internal and external. The categorization, however, was done with respect to the user's status. Dey and Abowd (Dey and Abowd 1999) and even Schilit (Schilit, Adams et al. 1994) categorize contextual information by levels. In the case of Dey's work, the primary level contains information that is related to the user's location, activity and time whereas with Schilit, the primary level refers to the user's environment, the physical environment and the computing environment. One more time, the contextual information considered in these categorizations did not sufficiently take environment context in depth. To respond to the problems raised in the previous categorizations, Razzaque (Razzaque, Dobson et al. 2005) proposed a finer categorization of contextual information. Dey's Context Toolkit (Dey, Salber et al. 2001) is one of the first architectures which considered three (3) important steps in works on context sensitivity (that is, the capture, representation and exploitation of context). In this architecture, the modeling of context uses an approach called sets of pairs of (entity, attribute).

Other approaches in context representation used *RDF* (Resource Description Framework) which is an extension of *W3C CC/PP* (World Wide Web Consortium Composite Capabilities/Preferences Profile) as in the work proposed by (Held 2002) and (Indulska, Robinson et al. 2003). *Ontology* was also used in context modeling in which approach context is considered as a set of entities having aspects describing its characteristics (Strang and Linnhoff-Popien 2003).

After modeling and storage, context needs to be disseminated to the application. Here, we draw our attention to the conceptual platforms of the architectural aspects of systems that are sensitive to context (Dey, Salber et al. 2001; Kindberg and Barton 2001). The works of (Indulska, Loke et al. 2001) and (Efstratiou, Cheverst et al. 2001) present service platforms related to providing necessary services to the user based on a given context. The interoperability environments dealing with the resolution of problem related to heterogeneity and mobility of a user are presented in (DeVaul and Pentland 2000) and

(Eustice, Lehman et al. 1999). Other works were oriented towards the development of distributed applications which deals with the conception of physical and logical infrastructure in developing distributed systems as in the case of works presented in (Banavar, Beck et al. 2000) and (Esler, Hightower et al. 1999). After the publication of the work of Weiser on distributed information systems (Weiser 1993), various works on context sensitivity in this genre of application has allowed the development of *ParcTab* (Schilit, Adams et al. 1993; Want, Schilit et al. 1995), *Mpad* (Kantarjiev, Demers et al. 1993), *LiveBoard* (Elrod, Bruce et al. 1992) and other interesting works (Dey 2001; Kephart and Chess 2001). The *Active Badge* project (Want, Hopper et al. 1992) of Olivetti Research and the *InfoPad* project (Truman, Pering et al. 1998) of Berkeley also embraced this axis of research on distributed computing, as in the case of other various centers of excellence, such as the *Carnegie Mellon University* (CMU_CS 2010), *IBM* (Horn 2001; Kephart and Chess 2001) and *Rutgers* (CS_Rutgers 2010), just to cite a few. We also note the works of (Kantarjiev, Demers et al. 1993), (Want, Schilit et al. 1995) and (Garlan, Siewiorek et al. 2002) which are some of the contributions in the research on adaptations of distributed applications on based on the given context. Also, an important work on the taxonomies of input devices include that of (Buxton 1983).

In perspective, in existing context-sensitive applications, very large efforts were expended by researchers in defining how to capture context and then disseminate it to the system. And yet, precise answer is still missing as to how the application itself will adapt to the given context. It is in this last direction that this work registers. Towards this end, we will present our proposed agents-based computing system that adapts accordingly based on the evolution of the interaction context.

Also, to obtain the full benefit of the richness of interaction context with regards to communication in human-machine interaction, the modality of interaction should not be limited to the traditional use of mouse-keyboard-screen alone. *Multimodality* (Dong, Xiao et al. 2000; Oviatt 2002; Ringland and Scahill 2003) allows for a much wider range of modes and forms of communication, selected and adapted to suit the given user's interaction context, by which the end user can transmit data with computer and computer responding or yielding results to the user's queries. In multimodal communication, the weaknesses of one mode of interaction, with regards to its suitability to a given situation, is compensated by replacing it with another mode of communication that is more suitable to the situation. For example, when the environment becomes disturbingly noisy, using voice may not be the ideal mode to input data; instead, the user may opt for transmitting text or visual information. Multimodality also promotes inclusive informatics as those with permanent or temporary disability are given the opportunity to use and benefit from information technology advancement. With mobile computing within our midst coupled with wireless communication that allows access to information and services, pervasive and adaptive multimodality is more than ever apt to enrich communication in human-computer interaction and in providing the most suitable modes for data input and output in relation to the evolving interaction context. A look back at recent research works inform us that much research efforts on ubiquitous computing were devoted on various application domains (e.g. identifying the user whereabouts, identifying services and tools, etc.) but there is barely, if ever, an effort made to make multimodality pervasive and accessible to various user situations. In this regard, this work fills the gap.

The solution that will be presented in this chapter is different from the rest of previous works in the sense that while others capture, disseminate and consume context to suit its preferred domain of application, this new multi-agent system captures interaction context and reconfigure its system architecture dynamically with the aim of providing the user with an infrastructure that will enable the user continue working on his task anytime, anywhere. The multi-agent system that will be presented, along with all of its mechanisms being generic in design, can be adapted/integrated into various computing systems in different domains of applications with ease or little amount of modification.

3. Agents, multi-agent system and interaction context

Our goal is to design a paradigm of a multimodal multimedia computing system capable of undergoing dynamic reconfiguration based on the given user's interaction context. To this end, we propose automation solution which will reinforce the system's adaptability to the user's situation as well as to support system decision in general and multimodal multimedia in particular. The proposed solution is an automated mechanism for the selection of modalities and supporting media devices that suit the given interaction context. This pertains to finding optimal configuration and quantifying it. The diagram demonstrating these proposed solutions is shown below (see Fig. 1).

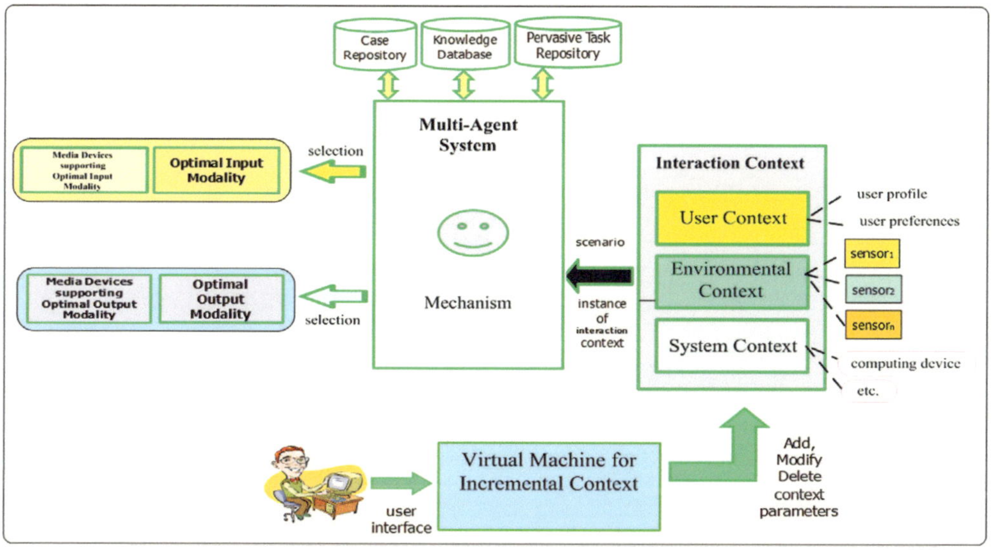

Fig. 1. The overall structure of our proposed multimodal multimedia computing system

In the proposed solution, the selection of optimal configuration is based on a compromise in which we take into account the constraints related to the user, his material environment, software and other factors. This contextual information represents the interaction context of the user. This context is the combination of situations that exist while the user undertakes an activity. These situations are real-time, existing from the time the user starts working on a task up to the time of its completion. During the execution of this activity, some situations remain stable while others change or evolve. Briefly, the interaction context is made up of the context of the user, of his environment and of his computing system. A change in the interaction context may result in the modification of appropriate modalities (and therefore of the media devices that support the modalities). We examined how an ever changing

interaction context affects the stability of the multimodal multimedia computing system so as it will continue providing services to the user.
The discussion that follows discusses the architectural framework and the design of the mechanism of the system's adaptation to the given interaction context.

3.1 The multi-agent system's architectural framework

The structure presented above (Fig. 1) is to be redrawn to make it a multi-agent system. The rationale behind this is due to the fact that given that the proposed mechanism is complex, it is preferable that the overall task is broken down into smaller pieces of works, and each work is to be delegated to an *agent*. **Why adapt agency?** The various tasks listed below are complicated and implementing them by just using objects or functions will not suffice. On the other hand, *agents* are *persistent, autonomous, social* and *reactive* entities, capable of learning, that they suit as **solutions** to implement our proposed solution.

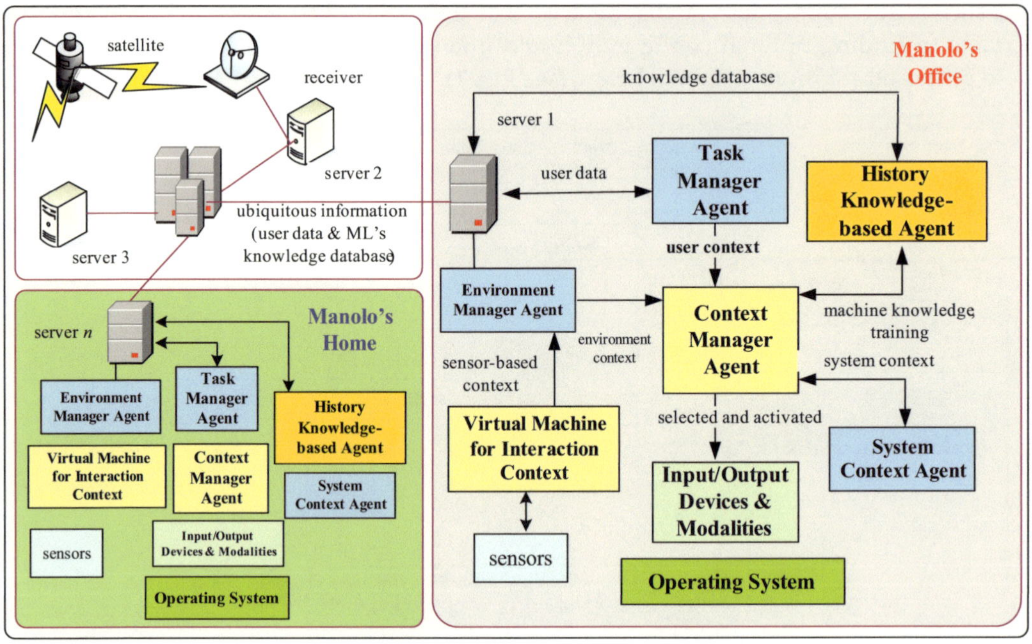

Fig. 2. Architecture of interaction context-sensitive pervasive multimodal multimedia computing system

The resulting multi-agent based multimodal system adaptive to the user's interaction context is shown in Fig. 2. The overall task is now distributed as smaller tasks to different agents. The components of this multi-agent system and their tasks are as follows:

- **The Task Manager Agent** (TMA) – manages user's profile, task and related data and their deployment from a server to the user's computing device, and vice versa.
- **The Context Manager Agent** (CMA) – detects interaction context taken from sensors and user profile, environment and computing system and select the modality and its supporting media devices that are most suitable to the given context.
- **The History and Knowledge-based Agent** (HKA) – responsible for machine learning training and knowledge acquisition.

- **The Virtual Machine for Interaction Context** (VMIC) - detects sensor-based context and allows the incremental definition of context by considering one context parameter at a time.
- **The Environmental Manager Agent** (EMA) - detects available and functional media devices in the user's environment.
- **The System Context Agent** (SCA) - detects the status of available computing devices and computing resources (e.g. bandwidth, CPU, memory and battery).

As shown in the diagram, a user (i.e. Manolo) may work at home, logs off and later on reconnects to a computing device in order to continue working on an interrupted task whenever and wherever he wishes. Due to user's mobility, there are variations in the user's interaction context as well as on available resources; these variations are compensated by corresponding variations in the selection of modalities and activation of supporting media devices.

As shown in Fig. 3, different parameters make up the interaction context. The User Context Agent detects the user's context; the Environment Context Agent in coordination with VMIC agent detects the context of the user's environment and the System Context Agent detects the available computing resources. All these parameters are consolidated and form the *overall interaction context* at that particular instance.

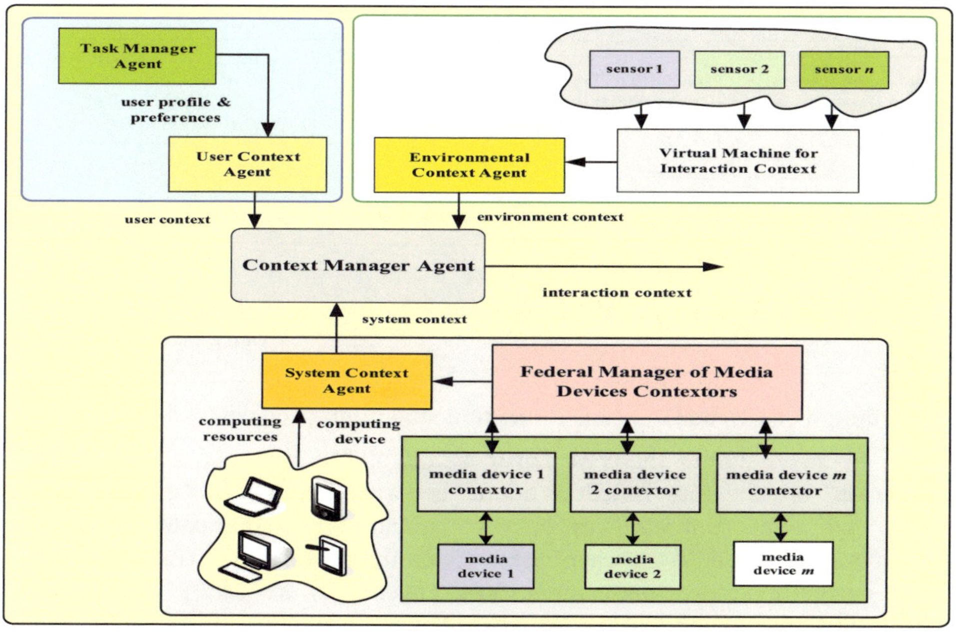

Fig. 3. The parameters that are used to determine interaction context

3.2 The virtual machine for incremental interaction context

To realize *incremental context* that is sensor-based, meaning that certain context parameters are interpreted based on the values obtained from certain sensors, we developed the VMIC using layered architectural approach (see Fig. 4). These architectural layers interact with one another; specifically the adjacent layers do interact with one another directly. *Layering* is a technique that is used to prevent possible cascading of errors or ripple effect whenever one wishes to debug or modify an element of a particular layer. Whenever possible, layering is chosen as a design consideration due to this benefit. Generally, in this structure, the *top* layer is associated with the interface interacting directly with an end user while the *bottom* layer is usually associated with gadgets or hardware elements.

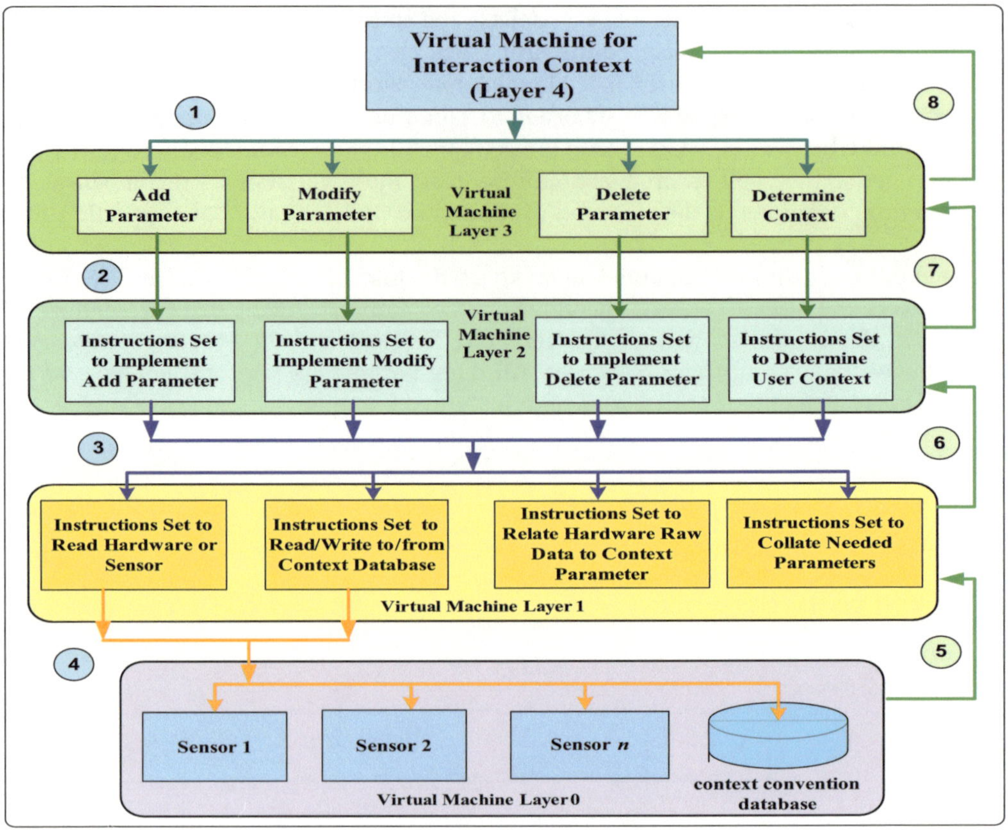

Fig. 4. The design of a virtual machine for incremental interaction context

As shown in the diagram, the **VM Layer 4** acts as the human-machine interface; its *"instruction set"* are the four functions found in **Layer 3** – the *"add parameter"*, *"modify parameter"*, and *"delete parameter"* are basic commands that manipulate the sensor-based context parameters while *"determine context"* yields the sensor-based context based on the values of currently-defined parameters. **VM Layer 2** is a *"library of functions"* that collectively supports Layer 3 instructions while **Layer 1** is another *"library of functions"* that acts as a link between Layer 2 and Layer 0. **Layer 0** is assigned to a collection of sensors (or machines or gadgets) that generate some raw data representing the value of a certain context parameter. Each lower layer supports the upper layer by providing the results to the functions demanded by the latter. This interdependence continues top down up to the very last layer. Consequently, the transfer of resulting data is propagated bottom up (meaning from layers 0 to 4). Layers 4, 3 and 2 are robust: the functions in these layers are independent of the context parameters, and therefore could be used by any system that deals with sensor-based context. If a new parameter needs to be added, then a minor modification may be needed in the functions in Layer 1 and the probe, one that will supply raw data for a certain parameter, may be need to be installed in layer 0. For example, the interactions among the layers to add a new context parameter (i.e. Noise Level) are shown in Fig. 5, the deletion of a context parameter in Fig. 6 and the detection of the sensor-based context in Fig. 7. Further details on how to add, modify and delete a context parameter as well as the detection of the current sensor-based context are provided in our work in (Hina, Tadj et al. 2009). These tools are designed in generic fashion such that they can be used and integrated into any kind of system, independent of the system's application.

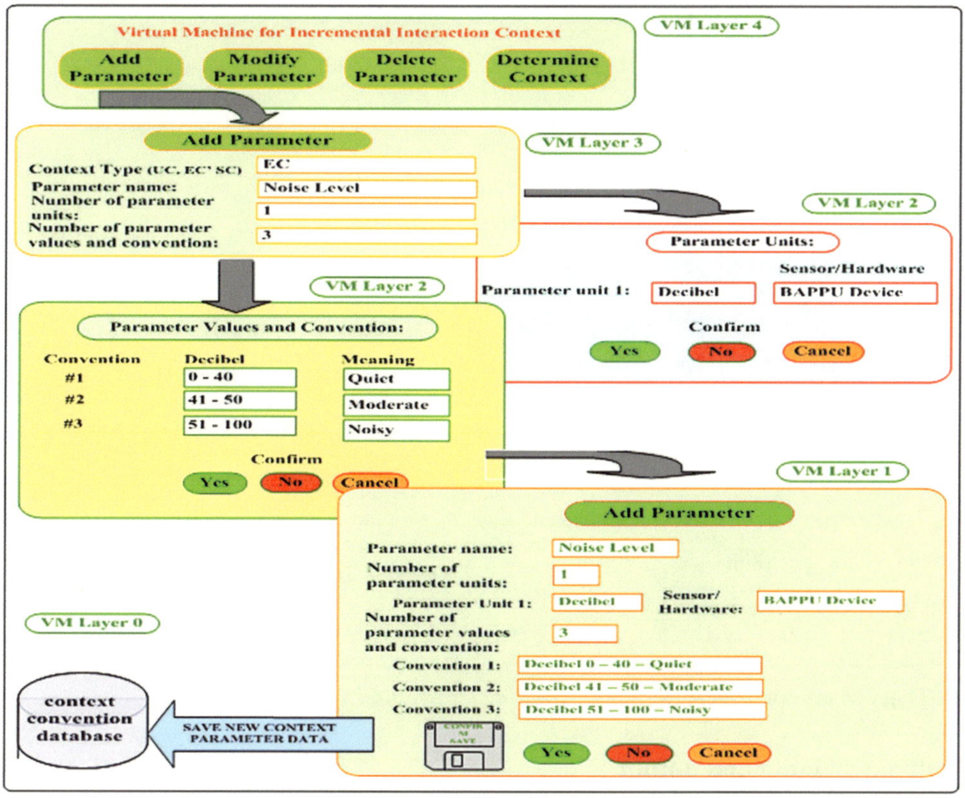

Fig. 5. The interactions among layers to add new context parameter: "*Noise Level*"

Why a virtual machine? The rationale for designing a virtual machine is always to come up with an efficient, isolated duplicate of a real machine. The *real machine* is always complicated, difficult to understand, and its behaviour is usually controlled by its designer. The aim therefore of *virtual machine* is to provide regular users ways of controlling and using the real machine without the necessity of having to know the intricacies of the actual machine. The end users, therefore, control the actual machine, asks it to do something for him/her using very simple instructions.

4. Modality and multimodal computing system

Multimodal interaction provides the user with multiple modes of interfacing with a computing system. Multimodal user interfaces are a research area in *human-computer interaction* (HCI). In the domain of multimodal interfaces, two groups have emerged - the multimodal input and the multimodal input and output.

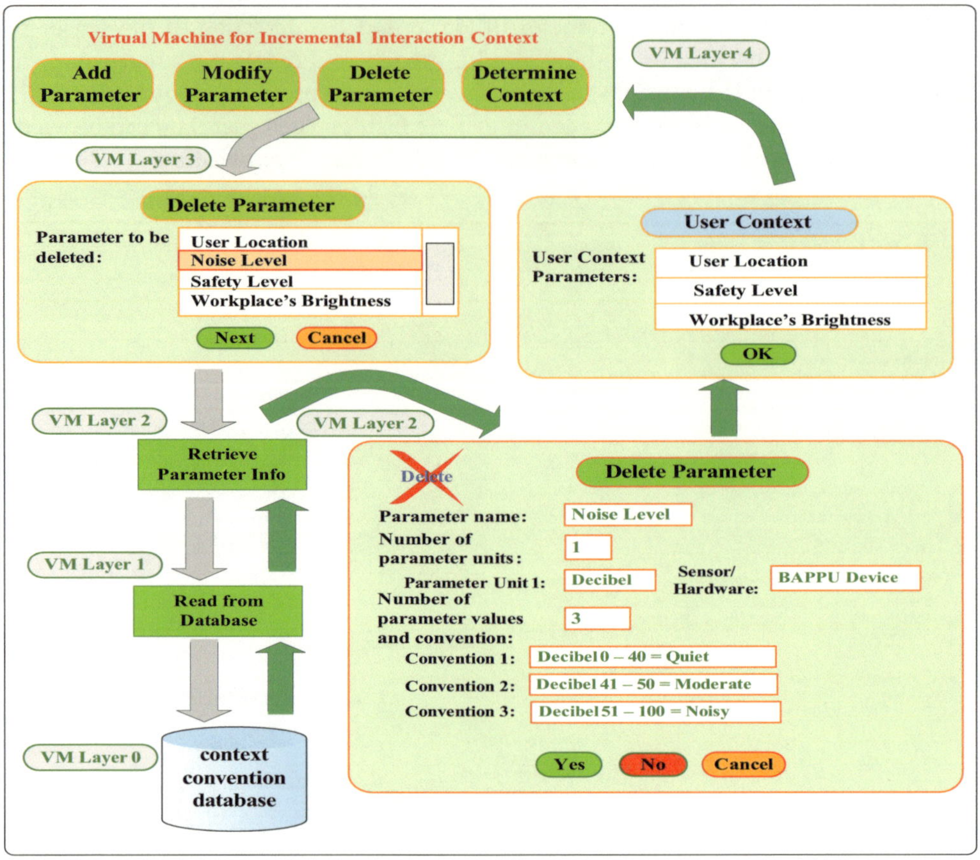

Fig. 6. The VM layers interaction to realize *"deleting a user context parameter"*

4.1 Multimodal input and output

The first group of multimodal interfaces combine various user input modes, beyond the usual keyboard and mouse input/output, such as speech, pen, touch, manual gestures, gaze and head and body movements. The most common of such interface combines a visual modality (e.g. a display, keyboard, and mouse) with a voice modality (speech recognition for input, speech synthesis and recorded audio for output). However other modalities, such as pen-based input or haptic input/output may be used. A sample detailed work in which mouse and speech were combined to form a multimodal fusion of input data is that of (Djenidi, Ramdane-Cherif et al. 2002; Djenidi, Ramdane-Cherif et al. 2003; Djenidi, Lévy et al. 2004).

The second group of multimodal systems presents users with multimedia displays and multimodal output, primarily in the form of visual and auditory cues. Other researchers also started to make use of other modalities, such as touch and olfaction. Proposed benefits of multimodal output system include synergy and redundancy. The information that is presented via several modalities is merged and refers to various aspects of the same process.

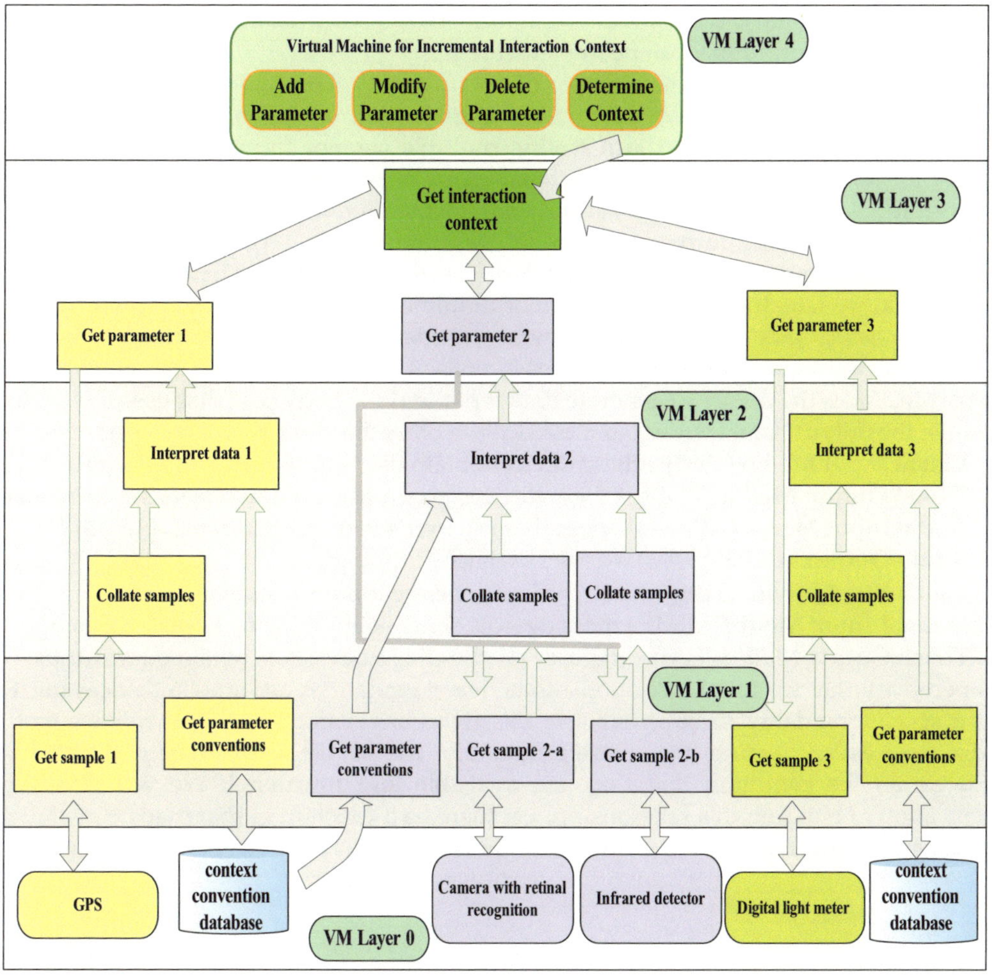

Fig. 7. VM layers interaction in detecting the current interaction context using specimen sensors

4.2 Modalities and media devices and their relationships

In this work, *modality* refers to the *logical* structure of man-machine interaction, specifically the *mode* for *data input* and *output* between a user and computer. Using natural language processing as basis, we classify modalities into 6 different groups:

1. **Visual Input** (VI_{in}) - the user's eyes are used as mechanism for data entry.
2. **Vocal Input** (VO_{in}) - voice or sound is captured and becomes the source of data input.
3. **Manual Input** (M_{in}) - data entry is done using hand manipulation or human touch.
4. **Visual Output** (VI_{out}) - data output is presented in the form as to be read by the user.
5. **Vocal Output** (VO_{out}) - sound is produced as data output; the user obtains the output by listening to it.
6. **Manual Output** (M_{out}) - the data output is presented in such a way that the user would use his hands to grasp the meaning of the presented output. This modality is commonly used in interaction with visually-impaired users.

To realize multimodality, there should be at *least one* modality for data input and at *least one* modality for data output that can be implemented.

There are *two* different meanings of *multimedia.* The *first* definition is that multimedia is media and content that uses a combination of different content forms. The term is used to describe a medium having multiple content forms. The term is used in contrast to media which only use traditional forms of printed or hand-produced material. Multimedia includes a combination of text, audio, still images, animation, video, and interactivity content forms. The *second* definition is that of multimedia describing electronic media devices used to store and experience multimedia content.

In this work, we take the *second* definition of multimedia and refer to the individual media as physical device that is used to implement a modality. Regardless of size, shape, colour and other attributes, all media devices - past, present or future - can be classified based on our part that uses the device to generate data input and the body part that uses the device to consume the output data. Hence, our classification of media devices is as follows:

1. **Visual Input Media** (VIM) - these devices obtain user input from human sight,
2. **Visual Output Media** (VOM) - these devices generate output that is meant to be read,
3. **Audio Input Media** (AIM) - devices that use user's voice to generate input data,
4. **Audio Output Media** (AOM) - devices whose output are meant to be heard,
5. **Touch Input Media** (TIM) - these devices generate input via human touch,
6. **Manual Input Media** (MIM) - these devices generate input using hand strokes, and
7. **Touch Output Media** (TIM) - the user touches these devices to obtain data output

It is necessary that we build a relationship between modalities and media devices for if we find a specific modality to be suitable to the given interaction context, it follows that the media devices supporting the chosen modality would be automatically selected and activated on the condition that they are available and functional. We will use formal specification in building this relationship. Let there be a function g_1 that maps a modality to a media group, given by $\mathbf{g_1}$**: Modality → Media Group**. This relationship is shown in Fig. 8.

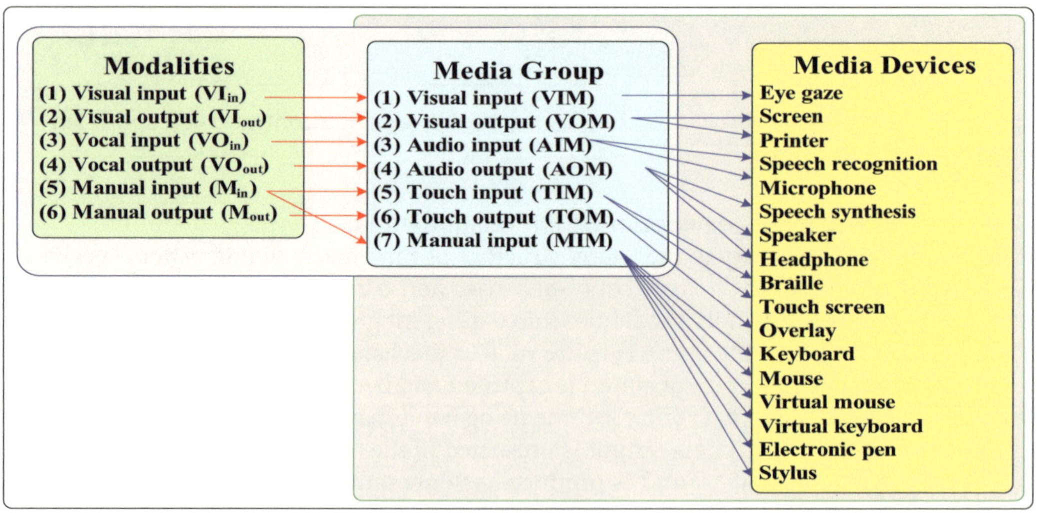

Fig. 8. The relationship between modalities and media, and media group and media devices

Often, there are many available devices that belong to the same media group. If such is the case then instead of activating them all, devices activation is determined through their priority rankings. To support this scheme, let there be a function g_2 that maps a media group to a media device and its priority rank, and is denoted **g_2: Media Group → (Media Device, Priority)**. Hence sample elements of these functions are:

g_1 = {(VI_{in}, VIM), (VI_{out}, VOM), (VO_{in}, AIM), (VO_{out}, AOM), (M_{in}, TIM), (M_{in}, MIM), (M_{out}, TOM)}

g_2= {(VIM, (eye gaze, 1)), (VOM, (screen, 1)), (VOM, (printer, 1)), (AIM, (speech recognition,1)), (AIM, (microphone, 1)), (AOM,(speech synthesis, 1)), (AOM, (speaker, 2)), (AOM, (headphone, 1)), etc.}.

It must be noted, however, that although media technically refers to a hardware element, we opted to include a few software elements without which VO_{in} and VO_{out} modalities could not possibly be implemented. These are the speech recognition and speech synthesis software.

4.3 Ranking media devices

The priority ranking of media devices is essential in determining which device would be activated, by default, when a certain modality is selected as apt for a given interaction context. Here, we outline the rules for prioritizing media devices:

1. The priority ranking of media devices shall be based on the relationship **g_2: Media Group → (Media Device, Priority)** and the elements of the function g_2.
2. When two or more media devices happen to belong to one media group, the priority of these devices would be based on these rules:

a. If their functionalities are identical (e.g. a mouse and a virtual mouse), activating both is incorrect because it is plain redundancy. Instead, one should be ranked higher in priority than the other. The most-commonly-used device gets the higher priority.

b. If their functionalities are complementary (e.g. a mouse and a keyboard), activating both is acceptable and their priority is identical.

c. In case that one device is more commonly used than the other (i.e. they do not always come in pair), then the more-commonly-used one gets the higher priority.

d. If both devices always come together as a pair, then both are ranked equal in priority.

Media Group	Media Devices				
	Priority = 1	Priority = 2	Priority = 3	...	Priority = *n*
Visual Input	Eye Gaze				
Audio Input	Microphone, Speech Recognition				
Touch Input	Touch Screen	Braille Terminal			
Manual Input	Mouse, Keyboard	Virtual Mouse, Virtual keyboard	Electronic Pen	Stylus	Braille
Visual Output	Screen	Printer	Electronic Projector		
Audio Output	Speaker	Headphone, Speech Synthesis			
Touch Output	Braille	Overlay Keyboard			

Table 1. A sample media devices priority table (MDPT)

In the early stage of setting up the pervasive multimodal multimedia computing system, it is essential that the end user provides this ranking. For example, in a quiet workplace, a speaker can be the top-ranked hearing output device. In a noisy environment, however, the headphone gets the top priority. An important component that implements this priority ranking is the *media devices priority table* (MDPT). See Table 1.

5. System adaptation to interaction context

In this section, we will present our proposed system's adaptation mechanism to the given instance of interaction context. To do this, we will derive the tools, relationships and mathematical formulas that the system has to learn and apply.

5.1 The History and Knowledge-based Agent (HKA)

As shown in Fig. 9, HKA is the agent tasked with the selection of modalities, of supporting media devices, and of the applications configurations based on the given instance of interaction context. Here, we discuss the concept behind HKA's knowledge acquisition. A *scenario* is the base of such knowledge.

Fig. 9 shows the generic diagram demonstrating how knowledge is acquired by HKA. The input to the *machine learning* (ML) component (responsible for analysis) is called the *pre-condition scenario* while the resulting output is called the *post-condition scenario*. The pre-condition scenarios as well as those of the post-condition scenarios are stored in a storage called *scenario repository* (SR). Whenever the ML component encounters a situation, it takes into account the parameters involved in the pre-condition scenario as well as consult its *initial knowledge* (also called *a priori knowledge*) or other previously-stored knowledge. If the pre-condition scenario is already found similar (or identical) to the one held in the scenario repository, the ML component simply takes in the corresponding post-condition scenario which is then taken as the necessary output that is bound for implementation.

In this work, we proposed the use of *case-based reasoning with supervised learning* (CBR) as a learning tool in order to automate the system's adaptation. If no knowledge is found (meaning, the scenario is new), the ML component performs calculations, determining the corresponding post-condition scenario which afterwards will be stored in the scenario repository. Over time, the ML component will accumulate enough knowledge that it will be able to "*learn*" most situations and that it will be able to react accordingly in the future.

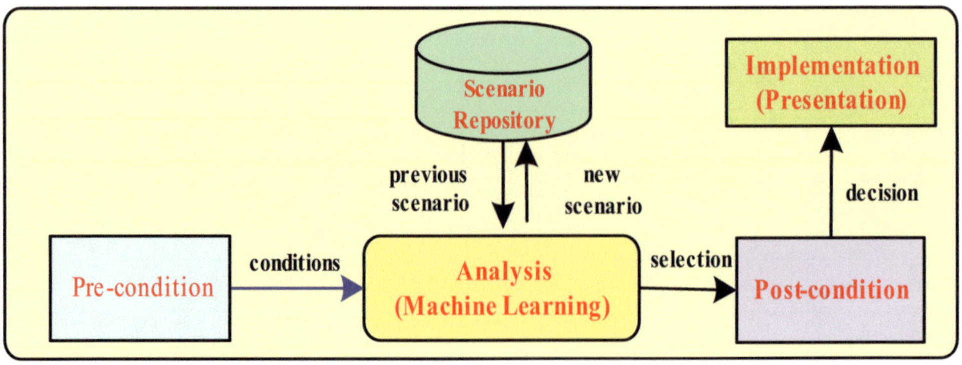

Fig. 9. Diagram showing knowledge acquisition within HKA

Using **CBR** makes it possible to find scenarios of related case. The technique, however, necessitates that a case must be identified. To use this approach, we need to model a *case* in such a way that we will end up finding a solution to the problem on hand. As stated by Kolodner (Kolodner 1993), a *case* is always composed of the same components, regardless of whatever application domain is in consideration. Its components are made up of a problem, a solution and an eventual evaluation:
The problem – this corresponds to the pre-condition scenario.
The solution – this corresponds to the resulting post-condition scenario
The evaluation – this would refer to the rate of relevance of the proposed solution.
The process of reuse consists of, for a new case, recovering a previously stored similar case, evaluate it and then store the new case onto the repository. This process is made up of the following steps:
Problem representation – For every scenario that is sent to HKA, we consult an identical case or cases that are most similar to the one in question. To do this, we need to formalize the problem part as if it is a new case in order to compare it against others that are already stored in the repository.
Similarity calculation – the case that is most pertinent is generally found through its similarity score with the new case. In order to do this, we come up with similarity calculation algorithm that helps in facilitating the search for similar cases.
Search of pertinent result – the search is based on the highest similarity score.
Memorization – the memorization is a choice that is usually left to the end user to decide since he is the most apt in deciding if the new case needs to be remembered or not. Even then, we proposed to the user to memorize his case.
Inspired by (Lajmi, Ghedira et al. 2007), we modify the similarity scoring scheme to reflect the needs of our system. Hence, given a *new case* (NC) and an individual case stored in the knowledge database, also called *memorized case* (MC), the similarity of the problem between the two cases (i.e. subscript indicates which case is considered) is equal to their *similarity* in their interaction context (**IC**) parameters. This relationship is given by:

$$Sim(IC_{NC}, IC_{MC}) = \frac{\sum_{i=1}^{NCC} Sim(IC_{i_{NC}}, IC_{MC})}{\max(IC_{NCC}, IC_{MCC})} \tag{1}$$

where IC_{NC} and IC_{MC} are the interaction context of the new case and the memorized case, respectively. NCC and MCC are the total number of community (i.e. total number of parameters) of the new case and the memorized case, respectively. Hence, IC_{NCC} tells us the number of community (i.e. parameters) that makes up the interaction context of the new case while IC_{MCC} denotes the number of community (i.e. parameters) that makes up the interaction context of the memorized case. The term IC_{iNC} denotes the ith interaction context parameter of the new case where *i* is a variable that loops from 1 to NCC. The expression $\max(IC_{NCC}, IC_{MCC})$ takes whichever is greater between the number of parameters of NC and MC. $Sim(IC_{iNC}, IC_{MC}) = \max_{j=1 \ldots MCC} Sim(IC_{iNC}, IC_{jMC})$ where $IC_{jMC} \in$ ICMC and $Sim(IC_{iNC}, IC_{jMC}) \in [0, 1]$ is the similarity between parameter *i* of NC and parameter *j* of MC.
For the comparison of parameter *i* of NC against parameter *j* of MC, we need to compare how similar they are in terms of their names and values. Hence, the similarity between parameter *i* of NC and parameter *j* of MC is given by:

$$Sim(ICi_{NC}, ICj_{MC}) = Sim(IC_{iName_{NC}}, IC_{jName_{MC}}) * Sim(IC_{iValue_{NC}}, IC_{jValue_{MC}}) \tag{2}$$

The numerical value associated to the results of the comparisons of the names and values of parameters *i* of NC and *j* of MC is given below:

$$Sim(IC_{iName_{NC}}, IC_{jName_{MC}}) = \begin{cases} 0 \text{ if } ICi_{Name_{NC}} \neq ICj_{Name_{MC}} \\ 1 \text{ if } ICi_{Name_{NC}} = ICj_{Name_{MC}} \end{cases} \tag{3}$$

The relationship above indicates that when the parameter name of *i* of NC and parameter name of *j* of MC are different, the similarity score between the two is zero. That means, if we compare, for instance, the parameter name "*temperature*" against parameter name "*noise level*", the similarity between them is automatically zero.

If and when the two parameters have the same name, their values do matter. The relationship is given by:

$$Sim(IC_{iValue_{NC}}, IC_{jValue_{MC}}) = 1 - \left(\frac{\left| ICj_{Value_{MC}} - ICi_{Value_{NC}} \right|}{\left| ICj_{Value_{MC}} - ICi_{Value_{NC}} \right| + 1} \right) \tag{4}$$

Hence, if we compare the name of the parameter of NC against the name of the parameter of MC and both are found to be identical, say both parameters are named "*noise level*", then the similarity score for their names is 1 and we will then proceed to comparing their parameter values.

In this work, each context parameter has a name and a value, and such value (or range of values) is associated with a convention number. For example, for noise level (see Fig. 5), if the measured or sampled value is 0 to 40 dB, we say that noise level = "*quiet*" (this is considered convention 1), noise level is from 41 to 50 dB, the noise level = "*moderate*" (this is convention 2) and noise level is 51 dB or more, then noise level = "*noisy*" (this is convention 3). Indeed, for every given context parameter, it is associated with one or more conventions. In our work, as a rule of thumb, if the convention number is 1, the value of the context parameter is ideal to the user. As the convention number increases in numerical value, the context parameter is beginning to shift to the unwanted condition. For example, taking into account the conventions, if noise level = 1, then the working environment is quiet, whereas if the noise level = 3, the working environment is noisy. The convention number associated with a context parameter will be used in measuring the similarity score of two parameters being compared.

If the name of the parameter in NC and the name of the parameter of MC are the same, we then proceed to determining their similarity score with regards to their values. Consider the following cases:

Case 1: Parameter of NC: Noise level = 1. Parameter of MC: Noise level = 1. In this case, $Sim(Name_{NC}, Name_{MC}) = 1$ and $Sim(Value_{NC}, Value_{MC})$ will be computed as follows: 1 – (1-1)|/|1-1|+1) = 1 – (0/1) = 1 – 0 = 1. They are completely the same, both in names and values.

Case 2: Parameter of NC: Noise level = 1. Parameter of MC: Noise level = 2. Again, their names are the same, Sim($Name_{NC}$, $Name_{MC}$) = 1. Sim($Value_{NC}$, $Value_{MC}$) will be computed as follows: 1 – (|1-2|/|1-2|+1)| = 1 – (1/2) = 0.5. The value indicates that they are quite closed enough (i.e. 50% similar with each other).

Case 3: Parameter of NC: Noise level = 1. Parameter of MC: Noise level = 3. Again, their names are the same. Sim($Value_{NC}$, $Value_{MC}$) will be computed as follows: 1 – (|1-3|/|1-3|+1)| = 1 – (2/3) = 1/3. The value indicates that they are quite far from each other and is 33.3% similar with one another.

Case 4: Parameter of NC: Noise level = 2. Parameter of MC: Noise level = 3. Again, their names are the same. Sim($Value_{NC}$, $Value_{MC}$) will be computed as follows: 1 – (|2-3|/|2-3|+1)| = 1 – (1/2) = 1/2. The value indicates that they are quite closed to each other (50% similar).

In general, the similarity value of two parameters having identical names is 1/distance between them. It means, if they have the same value, their similarity score is 1; if they are 2 values apart, their similarity score is ½. If they are 3 values apart, their similarity score is 1/3, and $1/n$ if they are n values apart from each other.

Previously, we had specified that interaction context (**IC**) is actually the composition of all the elements of user context (**UC**), environment context (**EC**) and system context (**SC**). In this respect, we made a decision that the weight of **UC**, **EC** and **SC** in the composition of IC is identical (meaning, UC = EC = SC = 1/3 of IC), hence the similarity formula specified in Equation 1 becomes:

$$Sim(NC, MC) = \tfrac{1}{3}Sim(UC_{NC}, UC_{MC}) + \tfrac{1}{3}Sim(EC_{NC}, EC_{MC}) + \tfrac{1}{3}Sim(SC_{NC}, SC_{MC}) \quad (5)$$

The similarity between the UC of NC vs. the UC of MC is given by:

$$Sim(UC_{NC}, UC_{MC}) = \frac{\sum_{i=1}^{UC_{NCC}} Sim(UC_{i_{NC}}, UC_{MC})}{\max(UC_{NCC}, UC_{MCC})} \quad (6)$$

For the similarity measures of **EC** and **SC** of NC vs. MC, the same principle as Equation 3 must be applied, with the formula adjusted accordingly to denote **EC** and **SC**, respectively, yielding:

$$Sim(EC_{NC}, EC_{MC}) = \frac{\sum_{i=1}^{EC_{NCC}} Sim(EC_{i_{NCC}}, EC_{MCC})}{\max(EC_{NCC}, EC_{MCC})} \quad (7)$$

$$Sim(SC_{NC}, SC_{MC}) = \frac{\sum_{i=1}^{SC_{NCC}} Sim(SC_{i_{NC}}, SC_{MC})}{\max(SC_{NCC}, SC_{MCC})} \quad (8)$$

where UC_{NCC} denotes the total number of community (parameters) in the **UC** of NC. The same principle applies to EC_{NCC} (total number of **EC** parameters in NC) and SC_{NCC} (total number of **SC** parameters in NC). This also applies to UC_{MCC}, EC_{MCC} and SC_{MCC}. Note that

the number of community (number of parameters) of a new case is equal to the sum of all of its community (i.e. parameters) in **UC**, **EC** and **SC**. That is, NCC = UC_{NCC} + EC_{NCC} + SC_{NCC}. Similarly, MCC = UC_{MCC} + EC_{MCC} + SC_{MCC}.
As shown in the above relationship, we are in the assumption that the weights of **UC**, **EC** and **SC** are equal (each is 33.3%) but this figure can be easily adjusted by the expert (i.e. end user) to suit his needs.
For simplicity of discussion, we revert back our discussion of **IC** (rather than the individual components **UC**, **EC** and **SC**) to simplify the issue of finding scenarios that are similar to the new case in consideration. The formula given in Equation 1 is used to compare its similarity against other scenarios that are within its "*neighborhood*". Those considered *neighbours* are actually *scenarios* that are very close to the case in question with respect the values of its interaction context parameters. Using these parameters, we can identify the index of the case in question within the database of scenarios. We call this index "*scenario number*" or *scenNum*. For example, if scenario *i* is composed of individual interaction context parameters IC_1, IC_2, …, IC_{max}, that is IC_i = (IC_1, IC_2, …, IC_{max}), the scenario index assigned to this specific case is given by:

$$ScenNum = IC_{\max} + \sum_{i=1}^{\max-1} ((IC_i - 1) \bullet \prod_{j=i+1}^{\max-1} card(IC_j)) \quad (9)$$

where card(IC_j) is the cardinality of the total number of values for the convention of a specific interaction context parameter j.
In the discussion that will follow, we will elaborate on the learning and adaptation mechanisms that are used by the HKA agent.

5.2 Selection of modalities and supporting media devices suitable to the instance of interaction context

Let *interaction context*, **IC** = {IC_1, IC_2,…, IC_{max}}, be the set of all parameters that manifest the user's interaction context. At any given time, a user has a specific interaction context *i* denoted as IC_i, $1 \le i \le max$, which is composed of variables that are present during the conduct of the user's activity. Each variable is a function of the application domain which, in this work, is multimodality. Formally, an **IC** is a tuple composed of a specific user context (**UC**), environmental context (**EC**) and system context (**SC**). An instance of **IC** is given as:

$$IC_i = UC_k \otimes EC_l \otimes SC_m \quad (10)$$

where $1 \le k \le max_k$, $1 \le l \le max_l$, and $1 \le m \le max_m$, and max_k, max_l and max_m = maximum number of possible user contexts, environment contexts and system contexts, respectively. The Cartesian product (symbol: ⊗) denotes that **IC** yields a specific combination of **UC**, **EC** and **SC** at any given time.
The user context **UC** is composed of application domain-related parameters describing the state of the user during his activity. A specific user context *k* is given by:

$$UC_k = \bigotimes_{x=1}^{\max_k} IC_{kx} \quad (11)$$

where IC_{kx} = parameter of UC_k, *k* = the number of **UC** parameters. Similarly, any environment context EC_l and system context SC_m are specified as follows:

$$EC_l = \bigotimes_{y=1}^{\max_l} IC_{ly} \tag{12}$$

$$SC_m = \bigotimes_{z=1}^{\max_m} SC_{mz} \tag{13}$$

The first knowledge that the ML component must learn is to relate the interaction context to appropriate modality. Let function $\mathbf{s_1}$**:** $\mathbf{IC} \rightarrow \mathbf{M}$ maps interaction context with appropriate modalities. This function takes an instance of $\mathbf{IC}$ = $\{IC_1, IC_2, \ldots, IC_{max}\}$ as pre-condition scenario input to HKA and as a result returns a set of optimal modalities $M_o = \{m_1, m_2, \ldots, m_{max}\}$as post-condition output.
Let $\mathbf{M} = \{VI_{in}, VO_{in}, M_{in}, VI_{out}, VO_{out}, M_{out}\}$ be the set of modalities. Modalities are possible when the following condition holds:

$$Modality\ Possible = (VI_{in} \vee VO_{in} \vee M_{in}) \wedge (VI_{out} \vee VO_{out} \vee M_{out}) \tag{14}$$

Consequently, modality fails under the following condition:

$$\begin{aligned} Modality\ Failure = {} & ((VI_{in} = Failed) \wedge (VO_{in} = Failed) \wedge (M_{in} = Failed)) \vee \\ & ((VI_{out} = Failed) \wedge (VO_{out} = Failed) \wedge (M_{out} = Failed)) \end{aligned} \tag{15}$$

wherein symbols $\wedge$ and $\vee$ represent logical AND and OR, respectively.
Let M_j = element of the power set of **M**, that is, $M_j \in \mathbb{P}(\mathbf{M})$ where $1 \le j \le mod_{max}$ (maximum modality). Also, let $\hat{M}$ = the most suitable M_j for a given interaction context IC_i. This set is given by the following relationship:

$$\hat{M} = \arg\max_j \mathrm{P}(M_j \mid IC_i) \tag{16}$$

To simplify calculation, Bayes Theorem (Kallenberg 2002), given below, can be adopted, and $P(M_j/IC_i)$ becomes:

$$P(M_j \mid IC_i) = \frac{P(IC_i \mid M_j) \times P(M_j)}{P(IC_i)} \tag{17}$$

The implementation of *Bayes Theorem* leads to the *Naive Bayes algorithm* (Mitchell 1997). The Naive Bayes algorithm is a classification algorithm that assumes that the IC_i attributes $IC_1, \ldots, IC_{max}$ are all conditionally independent of one another given a post condition M_j. The representation of $P(IC_i \mid M_j)$ becomes:

$$\begin{aligned} P(IC_i \mid M_j) &= P(IC_1, \ldots, IC_{max} \mid M_j) \\ &= P(IC_1 \mid M_j) \times \ldots \times P(IC_{max} \mid M_j) \\ &= \prod_{i=1}^{max} P(IC_i \mid M_j) \end{aligned} \tag{18}$$

Here, our goal is to train a classifier that, given a new IC_i to classify, will provide the probability distribution on all possible values of **M** (i.e. $M_1, M_2, \ldots, M_{max}$). Given that $IC_i = (IC_1, IC_2, \ldots, IC_{max})$, then the equation above becomes:

$$P(M_j | IC_1...IC_{max}) = \frac{P(M_j)P(IC_1...IC_{max} | M_j)}{\sum_{k=1}^{m} P(M_k)P(IC_1...IC_{max} | M_k)} \quad (19)$$

The above equation can also be written as:

$$P(M_j | IC_1...IC_{max}) = \frac{P(M_j)\prod_{i=1}^{max} P(IC_i | M_j)}{\sum_{k=1}^{m} P(M_k)\prod_{i=1}^{max} P(IC_i | M_k)} \quad (20)$$

which is the fundamental equation for the *Naive Bayes classifier*. Given a new instance of interaction context $IC_i = (IC_1, \ldots, IC_{max})$, the equation shows how to calculate the probability that M_j will take given the observed attribute values of IC_i and given that the distributions $P(M_j)$ and $P(IC_i | M_j)$ are estimated values taken from training data (SR). If we are interested only in the most suitable value of M_j, then we have the *Naive Bayes classification rule*:

$$\hat{M} = \arg\max_j \left(\frac{P(M_j)\prod_{i=1}^{max} P(IC_i | M_j)}{\sum_{k=1}^{m} P(M_k)\prod_{i=1}^{n} P(IC_i | M_k)} \right) \quad (21)$$

Given that the denominator does not depend on parameter j, then the above equation becomes

$$\hat{M} = \arg\max_j \left(P(M_j)\prod_{i=1}^{max} P(IC_i | M_j) \right) \quad (22)$$

Given that IC_i is composed of elements of **UC, EC** and **SC**, then $P(IC_i/M_j)$ can be written as:

$$P(IC_i | M_j) = P(UC_k | M_j) \times P(EC_l | M_j) \times P(SC_m | M_j) \quad (23)$$

Note that in IC_i, the parameters $IC_1, \ldots IC_{max}$ are mutually exclusive. Using Equation 11, Equation 12 and Equation 13, we replace each element of IC_i with the corresponding value. For example, the relationship involving user context UC_k given the modality M_j is given by:

$$P(UC_k | M_j) = \prod_{i=1}^{uc_{max}} P(UC_i | M_j) \quad (24)$$

In conclusion, the **optimal modality** for whatever instance of interaction context is given by:

$$\hat{M} = \arg\max_j \left(\left(\prod_{k=1}^{uc_{max}} P(UC_k | M_j) \times \prod_{l=1}^{ec_{max}} P(EC_l | M_j) \times \prod_{m=1}^{sc_{max}} P(SC_m | M_j) \times P(M_j) \right) \right. \quad (25)$$

where $P(Mj)$ = frequency count of M_j in scenario repository (SR) ÷ cardinality of SR and uc_{max}, ec_{max} and sc_{max} are, respectively, the total number of **UC** parameters, **EC** parameters and **SC** parameters within the interaction context being considered.

To illustrate the usage of the derived equation above, let us consider, for example, an interaction context that is composed of the following parameters: **IC** = (IC_1, IC_2, IC_3, IC_4, IC_5, IC_6, IC_7) wherein

- IC_1 = {true | false} = if user is manually disabled,
- IC_2 = {true | false} = if user is mute,
- IC_3 = {true | false} = if user is deaf,
- IC_4 = {true | false} = if user is familiar with Braille,
- IC_5 = {quiet | noisy} = environment's noise level,
- IC_6 ={silence required | silence optional} = environment's noise level restriction, and
- IC_7 = {PC or Laptop or MAC | PDA | Cell phone} = user's computing device.

Let us assume further that the intended user is a **visually-impaired** one. In this case, $\mathit{Modality\ Possible} = (VO_{in} \vee M_{in}) \wedge (VO_{out} \vee M_{out})$ wherein there are only 4 suitable modalities, namely *vocal* input and output and *tactile* (or manual) input and output.

Given the above constraints, the set of possible modalities is given by **M** = {M_1, M_2, M_3, M_4, M_5, M_6, M_7, M_8, M_9} wherein M_1 = {M_{in}, M_{out}}; M_2 = {M_{in}, VO_{out}}; M_3 = {VO_{in}, VO_{out}}; M_4 = {VO_{in}, M_{out}}; M_5 = {VO_{in}, M_{out}, VO_{out}}; M6 = {M_{in}, M_{out}, VO_{out}}; M_7 = {M_{in}, VO_{in}, VO_{out}}; M_8 = {M_{in}, VO_{in}, M_{out}}; M_9 = {M_{in}, VO_{in}, M_{out}, VO_{out}}. In this example, let us assume the following interaction context: (a) **user context**: blind with no further handicaps, familiar with Braille; hence IC_1 = False, IC_2 = False, IC_3 = False, IC_4 = True; (b) **environmental context**: the user is in a classroom, then IC_5 = noisy, IC_6 = silence required (c) **system context**: the user works on a laptop; IC_7 = Laptop.

The system now finds the modality that suits the given interaction context. Let us assume that a certain multimodal computing system's SR contains recorded scenarios as shown in Fig. 10. The given figure is generated by using WEKA (*Waikato Environment for Knowledge Analysis*) (Witten and Frank 2005) which is a collection of machine learning algorithms for data mining tasks. It is used in testing a machine learning algorithm as it contains tools for data pre-processing, classification, regression, clustering, association rules, and visualization.

As shown in the diagram, there are already 15 scenarios representing the system's acquired knowledge. The 16th scenario represents a new case. Using Equation 22, and with reference to the given interaction context and SR, the suitability score of Mj (where j = 1 to 9) can be calculated. Let us consider, for instance, the calculations involved with modality $\mathbf{M_1}$:

Suitability_Score (M1) = $P(IC_1 = False \mid M_1) * P(IC_2 = False \mid M_1) * \ldots * P(IC_7 = Laptop \mid M_1) * P(M_1) = 1 * 0.5 * 0 * \ldots * 2/15 = \mathbf{0}$

wherein $P(IC_1 = False \mid M_1) = 2/2$, $P(IC_2 = False \mid M_1) = ½$, $P(IC_3 = False \mid M_1) = 0/2$, $P(IC_4 = True \mid M_1) = 2/2$, $P(IC_5 = Noisy \mid M_1) = ½$, $P(IC_6 = silence\ required \mid M_1) = ½$, and $P(IC_7 = Laptop \mid M_1) = ½$. Also, $P(M_1) = 2/15$.

Similarly, we do calculate the suitability score of all other remaining modalities. Using the same procedure, the modality that yields the highest suitability score is $\mathbf{M_6}$:

Suitability_Score (M_6) = $P(IC_1 = False \mid M_6) \times P(IC_2 = False \mid M_6) \times \ldots \times P(IC_7 = Laptop \mid M_6) \times P(M_6) = 1 \times 2/3 \times 1 \times 1 \times 2/3 \times 1/3 \times 1/3 \times 3/15 = \mathbf{0.00976}$.

By applying the ML algorithm (see Fig. 11), $\mathbf{M_6}$ appears to respect the conditions on possibility of modality; hence, it is chosen as the *optimal modality* for the given **IC**. This new scenario will be added to SR as a newly-acquired knowledge (i.e. as scenario #16 in SR).

ARFF-Viewer - D:\JMM\SR.arff

File Edit View

SR.arff

Relation: Selection_of_Modality

No.	A1 Nominal	A2 Nominal	A3 Nominal	A4 Nominal	A5 Nominal	A6 Nominal	A7 Nominal	class Nominal
1	False	False	False	False	Noisy	Optional	CellPhone	M2
2	True	False	False	False	Quiet	Optional	Laptop	M3
3	False	False	False	True	Noisy	Required	PC	M6
4	False	False	True	True	Quiet	Required	PC	M1
5	False	True	False	True	Quiet	Optional	Laptop	M6
6	False	False	False	True	Quiet	Optional	PC	M9
7	False	False	False	False	Quiet	Optional	PC	M7
8	False	True	True	True	Noisy	Optional	Laptop	M1
9	False	False	False	True	Quiet	Optional	CellPhone	M7
10	False	False	True	True	Quiet	Optional	MAC	M8
11	True	False	False	False	Quiet	Optional	PDA	M3
12	False	False	False	True	Quiet	Optional	Laptop	M9
13	False	False	False	True	Noisy	Optional	PC	M6
14	False	False	True	True	Quiet	Optional	PC	M8
15	False	True	False	False	Quiet	Optional	Laptop	M2
16	False	False	False	True	Noisy	Required	Laptop	???

Fig. 10. A sample snapshot of a scenario repository (SR)

Fig. 11 shows the algorithm in finding the optimal modalities given an instance of interaction context. The first algorithm calculates the suitability score of each element of the power set of **M**, $\mathbb{P}$(**M**) for the given context. The second algorithm finds the optimal modality.

Suitability Score of Modality M_j
Input:
1. Interaction Context IC_i.
2. Modality M_j
3. Scenario repository SR

Output: Suitability score of M_j
Procedure:
1. get IC_i, UC_{max}, EC_{max} and SC_{max}
2. for each UC Parameter UC_i do
3. $P(UC_k/M_j) = P(UC_k/M_j) * P(UC_i/M_j)$
4. endfor
5. for each EC Parameter EC_i do
6. $P(EC_l/M_j) = P(EC_l/M_j) * P(EC_i/M_j)$
7. endfor
8. for each SC Parameter SC_i do
9. $P(SC_m/M_j) = P(SC_m/M_j) * P(SC_i/M_j)$
10. endfor
11. $P(M_j) = \#(M_j)/card(SR)$
12. $Suitability\_Score\_M_j = P(UC_k/M_j)*P(EC_l/M_j)*P(SC_m/M_j)*P(M_j)$
13. Return Suitability_Score_M_j

Endprocedure

Finding_Optimal_Modality
Input:
1. Interaction Context IC_i.
2. Modality set M
3. Scenario Repository SR

Output: Optimal modality
Procedure:
1. get IC_i and Modality set M
2. init = 1
3. Max = Suitability Score of modality M_{init}
4. Optimal_modality = M_{init}
5. for each element M_j of power set of M
6. if (VI_{in} OR VO_{in} OR M_{in}) $\in M_j$ AND (VI_{out} OR VO_{out} OR M_{out}) $\in M_j$ then
7. if Suitability Score of M_j > Max then
8. Max = Suitability Score of M_j
9. Optimal_modality = M_j
10. endif
11. endif
12. endfor
13. Return Optimal_modality

Endprocedure

Fig. 11. Algorithms: (Left) Given an interaction context IC_i, the algorithm calculates the suitability score of each modality M_j belonging to the power set $\mathbb{P}$ (**M**), (Right) Algorithm for finding the optimal modality

Once the optimal modalities for data input and output to the instance of interaction context are chosen, we then proceed to determining whether there are sufficient media devices that will support the selected modalities. If such is the case, then the concerned media devices are activated, otherwise, the optimal modality that was chosen earlier needs to be updated. That is to say that the modality that cannot be supported by available media devices is taken out from the list. This results in the HKA's evaluation if Equation 11 still holds true. If the result is affirmative, then modality is possible, the replacement modality is calculated and the newly found optimal modality is implemented. Otherwise, there is a failure of modality. Generally, there is more than one media device that supports a specific modality. Consequently, when too many devices are available to support the chosen modality, then only the top-ranked media device needs to be activated. Moreover, the ranking of media devices also serves purpose in finding replacement to a failed device. When a top-ranked device is malfunctioning or not available then the device that is next in priority ranking is activated. Given a specific media device D_i ($1 \le i \le n$), where i is priority index and n is the number of media devices that can support the chosen modality M_j, then the probability that it is adopted to implement the chosen modality is given by:

$$P(D_i \mid M_j) = 1 - \sum_{1}^{i-1}(1/n) \tag{26}$$

To demonstrate the essence of the above equation, supposed that there are 3 media devices ($n = 3$) supporting modality M_j, denoted by D_1 (first priority), D_2 (second priority) and D_3 (third priority). The probability that D_1 is selected for implementation of modality M_j is $1 - 0 = 1$, that of D_2 is $1 - 1/3 = 2/3$ and that of D_3 is $1 - (1/3 + 1/3) = 1 - 2/3 = 1/3$. Note that in this work, the numerical subscripts of those devices with higher priority are numerically smaller than the numerical subscript of those with lower priority. Example is device D_1 (subscript is 1) has a higher priority than device D_2 (subscript is 2).

The *media devices priority table* (MDPT) is a tool that we used in implementing the media devices' priority ranking. In MDPT, devices are grouped based on their category and ranked by priority. The top-ranked media device is always chosen for activation. When the highly-ranked device is found defective, the MDPT helps in determining which one replaces the defective one.

When a new media device d_{new} is added or introduced to the system for the first time, the device is associated to a modality and is given a priority ranking r by the user. What happen to the rankings of other devices d_i, ($1 \le i \le n$, and n = number of media devices) which are in the same modality as d_{new} in the MDPT? Two things may happen, depending on the user's selection. The *first possibility* is that after having the new device's priority **Priority(d_{new})** set to r then the priority of the other device i, ($1 \le i \le n$) denoted **Priority(d_i)**, remains the same. The *second possibility* is the priority rankings of all media devices ranked r or lower are adjusted such that their new priority rankings are one lower than their previous rankings. Formally, in Z (Lightfoot 2001), this is specified as: $\forall i, \exists r: \mathbb{N}_1; \forall d_i, \exists d_{new}$: **Devices | (Priority($d_{new}$) = r $\wedge$ Priority(d_i) $\ge$ r) $\Rightarrow$ Priority(d_i)′ = Priority(d_i) + 1**.

We also proposed mechanism for dynamic reconfiguration of the system to make it more fault tolerant, keeping the system persistent and able to resist breakdown in case certain media devices supporting chosen modalities are found to be missing or malfunctioning. Fig. 12 shows how a MDPT is assigned to a specific scenario. Fig. 13 demonstrates how the system finds a replacement to a missing or defective media device.

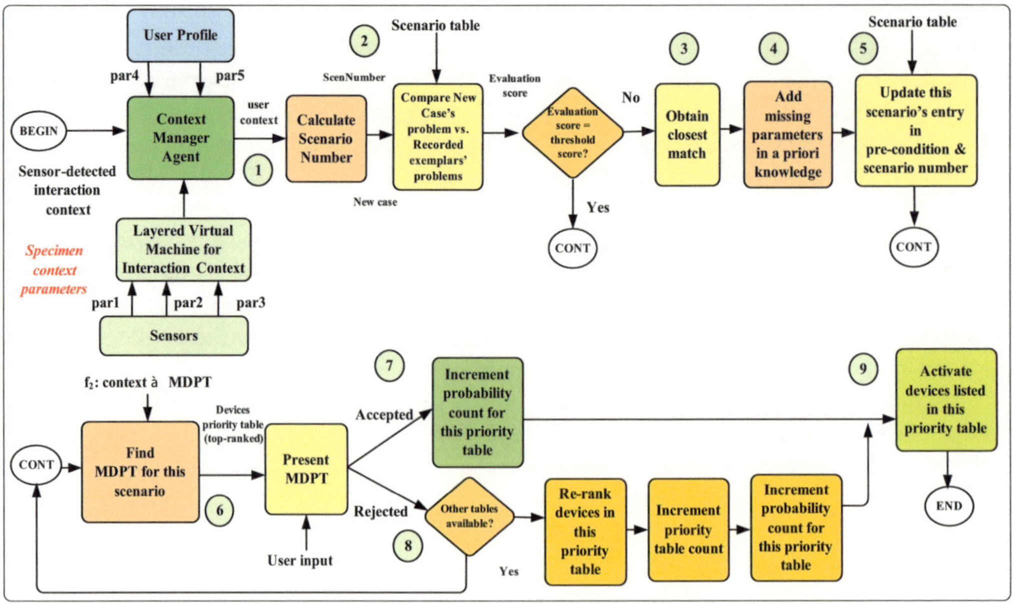

Fig. 12. The training for choosing appropriate MDPT for a specific context

6. Conclusion

This work - **A multi-agent based multimodal system adaptive to the user's interaction context** - is an intelligent system design. It supports pervasive computing, multimedia and multimodal computing, dynamic configuration of software architecture and machine learning. It is a contribution in the domain of the advancement of pervasive multimodality.

Our work supports *transparency* and *calm technology*, realizing Marc Weiser's vision of *ubiquitous computing*. In our work, the computer, as it takes its dynamic configuration to adapt itself to the current instance of interaction context, becomes an information tool that does not demand the focus and attention of the user. The adaptation of the system to provide the end user with the necessary and suitable modality of human-machine communication, supported by its associated media devices yields a result in which the end user concentrates on his computing task and not bothers himself with the intricacies of context awareness and the system's adaptation to it. In effect, the realization of this concept renders the computer to become servant to the user needs rather than the user spending time and effort to serve the needs of the computer.

In connection with our idea that context should be inclusive - meaning that it will fit all definitions of context given by previous researchers - we broaden the notion of context to become interaction context. *Interaction context* refers to the collective context of the user (i.e. user context), of his working environment (i.e. environment context) and of his computing system (i.e. system context). Each of these interaction context elements - user context, environment context and system context - is composed of various parameters that describe the state of the user, of his workplace and his computing resources as he undertakes an activity in accomplishing his computing task, and each of these parameters may evolve over time. To realize the incremental definition of incremental context, we developed a tool called layered *virtual machine for incremental interaction context* which can be used to add, modify and delete a context parameter on one hand and determine the sensor-based context (i.e. context that is based on parameters whose values are obtained from raw data supplied by sensors) on the other.

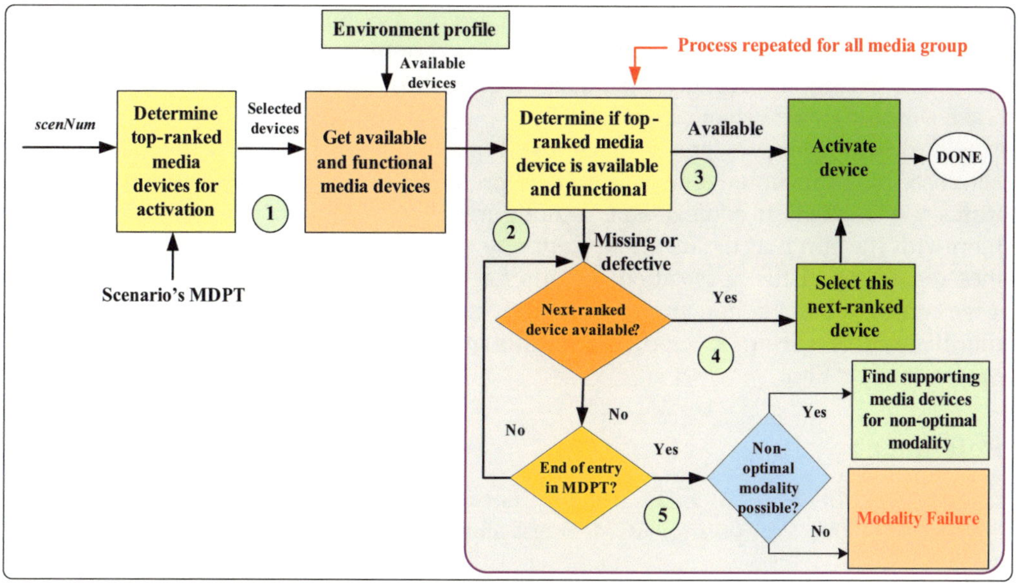

Fig. 13. The process of finding replacement to a failed or missing device

To benefit from the richness of interaction context with regards to communication in human-machine interaction, we invoke the adoption of multimodality which allows for a much wider range of modes and forms of communication, selected and adapted to suit the given user's interaction context. In multimodal communication, multimodality is beneficial to the end user because with multimodality, the weaknesses of one mode of interaction, with regards to its suitability to a given situation, is compensated by replacing it with another mode of communication that is more suitable to the situation. Multimodality also promotes inclusive informatics as those with permanent or temporary disability are given the opportunity to use and benefit from information technology advancement.

In our investigation of the current state of the art, we realize that a great deal of efforts were exerted in defining what context is all about, how to acquire it, how to disseminate it within the system and use it to suit the needs of a system in a specific domain of application (e.g. healthcare, education, etc.). Also, a great deal of efforts on ubiquitous computing were devoted on some application domains (e.g. identifying the user whereabouts, identifying services and tools, etc.) but there was no effort made with regards to making multimodality pervasive and accessible to various user situations. To this end, our work provides for the much needed solutions and answers. Our work is an architectural design that exhibits adaptability to a much larger context called interaction context. It is intelligent and pervasive, adaptive even when the user is stationary or mobile. It has mechanisms serving a specific purpose. That is, given an instance of interaction context, one which evolves over time, our system determines the optimal modalities that suit such interaction context. By optimal, we mean the selection is based on the trade-offs on appropriate multimodality after considering the given interaction context, available media devices that support the modalities and user preferences. We designed a mechanism (i.e. a paradigm) that does this task and simulated its functionality with success. This mechanism employs machine learning and uses case-based reasoning with supervised learning. An input to this decision-making component is an instance of interaction context and its output is the most optimal modality and its associated media devices that are for activation. This mechanism is tasked to continuously monitor the user's interaction context and on behalf of the user continuously adapts accordingly. This adaptation is through dynamic reconfiguration of the pervasive multimodal system's architecture.

Our work differs from previous works in the domain in the sense that while others capture, disseminate and consume context to suit its preferred domain of application, our system captures the interaction context and reconfigures its architecture dynamically in generic fashion with the aim that the user may continue working on his task anytime, anywhere he wishes regardless of the application domain he wishes to undertake. In effect, the system that we come up with, being generic in design, can be integrated with ease or little amount of modification to various computing systems of various domains of applications. This is our main contribution.

7. References

Abowd, G. D. and Mynatt, E. D. (2000). Charting Past, Present and Future Research in Ubiquitous Computing. *ACM Transactions on Computer-Human Interaction* 7(1): pp. 29 - 58.

Banavar, G., Beck, J., et al. (2000). Challenges: An Application Model for Pervasive Computing. *6th Annual Intl. Conf. on Mobile Computing and Networking* (MobiCom 2000), Massachusetts, USA.

Bennett, F., Richardson, T., et al. (1994). Teleporting - Making Applications Mobile. *IEEE Workshop on Mobile Computing Systems and Applications*. Santa Cruz, California: pp. 82 - 84.

Buxton, W. (1983). Lexical and Pragmatic Considerations of Input Structures. Computer Graphics *Journal of the ACM* 17(1): pp. 31 - 37.

Chen, G. and Kotz, D. (2000). A Survey of Context-Aware Mobile Computing Research. *Technical Report*, Department of Computer Science, Darmouth College.

CMU_CS. (2010). Speech at CMU. from www.speech.cs.cmu.edu.

Coutaz, J., Crowley, J. L., et al. (2005). Context is key. *Communications of the ACM* 48(3): pp. 49-53.

CS_Rutgers. (2010). The Vision, Interaction, Language, Logic and Graphics Environment. from http://www.cs.rutgers.edu/~village/.

DeVaul, R. W. and Pentland, A. S. (2000). The Ektara Architecture: The Right Framework for Context-Aware Wearable and Ubiquitous Computing Applications. *MIT Technical Report*.

Dey, A. K. (2001). "Understanding and Using Context " *Springer Personal and Ubiquitous Computing* 5(1): pp. 4 - 7.

Dey, A. K. and Abowd, G. D. (1999). Towards a Better Understanding of Context and Context-Awareness. *1st Intl. Conference on Handheld and Ubiquitous Computing*, Karlsruhe, Germany, Springer-Verlag, LNCS 1707.

Dey, A. K., Salber, D., et al. (2001). A Conceptual Framework and a Toolkit for Supporting the Rapid Prototyping of Context-Aware Applications. *Human- Computer Interaction Journal* 16(2-4): pp. 97-166.

Djenidi, H., Lévy, N., et al. (2004). Generic Multi-Agents Architecture for Multimedia Multimodal Software Environment. *International Journal of Object Technology* 3(8,): pp. 147-168.

Djenidi, H., Ramdane-Cherif, A., et al. (2002). Dynamic Multi-agent Architecture for Multimedia Multimodal Dialogs. *IEEE Workshop on Knowledge Media Networking.*

Djenidi, H., Ramdane-Cherif, A., et al. (2003). Generic Multimedia Multimodal Agents Pradigms and their Dynamic reconfiguration at the Architecture Level. Architecture for Software Environment. *Eurasip : European Journal of Applied Signal Processing- Special Issue on Multimedia Apllications.*

Dong, S. H., Xiao, B., et al. (2000). Multimodal user interface for internet. Jisuanji Xuebao/*Chinese Journal of Computers* 23(12): pp. 1270-1275.

Efstratiou, C., Cheverst, K., et al. (2001). An Architecture for the Effective Support of Adaptive Context-Aware Applications. *2nd Int. Conf. in Mobile Data Management* (MDM'01), Hong Kong.

Elrod, S., Bruce, R., et al. (1992). Liveboard: a large interactive display supporting group meetings, presentations and remote collaboration. *ACM Conference on Human Factors in Computing Systems*, Monterey, CA, USA.

Esler, M., Hightower, J., et al. (1999). Next Century Challenges: Data-Centric Networking for Invisible Computing. *5th Annual Intl. Conference on Mobile Computing Networking* (MobiCom'99), Seattle, WA, USA.

Eustice, K., Lehman, T. J., et al. (1999). A Universal Information Appliance. *IBM Systems Journal* 38(4): pp. 575-601.

Garlan, D., Siewiorek, D., et al. (2002). Project Aura: Towards Distraction-Free Pervasive Computing. *IEEE Pervasive Computing, Special Issue on Integrated Pervasive Computing Environments* 21(2): pp. 22 - 31.

Gwizdka, J. (2000). "What's in the Context?". Workshop on Context-Awareness, *CHI 2000, Conference on Human factors in Computing Systems*, The Hague, Netherlands.

Held, A. (2002). Modeling of Context Information for Pervasive Computing Applications. *6th World Multiconference on Systemics, Cybernetics and Informatics* (SCI2002), Orlando, FL.

Hina, M. D., Tadj, C., et al. (2009). Autonomic Communication in Pervasive Multimodal Multimedia Computing System. Book "*Autonomic Communication*". Vasilakos, A. V., Parashar, M., Karnouskos, S. and Pedrycz, W., Springer: pp. 251 - 283.

Horn, P. (2001). Autonomic Computing: IBM's Perspective on the State of Information Technology, *IBM Research*: pp. 1 - 22.

Indulska, J., Loke, S. W., et al. (2001). An Open Architecture for Pervasive Systems. *3rd Intl. Work. Conf. on Distributed Applications and Interoperable Systems* (DAIS 2001), Kraków, Poland.

Indulska, J., Robinson, R., et al. (2003). Experiences in Using CC/PP in Context-Aware Systems. *4th Intl. Conf. on Mobile Data Management*, Melbourne, Australia.

Kallenberg, O. (2002). *Foundations of Modern Probability*, Springer.

Kantarjiev, C. K., Demers, A., et al. (1993). Experiences with X in a wireless environment. Mobile & Location-Independent Computing *Symposium on Mobile & Location-Independent Computing*, Cambridge, MA, USA.

Kephart, J. O. and Chess, D. M. (2001). The Vision of Autonomic Computing, *IBM Thomas J. Watson Research Centre*: pp. 41 - 50.

Kindberg, T. and Barton, J. (2001). A Web-Based Nomadic Computing System. *Elsevier Computer Networks* 35(4): pp. 443-456.

Kolodner, J. (1993). *Case-Based Reasoning*. San Mateo, CA, Morgan Kaufman.

Lajmi, S., Ghedira, C., et al. (2007). Une méthode d'apprentissage pour la composition de services web. *L'Objet* 8(2): pp. 1 - 4.

Lightfoot, D. (2001). *Formal Specification Using Z*, 2nd ed., McMillan Press.

Mitchell, T. (1997). *Machine Learning*, McGraw-Hill.

Oviatt, S. (2002). *Multimodal Interfaces: Handbook of Human-Computer Interaction*. New Jersey, USA, Lawrence Erbaum.

Pascoe, J. (1998). Adding Generic Contextual Capabilities to Wearable Computers. 2nd *IEEE Intl. Symposium on Wearable Computers* Pittsburg, IEEE Computer Society.

Prekop, P. and Burnett, M. (2003). Activities, context and ubiquitous computing. *Computer Communications* 26(1): pp. 1168-1176.

Razzaque, M. A., Dobson, S., et al. (2005). Categorization and Modelling of Quality in Context Information. IJCAI 2005 *Workshop on AI and Autonomic Communications*, Edinburg, Scotland.

Ringland, S. P. A. and Scahill, F. J. (2003). Multimodality - The future of the wireless user interface. *BT Technology Journal* 21(3): pp. 181-191.

Schilit, B., Adams, N., et al. (1994). Context-aware computing applications. *First Workshop on Mobile Computing Systems and Applications*, WMCSA 1994, Santa Cruz, California, USA, .

Schilit, B. N., Adams, N., et al. (1993). The PARCTAB mobile computing system. *Fourth Workshop on Workstation Operating Systems* (WWOS-IV), Napa, CA, USA.

Schilit, B. N. and Theimer, M. M. (1994). Disseminating Active Map Information to Mobile Hosts. *IEEE Network* 8(5): pp. 22 - 32.

Strang, T. and Linnhoff-Popien, C. (2003). Service Interoperability on Context Level in Ubiquitous Computing Environments. *Intl. Conf. on Advances in Infrastructure for Electronic Business, Education, Science, Medicine, and Mobile Technologies on the Internet* (SSGRR 2003), L'Aquila, Italy.

Truman, T. E., Pering, T., et al. (1998). The InfoPad multimedia terminal: a portable device for wireless information access. *IEEE Transactions on Computers* 47(10): pp. 1073-1087.

Want, R., Hopper, A., et al. (1992). Active badge location system. *ACM Transactions on Information Systems* 10(1): pp. 91-102.

Want, R., Schilit, B. N., et al. (1995). Overview of the ParcTab ubiquitous computing experiment. *IEEE Personal Communications* 2(6): pp. 28-43.

Weiser, M. (1991). The computer for the twenty-first century. *Scientific American* 265(3): pp. 94 - 104.

Weiser, M. (1993). Some computer science issues in ubiquitous computing. *Communications of the ACM* 36(7): pp. 74-84.

Weiser, M. and Brown, J. S. (1996). Designing Calm Technology. *Powergrid Journal* 1(1): pp. 94 - 110.

Witten, I. H. and Frank, E. (2005). *Data Mining: Practical Machine Learning Tools and Techniques*, 2nd ed. San Francisco, Morgan Kaufmann.

3

Scenario-Based Modeling of Multi-Agent Systems

Armin Stranjak[1], Igor Čavrak[2] and Mario Žagar[2]
[1]*Software Centre of Excellence, Rolls-Royce Plc., Derby*
[2]*University of Zagreb, Faculty of Electrical Engineering and Computing*
[1]*United Kingdom*
[2]*Croatia*

1. Introduction

Constant expansion of network-centric services inevitably led into development of new software technologies that would enable seamless and transparent access to the expanding amount of information. The software agent-oriented model fits convincingly well within this context as a better-suited technology over typical modular, client-server approach. This model offers concepts like autonomous behavior, competitive or collaborative interactions, and seamless integration with the legacy systems (Jennings et al., 1999). Based on their capabilities and predefined and/or accumulated knowledge, agents can react to changes by adapting to the new circumstances if a better approach is identified. This results in a dynamic system, well suited to coping with an ever-changing environment. Agents individually choose to co-operate or compete with other agents in order to satisfy their own objectives, but by setting goals appropriately, their collective behavior can be engineered to achieve global system-wide objectives. This approach is an efficient way of handling the complexity of many modern software systems.

Within the competitive market context, agents interact with each other in order to win access to the shared resources, to get a better price or to bet for more processing power, etc. while trying to fulfill their plans by achieving given goals. Alternatively, cooperative environment promotes such agents that will perform their goals in the interest of the wider community or the authoritative entity that secures the fulfillment of the global goal. Typical examples would be applications for task planning and resource scheduling, search engines, or any other where the emergent behavior is influenced by collaborative and mutually non-exclusive individual goals.

Regardless of the environment characteristics used, agent's communication is achieved through asynchronous and message-oriented interactions. In addition to physical connection, it requires semantics in order to enable agents to reach the concluding state of the interaction through common understanding of the messages and their meanings. Consequently, the dialogue ontology and conversational semantics has to be defined within the framework of a conversation space. This space is defined as a sequence of messages exchanged between agents following a (set of) defined dialogue protocol(s). Dialogue protocols enable agents to take part in conversations by committing to the shared protocol semantics and defined conversation space within which agents are enabled to act, still preserving their decision-making autonomy (Greaves et al., 2000). The space boundary is defined by the definition of (1) an ontology of common terms that agents need to agree upon, (2) a language for ontology description, and (3) a language for a conversation description.

There are several conversation models identified in existing literature. A Belief-Desire-Intention (BDI) scheme is described in (Bratman et al., 1988) but it suffers from the semantic verification problem (Wooldridge, 2000). Although the MAP (Walton, 2002) language introduces an interesting concept of scenes and roles, its agent-centric nature increases complexity of conversation verification where inconsistent and unstructured protocols are not easy to detect. (Endriss et al., 2003) introduces the idea of protocol definition within the agent's own business logic. The similar idea is present in the IOM/T (Doi et al., 2005) language where the main focus is on message flow between agents. On the other hand, the language relies on a particular agent runtime platform which prevents it to be considered for large-scale adoption.

In this paper, we introduce a SDLMAS language for scenario description in multi-agent systems. The language is independent of the agent runtime platform and implementation language, and it is focused on a definition of message flow between agents providing intuitive scenario description. The paper also addresses corresponding SDLMAS platform purposely built for rapid design and development of agent-based systems. The platform includes a code generator from the SDLMAS language into a target implementation language and an agent platform. The generated code integrates seamlessly with the rest of the platform that provides scenario execution runtime framework, leaving complexity of interactions and message propagation hidden from the developer. Obviously, the agent's own business logic which is domain specific, provided as a generated code skeleton, needs to be populated manually with the desired functionality.

The SDLMAS language was developed in support of multi-agent simulation system for prediction and scheduling of engine overhaul in aerospace industry (Stranjak et al., 2008). Complexity of scenario descriptions between engine fleet managers and engine repair stations required significant design, development and testing efforts. Such difficult problem would require a declarative language for conversation framework definition within which simultaneous interactions would occur without explicit specification of their ordering or timing. In addition to this, a requirement to define intertwining protocols was necessary to enable cross-scenario communication. In other words, this would allow agents to achieve given tasks or gather required information within one scenario and to communicate them to the other. These agents would need to maintain several conversations simultaneously during negotiations for the best shop visit time and repair slot while utilizing balance between revenue earned from the engines in service and an acceptable risk of disruption. Current scenario description languages cannot satisfy given requirements and therefore it was necessary to define a new interaction description language and to build a corresponding platform.

The SDLMAS platform was developed as a development and runtime environment for the multi-agent systems whose scenarios are described using the SDLMAS language. The platform equips a designer with the mechanisms to define negotiation scenarios and a developer with the automatically generated components for message passing, execution of scenario actions and invocation of given business procedures, allowing him or her to concentrate only on development of domain specific actions that agent needs to perform during conversations. This way, the development cycle was shorten several times with significantly increased reliability of the system after deployment.

2. Related work

As a part of an initiative to formalize and define the process of design and implementation of multi-agent systems, numerous models and methodologies (Gomez-Sanz et al., 2003) (Wood et al., 2000) (Wooldridge et al., 2000) were developed in the last several decades. Agent interactions are ingredient element of design, development and deployment of such systems.

Agent UML is one of the popular models to visually represent agent interactions (Paurobally et al., 2003a). It is based on the UML standard in order to mitigate a paradigm shift from object-oriented to agent-based concepts, and to enable standardized notation for analysis, design and implementation of agent systems. In order to include concepts of roles and behaviors, UML class and sequence diagrams are extended by specificities of agent interactions. Since AUML is a visual language, it is necessary to define the ways of its transformation into textual notation of protocols in order to achieve practical usability, and various language transitions are proposed (Warmer et al., 1999) (Winikoff, 2005). In spite of these efforts, AUML lacks enough representation capabilities of agent's states, which causes an inability to define conditions under which messages can be received or sent by an agent. Additionally, it lacks the expressiveness and clarity, especially in case of complex multi-lateral scenario definitions. Although AUML lacks some features mentioned above, it has influenced other language designs (Warmer et al., 1999) (Winikoff, 2005) (Dinkloh et al., 2005) (Huget, 2002) and modeling frameworks (Quenum et al., 2006). The OCL language (Warmer et al., 1999) is the way to represent UML in a textual format and it can be used to represent AUML too but it was shown to have limited usability (Richters et al., 1998).

Petri Nets (Cost et al., 1999) also offers interesting perspective on agent-based scenario definitions, but due to lack of clarity and scalability for medium-to-complex scenarios, it is not very appropriate for description of agent conversations, especially for popular protocol like Contract-Net (Purvis et al., 2002).

Belief-Desire-Intention (BDI) scheme (Bratman et al., 1988) is another popular model for description of agent's functionality through definition of agent's goals that should be fulfilled by executing tasks based on knowledge base about its immediate environment. Although the model influenced definitions of widely accepted FIPA and ACL (FIPA) standards, it suffers from the "semantic verification" problem (Wooldridge, 2000) where it is not possible to guarantee the equal understanding of ontology terms by all agents involved.

The MAP language (Walton, 2003) for dialogue protocol definition is based on the principles found in Electronic Institutions (Estava et al., 2001) while its semantics is inspired by logic which is basis for communication and parallel systems (Milner, 1989). The language organizes dialogue definitions in scenes, an interaction context within which agents are communicating with each other. Another key concept is an agent's role, a certain set of behaviors that an agent will adopt during interactions. An interaction protocol is adopted by an agent based on the role agent plays. The MAP language is not based on message flows as the way how protocol is defined but on agent-centric approach. This means that agent's action is defined separately for every agent which implies significant effort of protocol validation and analysis since the protocol definition is scattered across several agents.

The IOM/T language (Doi et al., 2005) introduces a formal way of mapping interaction protocol from AUML and in general emerged from a tendency to strictly define protocols in a textual notation. Unlike the MAP language, the language is based on message flow which means the definitions of protocol-related agent activities are not separated but defined in the single definition. Unfortunately it lacks some important characteristics related to scenario descriptions.

Firstly, there is no explicit definition of message performative used in conversations. A protocol is defined as a sequence of messages whose character is determined by corresponding performatives. If the language lacks formal explicit definition of message performatives, message validity needs to be performed within the agent's business logic. This increases the complexity of the logic implementation with additional performance penalties since irrelevant or protocol-incompatible messages will not be immediately rejected after their arrival but during their processing. Furthermore, it is not possible to determine the differences between conversational and terminating performatives which prevents an agent to explicitly recognize a conversation completion. Since there is no clear distinction between performative types, it is also not possible to define conditions under which messages can be forwarded to the business logic or just ignored.

Secondly, the cardinality of agent instances is bound to the protocol implementation inside agent's internal logic. The protocol description is linked with the given scenario and the number of agent instances in a dialogue. If it is required to change a cardinality of agent instances, the protocol description needs to be modified too in order to reflect this update since the business logic defines the interaction description including agent instance cardinality. Consequently, it is not possible to change number of instances of a particular agent without re-implementing the internal implementation.

Thirdly, an implementation of agent's internal logic is language-dependent on the JADE agent platform (JADE), which disables possibility of usage IOM/T language in another agent platform.

Q Language (Ishida, 2002) is another language for interaction protocol definition in a textual form. Its main purpose is to define interactions with a user or other agents on behalf of a user. Consequently, it is not based on message flows in the way that SDLMAS is. Typically, scenario description will be considered only from the point of view of one agent who is supposed to interact with other parties assuming their prior knowledge about the scenario they are supposed to follow.

Popularity of scenario-based development of multi-agent systems is increasing and several interesting applications can be found in rescue simulation (Shinoda et al., 2003), interactive TV program (Shirai et al., 2007), modeling and simulations (Donikian, 2001), etc.

3. Scenario description language

The SDLMAS scenario description language, together with the SDLMAS run-time framework, represents the core component of the SDLMAS platform. The language has been designed with the main purpose of rapid design and development of multi-agent systems. In order to fulfill those goals three main language properties had to be achieved:

- Simple and intuitive creation of scenarios in multi-agent systems but yet capable enough to support complex agent interaction descriptions,
- Expressive language for strict and flexible interaction within the described multi-agent system,
- Abstraction of run-time environment in order to protect its users from run-time complexities related to interaction management within a large multi-agent system.

The SDLMAS language is a declarative, interaction-centric description language, designed with the purpose of defining permitted sequences of messages (communicative acts) exchanged among interaction participants (agents in a multi-agent system). An interaction protocol is defined implicitly, as a sequence of agent actions where order of those actions is important, thus achieving a sequential approach in protocol definition. The language describes conversations among agents as a sequence of conversation actions, where actions define a conditional mapping between incoming and outgoing messages, and an agent's internal logic. Conditions for reception and transmission of messages are defined explicitly as a part of a conversation protocol definition. An elementary action of the language is defined as a procedure that will be executed as a consequence of a condition being satisfied following reception of one or more messages. A scenario is formed of a logically complete sequence of conversation actions aimed at achieving some rational effect in the multi-agent system.

The language is restrained to a communication aspect of multi-agent systems, thus enforcing strict separation between conversation actions and internal agent logic implementing agent reasoning. Although direct influence on agent decision process is not possible, inadequate expressiveness could indirectly restrict or bias the way agent reasons or acts, or simply fail the attempt to model interactions of required complexity. The SDLMAS language provides adequate expressiveness through achievement of the following:

- Parallelism in agent interactions, defining synchronization communication points,
- Definition of conditions on incoming and outgoing messages, including complex logical expressions based around message types and agents as sources or targets of incoming and outgoing messages,
- Controlled variations in message exchanges during scenario execution, effectively defining a set of allowed scenario instances from one scenario definition,
- Complex runtime interaction within non-trivial multi-agent systems are mainly caused by following requirements:
    - To support many scenario instances an agent can concurrently participate in,
    - To handle simultaneous conversations with several agents within potentially several scenario instances of the same scenario, and to ensure conversation adherence to scenario defined rules,
    - To maintain conversation state with a particular agent within a scenario instance and correctly terminate conversations,
    - To correctly handle exceptions during conversation, both at the execution and at the protocol level.

Most of these required system properties are hidden from the developer by the built-in platform run-time mechanisms. Developed scenarios are completely independent of the agent platform and implementation language due to language's declarative nature and strict separation of communication aspects of multi-agent system from implementation of agents' internal business logic. As such, they allow relatively simple analysis and consistency validation, as well as transformation into alternative models. As the final step in the process of modeling and designing interactions within a multi-agent system, defined interaction scenarios are transformed into a program code for target agent platform and implementation language.

3.1 Example scenarios

In this chapter two example agent interaction scenarios are given in order to present the key elements and characteristics of the SDLMAS language. The examples are focused on a multi-agent system concerned with electrical power consumption planning and run-time power reallocation. All the power consumers, producers and brokering system elements are represented as one or more intelligent agents forming a virtual energy market. The main focus of the system is to ensure short and long term power allocation among consumers and power usage patterns such that the goals of the system can be fulfilled as optimally as possible, depending on variable internal and external system conditions. The three presented scenarios are just a small subset of scenario definitions required to completely define a conversational behavior of the system.

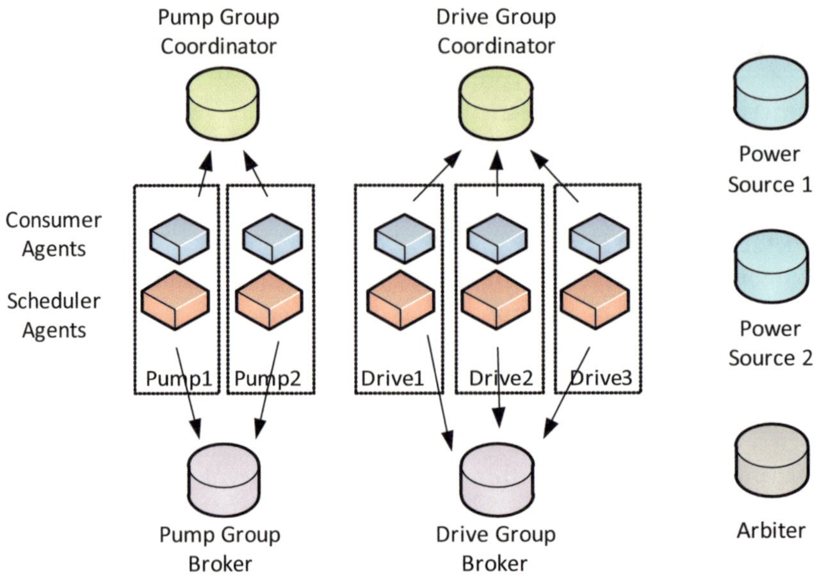

Fig. 1. Example multi-agent system

The structure of the described multi-agent system is depicted on Figure 1 including all agent types, their relations and mapping of agent types to physical system components. Each physical power consumer within the described system is represented by one Consumer type agent, concerned with current and near-future power consumption, and one Scheduler type agent in charge of power consumption planning and power allocation. Power consumers are organized into consumer groups of similar characteristics and managed by Coordinator agents. Pre-allocated power reservations from various system power sources are held by Coordinator agents allowing them to immediately serve consumer demands for additional power, if existing allocations suffice. If not, additional power is sought by coordinators from two agent types: Broker agent types and Power Source agent types. Such a process requires complex and simultaneous negotiations among many power sources and coordinator agents in order to identify the best offer or a combination of offers that would meet the initial request at an acceptable price. Broker agents negotiate power requests originated from Coordinator agents, examine and coordinate power reservation changes with Scheduler agents within their coordination group, and sell power surpluses in exchange for future power reservations or an immediately collected fee. Power Source agents represent various power sources in the system and their inherent characteristics (availability, current price etc).

The DynamicPowerRequest scenario depicts a situation where a consumer, a high-pressure pump, is required to complete an unplanned action and requires additional power to perform it. Such power reallocation must be negotiated in a specified time frame and with minimal impact on other system functions.

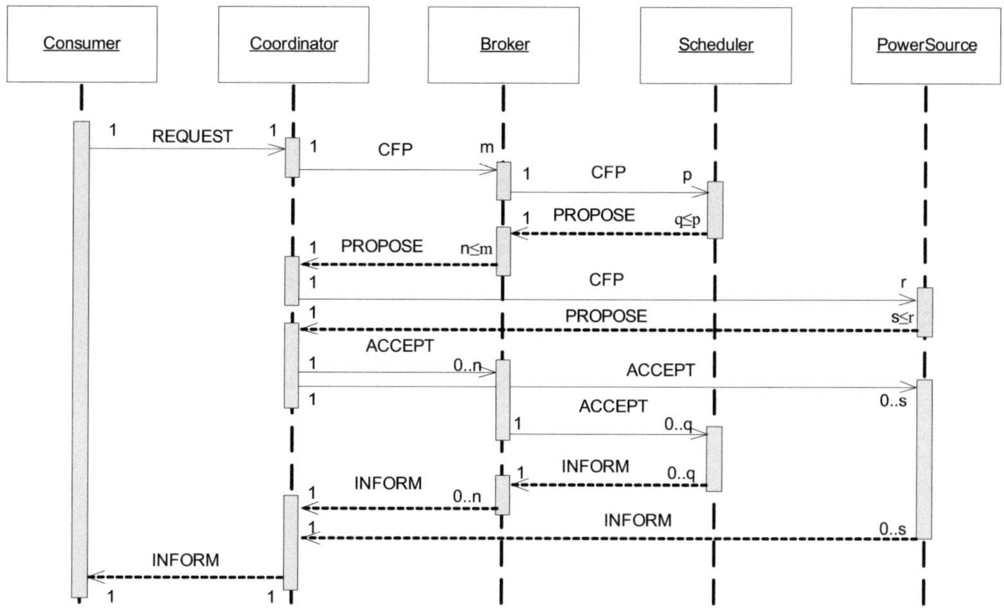

Fig. 2. Sequence diagram of the DynamicPowerRequest interaction scenario

Request for additional power is delivered to the agent's group Coordinator agent, where a decision is made based on a locally available pre-allocated power surplus. A requested amount of power can immediately be allocated to the pump if the sufficient amount of power is available to the coordinator, or the power can be sought from other sources such as other consumer groups and active power sources. In order to obtain additional power a CFP is issued by the coordinator agent to all the other coordinators in the system (represented by Power Broker agents). Power Broker agents can immediately deny or propose release of their pre-allocated power surpluses for compensation, or they can consult their managed Scheduler agents, by issuing a CFP, for any excess power or plan rescheduling. In any case, an offer or a refuse message is returned to the requesting Coordinator agent, determined on the basis of availability of pre-allocated Power Broker power or willingness of consumers within a Power Broker coordinated groups to release (sell) their power reservations. A call for proposal is also issued by the Coordinator agent to all of the system's active power sources and power production proposals collected. All the received offers are evaluated on the basis of their temporal characteristics and compensation requested from the originating source (both in form of future power allocations and immediate fees), and the most affordable one is selected.

The result of this complex interaction among the system's actors is finally relayed to the requesting high-pressure pump power consumer. If no satisfactory offer has been received, the requested unplanned action cannot be performed. Figure 2 contains a very simplified sequence diagram of the described interactions, lacking most of the details concerning alternative conversation paths and hiding a large amount of possible variations within the execution of scenario. The key characteristic of the presented interaction that makes

(A)UML sequence diagrams less suitable is its intertwining description of three contract net protocols where results from one protocol influence execution of other protocols. In addition, there are large sections of parallel conversations among agents and optional executions of certain scenario parts, that makes rendering of their description in UML very complicated and hard to interpret.

The *PowerAuction* scenario describes a simplified version of the regular power allocation mechanism to all interested Broker agents (details of interactions between Broker and Scheduler agents have been omitted for clarity reasons). A Power Source agent with available power within a certain time frame announces power availability to all Broker agents within the system. Such an announcement must be approved by the Arbiter agent (only one instance of Arbiter agent is present in the system). In the first step, Broker agents express their interest by submitting the first bid or leave the auction scenario immediately. As the next step a variant of English auction is employed to allocate available power to one or more highest bidders. At the end of auction participating Broker agents are informed of the final auction result by the Power Source agent. A simplified UML diagram of the interactions is presented in Figure 3.

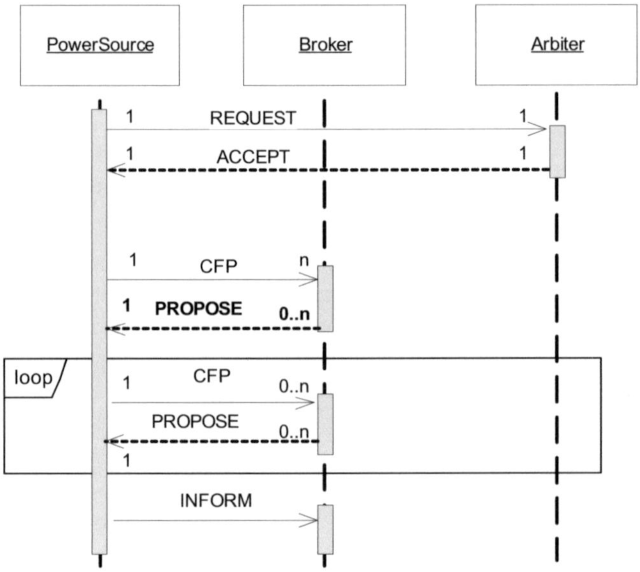

Fig. 3. Sequence diagram of the Power Auction interaction scenario

3.2 SDLMAS Scenario definition example

```
agent @consumer        : Consumer
agent $coordinator     : Coordinator;
agent @coordinator     : Broker;
agent $consumer, $localConsumers : Scheduler;
agent @psource         : PowerSource;
agent arbiter          : Arbiter;

scenario DynamicPowerRequest [reentrant=no] {
```

```
action Consumer in powerRequest() {
  msgSnd : (REQUEST -> $coordinator);
}

action Coordinator in rcvPowerRequest() {
  msgRcv : (REQUEST <- @consumer);
  msgSnd : (CFP -> <Broker>) |
           (#INFORM_DONE -> @consumer);
}

action Broker in rcvPowerReleaseCFP() {
  msgRcv : (CFP <- @coordinator);
  msgSnd : (CFP -> <$localConsumers>) |
           (PROPOSE | #REFUSE -> @coordinator);
}

action Scheduler in rcvPowerReleaseCFP() {
  msgRcv : (CFP <- @coordinator);
  msgSnd : (PROPOSE | #REFUSE -> @coordinator);
}

action Broker in collectPwrReleaseRsp(){
  msgRcv : (PROPOSE | #REFUSE <- <$localConsumers>);
  msgSnd : (PROPOSE | #REFUSE -> @coordinator);
}

action Coordinator in collectPwrReleaseRsp() {
  msgRcv : (PROPOSE | #REFUSE <- <Broker>);
  msgSnd : (CFP -> <PowerSource>);
}

action PowerSource in processPwrRequestProposal() {
  msgRcv : (CFP <- @coordinator);
  msgSnd : (PROPOSE | #REFUSE -> @coordinator);
}

action Coordinator in decideOnPwrAllocationOffers() {
  msgRcv : (PROPOSE | #REFUSE <- <PowerSource>);
  msgSnd : (ACCEPT | #REJECT -> <Broker>) &
           (ACCEPT | #REJECT -> <PowerSource>);
}

action PowerSource in allocatePower() {
  msgRcv : (ACCEPT | #REJECT <- @coordinator);
  msgSnd : (#FAILURE | #INFORM_DONE -> @coordinator);
}

action Broker in releasePower() {
  msgRcv : (ACCEPT | #REJECT <- @coordinator);
  msgSnd : (ACCEPT | #REJECT -> <$localConsumers>);
```

```
  }

  action Scheduler in confirmPwrRelease() {
    msgRcv : (ACCEPT | #REJECT <- @coordinator);
    msgSnd : (#FAILURE | #INFORM_DONE -> @coordinator);
  }

  action Broker in collectConsumerCommits() {
    msgRcv : (#FAILURE|#INFORM_DONE <- <$localConsumers>);
    msgSnd : (#FAILURE | #INFORM_DONE -> @coordinator);
  }

  action Coordinator in collectPwrAllocationCommits() {
    msgRcv : (#FAILURE|#INFORM_DONE <- <Broker>) &
             (#FAILURE |#INFORM_DONE <- <PowerSource>);
    msgSnd : (#REFUSE | #INFORM_DONE -> @consumer);
  }

  action Consumer in receivePwrAllocationRsp() [timeout=2000] {
    msgRcv : (#REFUSE | #INFORM_DONE <- $coordinator);
  }
}

scenario PowerAuction {

  action PowerSource in requestAuction() {
    msgSnd : (REQUEST -> arbiter);
  }

  action Arbiter in auctionRequest() {
    msgRcv : (REQUEST <- @psource);
    msgSnd : (ACCEPT | #REJECT -> @psource);
  }

  action PowerSource in initialCFP() {
    msgRcv : (ACCEPT | #REJECT <- arbiter);
    msgSnd : (CFP -> <Broker>);
  }

  action Broker in auctionStart() {
    msgRcv : (CFP <- @psource);
    msgSnd : (PROPOSE | #REFUSE -> @psource);
  }

  loop {
    action PowerSource in cfp1() {
      msgRcv : (PROPOSE | #REFUSE <- <Broker>);
      msgSnd : (CFP -> <Broker>);
    }

    action Broker in loopProps() {
```

```
111       msgRcv : (CFP <- @psource);
112       msgSnd : (PROPOSE | !REJECT -> @psource);
113     }
114 
115     action PowerSource in cfp2() {
116       msgRcv : (PROPOSE | !REJECT <- <Broker>);
117       msgSnd : (#INFORM -> <Broker>);
118     }
119   }
120 
121   action Broker in endAuction() {
122     msgRcv : (#INFORM <- @psource);
123   }
124 }
```

3.3 SDLMAS elements

SDLMAS language describes conversational behavior of multi-agent systems based on a number of agent types (roles), agent references and a set of interaction scenarios. Each scenario involves all or a subset of defined agent references in a sequence of conversational actions performed by involved agents. SDLMAS scenario descriptions are stored in a form of a text file where the header part contains the definitions of agent types and agent references, while the rest of the file (body) contains one or more scenario definitions.

3.3.1 Roles, scenarios and conversation actions

SDLMAS defines roles as standardized patterns of behavior required of all agents participating in conversations. SDLMAS employs an implicit approach to role behavior definition, as opposed to commonly used explicit state-based agent-centric approach. Each agent role behavior is defined by a number of role belonging conversational actions within all scenarios.

Inter-agent communication is not addressed on the single agent level, but defines communication patterns among different agent roles, thus leaving concrete scenario execution to adapt to current system structure. A single agent within a concrete multi-agent system can be assigned more than one role, and can participate in many parallel scenario instances. A metadata mechanism can be used to control specific execution behavior of scenarios, roles or actions in such a case.

At line 5 of the example the Power Source role is declared together with an anonymous reference of the same type. Power Source role behavior is defined by a sequence of conversation actions processPwrRequestProposal and allocatePower from DynamicPowerRequest scenario and requestAuction, initialCFP, cfp1 and cfp2 conversation actions from PowerAuction scenario.

SDLMAS scenario is defined by a unique scenario name and a sequence of conversation actions implicitly defining one interaction protocol. In a given SDLMAS example, scenario declarations start at lines 8 and 83.

Conversation actions are defined within scenario scope and are attached to agent roles. Each conversation action defines a procedure and two communication conditions. The procedure represents an internal agent logic function, and is invoked by the SDLMAS runtime framework upon satisfaction of communicative preconditions. Communicative postconditions ensure that all messages generated by internal agent's procedure conform to message transmission conditions. Regular conversation actions are defined using both preconditions and postconditions, but other types can have incomplete conversation conditions: scenario triggering action (first scenario action) does not define a precondition and conversation terminating action (last scenario action) does not define a postcondition.

Communicative preconditions and postconditions are defined with respect to message performative(s) and message originating agent role(s). A communicative precondition defines circumstances under which a received message or a set of received messages are being passed to an internal procedure implementing agent logic. A condition consists of a list of expected message performatives and their originating agent roles, and can form expressions using logical operators. Communicative postcondition lists messages and their performatives, generated by an execution of an internal agent logic procedure, to be sent to corresponding agent roles.

A simple communicative action condition is formed of an atomic communicative condition consisting of a required message performative and a target or source agent reference (examples on lines 38 or 86). A more flexible atomic condition definition is allowed by stating a list of required performatives separated by *or* operator symbol '|', defining "one of" semantics (line 28). Complex conditions are formed of a number of atomic conditions combined using logical operators *or* and *and* (symbol '&') in conjunction with parenthesis as grouping operator (line 22).

Sequential nature of conversations among agents can be described using only simple conditions. In the example scenario PowerAuction, a Power Source agent first requests a clearance from arbiter agent (line 86), and only after the clearance is granted (ACCEPT performative received) call for proposal messages are sent to all Broker agents in the system (line 96). Achieving conversation parallelism among agents of differing roles requires usage of complex conversation conditions. For example, Coordinator agent accepts or rejects Broker and PowerSource proposals in parallel (lines 48 and 49), effectively defining a "span" point (decideOnPwrAllocationOffers) and a corresponding "join" point in action collectPwrAllocationCommits (lines 73 and 74).

3.3.2 Conversation context

A conversation context represents a scenario instance execution within an agent. It encapsulates all the elements that define the scenario instance state, such as state of the conversation (current conversation action), communicative conditions and active constraints, values of agent references etc. A new conversation context is created as a consequence of two different communication events. The first event is the activation of the scenario triggering action, regardless of the activation method used (external or internal). Created conversation context is called a root conversation context and is a parent context to all the conversation contexts created during the scenario instance execution. In this case the initiator and the owner of the context is the agent that triggered the scenario. A conversation context is also created when an agent receives a message that activates the first conversation action in a scenario for a role the agent plays. The initiator of this context is the agent that initiated the conversation (triggered the context creation). A parent-child context relation is created in this case, forming the tree structure of conversation contexts with root context as the owner. Termination of a parent context implies termination of all contexts in the parent context sub tree. On Figure 4 a complete conversation context tree is presented for a

DynamicPowerRequest scenario execution, where pump1 Consumer agent requests additional power.

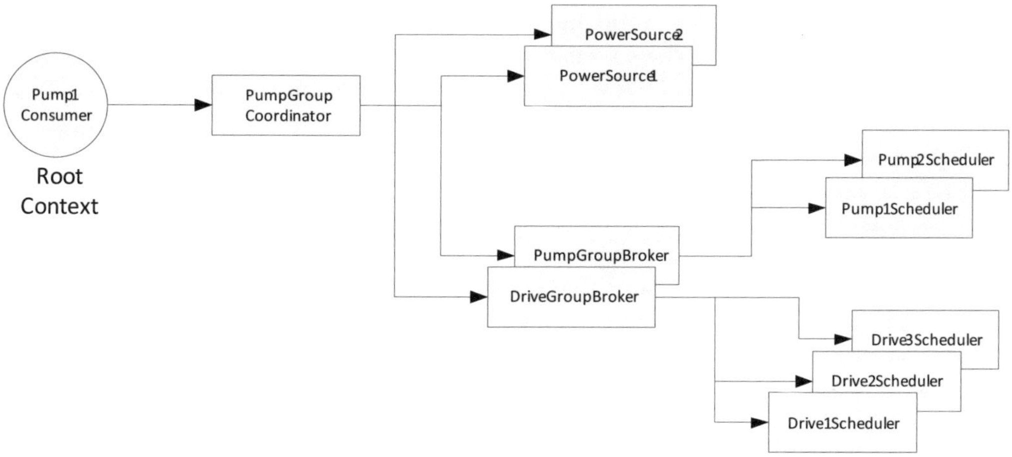

Fig. 4. Conversation context tree for Dynamic Power Request scenario execution

A single agent can be simultaneously involved in more than one scenario execution, thus having more than one active conversation context. In case an agent is assigned more than one role, and those roles participate in the same scenario, a situation can occur where the same conversation context is recursively activated (reentrant context). Reentrancy can be disabled on the scenario level by explicitly setting scenario property using metadata mechanism (line 8).

3.3.3 Conversation loops

In SDLMAS, a sequence of recurring conversational actions is defined as a loop. In scenario definition, recurring actions are isolated within a loop scope, defined by a loop keyword and curly braces (lines 104-123). Loops are a special version of nested scenarios, not addressed in this text. Additional requirements and semantics are defined for loop scoped conversation actions:

- The first and the last conversation action must be attached to the same agent role,
- Loop must be terminated by loop context termination (exchange of loop terminating performatives) or scenario context termination (exchange of scenario terminating performatives),
- Communicative precondition of the first conversation action and the postcondition of the last action are not part of the loop,
- The first action precondition is evaluated only once, upon start of the loop scenario execution. At line 106, PROPOSE or #REFUSE performatives are received from Broker agents only once, and CFP sent (line 107) to those who had not left the scenario with terminating performative #REFUSE,
- The last action postcondition is evaluated only once, upon loop termination by exchange of loop terminating performatives (lines 112 and 116), when all Broker agents refuse to submit a new bid,
- On all but first loop cycle, communicative precondition of the last action is effectively treated as the precondition of the first action (i.e. line 116 is 'copied' to line 106).

A loop conversation context is created upon when scenario execution enters the loop. All reference values are copied to the loop conversation context. Depending on the performative type used, group membership modifications are either confined to loop scope (loop terminating performatives) or propagated to scenario conversation context (scenario terminating performatives). When scenario execution leaves the loop, loop conversation context is collapsed, and original scenario context is again declared the active one.

3.3.4 Agent references

Agent references represent a single agent or a group of agents of a specified role. All agent references must be declared in the head section of SDLMAS file. A reference is characterized by its role, cardinality (single or group) and binding method. Five agent reference types are used in the current version of the SDLMAS language: *verbatim, variable, anonymous, group* and *group variable* references. Multiple conversation contexts active on the same agent have distinct reference bindings. All but verbatim references retain their bindings only for the duration of their enclosing conversation context.

Verbatim reference value is fixed at scenario definition and represents a specific agent within the system (usually references a singleton role agent). The example system hosts only one agent of role Arbiter, whose verbatim reference 'arbiter' is defined on line 6. Line 86 contains usage of that reference, where REQUEST performative is sent by a PowerSource role agent to the 'arbiter' agent.

Variable reference value must be bound by the agent logic during a new conversation context initialization and retains its initial value throughout the context lifetime. Example declarations of variable references (reference name prefixed by '$' symbol) can be found on lines 2 and 4. In powerRequest action (line 11) an agent of type Consumer initiates a DynamicPowerRequest scenario by sending a REQUEST message to its coordinator agent (each Consumer agent must be aware of its Coordinator agent).

Anonymous reference (names prefixed with '@' symbol) value binding is performed by the framework during creation of a new child conversation context - triggered by the reception of a scenario-triggering message. Lines 1, 3 and 5 contain declarations of anonymous references. Line 27 contains an example of an anonymous reference binding, where a new child conversation context is created in one of Scheduler agents and reference @coordinator is assigned to agent of type Broker, the one who dispatched a CFP message to the particular Scheduler agent. Anonymous reference value is preserved throughout the conversation context lifetime. Lines 63 and 64 contain an example of anonymous reference usage during the conversation context lifetime. As the reference value is invariable, reception and transmission of messages with @coordinator agent is performed with the same agent who triggered the conversation context creation at line 27.

Group references refer to more than one agent at a time. There are two types of group references defined in the current version of SDLMAS; *role group* references and *variable group* references. Both group references are populated at the time of conversation context creation. During conversation context lifetime agents can retain or leave the membership of a group reference, but new agents cannot be added to once initialized group reference. Agents leave a membership as a consequence of explicit exchange of scenario- or loop-terminating performatives, or an implicit reception of #TIMEOUT performative.

Role group reference name is enclosed within angled brackets and denotes all agents of a particular type (role) present in the system at the moment a group population is bound to a reference. Population identification and binding is performed by the SDLMAS platform during runtime and is hidden from scenario designers and developers. Line 16 of the DynamicPowerRequest scenario contains an example where a Coordinator agent dispatches a CFP message to all of the Broker agents, and at line 37 collects responses. Broker agents that terminated a conversation by returning a #REFUSE message are removed from the group reference membership.

Variable group reference name is prefixed with '$' symbol and enclosed within angled brackets. Those references differ from role group references only in the method of agent biding; while role group references are populated externally (by the SDLMAS runtime), group variable references are populated by internal agent logic, and follow the same philosophy as variable references. Group variable reference usage example can be found at line 59, where a Broker agent sends an ACCEPT or #REJECT message to all the Scheduler agents currently bound to the group variable.

3.3.5 Performatives

SDLMAS differentiates among four performative types: *conversational, scenario-terminating, loop-terminating* and *implicit performatives*. Conversational performatives preserve the active conversation context. All performatives not prefixed with special symbols '!' and '#' are conversational performatives.

Scenario-terminating performatives, prefixed with '#' symbol, explicitly denote an end of conversation between two or more agents within an active scenario instance. Run-time effect of scenario-terminating performative is determined by the hierarchical relation between affected conversation contexts: child context is being terminated and parent context performs revision of group reference memberships and, if, necessary, constraint elimination process. If the result of the constraint elimination process is an empty constraint structure, parent scenario instance is also being terminated. Termination of root context implies a scenario instance termination. An example of scenario-terminating performative usage can be found on line 43, where PowerSource role agent communicates a PROPOSE (conversational) or #REFUSE (scenario-terminating) performative to the requesting Coordinator role agent.

Loop-terminating performatives, prefixed with '!' symbol, explicitly denote an end of loop scoped conversation between two or more system agents. In case of loop terminating performative being communicated, child loop conversation context is being collapsed and parent loop context undergoes a procedure similar to one in case of scenario-terminating performative. The major difference between scenario-terminating and loop-terminating performatives is that termination (collapse) of loop contexts does not affect states of base conversation context references and constraints (their values are restored after the loop scoped interaction is terminated), but scenario-terminating performatives do. If the PowerSource agent (line 106) receives a #REFUSE performative from one of the Broker agents, that agent is evicted from the <Broker> group reference until the end of scenario execution. But if PowerSource receives a !REJECT performative from another Broker agent (line 116), that Broker agent is temporarily evicted from the <Broker> group reference only until the end of active loop. Consequently, #INFORM performative (line 117) will be sent to all Broker agents that had not communicated a #REFUSE performative or whose response had been timed out and replaced with implicit #TIMEOUT performative.

Implicit performatives are performatives generated by the runtime SDLMAS system in response to a specific event. Implicit performatives can be conversational (explicitly defined using scenario metadata mechanisms) or scenario-terminating. #TIMEOUT performative is generated by the SDLMAS runtime every time a message from a certain agent is not received within an expected time frame. On line 79, if #REFUSE or #INFORM_DONE performative is not received within 2 seconds from sending the REQUEST performative to the $coordinator agent (line 11), the Consumer agent will receive a #TIMEOUT performative instead.

3.3.6 Metadata

In order to provide a system designer with a mechanism to express required runtime scenario execution properties, a concept of scenario metadata definition has been introduced in the SDLMAS language. Metadata is expressed in form of a sequence of semicolon separated name-value pairs enclosed in square brackets and are placed immediately beside declarations of affected scenario elements. Line 78 of the example contains a timeout metadata definition, effectively forcing a #TIMEOUT performative to be generated if no response has been received from $coordinator agent within 2 seconds after the REQUEST performative had been issued (line 11). Metadata properties are defined on a per-language element basis (role, scenario, action).

4. SDLMAS platform

SDLMAS platform provides tools and a framework for implementation and runtime support of multi-agent systems whose interactions are modeled using SDLMAS language.

4.1 SDLMAS platform components

The following components make a set of core elements of a multi-agent system that is developed using the SDLMAS platform: a generic SDLMAS component (Management agent), application-specific SDLMAS components (Application agents) and underlying agent platform components (ORB and Naming Service agent).

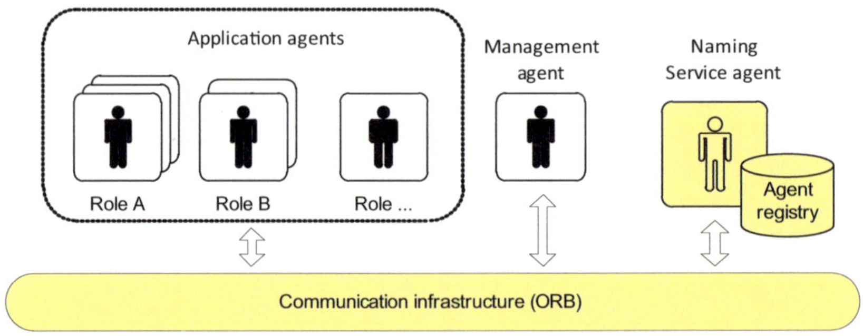

Fig. 5. SDLMAS Platform

The SDLMAS platform (Cavrak et al., 2009) relies on core functionality provided by target agent platform such as agent creation and multithreaded execution of agents, FIPA compliant messaging, agent container management, naming service as a central storage of agent references, etc. Upon their successful initialization, all agents are required to register with the Naming Service agent, and to deregister prior to their deactivation. Accurate information stored in the registry is crucial for correct behavior of late agent reference binding mechanism:

- Agent's type (role) is verified using the information from the registry in order to bind an anonymous reference to a real agent reference,
- All agents of the required type (role) are collected from the registry in order to bind a group reference to a list of acquired agents references.

Management agent, a mandatory system element, provides a support for bootstrapping and initialization of a multi-agent system based on provided global and agent-specific configurations.

Functionality of a multi-agent system is based on individual functionalities of system-constituting entities and on effects of interaction among those entities. A SDLMAS application agent plays a particular role in the system as it is defined in the scenario description. Conformance to the given role is guaranteed by generated program code from the description and must not be modified by an agent developer. Other portions of agent code, related to internal agent logic, are partially generated code skeletons where a developer is required to only implement agent's procedures within already predefined procedure signatures and parameter definitions.

System start-up procedure is as follows: (1) Naming Service Agent and Management Agent are started, (2) based on system configuration and scenario descriptions, the Management Agent starts a number of Application Agents, (3) Application Agents register at the Naming Service Agent, (4) a number of scenarios are initiated by the Management Agent based on scenario descriptions, with specified application agents as their initiators.

4.2 Automatic code generation

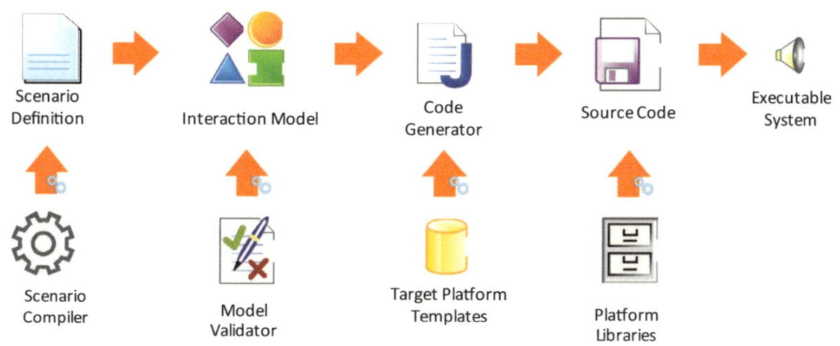

Fig. 6. SDLMAS Code Generation

The process of converting a SDLMAS scenario definition to a source code for a target agent platform is depicted on Figure 6. A text file containing agent type declarations and scenario definitions is converted to an internal model, suitable for both scenario validation and code generation. Platform-specific set of code templates are used to generate source code for the target agent platform. This way, the flexibility and transparency in choosing another target agent platform or implementation language is achieved as this approach allows easy retargeting of generated agent code by using different code templates. Generated source entities are divided into two main categories: model-level entities, shared among many system components, and scenario-level entities, containing role- and scenario-specific implementation of agent communication behavior.

SDLMAS scenario definition can be converted into platform code in two ways: a command line based tool and an Eclipse plug-in. The plug-in allows for easier syntax checking, model transformation and validation, as well as navigation between scenario definition and generated implementation code. Internal interaction model is stored in an EMF-based model and JET templates are used for generating the Java code. Currently the JADE platform (JADE) is supported.

A SDLMAS agent implementation can be divided into three main layers: Platform Abstraction Layer (PAL), SDLMAS Platform Layer (SPL) and Application Logic Layer (ALL).

PAL abstracts the specificities of the target platform programming interfaces and semantics and provides the SDLMAS platform with the generic interface towards the target platform resources. This layer is clearly dependent on the target platform and it must be developed for each platform the SDLMAS is ported to.

SPL consists of two sets of components: generic components and scenario-dependent components. Generic components provide support for scenario- and role-independent functionality and is provided in a form of a library. Scenario-dependent components are automatically generated from SDLMAS scenario description and it contains necessary functionality for tracking conversation progress and its contexts, enforcing message reception and transmission conditions and invoking internal agent logic procedures.

ALL encapsulates agent's internal application logic. It is partially automatically generated and it requires developer's further intervention to implement agent's internal procedures that will handle incoming messages and create outgoing messages during conversation progress, based on the agent's action definition in the scenario description(s).

5. Conclusion

Complex interactions within all but most simple multi-agent systems present a serious challenge during system design, implementation, testing and runtime analysis. Several approaches addressing those challenges have been employed so far and their strengths and weaknesses are outlined in this text. A scenario-based approach to modeling interactions in multi-agent systems is described, based on a notion of sequences of conversation actions, grouped into scenarios, describing conversational behavior of interacting agents. Scenarios are described by system designers using a proposed SDLMAS declarative language. The effect of using SDLMAS language and platform should be reflected in the significantly reduced effort invested during design and development of the communication aspect of a new multi-agent system, as well as in maintenance phase. A new version of SDLMAS allows for both linear and non-linear conversation sequences (loops), as well as increased runtime behavior control using metadata specification within scenario definitions.

Valid scenario models, resulting from processing of SDLMAS descriptions, are used for executable agent code generation for supported target agent platforms. SDLMAS Runtime framework provides runtime support for execution of SDLMAS based multi-agent systems and for gathering runtime behavioral data and its off-line analysis for profiling and optimization purposes.

6. References

Bratman, M. E., Israel, D. J., Pollack, M. E. (1988). Plans and Resource-Bounded Practical Reasoning. *Computational Intelligence*, 4 (1988), pp. 349-355.

Cavrak I., Stranjak, A., Zagar, M. (2009). SDLMAS: A Scenario Modeling Framework for Multi-Agent Systems. *Journal of Universal Computer Science,* Vol. 15, No.4, (June 2009), pp. 898-925.

Cost, R., Chen, T., Finin, T., Labrou, Y., Peng, Y. (1999). Modeling Agent Conversations With Colored Petri Nets. *Proc. Workshop on Specifying and Implementing Conversation Policies,* Seattle, USA (1999), pp. 59-66.

Dinkloh, M. Nimis, J. (2003). A Tool for Integrated Design and Implementation of Conversations in Multiagent Systems. *Proc. AAMAS03 PROMAS Workshop on Programming Multi-Agent Systems Selected Revised and Invited papers,* Melbourne, Australia (2003), pp. 187-200.

Doi, T., Tahara, Y., Honiden, S. (2005). IOM/T: An Interaction Description Language for Multi-Agent Systems. *Proc. 4th International Joint Conference on Autonomous Agents and Multiagent Systems* (AAMAS'05), Utrecht, Netherlands (2005), pp. 778-785.

Donikian S., (2001). HPTS: A Behaviour Modelling Language for Autonomous Agents, *AGENTS'01,* May 28 - June 1, 2001, Montreal, Quebec, Canada

Endriss, U., Maudet, N., Sadri, F., Toni, F. (2003). Protocol Conformance for Logic-based Agents. *Proc. 18th International Joint Conference on Artificial Intelligence* (IJCAI-2003), Acapulco, Mexico (2003), pp. 679-684.

Estava, M., Rodriguez, J. A., Sierra, C., Garcia, P., Arcos, J. L. (2001). On the Formal Specifications of Electronic Institutions. In *Agent Mediated Electronic Commerce,* The European AgentLink Perspective, Lecture Notes In Computer Science vol. 1991. Springer-Verlag, London (2001), pp. 126-147.

FIPA: Foundation for Intelligent Physical Agents. Available at: http://www.fipa.org

Gomez-Sanz, J. J., Fuentes, R. (2003). Agent Oriented Software Engineering with INGENIAS. *Proc. 3rd International Central and Eastern European Conference on Multi-Agent Systems CEEMAS 2003,* Prague, Czech Republic (2003), pp. 394-403.

Greaves, M., Holmback, H., Bradshaw, J. (2000). What Is a Conversation Policy? In *Issues in Agent Communication,* F. Dignum and M. Greaves, Eds. Lecture Notes In Computer Science, vol. 1916. Springer-Verlag, London, UK (2000), pp. 118-131.

Huget, M. P. (2002). A Language for Exchanging Agent UML Protocol Diagrams". Technical Report ULCS-02-009, The University of Liverpool, Computer Science Department, UK (2002).

Ishida, T., Q. (2002). A Scenario Description Language for Interactive Agents. *Computer,* 35, 11 (2002), pp. 42-47.

JADE: Java Agent Development Framework. Available at: http://jade.cselt.it

Jennings, N. R., Wooldridge, M. (1999). Agent-Oriented Software Engineering. *Proc. 9th European Workshop on Modeling Autonomous Agents in a Multi-Agent World: Multi-Agent System Engineering* (MAAMAW-99), Valencia, Spain (1999), pp. 1-7.

Milner, R., (1989). Communication and Concurrency. Prentice-Hall International (1989).

Paurobally, S., Cunningham, J. (2003). Achieving Common Interaction Protocols in Open Agent Environments. *Proc. 2nd international workshop on Challenges in Open Agent Environments* (AAMAS 03), Melbourne, Australia (2003).

Purvis, M. K., Cranefield, S., Nowostawski, M.,Ward, R., Carter, D., Oliviera, M. A. (2002). Agent Cities Interaction Using the Opal Platform. *Proc. Workshop on Challenges in Open Agent Systems, The 1st International Joint Conference on Autonomous Agents and Multiagent Systems* (AAMAS02), Bologna, Italy (2002).

Quenum, J. G., Aknine, S., Briot, J-P, Honiden, S. (2006). A Modelling Framework for Generic Agent Interaction Protocols. *Proc. 4th International Workshop on Declarative Agent Languages and Technologies*, Hakodate, Japan (2006), pp. 207-224.

Richters, M., Gogolla, M. (1998). On Formalizing the UML Object Constraint Language. *Proc. 17th International Conference on Conceptual Modeling*, Singapore (1998), pp. 449-464.

Stranjak, A., Dutta, P. S., Ebden, M., Rogers, A., Vytelingum, P. (2008) A Multi-Agent Simulation System for Prediction and Scheduling of Aero Engine Overhaul. *Proc. 7th International Conference on Autonomous Agents and Multiagent Systems: industrial track* (AAMAS2008), Estoril, Portugal (2008), pp. 81-88.

Shinoda, K., Noda, I., Ohta, M. (2003). Application of Parallel Scenario Description for RoboCupRescue Civilian Agent. *RoboCup 2003 International Symposium*, Padua, Italy July 10-11, 2003.

Shirai, T., Takano, M., Miyahara, H., Tajima, K., Kandori, K., Shimojo, S. (1999). Agent Enabled Scenario Language for Production of Interactive TV Program. *IEEE Pacific Rim Conference on Communications, Computers and Signal Processing* (PACRIM 1999), 22 Aug 1999 - 24 Aug 1999.

Walton, C. D. (2003). Multi-Agent Dialogue Protocols *Proc. 8th International Symposium on Arti_cial Intelligence and Mathematics*, Fort Lauderdale, Florida (2003).

Warmer, J., Kleppe, A. (1999). OCL: The Constraint Language of the UML Journal of Object-Oriented Programming (1999), pp. 10-13.

Winikoff, M. (2005). Towards Making Agent UML Practical: A Textual Notation and a Tool *Proc. 5th International Conference on Quality Software* (QSIC'05), Melbourne, Australia (2005), pp. 401 - 412.

Wooldridge, M. (2000). Semantic Issues in the Verification of Agent Communication Languages. *Autonomous Agents and Multi-Agent Systems*, 3, 1 (2000), pp. 9-31.

Wood, M. F., DeLoach, S. A. (2000). An Overview of the Multiagent Systems Engineering Methodology *Proc. 1st International Workshop on Agent-Oriented Software Engineering*, Limerick, Ireland, 2000., pp. 207-221.

Wooldridge, M., Jennings, N. R., Kinny, D. (2000). The Gaia Methodology for Agent-Oriented Analysis and Design. *Autonomous Agents and Multi-Agent Systems Archive*, 3, 3, pp. 285-312.

4

Modelling Multi-Agent System using Different Methodologies

Vera Maria B. Werneck[1], Rosa Maria E. Moreira Costa[1] and Luiz Marcio Cysneiros[2]
[1]*Universidade do Estado do Rio de Janeiro,*
[2]*York University,*
[1]*Brazil*
[2]*Canada*

1. Introduction

The increasing use of multi-agent systems brings challenges that have not been studied yet, such as: how we should adapt requirements elicitation to cope with agent properties like autonomy, sociability and proactiveness. The agent-oriented modelling is proposed as a suitable software engineering approach for complex organizational application domains that deal with the need for new applications. These requirements are not broadly considered by current paradigms. Autonomy and sociability aspects such as the dependency of an agent on another, and how critical this condition should be, have to be analysed from the early stages of the software development process (Wooldridge & Jennings, 1997).

This research work is included in the Agent-oriented Project that has been developed by the Informatics and Computer Science Department of State University of Rio de Janeiro (UERJ) and the School of Information Technology of York University (Toronto). This project aims at studying and comparing agent-oriented software development methods and techniques based on attributes and norms and by the models construction based on an exemplar. These experiments enabled the development and construction of Multi-Agent Systems applied to Health and Education areas, providing research on Systems (MAS) especially on the agent proliferation of control, communication and availability of information and knowledge in different computing environments.

The construction of Multi-Agent Systems allows experiments on the agent-oriented technology in relation to development methodologies with regard to agent-oriented programming environments. It also allows us apply this technology in practical and real applications in Health and Education Domains. The Glycemic Monitor System based on the Guardian Angel for aiding the diabetes treatment (Tavares et al., 2010) and the Educ-MAS (Education Multi-Agent System) (Gago et al., 2009), (Dantas et al., 2007), a learning education environment with multi-agents helping the teaching process on a specific topic, are two examples of Multi-Agent Systems that have been developed in the project Oriented Agents.

Many methodologies applying agent-oriented concepts to software development have been proposed however, the evaluation of these methodologies is not an easy task specially to choose the best method to be adopted in a MAS project. In this project, we have used an exemplar proposed by Yu & Cysneiros (2002) to evaluate some methodologies and language methods (Gaia, MESSAGE, Tropos, Adelfe, MAS-CommonKADS, MaSE, Ingenius, KAOS, AUML) (Souza et al., 2010), (Souza et al., 2009), (Werneck et al., 2008), (Werneck et al., 2007), (Werneck et al., 2006), (Coppieters et al., 2005), (Cysneiros et al., 2005), (Cysneiros et al., 2005a). This exemplar is rich and complex enough to guide us to investigate to understand them better. Now we are compiling the experiences we gathered from all the methodologies we evaluated to try and understand where most methodologies need to improve and where most of them are well developed. This knowledge will be modelled into an ontology and will be used to define an Agent-Oriented Methodology Approach based on the Situation Method Engineering (SME) that provides a flexible way of constructing a methodology based on a set of method fragments and the situation of the project requirements. This idea of using SME for constructing Agent-Oriented Methodology was also proposed by Henderson-Sellers & Ralyté (2010) that describes some experiences of using SME in MAS and object oriented methods.

This chapter provides a deep modelling overview of two different Multi-agents systems in two different Agent-Oriented Methodologies. Our objective is to demonstrate how modelling the problem with a methodology can improve quality and be a guide for further MAS development.

This chapter is organized into 5 sections. Section 2 gives an overview of Multi-Agent Systems methodologies describing the Adelfe (Bernon et al., 2003) (Henderson-Sellers & Giorgini, 2005), and Mase (Deloach, 2001), (O'Malley et al., 2001), (Dileo et al., 2002), (Henderson-Sellers & Giorgini, 2005) methodologies that will be shown in the next two sections. Section 3 describes the modelling of Guardian Angel System in Adelfe focusing on the mains aspects of agent oriented. Section 4 presents the modelling of the Educ-MAS using MaSE. Finally section 5 analyses the systems development with those methodologies concluding the work and also presents correlated and future works.

2. MAS methodologies

Many agent-oriented methodologies have been proposed based on a variety of concepts, notations, techniques and methodological guidelines. Some of these methodologies rely on standard methods or modelling languages as CommonKADS (Schreiber et al, 1999) and UML (Rumbaugh et al., 2004). The MAS-CommonKADS (Iglesias & González, 1998), (Henderson-Sellers & Giorgini, 2005) and AUML (2007), (Odell et al., 2001) extended CommonKADS (Schreiber et al., 1999) and UML (Rumbaugh et al., 2004) respectively to meet the multi-agent systems.

The agent-oriented methodologies have multiple roots (Figure 1). Some are based on the idea of artificial intelligence coming from the knowledge engineering (KE). Other methods originate from software engineering and they are extensions of object-oriented (OO) paradigm. There are still those that use a mix of concepts based on these two areas and some are derived from other agent-oriented methodologies.

Although we are going to present two methodologies based on Object Oriented in this chapter, both Adelfe and MaSE methodologies were chosen because they are based on common agent concepts and they are easy to understand having a good methodology guide and a tool support. A tool is a very important issue that can be a differential in the software development.

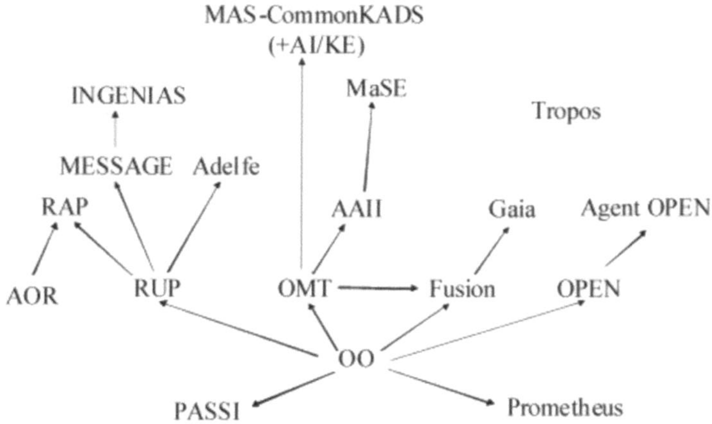

Fig. 1. Influences of Object-Oriented Methodologies on Agent-oriented Methodologies (Henderson-Sellers & Giorgini, 2005)

2.1 The Adelfe methodology

Adelfe is an acronym that translated from French means "framework to develop software with emergent functionality" (Adelfe, 2003), (Bernon et al., 2003), (Henderson-Sellers & Giorgini, 2005) and was developed to deal with open and complex agent problems. These systems work with composed agents that have cooperative interactions with each other and are called Adaptative Multi-Agent Systems (AMAS). .

Adelfe uses AUML principle (Odell et al., 2001), (AUML, 2007) together with UML (Rumbaugh et al., 2004) to express agent interaction protocols.

The development process of Adelfe is based on RUP (Rational Unified Process) (Krutchen, 2000) with some additions considering AMAS Theory specificities. For example, the environment characterization of the system and the identification of cooperation failures are some characteristics included in this process.

Adelfe provides some tools including one to estimate the AMAS technology adequacy. This can be a great support to inexperienced developers in the AMAS system field. The adequacy is studied at two levels: the global (the system) and the local (the components). Eight parameters are taken into consideration for the global level while for the components there are other three parameters.

Two other tools (Open Tool and Interactive Tool) are available to integrate the framework. The Open tool is a graphic modelling tool which supports Adelfe notation to construct the artefacts proposed in this method such as some UML diagrams and protocols of AUML interaction. The Interactive Tool provides the developer with a guide throughout the process application.

The Adelfe process covers all the phases of a classical software process from the requirements to the deployment based on the RUP process adapted to AMAS. Only the work definitions (WD) of requirements, analysis and design require modifications to be adapted for the AMAS. The rest of the RUP can be applied without modifications.

2.1.1 Preliminary and final requirements (WD1 e WD2)

The preliminary requirements work definition (WD1) of Adelfe (Adelfe, 2003), (Bernon et al., 2003), (Henderson-Sellers & Giorgini, 2005) is the same as proposed by the RUP (Table

1). The aim still consists of studying the stakeholders' needs to produce a document of the stakeholders and the developers´ agreement.
The activity of the environment characterization (A6) of the final requirements (WD2) (Table 1) was added to the RUP because the environment is a very important concept in AMAS theory. The environment has to be well comprehended and the A6 activity has the following tasks: determine the entities, define the context and characterize the environment. The characterization begins by the identification of the entities which interact with the system and the restrictions of these interactions (A6-S1). An entity in Adelfe is an actor classified as passive or active. An active entity can act in an autonomous and dynamic way with the system. A passive entity is considered a resource of the system that can be used or modified by active entities. The classification of the entities is essential in AMAS since the agents will be part of the system treated as active entities.
Define context (A6-S2) is an activity that analyses the environment through the interaction among entities and the system by defining UML sequence and collaboration diagrams. The information flow of passive entities and the system are expressed by collaboration diagrams, while interactions among active entities and the system are described by sequence diagrams. The Adelfe methodology defines these diagrams based on the result of the previous step (A6-S1) where the entities were pre-defined with the support of the set of keywords provided in (A4).

WD_1: Preliminary Requirements	**WD_2: Final Requirements**
• A_1: Define user requirements	**A6: Characterize environment**
• A_2: Validate user requirements	• S1: Determine entities
• A_3: Define consensual requirements	• S2: Define context
• A_4: Establish keywords-set	• S3: Characterize environment
• A_5: Extract limits constraints	A7: Determine use cases
	• S1: Draw inventory of use cases
	• **S2: Identify cooperation failures**
	• S3: Elaborate sequence diagrams
	A8: Elaborate UI (user interface) prototypes
	A9: Validate UI prototypes

Table 1. WD1 and WD2– Preliminary and Final Requirements in Adelfe (2003)

Completing the environment characterization, the developer performs the Step A6-S3 describing the environment in terms of being accessible (as opposed to "inaccessible"), continuous (as opposed to "discrete"), deterministic (as opposed to "non-deterministic"), or dynamic (as opposed to "static").
Cooperative agents are a central concept in Adelfe so the developer can be able to construct AMAS. The analysis of all the unexpected and harmful events is important to realize what the causes and consequences of non-cooperative situations are for the agents. These cooperation failures are exceptions. Taking this aspect into account, the determination of the use cases is modified by adding the step (A7-S2) in which cooperation failures must be identified using specific notation.
The elaboration of user interface (UI) prototypes activity (A8) models the graphic users interface (GUI) specifications used in the interactions defined in A6 and A7. GUIs are evaluated in A9 as functional or non-functional (ergonomics, design, ...) requirements. Sometimes in this phase it is necessary to go back to activity A8 to improve UI.

2.1.2 Analysis (WD3)

Adelfe Analysis phase (Table 2) is composed by three activities: (i) AMAS adequacy verification activity (A11) to identify agents and interaction among the entities, (ii) agents identification activity (A12) to analyse the entities defined in A6 that will be considered an agent in the system and (iii) the study of the interactions between entities activity (A13) to analyse all different types of interactions between active/passive entities, between active entities and between agents (Adelfe, 2003), (Bernon et al., 2003), (Henderson-Sellers & Giorgini, 2005).

The Adelfe AMAS technology adequacy verification of the system activity (A11) is performed using the adequacy tool which considers two levels of study: global (A11-S1) and components (A11-S2). The Global analysis answers the question: "Is an AMAS technology implementation to the system necessary?" For the local level the question is "Does any component need to be implemented as AMAS?" If the tool answers the first question positively, the developer can continue applying the process. If the second answer is also affirmative, the Adelfe methodology should be applied on the components considered as AMAS since they require evolution.

The developer identifies the components of the system studying use cases and scenarios previously elaborated in the domain analysis (Adelfe, 2003), (Bernon et al., 2003), (Henderson-Sellers & Giorgini, 2005).

A10: Analyse the Domain • S1: Identify classes • S2: Study interclass relationships • S3:Construct preliminary class diagrams **A11: Verify the AMAS adequacy** • S1: Verify it at the global level • S2: verify it at the local level.	**A12: Identify Agents** • S1: Study entities in the domain context • S2: Identify potentially cooperative agents • S3: Determine agents **A13: Study Interactions between Entities** • S1: Study active/passive entities relationships • S2: Study active entities relationships • **S3: Study agents relationships**

Table 2. WD3 - Analysis in Adelfe (2003)

The cooperative agents are a central concept of AMAS system. In Adelfe the agents are cooperative entities that satisfy at least the autonomy requirements, the local objective and the interaction with other entities. After assessing all the possible agents, the classes are marked with the cooperative agent stereotype.

In Adelfe, agents are not previously known thus the developer must identify them (A12). Entities which demonstrate properties such as autonomy, local objective to pursue, interaction with other entities, partial view of its environment and the ability to negotiate are the ones to be considered as potential agents. To effectively turn into a cooperative agent, the potential cooperative agent must be prone to cooperation failures. By studying its interactions with its environments and with other entities, the developer has to determine if this entity may encounter such situations that will be considered as non-cooperative situations at the agent level. The entities meeting all these criteria will be identified as agents and the classes related to them marked as agents.

The study of the interactions between entities (A13) analyses the interactions between entities and is represented by Collaboration and Sequence Diagrams. The agents' interactions are described by AUML Protocol Diagram.

2.1.3 Design (WD4)

The Adelfe design process (Table 3) starts by analysing the different possibilities of detailed architecture of the system, creating packages sub-systems, objects, agents and the relationships among them and producing the class diagrams with the new elements (Cooperative Agent Class and the Cooperative Agent stereotype) (Adelfe, 2003), (Bernon et al., 2003), (Henderson-Sellers & Giorgini, 2005).

A14: Study detailed architecture and multi-agent model • S1: Determine packages • S2: Determine classes • S3: Use design-patterns • S4: Elaborate component and class diagrams **A15: Study interaction languages**	**A16: Design Agents** • S1: Define skills • S2: Define aptitudes • S3: Define interaction languages • S4: Define representations • S5: Define Non-cooperative situations A17: FAST Prototyping A18: Complete design diagrams • S1: Enhance design diagrams • S2: Design dynamic behaviours

Table 3. WD4 - Design in Adelfe (2003)

In the activity A15 the developer studies the interaction languages to be able to define the protocols used by agents to communicate between themselves. This information exchange between agents has to be described. For each scenario defined in the A7 and A13 activities, these exchanges are described using AUML protocol diagrams. The protocols diagrams are attached to package (not classes) because they are generic. The language definition is not necessary when the agents' communications are via the environment.

The Design Agents (A16) activity is an Adelfe methodology specific activity and allows the developer to refine the CooperativeAgent stereotyped classes identified in the A12 and A14 activities. The different modules of an agent must be defined in these activities by describing its skills, aptitudes, interaction languages, design representations, design characteristics and design non-cooperative situations.

Methods and attributes can describe the skills of an agent with a stereotyped notation <<skill>>. Skills are the system knowledge that allows the agent to perform an action. The representation of aptitudes, interaction languages, design representations and design characteristics is defined similarly to skills with a stereotyped notation. Aptitudes are the agent´s capability to reason about a specific knowledge of the system or about a real situation.

The developer analyses protocols defined in A15 activity and those assigned to an agent are associated to a state-machine. The methods and attributes link with an interaction protocol must be stereotyped <<interaction>>. The methods and attributes related to perception and action phase are represented by <<perception>> and <<action>> respectively in (A16-S3).

The step Design Non-Cooperative Situations (NCS) (A16-S6) is the most important in the design agents' activity (A16), because this is a specific ability of cooperative agents. A model guides the developer in the definitions of all situations that seem to be "harmful" for cooperative social attitude of an agent. The table lists some types of situations like ambiguity, incompetence, uselessness and conflict. The developer should fill up the conditions described for each NCS. The table contains the state of this agent when detecting the NCS, a NCS textual description, conditions permitting local detection of NCS and actions linked to this NCS.

The Fast Prototyping activity (A17) uses OpenTool (Adelfe, 2003), (Henderson-Sellers & Giorgini, 2005) to test the agents´ behaviour previously defined. The customized version of OpenTool can automatically transform a protocol diagram into a state-chart that can be run to simulate the agents' behaviour. Some methods can be implemented using a OTscript language that is a set-based action language of OpenTool.
The last activity of design is to complete the detailed architecture enriching the class diagrams (A18-S1) and developing the state chart diagrams required to design the dynamic behaviours (A18-S2). The objective is to reflect the different changes of an entity state when it is interacting with others.

2.2 MaSE methodology

The Multi-agent System Engineering (MaSE) methodology aims at supporting the designer to catch a set of initial requirements, to analyse models and implement a multi-agent system (MAS). This methodology is independent of any agent's architecture, programming language, or communication framework. The MaSE's agents are considered object specializations that instead of simple objects, with methods that can be invoked by other objects, are agents that talk among themselves and act proactively in order to reach goals (MaSE, 2010), (Deloach, 2001).
MaSE is a traditional software engineering methodology specialization with two phases (Analysis and Design) and several activities which are shown in Figure 2 (Deloach, 2001). The MaSE Analysis phase has three steps: Capturing Goals, Applying Use Cases, and Refining Roles. The Design phase has four activities: Creating Agent Classes, Constructing Conversations, Assembling Agent Classes and System Design. The highlighted items represent the resulting models of each phase.
The first step in MaSE analysis is to capture goals that express what the system is trying to achieve. These goals generally remain stable throughout the rest of the Analysis and Design phases. A decomposition of goals in a hierarchy form is the MaSE goal representation.
After the goals were defined, the functional requirements are identified and represented into use cases. Use Cases describe the behaviour of agents for each situation in MAS. In the step Applying Use Cases, situations of the initial requirements are elicited and expressed into Use Cases Diagrams and Descriptions, and UML Sequence Diagrams. The Sequence Diagrams are applied to express the sequences of roles events and they represent the desired system behaviour and its sequences of events.
The last step of Analysis phase defines a set of roles (Role Diagram) that can be used to achieve the goals of the system level. A role is an expected abstract description behaviour of each agent that aids in reaching the system goals. These roles are detailed by a series of tasks, which are described by finite-state models (Concurrent Tasks Diagrams).
The Role Diagram associates at first the goals to a role by listing them below the role name. Often, these goals are represented by numbers used in the Goal Diagram. Then the Role Diagram is detailed by associating a set of tasks for each role, representing the expected role behaviour. Communications between roles are expressed by the roles´ association and their associate tasks.
The tasks definitions are built in Concurrent Tasks Diagrams based on finite automata states. By definition, each task must be executed concurrently, while communicating with other internal or external tasks. A concurrent task is a set of states and transitions. The states represent the internal agent mechanism, while the transitions define tasks communications. Every transition has an origin and a destination state, a trigger, a guard condition and a transmission (Deloach, 2001).

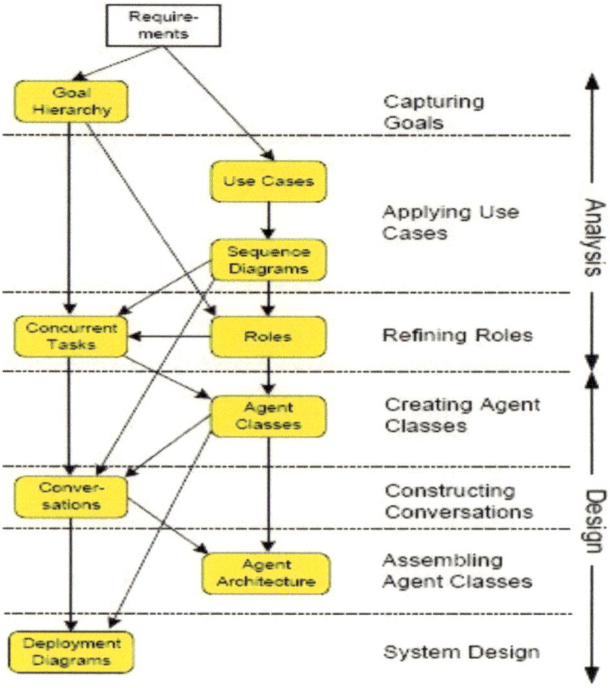

Fig. 2. MaSE Methodology Phases (Deloach, 2001)

In general, the events that are sent as broadcasts or triggers are associated with events sent to work in the same role instance, requiring an internal coordination of each task. The messages representation sent between agents uses two special events: (i) send event that represents the message sent to another agent and is denoted by send (message, agent) and (ii) receive event which defines the message received from another agent denoted by receive (message, agent).

The four diagrams proposed in the MaSE Design phase are Agent Classes, Conversations, Agent Architecture and Deployment Diagram.

The first step in the design process involves the definition of each agent class in an Agent Class Diagram. The system designer maps each role defined in the Roles Diagram to at least one Agent Class because this guarantees the goals will be implemented in the system and there is at least one agent class responsible for meeting this goal. The agent classes can be thought of as templates defined in terms of the roles they play and as the protocols they use to coordinate with other agents (O'Malley et al., 2001), (Gago, 2008).

The next step in the Design phase details the conversations between the agent classes and defines a coordination protocol between two agents. A conversation consists of two Communication Class Diagrams that represent the initiator and the responder. This diagram is a finite state automation defining the conversation states of the two agent classes using a similar syntax of the analysis phase:

rec-mess (args1) [cond] / action ^ trans-mess (args2)

This syntax defines: "if the message rec-mess is received with the arguments args1 and the condition cond holds, then the method action is called and the message trans-mess is sent with arguments args2. All elements of the transition are optional."

The third step in the Design phase is the definition of the agent architecture that is performed in two steps: (i) definition of the agent architecture and (ii) its components. The designer can choose the agent architecture, such as Belief-Desire-Intention (BDI), Reactive or Knowledge Base (Bryson & Stein, 2001).
The last activity in the Design Phase is defining the Deployment Diagram. In MaSE this diagram shows the agents´ number, types and location in the system. The diagram describes a system based on agent classes, and it is very similar to the UML Deployment Diagram. This diagram defines different agents' configurations and platforms to maximize the processing power and a network bandwidth.
MaSE can be developed using the AgenTool (2009) tool created by Air Force Institute of Technology (AFIT). AgenTool helps the system designer to create a series of models, from higher level goals definition to an automatic verification, a semi-automatic generation design and finally code generation.

3. Guardian Angel System Adelfe modelling

The Guardian Angel Project (Szolovits, 2004) was proposed as an information system centered on the patient, rather than the service provider. The software agents group explains the name "guardian angels" (GA). This "guardian angels" support functions for the patient's health, including the patient's medical considerations, legal and financial information.
Each GA is an active process which performs several important functions: (i) verification, interpretation and explanation of patient data collection, relevant facts or medical plans; (ii) recommendations with the acquired experience and patient's preferences; (iii) feasibility study, regarding the medical effectiveness, diagnostics cost and therapeutic planning; (iv) patient's health progress monitoring; (v) communications with other service providers software agents; (vi) education, information and support to the patient. All these facilities help to improve the medical diagnosis quality, increases the patient's commitment and reduces the disease effects and medical errors.
The Adelfe Guardian Angel (GA) modelling was developed using the Work Definitions for the early and final requirements, analysis and design, the AMAS Adequacy tool and OpenTool (Adelfe, 2003), (Henderson-Sellers & Giorgini, 2005). The Adelfe models presented in this section were developed by Kano (2007) and they were also improved and presented in Werneck et al. (2007).

3.1 Preliminary requirements

The following functional requirements were defined in the preliminary requirements phase: (i) allow the user to make different query to databases; (ii) allow to communicate with others sub-systems connected in the net; (iii) monitor the progress of the patient health conditions and the effect of the treatment; (iv) periodically verify the data integrity to find violations based on the user expectative and collateral effects; (v) expose the colleted data from auxiliary bases to user offering a maximal context comprehension to the user involved; (vi) customize services allowing the user objectivity, adequacy and efficiency; (vii) improve education functionalities to the user like access to encyclopaedias and universities researches to find knowledge from their diseases; (viii) provide alert and agenda functions remembering the patients their appointment, dosage and contraindications of medicines; (ix) offer to the patient the possibility to be in contact with support groups, forums and the main medicines laboratories; (x) be able to organize of the illnesses and diseases in a hierarchal structure using decreasing levels of severity, in order to make possible to apply together different techniques to the patients.

In this phase, the following non-functional requirements were also defined: (i) to be able to store physical and logical information using an enormous data volume; (ii) to make use of visual, sonorous and touch communication capacity; (iii) the system should be available 24 hours along the 7 days of the week, 365 days per year; (iv) be multi-task and allow to answer to several data request simultaneous at a certain average time; (v) to be conceptually distributed (the small parts inside inhabit all the same environment, however they represent, separately, concepts and well distinct parts); (vi) to allow the sudden appearance and the abrupt disappearance of its components; (vii) to allow the adaptation and evolution of its components.

The key words defined in this phase are: Monitoring, GA, Patient, Communication, Health Professional, Insuring, and History Information.

One of the GA constraints relates to maintenance routines when the system will not be available. Another restriction is the subnets functionality with which the system interacts. The case of eventual problems in one of these subnets the user will be unable to access them until they become again in operation.

3.2 Final requirements

The environment characterization activity (A6) identified the following passive entities: World Wide Web, Library, Hospital Stay, Illness Organism Information, Idiopathic Cause and Therapy. The active entities list are: Patient, Family, Support the Patient Group, Government, Health Plan Insurance, Laboratory, Health Professional, Hospital, Clinic, Pharmaceutical Industry, Ambient Factors and the proper Guardian Angel.

The central entity of the Guardian Angel is the Patient that has the ability to activate any events in any circumstance that will be convenient, dynamically interacting with the system. The Family is another entity that can modify the patient treatment routine depending on the treatment results and satisfaction degree, being able to dynamically interact with the system. The Health Professional entity has the power to trace treatment plans, to request examinations and to prescribe medicines, dynamically interacting with the system.

The Guardian Angel can be seen as "processing cells" of the system that interact dynamically in accordance with the recurrently perceptions of the environment. This entity was divided in 4 specializations: (i) Analyser - GA directed towards the tasks which require analyses, interpretation and understanding of data in one determined context; (ii) Inspector - GA directed towards the monitoring/inspection of specific states in the system; (iii) Diplomat - GA directed towards the reduction and treatment of Non-Cooperative Situations. The GA Diplomat is responsible for using its "diplomacy" together with a GA Analyser that helps to determine the priorities of the GAs´ execution, and (iv) Worker - the GA worker is the basic processing cell with the physical operations required to modify data/state of the system.

The Collaboration Diagrams for passive entities and the Sequence Diagrams for the active entities were built (Kano, 2007) and figure 3 presents an example of Customize Setting to Adapt Treatment to Patient's Reality.

The Guardian Angel system activity of characterizing environment (A6-S3) was classified as: (i) inaccessible because several users can be logged and they can modify data at anytime; (ii) continuous because the users are free to make their own actions; (iii) non-deterministic because the prescription of a treatment can be different for the same disease in different patients, and (iv) dynamic because the system depends on the environment and that can not be predicted by the system.

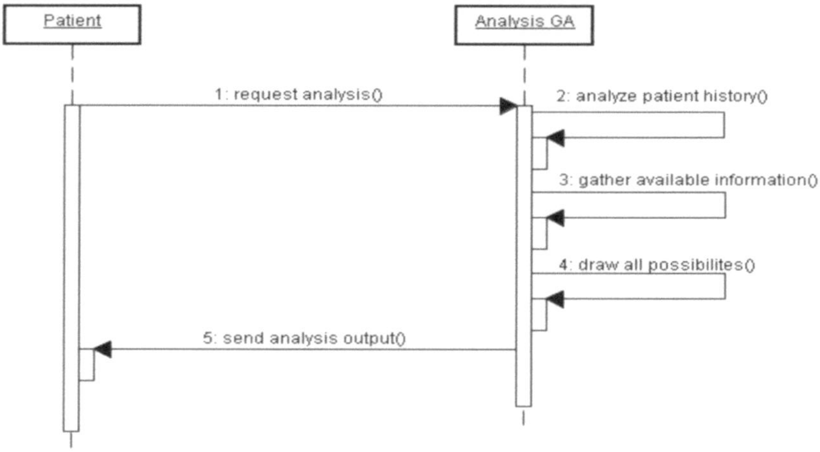

Fig. 3. Sequence Diagram: Customize Setting to Adapt Treatment to Patient's Reality (Kano, 2007)

Then the use case diagrams were defined and divided in five groups: GA Domain, Patient, Institutions, Administrative and Service. For each group a Use Case Diagram was modeled involving several use cases and then for each Diagram some NCS were identified as shown in Figure 4.

3.3 Analysis

In the GA Domain Analysis four new passive entities (Idiopathic Cause, Therapy, Hospital Stay and Disease-Causing Organism) were found and some diagrams and documents developed during previous steps had to be modified.

The classes identified in this phase were: User, People, Patient, Family, Health Care Professional, Doctor, Guardian Angel (Analyser, Diplomat, Inspector and Worker), Data Source, Clinic, Insurer, World Wide Web, Library, Government, Laboratory, Pharmacy Industry, Hospital, Patient Support Group, Environmental Factor, Idiopathic Cause, Therapy and Hospital Stay.

In the AMAS technology adequacy activity, the GA got the following reply from the tool in relation to the global criterion; "Your application possesses, with a high degree, almost all the characteristics that can justify - without any ambiguity- using AMAS". In the components evaluation the tool reply was: "Even if your application needs using AMAS some of its components must also be designed using this technology. We recommend you to apply as many times as necessary the methodology to specify all those components".

The agents identify activity (A12) studied active entities and for each one a form was defined as shown in Table 4. Thus four cooperative agents have been identified.

3.4 Design

The Design phase defined the packages and classes by elaborating the classes and collaboration diagrams. No design pattern was applied and the activity A17 of Fast prototype was not realized because the JAVA version of the tool does not work in the project computer because of some incompatibility that we could not fix.

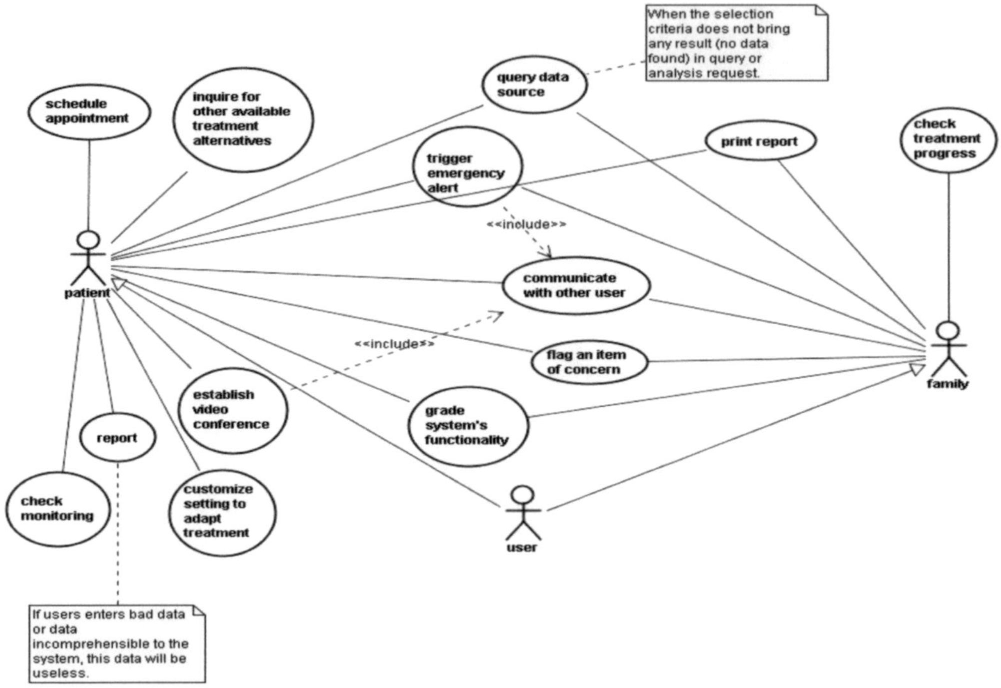

Fig. 4. Non-Cooperation Situations: User (patient) (Kano, 2007)

Guardian Angel	
Autonomy:	Has autonomy because can make decisions based only on its knowledge
Local Goal:	The local goal is to perform a task that was assigned to it.
Interactions with other Entities:	Interact with other Guardian Angels and Patient.
Environment Partial Overview:	Limited overview of the system
Negotiation Abilities:	Capable to Negotiate with other entities.
Potential agent:	An agent in potential according to Adelfe´s definition.
Dynamic environment:	Yes – it is not possible to prevent in which circumstances its actions are taken.
Face NCS	Yes - can request a service that is not available
Treat NCS	Yes- For example when a GA does not receive an answer to a feedback request.

Table 4. WD4 – Design in Adelfe (Werneck et al., 2007)

In the activity A15 the interactions between the agents were studied and for each an AUML Protocol Diagram was defined (an example is shown in figure 5). For each Guardian Angel the abilities, aptitudes, representations and characteristics were identified and also defined the protocols used in A15 activity which will be used by the agents. Finally the NCS in a form (Table 5) were defined.

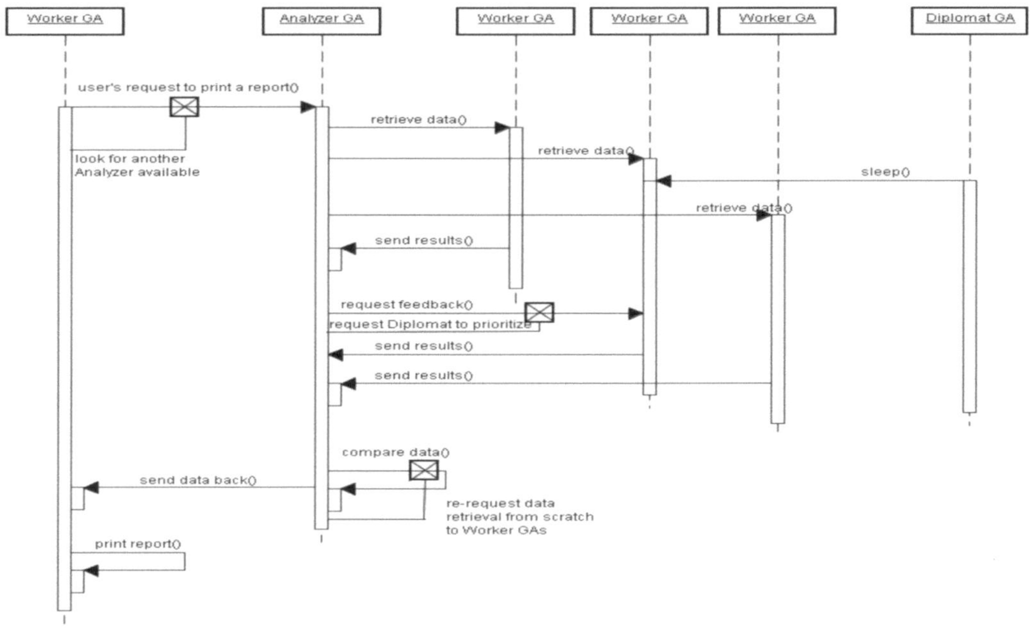

Fig. 5. Protocol Diagram of GA (Kano, 2007)

Name	Permission denied
State	Execute the activity
Description	An agent faces this situation when the activity that it intends to execute cannot be accomplished with the permissions of the user in question
Conditions	User with no knowledge about the system.
Actions	The agent must supply to the user a list of all the users who have connection with this and that they have permission to execute the task.

Table 5. The Identification of NCS Form (Kano, 2007)

The diagrams in the last activity (A18) were detailed and the dynamic behaviours were also completed by designing the State Chart Diagram where the attributes and methods were specified to express the agents' state, conditions and actions.

4. Educ-MAS MaSE modelling

The Educ-MAS (Educational Multi-Agent System) is a learning education environment with multi-agents that aims at helping the teaching process on a specific topic. The modelling presented in this chapter was improved from Gago (2008) and Gago et al. (2009).

The first step in the MaSE analysis requirements modelling is to define the Goal Hierarchy Diagram. Then the goals are decomposed in sub-goals until they can be expressed as functions as shown in Figure 6. The main goal Promote Individual Learning was structured based on the Intelligent Tutoring Systems classical architecture that considers four models: Pedagogic, Expert, Student and Interface. Each model reflects the ability and the characteristics of the Educational System (Viccari et al., 2003), (Wooldridge & Jennings, 1997): Explore Student, Plan Course, Manage Knowledge and Manage Teaching. The goals are also decomposed into other goals. For example the goal Plan Course was partitioned into two sub-goals (Consult Defined Goals and Define Course Plan) and the sub-goal Define Course Plan has two sub-goals named Define Content of the Modules and Define the Plan Presentation of the Module.

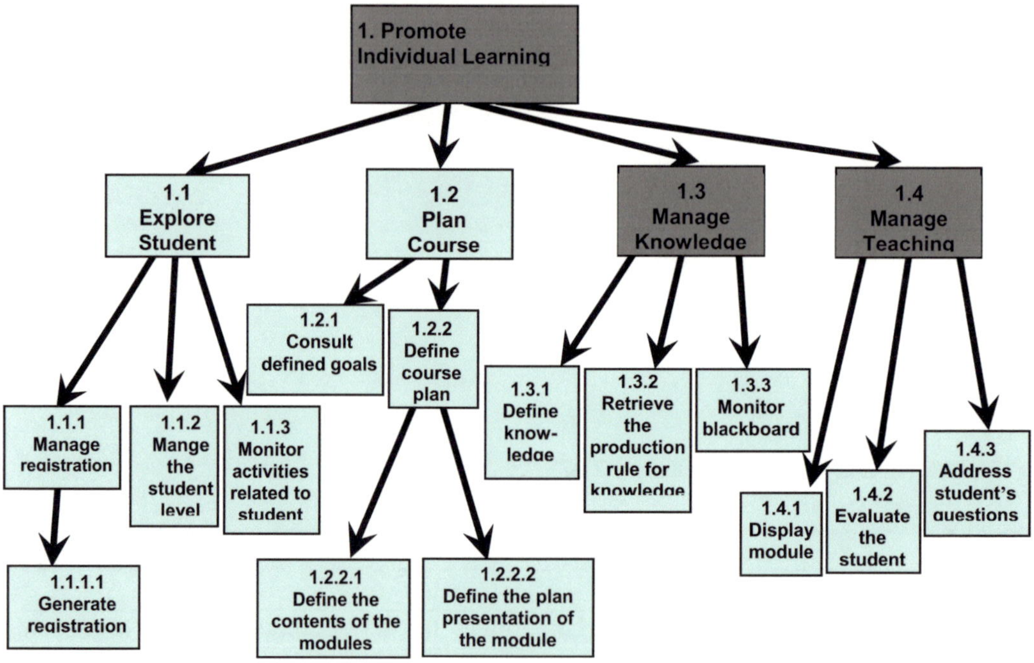

Fig. 6. Educ-MAS Goal Diagram adapted from Gago et al (2009)

Then the goals and sub-goals were translated into use cases. Figure 7 presents an example of Educ-MAS use case and the respective sequence diagram for the functional requirement Teach Class, its description and also the name of Sequence Diagrams that retracts the scenarios of this use case. The scenarios are Student's Class, Questions Resolved and Questions Not Resolved. For each one a Sequence Diagram has to be built showing how the system behaves. Figure 8 shows the agent behaviour with the third scenario of the case Teach Class The whole specification of Educ-MAS can be found in Gago (2008).

The next activity is to develop a set of roles and tasks showing how the goals are reached based on the Goals, the Use Cases (diagrams and descriptions) and the Sequence Diagrams. Figure 9 represents the Preliminary Role Diagram where the goals were mapped to system roles. For example, the System Administrator role (Fig.9) achieves the goals Explore Student (goal 1.1 in the Goal Diagram), Manage Registration (goal 1.1.1 in the Goal Diagram),

Generate Registration (goal 1.1.1.1 in the Goal Diagram), and Monitor (goal 1.1.3 in the Goal Diagram), activities related to student.

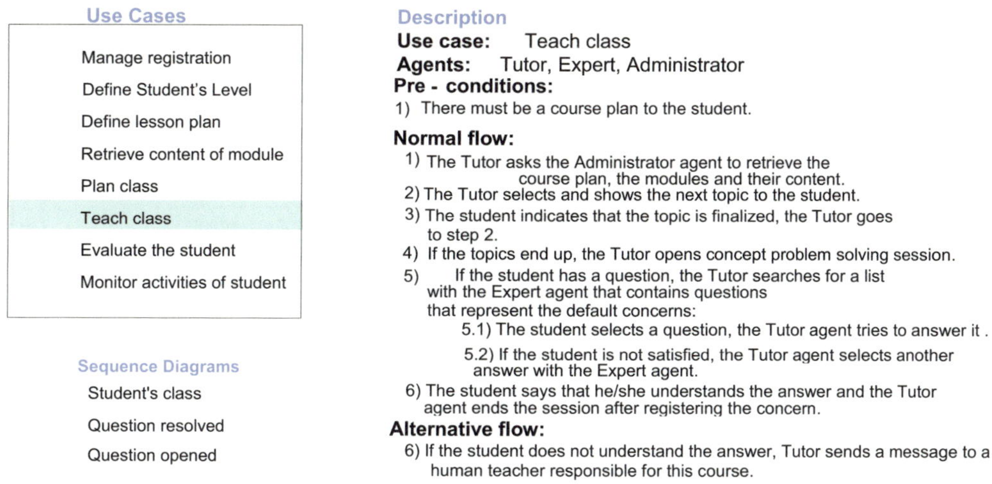

Fig. 7. Use Case Teach Class adapted from Gago et al (2009)

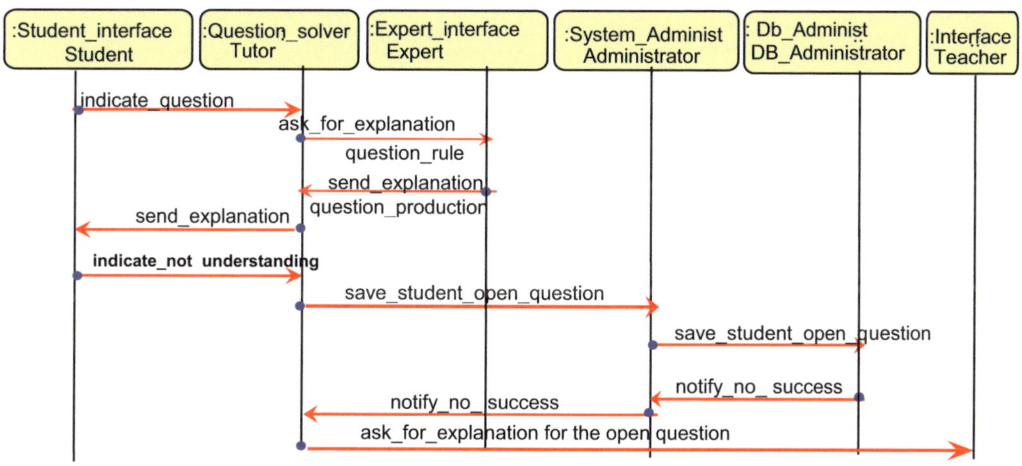

Fig. 8. Question Opened Sequence Diagram adapted from Gago et al (2009)

In the complete Role Diagram the tasks responsible for the roles and the associations among themselves were introduced to reach the responsible goal roles. Continuing the Analysis phase the Concurrence Task diagrams have to be built for each task as shown in Figure 10 for the task Monitor Blackboard. This task is associated to the Expert interface role which is responsible for the goal with the same name. This task monitors the blackboard in order to interface the knowledge base introducing the questions and their contents.

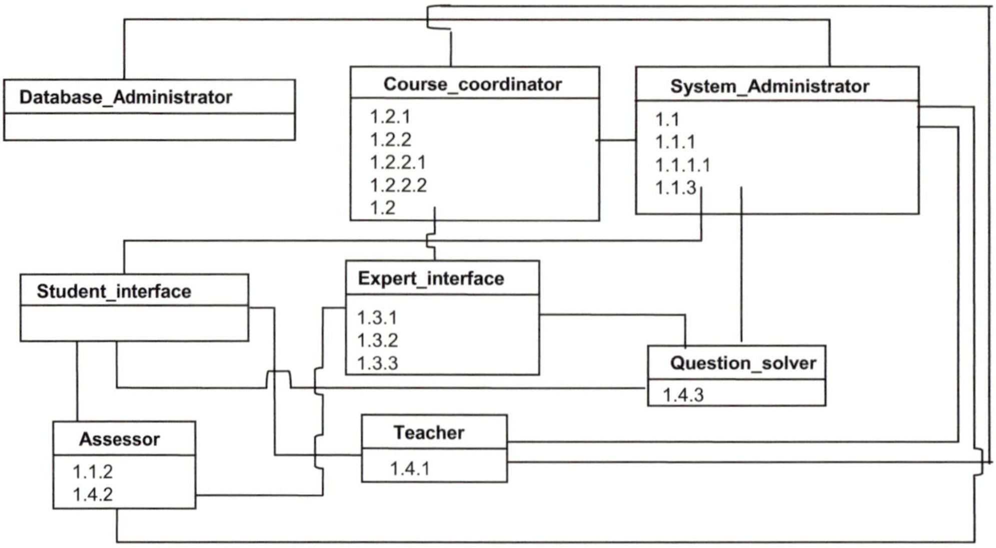

Fig. 9. The Educ-MAS Partial Role Diagram (Gago et al., 2009)

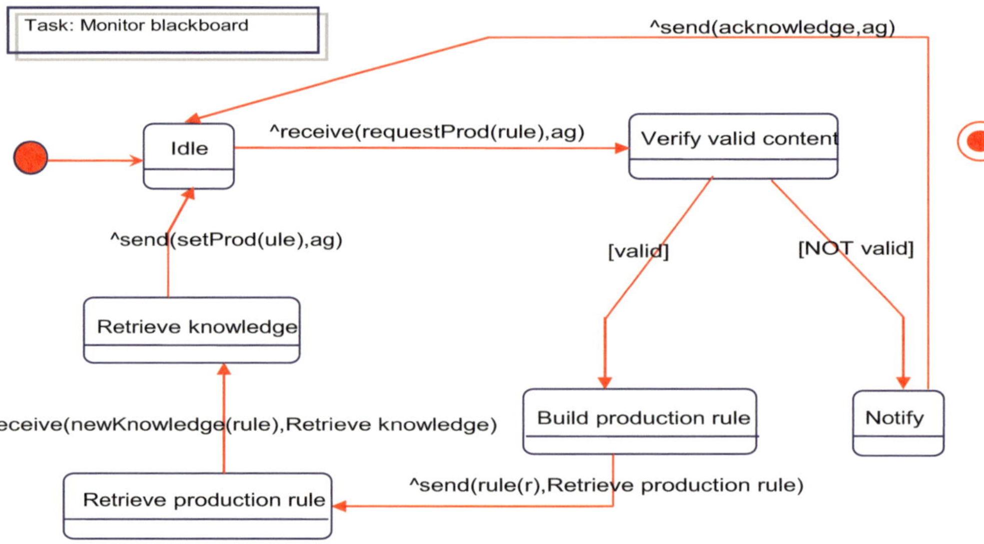

Fig. 10. Concurrent Task Diagram for the task Monitor blackboard (Gago et al., 2009)

In the Design phase the Role Diagram and the Concurrence Task diagrams have to be used to design the individual components of the agent classes as presented in Figure 11. The agent architecture chosen was a simple BDI (Belief-Desire-Intention) agent architecture and Figure 12 presents an example of a Tutor agent class partial structure components. The last step in the Design phase has to develop an overall operational design by designing the Deployment Diagram (Gago et al., 2009). The Tutor, Administrator, Coordinator and Expert Agents are defined in an environment as a system. The Interface (Student Model) starts at the student's computer while the Database Management and the other part of the system are in network computers.

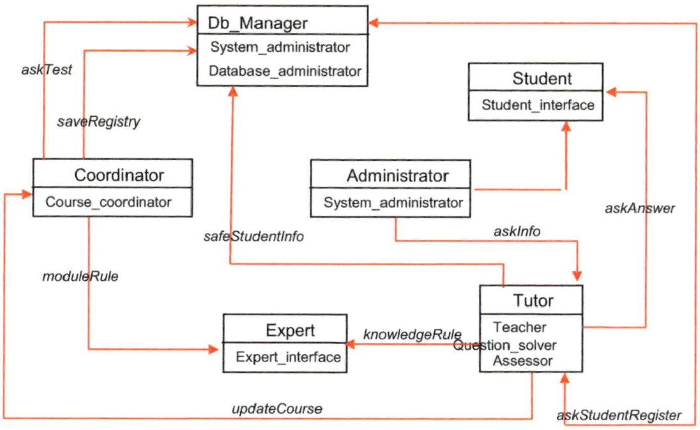

Fig. 11. The Educ-MAS Agent Class Diagram (Gago et al., 2009)

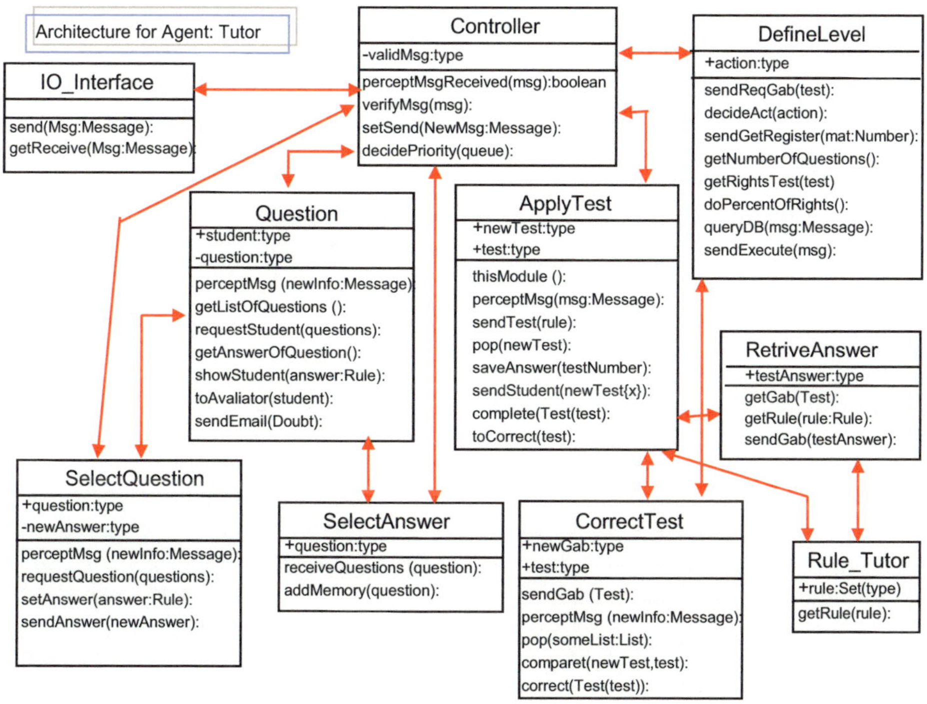

Fig. 12. Tutor Agent Class Partial Structure Component (Gago et al., 2009)

5. Conclusions

This work is part of a broader project which aims at analysing important aspects of modelling and developing different Multi-Agent Systems using several methodologies. The first system modelled presented was a classical Multi-Agent System case study in a Medical Domain using Adelfe methodology.

Adelfe is a methodology originated from object orientation based on UML (Rumbaugh et al., 2004) that incorporated AUML (2007) protocols diagram and the development process RUP (Krutchen, 2000). The Adelfe process covers the requirements, analysis and project phases with a well defined process. Adelfe can be a powerful methodology in terms of cooperative agents' concepts centred in Non-Cooperative Situations. This method allows the definition of important agent concepts as autonomy, proactivity and autonomy reason. However, the methodology needs to improve some aspects of characterized environment by adding new diagrams that can model goals, plan and organization.

The second Multi-Agent System modelled was a learning education environment in the MaSE that is an object-oriented methodology that supports analysis and design phases using agent-orientated techniques. MaSE can also be considered a powerful methodology in terms of cooperative agents' concepts (definition of autonomy, proactivity and autonomy reason and the agent concepts are centred in the Roles Diagram and in Goal orientation. However, this methodology is not completely defined, especially for the Early Requirements phase it lacks on capturing, understanding and registering terminology. In DiLeo et al. (2002) they propose to integrate ontology representation to MaSE that can solve this weakness. Another point to be improved is related to non-functional requirements that are not mentioned in the methodology and the MaSE protocols representation that is divided into two diagrams so both diagrams have to be seen to understand the agent communications.

In the future we are going to compile these experiences from all MAS development and define a knowledge base for an Agent-Oriented Methodology Approach based on the Situation Method Engineering (SME). This knowledge will provide a flexible way of developing a Multi-Agent System using a methodology based on strengths and examples of models of each method fragments and also situations when applying a respective method artefact.

6. Reference

Adelfe (2003). Atelier de Développement de Logiciels à Fonctionnalité Emergente) at *http://www.irit.fr/ADELFE.*

Agent Tool (2009). at *http://macr.cis.ksu.edu/projects/agentTool* , Last Updated October 2009.

AUML (2007). at *http://www.auml.org/auml/* Last updated on 17 June 2007.

Bernon, C., Camps, V., Gleizes, M. P. and Piscard, G. (2003). ADELFE: A Methodology for Adaptive Multi-agent Systems Engineering; In: *Lecture Notes in Computer Science,* Volume 2577, Springer Berlin Heidelberg, ISSN: 0302-9743, pp. 156-169.

Bryson, J. & Stein, L. (2001). Modularity and design in reactive intelligence, In: *International Joint Conference on Artificial Intelligence,* IJCAI-2001, Seattle (USA), pp 1115-1120.

Coppieters, A. M., Marzulo, L.A.J., Kinder, E. And Werneck, V.M. (2005). Modelagem Orientada a Agentes utilizando MESSAGE, In : *Cadernos do IME-Série Informática,* Rio de Janeiro, v.18, ISSN 1413-9014, pp. 38-46 in portuguese.

Cysneiros, L. M., Werneck, V. M. B., Amaral, J., Yu, E. (2005). Agent/Goal Orientation versus Object Orientation for Requirements Engineering: A Practical Evaluation Using an Exemplar, In: *Proc. of VIII Workshop in Requirements Engineering,* Porto, ISBN 972-752-079-0, pp.123-134.

Cysneiros, L. M., Werneck, V. M. B.; Yu, Eric (2005a). Evaluating Methodologies: A Requirements Engineering Approach Through the Use of an Exemplar. In: *Journal of Computer Science & Technology*, ISSN: 1000-9000, USA, v. 5, n. 2, pp. 71-79.

Dantas, T. C.; Soares, G. E. ; Costa, Rosa Maria Esteves Moreira Da Werneck, Vera M. B. ; Castro, M. C. S. (2007). AprendEAD: Ambiente para Educação à Distância Apoiado em Agentes; In: *Cadernos do IME. Série Informática*, v. 23, p. 16-23, ISSN 1413-9014, in portuguese.

Deloach, Scott A. (2001). Analysis and Design using MaSE and agentTool. In:*12th Midwest Artificial Intelligence and Cognitive Science Conference* (MAICS 2001), Miami University, Oxford, Ohio.

Dileo, Jonathan; Jacobs,Timothy; Deloach, Scott. (2002). Integrating Ontologies into Multiagent Systems Engineering. In*: Fourth International Bi-Conference Workshop on Agent-Oriented Information Systems (AOIS-2002*).

Gago, I. S. B. ; Werneck, Vera M. B. & Costa, Rosa Maria Esteves Moreira da . (2009). Modelling an Educational Multi-Agent System in MaSE. In : *Lecture Notes in Computer Science*, v. 5820, ISSN: 0302-9743, p. 335-346.

Gago, I., Utilização da metodologia MaSE na modelagem de Sistema Tutor Inteligente Dissertation on Informatics Technology, UnderGraduation, UERJ, Rio de Janeiro, 2008 pp 114 in portuguese.

Henderson-Sellers, Brian & Giorgini, Paolo (ed). (2005). *Agent-oriented Methodologies.* 1ed: Idea Group Inc, London, UK, ISBN 1-59140-581-5, p412.

Henderson-Sellers, Brian & Ralyté, Jolita. (2010). Situational Method Engineering: State-of-the-Art Review, In: *Journal of Universal Computer Science*, vol. 16, no. 3, DOI: 10.3217/jucs-016-01, 424-478.

Iglesias, C.A. & González, J.C. (1998). A Survey of Agent-Oriented Methodologies In *Proceedings of the 5th International Workshop on Agent Theories, Architectures and Languages (ATAL'98),* LNAI n1555, Springer Verlag, Paris, France, 317-330.

Kano, Abrahão Yehoshua Kano, Modelagem orientada a agentes do Sistema Guardian Angel: Sistema de Informação de Saúde centrado no Paciente. *Dissertation on Informatics Technology UnderGraduation*, UERJ, Rio de Janeiro, 2007 pp 247 in portuguese.

Krutchen, P. (2000) *The Rational Unified Process: An Introduction*, Reading, MA, Addison Wesley.

MaSE (2010} at *http://macr.cis.ksu.edu/projects/mase.htm* access at August, 2010

O'Malley , Scott A.; Deloach, Scott A. (2001). Determining When to Use an Agent-Oriented Software Engineering Paradigm. In : *Proceedings of the Second International Workshop On Agent-Oriented Software Engineering (AOSE-2001*), Montreal, Canada.

Odell, J., Parunak, H., Bauer, B. (2001). Representing agent interaction protocols in UML, In: *First International Workshop on Agent-Oriented Software Engineering,* (AOSE 2000), Ciancarini, P., Wooldridge, M., Eds., LNCS 1957 Springer, Limerick, Ireland, 121-140.

Rumbaugh, J., Jacobson, I. & Booch, G. (2004). The Unified Modelling Language Reference Manual, Second edition, Addison,-Wesley.

Schreiber, G., Akkermans, H., Anjewierden, A. Hoog, R. de, Shadbolt, N., Velde, W.Van de, Wielinga, B. (1999). *Knowledge Engineering and Management: The CommonKADS Methodology*, Cambridge, MA, ISBN: 0262193009 .

Sousa, R.; Araújo, Alex L. de, Gomes Junior, Carlos A.; Costa, Rosa Maria Moreira da, Werneck, V. M. B. (2009). Modelagem de Requisitos Orientada a Agentes utilizando MaSE; Cadernos do IME. Série Informática, v. 28, ISSN 1413-9014, in portuguese.

Sousa, R.; da Cunha, A. L. F.; Martins, R. F. A. Cysneiros, L.M., Werneck, V. M. B. (2010). Evaluating MaSE Methodology in the Requirements Identification; In : *Proceedings of Proceedings of the 33nd Annual IEEE Software Engineering Workshop.*: IEEE Computer Society Press, Skovde.

Szolovits, P., Doyle, J., Long, W.J., Kohane, I. e Pauker, S. G. (2004). *Guardian Angel: Patient-Centered Health Information Systems,* Technical Report MIT/LCS/TR-604, at http://groups.csail.mit.edu/medg/projects/ga/manifesto/GAtr.html

Tavares, D. G.; Eichler, J.; Pereira, L. F.; Silva, T. S.; Da Cunha, A. L. F.; Martins, R. F. A. Cysneiros, L.M., Werneck, V. M. B. (2009). Processo de Desenvolvimento do Sistema Multi-Agentes Monitor Glicêmico; Cadernos do IME. Série Informática, v. 28, ISSN 1413-9014, in portuguese.

Viccari, Rosa M., Floresa, Cecilia D., Silvestrea, Andre´ M., Seixasb, Louise J., Ladeirac, Marcelo, Coelho, Helder (2003). A multi-agent intelligent environment for medical knowledge, In: *Artificial Intelligence in Medicine,* 27, ISSN: 0933-3657, 335–366.

Werneck, V. M.; Pereira, L. F.; Silva, T. S.; Almentero, E. K.; Cysneiros, L. M. (2006). Uma Avaliação da Metodologia MAS-CommonKADS, In: *Proceedings of the Second Workshop on Software Engineering for Agent-oriented Systems,* (SEAS´06), Florianópolis, Brazil, ISBN: 0164-1212; 13-24, in portuguese.

Werneck, Vera M. B. ; Cysneiros, Luiz Marcio ; Kano, A. Y. (2007) Evaluating Adelfe Methodology in the Requirements Identification. In: *Proceedings of 10TH Workshop on Requirements Engineering*. Toronto , York University Printing Services, v. 1. 13-24.

Werneck, Vera M. B. ; Cysneiros, Luiz Marcio ; Kano, A. Y. ; Coppieters, A. M. ; Fasano, A. L. ; Marzulo, L. A. J. ; Furtado, L. O. ; Pereira, L. F. ; Lopez, M. A. C. ; Pereira, Ricardo Augusto Gralhoz, Rafael Barros; Silva, T. S. ; Santos, T. R. M. (2008). Metodologias Orientadas a Agentes. Cadernos do IME. *Série Informática,* v. 26, , ISSN 1413-9014. 7-16, in Portuguese.

Wooldridge, M. & Jennings, N. (1997). *Intelligent Agents: Theory and Practice,* at http://www.doc.mmu.ac.uk/STAFF/mike/ker95/ker95-html.html.

Yu, E. & Cysneiros, L.M. (2002). Agent-Oriented Methodologies-Towards a Challenge Exemplar, in *Proc of the 4th Intl. Bi-Conference Workshop on Agent-Oriented Information Systems (AOIS 2002),* Toronto, pp.47-63.

5

The Agent Oriented Multi Flow Graphs Specification Model

I. D. Zaharakis[1,2]

[1]*Department of Informatics Applications in Management and Economy, Technological Educational Institute of Patras,*

[2]*Research Academic Computer Technology Institute, Patras, Greece*

1. Introduction

The term agent is widely used in many areas with diverse meaning. In this work, agents have been used as they have been defined in the context of AI. In this context, many researchers use notions to describe an agent that are normally applied to humans, such as knowledge, beliefs, desires, intentions, capabilities, choices, commitments or obligation, (Shoham, 1993; Cohen & Levesque, 1990; Rao & Georgeff, 1991a) or even emotions (Bates, 1994). Wooldridge in (Wooldridge, 1999) uses a broader definition and argues that an agent denotes a hardware or software-based system that exhibits properties such as autonomy, social ability, reactivity, and pro-activeness. Several other agent properties that have been suggested include mobility, veracity, benevolence and rationality.

This work shares the need of the above properties and in order to express them an agent is considered as an *intentional system* based on the description of the philosopher Daniel Dennett. He proposed the *intentional stance* from which systems are ascribed mental qualities. Using this term, he describes entities "whose behaviour can be predicted by the method of attributing belief, desires and rational acumen" (Dennett, 1987). The intentional stance deals mainly with the behaviour of the described entities and helps to avoid paradoxes and clashes of intuition (Russell & Norvig, 2003). Its main disadvantage is that it cannot distinguish among implementations since any given behaviour can be implemented in many different ways and does not imply anything about the system's internal workings or representation. However, from an engineering point of view, it allows the better understanding and consequently the description of a complex system and for this reason is adopted by this work. Concluding that an agent is a system that is most conveniently described by the intentional stance, Wooldridge and Jennings (Wooldridge & Jennings, 1995) consider that the appropriate attitudes for representing agents are classified in *information attitudes* (belief and knowledge) which are related to the information that an agent has about the world it occupies, and *pro-attitudes* (desire, intention, obligation, commitment, choice etc.), which in some way guide the agents' actions.

More than one agent, who cooperate or deliberately act together in order to accomplish a task (usually common) constitute a multi agent system. Multi agent systems are inherently complex since "concurrency, problem domain uncertainty and non-determinism in execution together conspire to make it difficult to understand the activity within a distributed intelligent system" (Gasser et al., 1987). In order to solve the problem of complexity, there is a need for practical and helpful tools, which benefit a better understanding and managing of a multi agent system. Furthermore, there is a need of suitable and well-defined formalisms, which use appropriate attitudes for representing agents and can express the specific features of a multi agent system such as autonomy, concurrency, social ability and cooperation. Despite the development of several formalisms for this purpose, there are not many tools to embody a formalism and to turn it in a real system. The main reason for the gap between theories and real agent systems is due the abstract notions used and to the many unrealistic assumptions made about the agents' capabilities (Wooldridge, 1996). This work focuses on this issue and proposes the AOMFG model (*Agent Oriented Multi Flow Graphs*), which embodies and combines characteristics of agents' theories, Petri Nets and Cognitive Engineering.

Although formal specifications and methods have been the object of study since the late 1960s, they have not been widely used in software development nor have they been accepted as both worthwhile and practicable, even in mainstream computer science (Wooldridge, 1996). Formal specifications are expressed in a language whose vocabulary, syntax and semantics are formally defined. There are a number of reasons why one should use formal methods for system specification. The most significant among them are that they provide insights into and an understanding of the software requirements and the software design, they can be analyzed by mathematical methods and their consistency and their completeness can be proved, and finally they may be automatically processed.

In this direction and focusing on multi agent systems, some related attempts are reviewed. In addition, some methods describing human action and human computer interaction are examined. This is because several characteristics of human behaviour are ascribed to agents in order to simplify the reasoning about them. According to the agent definition that has been given, it seems that there is a need for a combination of the above methods in order to capture such mental notions, extend without losing specification expressiveness and to maintain the model simplicity to the greatest possible.

2.1 Structure of the paper

In the following sections, AOMFG a graphical formal model for agent specification is introduced. In the next section, several formalisms that have been used for the reasoning about multi agent systems as well as some formalism that are relevant with the scope of this work, are reviewed. Then, a description and a formal definition of the model are given in detail. Furthermore, the model execution is described as well as the model decomposition techniques. Finally, it is shown how an AOMFG can be transformed to a Petri Net. In the last section, the validation of the model is presented with the use of four examples: Shoham's algorithm, FIPA communication protocols, BDI related properties, and a multi agent tutoring system specification. The work concludes with a summary of the work and a description of model application.

3. Background

This section presents several attempts for reasoning about multi agent systems and other attempts in related subjects, which influenced the development of AOMFG model.

3.1 Models for multi agent systems

The most widely used formalism among those that have been developed for reasoning about multi agent systems is intentional logics, which are formalisms developed by researchers in AI and philosophy to describe systems with beliefs, goals, intentions and so on (Wooldridge, 1996). According to formalisms based on intentional logics, mental notions characterize an agent and reasoning about the system is carried out by attributing these notions (Cohen & Levesque, 1990; Hintikka, 1962; Konolige, 1986; Shoham, 1993). The mental notions correspond to a set of possible worlds with an accessibility relation between those worlds. However, because of the possible worlds interpretation, the well-known "logical omniscience" and "side effects" problems have emerged. These mean respectively, that an agent is a perfect reasoner and that it desires the logical consequences of its actions. Many attempts tried to settle these matters by grounding, weaken or even completely reject the possible worlds semantics. Although these efforts show some encouraging results, they are not clear on how attitudes such as desires or intentions can be expressed.

One of the most influential works in agent theory is due to Cohen and Levesque (Cohen & Levesque, 1990), who consider intention as a central notion and as a necessary characteristic for agent's reasoning and actions. Following this point of view, Rao and Georgeff developed a number of formalisms and decision procedures for multi agent systems based on the notion of beliefs, desires and intentions, which are known as the BDI formalism (Rao & Georgeff, 1991a; Rao & Georgeff, 1995). With respect of the intentional stance and in the spirit of speech act theory (Searle, 1969), Shoham proposed the agent oriented programming, as "... a new programming paradigm ... [which] promotes a societal view of computation..." (Shoham, 1993). Using choice as a primitive notion and an explicit reference to time in his formalism, he defines a simple programming language and its interpreter, showing in this way, how the theory comes to practice.

A more radical approach that rejects the possible worlds semantics altogether, is Konolige's deduction model of beliefs (Konolige, 1986), which models resource-bounded reasoners (agents as any real system have no unlimited resources) and allows logically incomplete reasoning via logically incomplete deduction rules. Later Wooldridge (Wooldridge, 1992), based on Konolige's model, developed a general model for the specification of realistic (resource-bounded) multi agent systems by using temporal logics. Temporal logics are used for reasoning about multi agent systems since the latter are reactive, concurrent and typically non-terminating. Although temporal logics seem to be powerful for describing past actions and for predicting the future actions of a reactive system according to changes in its environment, it seems to be a need of a combination with other notions such as those of intentional logics in order to become practical. The same holds for the process algebras, too. Process algebras are typically used for reasoning about concurrency in systems. In the case of multi agent systems, mental notions and conceptual properties must be described which are difficult to express using only methods of process algebras.

3.2 Models for human behaviour

Since many human characteristics are ascribed on agents, this section reviews the most important attempts in formal user representation (for details see (Kameas, 1995)) and, determines which of these methods and how may be applied in reasoning about multi agent systems. All these models approach users through Cognitive Engineering (Norman, 1987). In particular, users are considered to interact with computers in order to accomplish tasks that may contain subtasks. From this point of view, two model categories have been proposed: task analysis, which represents the task decomposition and, cognitive task modelling, which represents the tasks through the computer functionality and the interrelation between the physical and mental actions that are required for the task accomplishment.

According to task analysis (Johnson & Nicolosi, 1990), the user's actions are hierarchically decomposed into subtasks. There are abstract relations between the specifications of the accomplished tasks and their corresponding structures and a good understanding of these relations is required. The analysis techniques use natural language, are ambiguous and there are no specifications tools.

Cognitive task modelling regards human-computer interaction as an iterative procedure for the approximation of a goal through a strategy (Miller et al., 1960; Newel & Simon, 1972), and embodies two architectures. The Model Human Information Processor (Card et al., 1983) includes sensible, cognitive and applied processors together with a representation of the long and short-term memories. The Problem Space Model (Newel & Simon, 1972) treats the logical behaviour in a problem space, a set of situations representing the parts of problem solution and a set of actions provided to the user. According to this approach, a user has a goal, which represents the final state of the system. This goal is iteratively decomposed in subgoals that constitute action plans. The decomposition stops when actions take place for the achievement of the goals. Depending on the actions or the action plans, the cognitive models are divided into models of hierarchical representation of user tasks and goals, linguistic and grammar models and, models of device level. The latter two categories have only marginal interest for this work, so only the first one will be studied further.

A widely known representative of this category is GOMS model (Card et al., 1983), where the users have goals representing their intention for the achievement of a task, operators denoting the primitive actions, methods that are a sequence of actions and, selection rules that determine the choice of a method. Since a goal is decomposed into subgoals, a goal stack containing the intended goals is maintained and represents the users' long-term memory. Another approach is the model of Goal Structure Graphs (Kieras & Polson, 1985) as an application of Cognitive Complexity Theory (CCT). The specification with Goal Structure Graphs is a graphical representation of the system functionality as well as the reasoning of a user. In such a system the user's knowledge is represented as a set of production rules. The rules have a structure "if <condition> then <action>". The model provides mechanisms for the elaboration of the rules that produce a sequence of cognitive actions of the user.

3.3 Petri Nets based models

All the above models require a good understanding of their methods as well as an adequately deep knowledge of their theory. In many cases, it is difficult and infeasible to force software engineers to study specific mathematical models (such as temporal logic or process algebra) or even cognitive models (such as human psychology or user behaviour). On the contrary, it would be desirable to hide the complexity and the strict formalism of the model and to offer a friendlier tool that reflects the expressiveness of the model. In this way "... practitioners can learn from theoreticians how to make their models methodical, and theoreticians can learn from practitioners how to make their models more realistic" (Murata, 1989). Graphical tools with theoretical background satisfy some of these requirements and the best delegates are Petri Nets, which can specify systems that are concurrent/parallel, asynchronous, distributed, non-deterministic and/or stochastic. They have been used in a wide area of applications that include communication protocols, distributed systems, concurrent and parallel systems, formal languages, logic programs, human factors, and decision systems.

A Petri Net is a directed, bipartite graph and it consists of two kinds of nodes, called places and transitions. Directed arcs reside between the places and the transitions, which are labelled with their weights. The places maintain tokens, which are produced or consumed by transitions. The tokens are moved and distributed through the arcs. Every transition has a set of input and output places. Typically, a transition represents an event, input places represent preconditions and output places represent post-conditions. However, the interpretation of transitions and places is depending on the modelling concept used. For example, a transition may mean a clause in logic and input and output places may mean conditions and conclusions respectively, or a transition may mean a task and input and output places may mean resources needed and released respectively. A marking is an assignment of tokens to each place. A Petri Net has an initial marking (initial state) and this marking is changed according to a simple firing rule:

- A transition t is said to be enabled if each input place p of t is marked with at least $w(p, t)$ tokens, where $w(p, t)$ is the weight of the arc from p to t
- An enabled transition may or may not fire
- A firing of an enabled transition t removes $w(p, t)$ tokens from each input place p of t, and adds $w(p, t)$ tokens to each output place p of t.

By modelling a system with a Petri Net, one can study behavioural properties, which include reachability, boundedness, liveness, reversibility and home state, coverability, persistence, synchronic distance, and fairness, or structural properties, which include structural liveness, controllability, structural boundedness, conservativeness, repetitiveness, and consistency (Murata, 1989). Powerful analysis methods help the study of those properties and may be classified into the coverability tree method, the incidence matrix and state equation approach, and reduction or decomposition techniques. However, the classical Petri Nets have a series of restrictions, the major among them being the need of large nets in order to describe systems of medium complexity (Murata, 1989). In addition, the lack of formal treatment or of clear identification of individuals and the implicit structuring mechanisms used, made inevitable the introduction of new approaches, which are known as High-Level Petri Nets (HPN) (for an extensive review refer to (Gerogiannis et al., 1998)), and extend the classical Petri Nets from several perspectives.

Among all the HPN proposed, those of interest to this work are Predicate/Transition nets (PrTN) and Coloured Petri Nets (CPN). PrTN (Genrich & Lautenbach, 1981) are suitable for modelling logic programs since places play the role of predicates, transitions may associate logical formulas and tokens are predicate extensions. In addition, a PrTN may contain free variables, which are substituted according to the firing sequence. A variation of PrTN is the Predicate/Event Nets (PrEN) (Schmidt, 1991), which adopt methods of process algebra and are used to represent parallelism and concurrency. CPN (Jensen, 1981) associate colours with the tokens, the places, or the transitions. Typically, a colour is a data type assigned to the elements, which are handled by the model. In order to overcome some problems concerning the size of the CPN, an extension of the structuring mechanism has been proposed. This extension is the Hierarchical CPN (HCPN) (Jensen, 1997) consisting of interrelated subnets, called pages, and represent a substitution of transitions. PrTN and CPN are equivalent on computational power although their underlying formalism is

different since the PrTN are based on an algebraic notation while the CPN resemble the procedural programming languages.
Based on a hierarchically high level Petri net, Interactive Multi Flow Graphs (IMFG) (Kameas, 1995) embody characteristics of GOMS and CCT and in such a way combine into a Petri net-based formalism the more important features of state transition models with elements of cognitive models of user behaviour. IMFG is a process-based state transition model specially designed for the specification of interactive dialogue and interactive applications. It provides powerful analysis techniques, task decomposition formalism and event handling mechanisms. Along these lines, another modelling technique concerning the plan decomposition has been proposed (Kinny et al., 1996), however it uses different perspectives as it extends existing object oriented models and the decomposition is represented by state charts rather than Petri Nets. This technique models agents, which are based on BDI architecture, and employs (in some augmented way) object-oriented dynamic models as agents' plans, which are directly executable descriptions of agents' behaviour.

4. AOMFG model

Agent Oriented Multi Flow Graphs (AOMFG) model is a graphical model for the specification and design of multi agent systems. Its main purpose is to describe how the agents reason and act together in a dynamic environment for the accomplishment of common tasks. In essence, it is a high level Petri Net, which encapsulates notions of multi modal logic and reflects the modelling technique of agent systems based upon the BDI architecture. It constitutes a modification and an extension of IMFG model (Kameas, 1995) both in its philosophy and syntax. Although IMFG is a formal model that has been originally proposed for interactive dialogue description or for the specification of interactive applications (Kameas & Pintelas, 1997; Zaharakis et al., 1995), it is modified and extended for reasoning about multi agent systems. Its well-defined formalism for task decomposition and its event handling mechanisms are adjusted for the description of an agent's goal decomposition and for plan representation mechanisms as well as for the communication of messages between agents. The basic components of AOMFG reflect notions generally used by humans such as believes, desires and intentions that help in analysis and better understanding of complex computational systems. Indeed, the specification and design of those systems would be very difficult or even impossible without the use of such notions (Shoham, 1993). However, AOMFG is not intended to describe the human reasoning and behaviour or human social systems, so phenomena of human belief, communication and action are not the objects of this study.
The BDI architecture constitutes the theoretical background of the model and according to this, an agent in a multi agent system is viewed as having the three mental attitudes of belief, desire and intention (BDI). Beliefs are the information the agent has about the world it acts upon and the information it sends to the world. Desires are the tasks or the objectives that the agent is allocated or has to accomplish. Desires are usually referred as goals in the literature, although sometimes there is a distinction between these two notions, and goals have the meaning of the desires that are being pursued. However, this work does not distinguish them and they have the same meaning except when otherwise declared. Intentions are the agent's commitments to a desire. In addition, every agent contains a plan library. Plans are the possible ways that an agent can bring about an intention. In general, a plan is a partial commitment on how to achieve a desire. AOMFG explicitly represents the above notions in its structure.

4.1 General model description

The actions that an agent can execute, the alternative ways an action can be achieved, the perception of the environment and the communication with the environment, are all considered as a set of AOMFG. Every graph consists of two basic active entities, the *actors* (Fig. 1) and *links* (Fig. 2), corresponding to the transitions and the places of the Petri Nets respectively. These entities produce and consume *tokens*, which are the passive entities of the model and move along the connecting *edges* between actors and links.

Tokens

Tokens are transferred on the graph edges and represent data types, which are handled by the links and actors. Every token has an attached data type called *token colour*. The token colour may be a simple Boolean variable or an integer or even a complex structure such as a record. The token colour resembles the variables of programming languages and the value of token colour resembles the value assignment on the variables. In AOMFG, particularly, which is designed to express elements of multi modal logic, the tokens correspond to predicates or to the modal operators used. In graphical representation tokens are represented as black dots.

Actors

Actors represent the system processes and produce, consume or otherwise modify the tokens. Fig. 3 shows the internal structure of an AOMFG actor. Every actor has a *name,* which describes the actor. The interface part of an actor consists of a set of *input links* that provide the actor with tokens, and a set of *output links* that the actor supplies with tokens. In addition, every actor contains a set of firing *rules,* which determine the situations for the execution of an actor as well as the results of such an execution. Every rule has a left part that describes the pre-conditions for the rule firing and a right part that describes the post-conditions of the rule firing. The rules constitute the actor's behavioural part. The operations, which are carried out by the actor, are described with an *operation function* (it makes up the actor's functional part) and the binding of variables is done by a *binding function.* The *type* defines the meaning of the actor and consequently its allowed decomposition schemes. An actor may be:

- **action actor:** it represents a primitive action that an agent can execute and cannot be further decomposed. A primitive action may be **private** or **foreign**. A private action is executed by the agent himself. A foreign action is caused by the agent but its content is requested to be executed by another agent
- **context actor:** it represents a set of actions that lead to the achievement of a higher goal. A context actor is decomposed in sub-goals iteratively until it is refined into a set of action actors
- **library actor:** it represents the way a higher goal is decomposed and is executed in sub-goals. The goal decomposition is achieved with the directed distribution of the tokens. The library actors have inherent in their behaviour the laws of this distribution. The set of available library actors is predefined and the model determines their operation. Library actors play the role and correspond to the language structures of sequence, condition and iteration of high-level programming languages. Furthermore, they can be used to express and support non-determinism and concurrency issues. Depending on the way they manage and control the tokens, they are divided in:
    - **sequence library actor**, where the actors participating in the decomposition must be executed sequentially

    - **non deterministic choice library actor,** where (depending on the firing rule, which is described in the sequel) some actors are chosen and executed
    - **concurrency library actor**, where the actors participating in the decomposition are executed concurrently
    - **condition library actor,** where some actors are executed according to a contained firing condition
    - **iteration library actor,** where the actors participating in the decomposition are executed repeatedly until a termination condition is satisfied
- **group actor:** it has no computational meaning but is used for model clarity. Essentially, group actors are substitution transitions and work in a similar way as the *pages* in Coloured Petri Nets (Jensen, 1997).

As AOMFG is designed to specify concurrent tasks, it is usually necessary to reference time. This reference concerns how concurrent actions occur, when an action takes place or how long an action lasts. In addition, being a specification model, it has to be independent from the target platform where the specified application will be executed. Considering the above, AOMFG presumes time as a regular interval, which is not constant, but it is determined by the target platform (this approach has been originally proposed by (Shoham, 1993)). An executed action by an agent may need more than one regular interval. In addition, the amount of those regular intervals either is not known initially or it cannot be foreseen. However, in the current model version there is no explicit reference to time in actors; instead this can be described as a fact in actor's input links.

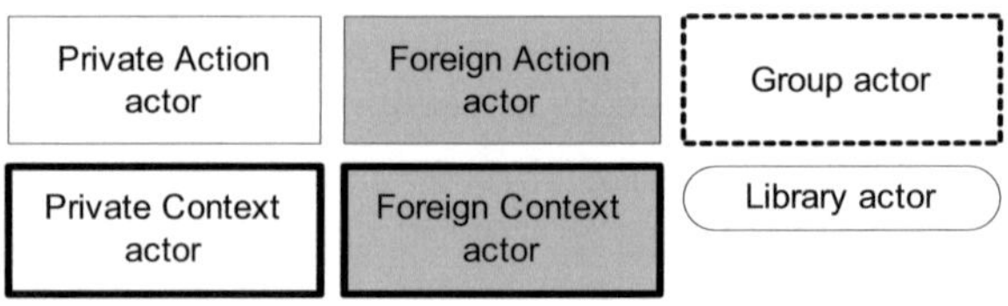

Fig. 1. The different actors provided by AOMFG

Links

Links represent the state that precedes or follows a process execution and they store, check and handle the tokens. Fig. 3 shows the internal structure of an AOMFG link. A link has a *name*, which describes the link, a set of *producing actors* that provide the link with tokens, and a set of *consuming actors* that the link supplies with tokens. The way a link is used is significant as it determines the role of the link inside the model and constitutes its behavioural part. In addition, a link can do several *operations* on a range of accepted coloured tokens. This establishes the link's computational part. Links correspond to the places of the Petri Nets and in AOMFG model represent notions of the BDI logic as well as some kinds of events. A link may be of one of the following types:

- **event link:** it reflects the caused events during the execution of the agent. Since, multi agent environments are populated by several agents, perhaps together with human participants, three kinds of events should be distinguished: those caused internally by an agent which concern exclusively himself, those concerning interaction between agents and those caused by the user of the system which are directed to the agents. Consequently, the event links are divided into
    - **system event links,** which are caused by the agent itself and represent the changes in the state of the system,

    - **system communication event links,** which are caused by the agent and are directed to other agent(s) in the environment in favour of a request for an action or a notification of an information (e.g. inform message),
    - **user event links,** which are caused by the user of the application. The model considers the user as an agent that generates events; thus its behaviour need not be further elaborated. The user event link is used for distinguishing between these events and the events of the system. This grading differentiates the agent's response towards the user to the interaction and communication between the agents (communication protocols etc.)
- **desire link:** it reflects the broader context where the several processes and the events of the system or the user take place. In essence, it represents the decomposition hierarchy where the corresponding actor belongs. The desire link when it is an input link of an actor, represents the starting point of an agent's goal, and when it is an output link of an actor, represents the ending point of an agent's goal. If an input desire link contains tokens, then it indicates the adopted intention of an agent to bring about the desire, and if an output desire link contains tokens then it indicates the drop of intention
- **belief link:** it is related to the information that an agent has about the environment it occupies and represents the information, which the agent handles or sends to the environment. In particular, the information, which must be sent to another agent, constitutes a subset of belief links and is represented by the **communication belief link**. The belief links can also be used as conditions that precede or follow an action of the system.

Fig. 2. The links provided by AOMFG

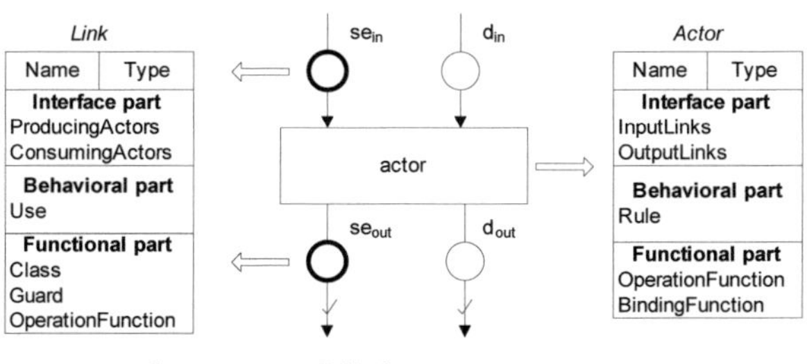

Fig. 3. The internal structure of actors and links

4.2 Formal definition of AOMFG

An AOMFG is a directed, bipartite graph combining text and graphics. It is described by the tuple AOMFG=(A, L, E, T), satisfying the following requirements:

- A is a non-empty set of actors
- L is a non-empty set of links
- E is a non-empty set of edges connecting the links and actors, where $E \subseteq (A \times L) \cup (L \times A)$
- T is a non-empty set of coloured tokens

- $A \cap L = \varnothing$ and $A \cup L \neq \varnothing$

The set of actors A is a non empty set such that

$A = ActionActor \cup ContextActor \cup LibraryActor \cup GroupActor$, where

$ActionActor = PrivateAction \cup ForeignAction$ and

$LibraryActor = SequenceLibraryActor \cup ConcurrencyLibraryActor \cup ConditionLibraryActor \cup NonDeterministicChoiceLibraryActor \cup IterationLibraryActor$.

In addition, the intersection between the members of A is the empty set, e.g.

$ActionActor \cap ContextActor = \varnothing$ etc.

Every actor $a \in A$ is a tuple

$a = (Name, InputLinks, OutputLinks, Rule, OperationFunction, BindingFunction, Type)$, where

Name is the name of the actor,

InputLinks is a function, which returns the set of input links and is defined as

$InputLinks: A \rightarrow \wp(L)$,

$InputLinks(a) = \{l \mid l$ is a link that is connected with an edge directed to the actor $a\}$ where

$\wp(L)$ is the powerset of L,

$\forall a \in A, InputLinks(a) \subset L$ and,

$\forall a \in A, \forall l \in InputLinks(a), \langle l, a \rangle \in E$

OutputLinks is a function, which returns the set of output links and is defined as

$OutputLinks: A \rightarrow \wp(L)$,

$OutputLinks(a) = \{l \mid l$ is a link that is connected with an edge directed from the $a\}$ where

$\wp(L)$ is the powerset of L,

$\forall a \in A, OutputLinks(a) \subset L$ and,

$\forall a \in A, \forall l \in OutputLinks(a), \langle a, l \rangle \in E$

Rule is a function, which returns the set of rules that describe the actor's behaviour during firing. As it is mentioned above a rule has a pre-condition part and a post-condition part. The functions *PreCond* and *PostCond* return the links that take place in the firing and in the firing results of the actor respectively. In addition, they return the tokens, which are consumed and produced respectively during actor firing. The domain of those functions is the set of rules R; the union of every actor's set of rules constitutes the R. The functions *PreCond* and *PostCond* are defined as

$PreCond: R \rightarrow (L \times T)$ and $PostCond: R \rightarrow (L \times T)$

where

$\forall (l, t) \in PreCond(r), l \in InputLinks(a), a \in A, t \in T$ and

$\forall (l, t) \in PostCond(r), l \in OutputLinks(a), a \in A, t \in T$

As a result the *Rule* function is defined as

$Rule: A \rightarrow \wp(R)$,

$Rule(a) = \{r \mid r \equiv PreCond(r) \Rightarrow PostCond(r)\}$, where $\wp(R)$ is the powerset of R.

OperationFunction is the function that describes the operations an actor does when its firing is caused

BindingFunction is the function that determines the binding of variables; essentially, it determines the colour value of each token that the actor handles

Type is a function that returns the actor internal complexity and is used during the decomposition of the actor. For example the returned value may be *ContextActor, PrivateAction, SequenceLibraryActor*, etc.
The set of links *L* is a non empty set such that

$L = EventLink \cup DesireLink \cup BeliefLink$, where

$EventLink = SystemEventLink \cup SystemCommunicationEventLink \cup UserEventLink$
and

$CommunicationBeliefLink \subseteq BeliefLink$.
In addition, the intersection between the members of *L* is the empty set, e.g.

$EventLink \cap DesireLink = \emptyset$ etc.
Every link $l \in L$ is a tuple

$l = \{Name, ProducingActors, ConsumingActors, Class, Use, Guard, OperationFunction, Type\}$,
where
Name is the name of the link,
ProducingActors is a function, which returns the set of producing actors, which supply the link with tokens and is defined as

$ProducingActors: L \rightarrow \wp(A)$,

$ProducingActors(l) = \{a \mid l \in PostCond(r), \forall r \in Rule(a), a \in A\}$, and

$ProducingActors(l) \subset A$,

where $\wp(A)$ is the powerset of A.
ConsumingActors is a function, which returns the set of the actors, which consume the tokens of the link and is defined as

$ConsumingActors: L \rightarrow \wp(A)$,

$ConsumingActors(l) = \{a \mid l \in PreCond(r), \forall r \in Rule(a), a \in A\}$ and

$\text{ConsumingActors(l)} \subset \text{A}$,

where $\wp(A)$ is the powerset of A.
Class is a function that returns a predicate, which describes the class of the link and determines the accepted colour of tokens
$Class(l) \in \{EventLink, DesireLink, BeliefLink\}$
Use is a function that returns a predicate, which describes the use that a link allows on its tokens. The returned value *Normal* refers to input links while the returned value *OK* refers to output links (graphically, the links of *Use=OK* are represented with a check mark on their edge)
$Use(l) \in \{Normal, OK\}$
Guard is a function that describes the accepted values of the coloured tokens
OperationFunction is the function that describes the operations a link does such as token integrity or error handling based on the value returned by the *Guard* function
Type is a function that returns the link's internal complexity and is used during the decomposition of the link. For example the returned value may be *SystemEventLink, DesireLink*, etc.

4.3 Model execution

The model execution is based on the notion of the state of a system, and of changes in state being caused by events. A *state* of an AOMFG represents the distribution of tokens over the system links at some moment in time and is defined as a function S, such that S: $L \rightarrow \{0, 1, 2, \ldots\}$. AOMFG has an *initial state* S_0 (initial marking), which is the initial assignment of tokens to the system's links. An AOMFG initial state is defined as S_0: $L \rightarrow \{0, 1, 2, \ldots\}$ and consequently an AOMFG together with its initial state is defined as (AOMFG, S_0).

Essentially, the above include the beliefs, desires and intentions of every agent the current moment; furthermore, describe what events are happening in the environment and how the whole multi agent system may evolve the next moment. As the behaviour of agents can be described in terms of agent states and their changes, AOMFG simulates this dynamic behaviour by *state transition*, which is a change from a state S_i to a state S_{i+1}. A state transition causes the redistribution of the tokens to links according to the actors' *firing rules*. The history of the model execution can be considered to be a sequence of states and state transitions.

A state changes according to the state transition function (firing rule). In addition, consider a weight function W on an arc $<x, y>$, where x is a link or an actor and y is an actor or a link, such that W: $E \rightarrow \{1, 2, \ldots\}$. For a link $l \in L$ and an actor $a \in A$, l is an input link l_{in} of a iff $<l, a> \in E$ (there is an arc from l to a), and l is an output link l_{out} of a iff $<a, l> \in E$ (there is an arc from a to l). Every firing rule contains at least one desire link and one event link in its left and right part and optionally some belief links. The AOMFG firing rule is as follows:

1. an actor $a \in A$ is *enabled* if there is a rule $r \in Rule(a)$ with an input desire link d_{in} on its left part ($d_{in} \in PreCond(r)$), which contains token. In this case the agent intends to bring about the specific desire,
2. an enabled actor $a \in A$ *fires* only if the input event link e_{in} of the rule $r \in Rule(a)$ ($e_{in} \in PreCond(r)$), contains token and the rest input links of the rule contain tokens,
3. the actor firing causes the consumption of tokens from all the input links l_{in}, ($l_{in} \in InputLinks(a)$, and $l_{in} \in PreCond(r)$), of the firing rule and tokens' production to all the output links l_{out}, ($l_{out} \in OutputLinks(a)$, and $l_{out} \in PostCond(r)$), of the firing rule, causing a state transition. The new state S' is defined as $\forall l$: $l \in L$ $S'(l) = S(l) + W(a, l) - W(l, a)$.

The above imply that i) actors with the same desire link belong to a certain desire and they all lead to the accomplishment of the same higher goal, ii) all the state transitions are caused by events and this reinforces the model with the properties of responsiveness and pro-activeness, and consequently iii) the undertaken actions lead to a certain goal that reflects a goal-directed behaviour. Furthermore, the history determines the state as previous beliefs (preconditions) are taken into consideration for the decision of the execution of an action.

The above firing rule stands in the general case, whilst according to the actor's type there are some parameters that alter the rule:

- the colour of the tokens determines which rules of an actor are going to fire. The check of the tokens' colour value is realized in the left part of the actor's rule and a new value assignment or production of new tokens is realized in the right part of the actor's rule in association with the binding function
- the consumption of tokens is instantaneous if the actor terminates its execution in one time regular interval. In a different case the tokens of input desire and system event links (d_{in}, e_{in}) are not consumed but they are retained until the actor terminates its execution. After actor termination these tokens are consumed and new tokens are produced in the output links

- every actor has an output desire link d_{out} and an output system event link e_{out} with *Use*(*l*)=*OK*. The d_{out} link means the termination of the pursued goal, and the e_{out} link means the successful processing of the event that caused the pursuing of the desired goal. It is mentioned that d_{out} contains no information about the achievement of the goal; instead such information is contained in the actor's output belief links. If tokens exist in the d_{out} and the e_{out} links then the execution of the actor is considered as successful.

Every AOMFG graph describes the alternative ways that an agent can bring about a desire that is the plans the agent has in order to accomplish a goal. Furthermore, considering that the way an agent reasons, or deliberates with the others of the environment where it exists, can be described by the plans that an agent has, then a multi agent system can be considered as the union of all the AOMFG, that is

$$\text{MAS} = \bigcup_i \left(\text{AOMFG}_i, S_{0_i}\right)$$

Considering that $\boldsymbol{L}$ is the set of all MAS links, and *MASS* is the state transition function of a the multi agent system such that *MASS*: $\boldsymbol{L}\rightarrow\{0, 1, 2, 3, \ldots\}$, then a system state transition is described as

$$MASS'(\boldsymbol{L}) = \bigcup (S(l)+W(a, l)-W(l, a)).$$

According to the firing rules, an actor is enabled when the input desire link of the behavioural rule contains token. This is very important for the model because it means that the agent has a goal and in addition it is committed to that goal; in other words, the agent intends the goal. All the actors that the agent intends are gathered in a list, which the model maintains, called *intention list*. The intention list comprises the third fundamental element of the BDI theory, the intentions. Thus, it is strongly connected with the theoretical model that the AOMFG is based upon. Only one of the actors residing in the intention list can be executed when the next event appears. Every new intended actor is placed at the head of the list and because of the head-to-tail examination of the list the head represents the current context. From the actors residing in the intention list those that belong in the current context are first examined and if no one recognizes the event then the rest of the list are examined. The actors remain in the intention list as long as their execution lasts. When the execution of the actor terminates, the actor is removed from the intention list. The above characteristics deal with the priorities between intentions and especially when an actor is more imperative than another. In the opposite case, belief links can be used as pre-conditions of the actor firing.

The intention list represents the commitments of an agent to the others and to itself. These are parts of its mental state, which is reviewed and updated in every regular time interval. When an actor's rule fires the contents of the intention list are changed according to the actor's type. Thus, the firing of a context actor puts all the contained actors in the intention list, whilst the firing of an action actor usually removes a set of actors from the intention list. This is expected since a context actor contains sub-goals that must be accomplished while the firing of an action actor means the termination of a set of goals. Furthermore, a context actor can represent a persistent goal; the goal persists until the sub-goals are accomplished. For instance, the persistent goal "I persist to avoid crash when I want to go somewhere by car", can be represented by a context actor "*avoid crash*" that is decomposed in several other actors such as "*driving a car*", "*driving a motorcycle*" and so on, and a belief link "*destination is reached*". The actor "*avoid crash*" is kept in the intention list until it is believed that destination is reached that is the execution of the actor "*driving a car*" terminates and the belief link "*destination is reached*" has a token with value true. The library actors administrate the intention list and depending on their type they add, remove or preserve goals and actions, which must be executed or have been already executed.

4.4 Decomposition

Since an AOMFG is an agent's plan that describes the necessary actions for the fulfilment of a desire, it is useful to support the composition and the decomposition of the plans in order to express higher goals and sub-goals respectively. This is realized with the use of special structures, in the style of dynamic logic (Harel, 1984), which determine the type of context actors and define the decomposition. The model supports goal decomposition and execution of the participating actions in the following ways:

- sequential (;), that is the actions are executed one after the other,
- non deterministic choice (|), that is one of the available actions may be executed,
- concurrency (||), that is the actions are executed in the same regular time interval,
- with test (?), that is proportionately on the conditions which may hold some actions are executed,
- iteration (*), that is the action is executed repeatedly until some termination condition is satisfied.

Actually, the above kinds of decomposition are operators that determine the execution of the plans (Table 1), where a, b are action or context actors and c is the value of a coloured token. The functionality of these operators is embodied in the AOMFG library actors.

a;b	a is executed and then b is executed
$a \mid b$	Either a or b is executed but not both
$a \| b$	a and b are executed concurrently
$c?;a \mid \neg c?;b$	If c holds then a is executed else b is executed
a*c and ca*	a is executed repeatedly until c is satisfied (*repeat-until* loop) and a is executed repeatedly if c is satisfied beforehand (*while-do* loop)

Table 1. Plan execution operators

4.5 Library actors

The decomposition capabilities of the model are supported with the help of the library actors. Library actors represent structure; they are in fact operators on computations. A library actor is in essence a pair of actors, where one of them constitutes the start (<*library actor name*>-S) of the decomposition and the other constitutes the end (<*library actor name*>-E). Those actors perform the stated actions of decomposition and supervise the correct distribution of tokens to the participating actors, and the correct termination of the execution. As participating actors, it is meant any combination of action, context or group actors. It is mentioned that when a context actor is decomposed then library actors represent this decomposition. The library actors provided by AOMFG are described in the sequel.

Sequence-S, sequence-E

When a token is produced in the input desire link of the sequence-S actor, then it produces tokens in the input desire links of the participating actors. The participating actors are placed in the intention list and remain there until the termination of the execution of the context actor. When a token is produced in the input event link of the sequence-S actor, then it produces tokens progressively in the input event links of the participating actors. The sequence-E actor produces tokens in its output desire and event links when it will receive tokens from all the output links of the participating actors. In addition, it removes the participating actors from the intention list.

Non-deterministic-choice-S, non-deterministic-choice-E

When a token is produced in the input desire link of the non-deterministic-choice-S actor, then it produces tokens in the input desire links of the participating actors. These actors are placed in the intention list and remain there until the termination of the execution of the context actor. When a token is produced in the input event link of the non-deterministic-choice-S actor, then it produces tokens non-deterministically in the input event links of the participating actors. The non-deterministic-choice-E actor produces tokens in the output desire and event links when it receives tokens from the respective output links of the participating actors. In addition, it removes the participating actors from the intention list.

Concurrency-S, concurrency-E

When a token is produced in the input desire link of the concurrency-S actor, then it produces tokens in the input desire links of the participating actors. The participating actors are placed in the intention list, and remain there until the termination of the execution of the context actor. When a token is produced in the input event link of the concurrency-S actor, then it produces tokens in the input event links of all the participating actors. The participating actors are executed concurrently. The concurrency-E actor produces tokens in the output desire and event links when it receives tokens from all output links of the participating actors. In addition, it removes the participating actors from the intention list.

Condition-S, condition-E

The condition-S actor contains condition "if…then…else" where it examines the conditions that must hold and produces tokens in the proper event links of the participating actors. However, it produces tokens in all the input desire links of the participating actors and it places all the actors in the intention list. The condition-E actor checks the termination of the actors' execution, and produces tokens in the output desire and event links. In addition, it removes the participating actors from the intention list.

Iteration-S, iteration-E

The iteration library actor is a kind of execution rather than a decomposition mechanism. Both iteration-S and iteration-E actors may have condition, which determines the start and the end of the execution repetition. In this way can be described loops such as "while…do" and "repeat…until". The same holds for the termination of the context actor, too. The participating actors determine the decomposition and administrate the intention list. If the termination condition of the iteration library actor is not satisfied then the tokens are not consumed from the input desire and event links of the context actor.

4.6 Transformation to Petri Nets

AOMFG is based on Petri Nets. Links resemble the places of Petri Nets. However, AOMFG provides a variety of link types and helps to the distinguishing of the different events that happen in a multi agent system, as well as to the reflection of the notions of an intentional system. Since Petri Nets are inherently event driven there is no representation of any kind of events. In order to transform an AOMFG to a Petri Net, the event links are eliminated without loss of expressiveness. Although action actors resemble the transitions of Petri Nets, context actors are more complex entities, as they are decomposition or composition structures. Since, the decomposition or composition of context actors is achieved via the library actors, their correspondence to the Petri Nets is presented in the sequel. The transformation of AOMFG model to equivalent Petri Nets makes it subject of analysis methods that imply on Petri Nets.

In Fig. 4, the sequence-S library actor sends tokens to the action actor t_2, and after the execution termination of the latter the action actor t_3 starts execution. In the correspondent Petri Net, the initial marking is at place p_1 and the transitions t_2 and t_3 are executed sequentially; the transitions t_1 and t_4 represent the sequence-S and sequence-E library actors respectively. The virtual transition t_v, simulates the operation of library actors that control the sequential execution.

In Fig. 5(a) either action actor t_2 or action actor t_3 is executed. The operation of the non-deterministic-choice-S actor is represented in Fig. 5(b) where either transition t_{v1} or t_{v2} fires. In addition, only one of the transitions t_{v3} or t_{v4} is needed to fire for the process termination.

In Fig. 6(a), the initial marking is in link p_1 and the concurrency-S library actor sends tokens to both action actors t_2 and t_3 so they can be executed concurrently. Similarly in Fig. 6(b) the transitions t_2 and t_3 fire simultaneously since transition t_1 provides with tokens both places p_2 and p_4.

In Fig. 7(a), the condition-S library actor sends a token to either action actor t_2 or action actor t_3 depending on the condition cond. Thus, only one of these action actors fires. In a similar way in Fig. 7(b) either transition t_2 or t_3 fires, and only one of the transitions t_{v1} or t_{v2} is needed to fire for the process termination. In Fig. 8(a) the action actor t_2 is executed repetitively until the satisfaction of the condition cond, and in a similar way in Fig. 8(b) transition t_2 does. In Fig. 9(a) if the condition cond=true then the action actor t_2 is executed repetitively, and in a similar way in Fig. 9(b) transitions t_2 does.

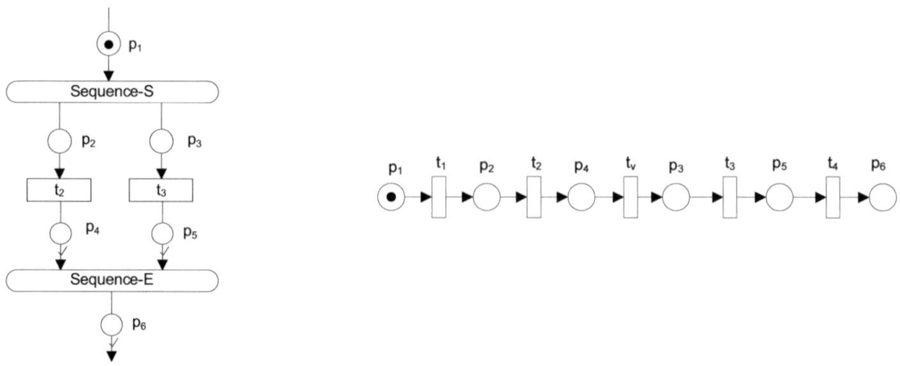

(a) (b)

Fig. 4. Sequential execution

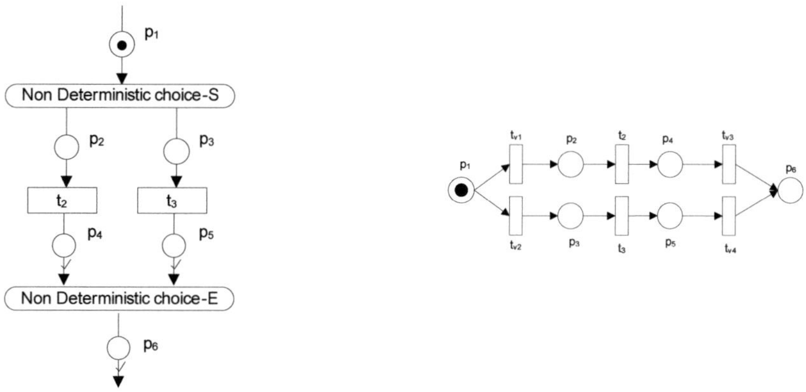

(a) (b)

Fig. 5. Non deterministic choice

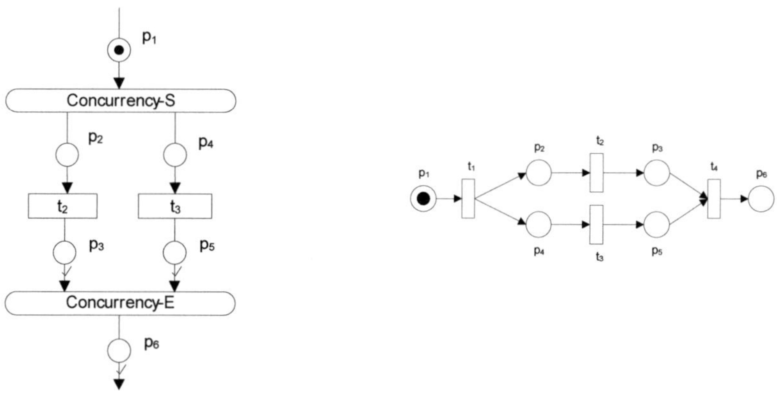

(a) (b)

Fig. 6. Concurrency

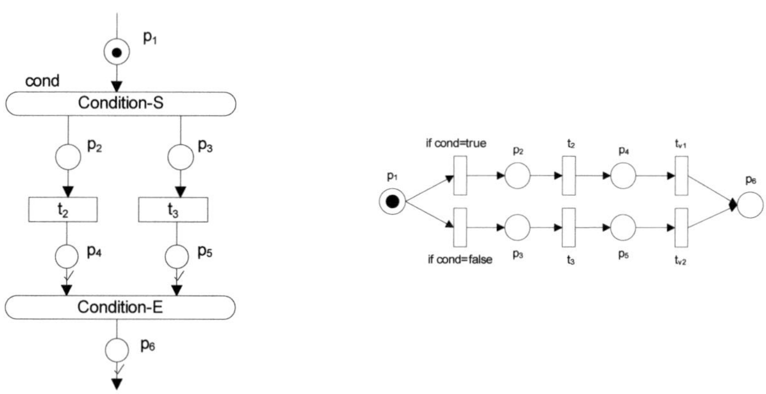

(a) (b)

Fig. 7. Condition

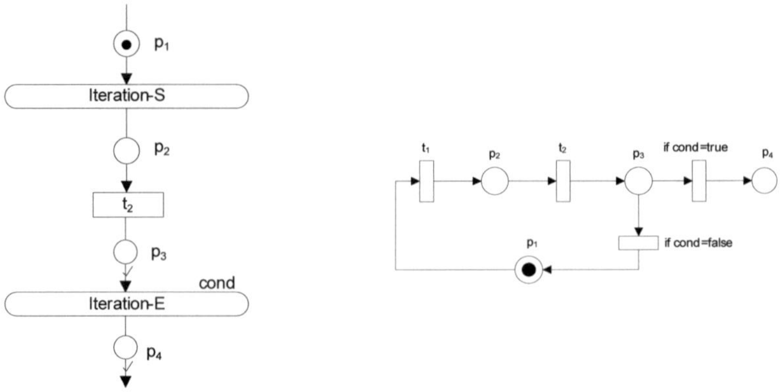

(a) (b)

Fig. 8. Iteration (repeat…until loop)

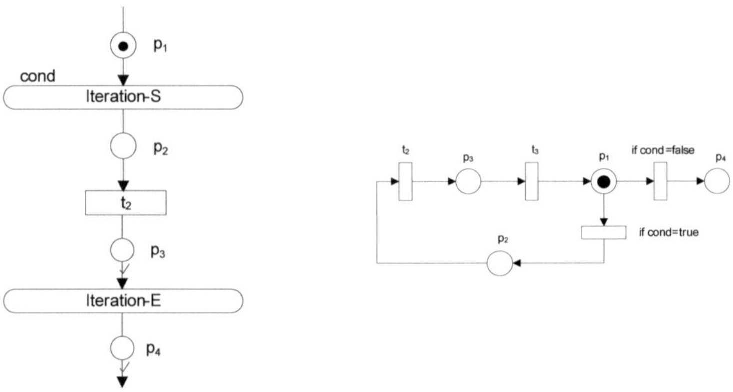

(a) (b)

Fig. 9. Iteration (while…do loop)

4.7 Discussion

The basic notions of BDI theory are embodied and represented by the structure of AOMFG. The beliefs are represented by the belief links that usually constitute the prerequisite or the results of an agent's actions. Thus, they are strongly connected to the planning of an agent's actions and decisions. The desires are described by the desire links and determine the context where the actions take place in order to achieve the agent's goals. The desires as input links determine the initiation of a higher goal and through the goal decomposition they determine the partially desires for the achievement of this goal. As output links, they examine and mark the successful termination of the executed actions that took place for the goals' achievement. The existence of the appropriate tokens in the desire links indicates the intentions to accomplish desires. All the enabled actors are placed in the intention list and point out the effort and the commitment of the agent to fulfil its desires as well as its obligations to the other agents. The communication between the agents is represented by the foreign action actors and as a part of the agent's actions is in accordance to the speech act theory. The communication belief links describe shared information, while the communication event links represent the triggering of communication and interaction events. The existence of foreign action actors and communication belief or event links, indicates the awareness of an agent about the capabilities and the needs of the other agents and it is an important factor for the role of every agent as a member of a team. In addition, this reflects implicitly nested mental states as in the example of the section "Specifying a real life system".

The model focuses on the description of the agent's goals and on the different ways they can be achieved. Thus, it does not represent desires, which cannot ever be accomplished. Instead, are represented desires that either can or cannot be accomplished based on the current situation of the environment or on the context they are performed. In this way, the intentions eventually drop. This is in accordance to the models of the Cognitive Engineering and especially those of Cognitive Complexity Theory that regard the human-computer interaction as iterative goal decomposition that leads to a sequence of actions; in addition, they maintain the goals and consequently the subgoals in a short-term memory, which represents the adopted intention to accomplish the goal or even the persistence of the goals. The capabilities of an agent are not represented explicitly by an element of the model but they are specified by the actions that an agent is capable to perform. The participation and the role of an agent in teamwork depend on its capabilities and its desires.

The graphical nature of the model makes it a user-friendly tool for formal specifications of multi agent systems. As it is, in essence, a HLPN, it inherits from Petri Nets many characteristics. Petri Nets are graphical formal specification models with strong mathematical background, powerful analysis techniques, and broad use in a range of applications. AOMFG model based on Petri Nets, incorporates principles of cognitive models and mental notions for the description of the behaviour of the agents, and results a model with theoretical background and an attractive, comprehensible tool, which visualizes the modelling and it is easy to be learnt and used by software engineers and software system designers.

5. Model validation

During specification process a software engineer focuses on those characteristics that he considers critical or not clear. As a result, a system specification may be viewed by different perspectives. In order to demonstrate the generality of AOMFG model and its potential use in many different ways for reasoning about multi agent systems, four different perspectives are used. The case studies that are used for model validation include an algorithmic one and especially Shoham' s algorithm for the generic agent interpreter presented in (Shoham, 1993), a cooperating problem solving one and especially a communication protocol from the standards of FIPA (Foundation for Intelligent Physical Agents) (www.fipa.org), BDI related properties described in (Rao & Georgeff, 1995), and finally the specification of the Dermatology Tutor system (Zaharakis et al., 1998).

5.1 Generic agent interpreter

Shoham proposed the agent-oriented programming (AOP) paradigm as a specialization of object-oriented programming paradigm. Particularly, "AOP specializes the framework by fixing the state (now called mental state) of the modules (now called agents) to consist of components such as beliefs (including beliefs about the world, about themselves, and about one another), capabilities, and decisions, each of which enjoys a precisely defined syntax.

Various constraints are placed on the mental state of an agent, which roughly correspond to constraints on their common sense counterparts. A computation consists of these agents informing, requesting, offering, accepting, rejecting, competing, and assisting one another" (Shoham, 1993, p.56). In AOP a multi modal formal language is introduced which describes the agents' mental state and a generic agent interpreter that describes the agents' behaviour. The interpreter works by consistently iterating between the following processes:

- read the current messages, and update your mental state, including your beliefs and commitments (the agent program is crucial for this update)
- execute the commitments for the current time, possibly resulting in further belief change (this phase is independent of the agent's program) (Shoham, 1993, p.68).

Time is counted in regular intervals determined by the target execution platform. According to the above algorithm there are two independent processes, which run iterative at regular intervals.

A private AOMFG action actor, *the update-mental-state,* and a context AOMFG actor, the *execute-commitment* can represent these processes (Fig. 10). The *update-mental-state* action actor checks and updates the agent's mental state according to the model that specifies its properties. The check and update mechanisms are not examined from the presented perspective; instead they can be implemented with the use of a programming language. The system event input link s_{in}=*sel1* and the desire input link d_{in}=*ums* represent the system qualification for the fulfilment of the goal to check or update its mental state. The system communication input event link ce_{in}=*"incoming messages"* represents the reading of incoming messages, which may be several requests or informs from other agents of the environment. The content of these messages is the subject that is examined by the mental state. The AOMFG model generates tokens in the s_{in}=*sel1* and the d_{in}=*ums.* When an incoming message exists a token is generated in the ce_{in}=*"incoming messages"*. When the action *update-mental-state* terminates then tokens are produced in the output belief link b_{out}=*"update results"*, which represents the conclusions of the check and update of the mental state, and in the system and desire output links s_{out}=*sel1.OK* and d_{out}=*ums.OK* respectively. The AOMFG model generates tokens in the s_{in}=*sel2* and the d_{in}=*ec* too, however the *"execute commitment"* context actor cannot start execution until b_{in}=*"update results"* contains tokens. The execute commitment process is represented by a context actor since it is a process that corresponds to many actions the agent is able to perform and may be decomposed to several other actions. Because of its general nature, it is not further decomposed here. When the process terminates, tokens are produced in the system and desire output links s_{out}=*sel2.OK* and d_{out}=*ec.OK* respectively. Any resulting information is stored in the belief link b_{out}=*"action results"*, and if there are messages for other agents then the communication event ce_{out}=*"outgoing messages"* is triggered.

AOMFG turned out to be a general enough model and capable of describing in a clear and straightforward way the two independent processes contained in the algorithm proposed by Shoham for his generic agent interpreter, which is the basis of the agents that can be built according to the AOP paradigm. The generality of the algorithm results in generality of the graphs, and lies mainly on the second process of the algorithm and consequently on the context actor "execute commitment". Nevertheless, in an implementation phase this context actor corresponds to a number of other actors that constitute instances of this actor. These instances can be executed concurrently or can be suspended as it happens in AGENT0 that implements Shoham' s algorithm. Furthermore, AOMFG can be used to describe the agent mental state and the alternative actions an agent may choose. However, the notion of time that is used explicitly in AOP cannot be represented in AOMFG in a straightforward way. Instead, the use of belief links as action preconditions can substitute the explicit reference to time.

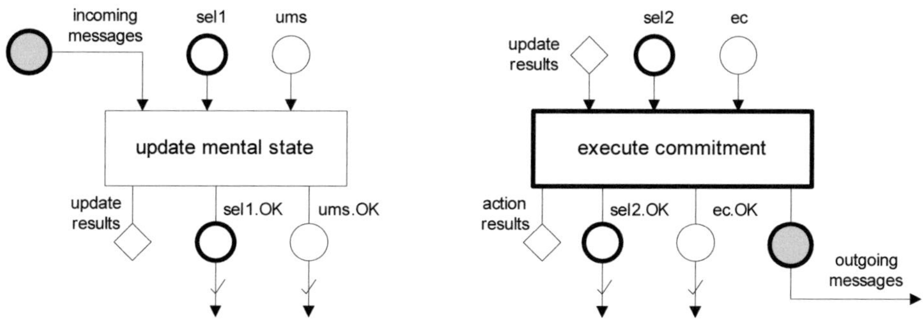

Fig. 10. Shoham' s generic agent interpreter

5.2 FIPA communication protocols

The Foundation for Intelligent Physical Agents (FIPA) has published a series of specification documents including the Communicative Act Library Specification (www.fipa.org). In this document, in addition to the formalism, a series of standard communication protocols between agents is presented. These protocols are based on *speech act theory* (Searle, 1969) and include communication actions such as request, request-whenever, request-when. Due to space limitations, the AOMFG is used to describe FIPA-request protocol only.

According to FIPA-request protocol, an agent requests an action from another agent and the latter either does not understand the message, or refuses the action and justifies the refusal, or agrees to perform the requested action and after the action termination it informs the requester agent about the results of the action.

For representing the FIPA-request protocol, two processes take place: the send process (Fig. 12), which is fired when a request is desired, and the receive process (Fig. 11), which is fired when a request has happened and there is a need for reaction. In essence, the AOMFG for the send process describes how an agent behaves after the request has been sent. The same holds for the receive process, i.e., after a request has been received. This concession has been done since it is trivial to describe these two processes e.g., by two single events.

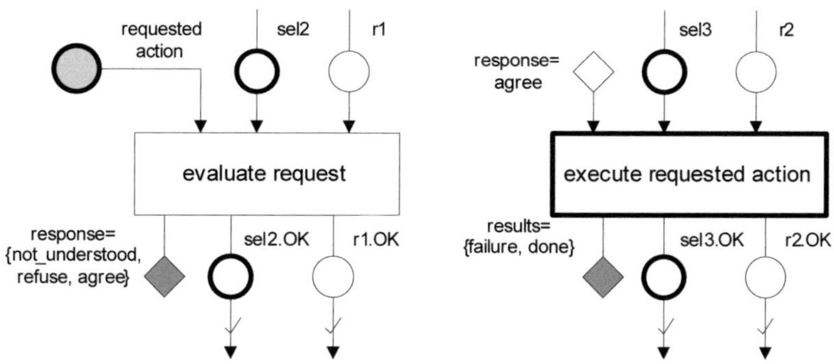

Fig. 11. FIPA-request protocol: receive process

Suppose that an agent (the receiver) received a request message from another agent (the sender). This is represented by the communication input event link ce_{in}=*"requested action"*. The receiver evaluates the request with action actor *"evaluate request"* and has to respond that it either did not understand the message, or that it refuses the action or that it agrees to perform the action. The response is represented as communication output belief link cb_{out}=*"response"*. It is mentioned that the values of cb_{out}=*"response"* are one among not_understood, refuse or agree. If the receiver agrees to perform the requested action then the context actor *"execute requested action"* is fired since there exist tokens in its entire input links. After the execution of the action, the receiver has to inform the sender about the results of the performed actions. Those results are represented by the cb_{out}=*"results"*, which may have the values failure or done.

Suppose now, that an agent (the sender) sends a request message to another agent (the receiver). After the evaluation of the request by the receiver, a communication event link represents receiver's response as ce_{in}=*"response"*. The whole process is specified by a condition library actor, which checks the content of ce_{in}=*"response"* and enables the appropriate action actor. In order to achieve this, the condition-S library actor contains the following rules:

i. if *response=not_understood* then (*sel1.1* and *ra1*)
ii. if *response=refuse* then (*sel1.2* and *ra2*)
iii. if *response=agree* then (*sel1.3* and *ra3*)

Since the successful termination of only one action actor is necessary, the condition-E library actor contains the rule:

if {(*sel1.1.OK* and *ra1.OK*) or (*sel1.2.OK* and *ra2.OK*) or (*sel1.3.OK* and *ra3.OK*)} then (*sel1.OK* and *ra.OK*)

The action actor *"wait until requested action terminates"* does not consume the tokens of its input links until it is believed that the action has been performed. The fact that something is believed can be modelled by another AOMFG that specifies the agent's mental state such as the one of Fig. 10.

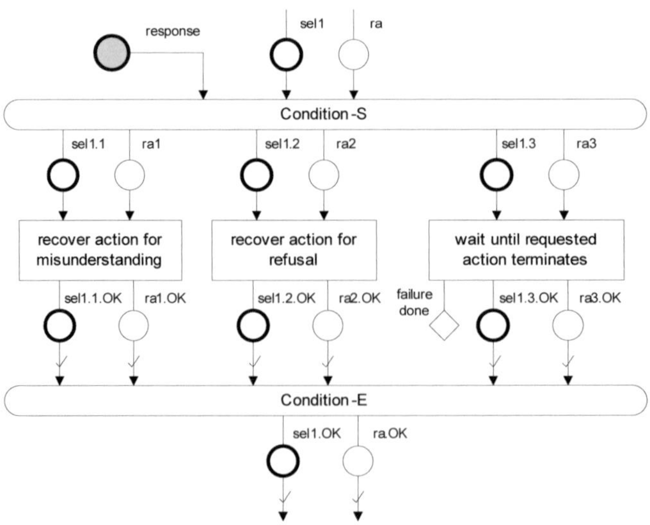

Fig. 12. FIPA-request protocol: send process

AOMFG was used to describe communication between agents in the sense of speech act theory. For this reason, the FIPA-request protocol was used as a test case. Although FIPA standards describe the communication process from an external observer's view, in this work the description is from an internal observer's view and focuses on the reactions of the agent in a communication action. This is due to the reasons of unity, uniformity, continuity and autonomy of the graphs and the specification method. Since AOMFG is used for the specification of the reasoning process and the actions of every agent separately, the communication should not be an exception. Besides, the model regards and manages the communication actions as physical actions. However, a different use of the model (external observer's perspective) is possible and this is due to the designer's choice.

5.3 BDI related properties

The AOMFG model reflects and explicitly represents the notions described by the BDI formalism, so this section attempts to represent some BDI related properties. The used BDI logic is a multi modal temporal logic based on the branching time logic CTL* (Emerson, 1991). The basic concept of the BDI logic is the transformation of a decision tree and the functions applied to it, to an equivalent model that represents beliefs, desires and intentions as accessibility relations over a set of possible worlds. Each world is a time tree with a single past and a branching future, with nodes corresponding to a possible system state and representing the options available to the system itself or the state of the environment which the system is embedded in, and with arcs (transitions) representing the different system actions for the achievement of an objective.
In this way, there are *belief-*, *desire-* and *intention-accessible worlds* corresponding to the states that the system believes to be possible, desires to bring about and intends to bring about, and *belief-*, *desire-* and *intention-accessibility relations* ($\mathcal{B}$, $\mathcal{D}$ and $\mathcal{I}$, respectively) which are the transitions between the worlds. The detailed syntax and semantics of the BDI logic are described in (Rao & Georgeff, 1995); in the following only its basic properties are briefly presented.

	Beliefs	**Desires**	**Intentions**
K-axiom	$\text{BEL}(p) \wedge \text{BEL}(p \supset q) \supset \text{BEL}(q)$	$\text{DES}(p) \wedge \text{DES}(p \supset q) \supset \text{DES}(q)$	$\text{INTEND}(p) \wedge \text{INTEND}(p \supset q) \supset \text{INTEND}(q)$
D-axiom	$\text{BEL}(p) \supset \neg\text{BEL}(\neg p)$	$\text{DES}(p) \supset \neg\text{DES}(\neg p)$	$\text{INTEND}(p) \supset \neg\text{INTEND}(\neg p)$
4-axiom	$\text{BEL}(p) \supset \text{BEL}(\text{BEL}(p))$		
5-axiom	$\neg\text{BEL}(p) \supset \text{BEL}(\neg\text{BEL}(p))$		

Table 2. The axioms of the KD45 system

The normal modal system KD45 (weak-S5) is adopted for beliefs, while the K and D axioms are adopted for desires and intentions. K-axiom states that if an agent believes (desires or intends) p and believes (desires or intends) that $p \supset q$ then it will believe (desire or intend) q. D-axiom says that the agent' s beliefs (desires or intentions) are not contradictory. 4-axiom and 5-axiom are respectively the positive and negative introspection axioms: 4-axiom states that an agent is aware of what it knows and 5-axiom says that an agent is aware of what it does not know. The axioms of the KD45 system are summarized in Table 2, where p, q are

propositions of the classical propositional logic, "$\wedge$" and "$\supset$" are the propositional connectives for conjunction and implication, and BEL, DES and INTEND are modal operators representing the agent's beliefs, desires and intentions respectively.
The necessitation rule is applied in beliefs, desires and intentions (Table 3)[1]:

	Necessitation rule
Beliefs	If $\vdash p$ then $\vdash$ BEL(p)
Desires	If $\vdash p$ then $\vdash$ DES(p)
Intentions	If $\vdash p$ then $\vdash$ INTEND(p)

Table 3. The necessitation rule for beliefs, desires and intentions

As the belief-, desire- and intention-accessible worlds are sets and in the same time are time trees, there are set relationships ($\subseteq$, $\cap$ etc.) and structure relationships (sub-world, identical or incomparable worlds) between them. Depending on the combinations of the above relationships and the axiomatizations of them, three constraints are under consideration: *strong realism* (Rao & Georgeff, 1991a), *realism* (Cohen & Levesque, 1990) and *weak realism* (Rao & Georgeff, 1991b). Structurally, AOMFG reflects the properties of realism since according to realism constraint an agent intends the actions it desires to bring about and it desires the actions it believes that can be achieved. In AOMFG model, the desires are represented by desire links and the intentions by desire links containing tokens. In addition, it is known the existence of the desire links a priori. Formally, $\mathcal{I} \subseteq \mathcal{D} \subseteq \mathcal{B}$, that is if an agent intends an action then it desires it and it believes it too.
However, AOMFG does not restrict the designer of an application to use one or another constraint. It is the designer's responsibility to use AOMFG in such a way that the properties of a constraint can be reflected. So, it is possible to reflect the properties of the other constraints too as this is depending on the broader concept in which, designer uses the model. Some of the characteristics of the weak realism are referred in the following, as it is the constraint for which some properties will be described by AOMFG. According to weak realism, the intersection between the belief-accessible worlds and desire-accessible worlds is not null and an agent does not desire a proposition the negation of which is believed. The same holds between desire- and intention-accessible worlds and between belief- and intention-accessible worlds. An agent does not intend a proposition the negation of which is desired or is believed (Table 4).

Semantic Condition	**Distinguishing Axiom**
$\mathcal{B} \cap \mathcal{D} \neq \varnothing$	BEL(p) $\supset \neg$DES($\neg p$)
$\mathcal{D} \cap \mathcal{I} \neq \varnothing$	DES(p) $\supset \neg$INTEND($\neg p$)
$\mathcal{B} \cap \mathcal{I} \neq \varnothing$	BEL(p) $\supset \neg$INTEND($\neg p$)

Table 4. The BDI modal system for weak realism

Some other properties that characterize the weak realism are the *asymmetry thesis* proposed by Bratman (Bratman, 1987) and extended by Rao and Georgeff (Rao & Georgeff, 1991b). Among them the intention-belief incompleteness ($\not\models$INTEND (p) $\supset$ BEL(p))[2], which is

[1] '$\vdash$' means that the formula which follows is valid

[2] '$\not\models$' means that the formula which follows is not satisfiable

allowed by weak realism, is selected to depict how this property can be represented by using AOMFG. In essence, it means that an agent intends to do an action but does not believe that it will do it. As a validation scenario is used the example referred in (Rao & Georgeff, 1995, p.33), in which Robbie the robot has an intention of opening the door when the bell rings but it does not believe that it will open the door when the bell rings because it might be serving beer.

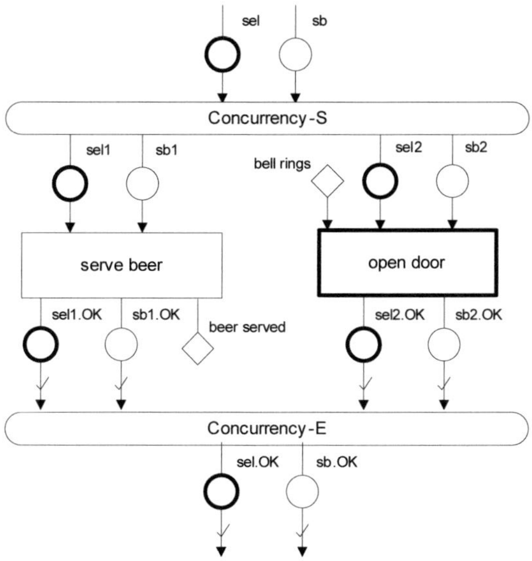

Fig. 13. Concurrent tasks for Robbie

Robbie serves beer while the bell rings (Fig. 13). The context actor *"open door"* is fired and is decomposed in the graph of Fig. 14. It is mentioned that both actors *"serve beer"* and *"open door"* may be in the intention list since Robbie might not have finished serving. In this case, the action actors *"move"* and *"open"* cannot fire since the condition link *"beer served"* contains no tokens and consequently no tokens can be produced in belief link *"door opened"*. So action actor *"do nothing"* fires and the context actor *"open door"* terminates its execution. It is mentioned that although *"do nothing"* is a void action it is considered as an action (in the flavour of speech act theory) that affects the environment as any other action does.

In the above, AOMFG was used to describe BDI related properties. Since it is based on BDI theory most of the properties are embodied in its semantics. Although the model structurally reflects the realism constraint, other BDI properties can be described too, but it is mentioned that is critical how the model will be used for such a purpose. This is not necessarily a drawback since even in theory there is a need of different logics in order to express the several constraints and their asymmetry thesis. It is mentioned that a primary aim of the AOMFG is to hide the complexity of strict formalisms from designers who are not experts in formal specification methods.

5.4 Specifying a real life system

General description of the Dermatology Tutor

The Dermatology Tutor (Zaharakis et al., 1998) is an intelligent tutoring system used for teaching Dermatology at the Department of Dermatology, School of Medicine, University of

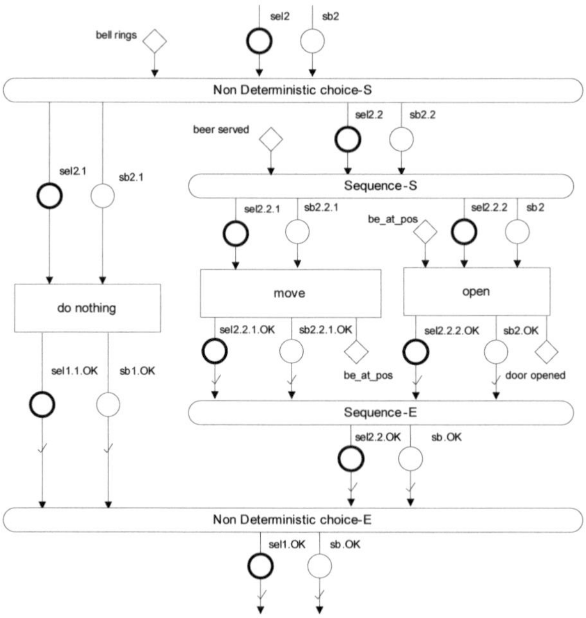

Fig. 14. Alternative actions according to Robbie's mental state

Patras. The Dermatology Tutor uses a self-organized society of autonomous software agents who have different capabilities or roles. In particular, the tutoring system for teaching dermatology consists of nine agents. A user can interact with the multi agent system through the user interface, which processes all the requests that come from the environment outside the system (i.e. the user). Depending on the event, this module (which has not been implemented as an agent) activates either the Dermatology Agent or the Help Agent. If they have a desire for the requested action and they believe that it is possible, then they adopt an intention about it. However, if there is a need to cooperate for task accomplishment then a structured society is constructed. As the architecture is composed for tutoring purposes, only the *Dermatology Agent* can act as an instructor; all the instructional strategies necessary for the tutoring process are contained in this agent's plans. The other agents populating the society called *medical agents*, can be members of a team formed by the Dermatology Agent and they can also communicate each other. Currently seven medical agents have been implemented: Histology, Physiology, Biology, Biochemistry, Microbiology, Radiology and Immunology agent. Each of them specializes on the corresponding medical domain and can provide knowledge and information about the domain matters. Furthermore, medical agents can request an action from third level agents (information agents) who may be local or remote and are responsible for information retrieval. The information agents are registered to the system and medical agents are aware of their existence. Although the information retrieval may be performed by a non-agent software system, their behaviour could be considered as one of an autonomous agent.

When the trainees use Dermatology Tutor, they have to select from a list of available actions, which includes "Teach", "Topic", "Search" and "Help". Each action causes the execution of one of the agent's high-level plans. For each trainee, a student environment is created, which records performance information. Currently, Dermatology Tutor creates a set of files for each trainee, where it records personal data, as name, year of study, specialty and performance data, as the goals accomplished, the learning units seen, the time spent on each plan or learning unit, the answers given and the score taken in each test, and the level of competence. In this way, Dermatology Tutor records the last position of the trainee, while performance information is used to decide the values of the preconditions of the agents' plans.

As described above, the plans specify the ways that an agent brings about its intentions. They refer to an agent's desires and they consist of actions that must be executed. There may exist more than one plan for each desire. Typically, plans have a name (plan name), pre-conditions that describe the plan triggering, and a body part, which describes the actions that will take part in the plan execution.

Using AOMFG for the specification of Dermatology Tutor

Suppose that the issue of psoriasis has to be taught. The Dermatology agent has a desire named "Teach psoriasis" and a plan in its plan library in order to carry out such a desire (Table 5). Each step of this plan constitutes a lower-level plan that can be further analyzed. The Dermatology agent is aware of the medical agents and can form teams in order to go through with its goals. In the following, the etiology and pathogenesis of psoriasis plan is examined. Dermatology agent adopts an intention about this goal and executes the corresponding plan (Table 6). In order to do this it needs to form a team with Biology, Biochemistry, Immunology, and Histology medical agents.

Plan name:	*Teach psoriasis*
Pre-conditions:	
Plan body:	Definition and Epidemiology
	Clinical View
	Histological View
	Etiology and Pathogenesis
	Treatment

Table 5. Dermatology agent plan for teaching psoriasis

Plan name:	*Etiology and Pathogenesis*	
Pre-conditions:		**Associated Agents**
Plan body:	Disorder of protein expression in keratinocytes	Biology, Biochemistry
	Antigenic stimulation and immunology activation	Immunology
	Proteases and intense mitotic activity	Biology, Biochemistry
	Metabolic disorders	Biochemistry
	Histopathologic changes of psoriasis	Histology

Table 6. Etiology and Pathogenesis plan of the Dermatology agent

The representation of "Etiology and pathogenesis" plan of the Dermatology agent with an AOMFG is depicted in Fig. 15. The plan is decomposed in foreign actions, which are requested from other agents. The context actor "Proteases and intense mitotic activity" is further decomposed in Fig. 16. The input desire link *ep* corresponds to the desire to teach the topic of etiology and pathogenesis of psoriasis, while the ep_i, i=1,…,5, correspond to the sub-goals which must be accomplished. When the agent adopts an intention to bring about this desire, a token is produced in the *ep* link. In addition, a token is produced in the system event link *sep*.

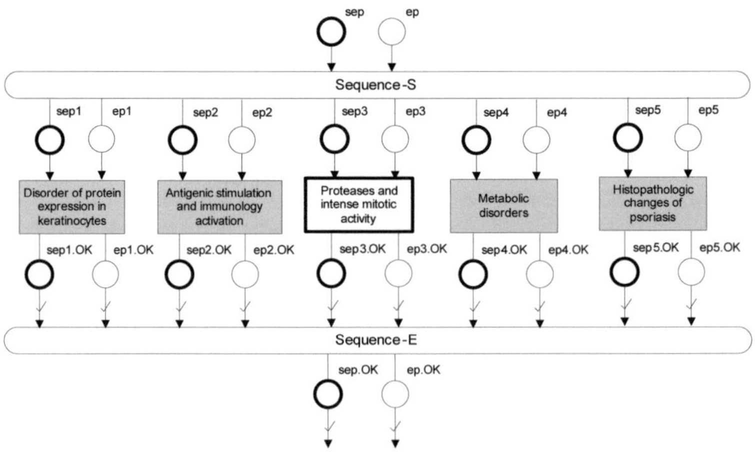

Fig. 15. Etiology and pathogenesis AOMFG

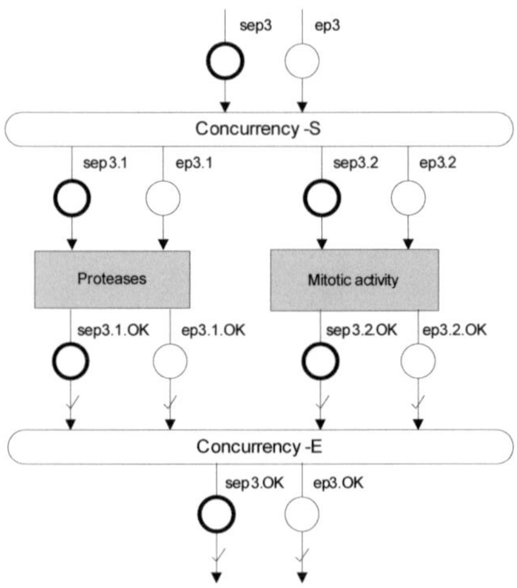

Fig. 16. Decomposition of "Proteases and intense mitotic activity" context actor

As the *sep* and *ep* input links contain tokens, the Sequence-S library actor produces tokens to every ep_i. All the actions are put in the intention list of the Dermatology agent as they are ready to fire (enabled). In addition, the Sequence-S library actor produces a token to the *sep1* and the action "Disorder of protein expression in keratinocytes" fires. When the execution of the action terminates, then the tokens of *sep1* and *ep1* are consumed and tokens are produced to *sep1.OK* and *ep1.OK*. Afterwards, the Sequence-S library produces a token to *sep2* and the same process follows. A concurrency library actor decomposes the context actor "Proteases and intense mitotic activity" and this means that when the actor fires, both actions "Proteases" and "Mitotic activity" are executed concurrently.

In order to fulfil its first partial goal ("Disorder of protein expression in keratinocytes") Dermatology agent requests the action from Biochemistry and Biology agents. As both Biochemistry and Biology agents have a desire about the requested action they adopt an intention about it (Table 7 and Table 8). AOMFG in Fig. 17 and Fig. 19 represent the plans of the Biochemistry and Biology agents respectively. The "Disorder of protein expression in keratinocytes" plans are detailed while the rest can be similarly represented. When both Biology and Biochemistry agents request this action, a token is produced in each input communication event links of the corresponding AOMFG in Fig. 18 and Fig. 20. Both agents adopt an intention, which means they produce a token to *kp* and *pe* desire links respectively. Furthermore, they produce a token to the *skp* and *spe*, respectively.

Plan name:	*Disorder of protein expression in keratinocytes: Keratinocyte proteins*	
Pre-conditions:		**Associated Agents**
Plan body:	Types of keratinocytes	
	Protein conformation	Biology
	Abnormal conformation	Biology
Plan name:	*Proteases*	
Pre-conditions:		**Associated Agents**
Plan body:	Proteases definition	
	Abnormalities	
Plan name:	*Metabolic disorders*	
Pre-conditions:		**Associated Agents**
Plan body:	Disorder of metabolic fermentations	
	• Disorder of metabolism of the cyclic nucleotides	
	• Disorder of metabolism of the arachidonic acid	
	• Disorder of metabolism of the polyamide	
	• Disorder of metabolism of the phosphatides	
	Vascular dysfunction	

Table 7. Plans of the Biochemistry agent

Plan name:	*Disorder of protein expression in keratinocytes: Protein expression*	
Pre-conditions:	*Protein conformation, Abnormal conformation*	**Associated Agents**
Plan body:	Normal expression of keratinoproteins	Biochemistry
	Abnormal expression of keratinoproteins	Biochemistry
Plan name:	*Mitotic acivity*	
Pre-conditions:		**Associated Agents**
Plan body:	Phases of mitotic activity	Immunology
	• keratinocytes	
	• macrophages	
	• lymphocytes	
	• mast cells	
	• neutrophilic cytes	
	Abnormalities of mitotic activity	

Table 8. Plans of the Biology agent

Biology agent cannot execute the first step ("Normal expression of keratinoproteins") of its "Disorder of protein expression in keratinocytes: Protein expression" plan, because it has to wait for precondition "Protein conformation" to become true. Neither can it execute the second step, due to precondition "Abnormal Conformation" being false. These preconditions are represented by the communication beliefs *Pc* and *Ac*. Biochemistry agent handles both preconditions. When the latter can infer the truth or the falsity of those facts, it will inform Biology agent about the results. This happens only after the execution of the actions "Protein conformation" and "Abnormal conformation" respectively, which cause the production of a token to each *Pc* and *Ac* communication belief links. Note that each medical agent that participates in a team is responsible for informing all other medical agents of the same team about all changes in its environment.

The above process indicates implicitly how AOMFG deals with some kind of nested beliefs. More precisely, Biology Agent cannot execute the actions "Normal expression of keratinoproteins" and "Abnormal expression of keratinoproteins" until it believes that Biochemistry agent believes that Pc and Ac are true, i.e.,

BEL("Biology Agent" BEL("Biochemistry Agent", "Pc"))
BEL("Biology Agent" BEL("Biochemistry Agent", "Ac"))

Equivalently, some kind of other nested mental states can be represented, for example, as described above, Dermatology agent requests the action "Metabolic disorders" from Biochemistry Agent and implicitly desires what Biochemistry agent desires, i.e.,

DES("Dermatology Agent" DES("Biochemistry Agent", "Metabolic disorders"))

When precondition "Protein Conformation" becomes true, then Biology agent executes the step "Normal expression of keratinoproteins". At the same time, the second precondition ("Abnormal Conformation") may become true, which means that Biology agent may execute the step "Abnormal expression of keratinoproteins". When both agents bring about their intentions they inform Dermatology agent for the results of the requested actions. Afterwards it attempts to fulfil the rest of its partial goals. After the execution of the "Etiology and pathogenesis" plan, Dermatology agent drops its intention for this plan and it continues with the next plan.

Thus, in order to validate AOMFG with a real system such as The Dermatology Tutor, the following steps were taken. Initially, the plans of all agents involved were analyzed. In this way, the agents' capabilities, desires and alternative ways of their achievement were expressed. Next, the agents' awareness of their environment and their interaction was

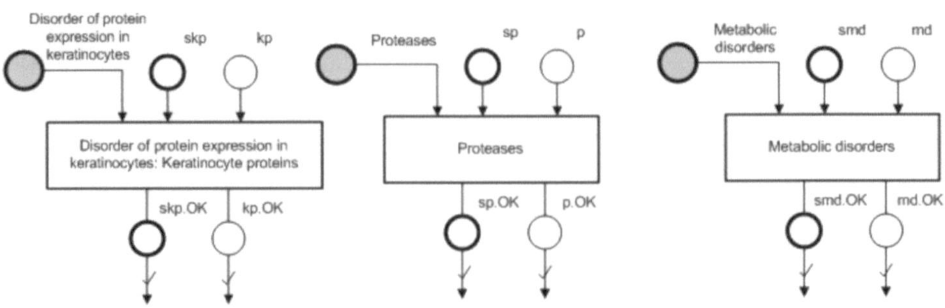

Fig. 17. AOMFG represents the plans of Biochemistry agent

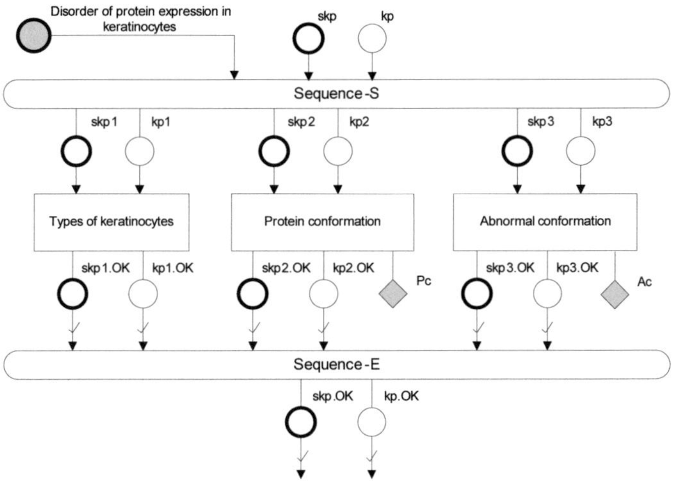

Fig. 18. Decomposition of "Disorder of protein expression in keratinocytes: Keratinicytes protein" plan

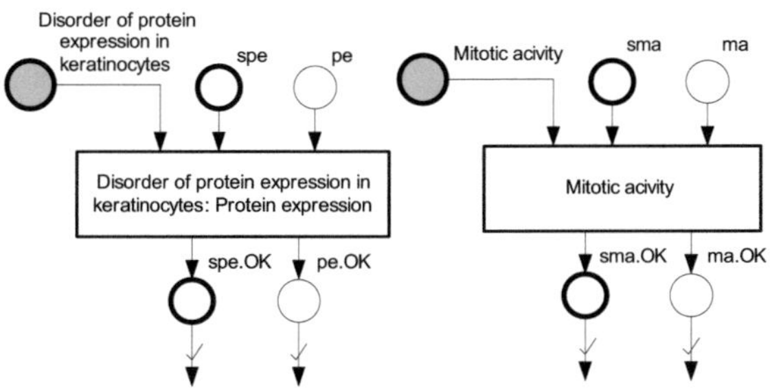

Fig. 19. AOMFG represents the plans of Biology agent

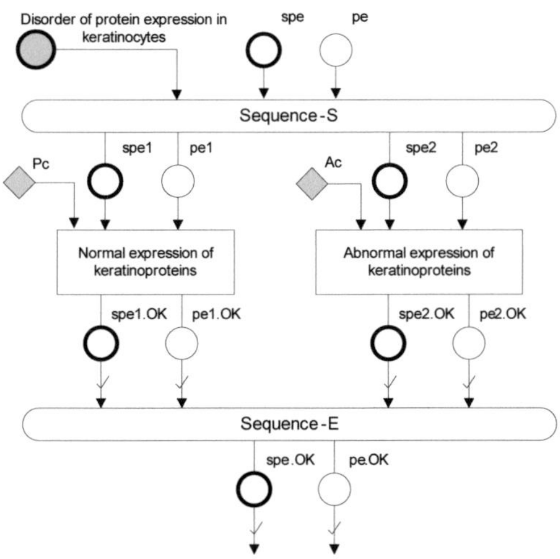

Fig. 20. Decomposition of "Disorder of protein expression in keratinocytes: Protein expression" plan

expressed with the use of the foreign action actors and communication event and belief links. Finally, their roles inside the formed teams according to their knowledge and capabilities were determined.
The design of the Dermatology Tutor was based on the description and the analysis of every agent separately and this gave a detailed view of the functionality and the participation in the team action. Thus, there are several autonomous design parts that relate with each other through communication actions, i.e. every agent is described by a set of graphs and the union of these graphs constitutes the whole system description. This approach does not allow a global and clear view of the composition and structure of the teams unless all the graphs are collected and studied. As a result, the team composition and the role of every agent are inducted from the foreign actors and the communication links. However, in the Dermatology Tutor the teams and the role of the agents are not determined at design time; instead the teams are formed dynamically depending on the tutoring process that justifies such a design approach.

6. Summary

Formal specifications are necessary for reasoning about multi agent systems. However, existing methods are not practical for wide use from designers and software engineers. In this work, AOMFG is introduced as a graphical model for formal specifications of multi agent systems. The model is based on well-defined formalism and possesses the mechanisms for expressing mental notions such as beliefs, desires and intention that are used for the description of the agents' behaviour. It provides ready to use mechanisms for goal decomposition and it also facilitates the expression of social activity of agents as it handles several kinds of events by providing reaction and communication mechanisms, and structures for the awareness of the environment.
In particular, AOMFG is based on the well-defined and broadly accepted BDI theory as well as on the principles of agent-oriented programming. The BDI theory has been chosen as the model underlying formalism because it reflects the intentional stance and employs a strong mathematical background. The principles of agent-oriented programming also reflect the intentional stance, in the same manner as the societal view of agents. In addition, AOMFG employs the most commonly used principles of state-based machines, programming languages, Cognitive Engineering and interaction specification models in a compact representation.
The presented model differs from the other related models in that it embodies in its building blocks the BDI and AOP concepts fused together with features taken from disciplines that relate to the design of applications based on multi agent systems. Furthermore, the graphical nature of AOMFG, which is based on High Level Petri Nets, provides a friendly way for multi agent systems specification by hiding from users the underlying use of mathematical formalism, which may be hard to use by non-specialists.
AOMFG is general enough to be used in a wide range of agent applications as well as to encapsulate other well-known agent theories. In the above sections, AOMFG model was used and validated under theoretical issues as well as in the description of a real system in order to provide evidence that it can cover the specification needs of both directions. In fact, as demonstrated, an AOMFG can be used for the specification of generic agent interpreters, FIPA communication protocols, and BDI properties as well as for the specification of real life systems. Furthermore, an AOMFG can be transformed to an equivalent Petri Net, which may then be subjected to formal analysis techniques. Other researchers and mainly practitioners in software specifications may use the model for easy and rapid specification and prototyping of multi agent systems. Programmers can also use the model as it embodies

programming structures familiar to them. The inclusion of an explicit representation of time in AOMFG is currently under investigation.

7. Acknowledgements

This work was initially carried out in Educational Software Development Laboratory, Department of Mathematics, University of Patras, Greece. I would like to thank Prof. A. D. Kameas and Prof. P. E. Pintelas for their support, their helpful comments and their valuable reviews.

8. References

Bates, J. (1994). The Role of Emotion in Believable Agents, *Communications of the ACM*, 37 (7) 122-125, ISSN: 0001-0782.

Bratman, M. E. (1987). *Intentions, Plans, and Practical Reason,* Harvard University Press: Cambridge, MA.

Card, S., Moran, T. P. & Newell, A. (1983). *The Psychology of Human-Computer Interaction,* Lawrence Erlbaum Associates Inc, ISBN: 0-898-59243-7, New Jersey.

Cohen, P. R. & Levesque, H. J. (1990). Intention is Choice with Commitment. *Artificial Intelligence*, 42 213-261, ISSN: 0004-3702.

Dennett, D. C. (1987). *The Intentional Stance,* The MIT Press, ISBN 0-262-54053-3, Cambridge, MA.

Emerson, E. A. (1991). Temporal and Modal Logic, In: *Handbook of Theoretical Computer Science,* J. van Leeuwen, (Ed.), 995-1072, The MIT Press, ISBN: 0-444-88074-7, Cambridge MA, USA.

Gasser, L. Braganza, C. & Hermann, N. (1987). MACE: A Flexible Testbed for Distributed AI Research, In: *Distributed Artificial Intelligence*, M. Huhns, (Ed.), 119-152, Morgan Kaufmann Publishers Inc., ISBN: 0-934-61338-9, San Francisco, CA.

Genrich H. J., & Lautenbach K. (1981). System Modeling with High-Level Petri Nets, *Theoretical Computer Science*, 13 109-136, ISSN: 0304-3975.

Gerogiannis, V. C., Kameas, A. D. & Pintelas, P. E. (1998). Comparative Study and Categorization of High-Level Petri Nets, *Journal on Systems and Software,* 43(2) 133-160, ISSN: 0164-1212.

Harel, D. (1984). Dynamic Logic, In: *Handbook of Philosophical Logic Volume II - Extensions of Classical Logic,* D. Gabbay and F. Guenther, (Eds.), 497-604, D. Reidel Publishing Company: Dordrecht, ISBN: 0-792-33097-8 The Netherlands.

Hintikka, J. (1962). *Knowledge and Belief,* Cornell University Press, NY.

Jensen, K. (1981). Coloured Petri Nets and the Invariant Method. *Theoretical Computer Science,* 14 317-336, ISSN: 0304-3975.

Jensen, K. (1997). *Coloured Petri Nets: Basic Concepts, Analysis Methods and Practical Use,* Vol. 2, Springer-Verlag, ISBN: 3-540-58276-2, Berlin Heidelberg New York.

Johnson, P. & Nicolosi, E. (1990). Task-based User Interface Development Tools, in: *Proceedings of the 3rd IFIP TC 13 International Conference on Human-Computer Interaction (INTERACT 90)*, pp. 383-387, August '90, Cambridge, UK.

Kameas, A. D. (1995). *A Formal Model for the Specification of Interaction and the Design of Interactive Applications,* Ph.D. Thesis, Department of Computer Engineering & Informatics, University of Patras, Hellas.

Kameas, A. D. & Pintelas, P. E. (1997). The Functional Architecture and Interaction Model of a GENerator of Intelligent TutORing Applications, *Journal on Systems and Software,* 36 (3) 233-245, ISSN: 0164-1212.

Kieras, D. E., & Polson, P. G. (1985). An Approach to the Formal Analysis of User Complexity, *International Journal of Man-Machine Studies*, 22 (4) 365-394, ISSN: 0020-7373.

Kinny, D., Georgeff, M. & Rao, A. (1996). A Methodology and Modelling Technique for Systems of BDI Agents, *Proceedings of the 7th European Workshop on Modelling Autonomous Agents in a Multi-Agent World (MAAMAW 96)*, pp. 56-71, ISBN:3-540-60852-4, Eindhoven, The Netherlands, January 22 – 25, 1996, Springer-Verlag New York.

Konolige, K. (1986). *A Deduction Model of Belief*, Morgan Kaufmann Publishers, ISBN: 0-934-61308-7, San Francisco, CA.

Miller, G. A., Galanter, G. & Pribram, K. H. (1960). *Plans and the Structured Behaviour*, Holt, Rinehart and Winston, ISBN 0-937-43100-1, New York.

Murata, T. (1989). Petri Nets: Properties, Analysis and Applications, in: *Proceedings of the IEEE*, 77 (4) 541-580 ISSN: 0018-9219.

Newell, A. & Simon, H. A. (1972). *Human Problem Solving*, Prentice-Hall, ISBN 0-134-45403-0, Upper Saddle River, NJ.

Norman, D. A. (1987). Cognitive Engineering – Cognitive Science, in: J. M. Carroll, (Ed.), *Interfacing Thought: Cognitive Aspects of Human-Computer Interaction*, 325-336, The MIT Press, ISBN 0-262-03125-6 Cambridge, CA.

Rao, A. S. & Georgeff, M. P. (1991a). Modeling Rational Agents within a BDI-Architecture, in: *Proceedings of Knowledge Representation and Reasoning (KR&R-91)*, R. Fikes and E. Sandewall, (Eds.), 473-484, Morgan Kaufmann Publishers: San Mateo, CA.

Rao, A. S. & Georgeff, M. P. (1991b). Asymmetry Thesis and Side-Effect Problems in Linear-Time and Branching-Time Intention Logics, In: *Proceedings of the Twelfth International Joint Conference on Artificial Intelligence (IJCAI-91)*, pp. 498-504, ISBN: 1-55860-160-0, Sydney, Australia, Morgan Kaufmann Publishers Inc., San Francisco, CA, USA.

Rao, A. S. & Georgeff, M. P. (1995). Formal Models and Decision Procedures for Multi-Agent Systems, *Technical Report 61*, Australian Artificial Intelligence Institute, Melbourne, Australia.

Russell, S. & Norvig, P. (2003). *Artificial Intelligence: A Modern Approach*, 2nd edition, Prentice Hall Inc, ISBN: 0-13-103805-2, Upper Saddle River, NJ.

Schmidt, H. W. (1991). Prototyping and Analysis of Non-Sequential Systems Using Predicate-Event Nets, *Journal on Systems and Software*, 15 (1) 43-62, ISSN: 0164-1212.

Searle, J. R. (1969). *Speech Acts: An Essay in the Philosophy of Language*, Cambridge University Press, ISBN: 0-521-09626-X, Cambridge, England.

Shoham, Y. (1993). Agent-Oriented Programming, *Artificial Intelligence*, 60 51-92, ISSN: 0004-3702.

Wooldridge, M. (1992). *The Logical Modelling of Computational Multi-Agent Systems*. Ph.D. Thesis, UMIST, Manchester, UK.

Wooldridge, M. & Jennings, N. R. (1995). Intelligent Agents: Theory and Practice, *The Knowledge Engineering Review* 10 (2) 115-152, ISSN: 0269-8889.

Wooldridge, M. (1996). Temporal Belief Logics for Modelling Distributed AI Systems, In: *Foundations of DAI*, G. M. P. O'Hare and N. R. Jennings, (Eds.), 269-286, Wiley Interscience, ISBN 0-471-00675-0, New York.

Wooldridge, M. (1999). Intelligent Agents, In: *Multiagent Systems: A Modern Approach to Distributed Artificial Intelligence*, G. Weiss (ed.), 27-77, The MIT Press, ISBN 0-262-23203-0, Cambridge, MA.

Zaharakis, I. D., Diplas, C. N., Kameas, A. D. & Pintelas, P. E. (1995). Specifying the Interaction with an Expert System Shell Using Interactive Multi Flow Graphs, *Proceedings of the 5th Hellenic Conference of Informatics*, pp. 601-613, Athens, Greece.

Zaharakis, I. D., Kameas A. D. & Nikiforidis, G. C. (1998). A Multi-agent Architecture for Teaching Dermatology, *Medical Informatics*, 23 (4) 289-307, ISSN: 1386-5056.

6

Multi-Agent Models in Workflow Design

Victoria Iordan
West University of Timisoara
Romania

1. Introduction

Many researchers have focused on the intelligent agent and multi-agent systems approaches as alternatives for e-business and enterprise integration applications. Agent approaches and technologies were developed and used in e-business applications business process management in (Jennings et al., 1996), (Jennings et al., 2000), (Papazoglu, 2008) supply chain management in (Huhns & Stephens, 2001) and enterprise integration in (Pan & Tenenbaum, 1991), (Sikora & Shaw, 1998) and (Sikora & Shaw, 2002). During the 1990s were developed ERP and EAI, the last one, involves the integration of various enterprise applications so that they can share information and processes freely in (Linthicum, 1999).
Workflow systems, enable the automation of a business process, in whole or part, during which documents, information or tasks are passed from one participant to another for action, according to a set of procedural rules as in (Fischer, 2000), (Aalst & Akhil, 2003). Processes have associated resources, in terms of participants and invoked applications. In turn these resources may have extended descriptions in terms of the organizational model, and application environment respectively. Validation of the process usually requires the knowledge of a domain expert on the underlying business rules, business process logic and many types of local constraints in (Sadiq et al., 2004). Manual validation for any reasonably complex process models is complex and hard to achieve with an adequate dose of accuracy. Furthermore, it is unrealistic to assume that domain experts would also carry expert knowledge on process modeling. One can expect that workflow designers and domain experts would typically be disjoint but collaborating users of the process technology. The validation, like structural verification is not intended to provide guarantees on the correctness and/or completeness of the process model against business requirements. It is rather intended to support the process modeling activity, by providing smart tools for cross checking process and activity properties, and identifying potential conflicting and redundant elements in the specification, thereby boosting user confidence in the deployment of the process model.
The areas like inter-organizational cooperation and virtual enterprises require new solutions due to the high dynamics in their interrelations. Since the process perspective has been within the center of interest, workflow management systems (WFMS) have had a revival in the context of the development of distributed applications. Most of the commercially available workflow management systems do not offer sufficient flexibility for distributed organizations that participate in the global market. These systems have rigid, centralized architectures that do not operate across multiple platforms (Purvis et al., 2004).

Modeling processes and workflow for complex systems constitutes a challenge for designers. The resources that are used in systems are in limited amounts and these must be shared between the processes and workflow instances activities.
Due to the complexity of real systems are needed more and sophisticated models. The multi agent models are widely used in order to use in an efficient manner the information, based on the reasoning of intelligent agents. The roles and their usage play an important place in the models with agents in the design of workflows.
Our considerations refer to the need of a data base in that the workflow constituents: instances and activities must be represented in a data base and also their time evolution.
We intend to propose a model for resource representation and allocation and as conclusion propose considerations concerning the design of processes, workflows and workflow management systems.

2. Integration requirements

A single work system or a single actor within a work system does not have the necessary knowledge, resources, and capability to solve such complex problem as is the integration. As a general goal is to integrate different work systems in order to solve the problems that span multiple work systems, coordinating the goals, tasks and resources of multiple work systems in order to achieve the overall system goals.
The main integration requirements are: work systems integration, data integration and technology integration and in addition to providing task and decision support within individual work systems.
The work systems integration is concerned with the key organizational aspects of goals, tasks of business processes, actors and resources. Work systems integration, considered as being coordination involves structuring workflow, allocating tasks and resources to actors, sharing resources, managing interdependencies (or simply dependencies) between tasks, resources and actors, and enabling communication across multiple work systems. The coordination as managing dependencies between activities if there are no interdependencies among activities then is no need for coordination in the system, as in (Malone & Crowston, 1994).
The coordination perspectives: managing dependencies, managing workflow and managing communication among various work systems use adequate analysis and modeling techniques.

3. Previous works

Concerning the coordination, many models were developed. The dependency perspective, which presumes that coordination problems are caused in the first place by interdependencies among various organizational actors, tasks, and resources, and that an effective coordination system should address and resolve these mutual interdependencies. For the dependency perspective were developed many models between we mention: Actor Dependency Model (Yu & Mylopoulus, 1996) and Dependency Network Diagrams that allow representing the essential elements of inter-organizational relationships based on resource dependency theory (Tillquist et al., 2002).
The Role Activity Diagrams (RAD) are presented in (Ould, 1995), as a set of graphic notations for modeling business processes these were frequently used. The RAD technique

represents a business process into a set of interacting roles. Each of these roles and group activities together might be carried out by a person, group or machine i.e., an actor or an agent. Roles have constructs to depict concurrent or parallel behaviors. They act in parallel and communicate and synchronize through interactions. RAD is essentially a state-based modeling technique and actions and interactions of a role move it from the current state to a new state.

The Workflow Intelligent Business Object (WIBO) approach can model and implement a workflow with intelligence, autonomy, collaboration and cooperation (Fakas & Karakostas, 1999). The workflow is modeled as a collection of interacting business objects that are able to manage themselves. These objects belong to meta-level classes or types: process, role, actor and resources. eXchangeable Routing Language (XRL), based on XML, is a language developed to support seamless routing of inter-organizational workflow (Aalst & Akhil, 2003). Most workflow modeling techniques lack capabilities to capture different aspects of a workflow system such as data, process and organization (resources) in a single consistent view (Bajaj & Ram, 2002). In (Basu & Blanning, 2000) was proposed a framework that integrates the informational, functional, and organizational perspectives of the workflow in a single model and in (Bajaj & Ram, 2002) was proposed State–Entity–Activity–Model using set theory.

A major problem is that of the ontology in every domain (Kishore et al., 2004). In (Fox et al., 1998) was proposed an organizational ontology for enterprise modeling. An organization is a set of constraints on the activities performed by organizational agents. An agent plays one or more roles. Each role is defined with a set of goals that the role is created to fulfill and is allocated with proper authority at the level that the role can achieve its goals. Agents perform activities in the organization, each of which may consume resources and there is a set of constraints that constrain agent activities. An agent can also be a member of a team set up in response to a special task, possesses skills and has a set of communication links that specify the other agents in the organization with who it can communicate.

In the IBIS model presented in (Kishore et al., 2006), the business enterprise has of a number of work systems each of which has been assigned certain goals to achieve that are derived from enterprise goals. The business enterprise can be a single business organization or it can be an extended, networked, or virtual organization or a strategic alliance consisting in a number of interacting partner firms who wish to integrate some of their work systems. Each work system contains multiple actors who are assigned sub-goals derived from work system goals, and who perform a number of tasks using some resources to achieve their goals, and in the process use or create some information objects. Accomplishment of actor goals contributes to the accomplishment of work system goals, which in turn contributes to the accomplishment of enterprise goals.

The above models and constructs include goals, roles, agents (actors), activities or tasks as components of processes, interactions, workflow, resources, data, and interdependencies. As was stated in (Kishore et al., 2006), the MAS paradigm provides an approach and suitable mechanisms for developing integrative business information systems to achieve the goal of creating an integrated enterprise.

In (Kishore et al., 2006), was proposed a conceptual framework for multi-agent-based integrative business information systems; was identified a minimal set of orthogonal ontological constructs in (Kishore et al., 2003) and (Sowa, 2000) that are central to the multi-agent-based integrative business information systems bounded discourse universe. In (Kishore et al., 2004) was given an approach of minimal ontological commitment and tried to identify those ontological constructs that are essential for conceptual analysis and modeling of multi-agent-based integrative business information systems.

4. Workflow modeling

The commercial community defined and standardized workflow languages that at least hold the potential of interoperability. Typical workflow scenarios include document lifecycle management, internal application workflow and business process management. A number of engines have been developed which revolve around well established protocols such as BPEL, BPEL4WS, XLANG, WSFL and many others. The Figure 1 illustrates the considerations based on the meta-model defined in (WfMC, 1999).

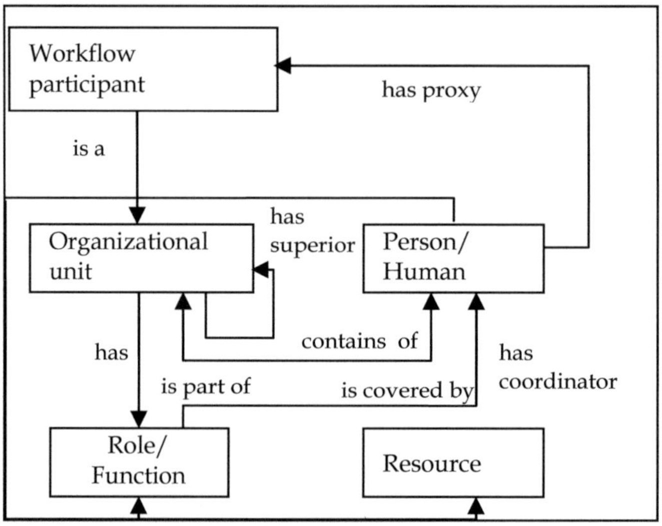

Fig. 1. Process instance state transitions meta-model

The activities that compose the process/workflow instances can gain various states and change each other during process instance. Activity state evolves as is illustrated in Fig. 2 (WfMC, 1999).

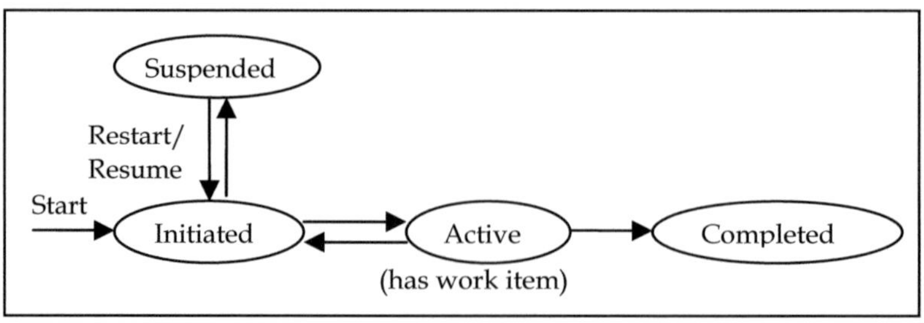

Fig. 2. Activity instance state transitions meta-model

In (Papazoglu, 2008) the Web Services are considered to be mandatory in conjunction with the specific languages (like BPEL4WS) based on numerous business process challenges such as coordinating communication between services, correlating message exchanges between parties, implementing parallel processing of activities, transforming data between partner interactions, supporting long running business transaction and providing consistent exception handling. These languages use many protocols and standards that allow representing the Business process management both inside and between the organizations, as is shown in Fig. 3. Web Services are frequently used in Workflow design in order to allow an expressive dynamic of the real processes (Papazoglu, 2008). Web services are not implemented in a monolithic manner, but rather represent a collection of several related technologies illustrated in Fig. 3.

<table>
<tr><td rowspan="10">Management</td><td colspan="3">Choreography</td><td rowspan="2">Business Processes</td></tr>
<tr><td colspan="3">Orchestration</td></tr>
<tr><td rowspan="3">WS-Reliability</td><td rowspan="3">WS-Security</td><td>Transaction</td><td rowspan="3">Quality of Service</td></tr>
<tr><td>Coordination</td></tr>
<tr><td>Context</td></tr>
<tr><td colspan="3">UDDI</td><td>Discovery</td></tr>
<tr><td colspan="3">WSDL</td><td>Description</td></tr>
<tr><td colspan="3">SOAP</td><td rowspan="2">Message</td></tr>
<tr><td colspan="3">XML</td></tr>
<tr><td colspan="3">HTTP, IIOP, JMS, SMTP</td><td>Transport</td></tr>
</table>

Fig. 3. Standards used for Business Process Management

Using Enterprise Application Integration technologies (EAI) companies share their information in distributed information systems and try to automate their Workflow Management Systems (WfMSs). Workflows are commonly modeled as activity diagrams. This approach to workflow modeling is called Activity-Based Workflow Modeling (AWM). An activity diagram comprises a set of discrete actions and the relationships among them.

One fundamental characteristic of activity diagrams is that all actions are treated equal regardless of real differences in their nature. For example, some actions are user-initiated while others may be system-generated notifications or triggers. Yet other actions may be business rule executions, often referred to in the AWM literature as automatic actions.

Another approach to workflow modeling is Contextual Workflow Modeling (CWM) (Nguyen, 2009). CWM is centered on a modified finite state machine running strictly in the context of a data environment. The data environment isolates the state machine such that the only way to effect a change in the running status of the state machine is through modifications to the data environment. Instead of focusing on the actions as in the case of AWM, CWM is primarily concerned with how the outcome of an action impacts the data environment. CWM is a rule-based system where all workflow events, ranging from state activation to participant assignments, are driven by user-defined business rules. These rules operate on data drawn from the data environment and form the bridge connecting the data environment to the state machine. On the other hand, the combination of the current workflow status and the participant roles determines who has the privilege and responsibility to modify which part of the data environment. The CWM approach provides a uniform mechanism through which external actors, whether human users or information systems, interact with the workflow model. There is no artificial distinction of user actions versus system actions in how they impact the data environment, and consequently the workflow status. As a result, integration and interchangeability of the different actor types

are much more seamless than in the AWM approach. CWM represents a departure from the typical AWM approach. By switching the modeling focus from actions to states and their driving business rules and by deriving action requirements dynamically from the workflow data content, CWM puts tremendous expressive power in the hands of the business process architect, allowing him to capture nuances that are simply beyond the reach of AWM. Workflow models in CWM tend to be streamlined, with the different action types organized logically according to their semantics. The semantic structure of CWM enhances comprehension of complex processes by giving analysts a top-level overview of a workflow and allowing them to drill down into particular areas of the workflow as necessary. Workflow systems are driven by the process models, which describe the workflow process. Workflow patterns were deeply analyzed and some main features are given in (van der Aalst & ter Hofstede, 2002). Adaptive workflows have been discussed for many years and many people have described what should be done (van der Aalst, 2001). Were proposed techniques to manage adaptability and only a small number of actual implementations have been made that tackle some aspects of adaptability. Transferring running work cases to a new model is still a difficult issue. Some adaptability can be provided by manual transfer of tokens in the new process model (van der Aalst & ter Hofstede, 2002). In (Purvis et al., 2004) was developed an agent-enhanced WfMS, where the work associated with running a WfMS has been partitioned among various collaborating agents that are interacting with each other by following standard agent communication protocols. The proposed model is developed in JBees and uses a CPN execution tool.
The architecture of proposed model from (Purvis et al., 2004) is illustrated in the Fig. 4.

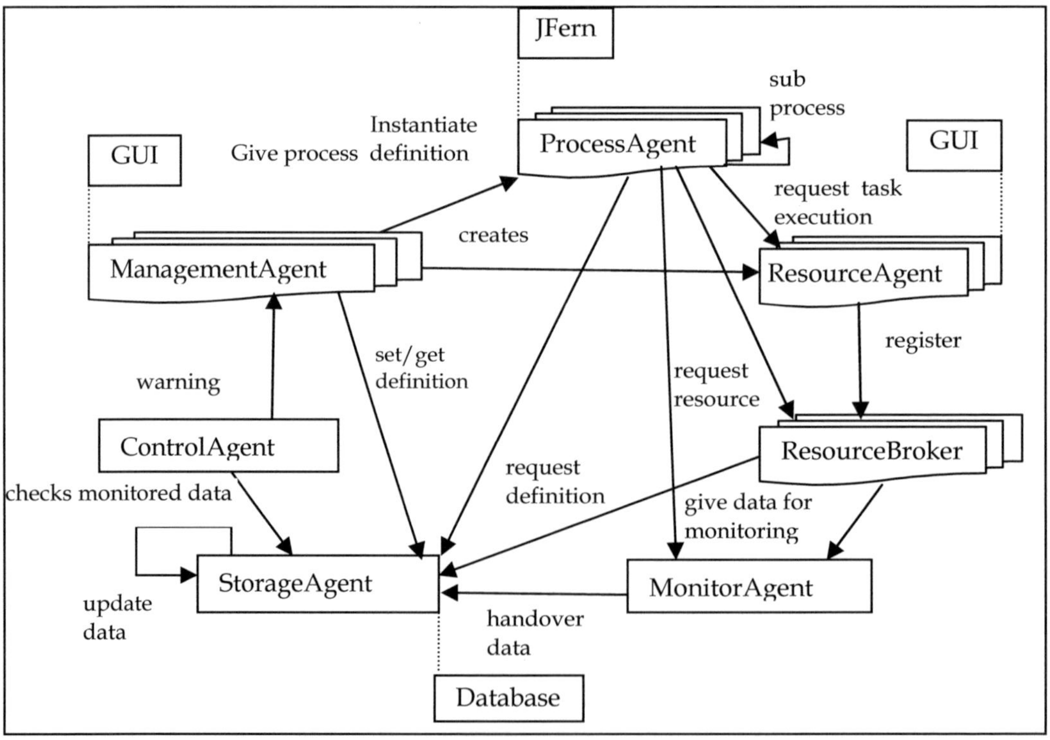

Fig. 4. The architecture of JBees

The flexibilities of workflow system enable to provide the support for distribution, adaptability, monitoring and controlling of processes. JBees supports the inter-organizational cooperation through the distribution of process.

5. Multi-agent systems

Multi-agent system can be considered a system that is composed of multiple autonomous agents and has the following characteristics presented in (Sowa, 2000), (Jennings et al., 1998) and (Aerts et al., 2002): (a) each agent has incomplete information or capabilities for solving the problem and, thus, has a limited viewpoint; (b) there is no global systems control; (c) data are decentralized; (d) computation is asynchronous.

An intelligent agent is autonomous, reactive, proactive, and social (Wooldridge, 2002). Agents are able to decide whether or not to execute an action after receiving requests (Yu & Mylopoulus, 1996).

In an agent-based system, agents use a common language with agent-independent semantics. There are different types of messages an agent can receive, and the agent is able to evaluate the received messages and decide what actions to perform. There are many agent communication languages between us mention KQML (Finin et al., 1995). Agent communication languages support several ways for agents to communicate, including direct communication, middle agent-mediated communication and broadcast.

Many coordination techniques have been developed in the intelligent agent and MAS literature. The coordination techniques include organizational structuring, metalevel information exchanging, multi-agent planning, contract net, negotiation, and market mechanisms depending on the domain were the agents are used. In (Kishore et al., 2006) is given a synthesis of developed technologies and their key constructs.

In (Yu & Schmid, 1999) is proposed a conceptual framework for agent-oriented and role-based workflow modeling. A workflow is viewed as a collection of agents interacting with others when they have interdependencies. The workflow is modeled a set of roles, which are further defined in terms of goals, qualifications, obligations, permissions and protocols. Interactions among roles are governed by protocols.

Roles are then assigned to agents based on the evaluation of qualification and capabilities. Once a role is assigned to an agent, the agent inherits the obligations and permissions specified in that role. Coordination of workflow is achieved by communication among agents. In (Sikora & Shaw, 1998) and (Sikora & Shaw, 2002) the enterprise information system is considered as consisting of multiple agents with different functionalities, and develop representational formalisms, coordination mechanisms, and control schemes necessary for integrating heterogeneous agents while meeting such performance criteria as overall effectiveness, efficiency, responsiveness and robustness. Based on a formal analysis, the same authors propose an agent-based framework for enterprise integration. In the framework, each process is modeled as an autonomous agent, which has its own well-defined goals and objectives. In (Jennings, 2001) and (Jennings, 2001) the business process is viewed as a community of negotiating agents. Was proposed the Advanced Decision Environment for Process Tasks (ADEPT) for conceptualizing, designing and implementing business process management systems.

Many of the following considerations are similar with those from (Kishore et al., 2006). In (Kishore et al., 2006), were presented conceptual similarities between integrated business enterprises and multi-agent systems in terms of their goal orientation (i.e., problem-solving orientation). In an integrated enterprise, actors interact with each other in a number of work systems in a highly coordinated manner to achieve their own and shared goals, thereby contributing to the work system and thereby overall enterpriser goals.

A multi-agent system is similar to an integrated enterprise because it is essentially a community of autonomous and problem solving agents who interact in computer network systems in a coordinated manner to achieve their own and shared goals. Therefore, in terms of the goal construct, the MAS paradigm is suitable for modeling and developing integrated enterprise applications.

The MAS paradigm is suitable approach for modeling integrative business information systems because unlike any other paradigm, agents in the MAS paradigm come closest to mimicking the characteristics of human actors in business organizations: those of intelligence, adaptive problem solving behavior, sociability and autonomy. The actors within multiple work systems in an integrated enterprise need to be coordinated to manage and resolve interdependencies between tasks they perform and resources they use during the course of performance of their tasks. Interaction (or communication) among actors, and therefore among work systems, is a fundamental concept for integrating work systems as it is one of the basic means for coordinating activities of actors and for resolving resource dependencies in an integrated business enterprise.

Interaction is also a fundamental concept in the MAS paradigm as agents interact/communicate one another to share resources, check for task/goal accomplishment, check for availability of other agents for performing certain tasks, negotiate prices and timelines, subcontract tasks to other agents, decide upon future courses of action, etc. Activities (or tasks) are also fundamental to the MAS because both actors in human organizations and agents in multi-agent communities perform tasks in order to accomplish their own and organizational/system goals. The notion of workflow is also central to the MAS paradigms because a coordinated flow of activities (work) performed by various actors/agents and it is necessary for achieving organizational/system goals.

Information is obviously a key construct in MAS domains. A variety of information is required for actors in business enterprises to perform their assigned tasks in order accomplish their goals. Information exchanges also take place between actors within and across work systems in integrated business enterprises as part of their interactions to coordinate their activities and resources. The same is the case with multi-agent systems. Agents within MAS also use information to perform tasks and exchange information with other agents as part of their interactions. Therefore, from the perspective of interactions, activities, workflow and information, the MAS paradigm is quite appropriate for the modeling and development of integrated system applications.

The concept of resources is a very important construct in integrative business information systems. Resources within business organizations are always finite, and one of the key goals of any business organization is to optimize on resource requirement and utilization to contribute directly to the profitability goal of the organization. When resources are distributed across multiple work systems, improving resource utilization requires their effective coordination for solving resource dependencies and sharing resources across multiple work systems. Thus, resources of a wide variety (e.g., technical skills, documentation, plant and equipment, computer systems, utilities, consumable supplies, tools, etc.) need to be explicitly modeled in integrative business information systems. Resources are also a key construct in the MAS paradigm as agents contend for and consume finite computational resources such as memory, processor time, communication bandwidth, etc. While the types of resources that agents in the MAS paradigm normally deal with are comparatively limited as compared to business enterprises, any type of physical or intellectual resource can be easily modeled using the MAS paradigm. Thus, the MAS paradigm appears to be suitable for modeling of integrated application systems from the perspective of resources as well.

The role has been used as a construct in many modeling techniques, for abstracting the tasks/activities that need to be performed by real human actors to achieve certain goals. These abstract roles are then assigned to real human actors who are expected to perform tasks (activities) included in these roles definition to achieve the goals the roles are designed to accomplish. While the MAS paradigm does not specifically deal with the notion of roles, it can be readily implemented by assigning abstract roles to intelligent agents within the MAS which are similar in a number of ways to human agents. Thus, from the perspective of roles as well, the MAS paradigm provides a suitable approach for modeling and implementation of integrated system applications. Also in (Kishore et al., 2006), was presented multi-agent-based integrative business information systems (MIBIS) and for it were proposed the following ontological constructs required for modeling systems in the MIBIS discourse universe: agent, role, goal, interaction, task, resource, information and knowledge. Every ontological construct was analyzed and motivated. Based on the above considerations, the MAS systems paradigm is suited for modeling and implementing a wide variety of integrative business information systems and also for workflow execution and modeling.

6. Agents and Roles in design of BPs and Wfs

The agent technology has been used in different ways. From a conceptual perspective workflows can be enhanced through the agent concept.

Agents offer a natural way to deal with open environments and are therefore of particular benefit for distributed systems. In some cases the agents fulfill particular roles that are required by different tasks in the workflow. In these cases the existing workflow is used to structure the coordination of these agents (Jennings et al., 2000), (Nissen, 2000).

An example of this approach is the work by M. Nissen in designing a set of agents to perform activities associated with the supply chain process in the area of e-commerce (Nissen , 2000). In other cases, the agents have been used as part of the infrastructure associated with the WfMS itself in order to create an agent-enhanced WfMS (Wang & Wang, 2002), (Stormer, 2001). These agents provide an open system with loosely coupled components, which provides more flexibility than the traditional systems. Some researchers have combined both of these approaches.

In (Purvis et al., 2004), an agent-based WfMS is used in conjunction with specialized agents that provide appropriate application-related services. We have taken the latter approach which provides sufficient flexibility required for a dynamic and adaptive system.

In (Reese et al., 2005) was developed a model that fragments the workflows for distributed execution with supporting protocols and architecture. This architecture is agent orientated, its formal basis is provided by Petri nets with a specific tool support. It allows the splitting of workflows into arbitrary fragments. These fragments, encapsulated by agents, are treated again as workflows and they can be executed at different locations using different workflow enactment systems, which are the conceptual platforms of the agents. Is provided a concept for a distributed and concurrent workflow management system, based on the FIPA compliant agent framework CAPA. The architecture is sketched in the Fig. 5.

Many specific techniques as input-process-output techniques, conversation-based techniques, and techniques based on role modeling, system thinking and system dynamics techniques, and constraint based representations techniques are used in BP modeling. Among these techniques, those based on role modeling have the advantage of supporting the well-known separation of duties principle (SoD) (Saidani & Nurcan, 2006).

The concept of role not only allows underlining the responsibility of each actor and reflects the organizational structure but also improves the understanding of the way responsibilities are achieved. Adopting role based methods to model BPs is useful, particularly if they are flexible enough to meet BP flexibility requirements, especially organizational, functional and operational requirements (Saidani & Nurcan, 2006).

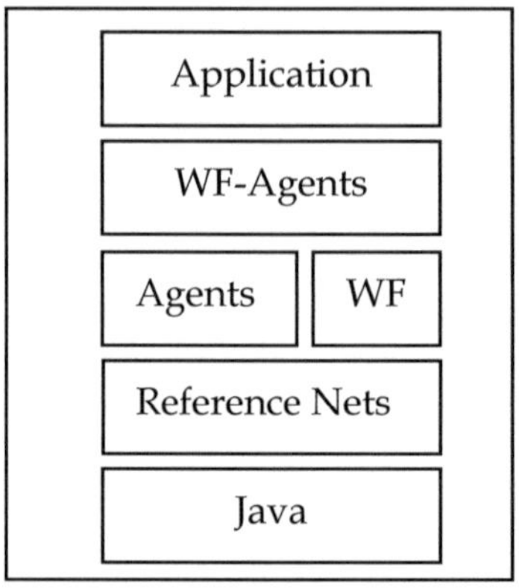

Fig. 5. The architecture of model proposed in (Reese et al., 2005)

The flexibility can be defined as the capacity of making a compromise between, first, satisfying, rapidly and easily, the business requirements in terms of adaptability when organizational, functional and/or operational changes occur; and, second, keeping effectiveness.

One of the main objectives of companies is to better and more quickly meet with the customer's requirements. In a changing environment, assuming that participants will always act as predefined is inaccurate, because it limits their autonomy and flexibility when changes make inapplicable some predefined conditions. The delegation concept is used in order to fulfill these requirements. Delegation is often defined as a substitution mechanism of all or a subset of the actor roles to one or more other actors. No actor can delegate a piece of role. However, in many cases an actor may want to delegate some missions from his/her role. What is more, in some cases, role-to-role delegation is needed. A flexible delegation model requires multiple forms of delegation, and supports flexible role, mission and operational goal level delegation.

The purpose of the separation of duties (SoD) is a policy to ensure that failures of omission or commission within an organization are caused only by collusion among individuals and, therefore, are riskier and less likely, and that chances of collusion are minimized by assigning individuals of different skills or divergent interests to separate tasks (Gligor et al., 1998).

In (Saidani & Nurcan, 2006) is detailed a model that allows to emphasize the flexibility in BP modeling and that will be sketched in the followings. The mission from (Saidani & Nurcan, 2006) is in our view the same as the task. Organizations can be viewed as being structured as networks of BPs in order to achieve their business goals. BP can be first analyzed in term of roles played by actors and holding tasks (missions). During the execution of a BP, actors perform tasks (missions) that specify the responsibilities and the work included in swim-lines in classical activity-oriented representation formalisms. During the execution of a BP, it is an actor who performs operations. Organization's roles and tasks (missions) are usually more static than actors and operations are. The central concepts are the role and the mission. A role is a semantic construct about which business rules and other concepts can be formulated. It can represent competency to realize particular missions, an engineer, and can embody authority and responsibility, a project supervisor.

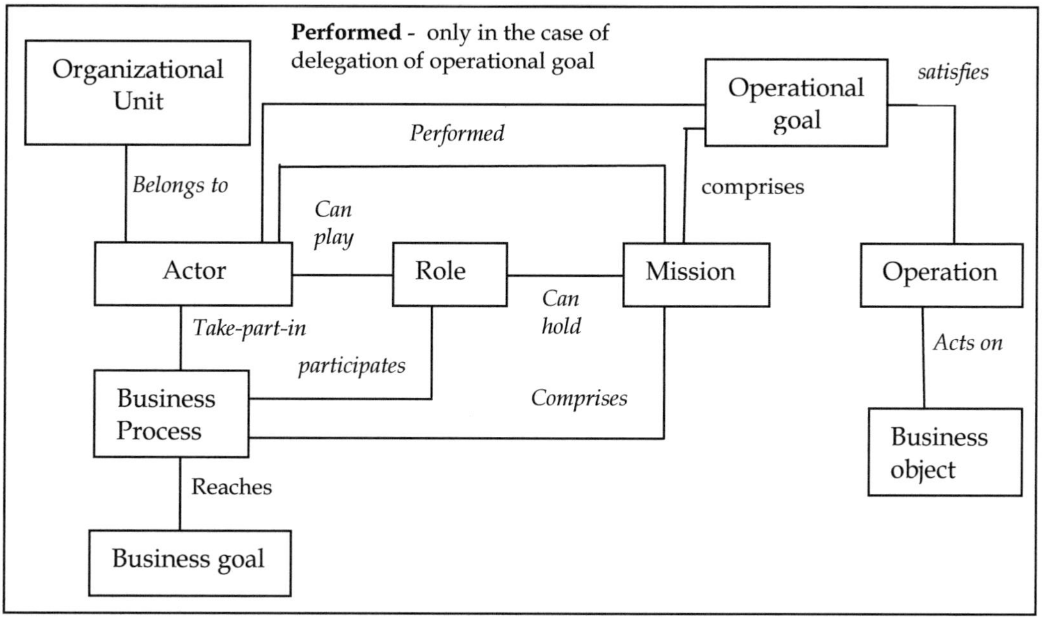

Fig. 6. The proposed model from (Saidani & Nurcan, 2006)

In Fig. 6 each actor belongs to at least one organizational unit and is assigned to appropriate roles based on his responsibilities and qualifications. The concept of task (mission) serves as a link between roles and operations: A task (mission) is defined as a collection of operational goals satisfied by achieving operations. A task (mission) can comprise several operational goals because it is not achieved performing straightforward and continuous operations without any interaction with other roles. The set of operations allowing a role (played by an actor during the process occurrence) to achieve an operational goal can be specified as an activity. The specificities of the model consist in the followings: (i) is defined the piece of responsibility of a role in the intentional level (operational goal), (ii) goes deeply in the specification of this operational goal (dealt with as a black box in usual workflow formalisms), and finally,

(iii) specifies the operations which performance acts on the business objects and allows achieving the operational goal.

Constraints on the relationships defining flexibility and Constraints in delegation model are representative in flexibility management. In order to deal effectively with the BP flexibility, relationships between the concepts (Fig. 7) should be controlled to ensure the usability of the provided flexibility mechanism. The figure Fig. 7 illustrates the model.

As a major constraint on the relationships between the concepts is the constraint controlling separation of duties: separation of duties is a business technique trying to minimize fraud by dispersing the authority and responsibility for an action over multiples actors. This can be ensured by defining mutually disjoint actor-to-role assignments with respect to sets of roles.

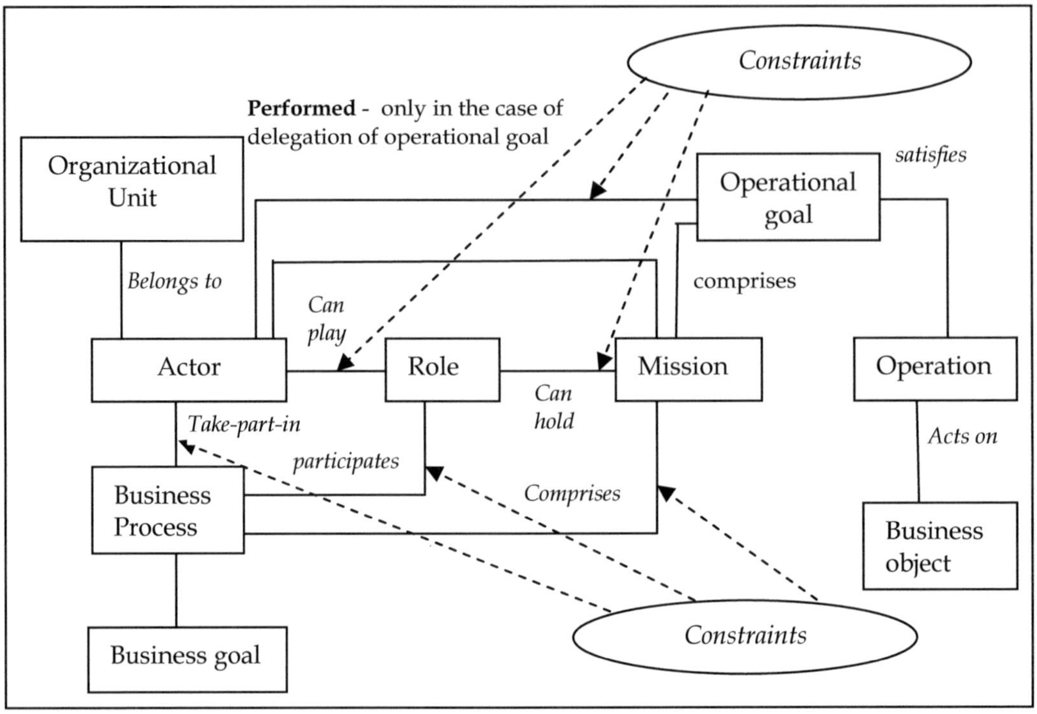

Fig. 7. Constraints for the control mechanism

Constraints can apply to actor-to-role, mission-to-role and operational-goal-omission assignments. They can limit, for instance, the number of members or missions of a role or the number of operational goals for a mission. Constraints can also apply to processes, and to talked-part-in and participates relationships associated with a BP. Constraints on BPs can limit the number of occurrences of a BP in which an actor can realize missions simultaneously. Constraints can precise if an actor or a role may participate to multiple business processes at the same time.

7. Reengineering failed workflows

In (Cicortas et al., 2006) and (Cicortas & Iordan, 2009a) was proposed a model that is based on a multi-agent system. The workflow and its constituents are preserved in a data base. Workflows especially for business processes are generally in a very high dynamic. So during the execution the state of the system and also of the workflow can change, or can fail. Whereas the system state is stable the workflow can evolve but while in some state the system changes in an unpredictable way the workflow will encounter particular cases (states) that were not developed. In such cases the workflow must be able to adapt to the new conditions. During the execution of an activity, of a workflow instance, a failure of the activity can appear. In this case the workflow will be stopped and its reply can be done, in the actual circumstances, or can be done only from its beginning.

As was stated in (Cicortas et al., 2006) we propose a model that allows using a multi-agent system that will be able to manage the failures in the execution of the workflow instances. For being able to do that, we need to develop some specific concepts and use an appropriate data bases. In (Cicortas et al., 2006) were given details that concern the activities and their results that eventually can be reused in the case of the reply of the workflow instance execution. For every activity it is needed some specific information that will be used in the case of a reply of the instance execution, after a failure. The information concerning the activity is placed into the Workflow Data Base (WfDB). The entity in this data base is the activity. Also for every workflow instance a specific data base it is needed, Workflow Instance Data Base (WfIDB), here the entity is the workflow instance. Due to the space of paper limitations some of the basic attributes of entities from the previous data bases are not given. The relation between the entities of WfDB and WfIDB can be easy imagined.

The Fig. 8 shows the proposed databases and the interaction of the agents with these data bases (Cicortas & Iordan, 2009a).

The multi-agent system (MAS) that is able to analyze the workflow instance that was blocked and based on its state to redesign the reminded part of the workflow instance that will be executed. This analysis must decide for every activity that its result can be or not can be used in the conditions that allow it, if we dispose for appropriate information. In a workflow, we have some activities whose result is in one of the following categories: the activity result can be retained and in future can be used, we can say it is "persistent"; the activity result is volatile in future, it does not be used, if we want the activity result in the future, we must reply it; the activity result has affected the real system state and the system state must be restored in the case if we want to replay this activity we must remove this "effect". If the workflow fails, then it fails due some activity that it failed.

The previous Workflow activities were executed and based on their result as previous analysis was done, we can find the activities whose results are reusable and are persistent. In the case of the replay of the Workflow we must make an analysis that: restores the activities that were affected in some way the system state, find the activities that have reusable and persistent results, reconstruct a new Workflow with the remained activities and reusable results. (The problem is that on every parallel branch we must have a reusable result). In the following we propose the steps that will allow constructing and using our proposed model:

a. For every activity the designer must decide if it has remanent result and the way that allow identifying and storing it;
b. For all activities it will specify if its result is volatile or the effect of the activity on the overall system, in the sense that it must be discarded (example: updating data bases with the cancellation of the activity effects).
c. During the execution of a workflow instance will be recorded in a data base, the activities (their results if there is in the case of the remanence) as soon as these are executed.
d. When a workflow instance fails due of an activity failure, then an analysis is done and it concerns the effects of activities on the system state; the last activities with remanent results will be retained. A mechanism for finding on every branch these remanent activities is required.
e. After the previous step when the workflow instance must be replied, a new variant of the workflow instance is constructed as follows: as input locations that enter in a transition are the locations of activities with remanent results (as it was given in (Cicortas et al. 2006)).
f. The new workflow instance that was constructed in the previous step can be started.

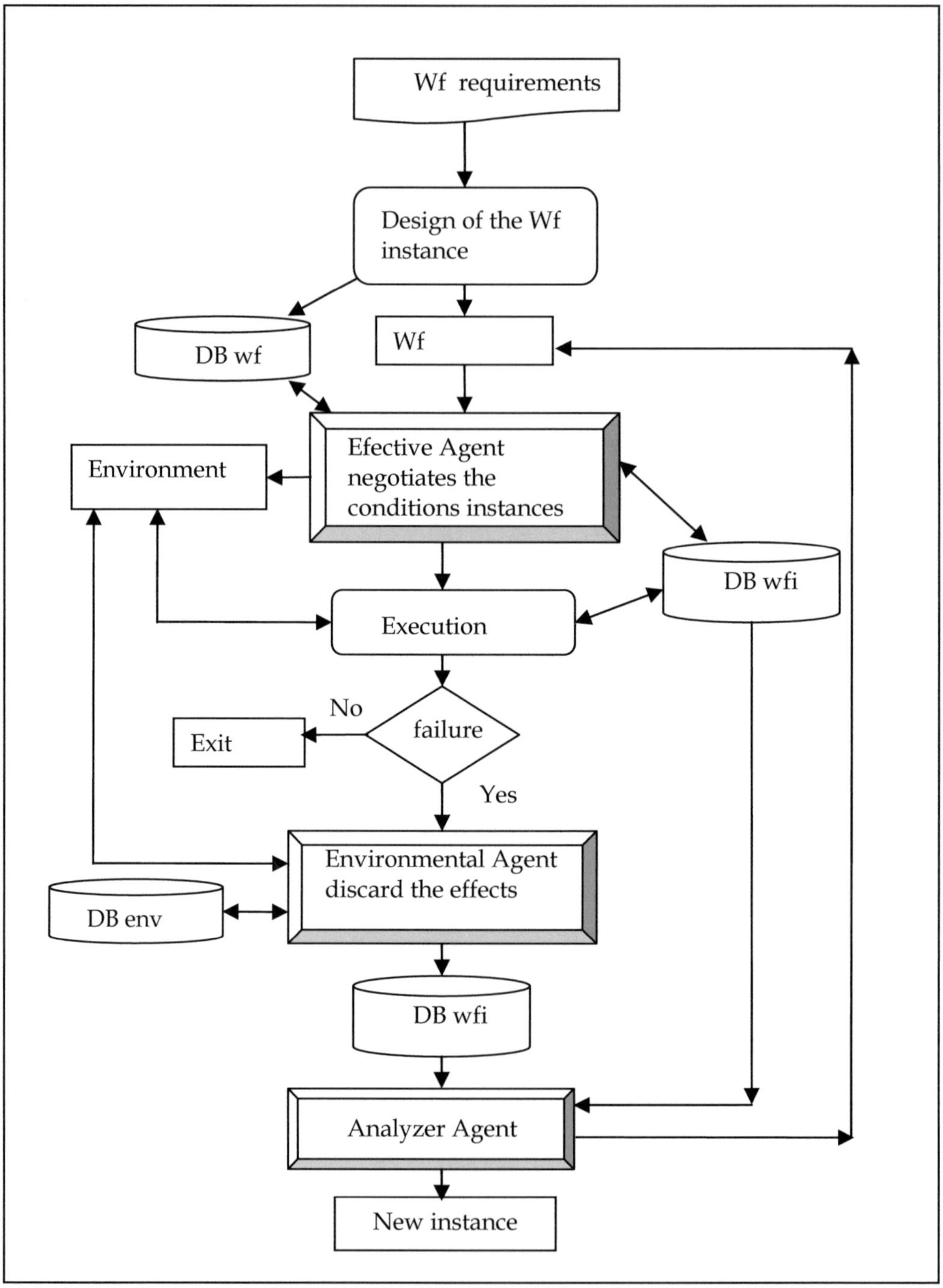

Fig. 8. Interaction of the agents with data bases

The agents of the proposed MAS act after the workflow was described as it was previous stated (i.e. a workflow description in that the activities were described).

In the case of a workflow instance failure the Analyzer Agent, make the analysis as follows: (a) all the activities on the every parallel branch are specified and their results are available; (b) for all the activities that affect the overall system state prepares their cancellation actions; (c) redesigns the new workflow instance.

The Environmental Agent executes the cancellation activities. The Effective Agent negotiates the conditions for the execution of the new instance of the workflow and launches it in execution. Decision for modelling is based on process complexity, failure of activities that can fail only the activity and "suspend" the process or fail all the process. The problem is to identify the reply of the process and its implications. Done to the process complexity the solution can be: restart the process from the beginning or reply the process from one of the previous "valid" states before its failure under some conditions. Needs for replies in a failure case are: (a) every activity must have specified its type concerning its result (persistent, affect the environment, insignificant); (b) during the execution every activity recalls somewhere (in a data base) its result and this result can be used depending of activity type in the future (if the activity is of reusable type). (Cicortas & Iordan, 2009b).

The Fig. 9 shows in short our proposal (Cicortas & Iordan, 2009a).

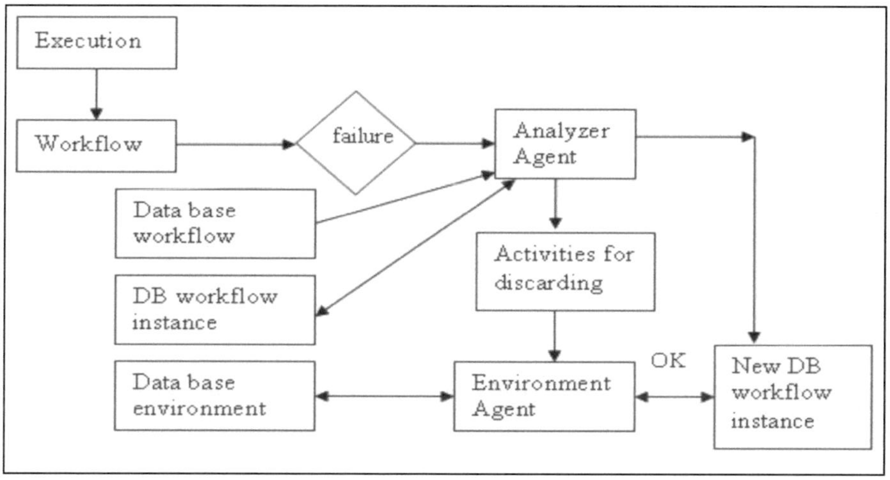

Fig. 9. The flow of actions

8. Conclusions

As was stated in the above considerations, we consider that as a main goal that argues and motivates the usage of MAS and the ontology constructs, are the following:

a. the dependency modeling, that supports goal dependencies, task dependencies, and resource dependencies. Here we outline that the same role must execute many tasks and the role can be played by the same agent and at one time instant and we dispose only for one such agent (i.e., many tasks need in the same time instant the same role that can be played by the same agent). Some constraints concern the dependencies between the orders of tasks execution in this case. Here an intelligent analysis must be done and it justify the multi-agent concept;

b. resource dependencies within and among roles and tasks can also be similarly captured and represented using the knowledge construct. The knowledge construct specifies which task performed by a particular role requires what resources. The knowledge construct can also be used to model the contention of resources and availability of resources can be signaled using messages and this message flow information (e.g., what message should be expected and from whom when a required resource becomes available) can be modeled using the knowledge construct;

c. the concurrency is mandatory and it is one of the main requirements in the area. The agents that will be used act in an independent manner and in the same time they must cooperate in order to attain their goals and the system objectives;
d. new features are needed for the workflow engines that will allow the deal with the process dynamic and with the flexibility.

9. References

van der Aalst, W.M.P. (2001). Exterminating the Dynamic Change Bug: A Concrete Approach to Support Workflow Change, Information Systems Frontiers, 3(3), pp. 297–317, (2001).

van der Aalst, W.M.P. & ter Hofstede, A.H.M. (2002). Workflow Patterns: On the Expressive Power of (Petri-net-based) Workflow Languages. In: Kurt Jensen (Ed.): Proc. of the Fourth International Workshop on Practical Use of Coloured Petri Nets and the CPN Tools, Aarhus, Denmark, August 28-30, 2002, pages 1-20. Technical Report DAIMI PB-560, August 2002.

van der Aalst, W.M.P. & Akhil, K. (2003). Xml-based schema definition for support of interorganizational workflow, *Information Systems Research*, Vol.14 (1), 2003, pp. 23-46.

Aerts, A.; Szirbik, N. & Goossenaerts, J. (2002). The flexible agent based infrastructure for virtual enterprises, *International Journal of Computers in Industry*, Vol. 49, No.3, 2002, pp. 311–328.

Bajaj, A. & Ram, S. (2002). Seam: a state–entity–activity–model for a well-defined workflow development methodology, *IEEE Transactions on Knowledge and Data Engineering*, Vol. 14, No.2, 2002, pp. 415– 431.

Basu, A. & Blanning, R.W. (2000). A formal approach to workflow analysis, *Information Systems Research*, Vol. 11(1), 2000, pp. 17–36.

Cicortas, Al.; Iordan, V.; Fortis, Al. & Fortis, F. (2006). Reengineering the Failed Workflows, *Annals of the Tiberiu Popoviciu Seminar*, Supplement international Workshop in Collaborative Systems, 2006, Vol. 4, ISSN 1584-4536, pp. 57-66.

Cicortas, Al. & Iordan, V. (2009a). Multi-agent models in workflow design, Proceedings of 5th International Symposium on Applied Computational Intelligence and Informatics SACI'09, Timisoara, Romania, pp. 527-532, ISBN 978-1-4244-4478-6, IEEE CFP0945C-CDR

Cicortas, Al. & Iordan, V. (2009b). Considerations on the Requirements for WFMS, Proceedings of the CSCS-17, 17-th International Conference on Control Systems and Computer Science, MASTS 2009, The International Workshop on Multi-Agent Systems Technology and Semantics, 26-29 May, Bucharest, Vol. 2, Ed. Politehnica Press, ISSN: 2066-4451, pp. 553-558.

Fakas, G. & Karakostas, B. (1999). A workflow management system based on intelligent collaborative objects, *Information and Software Technology*, Vol.41(13), 1999, pp. 907-915.

Finin, T.; Labrou, Y. & Mayfield, J. (1995). *Kqml as an agent communication language*, in: Jeff Bradshaw (Ed.), Software Agents, MIT Press, Cambridge, 1995.

Fischer L. (2000). *The Workflow Handbook 2001*, Association with the Workflow Management Coalition (WfMC), 2000.

Fox, M.S.; Barbuceanu, M.; Gruninger, M. & Lin, J. (1998). An organization ontology for enterprise modeling, in: M. Prietula, K. Carley, L. Gasser (Eds.), *Simulating Organizations: Computational Models of Institutions and Groups*, AAAI/MIT Press, Menlo Park CA, 1998, pp. 131–152.

Gligor, V.; Gavrila, S., & Ferraiolo, D. (1998). On the formal definition of separation-of-duty policies and their composition. In Proceedings of the 1998 IEEE Computer Society Symposium on Research in Security and Privacy (Oakland, CA, May), IEEE Computer Society Press, Los Alamitos, CA, 172–183.

Huhns, M.N. & Stephens, L.M. (2001). Automating supply chains, *IEEE Internet Computing*, Vol. 5 (4), 2001, (Jul/Aug), pp. 90–93.

Jennings, N.R.; Faratin, P.; Johnson, M.J.; Norman, T.J.; O'Brien, P. & Wiegand, M.E. (1996) Agent-based business process management, *International Journal of Cooperative Information Systems*, Vol. 2 and 3, 1996, pp. 105- 130.

Jennings, N.R.; Sycara, K. & Wooldridge, M. (1998). A roadmap of agent research and development, *Autonomous Agents and Multi-Agent System*, Vol. 1 (1), 1998, pp. 7- 38.

Jennings, N.R.; Norman, T.J.; Faratin, P.; O'Brien, P. & Odgers, B. (2000). Autonomous agents for business process management, *Journal of Applied Artificial Intelligence*, Vol. 14 (2), 2000, pp. 145- 189.

Jennings, N.R. (2001). An agent-based approach for building complex software systems, *Communications of the ACM*, Vol. 44 (4), 2001, pp. 35- 41.

Kishore, R.; Ramesh, R. & Sharman, R. (2003). Computational ontologies: foundations, representations, and methods, in *Proceedings of Ninth Americas Conference on Information Systems* (9th AMCIS), Association for Information Systems, Tampa, FL, 2003, pp. 3178- 3189.

Kishore, R.; Zhang, H.; Ramesh, R. & Helix, A. (2004). Spindle Model for Ontological Engineering, *Communications of the ACM*, Vol. 47 (2), Feb. 2004. pp. 69–75.

Kishore, R.; Zhang, H. & Ramesh, R. (2006). Enterprise integration using the agent paradigm: foundations of multi-agent-based integrative business information systems, *Decision Support Systems*, Vol. 42, 2006, pp. 48- 78.

Linthicum, D.S. (1999). *Enterprise Application Integration*, Addison-Wesley, Boston, MA, 1999.

Malone, T.W. & Crowston, K. (1994). The interdisciplinary study of coordination, *ACM Computing Surveys*, Vol. 26 (1), 1994, pp. 87–119.

Nissen, M.E. (2000). Supply Chain Process and Agent Design for E-Commerce, In 33rd Hawaii International Conference on System Sciences, 2000.

Nguyen, V. (2009). Contextual Workflow Modeling, http://www.macronetics.com/docs/CWM%20Whitepaper.pdf, accessed 10.03.09.

Ould, M.A. (1995). *Business Processes-Modeling and Analysis for Re-Engineering and Improvement*, Wiley, Chichester, 1995.

Pan, J.Y.C. & Tenenbaum, J.M. (1991). An intelligent agent framework for enterprise integration, *IEEE Transactions on Systems, Man and Cybernetics*, Vol. 21 (6), 1991, pp. 1391–1408.

Papazoglu, M. P. (2008). *Web Services: Principles and Technology*, Prentice Hall, ISBN 978-0-321-15555-9, 2008.

Purvis M.; Savarimuthu, B.T.R. & Purvis, M. (2004). Evaluation of a multi-agent based workflow management system modeled using Coloured Petri Nets, In M. Barley and N. K. Kasabov, editors, PRIMA, volume 3371 of LNCS, pp. 206–216. Springer, 2004.

Reese, C.; Ortmann, J.; Moldt, D.; Offermann, S.; Lehmann, K. & Carl, T. (2005). Architecture for Distributed Agent-Based Workflows. In: Proceedings of the Seventh International Bi-Conference Workshop on Agent-Oriented Information Systems (AOIS-2005). 2005; pp. 42–49.

Sadiq, S.; Orlowska, M.; Sadiq, W. & Foulger, C. (2004). Data Flow and Validation in Workflow Modeling, *ACM International Conference Proceeding*, Series; Vol. 52 archive, Proceedings of the 15th Australasian database conference, 2004, pp. 207-214.

Saidani O. & Nurcan S. (2006). A Role-Based Approach for Modelling Flexible Business Processes, *BPMDS*, 2006, pp. 111-120.

Sikora, R. & Shaw, M. (1998). A multi-agent framework for the coordination and integration of information systems, *Management Science*, Vol. 44 (11), 1998, pp. 65–78.

Sikora, R. & Shaw, M. (2002). Multi agent enterprise modeling, in: C. Holsapple, V. Jacob, H.R. Rao (Eds.), *Business Modeling*: A Multidisciplinary Approach Essays in Honor of Andrew B. Whinston, Kluwer Academic Press, 2002, pp. 169–185.

Sowa, J.F. (2000). Ontology, Knowledge Representation: Logical, Philosophical and Computational Foundations, Brooks/Cole, New York, NY, 2000, pp. 51–131.

Sycara, K.P. (1998), Multiagent Systems, AI Magazine, Vol. 19 (2), 1998, pp. 79– 93.

Stormer, H. (2001). AWA - A flexible Agent-Workflow System , In Workshop on Agent-Based Approaches to B2B at the Fifth International Conference on Autonomous Agents(AGENTS 2001), Montreal, Canada, 2001

Tillquist, J.; King, J.L. & Woo, C. (2002). A representational scheme for analyzing information technology and organizational dependency, *MIS Quarterly* , Vol. 26 (2), 2002, pp. 91–118.

Wang, M. & Wang, H. (2002). Intelligent Agent Supported Flexible Workflow Monitoring System, In Advanced Information Systems Engineering: 14th International Conference, CAiSE 2002, Toronto, Canada, 2002.

WfMC, (1999). *Workflow management coalition terminology & glossary. Workflow Management Coalition. Document status*, Issue 3.0, 1999.

Wooldridge, M. (2002). An *Introduction to Multiagent Systems*, John Wiley and Sons, West Sussex, England, 2002.

Yu, E.S.K. & Mylopoulus, J. (1996). Using goals, rules and methods to support reasoning in business process reengineering, *International Journal of Intelligent Systems in Accounting, Finance & Management*, Vol. 5 (1), 1996, pp. 1– 13.

Yu, L. & Schmid, B.F. (1999). A conceptual framework for agent oriented and role based workflow modeling, *Proceedings of International Bi-Conference Workshop on Agent-Oriented Information Systems*, Heidelberg, Germany, 1999.

7

Evolutionary Reduction of the Complexity of Software Testing by Using Multi-Agent System Modeling Principles

Arnicans G. and Arnicane V.
University of Latvia
Latvia

1. Introduction

1.1 A complex nature of software testing

Software testing is a fundamental component in the development of high-quality software. Research shows that 30-60% of the resources that are devoted to software development are focused on testing (Paradiso, 2001; Perry, 2006). Because of this major use of resources and the fact that results that are achieved are often less than adequate, specialists are dissatisfied with the current situation, and they are looking for ways of improving the testing process.
Causes which are often cited in relation to these problems include delays in the launch of testing, a lack of time, a shortage of specialists, and a lack of professionalism in testing. This is due to the fact that specialists from the business with poor IT knowledge are increasingly being put to work as testers, while other IT specialists are not available. There is also a shortage of budget for a proper testing environment, the necessary tools, and the wages of the necessary specialists.
Authors consider that the roots of many problems are found in the complex nature of testing processes. Software testing is a process which can be viewed as a complex system. This allows us to better understand the nature of software testing and to look for more non-traditional approaches toward the restructuring of the process. Our initial goal is to find ways of reducing the complexity of testing. That would make it possible to do the work far more efficiently, to reduce the necessary resources, and to improve the quality of the testing.

1.2 Looking at sociotechnical system by MAS design principles

The testing of software as system is a sociotechnical system. It includes the software, the testers, and the environment in which the testing occurs - the testware, additional software, hardware, and the necessary infrastructure (Joslyn & Rocha, 2000). The main element for the testing is the software system under test, along with the people who are doing the testing.
Testing as system can be considered as a complex system, because it consists of a large number of interacting components (agents, processes, etc.), with a large number of interactions and whose aggregate activity not always is derivable from the summations of the activity of individual components (Sherard & Mostashari, 2009). Complex systems can be described with a multi-agent model (Boccara, 2004; Russel & Norvig, 2003; Shoham & Leyton-Brown, 2009).

Multi-agent models and the architectures which are based upon them are used to design software which, in a simplified way, copies or simulates real-world objects and their behaviour. Designers of models mostly choose issues that are of fundamental importance to complex systems from the real world, and they represent a simplification of those systems.

In testing, as in other complex processes, organisation of the process is of critical importance so that the resources which come from the internal abilities and knowledge of the system can be used efficiently and so that we can adequately adapt these to the surrounding environment. Accordingly, we propose that more attention has to be paid to those organisational principles that are important in establishing multi-agent models to improve the management of testing processes. This approach may help to observe many important issues which we fail to notice in daily routine situations because of the complexity of the relevant system.

A great deal of long-term research has been done to identify the main issues of complex systems and to understand the most important principles on which they operate. The results have served as a foundation for various theories and methodologies which allow us to put together the model of a complex system. This is a simplified model of real life, maintaining only the most critical aspects that are needed to simulate that which occurs in reality. This involves transformation from the real world to an artificial model which can be used for several purposes, for instance, to design software.

We propose more seriously use approach which is based on the usage of knowledge about operation of complex system crystallized in the model as basis of evolving of complex system in the real world. The model covers the most important principles of the real world. If a complex system does not function with sufficient effectiveness, then model that bases on studies of effective systems can serve as an example for the level toward which the complex system should be evolved. The model can show not just the most important elements of the new system, but also undirectly points to unimportant things which the tester should get rid of lest the resources of the system be overburdened. This must be done carefully, however, because it is possible that the model does not take into account some key aspects that are necessary for the full and proper functioning of the system.

The approach toward the improvement of testing processes that we are considering here is just an example of how the principles of multi-agent system modeling can be brought to bear. This could apply to many situations in which it is necessary to address complicated problems related to the active and important participation of individuals. Here is the core question for such research: "How can human organisational principles be used for multi-agent architectures?" We have already noted here that we have chosen the opposite direction: "How can the architecture of a multi-agent system and the principles whereby that architecture is developed be used in order to organise the processes of real-life complex systems in a better way?"

One of the problems here is that there are comparatively few specialists who are familiar with the theories of complex systems and the ways in which they can be modeled. This applies to the modeling of multi-agent systems, as well. Developers or testers will not use methodologies which they don't understand and with respect to which they don't have the necessary skills. This means that the use of MAS modeling principles must be introduced gradually, beginning with the simplest elements. Models meant for the design of intelligent software are usually too complicated for non-specialists in the area of multi-agents. Preference, therefore, must be given to those models which can characterise a complex system or multi-agent system at the conceptual level. The existing situation in the industry, however, is one in which at least initially, the establishment of the model can be an informal process - even just a mental model in the brain of the person who is organising the testing if he or she does not wish to write it down (Sheard & Mostashari, 2009).

1.3 Managing of system complexity to evolve

A testing process is changing a great deal over the course of time. The software that is being tested is changing, as growing its level of readiness. There are be changes in the testing team, the testing environment, the tools that are brought to bear, the requirements that are applied, and the resources that are available during the period of testing of the newly developed software. This means that testers must constantly adapt to new circumstances by choosing different testing methods and approaches. That is why the testing model must evolve all the time in an iterative sense so that it is in line with reality. For instance, let's assume that we have multi-agent modeling principles that have been chosen and learned well or that have shown that they are no longer of use. In that case, we introduce new principles or supplement the collection of existing ones so that the model is once again in line with the situation at hand.

Because the system is constantly changing and the model has to be adjusted, the system in real life and the model should be more principle-based than rules-based inasmuch as this is possible. This ensures greater freedom for system elements, and the system can operate more effectively and securely whilst, at the same time, reacting in a better way to changes in its surrounding environment (Bar-Yam, 2003). At each moment we must formulate a few principles that allow agents to gain new knowledge and to rearrange themselves in line with the next condition of the system in its planned route of evolution. If testers understand the approach, then it is not necessary for them to be familiar with the model's precise details. It is enough for them to be aware of its most important elements, how they are linked, and how they operate. Formalism becomes important when the need is to replace a human agent with a software agent, as well as to ensure the necessary relationships between people and their computers.

We have observed that the divide-and-conquer principle, which is also known as decomposition, is not used to a sufficient degree. The MAS modeling principles suggest that there be small agents so that their work can be primitive. Larger jobs must be handled by groups of such primitive agents. The techniques, methods and activities of testing can be divided up into many smaller components, which make it possible to use the relevant testing resources more effectively. That particularly applies to the testers who are doing the basic work.

In our approach, the complexity of the testing process is reduced and effectiveness is increased by managing a large number of agents (the skills of employees) and the primitive assignments that are a part of the multi-agent system model. It must be noted that reduction in complexity is a relative concept, because we actually reduce the complexity of only one aspect that is causing problems in terms of the further evolution of the system. In fact, the overall complexity of the system may even increase. The multi-agent model helps us to find weaknesses, and it offers suggestions as to how the situation can be improved - create new agents by training employees, improve planning and co-ordination among agents, or present primitive tasks which can be automated. We believe that testers who are familiar with the most important principles that are described in this chapter can apply them successfully in their work without the establishment of a formal model. From here, we will sketch out ideas as to how MAS modeling principles can help to improve testing processes.

These ideas are based on the practical work of the authors in the field of software testing, including teaching testing processes to others, and organising testing processes.

2. Testing of software as a complex system

2.1 Complexity of software testing

The software that is being tested can be a complex system if it is made up of many autonomous, interlinked and collaborating components or services which are adapting to the environment in which their work is being done, the user who is doing the work, and the situation under which the work is progressing. For instance, such can be systems based on Service Oriented Architecture (Fiadeiro, 2007), as well as component-based software. The software is made up not of large, mutually integrated components, but instead of modular components among which there are many different ways of interaction. The complexity of software is determined not just by its structural or physiological complexity or its size. Also of importance is the social complexity which emerges from the number and intricacy of interactions which involve autonomic components (Fiadeiro, 2007). The tested software can be used in a computer which already has an operating system, with all of the relevant components, and there can be testware or other software used by users during their work. The interaction of all of these elements within a computer is complicated and not always predictable.

Testing processes are handled by people - testers, users and developers. Those who are a part of the testing team also establish a complex system. What is more, testing can involve several overlapping teams - testers, users and developers. There are links between these groups, but there are also links among the people themselves. Some people can be wearing different hats by being a part of different groups.

Testing is a system of systems (SoS) because it includes several complex systems itself - the software that is being tested and the people who are involved in the process. In practice, there are times when several software systems are tested simultaneously to test their mutual interfaces and other types of interaction. In that case, the testing is an even more complex system, because it contains several complex systems in and of itself, and all of the work that is planned and implemented must be balanced to an even greater degree.

The testing system is substantially affected by its environment and by external limitations in terms of the job that has been assigned, the schedule for the work, the budget, and the infrastructure in which the testing system operates - facilities, computers, computer networks, servers, and the like.

2.2 System and environment

2.2.1 Manifestations of system complexity

Complexity as a problem in software engineering is usually addressed by diminishing the complexity of the environment or by increasing the ability of the system to deal with complexity. A third option is complexity engineering or the approach of emergent engineering - using the complexity instead of fighting against it. Appropriate characteristics of complex systems in this regard are self-organizing, co-evolution and emergent behaviour (Heylighen, 2009).

The total complexity of complex systems cannot be described with a single metric. There are different types of complexity (Thorsten et al., 2006) - time, the level of organisation, as well as systemic complexities. Time-related complexities are static and dynamic. Dynamic complexity refers to the process of the system, the elements, the links among the elements, the number of properties, and changes in differences over the course of time. Static complexity, for its part, expresses these indicators at a specific moment in time. Organisational complexities relate to the structural complexity of the system - the number of elements, the diversity of elements, and the number of links and properties therein. Process-oriented complexity relates to the number and diversity of flows of processes. There can be internal and external systemic complexity. External complexity speaks to the incoming data and resources for the system from the environment which the system can handle and process. Internal complexity refers to the complexity of the model of the system. The boundary between internal and external complexity will depend on the limits of the system itself - what we include as parts of the system and what we leave as elements of the environment (Jost, 2004).

2.2.2 Internal complexity

The elements in a testing system include people, software and hardware. The team includes software testers, software developers and users. Software developers offer consultations to testers about the technological issues of the system and help to produce testware. Users are initially involved as consultants as to the relevant business processes, and later they test it in the system testing and accepttesting levels. The size of the testing team changes over the course of time, depending on the work that needs to be done at any given moment. Only a few users may be involved as consultants at first, while at the level of accepttesting there can be a far greater number of users so as to cut the amount of time that is needed to do the work. In other words, there are dynamic shifts in the structurally organisational complexity of the system (the number of people and links among them), as well as in the process-oriented complexity (the processes in which these people take part and the types of processes that there are).

The software that is being tested changes, as well. New functionality of software are gradually brought into the testing process, found faults are fixed, new requirements are identified and implemented. This changes the number of software modules and services, as well as links among them. This is reflected in the structurally organisational complexity of the system and in the process-oriented complexity thereof.

2.2.3 External complexity

The external complexity of a system is based on new or changed software units - the number and size of modules provided by the developers, as well as the demands from management as to what kinds of testing are expected and how quickly they must be performed. The incoming information and resources have an effect on the internal complexity of the system. If the budget for the system is increased, the elements of the system can be supplemented or changed - new people can be hired and new software can be purchased to improve the testing process.

Demands related to software testing and time limits are of a different nature. These demands change the process-oriented organisational complexity of the process in terms of the testing methods that are necessary and viable, as well as the issue of the scope of the testing - covering all of the software or just a segment thereof. In the latter case, the focus might be on the most critical usage scenarios and the most complicated calculations that are brought to bear.

The external complexity of the system is also based on the complexity of the artefacts which it changes or establishes - mistakes identified in the software, reports about problems, and documentation such as testing plans, samples, reports on testing and conclusions about the quality of the software that is being tested.

2.3 Organisational complexity of software testing and behaviour of testers

2.3.1 Role of organisation

Testing is a component of the life cycle of information system development projects. A study of several hundred projects of this type in North America found that the greatest effect on project performance indicators such as delivery time, cost, functionality and user satisfaction is had by the structurally organisational complexity of the process, as expressed through the complication and closeness of the various elements in the project's organisational environment, also not forgetting about project resources, support from managers and users, the attitudes of project personnel, and the level of professional skills among the personnel (Xia & Lee, 2004). There is reason to say, therefore, that the level of testing performance can also be affected substantially by structurally organisational complexity.

For that reason, particular attention in this chapter will be focused on ways of changing the organisationally structural complexity of a system by using the principles that are used in the modeling of complex systems.

2.3.2 Perception of system from inside

The complexity of a system depends on the subjective perceptions of the user. The system is viewed by the people who are involved therein. Often they seem just a part of the system, not the entire complexity thereof. It is important to make sure that the part of the system that a user needs to do his or her work is not so complicated from the user's perspective that the work simply becomes impossible.

From another perspective, it can be said that the complexity of complex systems is characterised by emergence, self-organisation, non-linear links among the components, openness and feedback loops (Grobbelaar & Ulieru, 2007).

2.3.3 Reaction of testers to the changes in the environment

Testing is a complex adaptive system. It must react to changes in the external environment and within the system itself.

In practice, it is typical that developers submit software for testing too late, while the deadlines for doing the work are not changed. The result is that testers often have far less time for their work than had been planned, and this will have an effect on the quality of testing. Often enough the work is not done at a sufficient level of quality. Our hypothesis is that if testing is to be more successful, testers must demonstrate skills related to emergence, self-organising, the ability to view synergetic effects, and the ability to handle different tasks related to the process. Then the testing system evolves on the basis of the laws of a complex system.

Testing processes typically have two different kinds of goals – finding mistakes on the one hand and making sure that there are no mistakes on the other. This process is arranged in different ways – in accordance with testing levels, risk priorities, the chosen testing techniques, etc. However, it is always a very creative process in which the individual decisions taken by testers in each specific situation are of great importance. The behaviour of testers is emergent. Testers do their work in a creative way, but they plan and organise it in accordance with management plans, their own experience, their motivations and their level of understanding as to the job at hand. As a result, their behaviour cannot always be predicted and controlled with any great precision.

2.4 Emergent evolving

The testing process can evolve and self-organise in a natural way. When the iteration of each testing process ends, there is an evaluation of what has been good and bad, what we can learn, what needs to be kept, what needs to be improved, and what is lacking. Also of use during the evaluation are measurements that have been taken during the testing and the systems thereof (Chen et al., 2004). The results of the evaluation show directions related to the growth of the process and the development of its participants.

Testing systems are imbued with a series of characteristics that are typical of complex adaptive and evolving systems - self-organisation, emergence, positive and negative feedback, states of equilibrium or absence thereof, the large amount of possibilities, co-evolution, and the nature and history of evolution.

Testing processes are in a stable condition near of the equilibrium when there is no need for new test cases. That usually happens when software is used for a long time without any change in the software or its environment. One or more stably regressive test cases are set up, and these are occasionally used to make sure that the software is continuing to operate in line with requirements. Each time that the software is changed, the testing process loses its condition of equilibrium to a greater or lesser degree, and as new test cases are established so as to stabilise the software, there is once again a permanent set of regression test cases, and the condition of equilibrium is renewed. At the beginning of the testing process, the situation is far from equilibrium, by contrast, and that is particularly true in the early stages of the process, when static analytical testing methods are brought to bear.

Positive feedback about testing processes changes their ecosystem and creates the need for evolution, learning and emergence (Heylighen, 2009). This leads to new versions of software, the identification of new mistakes, the setting out of new goals or missions for the testing, as well as changes in the supply of resources.

There are usually vast numbers of possibilities in testing. There are choices as to strategies, methods, test data and the order in which test cases are assessed. In some cases the method will identify the introductory values that are chosen, although in most cases the value must be chosen from an interval or a list of values.

A very characteristic aspect of testing processes is co-evolution. When one tester teaches another, they both evolve. The former trainer learns to teach others, while the latter person gains knowledge about testing. If a tester finds a mistake made by the software developer, then he gains experience as to how to find the mistakes, while the software developer learns about the mistake and can decide on what to do to make sure that that never happens again.

Testing processes have a history that is based on the situation, chances in terms of what could be done, and what is actually done.

Complexity can be absorbed as the system is adapting to circumstances of the environment and/or evolves.

3. Possibilities to deal with a system complexity

3.1 Exploring of complex systems

People have, for a long time, studied complex systems that exist in our perceived reality. The goals for such research can differ. For instance, there can be a focus on the operating principles of a system so as to:

- Use the principles in another sphere.
- Understand the operating of other complex systems.

- Model and forecast system operations in terms of time and external environmental circumstances.
- Replace the entire system or a part thereof with a technical system such as a computer which uses the relevant software.
- Create new systems which have not existed before.

These examples are based on a study of the general principles which exist in the operations of existing systems, analysis, understanding and the establishment of a model which describes the systems. There are various theories which make it easier to understand and model complex systems. Multi-agent systems are the basis for one such theory.

3.2 Modeling principles of MAS as nature of complex systems

Different methodologies and frameworks have been established on the basis of the multi-agent modelling theory which makes it possible to establish the necessary models more quickly and precisely. Multi-agent systems are based on the systems which make up living organisms, particularly people. The agent can be analogous to a human being, agents conduct the functions that are entrusted to them, they work together, they react to changes in the surrounding environment, and they are born, they die, they educate themselves, and they try to achieve their own goals and the global goals of the entire system.

Our view is that extensive research has made it possible to identify the principles and logic which determine the structure and operations of various complex systems. The identification of the most important things in the real world means that a more primitive model can be used to describe the way in which the system handles a job and exists in the real world while pursuing the mission that has been entrusted to it.

Let us take a look at the primary goal of multi-agent systems. Software that is based on the multi-agent model can intelligently replace an actual person or team in the handling of many different tasks. Here we use the transformation scheme "from the real world to the model", or "software that is based on a model." Our hypothesis is that the transformation can also occur in the opposite direction - "from the model to the real world". This means that we can take a system from the real world and identify the most important principles therein, getting rid of unimportant things that might even be a hindrance in real life. Thus we know the elements and processes of the system which are the most critically important ones - those which determine the results and effectiveness of the operations. We can call these elements the essence of the system.

3.3 Using of MAS models to evolve

3.3.1 Learning from MAS design principles

Complex sociotechnical systems can have different stages of development as determined by their internal structure, organisation, processes and knowledge. We can say that a system is at a higher level of development if it can handle more work or more complicated work at a higher level of effectiveness in terms of the resources that are used. System development usually requires a long time, and it is handled via evolutionary mechanisms. A system can also exist in very different conditions that are dependent on the external environment. One of the key aspects of development and adaptation in a specific environment is self-learning. That is particularly true in the case of systems with little "experience" - i.e., those that are at a low level of development or that are unaware of the best forms of adaptation when there are unexpected changes in the external environment.

Training processes are much quicker and more effective if there are examples from other systems in terms of how to develop the system, the goals that should be pursued, and what to do in various situations that can occur in life. This approach is often the foundation for training about many existing systems. For instance, when we need to improve software testing processes, we can study books which contain information about the experience of others in this regard, as well as recommendations that have proven their validity over the course of time.

We propose a more non-traditional approach to system training and development on the basis of the principles whereby multi-agent systems are developed. If we are familiar with those, we can concentrate on very important issues and speed up the training. We make far more rational use of the resources that are available for the training and for the most typical elements therein. We also can be quite sure that we know the way in which the system will evolve. This is an approach which allows us, in a natural and comparable way, to gain domain-specific knowledge. In our case, that relates to knowledge about software testing.

3.3.2 The evolution of a complex system

When we put together a multi-agent system the plan is that in future it will be changed or will change itself on the basis of new circumstances. If the surrounding environment does not change much and there are no fundamental changes in terms of the requirements that are levelled against the system, then the planned mechanism ensures development and evolution along with changes that occur. If an existing system needs to be changed, however, there is a different approach:

1. We identify the vision and goals so that we know the situation that we want to achieve in terms of the system and its environment.
2. We identify the current condition of the system.
3. We think about strategies in pursuit of the goal and choose the best one.
4. We plan activities in pursuit of the chosen strategy.
5. We do the work in accordance with plans, and we iteratively repeat the whole process from time to time.

In real life, in most cases, complex systems adapt to surrounding circumstances in a gradual and evolutionary way. Revolutionary, major and rapid changes are less common. Revolutionary changes in software testing may occur if the company decides to outsource the testing, as opposed to doing it in house. In that case, a key component of the system has been changed, and links to other external systems must also change (e.g., there must be formal and legal relations between the recipient and the supplier of the testing services).

Let us look at a typical situation in which a system develops gradually so as to ensure a situation that is better for the surrounding environment and for the global goals and demands that relate to the system. In the multi-agent model, we have various ways in which a system can adapt to a new situation. Agents can educate themselves and change their operations. Alternatively, old agents "die" and are replaced by new and more appropriate ones. The operations of agents will also change in accordance with existing knowledge and skills which are the result of a monitoring of changes in the system. This is because the agent may seek to achieve its own goals and those of the entire system with a lesser usage of resources.

The key role of agents in testing processes is performed by people. It is very hard to change people rapidly, and a gradual process is needed instead (Arnicans & Arnicane, 2009). A more revolutionary approach can be taken toward software agents, because the computer does what it is instructed to do without "thinking." There will be greater problems if software agents become more intelligent, because then they will adopt the shortcomings that relate to human agents. What is more, any revolutionary changes in a complex system are difficult to forecast, because this is a property of complex systems as such.

There are different driving forces behind evolution. There can be planned development in which someone comes up with the correct scenario for development and forces the entire system to pursue it. Another option is to make use of the advantages of a self-adaptive system, which means that the components of the system can be quite free in taking decisions. In that case, the system seeks a status of balance at which it can handle the relevant requirements whilst minimising the resources that are consumed. This approach may ensure an optimal situation at the local level, but it may be that there are other opportunities for implementing requirements even more efficiently. The principles of multi-agent systems make it possible to come up with different strategies for functioning. Most agents may be reactive and only obey commands, but agents can equally be intelligent and proactive in terms of adapting themselves to the situation at hand.

3.3.3 Problem with information entropy

The complexity of a complex system (i.e., a testing system) cannot be stated in absolute measurement units, but it is possible to analyse the characteristics of different complexities during periods of change.

Scientists and practitioners have been dealing with attempts to reduce the complexity of software testing in direct and indirect ways for more than 30 years now, ever since the 1970s. Lots of books and articles have been written about software testing. Initially, the issue had to do with testing techniques, but later authors began to focus more on the organisation and management of testing processes. Our observation is that literature about software testing reflects its complexity and the nature of a complex system quite well. There are many good books for practical use, although each author or group of authors will have different views about testing. The numbers are very different, because they show what the author or authors think about testing and its various aspects.

The excess of literature and the complexity of testing mean the following problems:

- There is no single source of literature which is good enough in terms of demonstrating the essence of testing. Indeed, no such source is possible, because a very complicated system cannot be described in a single book.
- Short books do not offer enough information.
- Excessively thick books sometimes keep readers from studying them fully because they lack time to do so.
- If a reader has absorbed a great deal of literature, then the content can be hard to understand in terms of separating the important from the unimportant. This creates problems in choosing the right strategy or testing technique for the specific situation.

This problem is particularly evident when non-IT specialists become involved in testing as a temporary job that management forces them to do. They usually don't have the motivation to understand the essence of testing, nor do they have the ability to learn about these matters.

In order to change the situation, we must understand the nature of a complex system and the ways in which we can at least reduce the complexity of understanding it.

3.3.4 Design complexity and control complexity

According to Casti, "*... complexity cannot be thought of as an intrinsic property of an isolated (closed) system; it is only made manifest by the interaction of the system with another, usually in the process of measurement and/or control. In this sense, it is probably more meaningful to consider complexity more as a property of the interaction than of the system, although it is clearly associated with both. (..) System complexity is a contingent property arising out of the interaction I between a system S and an observer/decision-maker O*" (Casti, 1986). Here we can talk about the complexity of the system S for the observer O, which is described as design complexity, or about the complexity of the observer O for the system S, which is called control complexity. The two complexities need to be in balance.

If we look for ways of reducing system complexity, we need to understand what a simple system is. Casti (1986) also mentions several characteristics of simple systems:

- Predictable behaviour: We understand the system's behaviour and our ability to forecast its reaction to specific entry data or to the surrounding environment.
- Few interactions and feedback/feedforward loops: The system has a few components among which there few and understandable interactions. The interaction links of the components should not lead to radical changes in the system.
- Centralised decision-making: The behaviour of the system determines by one or only a few decision-makers.
- Decomposability: The system consists of clearly evident components among which there are weak links. Each component is independent in relation to other components.

3.3.5 Simplification of system by MAS models

One of the primary duties in modeling multi-agent systems is to describe the operations of a complex system as simply as possible. Because the basic thought in this is about software design, the recommendation is to use the following techniques to reduce complexity (Booch, 2004):

1. Decomposition: The larger problem is divided up into smaller sub-problems to the point at which the sub-problems can be understood and resolved more easily in isolation from other sub-problems. Complexity is reduced, because each phase in the solution is understood, the solution is simpler, and it can be implemented in a safer and more high-quality way.
2. Abstraction: We use different simplified models to emphasise that which is most important and to hide the details that are not important at the specific level. Complexity is reduced, because we can concentrate on the fundamental aspects of the problem. We can have a conceptual understanding of what is happening, choose the best solution or strategy, and reduce the likelihood of serious mistakes.
3. Hierarchy and organisation: We identify and manage relations among the components which underpin the solution. These can be grouped and seen as a more universal and homogeneous component at a higher level. There are techniques for organising co-operation among components in pursuit of solutions to a complicated issue. Duplication of effort, moreover, can be minimised.

These are effective techniques, but we must keep in mind that when there is a certain level of interdependency in a complex system, the techniques become ineffective. The decomposition of an object is possible only if its behaviour represents a merger of the behaviour of its components. Abstraction can be brought to bear if the description of the object can be prepared independently from other objects in the system. Because a complex system is basically made up of elements with behaviour that cannot be described as the sum of the behaviour of all of its components, and also because there are elements which cannot be described apart from other elements in the system, these techniques of simplification in complex systems can only be used to a certain degree.

3.3.6 Using of ontologies

Now let us return to the problem of vast and diverse information about software testing. Setting up of multiagent systems can be fundamentally improved if the ontology of modeled system or problem is created. This reduces the complexity of understanding the system, because there are fewer concepts and links among them. It is only natural, then, to hope that the ontology will make it possible to access further and more detailed information that is necessary to deal with the problem at hand. Sadly, no such ontology has been created at this time. That may be a consequence of the complex nature of testing - the ontology would be massive, and it would probably not satisfy all specialists, because each specialist will have a different view of the complex system.

3.3.7 Conservation of complexity

Another opportunity is to reduce the complexity of one part of the system, remembering, then, that the complexity of another part will increase. In a testing system, for instance, it will mean that the complexity will move from testers to software designers, users and managers.

For instance, let's assume that we simplify testing to the point where software is essentially tested only by end users who use it, while even the software developers don't do anything more than elementary unit testing. These users cannot be seen as a part of the testing system in this case, because they are really only software users who encounter various problems therein. As a result, for instance, several million users start to complain about problems to management if it is business software, to the development company or to the development team. This means lots of new links between users and software developers, after which software developers start to look for new processes in approaching each problem, and new processes are used in new versions of the software that is delivered to users. So by simplifying testing we get that the overall complexity of development and use of the software increases. This means that we need to think about ways of affecting the complexity of the system within itself and in the complex system in which our system is a component. A similar situation often exists within a single complex system. When reducing complexity in one aspect, we increase complexity in other aspects.

3.3.8 Reducing of complexity by primitive agents to promote whole system evolving

Our proposal is based on the principle that a complex system - in this case, software testing - teaches itself, adapts to new situations and evolves to the point where it serves its mission whilst using as little in the way of resources as possible. This can be called system evolution, and it means that when we talk about reduced complexity, we are actually thinking about simplifying the system from a fixed perspective so as to ensure its evolution over the course of a longer period in time. When we use the principles of multi-agent systems, we can transfer complexity from one aspect to another.

The overall trend is to ensure that each person who is involved in the testing process has many local and simple views or simple sub-systems which the person already understands.

Each such sub-system must maximally satisfy the needs for simple systems - it consists of simple components that can be decomposed, it has few interactions, there is centralised decision-making process, and the behaviour of this system is predictable. This makes it easier to learn new knowledge and skills so as to do the entrusted job effectively in the context of this small and simple sub-system. The effectiveness of the system may then increase gradually. The overall complexity of the system will certainly increase if it was at a low level before, but the higher effectiveness of the testing process should reduce the complexity of other complex systems that relate to software testing by, for instance, the team of software developers.

4. Using the principles of an agent-based modeling

There are many various frameworks and methodologies that describe the architecture and principles of development of multi-agent systems (Giorgini , 2005).
An explanation of the essence of our approach could be based on any framework that seems acceptable and understandable, because the basic concepts and principles therein are comparable.
We are using the frameworks proposed in (Aart, 2005; Jennings, 2000), because they are based on human organisational principles. Lets us look on the most important concepts that we are holding for our model.

4.1 A Principles based approach

When establishing a model for a testing system and trying to simplify it, we have to keep in mind that it is important to allow the testing system to operate as a complex system, i.e., it is important to create contexts in which they can self-organise to serve our needs without direct design or specification.
Let us take a look at the most importance principles that have been adapted from multi-agent systems and the techniques of establishing them. We can also look at the experience which these authors have had in the area of software testing.
It is hard to define requirements which underpin a complex adaptive system. Far more useful in this regard is a principles-based approach, as opposed to the rules-based approach that is used far more often in describing such systems (Polacek & Verma 2009). Former US Treasury Secretary Henry Paulson has had this to say: *"One important of the IFRS accounting system is that it is principles-based, rather than rules-based. By 'principles-based,' I mean that the system is organised around a relatively small number of ideas or concepts that provide a framework for thinking about specific issues. The advantage of a principles-based system is that it is flexible and sensible in dealing with new or special situations. A rules-based system typically gives more specific guidance than a principles-based system, but it can be too rigid and may lead to a 'tick-the-box' approach. (Paulson, 2006)"* In this case, the IFRS accounting system is a complex system.
The principles-based approach involves a small number of principles related to the specific system in the interest of emergence and evolution. Once the system or the surrounding environment changes, the principles are reviewed, and the set of principles is updated with new ones. The principles for each specific system will differ. The testing system for every piece of software differs from other systems in terms of the job that is to be done, the software that is tested, the knowledge and skills of the testers, and other parameters. We can look at a few examples adapted from (Arnicane & Arnicans, 2008) in terms of sets of principles that could be used by a company which engages in software testing. The

principles therein are sufficiently universal to ensure that they can be used in systems with qualified testers or with testers who do not have special knowledge about software testing and IT. We chose these principles first of all because our practical experience with many projects relates to the organisation of testing projects and to the testing itself. Second, we have made use of our knowledge about complex systems and, particularly, the modeling of complex systems with the help of multi-agent systems.

4.2 Agents

In society, an agent is a person operating in someone's interests (Sterling & Taveter, 2009). In a testing system, that can refer to the tester, the user, the manager or the software developer, all of whom are acting on the basis of the goal of producing high-quality software. The status of an agent can also, however, be assigned to a robot or to software which can operate flexibly and autonomously with the aim of fulfilling its goals (Aart, 2005). We propose to look at a person in a slightly different way. A person is a complex system which can be modeled as a multi-agent system. We could identify agents that are responsible for various primitive parts of the testing process. Other agents within the person need not be identified directly as long as they are not important for the testing process. Thus we can say that the set of agents which represent a person can be seen as an agency at which agents satisfy most of the classical requirements for agents, apart from those properties that apply only to software-agent type agents. The set of human agents who are useful in testing processes can change. The situation improves if the individual gains new knowledge and/or skills about testing methods, for instance.

It can equally be true that human skills among people who are not defined as agents may become necessary in the testing process, and so these people must be identified as new agents. For instance, a tester can be familiar with bookkeeping, and at some point the software needs to be tested in terms of a bookkeeping-related functionality.

At the same time, however, we can look at people not as agencies of independent agents, but instead as a holonic multi-agent system (HMAS). That is because we can say that all external communications occur only through one special agent - the head of the holon. The HMAS has different characteristics that need to be taken into account. When it comes to communications with other agents, for instance:

- Even though the communications pass through a single agent, it is possible to communicate in many different ways (all of the types of communications and the techniques/languages of information transmission which the specific individual can accept on the basis of his or her senses, skills and knowledge).
- The holon may perceive received reports differently in semantic terms than had been intended by the sender.
- The forms of communication that are accepted by the holon may change over the course of time (e.g., people are in different conditions depending on the time of day or night, and there can also be differences in technical resources or in the desire of others to engage in communications).

There are also nuances when it comes to the internal agents of the holon:

- The agent has limited opportunities to do specific work, because the holon is limited – agents tend to operate in a specific sequence of tasks, because there are few people who do different kinds of work simultaneously.
- The work of the agent may be stopped at any time and for an unpredictable and unknown duration.

- It is difficult for the agent to return to work after an interruption if the pause has been very long (people can forget the precise situation in which they were, or it proves impossible to regain the previous condition).
- The agent's results in relation to a single task can differ from one case to the next.
- The agent can submit the results of work that has not been completed.
- The agent can do several jobs at the same time, suspending and then resuming them.
- The reaction of other agents in the holon cannot be predicted if a job is assigned to a specific agent of the holon (the holon involves the emotional and psychological characteristics of a human being).

This means that people, as multi-agent systems, have a dual nature. On the one hand, we can say that we can take different relatively independent agents that can be organised in a new and virtual multi-agent system, but on the other hand, the holon of a person encapsulates all of its agents and determines their availability and the specifics of their use.

If we consider all of the people who are involved in a testing process to be agencies, then we obtain a great many different agents, indeed. This makes it possible to establish a new virtual multi-agent system (VMAS). The more primitive and simple the agents that we have identified in the person, the greater will be the possibility to organise those agents in pursuit of a major task. Now let's look at all of the agents in our VMAS. Several of them will be similar. For instance, the writers of problem reports are agents. Still, each one will be different, because each person will write the report a bit differently. The point is that all agents in a VMAS are unique. We can only assemble groups of similar agents from whom we expect a similar reaction and results.

The quality of results among the agents in a single group can differ very substantially. For instance, an expert will write up a much better problem report than a beginner will do. The agents who come up with the strategy and relevant missions need to keep this in mind before assigning tasks in pursuit of the desired goals. Additional problems for planning agents are based on the fact that available agents are in holons, and that limits the use of these agents at any given moment.

Our hypothesis here is that by using a VMAS, we can affect the complexity in the complex system of software testing. If we simplify the necessary sub-systems, then we can achieve faster and better evolution of the system so that it does its work more effectively and is more likely to adapt to the changing environment. In the context of this hypothesis, we consider a complex system to be software testing, but we also feel that there are other complex systems to which the same hypothesis could apply. Let us look on principles that we propose. For the sake of readability of following explanation we add identifiers to the essential principles, using a different letter for each one according to the perspectives of our model - A (Agents), T (Tasks), O (Operations), S (Structure of organisation), C (Co-ordination), and F (Functioning, which refers to the agent's capabilities).

A1: The agents who will do the work are as primitive as possible. An agent is a person or software that performs a specific task. For instance, agents can be handlers of test cases, evaluators of the results of a test case, the designers of test cases in accordance with criterion C1, documenters of failures that are identified.

A2: Agents are grouped into typical classes or groups, and relations among them or within them are defined. The subordination of agents is specified (leader/subordinate), the upper level specialisation of the agent is defined (operator, manager, planner, resource manager), the lower level specialisation is also defined (evaluator of test results, preparer of reports about failures, designer of test cases), and the participants which will handle specific tasks (e.g., regression testing, testing of scenarios, testing of performance) are identified.

A3: Agents which exist in a single individual or computer are merged into an agency (holon). According to the A1 principle, a person or computer can contain many primitive agents. Accordingly, the activities of the agents are limited - one agent acts under the framework of the assigned time slot. The parallel activities of several agents, however, can be simulated within the framework of a single agency.

A4: The agencies that are available to us and the agents residing therein must regularly be identified. This means that we are aware of the resources that are available to us, and we can plan specific activities - we choose the operations that can be handled with the available resources, we seek opportunities to gain a new agency with a necessary agent, or we establish a new agent in the existing agency.

A5: We determine the ability of each agency to create new agents. We must be familiar with the ability of each employee to gain new skills (i.e., create a new agent in himself). We must also be familiar with the computer and its software in terms of opportunities to use or configure these or to create opportunities for automatic adaptation of the software).

A6: Planning the effective use of the agency. Each agency has its operating costs. We use employees with a low level of qualifications to handle primitive and standardised tasks. The computer is what handles operations that are frequently repeated and can be computerised - this makes the testing automatic. Highly qualified employees must be used for non-standard and innovative operations, and they should not be assigned tasks that can actually be handled by employees who are lower on the ladder of qualifications.

4.3 Tasks

A task or action is something done to achieve the aims of global and individual agents. Higher-level tasks are usually so complicated that even fine specialists have problems in handling them. These are simplified via decomposition. Tasks are divided up into sub-tasks to the point where they become quite primitive and it is clear how they can be handled or, alternatively, that they cannot be split up any further unless the quality of the process can be lost.

Decomposition leads to a hierarchy of the tasks that must be done. Different links can be made among the tasks and sub-tasks to create a graph or network of dependency.

Task related principles are following.

T1: We divide up the tasks to get primitive sub-tasks. There must be harmony here with the A1 principle. The more primitive the tasks and the agents that handle them, the less complex the system will be. We assume that the system's "complexity of understanding" declines more rapidly than the "complexity of the quantity of components" increases, because we can make use of resources that are offered by abstraction and grouping. Here we have great opportunities for optimal operations, because major tasks can be handled by more than one agent.

T2: Determination of critical tasks. In evaluating risks and the interests of various stakeholders (the client, the agent doing the work, the user), we can prioritise the tasks that are necessary. We start this evaluation by the highest-level tasks. Evaluation of sub-tasks is conducted only for the critical upper tasks. This helps us to define our testing strategy, to decide whether new tasks must be created, and to come up with conditions for the establishment of a plan to perform the tasks.

T3: Defining those groups of tasks which will require a lot of time to perform. Here we determine which tasks are interdependent on the basis of various criteria that will affect the total amount of time that is needed (the tasks have to be handled in sequence, they consume one and the same resource, etc.).
T4: Determining those tasks which only a limited number of agents can handle. Usually there will be tasks which require someone with a high level of qualifications to handle them, and that means that there is a deficit of appropriate agents and agencies. Such agencies must be reserved for these critical functions, keeping them from doing other, simpler work.

4.4 Operations

The operations are handled by aǵents in order to fulfill the task. Operations use objects that are available, for instance, data, information, knowledge, tools, data bases, or material resources. Typical operations with objects are creating, modifying, destroying and consuming of them. Let us also note that operations can be described with a precise algorithm, or they can be also ones in which the agent must come up with its own innovative solution in each specific situation.
A typical operation in a testing system is the handling of a test case related to the software that is being tested. The tester initiates the work, ensures the necessary data, receives the results, and then compares them to correct result produced by the oracle to see whether the output data are correct. Operations related principles:
O1: We divide up the operation into primitive sub-operations. As was the case with principle T1, we reduce the complexity of the overall job and make it more possible to manoeuvre with the selection of agencies for each sub-operation. It is also easier to monitor the performance of the work.
O2: We define the most important classes of operations and specify their operational algorithm. Typical solutions are identified for those operations that are more important and must be handled more often. Templates help us to describe the way in which the operation is to be conducted. Those operations that can be performed on the computer can later be programms, and the relevant software agents can be created.
O3: Protection against deadlock. Because most agencies will be human beings who have a great deal of freedom in taking decisions, we must make sure that there are controls to ensure that the work is done. In practice, an agency can make some of his agents passive or fail to give them the time that is necessary to do the work. The result is that work on an operation can come to a halt, and that will have an effect on the behaviour of other agencies. When the agent is actually software, the work is easier to adjust and forecast.

4.5 Organizational structure and relationships therein

Testing jobs can often be handled more quickly and successfully if agents handle them not alone, but in partnership with other agents. This means teamwork among agents. A new team of agents can be set up for every task.
Here is what is typical for teamwork in multi-agent environments (Dunin-Kepli & Verbrugge, 2010):

- The agents work together in pursuit of a common goal.
- They monitor the progress of the group's work.
- They help each other as necessary.
- They co-ordinate the work of agents so that they do not hinder each other's work.

- They analyse and discuss successes and failures because that helps to improve the work that the team does.
- They do not compete amongst one another in pursuit of the common goal.

Organizatorial structure related principles are following.

S1: We select the best organisational structure for each class of tasks. We have an official organisational structure for our agencies, and that must be taken into account. At the same time, however, there are also informal relations among agencies. We can choose and govern both formal and informal structures. This must be in line with principle C1.

S2: We use existing organisational structures. The analogue is with principle C3.

4.6 Coordination and its mechanisms

Each team has certain co-ordination mechanisms. Coordination can be vertical with the leader and subordinates or horizontal when agents have equal rights. Coordination can be implemented depending on the environment, the activities that are to be pursued, and the organisational structure that is at hand:

- Direct supervision underpins vertical co-operation, with the manager overseeing the work of subordinates.
- Standardisation of work, where co-operation is based on precise standards or instructions as to the co-operation and the work that is being done.
- Mutual adjustment, with agents agreeing among themselves on their co-operation without any encouragement from the outside.

There are organizatorial structure often established in company determining groups of system's elements and their „legal interactions". Like each employee has its position in company with his duties and rights, each agent also acts in some position or role.

Coordination related principles:

C1: We specify the best possible co-ordination mechanism for each task. Depending on our strategy for ensuring the testing process and the agencies that are available, we define the best co-ordination mechanisms among agents and among agencies. The testing process is very flexible and dynamic. It depends on the project phase and the testing methods that are used. This means that many different versions of co-operation will be used simultaneously in the system.

C2: Promoting co-operation among agents and agencies. We set up opportunities for co-operation, show why they should be used, ensure an environment for the pursuit of global goals, and then let agencies themselves decide on co-operation as such. The goal could be to set up a self-organising system, because such a system is far more effective and viable under critical circumstances. Let's be careful, however, to make sure that the agencies do not get too carried away with private goals and ignore the system's goals.

C3: Use of existing co-operation mechanisms. The cornerstone for the testing process, at the end of the day, will involve living people, and the organisation will have specific co-operation models for specific individuals. There is no ideal co-ordination mechanism among people, because each person prefers his own desired mechanism or a combination of mechanisms. This will depend on the individual's personal characteristics, the level of the individual's maturity, and the goals which the individual sets. People don't like to accept rapid changes in their lives, and that's why we need to try to use the existing co-operation model, gradually transforming it in the desired direction.

4.7 Capabilities

An agent has to have necessary capabilities in order to handle the tasks that are assigned to it. We have chosen the Five Capabilities model for the modeling and management of the abilities of agents (Aart, 2005). The capabilities grouped therein include communication, competence, self, planner, and environment. These are the most important considerations if the agents are to be a capable as possible in handling tasks in our system.

Communication ensures co-operation between one agent and others, as well as with the surrounding environment and the maintenance of the necessary knowledge. *Competence* (knowledge and methods) ensure that the job can be done in technical terms. *Self* supports the agent's "intimate life" - the agent maintains its goals, the work that needs to be done and the opportunities that are at hand, it supervises, maintains and improves itself, and it manages its operations. *Planner* refers to the ability of the agent to decide on operating strategies, the order in which tasks are to be handled, what techniques are to be used, etc. - in other words, the agent plans its own operations. Finally, the capabilities under the heading of *environment* enable the agent to gain information about the surrounding environment, other agents, and the processes which are occurring.

Capabilities related principles are following:

F1: We determine the most important skills of agents and agencies. We must know the resources that are available to us before we can plan our testing strategy and activities.

F2: We determine the most important skills of agencies that are needed for the most critical tasks. This has to be harmonised with the results that we get when applying principles T1, T2 and T3. We can define the missing skills, which will be the difference between those abilities found with principle F1 and those found with principle F2.

F3: Seeking out alternative skills. We look for ways of replacing those skills that are missing with others, perhaps looking for entirely different solutions to the problem. Testing is a process in which different methods can be used to achieve the same goal, and that also means different functions. This represents dynamic adaptation to the circumstances which prevail.

F4: Developing new skills. We look at ways of ensuring those skills which are missing and ensure that they are gradually developed. This means creating new agents by training employees, obtaining new software, or configuring existing software.

4.8 Evolving by choosing the other principles

The most important prerequisite in the application of principles in practice is to do so gradually and moderately. First choose some principles which you understand and believe can be implemented without much difficulty. After awhile, these may become principles that are automatically understood. Use them until they are not longer actual according to the new circumstances. When some principles prove to be of no more use, replace them with others. Thus the testing team gradually learns about the basic principles and evolves in its work. If the choice of principles is repeated in a cyclical way in support of further development, then it is necessary to review other general principles related to complex systems and to choose the appropriate ones. For instance, typical principles for the establishment of complex systems can be found in (Polacek & Verma, 2009). It is also important to take into account domain-specific principles. For software testing, basic principles can easily be adapted from (Kaner et al., 2002), for instance. That is a source which offers several hundred principles and recommendations that are important for testing, have been examined in practice, and can be used successfully in combination with MAS modeling principles.

5. The evolution of the work of testers

5.1 A lack of qualified testers

In 2000 study by the European Systems and Software Initiative found that 70% of all software has been designed by organisations which do not specialise in software design (Haugh, 2001). There is no reason to think that this share has dropped. The organisation particularly looked at problems related to the quality of software and to testing. It found that testing was not being done at an adequate level. The main cause, according to the specialists, was a shortage of good testing specialists. Instead, there was intensive use of employees with good business knowledge, but poor knowledge about IT in general and software testing in particular (Marick, 2001). Problems related to the intensive use of non-IT testers are described in (Arnicane, 2007).

Let us look at a fairly typical situation which the authors have encountered at non-IT companies. Testing is often organised on the basis of a simple and understandable principle - each functional part of the software involves a tester who has to test that particular area. There is a fundamental shortcoming here, however. A tester without proper qualifications usually limits the work just to typical test cases, and that is usually not effective. Sometimes nothing in this regard changes over the course of many years.

5.2 Towards MAS paradigm

Companies are not satisfied with this, and so they bring in one or more testing specialists. A good specialist can plan a more or less optimal testing strategy on the basis of his capabilities and knowledge. Alas, there is a lack of human resources to pursue these plans. An unqualified tester cannot be assigned a high-level task, because he simply will not know what to do with it.

Testing is much improved if the activities are divided up into atypically small sub-activities that are comparatively primitive. Small and understandable tasks are delegated to non-IT testers, with the necessary individual training that can usually be completed in a short period of time. The testing professional handles only those primitive tasks which are nevertheless too complicated for non-IT testers. What's more, the specialist basically has to deal only with strategic planning, the detailed delegation of tasks, training, and monitoring of the work that is done. The professionalism of non-IT testers gradually increases, they can be given less detailed tasks, and the effectiveness of the total team is enhanced. When fundamentally different or new circumstances occur, the activities are once again split up into a greater number of parts, and training begins anew.

This process can be described very well with multi-agent system models. The advantage of the multi-system approach is that the same principles can be used to describe the co-operation or symbiosis between people and computers in pursuit of common goals. This makes it easier to replace computer operations with human work, as well as to formalise operations, describing them with algorithms so that it becomes possible to establish software-based agents.

5.3 A Sample of strategy to apply the MAS principles

Let's assume here that a company has found a good testing specialist. At the conceptual level, let us see how the aforementioned principles are used to restructure the software testing. We'll list the strategic activities which yielded positive results in real projects. In line with MAS principles, these can be handled simultaneously and in parallel. Each activity is pursued until such time as the internal condition of the system or the surrounding environment has changed:

- When a new person (agent) arrives at the company, the organisational situation is determined along with relations among employees so as to better integrate into the company and to make changes gradually and without major revolutions (S2). We look at the organisational structures that are best for reaching each fundamental testing goal, i.e., at how to work with agents more effectively (S1). We must assess the group of testers (the interior part of the system), as well as the company's other departments, partners, and users of the tested software (the environment for the software).
- We consider employees to be holonic agents who work together with other agents (A3), and we gradually identify the available people and their abilities, as well as the software, its functionality (A1, F1), and the way in which they work together (F1, C3). Accordingly, we can identify the testing tasks that we can achieve, and in the case of the simplest tasks, we can set deadlines and determine necessary levels of quality. We can plan the testing strategy, as well as a strategy for further training.
- We plan the testing strategy, and we divide up all of the tasks (T1) and processes (O1, O2). We divide them up into tasks and processes that are as small, simple and elementary as possible, the aim being to make sure that the available agents can handle them. We reject work that cannot be done, or we look for new and necessary agents to do that work.
- We determine which agent can handle each elementary task (A2, A3), judge whether quick training is needed (A5, F2, F4), assess the speed and quality of the work (A6, T1, T3), and determine the order of the tasks and the deadline for completing them (T1, T2). In a worst-case situation, we initiate training of employees to create new agents, or we look for ways of doing the job in a different way (F3).
- We assign the work to agents directly or create conditions in which employees are motivated to do the necessary work on their own (C1, C2, C3).
- We evaluate the risks which are associated with the most important tasks (A4, A5, T2, T3, T4, O3) and facilitate restructuring of the testing process if the performance of important tasks is endangered.
- We monitor the overall process and the achievements of each agent (O2, O3, C2, C3).
- We constantly improve the operating model and create new agents by training employees or designing appropriate software (A4, A5, T4, O2, F4).

5.4 Obtaining of New Skills and Agents

If the system is evolving more quickly, it is critically important to make sure that there are at least a few capable agents and that at least one of the agents has the necessary critical knowledge. Otherwise the system will be developed slowly, or it may not develop at all. In that case, there is the risk that as circumstances change, the system will not be able to handle even its most basic functions. In this case, the professional testing specialist who is brought into the process will require many different skills and areas of knowledge.

It is possible to organise an increase in the number of agents by hiring new employees and training them or by training existent employees - testers. Here is the technique that should be used for training: The future agent should first be allowed to handle the task as best he or she can. Then the work is corrected or completed by a professional agent, after which the trainee compares his or her results to the work of the professional agent. That helps people to learn.

5.5 A complexity for the key testers

Evolution of the system is achieved by reducing the complexity for the majority of employees who are involved in the testing, because that gives them a better understanding of the work that is done. They only are assigned tasks which they can achieve, they constantly learn new skills, and co-operation is basically informal in the context of a higher-level task, as opposed to being subordinated to the official structure of the company. The overall structure of the process does not disappear, however, because the complexity of the work of the professional tester is increased substantially. The tester is forced to devote more time to planning, training and organisational aspects of the work, as opposed to the testing process itself. One such employee can work with a small number of non-IT employees. Otherwise, the speed of development diminishes substantially.

6. Conclusions

There is discussed software testing as a complex system and considered ways of reducing its complexity in this chapter. Complexity is an inherent characteristic of complex systems, and it is not, therefore, possible to reduce their overall complexity. It is, however, possible to reduce the complexity of individual aspects of the system so as, for instance, to ensure that the work of people who are involved with the system becomes simpler, easier and more likely to be handled in a high-quality way.

A set of principles is offered based on ideas from multi-agent modeling methodologies and author's expierence in software testing. By gradually putting these into practice, it is possible to ensure that the work of the testers gradually evolves because the complexity of the testing is reduced insofar as many of the people in the process are concerned.

In order to model testing system there are used the basic concepts of multi-agent systems – agent, task, operation, co-ordination and organisational structure. Traditionally, people are modeled as agents. It was handy to perceive people as complex systems with agents as elements that are responsible for various primitive aspects of testing processes. Other agents are not identified within people as long as they are not proven to be important as participants in testing process. Each testing job is done by one or more agents. Agents can belong to one or more individuals who are doing the testing work. This work is based on principles from the theory of modelling multi-agent systems. Testing systems are very different – by SUT, testing team, constraints, priorities and accordingly by sets of principles. There are considered those principles in this chapter which relate to improvement of the management of testing processes, because it is one of the ways how to achieve improvements in testing process with relatively small effort.

There are not discused principles which could be used to ensure adequate and effective testing in this chapter, for instance, a minimal set of test cases that can be handled with minimal effort, that have results that can be evaluated precisely, and that allow for the conclusion that the handling of the consequences of remaining potential errors could be cheaper than the resources that would be needed for additional testing.

The sense of testing as a complex system allows explain why there have been so many failures in practice in this regard – money and time have been expended, work and effort have been invested, but the result is not achieved in that there remain numerous problems in the software under test. The errors are found as the software is used. The complexity of testing systems means that it is hard to evaluate the effort, time and money that will be needed for the work when the testing process is being planned.

Another result of the fact that testing is a complex system is that it is basically not possible to define or to describe the work of testers with procedures and then control the compliance of the work that is being done with these procedures. It is necessary to allow testers to ensure emergence, self-organisation and flexible behaviour that will lead allow them to deal with the situation at hand.

Historically, the complexity of testing systems has been limited by limiting the freedom of its elements and ensuring as much order as possible. This is done by implementing limitations such as the demand for plans, the strict adherence to the plans, and the observance of written procedures related to the work. In many cases, however, there can be plans, reports and a lot of bureaucracy, but the results will nonetheless be far from perfection. Perhaps that is because of all of the major limitations. Testing is a creative process.

Further research is needed into how an environment can be set up for a testing system in which it can make use of all of its advantages as a complex system – the ability to deal with complicated tasks in a creative way whilst, at the same time, not complicating the work of others who are involved in software development - developers, users and managers. Testing which is highly restricted by procedures and rules is more advantageous to management, because it is more predictable, and it is easier for managers to reject the idea that they are responsible for failures. In such cases, however, testing is no longer a complex system, it is just a complicated one. The greater the level of freedom in the elements of the testing system, the more the testing system behaves like a complex system which is harder to understand, describe and predict. Research is needed into ways of balancing risks that come from the unpredictability of the system with the benefits that the complex system provides.

Even though it seems that there is no real chance to set up formal models at this time, it is worth looking at whether there cannot be special tools and methodologies which make it easier to observe the principles of establishing a multi-agent system in testing processes.

In conclusion, it has to be stressed that the use of the ideas described in this chapter will largely depend on whether the testing team has at least one specialist who understands fundamentals of multi-agent systems and has good knowledge about software testing. There are no empirical data collected yet whether there can be fundamental improvements to testing processes if this is not the case.

The critical need is for a specialist who can imagine the testing system as a set of many primitive agents which engage in small tasks in pursuit of the overall goal, as well as can establish and constantly renew the concrete model for the specific project at least in a mental and informal way, the goal always being to allow the testing system to evolve gradually toward reduced complexity, at least insofar as testers who are involved in the system are concerned.

7. Acknowledgement

This work has been supported by the European Social Fund Project No. 2009/0216/1DP/ 1.1.1.2.0/09/APIA/VIAA/044. We wish to thank Karlis Streips for improving the English of this chapter.

8. References

Aart, C. (2005). *Organizational Principles for Multi-Agent Architectures*, Birkhauser Verlag, ISBN 3764372133, Basel Boston Berlin

Arnicane, V. & Arnicans, G. (2008). Using the Principles of an Agent-Based Modeling for the Evolution of IS Testing Involving Non-IT Testers, *Proceedings of 8th International Baltic Conference on Databases and Information Systems (Baltic DB&IS 2008)*, pp. 129-140, ISBN 978-9985-59-789-7, Tallinn, Estonia, June 2008, Tallinn University of Technology Press, Tallinn, Estonia

Arnicane, V. (2007). Use of Non-IT Testers in Software Development, *Proceedings of 8th International Conference on Product Focused Software Process Improvement (PROFES 2007)*, pp. 175–187, ISBN 3-540-73459-7, Riga, Latvia, July 2007, Berlin: Springer, (LNCS), Riga, Latvia

Arnicans, G. & Arnicane, V. (2009). Opportunities to Improve Software Testing Processes on Basis of Multi-Agent Modelling, In : *Databases and Information Systems V: Selected Papers from the Eighth International Baltic Conference, DB&IS 2008 - Volume 187 Frontiers in Artificial Intelligence and Applications,* Haav H. M., & Kalja, A., (Ed.), 143-156, IOS Press, ISBN 1586039393, Amsterdam Berlin Oxford Tokyo Washington DC

Bar-Yam, Y. (2003). When systems engineering fails-toward complex systems engineering, *Proceedings of IEEE International Conference on Systems, Man and Cybernetics*, Vol.2, pp. 2021-2028, ISBN: 0-7803-7952-7, Oct., 2003, USA

Boccara, N. (2004). *Modeling Complex Systems,* Springer, ISBN 0-387-40462-7, New York Berlin Heidelberg Hong Kong London Milan Paris Tokyo

Booch, G. (2004). *Object-Oriented Analysis and Design with Applications,* Addison Wesley Longman Publishing Co., Inc., ISBN 020189551X, Redwood City, CA, USA

Chen, Y., Probert, R. L. & Robeson, K. (2004). Effective test metrics for test strategy evolution, *CASCON '04: Proceedings of the 2004 conference of the Centre for Advanced Studies on Collaborative research,* pp. 111-123, ISBN , Markham, Ontario, Canada, October, 2004, IBM Press, Markham Ontario Canada

Dunin-Kepli, B. M. and Verbrugge, R. (2010). *Teamwork in Multi-Agent Systems: A Formal Approach*, Wiley, ISBN 0470699881

Fiadeiro, J. L. (2007). Designing for Software's Social Complexity, *Computer,* Vol. 40, No. 1, (Jan. 2007), 34-39, ISSN 0018-9162

Giorgini P. (2005). Agent-Oriented Methodologies: An Introduction, In: *Agent-oriented Methodologies,* Henderson-Sellers B. & Giorgini P., (Ed.), 1-19, Idea Group Publishing, ISBN 1591405815, Hershey London Melbourne Singapore

Grobbelaar, S. & Ulieru, M. (2007). Complex networks as control paradigm for complex systems, In: *Proceedings of IEEE International Conference on Systems, Man and Cybernetics (SMC),* pp. 4069-4074, ISBN 978-1-4244-0991-4, Montreal, QC, Canada, Oct. 2007

Haug, M. (2001). Software Process Improvement: A European View, In: *Software Quality Approaches: Testing, Verification, and Validation*, Haug, M., Olsen, E. W. & Consolini, L. (Ed.), 3-14, ISBN 3540417842, Berlin Heidelberg New York Barcelona Hong Kong London Milan Paris Tokyo

Heylighen F. (2009). Complexity and Self-organization, In: *Encyclopedia of Library and Information Sciences,* Bates, M. J. & Maack M. N., (Ed.), CRC Press, ISBN 084939712X

J. Casti, J. L. (1986). On System Complexity: Identification, Measurement and Management, In: *Complexity, Language and Life: Mathematical Approaches,* Casti, J. L. & Karlqvist A., (Ed.), 146 - 173, Springer-Verlag, ISBN 3-540-16180-5, Berlin Heidelberg NewYork Tokyo

Jennings N. R. (2000). On agent-based software engineering. *Artifical Intelligence,* Vol. 117, No. 2, 277-296, ISSN 0004-3702

Joslyn, C. & Rocha, L.M. (2000). Towards semiotic agent-based models of socio-technical Organizations, In: *Proceeding of AI, Simulation and Planning in High Autonomy Systems (AIS 2000),* pp. 70–79, Tucson, Arizona, USA

Jost, J. (2004). External and internal complexity of complex adaptive systems, *Theory in Biosciences,* Vol. 123, No. 1, (June 2004), 69-88, ISSN 431-7613

Kaner, C., Bach, J. & Pettichord B. (2002). *Lessons Learned in Software Testing: A Context-Driven Approach,* Wiley Computer Publishing, ISBN 0-471-08112-4, New York Chischester Weinheim Brisbane Singapore Toronto

Marick, B., (2001). Classic Testing Mistakes, In: *Software Quality Approaches: Testing, Verification, and Validation,* Haug, M., Olsen, E. W. & Consolini, L. (Ed.), 57-82, Springer-Verlag, ISBN 3540417842, Berlin Heidelberg New York Barcelona Hong Kong London Milan Paris Tokyo

Paradiso, M. (2001). Software Verification & Validation Introduced, In: *Software Quality Approaches: Testing, Verification, and Validation,* Haug, M., Olsen, E. W. & Consolini, L. (Ed)., 36-45, Springer-Verlag, ISBN 3540417842, Berlin Heidelberg New York Barcelona Hong Kong London Milan Paris Tokyo

Paulson, H. M. (2006). Remarks of Treasury Secretary Henry N. Paulson on the competitiveness of U.S. Capital marlets Economic Club of New York, retrieved September 20, 2010, from http://www.ustreas.gov/press/releases/hp174.htm

Perry, W. E. (2006). *Effective Methods for Software Testing,* Wiley Publishing, Inc, ISBN 0-7645-9837-6, Indianapolis, Indiana

Polacek, G. A. & Verma, D. (2009). Requirements Engineering for Complex Adaptive Systems: Principles vs. Rules, *Proceedings of the 7th Annual Conference on Systems Engineering Research CSER 2009,* ISBN 978-0-9562440-0-0, Loughborough University, UK, April 2009, Research School of Systems Engineering, Loughborough University, Loughborough, UK

Russell, S. J. & Norvig, P. (2003). *Artificial Intelligence: a Modern Approach,* Prentice Hall, ISBN 0-13-080302-2, London Sidney Singapore Hong Kong Toronto Tokyo New Jersey

Sheard, S. A. & Mostashari, A. (2009). Principles of complex systems for systems engineering, *Systems Engineering,* Vol. 12, No. 4, (Nov. 2009), 295-311, ISSN 1098-1241

Shoham, Y & Leyton-Brown K. (2009). *Multiagent Systems: Algorithmic, Game-Theoretic, and Logical Foundations,* Cambridge University Press, ISBN 0521899435, Cambridge New York Melbourne Madrid Cape Town Singapore Sau Paulo Delhi

Sterling L. & Taveter K. (2009). *The Art of Agent-Oriented Modeling,* The MIT Press, ISBN 978-0-262-01311-6, Cambridge, Massachusetts London, England

Thorsten, P., Bose, F. & Windt, K. (2006). Autonomously controlled processes - characterisation of complex production systems, In: *Proceedings of 3rd International CIRP Conference on Digital Enterprise Technology (DET),* Setubal, Portugal, Sept. 2006

Xia, W. & Lee, G. (2004). Grasping the complexity of IS development projects. *Commun. ACM,* Vol. 47, No. 5, (May 2004), 68-74, ISSN 0001-0782

8

An Approach to Operationalize Regulative Norms in Multiagent Systems

Carolina Howard Felicíssimo[1,2], Jean-Pierre Briot[2]
and Carlos José Pereira de Lucena[1]
[1]*DI/PUC-Rio, Rua Marquês de São Vicente 225, 22453-900, RJ,*
[2]*LIPVI/ParisVI, Avenue du Président Kennedy, 75016, Paris*
[1]*Brazil*
[2]*France*

1. Introduction

Multiagent systems have emerged as a promising approach to develop information systems that clearly require several goal-oriented problem-solving entities [Jennings *et al.*, 1998]. Following this direction, it is believed that upcoming information systems will be implemented as *open* multiagent systems, in which agents (their entities) can freely migrate among those systems in order to obtain resources or services not found locally.

A multiagent system(s) (hereinafter referenced as MAS[1]) is/are an example of an open system in which the actions of heterogeneous, self-interested agents may deviate from the expected behavior in a context. Openness has led to dynamic software systems that have no centralized control and that are composed of autonomous entities [Hewitt, 1991]. Key characteristics of such systems are heterogeneity, conflicting individual goals and limited trust [Artikis *et al.*, 2002].

As stated in [Esteva *et al.*, 2004], "*openness without control may lead to chaotic behavior*". In order to be a viable solution for dynamic software systems, MAS must be enhanced with norms for defining which actions are *permitted, obliged* and *prohibited* to be performed by agents so that the system does not reach an undesirable state. A *permitted* norm defines that an action is allowed to be performed; an *obliged* norm defines that an action must be performed; and, a *prohibited* norm defines that an action must not be performed.

Permissions and prohibitions are used to describe positive/negative authorizations, whereas obligations are used to describe responsibilities [Kagal and Finin, 2007]. These three types of norms represent the three fundamental *deontic statuses* of an action [Alberti *et al.*, 2006] from deontic logic [Wright, 1951] and they are logically connected as presented by the following statements:

- If an action is *permitted*, then, it is *not prohibited;*
- If an action is *obligatory*, then, it is *permitted* and it is *not prohibited;*
- If an action is *prohibited*, then, it is *not obligatory* and it is *not permitted;*

---

[1] Through all the text of this chapter, when the characteristic of open systems is important to be outlined, then, we will explicitly use the 'open MAS' expression instead of simply 'MAS'.

- If an action is *not permitted not to perform*, then, it is *obligatory*;
- If an action is *prohibited not to perform*, then, it is *obligatory*;
- If an action is *obligatory not to perform*, then, it is *prohibited*;

Deontic logic enables addressing the issue of explicitly and formally defines norms and deals with their possible violation [Alberti *et al.*, 2006]. In such way, deontic logic could be used in the agents' logics and architectures when norms can be violated and agents have to explicitly reason about those violations and their consequences [Jones and Sergot, 1993].

This means that agents should be able to take into account the existence of social norms in their decisions (either to follow or violate a norm) and to react to violations of the norms by other agents [Castelfranchi *et al.*, 1999].

Important works concerning normative MAS (*e.g.*, [Vázquez-Salceda *et al.*, 2005; Esteva, 2003; Hübner *et al.*, 2002; Minsky_LGI, URL; Chopinaud *et al.*, 2006]) have been proposed recently. A normative MAS is a system that conforms to or is based on norms [Boella *et al.*, 2006b]. That type of system must allow some facility for the system developer, while he is describing and evolving the norms of his system, and also allow some facility for agents' reasoning about applied norms.

We agree that current solutions for normative MAS usually have the following drawbacks: (i) they consider norms with a valid universal meaning in an application domain; (ii) they do not support the direct design and implementation of norms specific to the application domain (*e.g.*, political, economical, religious norms); (iii) they do not support the management of norms during system execution (*i.e.*, norm description off-line and norm enforcement on-line); and (iv) they expect that agents must be already aware of the (*predefined*) system norms.

The motivation for our research came forth from the need to resolve those challenges, providing an approach applicable in open systems, in which norms can be effectively applied to their agents and easily managed. In such systems, heterogeneity and autonomy rule out any assumption concerning the way third-party entities are implemented and behaved. Thus, a viable solution for regulation in MAS should not be hard coded inside agents' original implementations and must allow, for some degree of precision and flexibility, to update data (*e.g.*, norms) during the system execution.

Our research intends to bridge the gap between the theoretical work on norms and practical normative systems by proposing our DynaCROM approach [Felicíssimo *et al.*, 2008b and 2008c]. DynaCROM stands for *Dynamic Contextual Regulation Information Provision in Open MAS* and it aims to operationalize regulative norms in open MAS.

From the individual agents' perspective, DynaCROM is an information mechanism that makes application agents aware of the norms they are bound to at a given moment. From the system developers' perspective, DynaCROM is a methodology for the application and management of norms in open MAS so developers are able to embody abstract norms with domain values. Therefore, norms are contextualized in the application domain wherein they hold, facilitating regulation through norm enforcement mechanisms.

By 'context', DynaCROM follows the definition of [Dey, 2001] stating that "context is any implicit information that can be used to characterize the situation of participants and to provide relevant information and/or services to them, where relevancy depends on participants' tasks".

Regarding '*situation of participants*', DynaCROM is concerned with the issue of regulation in complex systems, which follows [Simon, 1996] in his definition stating that: "*complexity frequently takes the form of a hierarchy. That is, a system is composed of interrelated subsystems, each of which is in turn hierarchic in structure, until the lowest level of elementary subsystem is reached*".

In the remaining sections, the research involved to conceive our DynaCROM approach is presented. The theoretical fundamentals of DynaCROM are the main goal of the chapter. Further practical information related to the applicability of DynaCROM can be found via two motivating scenarios: in [Felicíssimo *et al.*, 2008a], through the domain of multinational organizations, and in [Felicíssimo, 2008d], through the television domain.

2. Dynamic contextual regulation information provision

Open MAS can be extremely dynamic due to heterogeneous agents that migrate among those systems for obtaining resources or services not found locally. In order to prevent malicious actions and to ensure agent trust, open MAS should be enhanced with normative mechanisms. However, it is not reasonable to expect that *foreign* agents will know in advance all the norms of the MAS in which they will execute.

In the following section, the DynaCROM methodology developed to support the system developer in the tasks of implementation, management and evolution of the norms of his MAS is explained. The methodology includes the phases of contextualization, concretization, representation and composition of norms.

2.1 From abstract to concrete norms in MAS

A major challenge in MAS is how norms can be effectively applied to their agents and, then, easily managed and evolved. The application of norms in MAS is not a straightforward task, since heterogeneity and autonomy rule out any assumption concerning the way that heterogeneous agents are implemented and behave in MAS [Grizard *et al.*, 2006].

In [Gaertner *et al.* 2007], the authors of the paper propose to extend the coordination level of a MAS with a normative level, so that, norms can be integrated during the design and execution time of the system. DynaCROM follows their proposition but, furthermore, it also proposes to extend the normative level with, what we called, a *contextual normative level*. In this level, abstract norms are concretized (*i.e.*, embodied) with domain values according to the context wherein they hold. The proposition for contextual classification of norms follows the ideas first proposed by Dignum in [Dignum, 2002] and, then, refined in [Grossi and Dignum, 2004]. However, their works mainly address formal issues while our approach addresses the practical ones, providing DynaCROM – an implemented solution as a proof-of-concept for the ideas proposed.

In order to illustrate the DynaCROM proposal, Figure 1 presents the *Coordination, Normative* and *Contextual Normative Levels* of a simplistic supply-chain scenario in which activities (illustrated by linked ellipses) are represented on the three layers (connected by dashed arrows). Norms (illustrated by vertical arrows) are applied at the second and last levels. Contextual norms (illustrated by diagonal arrows) are applied at the last level.

In order to exemplify how norms are concretized in normative levels, the *Negotiation* activity of Figure 1 is considered. A *Negotiation* summarizes a set of more specific activities performed between customer and seller agents (*e.g.*, a customer asks a seller how much a product costs; the seller states his price, with or without discounts; the customer accepts the seller's price). The *Negotiation* activity is linked to the *Payment* one and both activities might be translated in the normative level to:

A Payment Norm for Effecting a Negotiation: Negotiations are obliged to be paid by using the national currency of the seller's country.

The payment norm presented above is abstract and vague, and therefore, applied only for general purposes. In order to cause any effect in a regulated system, abstract norms must be translated into concrete norms [Grossi and Dignum, 2004]. Thus, the abstract payment norm might be contextualized, by the system developer, as an environment norm and, then, concretized in its MAS. For example, in *American* and *Japanese* supply-chain domains, the environment norm could be concretized with the following instantiations:

A Concrete Environment Norm for Effecting a Negotiation: Negotiations are obliged to be paid (i) in *USA*, with *American dollars* (*USD*); and, (ii) in *Japan*, with *Japanese Yen* (*JPY*).

In the DynaCROM contextual normative level, the classificatory reading of *'counts-as'* from [Grossi *et al.*, 2006] is applied. The reading states that if "A counts-as B in context c", then, it is interpreted as "A is a sub-concept of B in context c". In this sense, *'counts-as'* statements work as *'contextual classifications'*.

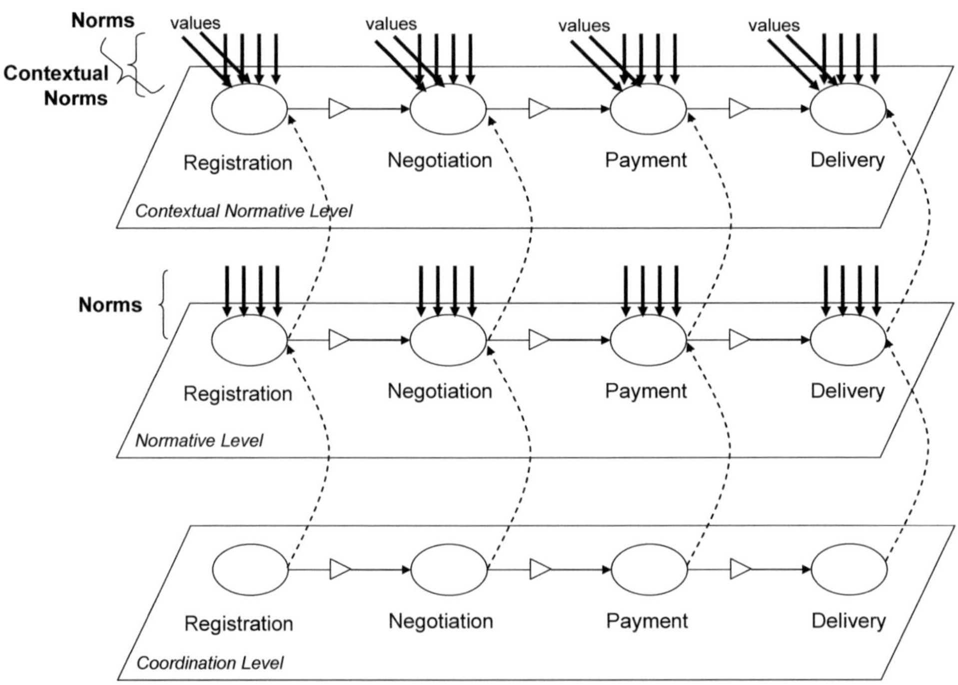

Fig. 1. Activities, regulated activities and contextual regulated activities represented in their specific layers, based on [Gaertner et al., 2007]

For instance, considering the payment norm exemplified above, its reading is done as follows: "*USD* counts-as a *valid currency* in the context of the *USA environment*"; and, its interpretation is done as follows: "*USD* is a sub-concept of a *'valid currency'* concept in the context of the *USA environment*".

Figure 2 illustrates part of the *Contextual Normative Level* of Figure 1 in which the *'valid currency'* variable of the *Negotiation* activity is instantiated for the payment norm according to the *American* and *Japanese* environments.

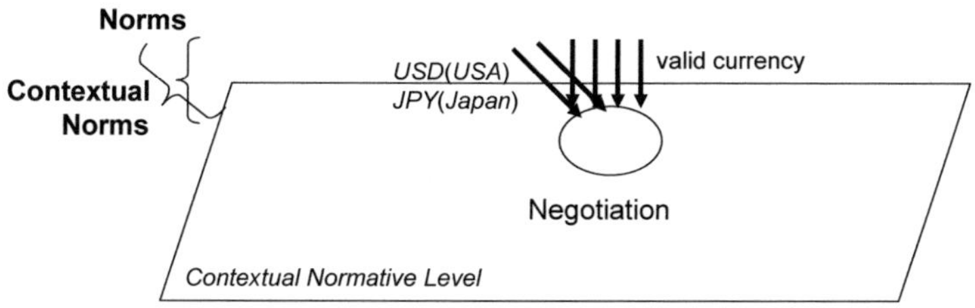

Fig. 2. Contextual classifications for a payment norm

Moreover, besides the instantiation of contextualized variables, DynaCROM consideres that activities, in the contextual normative level, can also have different predefined conditions. For instance, *Give discount* (a possible sub-activity of *Negotiation*) states that, in an organization, discounts can be given (a) by subtracting *10%* of the price value for *orders paid in cash*, or (b) by subtracting *15%* of the price value for *products bought in bundles.*

2.2 Contextual norm classification

Basically, a MAS consists of environments, organizations and agents playing roles and interacting [Jennings, 2000]. As environments, organizations, roles and agent interactions are important concepts for the understanding of the text, the meaning in which they are used in this chapter is characterized below.

Environments [Weyns *et al.*, 2007] are discrete computational locations, similar to places in the physical world, which provide conditions for agents to inhabit it. Environments can have refinement levels, such as a specialization relationship (*e.g.*, country and state), but there cannot be overlaps (*e.g.*, there cannot be two countries in the same place). An environment can also have many organizations.

Organizations [Ferber *et al.*, 2003] are social locations in which groups of agents play roles. An organization can embody many sub-organizations, but each organization belongs to only one environment [Silva and Lucena, 2004b]. Agents can execute in different organizations and they can also migrate among environments and organizations in order to obtain resources or services not found locally.

Roles [Thomas and William, 2005] are abstractions that prescribe a set of related tasks, which agents must perform in order to achieve their designed goals. Roles are defined by organizations independently of agents' individual identities.

An agent can interact with any other agent in a MAS, for example, by exchanging messages.

Environments, organizations, roles and interactions suggest different contexts for regulation in MAS. *Context-aware computing* means to be software that "*adapts according to its location of use, the collection of nearby people and objects, as well as changes to those objects over time.*" [Schilit and Theimer, 1994]. Although contexts are tacitly known by most people, they are normally hard to be identified and, therefore, not distinguishable for computing.

In order to help the system developer in his task of norm contextualization, DynaCROM follows directions taken by research in context-aware applications that suggest top-down architectures for classifying contextual information [Khedr and Karmouch, 1995; Henricksen and Indulska, 2005].

DynaCROM defines that norm information should be classified in a MAS according to the following contexts: *Environment*, *Organization*, *Role* and *Interaction*, which are differentiated by the boundaries of their data (*i.e.*, norms).

Environment Norms are applied to all entities in a regulated environment. Likewise, *organization norms* are applied to all entities in a regulated organization; *role norms* are applied to all agents playing a regulated role; and, *interaction norms* are applied to all agents involved in a regulated interaction.

Figure 3 illustrates an example scenario in which entities of a MAS are influenced by the application of norms (represented by arrows) from different levels of abstractions (represented by dashed boxes). In the *Environment Normative Level* (upper level), environment norms are directly applied to environment instances (*e.g., USA* and *Japan*). In the *Organization Normative Level,* organization norms are directly applied to organization instances (*e.g., Dellie, HPie* and *DellieJapan*); in the *Role Normative Level,* role norms are directly applied to role instances (*e.g., ADellieSeller, AHPieSupplier* and *ADellieJapanManufacturer*); finally, in the *Agent Normative Level,* interaction norms are directly applied to the agents that are interacting.

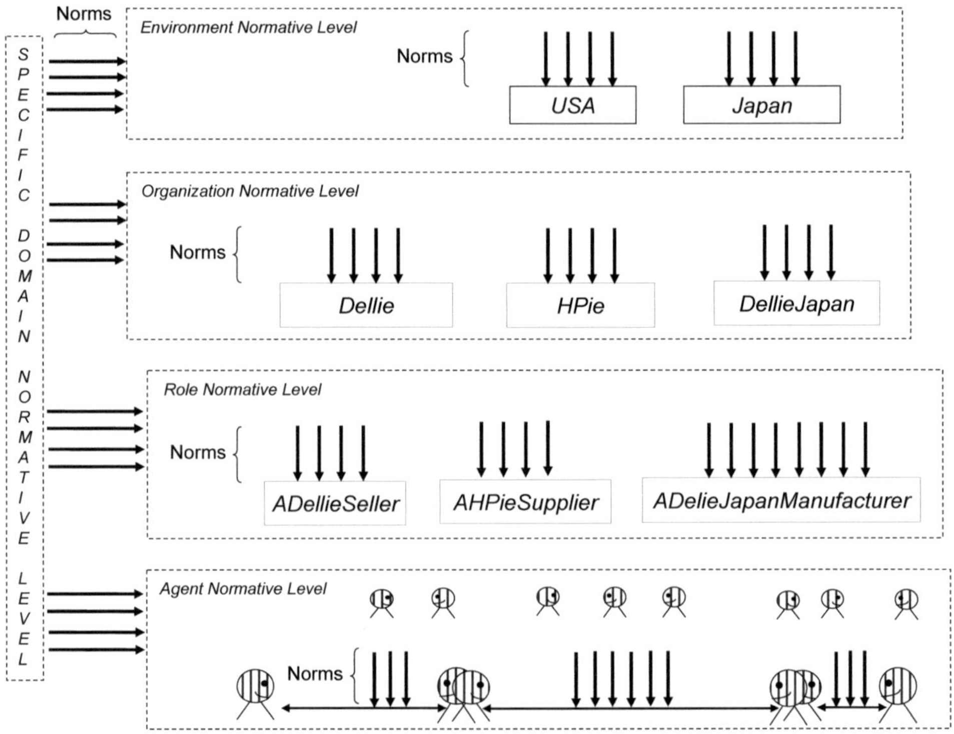

Fig. 3. Norms from different contextual normative levels

The four predefined normative contexts of DynaCROM are not targeted to a particular application domain; moreover, they rather represent a basic set for a general regulation in MAS. For a more precise regulation, this set should be improved through additions and refinements of application domain normative contexts and their respective norms. An example of a domain normative context and its norm might be, in the *Catholic* domain, a *Religious* concept that holds a (religious) norm stating that "*marriage is prohibited in the case that the man and/or the woman to be married made perpetual vows of chastity in a religious institute*".

DynaCROM states that specific[2] domain norms (*e.g.*, political norms) can be directly applied in any other normative level, as also illustrated in the Figure 5 (by the horizontal arrows from the vertical rectangle in the left side of the figure). For instance, the political norm: *"American and Japanese organizations are forbidden to deal with each other when their countries are undergoing political crisis"* can be directly applied in the *Organization Normative Level* of *American* and *Japanese* organizations (*e.g.*, in the *Organization Normative Level* of *Dellie* and *HPie*, from the *American* side, and in *DellieJapan*, from the *Japanese* side).

It is important to mention here that the extra effort of the system developer to classify norm information in more precise levels of abstraction is rewarded during the management phase and can also provide a fine-grained mechanism for norm enforcement solutions. Norms concretized in the contexts that directly affect the different MAS entities can be more easily found and updated because information is decoupled in predefined levels for norm classification. Besides that, each norm from the normative level of environments, organizations, roles or interactions can hierarchically influence each other, and each specific domain norm can transversally influence any norm from the other normative levels of a MAS.

2.3 Contextual norm representation

In order to represent norms in a meaningful way for heterogeneous agents, the formalism to be used in a MAS needs to be chosen. This choice must balance two major characteristics: *expressiveness* versus *efficiency*, and also should consider that, from a software engineering perspective, agent responses in MAS should be *quick*, *automatic* and *reliable* [Breitman *et al.*, 2004].

Speed is a requirement intrinsic to most systems. A *quick* response means that, once a request is sent by an agent, its response should be given at system runtime, even if the request may have been sent to multiple recipient agents, which compete for time of response.

Interoperability among agents in MAS lead to executions that must be *automatic*, *i.e.*, that cannot count with user intervention. One reason for that is, while the designer of a MAS is a domain expert, its human users may not be. Moreover, in open systems, a minimum level of *reliability* is mandatory in order to build trust for its participants.

The number of related norms involved in a negotiation among agents can be extremely high. In this case, it is not reasonable to expect that all system norms will be investigated in each negotiation, not in a reasonable time frame.

For the goal of our DynaCROM approach, it is accepted that the provision of a sub-set of relevant norms, where relevance is characterized by both agents' current contexts and actions performed, is a reasonable result if it is attained quickly, automatically and within reliable limits (predefined by the system developer). This way, information does not need to be stored since the relevant norms are provided, each time, at system/agents' requests.

Norm Representation by Using OWL

The *Web Ontology Language* (OWL) [Bechhofer *et al.*, URL], a Web standard from the *World Web Consortium* (W3C), was analyzed in order to verify its applicability for norm representation in open MAS. OWL was chosen mainly because of the two following reasons.

---

[2] 'Specific' meaning 'particular' and having 'general' as its antonym (definition from the Roget's New Millennium™ Thesaurus [OnLineDictionary, URL]).

The first reason is because OWL represents information in a meaningful way (*i.e.*, with a common understanding) for heterogeneous agents, supporting them in their processes of data retrieving and integration with different sources. This way, information can be understood by computer applications, instead of only by humans.
The second reason for choosing OWL is because it provides three sublanguages, which are differentiated by their levels of expressiveness: OWL Lite, OWL DL (includes OWL Lite) and OWL Full (includes OWL DL).
OWL Lite was designed for easy implementation and to provide users with a functional subset that permits a classification hierarchy and simple constraints.
OWL DL (where DL stands for *Description Logic*) was designed to support those users who want the maximum expressiveness without losing computational completeness (*i.e.*, all entailments are guaranteed to be computed) and decidability (*i.e.*, all computations will finish in finite time) of reasoning systems. OWL DL is so named due to its correspondence with description logics [Baader *et al.*, 2003], a field of research that has studied a particular decidable fragment of first order logic. OWL DL was designed to support the existing Description Logic business segment and to provide a language subset that has desirable computational properties for reasoning systems.
OWL Full is meant for users who want expressiveness with no computational guarantees. In this case, OWL Full relaxes some of the constraints on OWL DL so as to make available features which may be of use to many database and knowledge representation systems, but which violate the constraints of Description Logic reasoners. Thus, it is unlikely that any reasoning software will be able to support every feature of OWL Full.
Based on the characteristics of each OWL sublanguage, OWL DL was the one chosen for representing the domain data of the usage scenarios presented in this chapter. This is because, in those examples, OWL DL meets the software engineering requirements for responses in MAS (*i.e.*, expressiveness in computational completeness and decidability). Therefore, *formal* versus *non-formal* issues related to the examples are restricted to the available properties of the OWL DL sublanguage.

Declarative Specifications of Concrete Norms

DynaCROM proposes a *contextual normative ontology* for declarative specifications of norms, providing information with a common understanding about well-defined system regulation to heterogeneous agents.
An *ontology* is a conceptual model that embodies shared conceptualizations of a given domain [Gruber, 1993]; a *contextual ontology* is an ontology that represents localized domain information [Bouquet *et al.*, 2003] (*e.g.*, *USD* is the national currency of *USA*); and, a *contextual normative ontology* is a contextual ontology that has a *Norm* concept as its central asset. The *Norm* concept should be instantiated with norms contextualized differently according to the basic MAS entities (*i.e.*, environments, organizations, roles and agent interactions) or specific domain entities.
The DynaCROM contextual normative ontology, hereinafter the DynaCROM ontology, defines the following five related concepts, all in the same hierarchical level: *Role*, *Organization*, *Environment*, *Norm* and *Action*, as illustrated in Figure 4[3]. These concepts must be instantiated according to the application domain of its MAS.

[3] For readability purposes, all ontologies created for this chapter are presented graphically by using the Ontoviz graph plug-in for OWL [Ontoviz, URL].

In the DynaCROM ontology, the *Role* concept encompasses the instances of all regulated roles of the system and each role instance is associated with its norms (via the *hasNorm* property) and with its organization (via the *isPlayedIn* property). The *Organization* concept encompasses the instances of all regulated organizations and each organization instance is associated with its norms, with itself (via the *hasMainOrganization* property for representing its main organization) and with its environment (via the *isIn* property). The *Environment* concept encompasses the instances of all regulated environments and each environment instance is associated with its norms and with itself (via the *belongsTo* property for representing its owner environment). The *Norm* concept encompasses the instances of all norms and each norm instance is associated with its regulated actions (via the *regulates* property). The *Action* concept encompasses the instances of all regulated actions of a proposed system.

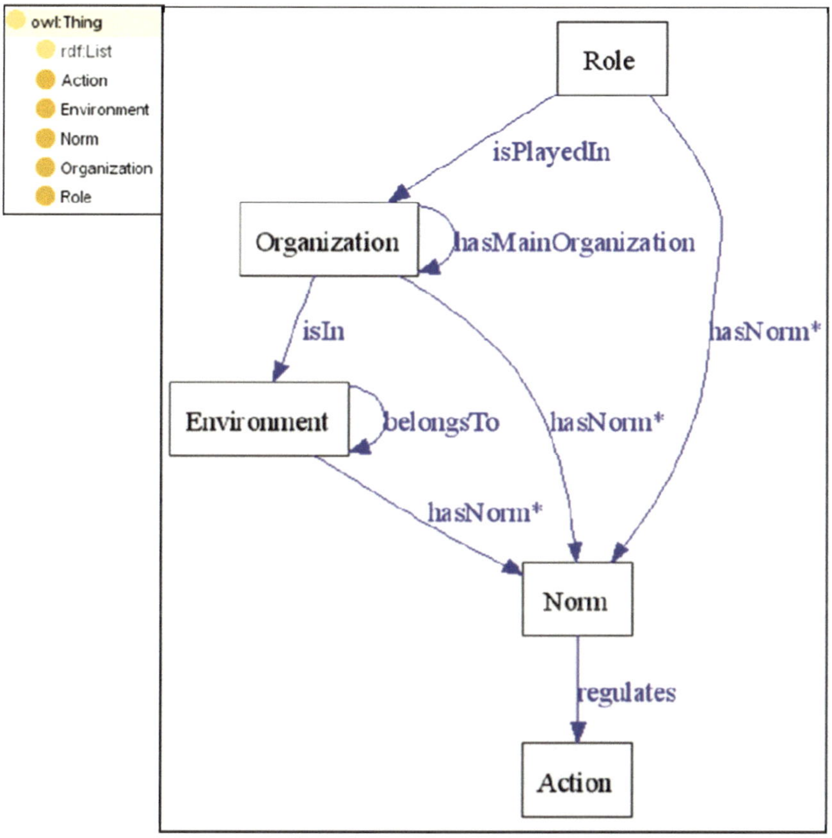

Fig. 4. The DynaCROM ontology

The DynaCROM ontology is an extensible one, *i.e.*, its basic concepts can be extended and/or new domain concepts can be created, both for representing classified contextual domain information. More precisely, the representation of a concrete norm in a DynaCROM ontology should be done by extending existing concepts or by creating new ones, then, instantiating the concept with norm information and, at last, linking the regulated instances to its related abstract norm (represented as a created norm instance).

For example, Figure 5[4] illustrates the *OblToPayWithNationalCurrency* norm instance that represents an abstract payment norm for effecting a negotiation. The norm is concretized in each environment by instantiating its domain datatype property *hasNationalCurrency* (*e.g.*, *JPY (Japanese Yen)* in *Japan* and *USD (U.S. Dollar)* in *USA*), which extends the DynaCROM *Environment* concept (originally presented in Figure 4).

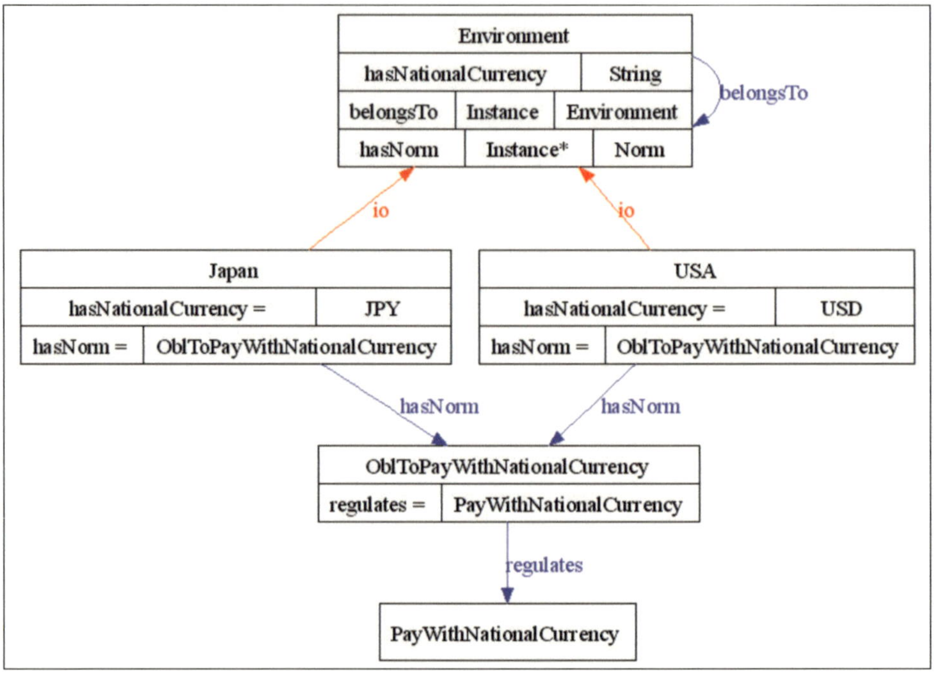

Fig. 5. An abstract payment norm concretized in *Japan* and *USA*

For a more precise regulation in MAS, specific domain contexts should be represented in an application domain DynaCROM ontology through additions and refinements of their related concepts and norms. An example of an application domain context and its norm can be:

> *A Political Norm for Regulating Deals:* organizations are prohibited from dealing with each other when their countries are undergoing political crisis.

The political norm presented above is an example of abstract interaction norm. In a DynaCROM domain ontology, interaction norms should be concretized by instantiating its *Norm* sub-concept, which must be already created for linking the other concepts from the relation (*i.e.*, reification of relationship). This solution follows the representation pattern presented in [Noy and Rector, URL].

Figure 6 illustrates the abstract political norm for regulating deals represented by the *PrhToDealWith* (a *Norm* sub-concept) and concretized in *AmericanOrganizations* by the *PrhToDealWithJapaneseOrganizations* norm instance. The concrete norm prohibits *AmericanOrgani-*

[4] In the Ontoviz graph plug-in, 'io' means 'instance of' and it is the label given for the link between a concept and its instance.

zations to deal with *JapaneseOrganizations* when their countries are undergoing political crisis.

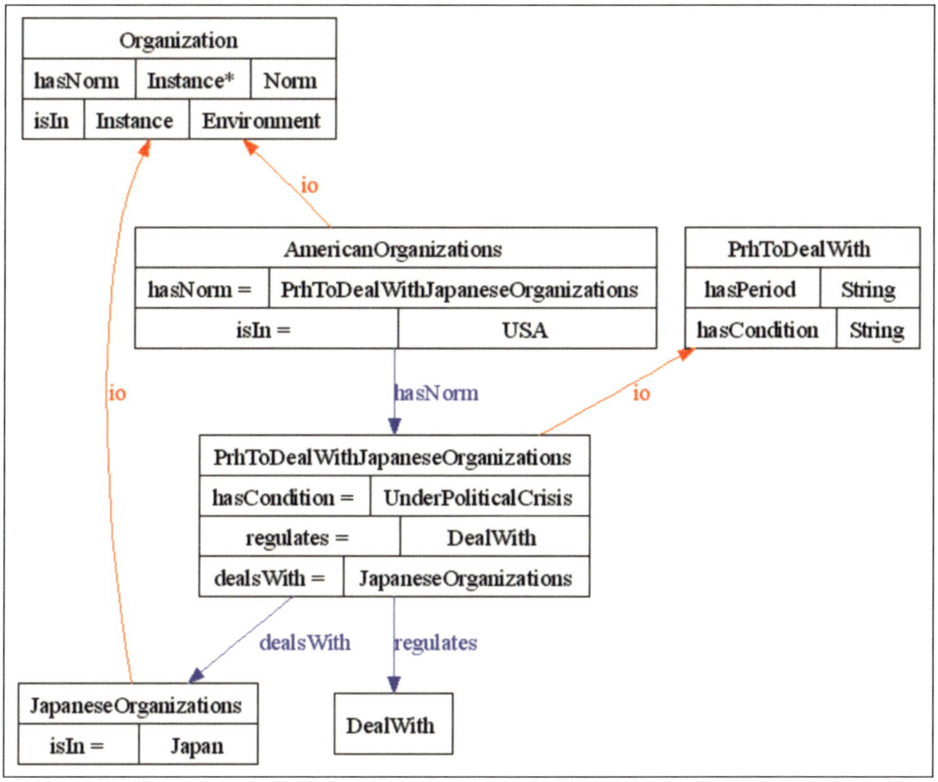

Fig. 6. A political norm concretized in *American* organizations

2.4 Contextual norm composition

After classifying and representing norms in precise levels of abstractions, contextual norms can be composed during system execution since, at any given moment, an agent may be related to norms defined at one or more normative contexts. Compositions of related contextual norms result in sets of independent norms, in which the semantic of one norm can influence the semantics of the others. For instance, the environment norm presented below is considered:

> *A Concrete Environment Norm for Calculating Prices:* a state corporate income tax rate of *6.25* in *Missouri* is obliged to be imposed on all sales.

Figure 7 illustrates the environment norm for calculating prices in *Missouri*. Although *Missouri* and *USA* are hierarchical environments (defined via their *belongsTo* relationship), a mechanism should be used in order to effectively compose their norms in a DynaCROM MAS.

DynaCROM follows rules to compose contextual norms. DynaCROM rules are *ontology-driven* rules, *i.e.*, they are created by the system developer, according to the ontology structure, and they are limited to the related concepts to which each concept is linked to.

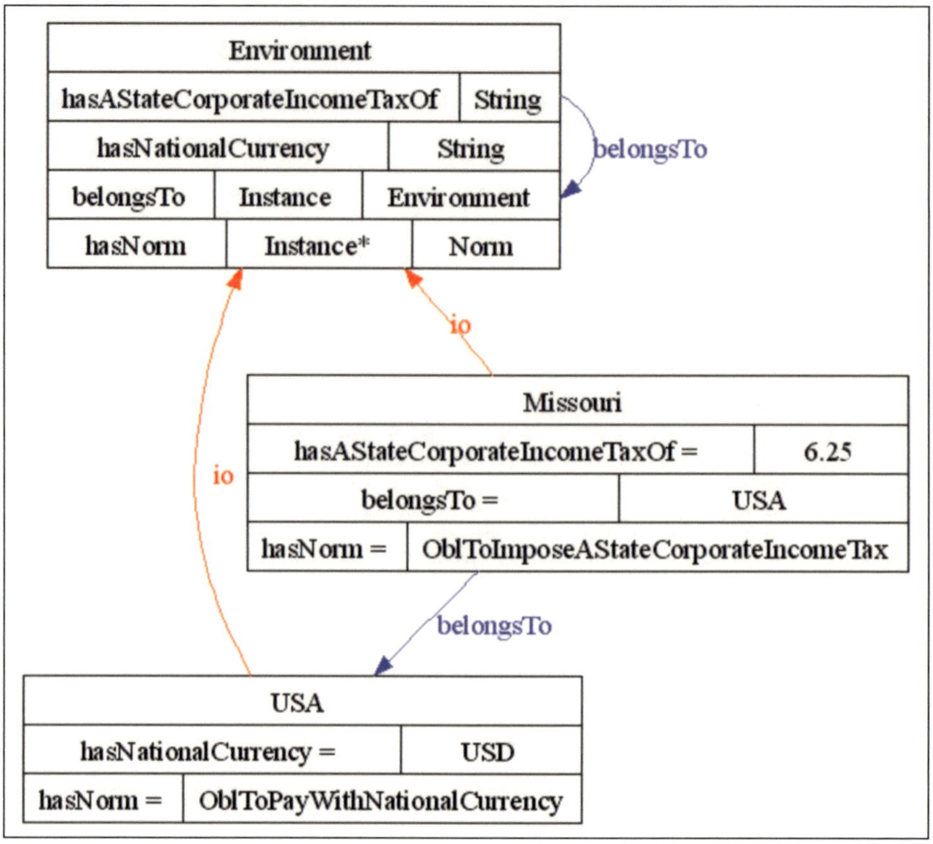

Fig. 7. The *Missouri* and *USA* hierarchical environments

Code 1[5] presents an example of rule that recursively compose the norms of hierarchical environments as, for instance, the norms of *Missouri* and *USA*. More precisely, considering *Missouri* as an example of the given environment, the following composition process is executed, according to the domain ontology instance illustrated in Figure 9: in (4), the '*?OEnv*' variable is instantiated with the *USA* inferred value, when the '*?Env*' variable is instantiated with the *Missouri* given value; in (3), the '*?OEnvNorms*' variable is instantiated with the *OblToPayWithNationalCurrency* inferred value; and in (2), the inferred norm is added as a new norm of *Missouri*.

The result of the norm composition process is that, in *Missouri*, all negotiations are obliged to be paid with *USD* and increased by a state corporate income tax of *6.25*.

```
(1)  [DynaCROMRule_EnvWithOEnvNorms:
(2)    hasNorm(?Env,?OEnvNorms)
(3)     <- hasNorm(?OEnv,?OEnvNorms),
(4)        belongsTo(?Env,?OEnv)]
```

Code 1. A DynaCROM rule to compose the norms of hierarchical environments

[5] The rules presented in this chapter are written following a simplified syntax for readability purposes.

DynaCROM predefines the rules to compose the norms of hierarchical environments (explained above) and also the others presented in Code 2. Inputs for these rules are domain instances of the *Organization* and *Role* concepts and their outputs are compositions of related contextual norms.

Following a norm composition process similar to the one explained for the '*DynaCROMRule_EnvWithOEnvNorms*' (presented in Code 1), the '*DynaCROMRule_OrgWithMOrgNorms*' (line 5 to 8 from Code 2) states that a given organization will have its norms composed with the norms of its main organization; the '*DynaCROMRule_OrgWithEnvNorms*' (line 9 to 12 from Code 2) states that a given organization will have its norms composed with the norms of its environment; and, the '*DynaCROMRule_RoleWithOrgNorms*' (line 13 to 16 from Code 2) states that a given role will have its norms composed with the norms of its organization.

```
(5)   [DynaCROMRule_OrgWithMOrgNorms:
(6)     hasNorm(?Org,?MOrgNorms)
(7)      <- hasNorm(?MOrg,?MOrgNorms),
(8)         hasMainOrganization(?Org,?MOrg)]

(9)   [DynaCROMRule_OrgWithEnvNorms:
(10)    hasNorm(?Org,?OrgEnvNorms)
(11)     <- hasNorm(?OrgEnv,?OrgEnvNorms),
(12)        isIn(?Org,?OrgEnv)]

(13)  [DynaCROMRule_RoleWithOrgNorms:
(14)    hasNorm(?Role,?OrgNorms)
(15)     <- hasNorm(?Org,?OrgNorms),
(16)        isPlayedIn(?Role,?Org)]
```

Code 2. DynaCROM rules to compose the norms of normative contexts

Rules can compose data from the same concept type (*e.g.*, the '*DynaCROMRule_EnvWithOEnvNorms*' and the '*DynaCROMRule_OrgWithMOrgNorms*') or from different concept types (*e.g.*, the '*DynaCROMRule_OrgWithEnvNorms*' and the '*DynaCROMRule_RoleWithOrgNorms*'). Rules can also compose data from concepts directly related (hierarchical form) or indirectly related (non-hierarchical form).

Code 3 presents an example of a rule that compose the norms of the DynaCROM *Role* and *Environment* concepts, which are examples of indirectly related concepts.

```
(17)  [DynaCROMRule_RoleWithOrgEnvNorms:
(18)    hasNorm(?Role,?OrgEnvNorms)
(19)     <- hasNorm(?OrgEnv,?OrgEnvNorms),
(20)        isIn(?Org,?OrgEnv),
(21)        isPlayedIn(?Role,?Org)]
```

Code 3. A rule for composing the norms of two indirectly related concepts

For the composition process, DynaCROM employs[6] an inference rule engine that executes the following tasks: (i) read an ontology instance to get data (*i.e.*, concept instances and their

[6] 'Employ' meaning "to make use of (an instrument, means, etc.); use; apply" [OnLineDictionary, URL]).

relationships), (ii) read a rule file to retrieve the information about how concepts must be composed; and then, (iii) infer an ontology instance based on the previous readings. An overview of this composition process is illustrated in Fig. 8.

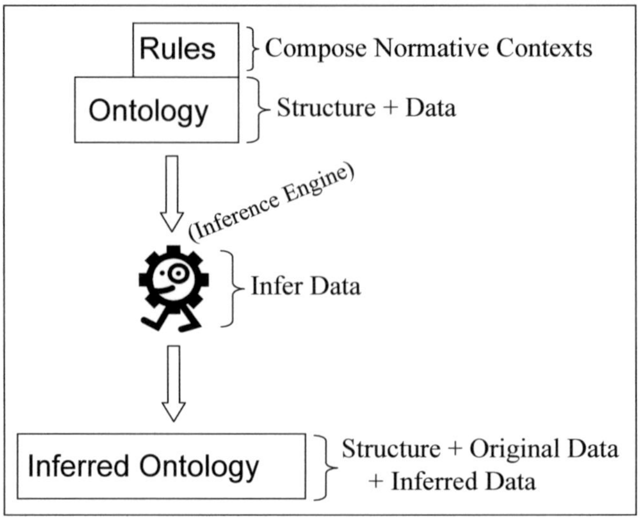

Fig. 8. The DynaCROM composition process

Once the domain ontology and/or rule file change(s), updated information is automatically forwarded to system agents in the next DynaCROM execution. This makes it possible for information management to be done at runtime, providing the dynamicity and flexibility necessary for regulation and also regarding social changes characteristic of MAS. These achievements are gotten because all norms provided by DynaCROM are applicable at a given moment.

In the current implementation of DynaCROM, the Jena rule-based inference engine [JENA, URL] is used for the composition process, however, other Semantic Web reasoners, like Racer [RACER, URL], Pellet [PELLET, URL] or FaCT [FACT, URL], can also be used.

In the composition process, it will still be the system developer's responsibility to write rules in the exact order he wants to compose his system data. Normally, the chosen inference engine will read/interpret those rules in sequence, from the top to the bottom of the file.

3. Contextual norm enforcement

DynaCROM is an approach for implementing dynamic MAS, in which norms can be updated at system runtime. In that way, agents are continuously supported with precise information about the current norms they are bound to in a given moment. Nevertheless, a regulated MAS should verify if a performed action is legal or illegal based on its defined norms, which might be enforced. However, it is the responsibility of the system developer to define if the norms of his MAS are allowed or not to be violated, by imposing the correct strategy for norm enforcement.

Norm enforcement in MAS can be carried out *a posteriori*, by punishing infringing agents, or *a priori*, by avoiding norm violation. *A posteriori* enforcement does not guarantee norm compliance, however, the implementation of punishments inhibits infringing agents. *A priori* enforcement guarantees norm compliance while enforcing the norms of the regulated actions of a MAS.

In the following two subsections, it is illustrated how DynaCROM supports the norm enforcement *a posteriori* and *a priori*, respectively. In subsection 3.3, an overview of the process on how DynaCROM works as an input mechanism to third-party enforcers is given. Finally, in the last subsection, it is exemplified how norms are enforced based on the agents' external and internal behaviors.

3.1 *A Posteriori* norm enforcement

The aim of any society and its norms is to provide a common space for the realization of individual and global objectives of its participants. Sometimes, depending on both the goals of agents and their priorities, the violation of norms is the best choice for agents (and also for the society). In this sense, norms act as a goal-oriented decision mechanism in regulated systems, being the means to achieve goals in a society. Hence, norms are allowed to be violated instead of being defined as constraints which unable any undesired behavior to happen.

In [Felicíssimo *et al.*, 2005b], it is given an example of a MAS, from the urban traffic domain, in which its norms might be violated. In the motivating scenario of the example, an agent playing a car driver role is going from his home in the city to his summer house on the mountains (see Figure 11). Suddenly, on the way, his pregnant wife begins to go into labor. Now, the goal of the driver agent to get to a hospital, as soon as possible, emerges as the one with the highest priority. Then, he considers violating some norms. In the emergency situation, the agent prefers to pay the fine for going through a red traffic light, if that will get him to the hospital faster. However, if pedestrians were crossing the street in front of the traffic light, then, the driver would not go through the red light. This is because of the risk of killing pedestrians and, thus, the fine he would have to pay would be too high. Both fines could be informed by DynaCROM, through requests from the car driver agent.

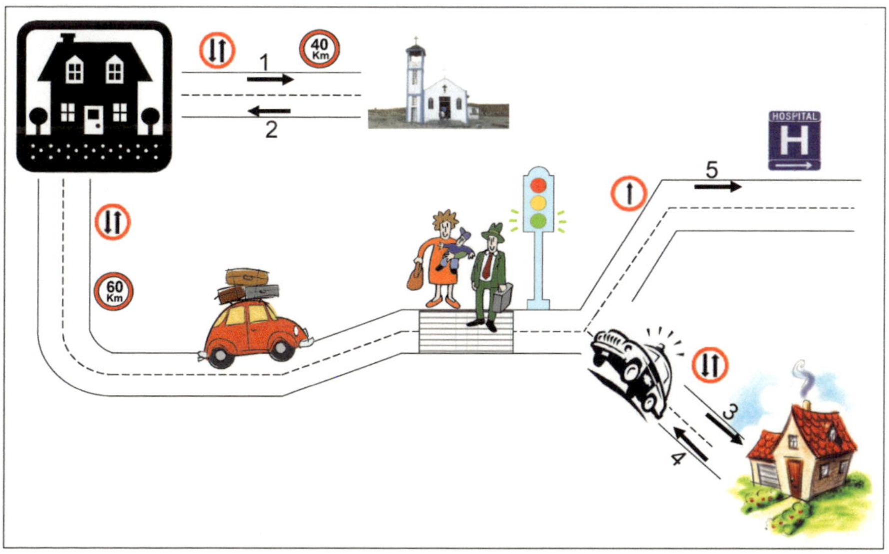

Fig. 9. An urban traffic's scenario

Another emergency situation which requires agent reasoning for norm violation is illustrated in Figure 12. An agent is driving down a road when he perceives that another driver agent is trying to pass his car on the left. Suddenly, a cow appears in front of his car. Now, what should the driver agent do? His decision must be based on the norms applicable to him, *i.e.*, on his contextual norms informed by DynaCROM.

If the situation of the motivating scenario occurred in an area in which the *Hinduism* religion is practiced, as in *India*, then, it would be better for the car driver to crash into the other car. This is because the fine of hurting a cow in a *Hindu* territory might be too high (*Hindus* believe that cows are sacred animals and, therefore, must be kept in safety). However, in *non-Hindu* countries, perhaps, it would be better to run over the cow instead of crashing into the other car. In both cases, if no risk to human lives was involved, then, the decision of the car driver would be based on how high a fine he would have to pay.

Fig. 10. A situation in which contextual norms must be considered

Sanction for *a posteriori* norm enforcement

A norm violation is a situation in which an agent breaks one or more norms, entering in an illegal (unsafe) state. In order to make agents legal again (*i.e.*, performing back in a safe state), sanction can be used in *a posteriori* norm enforcement. Sanction is a set of actions whose realization will remove the violation, by paying its consequences. In that way, agent are informed about the drawback of violating a norm. Sanction can be represented in the DynaCROM ontology inside a *Sanction* new concept, which holds the consequences of a violated norm.

Figure 13 illustrates an example that killing cows is prohibited in the *Hinduism* religion. In the example, the DynaCROM ontology was extended with the *Religion* and *Sanction* domain concepts; moreover, the DynaCROM *Environment* concept was extended with the domain object property *hasReligion*, for concretizing religions in each environment, and the DynaCROM *Norm* concept was extended with the domain object property *hasSanction*, for concretizing sanctions in each norm.

Figure 11 also illustrates the DynaCROM ontology instantiated for the example. The *India* instance represents the environment that holds the *Hinduism* religion, which, in turn, holds the *PrhToKillCows* prohibition norm. This norm regulates the *KillCows* action and has *A10YearPrisonSentence* as its sanction.

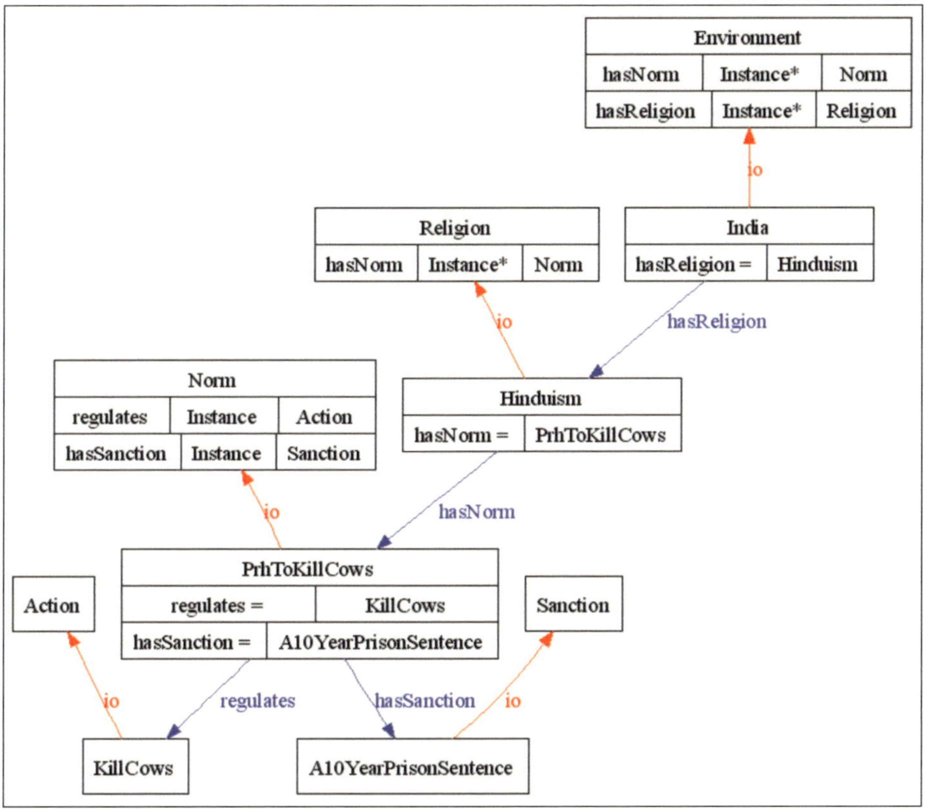

Fig. 11. A Hinduism religious norm concretized in the India environment

3.2 *A Priori* norm enforcement

In order to support *a priori* norm enforcement, DynaCROM has to be enhanced with an enforcer that will be in charge of guaranteeing norm compliance when there is an attempt to violate a norm.

Experiments were made integrating DynaCROM with SCAAR and MOSES, two solutions for norm enforcement. In SCAAR [Chopinaud *et al.*, 2006], the enforcement is done based on the internal behavior of agents; and in MOSES [Minsky_MOSES, URL], it is based on the external behavior of agents. For both solutions, DynaCROM works providing precise norm information as their input.

In the following section, an overview of how DynaCROM works as an input mechanism for norm enforcement solutions is presented. Then, in the two subsequent sections, the norm enforcement based on the agents' external and internal behaviors are explained. Because the enforcement solution is not the focus of DynaCROM, this chapter does not deal with the problems related to that part (*e.g.*, malfunction of the enforcer).

3.3 DynaCROM as an input mechanism for norm enforcement solutions

DynaCROM can be used for providing information as input to norm enforcement solutions. For this, each time an agent starts the execution of a regulated action, DynaCROM retrieves, in the domain ontology, the applicable norms according to the agent's current contexts and, then, sends those norms to be enforced by the chosen norm enforcement solution.

Figure 12 illustrates an overview of the process for contextual norm enforcement. Once an agent executes a regulated action, DynaCROM verifies, in the domain ontology instance, the norms of the action, according to the agent's current contexts. Then, DynaCROM concretizes those norms in a file that is used by the chosen enforcer as its input. The enforcer reads the input file and, then, enforces the norms of the performed action.

In the case of *a posteriori* norm enforcement, the information about the violated norms is sent back to DynaCROM for the application of sanction actions. In this phase, a third-party sanction system can be used for enhancing the DynaCROM solution. However, this idea is not developed in the text of this chapter, but in [Silva, 2008] more information about this issue can be found.

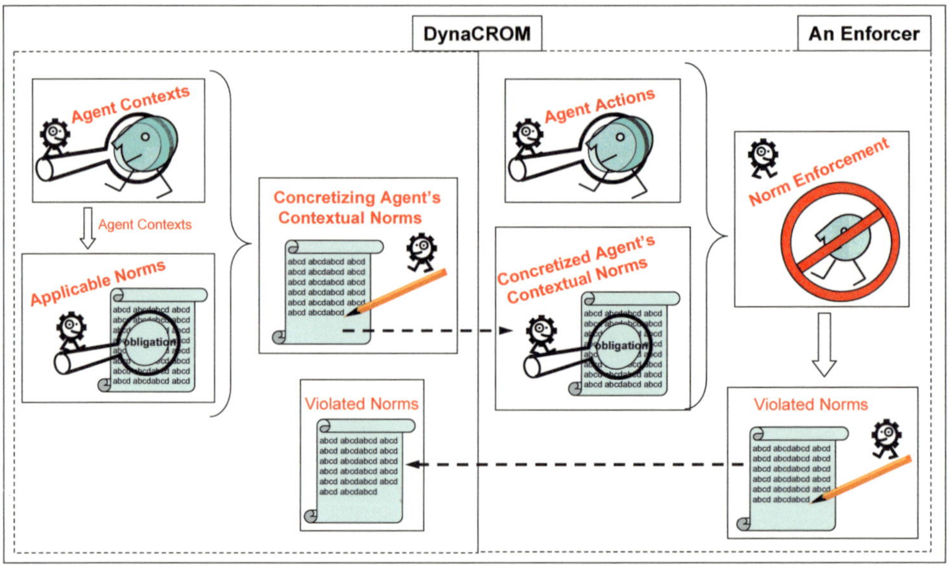

Fig. 12. DynaCROM providing contextual norm information as input to enforcers.

3.4 Contextual norm enforcement based on agents' behavior

Contextual norm enforcement can be done based on the agents' external or internal behavior. In order to exemplify both situations, the following simplification of the FIPA Contract-Net interaction protocol [FIPA_Contract-Net, URL] is considered:

1. A manufacturer wants to build 100 computers;
2. He issues a call for proposal (CFP) to computer suppliers;
3. Computer suppliers answer the CFP with their proposed price;
4. The manufacturer chooses one proposal among the ones he received and informs his decision to the chosen supplier.

In the example, the action of suppliers to 'propose a price' is regulated by the norm for effecting negotiations ("*negotiations are obliged to be paid by using the national currency of the seller's country*") and by the norm for calculating prices ("*a state corporate income tax rate is obliged to be imposed on all sales, for immediate delivery or if the deliver address is in North America*"). Both norms were previously mentioned in the text of this chapter. For the enforcement of the last norm, the base price of a computer is predefined to make it possible to calculate its acceptable minimum price.

Norm Enforcement Based on the Agents' External Behavior

An example in which the norms for payments are enforced by a created police agent, based on the agents' external behavior, is illustrated in Figure 13. In brief, the *MissourianManufacturer* (an agent playing the *manufacturer* role in the *Missouri* environment) sends a CFP to the *JapaneseSupplier* (an agent playing the *supplier* role in the *Japan* environment). The *JapaneseSupplier* answers the CFP message with a PROPOSE message in which the currency value is different from the one expected (*JPY* instead of *USD*, the national currency of *USA*).

When the message arrives at the *ManufacturerPolice* (the police agent created to enforce the system norms in the manufacturer agent), the *ManufacturerPolice* blocks the sending of the message to the *MissourianManufacturer* agent and sends an INFORM(*Nok,NationalCurrency*) message with the error occurred (*i.e.*, wrong currency) to the *JapaneseSupplier*. Then, the *JapaneseSupplier* sends a new PROPOSE message with the correct currency, however, he does not considered the state corporate income tax of *6.25* from *Missouri*. So, the *ManufacturerPolice* also enforces the other norm and sends an INFORM(*Nok, StateCorporateIncomeTaxOf*) message to the *JapaneseSupplier*, informing him that now the error is with the missing state corporate income tax.

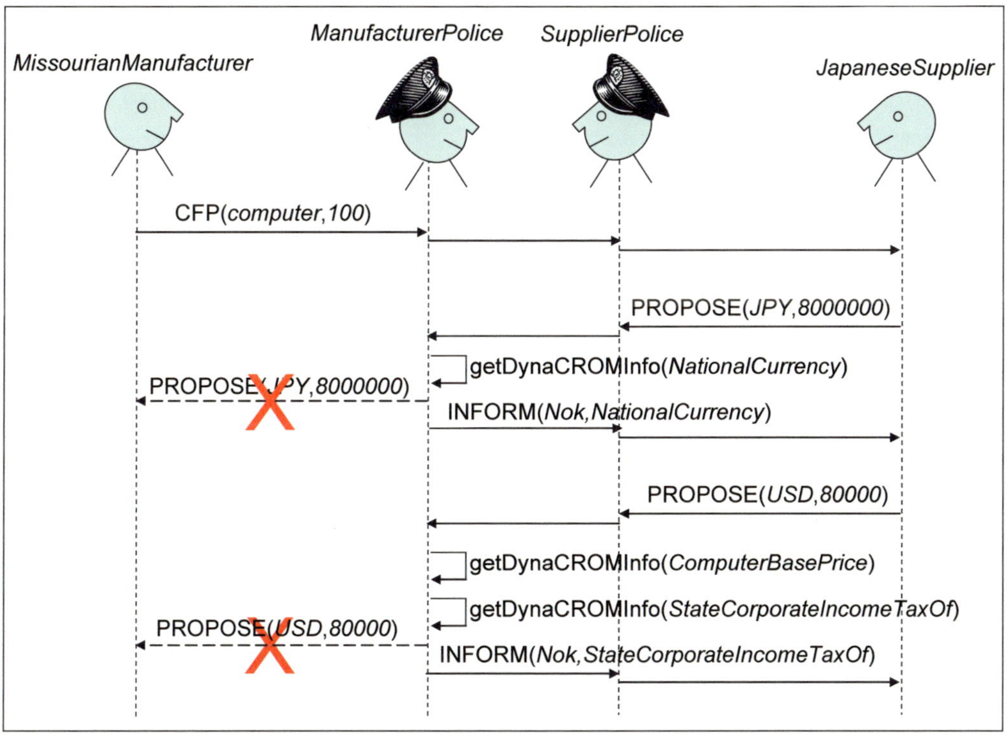

Fig. 13. An example of a police agent enforcing contextual norms for payments

Norm Enforcement Based on the Agents' Internal Behavior

An example in which the norms for payments are enforced by the agents themselves (*i.e.*, agents are self-regulated), based on their internal behavior, is illustrated in Figure 14. In brief, the *MissourianManufacturer* sends a CFP to the *JapaneseSupplier*. The *JapaneseSupplier* tries to answer the CFP message with a PROPOSE message, but, because the proposed currency value is different from the one expected (*JPY* instead of *USD*, the national currency of *USA*), the message is not sent due to the (self-)enforcement of the norm for payments with the national currency.
Then, the supplier agent tries to send a new PROPOSE message (now, with the correct currency), however, he does not consider the state corporate income tax of *6.25* from *Missouri*. Then, the message is not sent due to the (self-)enforcement of the norm for payments with the state corporate income tax.

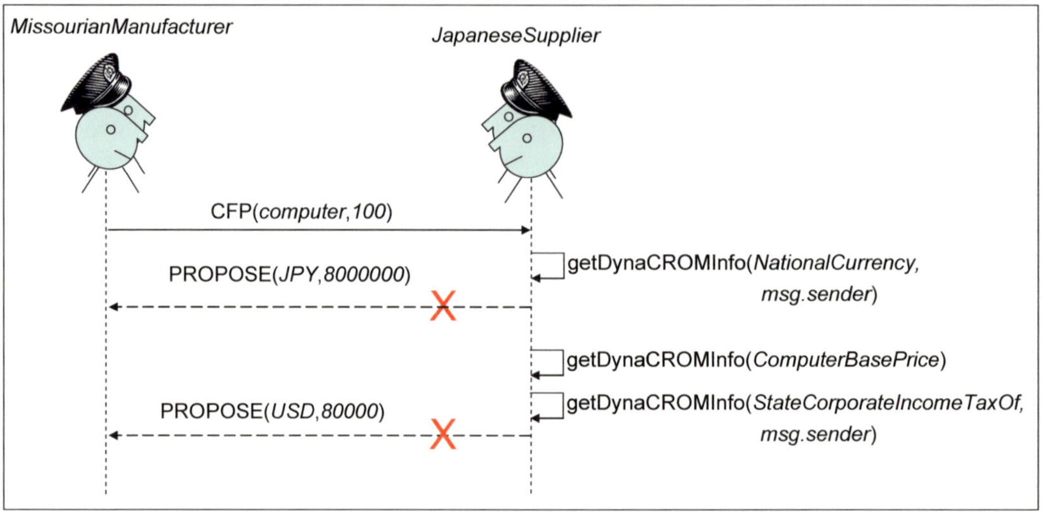

Fig. 14. Self-regulated agents enforcing contextual norms for payments

4. Related work

Despite all efforts made to move theory and practice of MAS from closed to open agent societies, current solutions do not yet explicitly support openness and its consequences. More precisely, methodologies, modeling languages and tools (*e.g.*, frameworks, platforms), needed for implementing open MAS, do not conveniently cover the aspects of regulation and domain representation for society differentiation.
Traditional modeling of MAS [Bresciani *et al.*, 2004; Cervenka *et al.*, 2005; Odell *et al.*, 2000; Wooldridge *et al.*, 2000] often assumes an individualistic perspective in which agents are considered as autonomous entities that pursue their individual goals, based on their own beliefs and capabilities. Even in this perspective, global behavior emerges from individual interactions and, therefore, the modeling has to be expanded to consider not only an *agent-centric* view, but also *societal* and *organizational-centric* views [Silva *et al.*, 2008]. Furthermore, the overall problem of analyzing the social, legal, economic and technological dimensions of an agent organization must be considered.

Agent-centered approaches can be useful for closed systems, composed of a small number of agents, but they fail to design open systems [Rodríguez-Aguliar, 2001; Esteva, 2003]. For instance, in critical applications such as those within business, environments or government agencies (hospitals, police, justice, etc.), the structural characteristics of the domain have to be incorporated. That is, the design of an agent society must also consider organizational characteristics such as stability over time, some level of predictability, commitment to aims and strategies, and so on.

The idea of modeling MAS as organizations was early proposed by [Gasser *et al.*, 1987; Pattison *et al.*, 1987; Corkill and Lesser, 1983; Werner, 1987] and it is still a major issue in the MAS research field, especially in applications on the areas of Service Oriented Computing, Grid Computing and Ambient Intelligence. Recently, the subject of MAS design from the organizational perspective has been mainly discussed in the COIN workshop (meaning workshop on *Coordination, Organization, Institutions and Norms* in agent systems) [COIN, URL].

The COIN workshop series started in 2005 during the ANIREM [Lindemann *et al.*, 2005] and OOOP [Boissier *et al.*, 2005] workshops held in AAMAS'05 [Kraus and Singh, 2005]. The series has been held yearly since then, as a dual event co-located within large international conferences of the area in different geographic regions (*e.g.*, in 2008, at AAAI'08 [Dignum and Matson, 2008] in the USA and at AAMAS'08 [Hübner and Boissier, 2008] in Portugal; in 2007, at AAMAS'07 [Ossowski and Sichman, 2007] in Hawaii and at MALLOW'07 [Noriega and Padget, 2007] in UK; in 2006, at ECAI'06 [Boella *et al.*, 2006a] in Italy and at AAMAS'06 [Dignum *et al.*, 2006] in Japan).

Even with this research effort, organizational approaches have not been a common use in MAS, which is usually seen as a pure aggregation of agents. The fact that organizational approaches have not been effectively adopted suggests that some work still needs to be done in providing better tools for the design and implementation of MAS. System developers need to be supported when dealing with MAS in which intrinsic characteristics of the application domain (*e.g.*, society structure) have to be considered. This necessity increases when considering open systems from particular 'cultures'[7].

According to [Jennings, 2001] there are two points that qualitatively differentiate agent interactions from those that occur in other software engineering paradigms. First, agent-oriented interactions generally occur through a high-level (declarative) agent communication language, which is often based on the speech act theory [Mayfield *et al.*, 1995]. Secondly, agents need the computational apparatus to make context-dependent decisions about the nature and scope of their interactions and to initiate (and respond to) interactions that were not initially foreseen.

Regarding these distinctions, an appropriate solution for regulating interactions among agents cannot be rigidly fixed at any system phase and should continuously support data updates according to the changing contexts of agents. Moreover, besides hierarchical relationships among participants in interrelated subsystems, non-hierarchical relationships is also relevant information for norm enforcement in MAS.

Thus, it makes it necessary to provide a contextual normative solution in which different types of relationships among agents can be dealt with in order to enable norm enforcement

[7] 'Culture' meaning "the predominating attitudes and behavior that characterize the functioning of a group or organization" [OnLineDictionary, URL].

in MAS. The solution should be flexible enough for supporting norm evolution and it should not be only based on the interaction level, but also on others domain levels.

5. Conclusion

Three main assumptions underlie this research. Firstly, MAS has emerged as a concrete solution to develop complex software systems in which monolithic architectures (based on objects) have been replaced by distributed ones (based on agents). Secondly, with the advent of the Semantic Web and its technologies (*e.g.*, new ontologies' languages as OWL), agents will be able to process information from different sources. In this way, they will be able to move around other MAS looking for resources and/or services not found locally. In this scenario, openness will be an intrinsic and mandatory characteristic of upcoming systems. However, openness without control leads to chaotic scenarios. The use of norms in MAS is a promising approach for achieving openness in a reliable way. So, the final assumption of this work is that MAS should be normative.

In this chapter, the theoretical fundamentals of the DynaCROM methodology developed to support the system developer in the tasks of implementation, management and evolution of the norms of his MAS is presented. The methodology includes the phases of: (i) contextualization, through a top-down classification for contextual norms; (ii) concretization and representation, through a contextual normative ontology; and, finally, (iii) composition of norms, through a norm composition process.

The top-down classification for contextual norms proposed by DynaCROM facilitates the tasks of elicitation, organization and management of norms. The DynaCROM contextual normative ontology supports heterogeneous agents with a common understanding about the system norms. The norm composition process defined by DynaCROM makes it easy to update system regulation by both evolving norms in a unique resource (an ontology) and/or by customizing particular rules for different compositions of contextual norms.

Although application agents can be informed about their current (contextual) norms, by using the DynaCROM behavior, agents' developers can implement their agents regardless of this information. In this case, agents need a solution that continuously informs them about system data, according to their current contexts, in order to deal with the applicable norms of each action performed by them.

The subject of contextual norm enforcement is also analyzed in this chapter. The achievement of a norm enforcement contextualized for each application agent is due to the integration of DynaCROM with third-party enforcers. The integration of MOSES with DynaCROM permits a contextual norm enforcement based on the agent's external behavior. The integration of SCAAR with DynaCROM permits a contextual norm enforcement based on the agent's internal behavior. For both cases, norm enforcement was done *a priori*. Nevertheless, *a posteriori* norm enforcement is presented in the beginning of the chapter, where an overview of a DynaCROM solution for it is also given.

As future work, DynaCROM should encompass a formal method amenable to rigorous verification of the system developer's specifications. In the current solution, *formal* versus *non-formal* issues in DynaCROM are restricted to the available properties of the chosen ontology and rule languages for norm representation and composition, respectively.

DynaCROM should also propose how to deal with constitutive, procedural and conditional norms. New examples of how those types of norms should be given to guide system developers interested in that solution. Other interesting future works are to consider time restrictions in DynaCROM, and suggest solutions for conflicting norms from the same or different levels of abstractions.

6. References

Alberti, M.; et al. Mapping Deontic Operators to Abductive Expectations. *Journal of Comput. Math. Organ.* Theory, v.12, Issue 2-3, p.205–225, 2006.

Artikis, A.; et al. Animated specifications of computational societies. *1st International Joint Conference on Autonomous Agents and Multiagent Systems*, ACM, Italy, p.1053–1061, 2002.

Baader, F.; et al. The Description Logic Handbook: Theory, Implementation, Applications. Cambridge University Press, UK, 2003. ISBN 0-521-78176-0.

Bechhofer, S.; et al. OWL Web Ontology Language Reference. Recommendation from W3C since February, 2004. URL: <http://www.w3.org/TR/owl-ref/>.

Boella, G.; et al. *Workshop on Coordination, Organization, Institutions and Norms at the 17th European Conference on Artificial Intelligence*, (COIN@ECAI2006), 2006a.

Boella, G.; et al. Introduction to normative multiagent systems. *Journal of Comput. Math. Organ. Theory*. v.12, Issue 2-3, p.71–79, 2006b, ISSN 1381-298X.

Boissier, O.; et al. International Workshop on Organizations in Multi-Agent Systems FROM ORGANIZATIONS TO ORGANIZATION ORIENTED PROGRAMMING IN MAS at the *4th International Conference on Autonomous Agents and Multiagent Systems* (OOOP@AAMAS2005), July, 2005, the Netherlands.

Bouquet, P.; et al. C-OWL: Contextualizing Ontologies. In: 2nd International Semantic Web Conference (ISWC-03), *Lecture Notes on Computer Science*, 2870, p.164–179, 2003.

Breitman, K.K.; et al. Using Ontologies to Formalize Services Specifications. In: *Multi-Agent Systems*, 3rd NASA - Goddard/ IEEE Workshop FAABS III, Formal Approaches to Agent-Based Systems. Greenbelt, MA. 2004.

Bresciani, P.; et al. Tropos: an agent-oriented software development methodology. *Journal of Autonomous Agents and Multi-Agent Systems*, v.8, n.3, p.203–236, 2004.

Castelfranchi, C.; et al. Deliberative Normative Agents: Principles and Architecture. In: *Agent Theories, Architectures, and Languages* (ATAL-99), p.364–378, 1999.

Cervenka, R.; et al. AML: Agent Modeling Language toward industry-grade agent-based modeling. *Agent-Oriented Software Engineering* V, Lecture Notes in Computer Science, v.3382, p.31–46, 2005.

Chopinaud, C.; et al. Prevention of harmful behaviors within cognitive and autonomous agents. *7th European Conference on Artificial Intelligence* (ECAI'06), 205–209, 2006.

COIN. Website of the Coordination, Organization, Institutions and Norms in agent systems workshop. URL: <http://www.pcs.usp.br/~coin/>.

Dey, A. Understanding and using context. *Personal and Ubiquitous Computing*, 5(1), p.4-7, 2001, ISSN: 1617-4909.

Dignum, F. Abstract Norms and Electronic Institutions. In: *International Workshop on Regulated Agent-Based Social Systems: Theories and Applications* (RASTA'02), p.93–104. Bologna, Italy, 2002.

Dignum, V.; et al. Workshop on Coordination, Organization, Institutions and Norms at the *5th International Conference on Autonomous Agents and Multiagent Systems* (COIN@AAMAS2006), May 09, 2006, Japan.

Dignum, V. and Matson, E. Workshop on Coordination, Organization, Institutions and Norms at the *23rd Conference on Artificial Intelligence* (COIN@ AAAI2008), July 13-14, 2008, Chicago, USA.

Esteva, M. Electronic Institutions: from specification to development. N. 19 in the Monograph Series of the Institut d'Investigació en Intelligència Artificial (IIIA), PhD thesis, Technical University of Catalonia, 2003.

Esteva, M.; et al. AMELI: An Agent-based Middleware for Electronic Institutions. In: *3rd International Joint Conference on Autonomous Agents and Multiagent Systems*, p.236–243, 2004.

FACT. Website of the Fast Classification of Terminologies. URL: <http://www.cs.man.ac.uk/~horrocks/FaCT/>.

Felicíssimo, C. H.; et al. Normative Ontologies to Define Regulations Over Roles in Open Multi-Agent Systems. *AAAI Fall Symposium: Roles, an Interdisciplinary Perspective: Ontologies, Programming Languages, and Multiagent Systems.* AAAI Press. v.1. p.68-72, 2005b.

Felicíssimo, C.; et al. Providing Contextual Norm Information in Open Multi-Agent Systems. *Post Proceedings of the 8th International Bi-Conference Workshop on AGENT-ORIENTED INFORMATION SYSTEMS* IV, Lecture Notes in Computer Science, v.4898, p.19–36, 2008a, ISBN: 978-3-540-77989-6.

Felicíssimo, C. H.; et al. Contextualizing Normative Open Multi-Agent Systems. In: *23rd Annual ACM Symposium on Applied Computing* (ACM SAC 2008), Fortaleza, Brazil, March 16-20, 2008b.

Felicíssimo, C.; et al. DynaCROM: An Approach to Implement Regulative Norms in Normative Multiagent Systems. In: *3th DEON'08 International Workshop on Normative Multiagent Systems of the 9th International Conference on Deontic Logic in Computer Science* (NorMAS@DEON'08). Luxembourg, 2008d.

Felicíssimo, C.; et al. How to Concretize Norms in NMAS? An Operational Normative Approach Presented with a Case Study from the Television Domain. In: *AAAI'08 International Workshop on Coordination, Organization, Institutions and Norms in agent systems* (COIN@AAAI'08). USA, 2008e.

Ferber, J.; et al. From Agents to Organizations: an Organizational View of Multi-Agent Systems. In: *Agent-Oriented Software Engineering* IV (AOSE, 2003), Lecture Notes in Computer Science, v.2935, p.214–230, 2003.

FIPA_Contract-Net. Website of the FIPA Contract Net Interaction Protocol Specification. URL: <http://www.fipa.org/specs/fipa00029/SC00029H.html>.

Gaertner, D.; et al. Distributed Norm Management in Regulated Multi-Agent Systems. In: *6th International Joint Conference on Autonomous Agents and Multiagent Systems*, p.624–631, 2007.

Gasser, L.; et al. Distributed Artificial Intelligence, chapter MACE: A flexible test-bed for distributed *AI research*, p.119–152, Pitman Publishers, 1987.

Grizard, A.; et al. A peer-to-peer normative system to achieve social order. In: *AAMAS'06 Workshop on Coordination, Organization, Institutions and Norms in agent systems* (COIN@AAMAS-2006), 2006, Japan.

Grossi, D. and Dignum, F. From Abstract to Concrete Norms in Agent Institutions. 3rd NASA Workshop on Formal Approaches to Agent-Based Systems (FAABS III). *Lecture Notes in Computer Science*, 3228, 12–29, 2004, ISBN: 978-3-540-24422-6.

Grossi, D.; et al. Classificatory Aspects of Counts-as: An Analysis in Modal Logic. In: *Journal of Logic and Computation*, v.16, n.5, p.613–643, 2006.

Gruber, T. R. A translation approach to portable ontology specifications. In: *Knowledge Acquisition*, 5(2), p.199–220, 1993, ISSN: 1042-8143.

Hewitt, C. Open Information Systems Semantics for Distributed Artificial Intelligence. *Artificial Intelligence*, v.47(1-3), p.79–106,1991, ISSN:0004-3702.

Hübner, J. F.; et al. A model for the structural, functional, and deontic specification of organizations in multiagent systems. In: Advances in Artificial Intelligence: 16th Brazilian Symposium on Artificial Intelligence (SBIA 2002). Brazil, 2002. *Lecture Notes in Artificial Intelligenc*, v.2507. p.118–128, Berlin, Springer. 2002.

Hübner, J.F. and Boissier, O. Workshop on Coordination, Organization, Institutions and Norms at the *7th International Conference on Autonomous Agents and Multiagent Systems* (COIN@AAMAS2008), May 12-13, 2008, Portugal.

JENA. Website of Jena - A Semantic Web Framework for JAVA. URL: <http://jena.sourceforge.net/>.

Jennings, N.; et al. A Roadmap of Agent Research and Development. *Journal of Agents and Multi-Agent Systems*, v.1, p.7–38, 1998.

Jennings, N. R. On Agent-Based Software Engineering. *Artificial Intelligence*, 117(2), p.277–296, 2000.

Jennings, N. R. An agent-based approach for building complex software systems. *Communications of the ACM*, 44(4), p.35–41, 2001.

Jones, A.J.I. and Sergot, M. On the characterization of law and computer systems: the normative systems perspective. *Deontic Logic in Computer Science*, 1993.

Kagal, L. and Finin, T. Modeling conversation policies using permissions and obligations. *Journal of Agents and Multi-Agent Systems*, v.14, p.187–206, 2007.

Khedr, M. and Karmouch, A. ACAI: Agent-Based Context-aware Infrastructure for Spontaneous Applications. *Journal of Network & Computer Applications*, 28(1), p.19–44, 1995.

Kraus, S. and Singh, M. In: *4th International Conference on Autonomous Agents and Multiagent Systems* (AAMAS2005), July, 2005, the Netherlands.

Lindemann, G.; et al. Agents, Norms and Institutions for Regulated Multiagent Systems at the *4th International Conference on Autonomous Agents and Multiagent Systems* (ANIREM@AAMAS2005), July, 2005, the Netherlands.

Mayfield, J.; et al. Evaluating KQML as an agent communication language. *Intelligent Agents* II, p.347–360, 1995.

Minsky_LGI. Website of the Law Governed Interaction (LGI): A Distributed Coordination and Control Mechanism (An Introduction and a Reference Manual), URL: <http://www.cs.rutgers.edu/~minsky/papers/manual.pdf>.

Minsky_MOSES. The MOSES toolkit. URL:<http://www.moses.rutgers.edu/>.

Noriega, P. and Padget, J. In: Workshop on Coordination, Organization, Institutions and Norms at the Multi-Agent Logics, Languages, and Organisations – *Federated Workshops* (COIN@MALLOW2007), p.3–4, 2007, Uk.

Noy, N. and Rector, A. (eds.): Defining N-ary Relations on the Semantic Web: Use with Individuals, 2007, URL: <http://www.w3.org/TR/swbp-n-aryRelations>.

Odell, J.; et al. Extending UML for agents. In: *Agent-Oriented Information Systems Workshop at the 17th National Conference on Artificial Intelligence*, p.3–17, 2000.

Ossowski, S. and Sichman, J.S. *Workshop on Coordination, Organization, Institutions and Norms at the 6th International Conference on Autonomous Agents and Multiagent Systems*, May 14-18, 2007, Honolulu, Hawaii, USA.

PELLET. Open Source OWL DL Reasoner. URL: <http://pellet. owldl.com/>.

RACER. Website of the Renamed Abox and Concept Expression Reasoner software. URL: <http://www.sts.tu-harburg.de/~r.f.moeller/racer/>.

Rodríguez-Aguilar, J.A. On the Design and Construction of Agent-mediated Electronic Institutions, PhD thesis, Universitat Autonoma de Barcelona, 2001.

Schilit, B. and Theimer, M. Disseminating Active Map Information to Mobile Hosts. In: *IEEE Network*, 8(5), p.22–32, 1994.

Silva, V. T. da and de Lucena, C.J.P. From a conceptual framework for agents and objects to a multi-agent system modeling language. *Journal of Autonomous Agents and Multi-Agent Systems*, v.9(1-2), p.145–189, 2004b, ISSN 1387-2532.

Silva, V. T. da. From the specification to the implementation of norms: an automatic approach to generate rules from norms to govern the behavior of agents. In: *Journal of Autonomous Agents and Multi-Agent Systems*, v.17(1), p.113–155, 2008, ISSN: 1387-2532.

Silva, V. T. da; et al. MAS-ML: a multiagent system modelling language. In: *International Journal of Agent-Oriented Software Engineering*, v.2(4), p.382–421, 2008.

Simon, H. A. The Sciences of the Artificial. MIT Press. 1996.

Thomas, G. and Williams, A. B. Roles in the Context of Multiagent Task Relationships. AAAI Fall Symposium "Roles, an Interdisciplinary Perspective: Ontologies, Programming Languages, and Multiagent Systems", ISBN: 978-1-57735-254-9, 2005.

Vázquez-Salceda, J.; et al. Organizing Multiagent Systems. In: *Journal of Autonomous Agents and Multi-Agent Systems*, 11(3), p.307–360, 2005.

Weyns, D.; et al. Environment as a first class abstraction in multiagent systems. In: *Journal of Autonomous Agents and Multi-Agent Systems* (JAAMAS, 07), v.14(1), p.5–30, 2007, ISSN: 1387-2532.

Wooldridge, M.; et al. The Gaia Methodology for Agent- Oriented Analysis and Design. In: *Journal of Autonomous Agents and Multi-Agent Systems*, v.3(3), p.285–312, 2000.

Wright, G.H.v. Deontic Logic. In: *Mind New Series*, v.60(237), p.1–15, 1951.

Part 2

Interaction and Decision Making on Agent Environments

9

Agent-Environment Interaction in MAS - Introduction and Survey

Joonas Kesäniemi and Vagan Terziyan
University of Jyväskylä
Finland

1. Introduction

Although agent and its environment have been inseparable concepts since the beginning of agent related research, there are quite a few opinions what the concept "environment" actually comprises in the context of multi-agent systems. Environment is often treated either in an implicit or ad hoc way, by referring basically anything outside the boundaries of an individual agent as the environment. Only recently environment has been considered as a first class abstraction with its own clear cut responsibilities apart from agents (Weyns et al., 2005). This progress has been made as part of the agent-oriented software engineering (AOSE) field, which aims at incorporating agent-oriented concepts into the disciplined processes of software engineering.

In the layered view of MAS with environment-based supports by Viroli et al. Viroli et al. (2007) the application level environmental abstractions are supported by specialized platform level infrastructure. Using this infrastructure, the environmental abstraction can interact with each other and with the agents. According to the classic definition of agenthood by Russell and Norvig [4], agents can receive information from the environment through sensors and affect it via actuators. This agent-environment interface will be the focal point of this chapter.

The goal of this chapter is two fold. First of all, we want to give an introduction to the relationship between agent and its environment. This age-old issue is covered from the perspective of individual agent and multi-agent system. Second, we focus on the agent-environment interface and survey the different aspects of agent-environment interaction. Survey emphasizes the engineering side of the multi-agent systems, as we go through the meta-models, methodologies and infrastructures presented in the recent research literature. However, details of any application-specific environmental infrastructures or agent's inner workings are out of the scope of this paper. We limit ourselves to the action and observation related issues that make it possible for an agent to perceive and affect its environment.

By turning the attention to the design and implementation details of agent-oriented systems, AOSE approach offers results that pave the way for turning agent systems from research prototypes into serious alternatives for mainstream software development. In order for this to happen, it is crucial to understand the different roles that agent related concepts, such as agent, environment and agent-environment interaction, play in the context of multi-agent systems.

2. Role of the environment

> "Agents cannot be considered independently of the environment in which they exist and through which they interact" (Müller, 1996)

This chapter elaborates the different aspects of environment in the agent related research literature. According to the survey by Weyns et al (Weyns et al., 2005) one of the main causes of confusion what is actually included to the environment, is brought about by the fact that the environment, as an abstract, logical concept of agent related theories and models, is mixed up with the environment as infrastructure for engineering agent based systems. This of course stems partially from the inherited generality of the term "environment" and the confusion can be alleviated by proper definitions for every given context. However, since one of the goals of this chapter is to contribute to the general discussion of the role of environment in multi-agent systems, we are going to have to mix it up and cover both theoretical and practical sides of the term. The main distinction is made between the artificial intelligence (AI) and agent-oriented software engineering (AOSE) related uses of the environment in an effort to facilitate the discussion about the relationship between agent and its environment in both MAS theory and systems engineering.

2.1 Agent and its environment

The "classic" agent research that can be classified under AI discipline has been quite agent centric. The research has concentrated on areas such as agent architectures, agent communication languages and agent coordination models based on direct agent-to-agent communication. In the process, the role of the environment has often remained ambiguous or implicit.

One of the classic definitions of agent-hood by Russell and Norvig (Russell & Norvig, 1995) defines agent as being "anything that can be viewed as perceiving its environment through sensors and acting upon that environment through effectors.", which in other words proposes that environment is basically anything outside the boundaries of an individual agent and that all the interaction in multi-agent system happens between agent and its environment. (Russell & Norvig, 1995) also describes some characteristics of the agent environments:

- Accessible vs. inaccessible: indicates whether agent can sense the complete state of the world or not.
- Deterministic vs. nondeterministic: indicates whether the state changes of the environment are completely determined by its current state or not.
- Episodic vs. non-episodic: indicates whether the agent's interaction sequences with its environment (or "episodes") can be though of as independent or not.
- Static vs. Dynamic: indicates whether the state of the environment can change while the agent deliberates or not.
- Discrete vs. continuous: indicates whether the agent's interactions with the environment are limited or not.

Back in the nineteen nineties, environment was generally handled in a application specific manner as demonstrated by examples of agent environment in (Russell & Norvig, 1995), which uses chessboard as an example of simple accessible, deterministic, episodic and discrete environment. Chess pawns are modeled as agents.

Another prominent definition from the mid-nineties comes from Maes, who describes agents as "computational systems that inhabit some complex dynamic environment, sense and act autonomously in this environment." (Maes, 1995). The same requirements for agent an being able to sense and act in the environment are present as in the previous definition by Russell and Norwig, but Maes emphasizes the complexity and dynamic nature of the environment.
Agent definition from Hayes-Roth et al. explicitly links the environmental state changes to the actions of the agents by stating that an intelligent agent "continuously performs three functions: perception of dynamic conditions in the environment; action to affect conditions in the environment; and reasoning to interpret perceptions, solve problems, draw inferences and determine actions"(Hayes-Roth, 1995). From the environment's perspective, this basic relationship between agent and its environment is nicely illustrated in the generic environment program (Russell & Norvig, 1995), which also takes in to consideration the dynamics of the environment (Listing 2.1).

Listing 1. Generic environment program (Russell & Norvig, 1995)

```
procedure RUN-ENVIRONMENT(state ,UPDATE-FN, agents , termination)
inputs :
  state , the initial state of the environment
  UPDATE-FN, function to modify the environment
  agents , a set of agents
  termination , a predicate to test when we are done

repeat
  for each agent in agents do
    PERCEPT[agent] <- GET-PERCEPT(agent , state)
  end
  for each agent in agents do
    ACTION[agent] <- PROGRAM[agent](PERCEPT[agent])
  end
  state <- UPDATE-FN(actions ,agents , state)
until termination(state)
```

The environment program first resolves perceptions for every agent based on the current state of the environment. The perceptions generated by agents are then turned into actions by feeding the perceptions back to the agents. Finally the state of the environment is updated using the actions of the agents and the actions resulting from the possible environmental processes running separately from agents.
The environmental processes was also covered in (Ferber & Müller, 1996), which presented a new model for agent-environment interaction in situated multi-agent systems. The details of the model are out of the scope of this chapter, but we want to highlight couple of the main concepts of the model that concern the agent-environment interface. First of all, the model distinguishes between action and the effect caused by that action. Ferber refers to the attempts of an agent to modify the state of its environment as influences. The actual state changes are referred as reactions, which are produced as the combination of influences from all the agents, the current state of the environment and the possible laws or other restrictions imposed by the environment. Another important concept presented in the article, is the decomposition of

the system into dynamics of the environment and the dynamics of the agents situated in that environment, effectively emphasizing the role of the environment as distinct and active entity in MAS.

Clear distinction between agent and environment was further promoted by Parunak, who in (Parunak, 1997) presented a set of general principles for emergent behavior in multi-agent systems inspired by natural systems such as ant colonies and flock of birds. He argues against agent-based functional decomposition of distributed MAS in favor of more multifaceted, yet still simple agents, so that the functions can emerge from the interactions between agents. He claims that functional decompositions appears most natural when the distinction between agents and their environment is overlooked. When it is recognized that environment's own processes mediate agent interactions, it is more difficult to assign agents to arbitrarily conceived functions. Although Parunak was concentrating on agents situated in physical environment, the principles presented in the paper have later been successfully applied to agents inhabiting also virtual environments (Mamei & Zambonelli, 2005).

Odell et al. (Odell, Parunak & Fleischer, 2003) defines the environment as something that "provides the conditions under which the an entity (agent of object) exits". The definition adds an important aspect to the role of the environment by including the management of other entities than just agents to the responsibilities of the environment. In an effort to present a more detailed view of environment in MAS, Odell et al. (Odell, Parunak & Fleischer, 2003) distinguish between three different environments: physical, communication and social. Physical environment provides the laws, rules, constraints, and policies that govern and support the existence of agents and objects that make up the system, just like the environment we humans live in, is constrained for example by the laws of physics. Even though the idea is modeled after natural physical environment, it does not rule out software agents and virtual environments. Communication environment provides 1) principles and processes that govern and support exchange of ideas, knowledge, information and data, and 2) the functions and structures that are used to enhance communication. Social environment is a subset of communication environment in which the agents interact in a coordinated manner. The social environment consists of 1) groups in which the agent participates, 2) roles of the agent, and 3) all the members who play roles in these social groups.

The support required by physical environment as defined in (Odell, Associates, Arbor & Parunak, 2003) would consist of three layers of platform level environmental support: 1) Application support required by the entities running in the environment, such as directory, ontology and security related services, 2) communication and data transfer facilities required by application abstractions, and 3) physical linkage, meaning the hardware such as sensors and actuators needed to affect and sense the physical world. Of course, for purely virtual systems, there is no need for physical linkage. (Odell, Parunak & Fleischer, 2003) lists similar requirements for communication environment, which should provide support for processes such as interaction management, policy enforcement, coordination services and services related to managing group and role based social environment. The article discusses a common processing platform that would provide a foundation upon which agent societies could be built to leverage their application specific environmental requirements. Next section zooms in to this notion of environment as common processing platform for MAS.

2.2 Environment in MAS

(Huhns & Stephens, 1999) considers the role of the environment in multi-agent systems as the computational infrastructure for enabling and ruling interactions. As depicted in the previous

section, this interaction can involve agent-to-agent communication, agent-to-environment actions and interactions induced by environmental processes. From the architectural perspective, infrastructure is usually modeled as a middleware layer providing some domain specific services between the entities implementing the application specific features and the hardware infrastructure.
Designing and implementing complex MAS environments calls for detailed discussion of the concrete features that should be part of the environment for MAS. But before going into environment architectures, let us get a look into different levels of support available from the environment and basic functionalities bestowed upon them.
It was not until the latter half of the first decade of the 21st century, when researchers started to promote environment as a legitimate abstraction of its own. Weyns et al. were the first to put forward the idea of environment as first class abstraction. (Weyns et al., 2006) defines environment as "first-class abstraction that provides the surrounding conditions for agents to exist and that mediates both the interaction among agents and the access to resources". In the context of information system science, first class abstraction is defined as a piece of software that provides an abstraction or information hiding mechanism so that the actual implementation can be changed without requiring changes to the other programs depending on it. Authors argue that the reasons behind this promotion of emphasized role of the environment are related to fact that agents are used as an interface to many services that should not conceptually be assigned to them (Weyns et al., 2006), for example communication and coordination infrastructures. Another important point is that the environmental aspects should be made explicit instead of relying on implicitly stated functionalities of the presumed environment and its ad hod implementations. (Weyns et al., 2006) argues also that by treating both agents and environment as first-class abstractions will contribute the separation of concerns, which in turn can help managing the complexity of building real-world applications. In an effort to get the role of the environment up to date, (Weyns et al., 2006) presents the following list of functionalities that the MAS environment should support.

- **Provide structure for the MAS:** Environment maintains relationships between entities in the environment and enforces rules to which the relationships must comply. Different forms of structuring include physical, communication and social structures.
- **Embed resources and services:** Environment acts as the source for resources and services.
- **Maintain dynamics:** This refers to the active nature of the environment.
- **Be locally observable:** Agents should be able to observe the state of environment. The observable environment might be limited by the current spatial, social or communication context of the agent. Providing observability can be seen as the environmental counter-part to the agent's ability to perceive its environment.
- **Be locally accessible:** Naturally, the agents must be able to act in their environment, but their actions might be constraint by their current context.
- **Define and govern environmental rules:** By enforcing the rules, whether they are restrictions imposed by the application domain at hand or arbitrary laws defined by designer of the system, environment attempts to keep the system in consistent state.

The degree of functionality provided by the environment can be categorized using three level model by Weyns et al. (Weyns et al., 2006) (see figure 1).

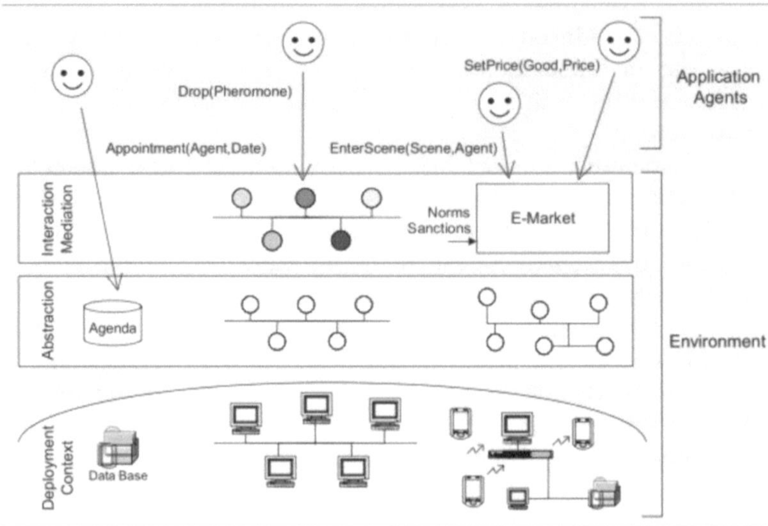

Fig. 1. Degrees of environmental support (Weyns et al., 2006)

The basic level of support is referred as the deployment context of MAS. It includes any hardware or software resources outside the boundaries of MAS. Examples of such resources are hardware sensors, databases and web services. Proving access to deployment context is one of the fundamental properties of the environment, but interacting directly with the deployment context forces agents to work with low-level details of both software and hardware environment and is not well suited for situations when the MAS is deployed in an unpredictable and highly dynamic environment. At the second level, the environment provides agents with abstractions that shield them from the low-level details of the deployment context. For example, instead of interacting with the humidity sensor directly using byte-level interface of the embedded software, agent can use a service to request a higher level representation of the state of the sensor. The abstractions are usually supported by some middleware software, which hides the possible complexity of the underlying deployment context. At the third level, the environment provides services for mediated interaction between agents. This requires environment to become an active entity that can change its state without any agent involvement. Examples of interaction-mediation level services are infrastructures for computational fields (Mamei & Zambonelli, 2005) and electronic institutions (Esteva et al., 2004).

We use FIPA (*FIPA: Foundation for Intelligent Physical Agents.*, n.d.) standards as a starting point for the more fine grained view of the responsibilities of the environmental infrastructure. The agent management reference model defines a logical MAS component called agent platform, which embeds agents as well as infrastructural components for agent communication, deployment and discovery. Figure 2 shows the reference model of the FIPA architecture.

Agent platform is responsible for running the agents. Agent management system (AMS) controls the life-cycle of agents in the system and takes care of life-cycle management services. It also maintains a directory of agent names and provides white-paper services for other agents. Message Transport System is responsible for providing ACL-based facilities for direct

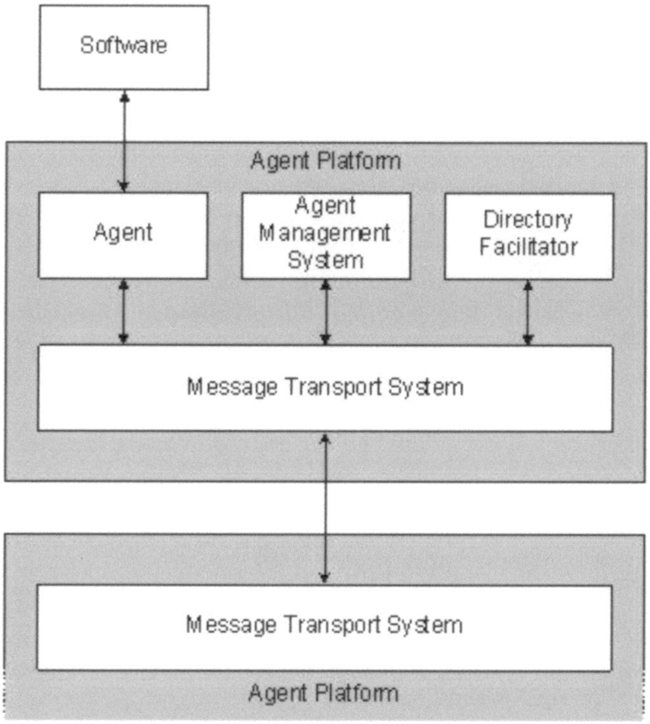

Fig. 2. FIPA abstract architecture (*FIPA: Foundation for Intelligent Physical Agents.*, n.d.)

agent-to-agent communication. Directory facilitator is an optional component that can used to discover agents based on their registered services.

FIPA reference model only covers the interaction between agents. However, reducing environment to a transfer medium of direct interaction underplays the potential of the environment as an active support for communication. Agents interact also with other entities in the environment using sensors and actuators. For example an agent can interact with a file system to sense any new files added to a certain directory, or it can call a web service to store some data to the database. Since there is no explicit abstraction for environment in FIPA reference model, agent-environment interaction is out of its scope.

Similarly as in (Weyns et al., 2006) where environment is divided into interaction-mediation and abstraction layers based on the degree of functionality provided, the survey conducted by Platon et al about the mechanisms for MAS environment (Platon et al., 2006) argues that infrastructures for environment can be classified into mechanisms that provide means for agents to interact with each other and mechanisms for agents to acquire and manage resources and contextual information. Two main classes of mechanisms are further divided in the following way: They further divide the two main classes of mechanisms in the following way:

- Interaction mediation
  - Environment-mediated interaction channels
  - Synchronization mechanisms
  - Overlay networks

- Resource and context management
  - Resources and context manager
  - Notification of contextual events
  - Overlay data structures

Different types are described using the same set of characteristics for easy comparison and evaluation. The examples given for each type range from quite low level infrastructures such as distributed hash tables (Rowstron & Druschel, 2001) and synchronization mechanisms to complete systems implementing digital pheromones, exemplifying the different layers of environmental infrastructures. For example, the pheromone infrastructure could depend on distributed hash table as its data management implementation. The higher the level of abstraction provided by the infrastructure is, the greater the potential benefits of adopting or reusing it are.

In the context of designing self-organizing emergent applications, to which many multi-agent systems can be included in, (De Wolf & Holvoet, 2006) catalogues mechanisms for de-centralized coordination using the design patterns as the basis for classification. Design pattern is a software engineering concept that captures the best practices and known solutions in a structured way. Patterns usually follow a common structure known to the mainstream software engineering, which includes sections such as context/applicability, problem/intent, solution, related patterns, examples and known uses (Meszaros & Doble, 1996). Presenting environmental mechanisms as designs patterns makes it easy to find, evaluate and compare possible solutions. It also integrates MAS infrastructures to the mainstream software engineering practices.

According to the 3-layer model for MAS by Weyns et al. (Weyns et al., 2005) both agents and environmental mechanisms are part of the MAS application layer . Other main layers include execution platform, which is composed of generic middleware infrastructure and virtual machines that run on top of operating system, and physical infrastructure that represent the hardware and network infrastructure that runs and connects the nodes hosting the MAS (see figure 3).

Application environment embeds agents that contain the application specific logic. MAS framework sub-layer includes infrastructures that offer agents high level programming abstractions for communication and agent-environment interaction. Low level infrastructures, such as distributed hash tables or synchronization mechanisms are then considered as part of the execution platform.

The 3-layer view for MAS (Weyns et al., 2005) successfully represents the role of the environment in the abstract architecture of MAS, but fails to take into account the possible middleware nature of the MAS infrastructures. The model was refined in (Viroli et al., 2007) by a) moving the environmental infrastructures down to the execution platform level, leaving only the abstractions they provide as part of the MAS application, and b) dividing the execution platform into MAS middleware and deployment context layers (see figure 4).

The logical view of the environment presented in (Viroli et al., 2007) emphasizes the role of the environment infrastructures as not necessarily application specific mechanisms built from scratch, but reusable and time-tested mechanisms selected to address certain problem in a more general domain of MAS environment. Their model also clearly separates the environmental abstractions and their interfaces from the infrastructure on top of which they are run. In other words, environmental abstractions are treated as first-class entities. The MAS middleware layer can consist of multiple agent and environment infrastructures. For example

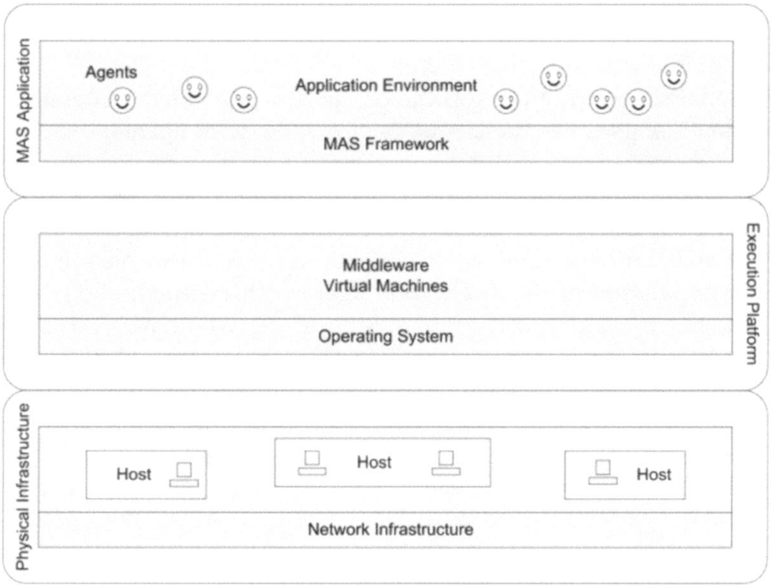

Fig. 3. 3-layer model for MAS (Weyns et al., 2005)

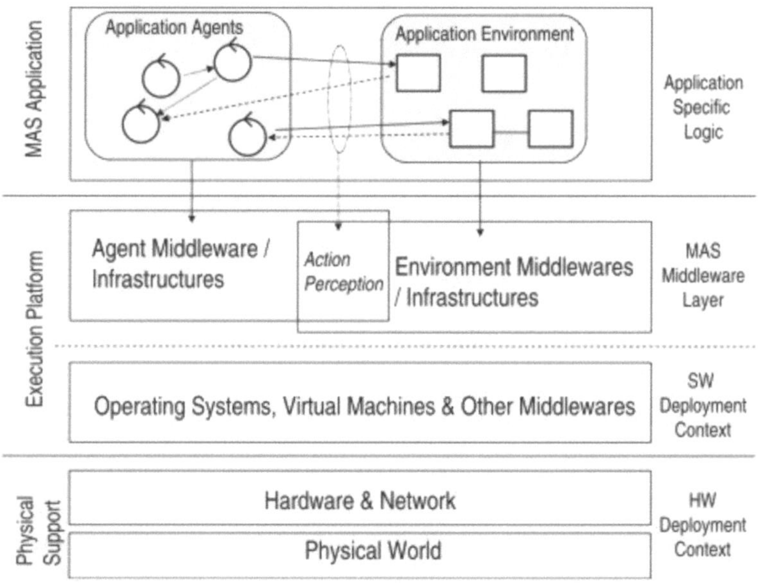

Fig. 4. MAS layers with environmental support (Viroli et al., 2007)

there could be agents running on JADE [1] and Cougaar [2] agent platforms that need to use tuple spaces, digital pheromones and electronic institutions to achieve their goals.

[1] http://jade.tilab.com/
[2] http://www.cougaar.org/

In figure 4, the arrows going from agents to environmental abstractions represent actions and the dashed lines in the opposite direction represent perceptions. We will focus on this agent-environment interface in the next section.
The resources modeled as part of the application environment are considered as passive and reactive. They don't exhibit the characteristics associated with agents, such as autonomous and pro-active behavior or social abilities (Omicini et al., 2008). If more intelligent environment is needed, nothing prevents us from creating another layer of application environment using special type of agents. These infrastructural agents can be organized as an intelligent and self-organizing environmental layer and can have for example some control over the population of the application agents. Infrastructural agents could be for example in charge of managing self-configuration of the whole MAS. The idea of agents as part of the environment is demonstrated in (Mili & Steiner, 2008), which presents a model of Agent-Environment Systems (AES) based on layered view of agents. (Mili & Steiner, 2008) defines AES as "as a system composed of a) a set of interacting social-agents, b) a distinct open environment in which these agents are situated, and c) a mechanism for social-agent/ environment interactions.". Open environment is split into cells that provide manageable division of large open MAS and social-agent/environment interaction is executed via specialized cell controller agents that form a middle layer between application environment and application agents (see figure 5).

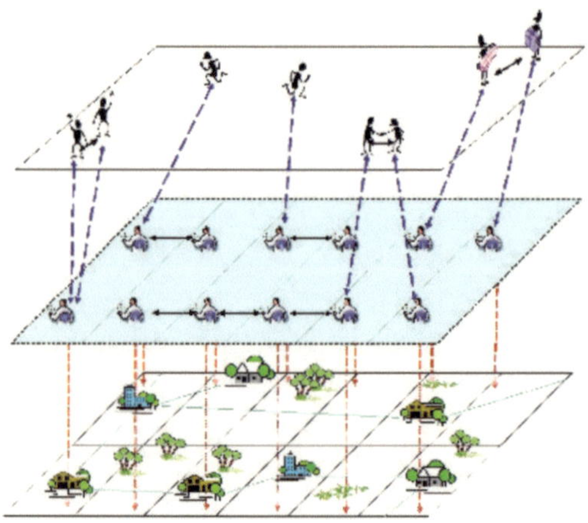

Fig. 5. AES layers (Mili & Steiner, 2008)

Social-agent can observe the state of the environment by querying the controller agents for perceptions. Controllers manage access to the environmental resources and provide synchronization services. Controller agents can also inform other controllers of any changes that may effect their cells or push the latest state of the environment to their local agents.
There is a need to model, develop and research infrastructures for both agents and environment. FIPA abstract architecture and related specifications are a popular way of modeling the agent platform, but they only cover the agent side of the execution context and miss the benefits of explicitly modeled environment. The environmental infrastructure can be seen as service to the agents that provides abstractions for engineering the environment. One of the main challenges of engineering service-oriented environments is the integration of services Weyns et al. (2007). Horizontal integration deals with problem of integrating services

at the same level of abstraction by allowing flexible composition of available services based on the application specific requirements. This could mean for example allowing environmental process running on infrastructure X to observe the state of the resources supported by infrastructure Y. Vertical integration concerns both the integration of domain-specific services upwards with the agents and downwards with the more general services. The former is critical to the interoperability between agent and its environment and the latter to the efficient engineering of infrastructures for environment (Weyns et al., 2007).

3. Agent-environment interaction

Based on the research presented in the previous section, it should be clear that environment can play an important part in MAS interaction when its role is extended beyond mere transfer medium for direct agent-to-agent messaging. The models and mechanisms for environmental support for indirect interaction extend the traditional means and models of interaction in MAS and provide valuable ways of managing complexity. On the other hand, infrastructural or middleware approach to engineering agent-based systems contributes to the creation of generic and reusable components for implementing MAS environments. Infrastructures use domain specific abstractions such as digital pheromones, co-fields or organizational concepts to tackle interaction problems. Each infrastructure usually also provides their own unique interface for agents to use. Complex and open MAS environments can utilize multiple infrastructures, all coming from different sources with their own usage interfaces. This infrastructural complexity of the environment leads to more complex agents, who have to be able to adapt to different ways of sensing and acting in the environment.

We argue, that it is crucial to keep the interface between agent and its environment as simple as possible, without sacrificing the benefits of the environment-mediated interaction. In an ideal situation, agent could sense and act in the environment through a single interface, which would provide access to the whole environment and the major integration task would be moved from the agent side to the side of the environment. This is a reasonable assumption, because although it is possible to think of environment as an unbounded, in practice it is implemented as a set of situated interaction spaces, confined by real-world or artificial restrictions. In other words, the agents explicitly enter and leave the environment. For example, for agents inhabiting a physical object, such as a mobile phone, entering an environment might mean that the object is carried inside a certain smart room. Virtual agent on the other hand might be required to present valid credentials before gaining access to a shared virtual environment. So, even though the environment could be made up of components from different sources it is usually maintained by a single stakeholder.

In contrast to the models and infrastructures presented in the earlier sections, this chapter raises the level of abstraction to generic perception and actions. So, instead of discussing about depositing and observing digital pheromones, we look into the problem of how agents can observe the environment in a generic way and discover, choose and perform any generic action that will help them to reach their goals. This must also include the modeling of the environment upon which the action are executed. The goal of this section is to provide a survey of the current research literature concerning the theory, design and implementation aspects of generic interface for agent-environment interaction.

The first sub-section covers artifacts as the unifying concepts of agent-environment interaction. Second subsection takes an AOSE approach and discusses the impact of explicit environment to the agent-based engineering methodologies. In the third subsection we discuss the context of agent actions. Fourth subsection present two infrastructures available that support the high level modeling concepts for resources and observation. Finally the last subsection discusses the semantic description of the environment.

3.1 Artifacts as unifying abstraction for engineering environment-mediated interaction

One of the most general approaches to modeling environment-mediated interaction comes from Ricci at al. (Ricci et al., 2006)in the form of artifacts as the functionality-oriented building block of the MAS environment. Artifact is used as a first-class abstraction to represent everything in MAS context that is not suitably modeled as an agent i.e. everything that is not characterized as goal- or task-oriented. The idea is that the same concept of artifact is used through out the whole process of developing MAS from modeling to implementation and all the way to deployment, where the artifacts are supported by suitable infrastructures. (Ricci et al., 2006) defines artifact as "a computational device populating agents' environment, designed to provide some kind of function or service, to be used by agents - either individually or collectively - to achieve their goals and to support their tasks". Multi-agent system is then defined as a computational system that consists of agents and artifacts (Omicini et al., 2008). Agents represent the pro-active and autonomous components of the system whereas artifacts are passive and reactive.
Figure 6 shows the abstract representation of an artifact. Artifact is described by its function, usage interface and operating instructions. The definition of artifact says nothing about its internals. Function describes the intended use of the artifact provided by its designer, but it doesn't necessarily determine the actual usage of the artifact. Usage interface is defined as the set of operations, observable states and events provided by the artifact.

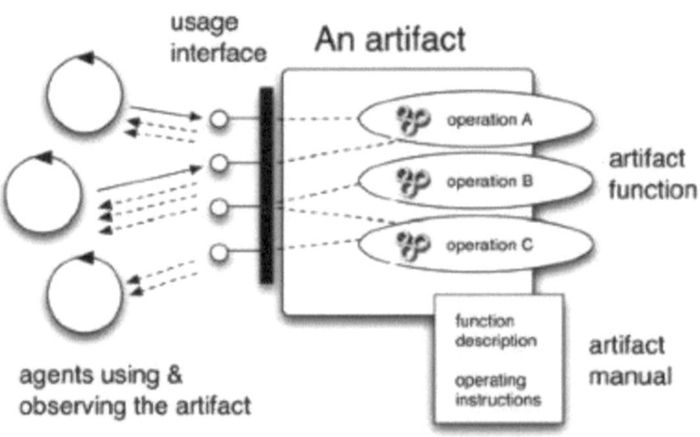

Fig. 6. Abstract representation of the artifact. (Ricci et al., 2007b)

Observable state consists of dynamic and persistent attributes that belong to the artifact and can be observed without interacting with the actual artifact. Observable events on the other hand are non-persistent information that carry information about the evolution of the artifact's observable state (Ricci et al., 2008).
(Ricci et al., 2006) presents some of the basic artifact types common in the context of MAS engineering: coordination artifacts, boundary artifacts and resource artifacts. Another

categorization is given in (Ricci et al., 2007b), which categorizes artifacts into resources and tools. According to (Ricci et al., 2007b) resources are the primary source and target of the agent activities, whereas the tools are used as means to achieve some goal. In other words, agent can interact directly with the resource or use an appropriate tool. (Viroli et al., 2005) divides artifacts into individual, social and resource artifacts as depicted in figure 7.

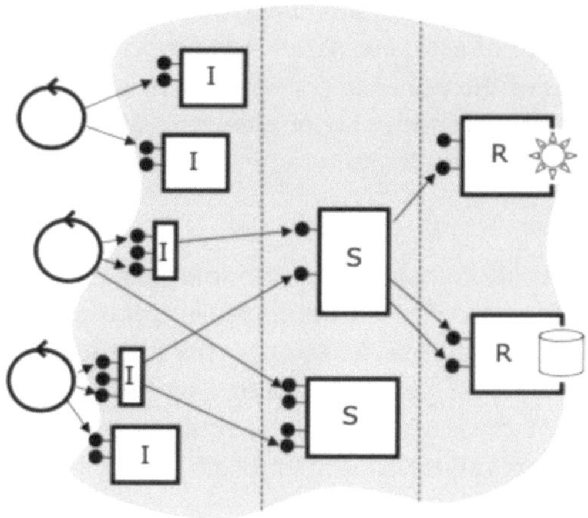

Fig. 7. Artifacts and the layered view of application environment. (Viroli et al., 2005)

Individual artifact are used by only one agent. They can be seen as the personal artifacts of the agent and can implement for example a private extension of agent's memory. As the name implies, social artifacts are used by two or more agents. They mediate interaction between agents and their functionality is usually geared towards the environmental goals instead of the goals of an individual agent. Examples of social artifacts include coordination services and shared repositories. Finally, resource artifacts are artifacts that wrap external resources such as legacy systems and physical sensors (Viroli et al., 2005). As part of the effort to further generalize the artifact based approach, Agents & Artifacts meta-model (Omicini et al., 2008) makes a distinction between artifacts that are used by cognitive and non-cognitive agents. Basically, a cognitive artifact must include the function, usage and operation instructions described above, whereas a basic artifact can be deployed without them.

Ricci et al. identify three main aspects of agent-artifacts relationship: 1) selection, 2) use and, 3) construction and manipulation (Ricci et al., 2006). The selection process relies on the observability of artifacts. Agent must be able to inspect the state and behavior of an artifact in order to be able to select the appropriate artifact for the task at hand. Agent uses artifacts to support their activities. Artifacts are situated in the environment, meaning that they are both the source and target of change in the environment. Being situated, the function of an artifact or what the artifact does when used by an agent is defined as the change it produces to the environment. Agent uses artifact through an interface, which is defined as a collection of operations. Operation changes the state of the artifact, activates it and produces the defined effects to the environment. Finally, construction and manipulation refers to linkability and malleability of the artifacts respectively. Linkability allows agents to combine them at runtime to create new and more complicated artifacts. Malleability refers to the characteristics of

artifacts that makes it possible for agent to change the behavior of an artifact at runtime in order to adapt it to the dynamic requirements of the open environment.
According to the Agents & Artifacts meta-model (Omicini et al., 2008), the agent actions in MAS can be classified in three categories: 1) Internal actions, which are actions that are part of the inner workings of an agent, 2) communicative actions, which are related to sending and receiving of ACL messages from other agents and 3) pragmatic actions that involve interaction with the environment via artifacts. Pragmatic actions cover the observation, usage, construction and modification of artifacts. A&A meta-model does not however provide any means for explicit modeling of the action itself, which it is left to the concrete models.
Artifacts represent a very general model for engineering MAS. The models presented in the following sections share many of the characteristics of artifacts and provide extra abstractions for more concrete modeling tasks.

3.2 Agent-environment interaction in AOSE methodologies

Although some of the modern AOSE methodologies emphasize the role of the environment, they rarely provide an explicit meta-model or concepts for modeling the agent-environment interaction for that matter. Even if the methodology would include tools for environmental modeling, the gap between design and implementation remains significant if the target deployment infrastructures are not taken into account.

3.2.1 GAIA

(Zambonelli et al., 2003) presents an updated version of the GAIA methodology with environment model, where the environment is modeled as set of abstract computational resources made available to agents for sensing, effecting and consuming. A simple model for agent-environment interaction is given as a list of resources each associated with the type of actions (read, change, and remove) agents can perform on it and possible informal textual descriptions of the actions. GAIA was one of the first methodology to include environmental modeling, but the proposed approach is too limited for any detailed discussion of the environmental responsibilities.

3.2.2 Agent Environment Interaction model

Agent Environment Interaction (AEI) (DeLoach & Valenzuela, 2007) is an extension to the O-MaSE methodology (Deloach, 2006) and it concentrates on the agent-environment interaction. The proposed model uses concepts from O-MaSE. AEI has three main components: Capability model, Environment model and Interactions between capabilities and the environment. Figure 8 depicts the main concepts of the model and their relationships.
Environment model is designed to support the modeling of active environment through Process entities. The environment itself is composed of objects, which can be connected with relations. Agents are considered as a special type of objects that can posses capabilities. Capability is defined as an entity that can perform one or more actions. Capabilities can be defined at different levels of abstraction based on the requirements of the application. AEI model also supports the creation of new capabilities as a composition of existing capabilities. This basically means that the new capability has access to all the actions defined in the capabilities it is composed of. Action is used to represent the actual sensor of actuator. It is defined via single operation that is used to invoke the action. The operation can be equipped with pre-conditions that must be met in order to execute it. There can also be post-conditions

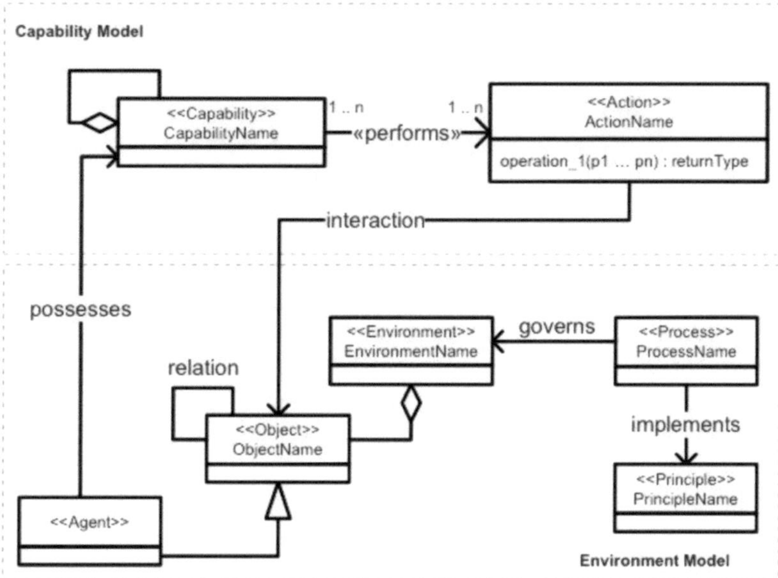

Fig. 8. Agent-Environment Interaction model. (DeLoach & Valenzuela, 2007)

that describe the desired state of the environment after operation execution. The dynamics of the environment can affect the state of the environment so that the post-conditions might not hold.

The viewpoint of the capability model is one of agent behavior as opposed to the artifact behavior emphasized by A&A meta-model. Instead of using environmental objects directly, agent is said to perform actions/operations on the environment as a whole, which may impact the state of one or more objects in the environment. There is no mention of general observability of the environment. Whether or not to allow agents to observe certain state of the environment is modeled as part of the actions. Of course, one could create a capability called Observe through which the agents could perform generic observation related actions with operations such as *getObservableObjectsByType(objectType)* and *getCurrentObservableState(objectID)*. Lack of explicitly defined observability also affects the definition of operations. In AEI every operation has a return value in contrast to the operation in artifact, which makes its new state available through asynchronously manifested observable events.

3.2.3 SODA

SODA (Societies in Open and Distributed Agent spaces) is an agent-oriented methodology that focuses on the inter-agent issues related to analysis and design of open agent-based systems (Omicini, 2001). SODA is one the few agent-based methodologies that deals with MAS environment explicitly. In the analysis phase resource model is created by expressing the environment as a set of services, each associated with a certain abstract resource. Resource model also includes abstract definitions for permissions associated with each role or group. The information flow between a service and its user is captured as part of the interaction model in the form of interaction protocols. Later, in the design phase, resources are mapped to infrastructural classes or components in order create concrete environment model. Each

component is associated with an interface, which is defined by its associated interaction protocol.
Original SODA methodology has been later extended with the notion of artifacts (see previous section) (Molesini et al., 2005). Artifacts in SODA are mainly considered at the design phase, although the authors do acknowledge their role in the analysis phase and especially to the interaction model. In the context of resource/environmental models the introduction of artifacts has two major consequences (Molesini et al., 2005). Replacing concrete resources with resource artifacts, which embody external resources, allows designers of MAS environment to raise the description of those resources up to the agent cognitive level. Another observation derived from the artifacts is the need for topological model. The authors argue that in order for the artifact to be applicable abstraction through out the whole engineering process from design to deployment, it is important to give the engineers of MAS environment the ability to model the topology of the system already at the design phase (Molesini et al., 2005). The interaction model is modified to coincide with the interaction categories of A&A meta-model (Omicini et al., 2008) by dividing interaction protocols into role interaction protocols that deal with the agent-to-agent communication and resource interaction protocols that are related to artifact usage.
MeNSA project [3] is an interesting initiative that has taken synthesizing approach at creating a new methodology by integrating methodologies under a new shared meta-model in order to produce as versatile meta-model as possible. (Dalpiaz et al., 2008) present the first result towards that goal by introducing the first version of MeNSA meta-model that combines strongest aspects from GAIA (Zambonelli et al., 2003), Tropos (Bresciani et al., 2004), SODA (Omicini, 2001) and PASSI (Cossentino, 2005) methodologies. Not surprisingly, MeNSA has adopted the environment model from SODA.

3.3 Environment as a context for agent actions

Agent actions are a fundamental part of the MAS and thus usually covered by AOSE methodologies either implicitly or explicitly. Action is always performed in some context and there should be a flexible way for modeling preconditions for the action in that context. In the current approaches, the context model for action usually does not take into consideration the state of the non-social part of the environment. EAI model (DeLoach & Valenzuela, 2007) has something in that direction, but based on the article, one can't conclude anything definitive about the scope of possible context for the preconditions of operations. In SODA (Omicini, 2001), the permissions regarding actions on resources are based on the role or group that the agent belongs to in the organization. This is enough for environments that don't contain many interconnected resources that might affect each others availability. For complex environments there might be requirement to include for example information about the topology of the environmental resources to context against which the preconditions of the action are evaluated.
The Environment as Active Support if Interaction (EASI) model by Saunier et al (Saunier et al., 2007) defines the context of MAS as the observable properties of all the entities in MAS. Agent's actions are therefore guarded by contextual conditions that take in to account the collective status of the whole MAS. Of course, this approach gets complicated when the environment is distributed, but then the contextual information can be restricted to the local state of the MAS. Similarly to EASI, Agent Observable Environment (Kesäniemi et al., 2009)

[3] http://www.mensa-project.org

infrastructure presented in the next section is designed to use the so called observable state of the local environment as the context for observation rules.

3.4 Infrastructural support for agent-environment interface

In the previous sections we have gone through methodologies and meta-models proposed for engineering and modeling environment and agent-environment interaction. In order to move the system from design to deployment, the design time models have to be transformed into an implementation. It is always at least theoretically possible to build the whole implementation from scratch but in practice that is rarely an acceptable route to take for obvious resource related reasons. That is why everything is usually built on top existing software, frameworks, libraries and infrastructures. MAS infrastructures have traditionally focused on supporting abstractions related to building different type of agents or facilitating agent-to-agent communication, while the environment part of the MAS, if included in the designs at all, has been left for ad hoc implementations or the infrastructural support has been for relatively low level functionality.

The recent promotion of environment as a first-class entity (Weyns et al., 2006) has fueled the development of more generic, adaptable and reusable infrastructures for environments. But the use of high level environmental infrastructures doesn't remove the fact that there is usually a conceptual gap between the abstract concepts used in the meta-model of the methodology and concepts provided by the infrastructure. The cause for this gap is argued to be in the different perspectives taken by the creators of methodologies and infrastructures (Dalpiaz et al., 2008). AOSE methodologies usually follow the top-down approach, moving from real life problems to architectures, whereas the infrastructure developers start from existing programming paradigms and work their way up to higher level programming constructs. In the end, there is usually mismatch between the approaches and some transformations or "glue" concepts must be developed to bridge the gap. Decreasing the gap would alleviate the challenges related to the vertical integration of domain specific infrastructures upwards to agents. In this section we focus on the particular type of environmental infrastructure that tries to minimize that gap in the context of agent-environment interaction.

3.4.1 CArtAgO

CArtAgO or Common "Artifacts for Agents" Open framework, is a Java based open source software [4] created in the university of Bologna. It provides development and run-time support for artifact-based (see section 3.1) computational environments (Ricci et al., 2007a). The three main components of the framework are 1) API for designers and implementors of the environment for defining artifact types, 2) API for agents for interacting with the artifacts, and 3) infrastructure for run-time support for artifact based working environments. CArtAgO is an environmental infrastructure and it is designed to be integrated with existing agent frameworks.

Figure 9 shows the abstract architecture of CArtAgO. In addition to artifacts and workspaces, two concepts coming from A&A meta-model, CArtAgO introduces a new concept called agent body, which works as the interface between agent and its environment. It is very similar to the softbody introduced by Platon et al. in (Platon et al., 2005). Agent body is created for every agent that inhabits CArtAgO environment and it contains the effectors and sensors of the agent. Agent controls its own body and can dynamically link and unlink different kinds

[4] http://sourceforge.net/projects/cartago/

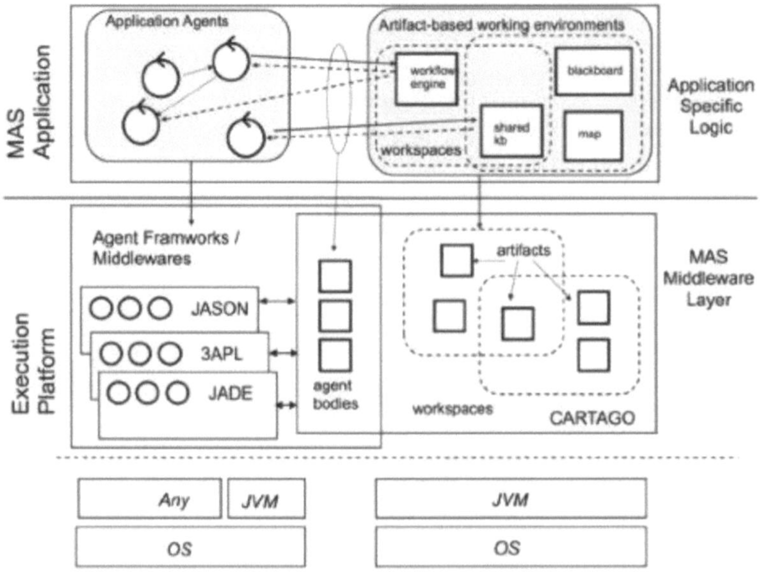

Fig. 9. Abstract representation of a MAS application using CArtAgO. (Ricci et al., 2007b)

of sensors to it. Agent-environment interaction happens through the construction, selection and use of artifacts and perception of observable event as described in section 3.1.

The agent side of the API, i.e. the way agent can interact with its environment, deals with the construction, disposal, selection, use and inspection of artifacts as well as sensor and workspace related management tasks. For example, agent can execute specific operation on a given artifact by using the action *execOP(ArtifactID, OperationName, Args, SensorID)*. The last two parameters are optional. Args refers to the parameters of the operation and SensorID to the sensor that is going to be used to collect the possible observable event generated by the action. On the artifact side the available actions deal with the generation of observable events and management of operations and observable state of the artifact. Detailed description of the API is available in (Ricci et al., 2007a).

3.4.2 Agent observable environment

Agent Observable Environment (AOE) is an infrastructure designed to support the observation process of an agent through observable softbodies (Kesäniemi et al., 2009). It separates the common Observable Environment (OE) from the domain-specific infrastructures. The idea is that all the MAS infrastructures use the same OE making it the principal source and target of observation for the whole MAS. In other words, AOE works as a integration middleware between various agent and environment infrastructures. It was designed with the notion of open MAS in mind, where both the agent population and services and resources of the environment can be very dynamic. In a dynamic environment, AOE would work as the lowest common denominator between the heterogeneous entities and facilitate the indirect interactions between them. It should be noted that AOE only accounts for observation side of the perception/action interface between agent and its environment.

Figure 10 shows the logical architecture of AOE using the layered presentation of MAS adapted from (Viroli et al., 2007). The observable part of the environment is modeled as a separate entity called Observable Environment, which contains soft-bodies and observation rules. Every soft-body is connected to either an agent or some environmental resource.

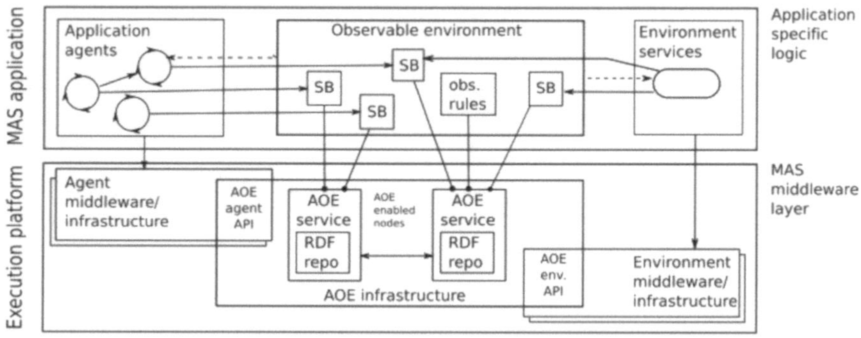

Fig. 10. Logical architecture of the AOE. (Kesäniemi et al., 2009)

Soft-body is further divided into owner and environment managed parts. The division means that the entity to which the soft-body belongs to has only partial control over its observable state. This is different from the agent body in CArtAgO, which is completely under agent's control. AOE supports both static and dynamic observation (Viroli et al., 2001). The result of a static observation is a snapshot of the observable state of the environment presented as observable items, whereas dynamic observation allows agent to observe the evolution of the state through observable events. In addition to agent initiated static or dynamic observation, AOE is able "push" observable items or events to the agents without explicit request from the agent. This behavior takes the environment controlled awareness provided by the EASI (Saunier & Balbo, 2007) even further and is considered as a potential source for emergent behavior in MAS. Observability of the soft-body can be restricted using observation rules. There are two kind rules: ones originating from the environments side and ones set up by the agents. Environmental rules, or "laws of nature", take precedence over rules set by the agent.

3.5 Semantic description of environment

All the approaches covered in the paper so far, have at some level conveyed the need to provide formal, machine processable descriptions of the environment to the software agents. Actual models for such descriptions have been out of their scope and the task has been delegated as part of the development process of a system. This easily leads to ad hoc and application specific descriptions, in the same way as the early MAS environments were implemented on a application to application basis. One way of fostering interoperability between diverse sources of environmental data is to use upper level core ontology (Doerr et al., 2003) from which the infrastructure specific concepts can be extended or to which they can be mapped or transformed. The use of ontologies also allows agents to reason about the state and behavior of their observable environment. This is especially important in open and dynamic environments where the agent might not have any prior knowledge about the environment before entering it.

Descriptions of environmental resources and services are an integral part of the A&A meta-model with the so called cognitive artifacts (Omicini et al., 2008). Cognitive artifact must include function, usage and operation instructions in some machine processable form. Agent Observable Environment can also be greatly enhanced with the use of ontologies. Since

AOE uses RDF [5] as the representation of observable environment it is easy to extends it with ontologies, which can be used to enable semantic observation capabilities (Kesäniemi et al., 2009). Acay et al. coined the term extrospection in (Acay et al., 2007), which refers to a sort of cognitive situatedness in agent's ability to discover, select, use and reason about environmental resources based on their formal semantic descriptions. They argue that the combination of artifact and its usage manual, or cognitive artifact, would benefit the MAS development by making it possible for agents to complete their design at run-time through the process of discovery, use and reuse of components and allowing domain independent meta-level reasoning to be built into agents (Acay et al., 2009). Next section describes their ontology based approach to environmental modeling.

3.5.1 OWL-T

OWL-T (OWL Tool) is an ontology for describing infrastructural components (Acay et al., 2007). The approach taken in the information modeling is pragmatic as opposed to epistemic, meaning that instead of trying to classify and label thing and relations between them, the goal of OWL-T has been define the functional nature of an object independent of its physical properties. For example both paddle and a sail affords to moving a boat on the water although they are not that similar in their physical properties. As the name implies, OWL-T uses Web Ontology Language (OWL) [6] or more precisely the OWL-DL variant of OWL, as its ontology language.

OWL-T can be divided into five mutually exclusive sub-models: ActionModel, ObjectModel, OrganizationModel, AgentModel, and AbstractConcept. We will shortly describe the ones that are most relevant to the topic at hand, namely the ActivityModel, ObjectModel, and AbstractConcept models. The AgentModel is out of the scope of this chapter because it deals with the inner workings of an agent.

Objects in OWL-T are divided into *Artifacts* and *Tools*. Tool is defined by its *PhysicalProperty* and *IdealProperty*. Former supports the spatial and shape characteristics of any object and the latter refers to the functionality of the *Tool* or in other words in what kind of activity it is useful. The usage interface is formalized as an *Interface*, which represent the actions supported for a given *Role*. OWL-T defines three types of agent behavior: *Process*, *Action* and *Activity*. *Process* in an atomic, reactive behavior whereas *Action* represent goal-oriented and non-atomic agent behavior. Completion of an action might require sequence of *Processes* to be executed before completion. The order of *Processes* required by the an *Action* is defined using *ProcessModel*. *Action* takes an *Artifact* as an input parameter and transforms it into output. *Process* can then be seen as working at the operation level of an *Artifact*. Finally, an *Activity* is used to encapsulate actions of multiple agents into to a group activity with a common, system level goal where every agent plays a certain role. Full description of the ontology and related formal semantic and pragmatic for it can be found in (Acay et al., 2007).

4. Conclusions

In this chapter, we provided an introduction to the different roles of environment in agent-based systems. We also presented a survey of different aspects of agent-environment interaction from the perspective of agent-oriented software engineering. The promotion

[5] http://www.w3.org/RDF/
[6] http://www.w3.org/TR/owlref/.

of environment as a first-class abstraction has led to research results in various fields of agent-oriented software engineering ranging from new or extended methodologies that include explicit environmental models to general infrastructures that can support application-independent concepts for building and integrating environments for MAS. There has also been efforts towards semantic description of infrastructural components.
At a very abstract level, agent-environment interaction can be reduced to agent actions performed via sensors and actuators and it basically has three ways of using them. First, it can use the sensors/actuators that are part of its own "body". The features of the agent's body can be static and decided by the designer of the agent, or they can be dynamically modifiable at run-time by the agent itself. Second, if the agent does not possess some required capability, it can try to ask some other agent to provide it. Third option is to use the resources available in the environment. The discovery and usage of environmental resources are the cornerstones or agent-environment interaction and are therefore covered at some level by all the surveyed models and infrastructures. One interesting extension that is not taken into account, is the possibility for agents to deposit their own actuators and sensors to the environment for others to use so that they would be available even if the agent that created them is no longer available. For example, a mobile agent could place a specialized messaging resource to the environment that would allow other agents and resources to interact with some previously unknown external system. In all of the three cases, sensors and actuators can be seen as a sort of a service, either provided by the agent's body itself, other agents or the environment. This kind of sensor/actuator as a service view of the agent-environment interaction could be used to create unified layer for discovery and usage, both direct of indirect, of sensors and actuators regardless of their source.

5. References

Acay, L. D., Pasquier, P. & Sonenberg, L. (2007). Extrospection: Agents reasoning about the environment, *3rd IET International Conference on Intelligent Environments (IE 07)*, pp. 220–227.

Acay, L. D., Sonenberg, L., Ricci, A. & Pasquier, P. (2009). How situated is your agent? a cognitive perspective, *Programming Multi-Agent Systems: 6th International Workshop, ProMAS 2008, Estoril, Portugal, May 13, 2008. Revised Invited and Selected Papers*, Springer-Verlag, Berlin, Heidelberg, pp. 136–151.

Bresciani, P., Perini, A., Giorgini, P., Giunchiglia, F. & Mylopoulos, J. (2004). Tropos: An Agent-Oriented Software Development Methodology, *Autonomous Agents and Multi-Agent Systems* 8(3): 203–236.

Cossentino, M. (2005). From Requirements to Code with the PASSI Methodology, *Agent-Oriented Methodologies*, Idea Group Publishing, pp. 79–106.

Dalpiaz, F., Molesini, A., Puviani, M. & Seidita, V. (2008). Towards filling the gap between AOSE methodologies and infrastructures: Requirements and meta-model, *in* M. Baldoni, M. Cossentino, F. De Paoli & V. Seidita (eds), *9th Workshop "From Objects to Agents" (WOA 2008) – Evolution of Agent Development: Methodologies, Tools, Platforms and Languages*, Seneca Edizioni, Palermo, Italy, pp. 115–121.

De Wolf, T. & Holvoet, T. (2006). A catalogue of decentralised coordination mechanisms for designing self-organising emergent applications, *Technical Report CW458*, Katholieke Universiteit Leuven, Department of Computer Science.

Deloach, S. A. (2006). Engineering organization-based multiagent systems, *LNCS*, Springer, pp. 109–125.

DeLoach, S. & Valenzuela, J. (2007). An agent-environment interaction model, *in* L. Padgham & F. Zambonelli (eds), *Agent-Oriented Software Engineering VII*, Vol. 4405 of *Lecture Notes in Computer Science*, Springer Berlin / Heidelberg, pp. 1–18.

Doerr, M., Hunter, J. & Lagoze, C. (2003). Towards a core ontology for information integration, *Journal of Digital Information* 4(1).

Esteva, M., Rosell, B., Rodriguez-Aguilar, J. A. & Arcos, J. L. (2004). Ameli: An agent-based middleware for electronic institutions, *AAMAS '04: Proceedings of the Third International Joint Conference on Autonomous Agents and Multiagent Systems*, IEEE Computer Society, Washington, DC, USA, pp. 236–243.

Ferber, J. & Müller, J.-p. (1996). *Influences and Reaction : a Model of Situated Multiagent Systems.*

FIPA: Foundation for Intelligent Physical Agents. (n.d.).
URL: *http://www.fipa.org*

Hayes-Roth, B. (1995). An architecture for adaptive intelligent systems, *Artif. Intell.* 72(1-2): 329–365.

Huhns, M. N. & Stephens, L. M. (1999). Multiagent systems and societies of agents, *in* G. Weiss (ed.), *Multiagent Systems: A Modern Approach to Distributed Artificial Intelligence*, The MIT Press, Cambridge, MA, USA, pp. 79–120.

Kesäniemi, J., Katasonov, A. & Terziyan, V. (2009). An Observation Framework for Multi-agent Systems, *2009 Fifth International Conference on Autonomic and Autonomous Systems* pp. 336–341.

Maes, P. (1995). Artificial life meets entertainment: lifelike autonomous agents, *Communications of the ACM* 38(11): 108–114.

Mamei, M. & Zambonelli, F. (2005). Programming stigmergic coordination with the tota middleware, *AAMAS '05: Proceedings of the fourth international joint conference on Autonomous agents and multiagent systems*, ACM, New York, NY, USA, pp. 415–422.

Meszaros, G. & Doble, J. (1996). MetaPatterns: A Pattern Language for Pattern Writing, *In 3rd Pattern Languages of Programming conference*, pp. 4—-6.

Mili, R. Z. & Steiner, R. (2008). Modeling agent-environment interactions in adaptive mas, pp. 135–147.

Molesini, A., Omicini, A., Denti, E. & Ricci, A. (2005). Soda: A roadmap to artefacts, *ESAW*, pp. 49–62.

Müller, J. P. (1996). *The Design of Intelligent Agents*, Springer Berlin / Heidelberg.

Odell, J., Associates, J. O., Arbor, A. & Parunak, H. V. D. (2003). Modeling agents and their environment: the physical environment, *Journal of Object Technology* 2: 43–51.

Odell, J., Parunak, H. V. D. & Fleischer, M. (2003). Modeling agents and their environment: The communication environment, *Journal of Object Technology* 2(1): 39–52.

Omicini, A. (2001). Soda: Societies and infrastructures in the analysis and design of agent-based systems, *in* P. Ciancarini & M. Wooldridge (eds), *Agent-Oriented Software Engineering*, Vol. 1957 of *Lecture Notes in Computer Science*, Springer Berlin / Heidelberg, pp. 311–326.

Omicini, A., Ricci, A. & Viroli, M. (2008). Artifacts in the A&A meta-model for multi-agent systems, *Vital And Health Statistics. Series 20 Data From The National Vitalstatistics System Vital Health Stat 20 Data Natl Vital Sta* (May): 432–456.

Parunak, H. V. D. (1997). " Go to the Ant ": Engineering Principles from Natural Multi-Agent Systems, *Artificial Intelligence* 4049: 1–27.

Platon, E., Honiden, S. & Sabouret, N. (2005). Oversensing with a softbody in the environment: Another dimension of observation, *Proceedings of Modeling Others from Observation at International Joint Conference on Artificial Intelligence*.

Platon, E., Mamei, M., Sabouret, N., Honiden, S. & Parunak, H. V. D. (2006). Mechanisms for environments in multi-agent systems: Survey and opportunities, *Autonomous Agents and Multi-Agent Systems* 14(1): 31–47.

Ricci, A., Piunti, M., Acay, L. D., Bordini, R. H., Hübner, J. F. & Dastani, M. (2008). Integrating heterogeneous agent programming platforms within artifact-based environments, *AAMAS '08: Proceedings of the 7th international joint conference on Autonomous agents and multiagent systems*, International Foundation for Autonomous Agents and Multiagent Systems, Richland, SC, pp. 225–232.

Ricci, A., Viroli, M. & Omicini, A. (2006). Programming mas with artifacts, *in* R. Bordini, M. Dastani, J. Dix & A. Seghrouchni (eds), *Programming Multi-Agent Systems*, Vol. 3862 of *Lecture Notes in Computer Science*, Springer Berlin / Heidelberg, pp. 206–221.

Ricci, A., Viroli, M. & Omicini, A. (2007a). Cartago: a framework for prototyping artifact-based environments in mas, *E4MAS'06: Proceedings of the 3rd international conference on Environments for multi-agent systems III*, Springer-Verlag, Berlin, Heidelberg, pp. 67–86.

Ricci, A., Viroli, M. & Omicini, A. (2007b). Give agents their artifacts: the a&a approach for engineering working environments in mas, *AAMAS '07: Proceedings of the 6th international joint conference on Autonomous agents and multiagent systems*, ACM, New York, NY, USA, pp. 1–3.

Rowstron, A. & Druschel, P. (2001). Pastry: Scalable, decentralized object location, and routing for large-scale peer-to-peer systems, *Middleware '01: Proceedings of the IFIP/ACM International Conference on Distributed Systems Platforms Heidelberg*, Springer-Verlag, pp. 329–350.

Russell, S. J. & Norvig, P. (1995). *Artificial Intelligence: A Modern Approach*, Prentice-Hall International.

Saunier, J. & Balbo, F. (2007). An Environment to Support Multi-Party Communications in Multi-Agent Systems, *Environment* pp. 52–61.

Saunier, J., Balbo, F. & Badeig, F. (2007). Environment as active support of interaction, *E4MAS'06: Proceedings of the 3rd international conference on Environments for multi-agent systems III*, Springer-Verlag, Berlin, Heidelberg, pp. 87–105.

Viroli, M., Holvoet, T., Ricci, A., Schelfthout, K. & Zambonelli, F. (2007). Infrastructures for the environment of multiagent systems, *Autonomous Agents and Multi-Agent Systems* 14(1): 49–60.

Viroli, M., Moro, G. & Omicini, A. (2001). On observation as a coordination paradigm: an ontology and a formal framework, *SAC '01: Proceedings of the 2001 ACM symposium on Applied computing*, ACM, New York, NY, USA, pp. 166–175.

Viroli, M., Omicini, A. & Ricci, A. (2005). Engineering MAS environment with artifacts, *in* D. Weyns, H. V. D. Parunak & F. Michel (eds), *2nd International Workshop "Environments for Multi-Agent Systems" (E4MAS 2005)*, AAMAS 2005, Utrecht, The Netherlands, pp. 62–77.

Weyns, D., Helleboogh, A., Holvoet, T. & Schumacher, M. (2007). The Agent Environment in Multi-Agent Systems : A Middleware Perspective, *Sciences-New York* (3): 1–20.

Weyns, D., Omicini, A. & Odell, J. (2006). Environment as a first class abstraction in multiagent systems, *Autonomous Agents and Multi-Agent Systems* 14(1): 5–30.

Weyns, D., Parunak, H. V. D., Michel, F., Holvoet, T. & Ferber, J. (2005). Environments for multiagent systems, state-of-the-art and research challenges, *Lecture Notes in Computer Science Series* 3374: 2–52.

Zambonelli, F., Jennings, N. R. & Wooldridge, M. (2003). Developing multiagent systems: The gaia methodology, *ACM Trans. Softw. Eng. Methodol.* 12(3): 317–370.

10

A Dependable Multi-Agent System with Self-Diagnosable Function

Keinosuke Matsumoto, Akifumi Tanimoto and Naoki Mori
Osaka Prefecture University
Japan

1. Introduction

In tandem with the penetration of the Internet, many information systems are connected to large-scale computer network systems or multi-processor systems. These distributed systems cooperate, negotiate, and solve problems by exchanging information each other. A multi-agent system (MAS) (Weiss, 1999) attracts attention as a solution to competition or cooperation in distributed systems. It is necessary that multi-agent systems operate for a long time without human's support from the viewpoint of dependable distributed system. Some techniques (Chiang & Chen, 1994) that assume failures beforehand have been developed for this problem. These techniques need another integrated system that managements all the agents for fault diagnosis. It is practically impossible to apply them to large-scale distributed systems.

We need a technique detecting faults autonomously in multi-agent systems. A self-diagnosable algorithm (Kohda et al., 1997) has been proposed for distributed systems. In this conventional simple highly structured system, all agents mutually diagnose all other agents. It has a problem that the more agents are included in a system, the more communication loads increase. To solve the problem, this paper proposes a new self-diagnosable multi-agent system that mitigates communication loads in the multi-agent system. Our method introduces middle agents that do not interaction with basic client agents to mitigate the communication traffics between agents.

2. Conventional self-diagnosable algorithm

This section describes a conventional self-diagnosable algorithm, which we call it as a simple highly structured system.

2.1 Faulty agent

An agent may malfunction in a multi-agent system and such an agent is called a faulty agent. Our research deals with the following three kinds of failure (Fedoruk & Deters, 2001):

a. Crash failure
b. Byzantine failure
c. Communication failure.

Where, crash failure refers to an agent that is stopped by a processor fault or shortage of system resources. Byzantine failure is a fault that does not assume faulty agents' behavior,

and it is caused mainly by unexpected state transitions or program bugs. Communication failure drops out all or some part of messages, or it cannot establish communication link between agents.
If these failures occurred simultaneously at two or more agents, a multi-agent system will malfunction because of interaction among agents. When faulty agents exist in a system, reliability of the system cannot be maintained without identifying the faulty agents and processing them properly.

2.2 T-fault one-step diagnosable system

Mutual diagnosis in a self-diagnosable algorithm (Preparata et al., 1967) is expressed by a directed graph as shown in Fig. 1. In this figure, a unit and testing correspond to a vertex and directed arc respectively. The system is defined as a directed graph G = [V, E], where V = {v} is a set of vertexes (units) and E = {(u, v)} is a set of directed arcs (u, v). The unit corresponding to starting point u and terminal point v of directed arc (u, v) are called a testing unit and tested unit respectively.
A test result a(u, v) is defined as shown in Table 1, and let it be a weight of the directed arc. This algorithm premises that it does not trust the test result if the testing unit is out of order and each unit does not test itself. As another self-diagnosable algorithm, t-fault one-step diagnosable system (Hakimi & Amin, 1974; Kohda, 1994) is proposed that can detect simultaneously multiple faults of up to t among n units from mutual diagnostic results of the system (hereinafter referred to as t-OD system).

2.3 Highly structured T-OD system

Definitions of a highly structured system and its characters as a t-OD system are described below:
[Definition 1] A system G = [V, E] is a highly structured system if an arbitrary unit v ($v \in V$) of the system G has a subsystem H(v; α, β) expressed in Fig. 2.

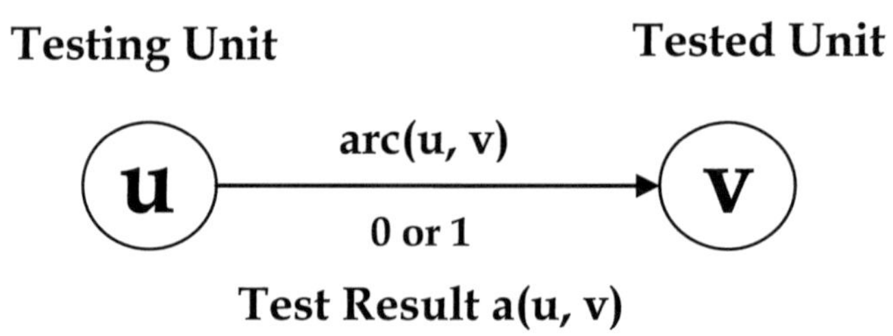

Fig. 1. Basic system component

Testing Unit **u**	Tested Unit **v**	
	Fault-free	*Faulty*
Fault-free	0	1
Faulty	*	*

*: don't care

Table 1. Test result a (u, v)

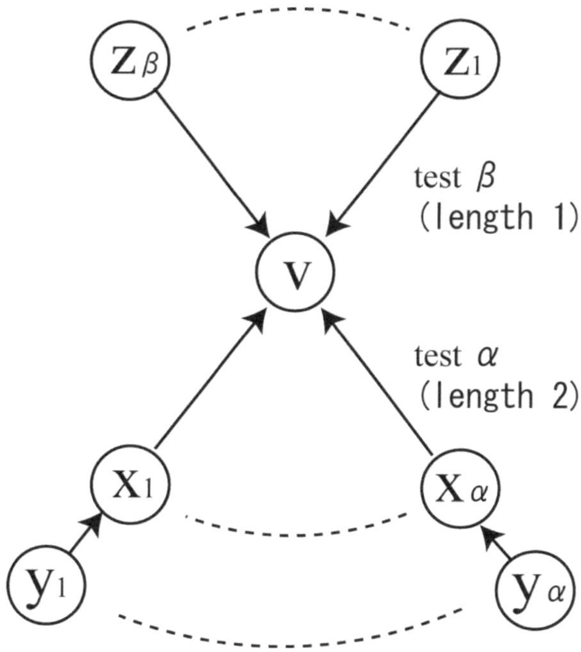

Fig. 2. A subsystem H(v; α, β)

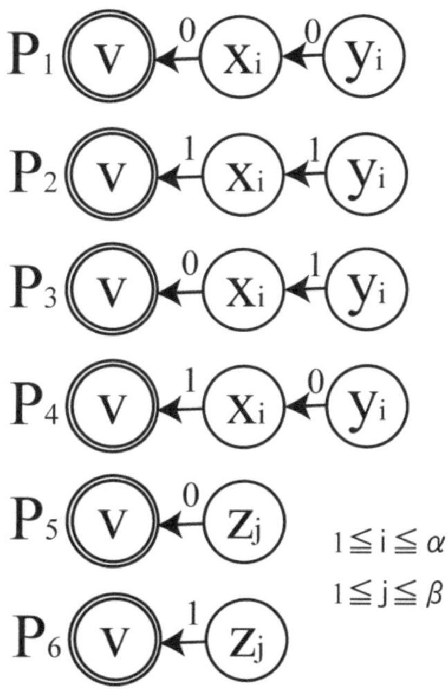

Fig. 3. Six test result patterns of type P_k in H(v; α, β)

The subsystem H(v; α, β) consists of a kernel unit v, (2α+β) other units, and (2α+β) testing links, where α is the number of testing links of length 2 and β the number of testing links of length 1. A highly structured system has the following character 1.

[Character 1] If every unit v ($v \in V$) of a system G = [V, E] has a subsystem H(v; α, β) of the definition 1 and

$$\alpha + [\beta/2] \geq t, \tag{1}$$

then G is a t-OD system.
Where, t > 0 and [x] means a maximum integer not exceeding x.
[Definition 2] A highly structured system satisfying (1) is called a highly structured t-OD system.
The following character 2 is suggested as an analyzing method of highly structured t-OD systems.
[Character 2] For an arbitrary unit v ($v \in V$) of a system G = [V, E] that satisfies the character 1, v is normal if and only if the following (2) is satisfied.

$$H(v; \alpha, \beta) \equiv p_1 + [\beta/2] - (p_4 + p_6) \geq 0 \tag{2}$$

Where, p_k is the number of test result patterns of type P_k shown in Fig. 3.

Mutual test results do not depend on the order of diagnosing each unit, and its character is a strong point of the highly structured t-OD system.

2.4 Problems of the self-diagnosable algorithm

The foregoing self-diagnosable algorithms have the following two problems: First, the more agents are included in a system, the more communication traffics increase. This is because the highly structured system (hereafter, it will be called a simple highly structured system in order to distinguish from our method) applies a simple mutual diagnosis for all units. Second, generation of mutual test results must synchronize for all units. If not all the mutual test results are completed, it does not satisfy the condition of t-OD systems. It means that faulty agents cannot be uniquely identified.

3. Self-diagnosable multi-agent system in consideration of load distribution

This section describes an approach to solving the problems that simple highly structured systems have.

3.1 System configuration

The problems can be solved by introducing not only distributed type of elements but also concentrate type of elements. Specifically, middle agents are introduced as elements. All agents of pure MAS are not controlled by any concentrated agents. But it is natural that a hybrid MAS (Hagras et al., 2003; Alur et al., 2003) exists as a middle class between a pure MAS and a pure concentrated system. There is a reason for existence of the hybrid MAS if some advantages could be obtained when it replaces the pure MAS. Middle agents are located in a different layer from a client agent's layer. Each middle agent has the following characters:

[Character 3]

- It is distinguished from basic client agents.
- It does not take part in interaction among basic client agents.
- It carries only information of mutual test results.

- It is assumed not to break down.

Our approach introduces middle agents that do not interaction with basic client agents to mitigate communications between agents. An initial system configuration is shown in Fig. 4. One middle agent is prepared for three client agents (they may become four client agents since a fraction is taken into consideration) that are the minimum composition of a t-OD system in order to keep domain of mutual tests to a minimum. They are grouped as a partial domain. The client agents carry out mutual tests within the group through the middle agent. In this group, only one faulty agent can be detected using (1).

We define middle agents that directly carry client agents' communication as a bottom layer, and another middle agent that carries communication between middle agents is defined as a top layer. This composition technique can limit range of mutual tests and mitigate each agent's load because communications between agents are carried within every local group in parallel.

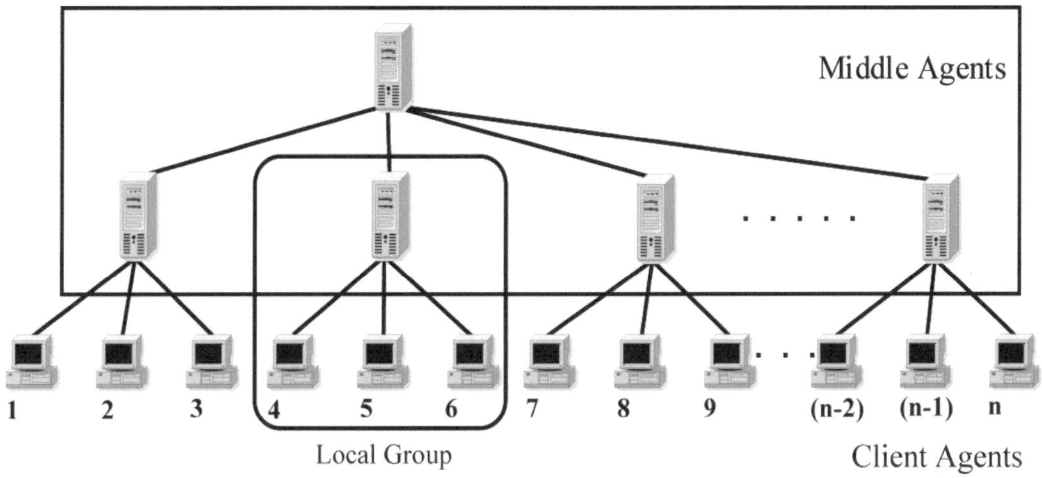

Fig. 4. Initial system configuration of the proposed system

3.2 Dynamic highly structured system

The proposed system can detect only one faulty agent for each group using (1). It is necessary to dynamically reconstitute a system configuration so that faulty agents may not be concentrated in certain groups. For that purpose, the number of branches of the middle agents at the bottom layer is fixed, and candidates of faulty agents are determined by rearranging client agents and changing groups.

Our dynamic highly structured system has the following four processes as shown in the Fig. 5:

1) *System reconfiguration*

At first, we fix a number of client agents that can be connected to a middle agent at the bottom layer. The middle agent exchanges the client agents of each group at random not to concentrate faulty agents in certain groups and to reconstruct mutual testing graphs. Because mutual tests can be conducted in parallel, faulty agents are detected for every group from the test results. These agents are regarded as candidates of faulty agents, and it is not decided to be faulty agents at this time.

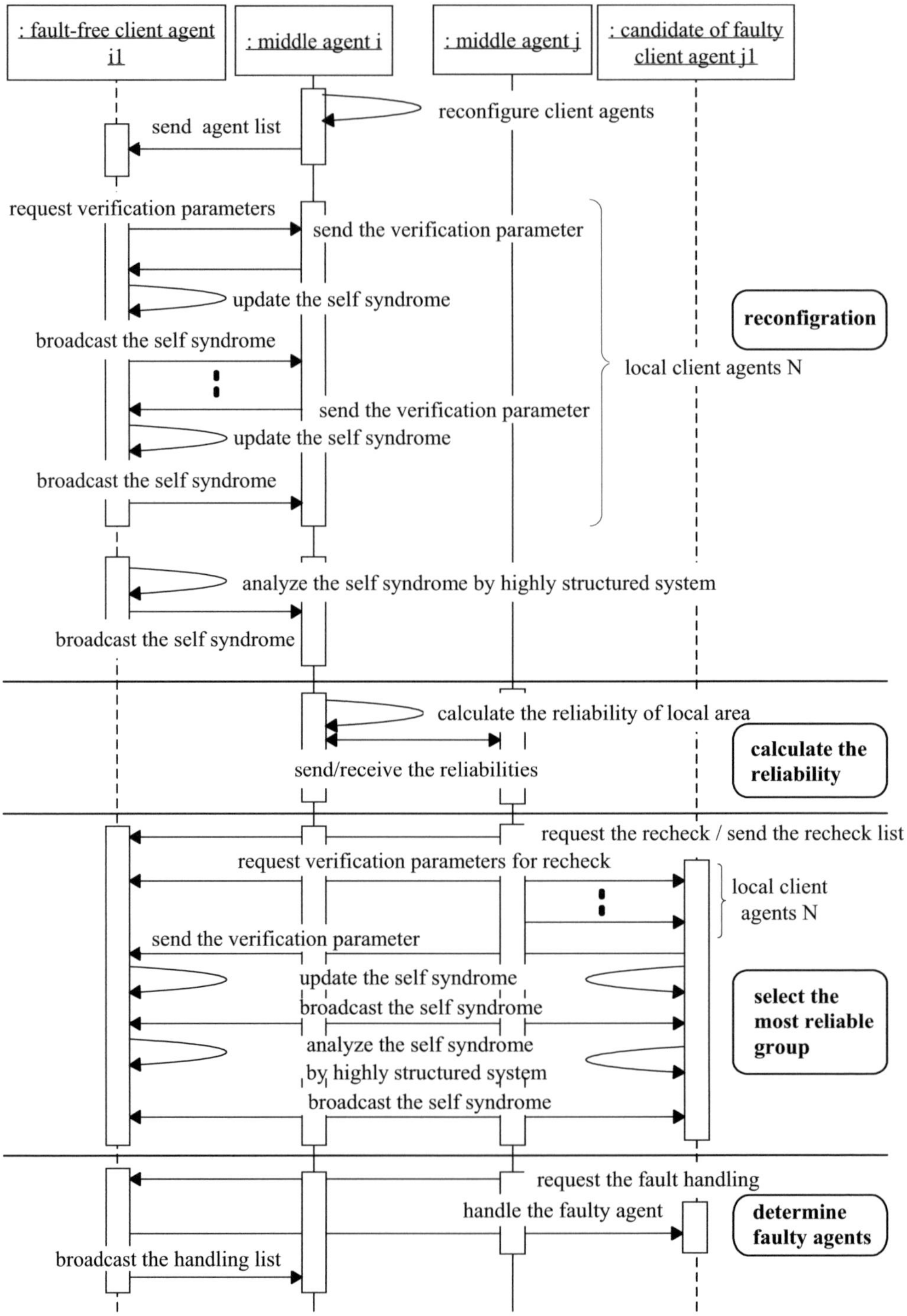

Fig. 5. A process of dynamic highly structured system

2) *Calculation of reliability*

Equation (3) is introduced here. It expresses reliability of a middle agent based on the number of doubtful agents within its group.

$$R(m_i) = 1 - \frac{Nm_i}{Am_i} \tag{3}$$

Where, m_i is an ith middle agent group, Nm_i is a number of faulty agent candidates that belong to m_i, and Am_i is a number of agents that belong to m_i. The value of this function $R(m_i)$ will go down if the number of faulty agent candidates increases. Each middle agent at the bottom layer computes (3) at each group and it shares the information among middle agents.

3) *Selection of the most reliable group*

We omit a group that has more than two faulty agent candidates, which means that it is not a t-OD system. We choose a group of the highest reliability value among the remaining groups. If there are more than two groups have the same value of $R(m_i)$, we give priority to a group whose value of H(v; α, β) in (2) is the largest. H(v; α, β) is a parameter showing allowable degree of failures.

4) *Determination of faulty agents*

Combining faulty agent candidates with agents connected to another middle agents having high reliability, mutual tests are performed again, and faulty agents are finally determined.

Because the number of times of mutual tests changes with the number of failures in an actual system, the dynamic highly structured system has feature that it is able to mitigate the communication loads between agents when all agents are trouble-free or a few agents are faulty. Unlike the conventional techniques, our approach has an advantage that it should synchronize generation of test results only within each local group.

Our self-diagnosable system conducts independent mutual tests only in a middle agent layer. This algorithm has restrictions that more than a half must be normal among the agents that constitute a mutual testing group. It can be said that the element of a meta-level does not need to guarantee high reliability because it is tested to be normal or faulty. Calculation amounts necessary for mutual tests are estimated for a simple highly structured system and a dynamic highly structured system. If the number of client agents is n, $O(n)$: orders of calculation to diagnose are as follows:

- Simple highly structured system

$$O(n) = n^2 - n \tag{4}$$

- Dynamic highly structured system

$$\begin{matrix} 2n \le O(n) & \le 8n - 12 \\ (t = 0) & \left(t = \left[\frac{n-1}{2}\right]\right) \end{matrix} \tag{5}$$

where, t is the number of faulty agents.

For the dynamic highly structured system, (5) shows that calculation orders in the cases in which the trouble is not completely occurring, and the number of faulty agents is fewer than half of all agents by one that is an upper limit of the number of faulty agents. The calculation order changes between these two values according to the number of faulty agents which exists in the system. The dynamic highly structured system needs synchronizing mutual tests only in each local group, but no necessity of synchronizing in all client agents. Therefore, the proposed system can reduce the communication traffics between agents.

4. Simulation results

Our approach has been applied to a multi-agent system (circle multi-agent system) that forms a circle autonomously, and compared with a simple highly structured system.

4.1 Circle multi-agent system

Initial conditions of the circle multi-agent system are shown below:

- Each agent knows a value of diameter that should be kept, and perceives other agents' locations.
- Each agent determines its action based on two distances to the furthest agent and to the nearest one.
- Each agent is placed at a two dimensional latticed space, and chooses one action among eight directions and no motion.

Behaviors of this system are shown in Fig. 6 to Fig. 8. Fig. 6 shows a normal state in which a circle can be formed in cooperation. Fig. 7 shows a faulty state that troubles arise at Agent1, Agent11 and Agent21, and they cannot obtain right location data of other normal agents. As a result, the cooperative target of forming a circle cannot be attained. On the other hand, in Fig. 8 a restoration system stops the faulty agents and the other normal agents form another circle. The experiment environment is as follows: CPU is Pentium4 (R) 2.4 GHz, OS Windows XP Professional, and the programming language Java JDK version 1.4.

4.2 Experiments on communication traffics between agents

The proposed system was incorporated to the circle multi-agent system, and some simulations were carried out. The experiment conditions are shown below:

- Byzantine failures happen at some agents and they cannot get right location data of other agents. It means that they fail to identify the environment.
- The experiments are carried out for two cases:
  1) 10% of agents are faulty, and
  2) 40% of agents are faulty, which means a fatal failure to the system.
- Faulty agents are selected by uniform random numbers.
- An agent is tested comparing location data of its own with the same location data that another agent has.
- A restoration system only stops faulty agents.

For a simple highly structured system and a dynamic highly structured system, the experiment measured the number of communication traffics between agents to detect faulty agents. For both systems, the number of agents was changed every ten agents from 10 to 100. Fig. 9 shows average values of ten trials.

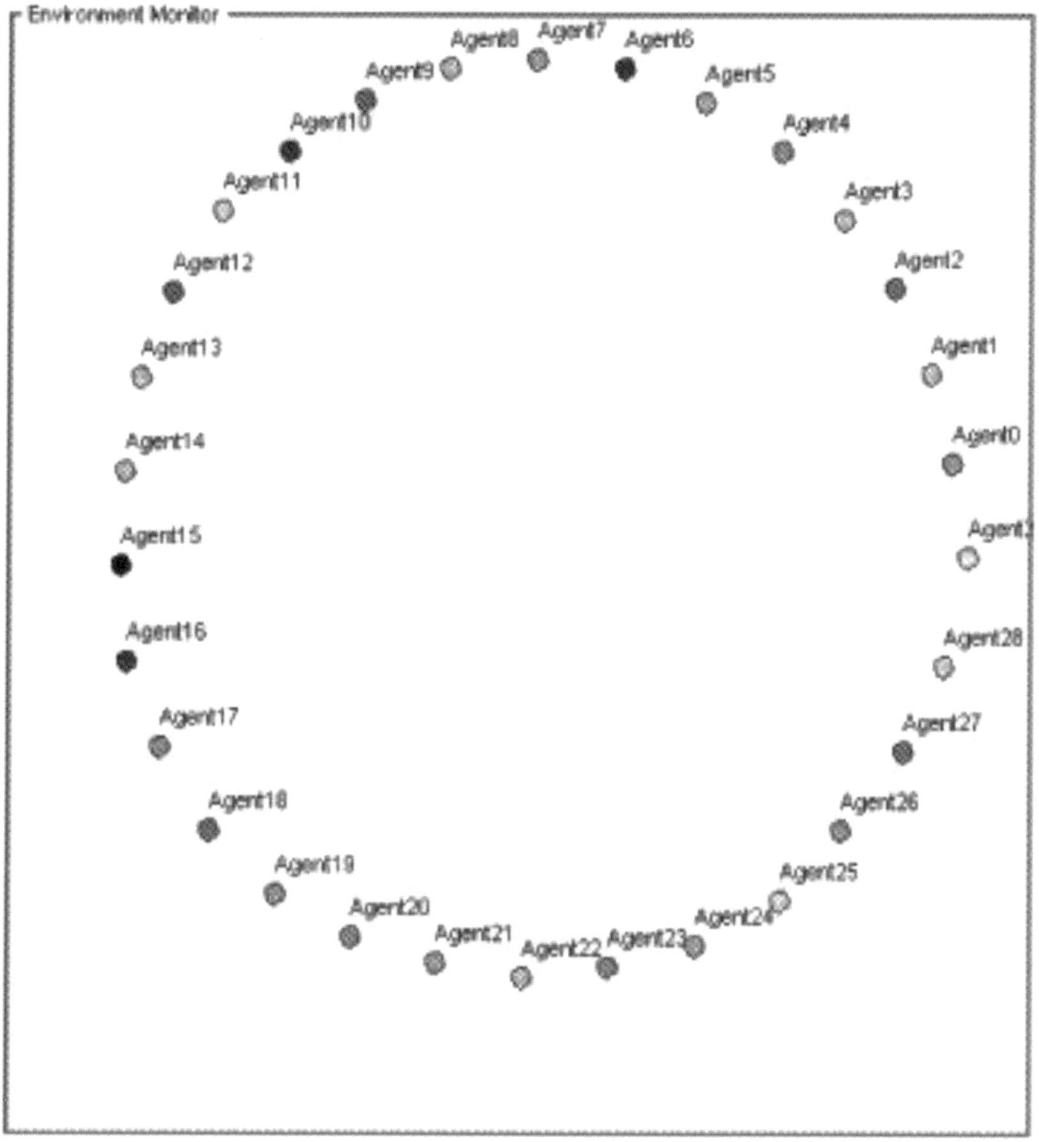

Fig. 6. A normal state of a circle multi-agent system

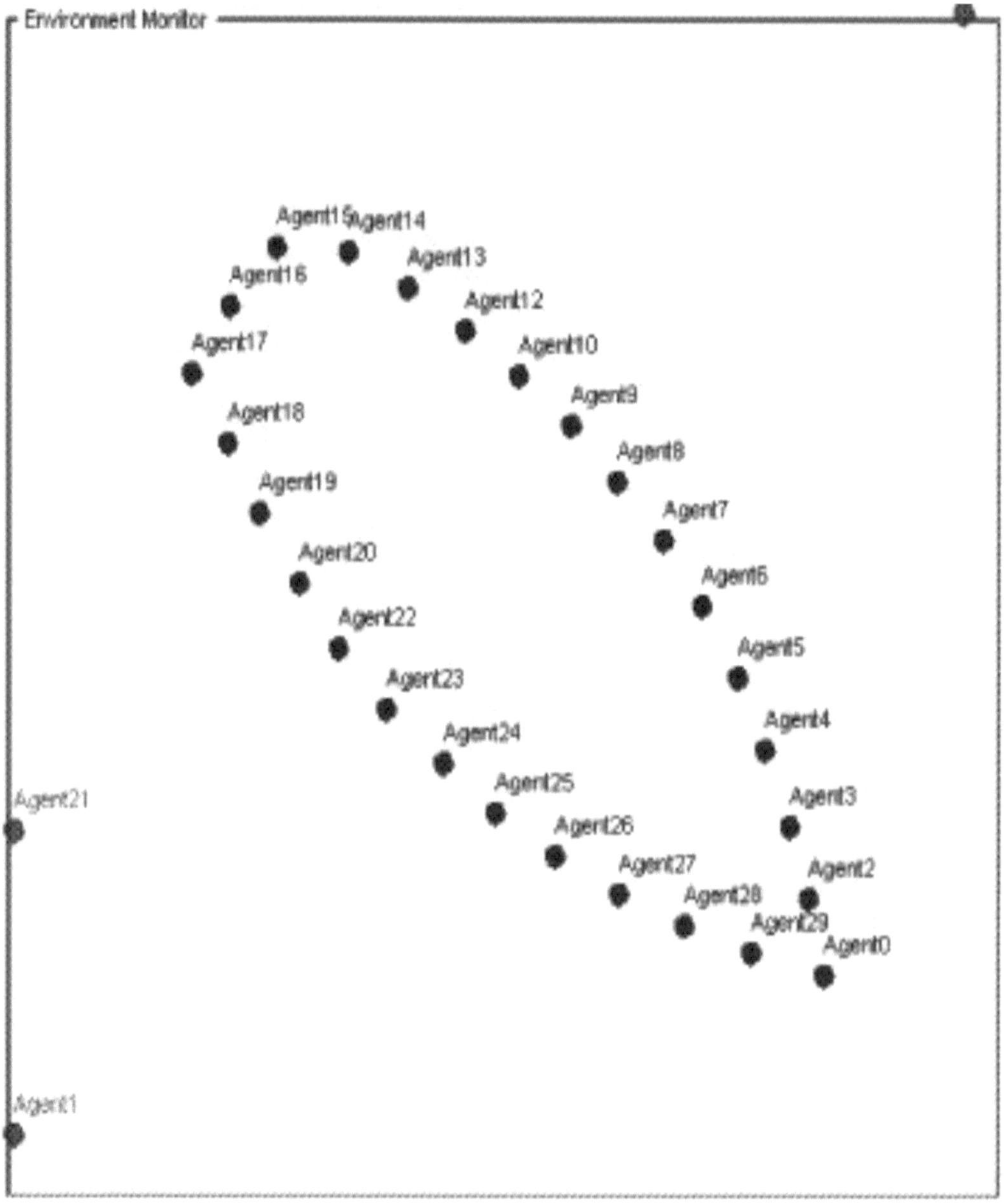

Fig. 7. A state after Byzantine failure

Fig. 8. A state after restoration

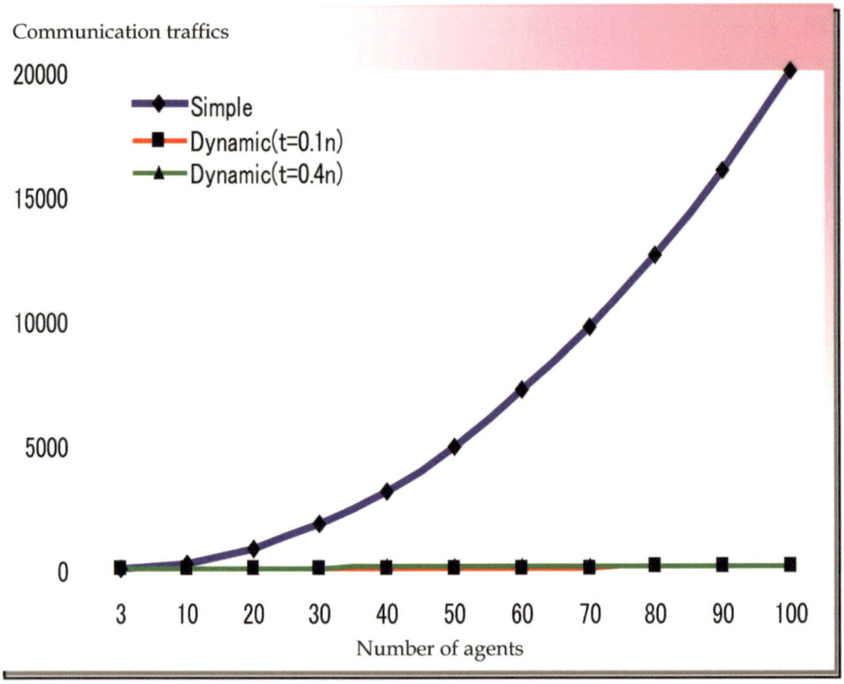

Fig. 9. Communication traffics

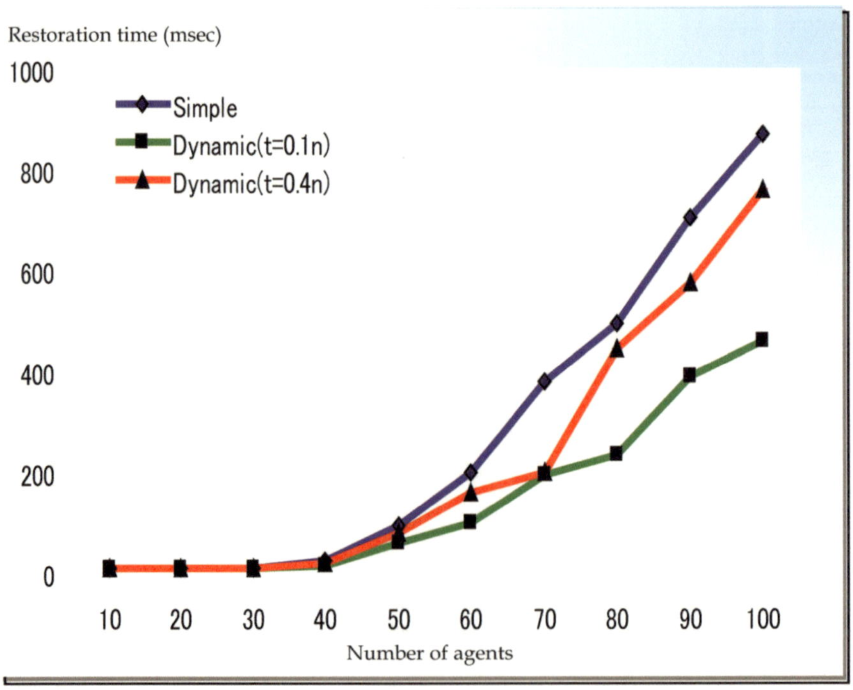

Fig. 10. Restoration time

Fig. 9 proves that the proposed system needs only a few times to communicate while the simple highly structured system remarkably increasing times with the number of agents. It means that mutual tests are carried out in parallel in dynamic highly structured system. Small communication frequencies make the load of the agents reduce.
As for failure processing, we measured the restoration time from occurring of failure to stopping faulty agents. Fig. 10 shows the results. The more faulty agents exist, the longer the restoration time is. The restoration time of the conventional system has exceeded that of the proposed system for both cases of failure rate 10% ($t = 0.1n$) and 40% ($t = 0.4n$). The cause is that the proposed system can be processed in parallel and synchronizing only in each local group.

5. Conclusion

This paper has proposed a self-diagnosable multi-agent system that uses a dynamic highly structured system for fault diagnosis and a restoration system. Some experiments have demonstrated the validity of the proposed system. Future works to be done are as follow: development of a more accurate reconstituting algorithm of basic client agents, a more advanced restoration algorithm, and a reliability improvement method of middle agents.

6. Acknowledgment

This work was partially supported by JSPS KAKENHI 21560430.

7. References

Alur, R.; Thao Dang; Esposito, J.; Yerang Hur; Ivancic, F.; Kumar, V.; Mishra, P.; Pappas, G.J., & Sokolsky, O. (2003). Hierarchical Modeling and Analysis of Embedded Systems, *Proceedings of the IEEE*, Vol.91, No. 1, pp. 11- 28.

Chiang, W. K. & Chen, R. J. (1994). Distributed Fault Tolerant Routing in Kautz Networks, *Journal of Parallel and Distributed Computing*, Vol. 20, No. 1, pp. 99-106.

Fedoruk, A. & Deters, R. (2001). Improving Fault Tolerance by Replicating Agents, *Proceeding of the First International Joint Conference on Autonomous Agents and Multi-Agent Systems*, pp. 737-744, Bologna, Italy.

Hagras, H.; Callaghan, V.; Colley, M. & Clarke, G. (2003). A Hierarchical Fuzzy–Genetic Multi-Agent Architecture for Intelligent Buildings Online Learning, *Adaptation and Control, Information Sciences*, Vol.150, No. 1-2, pp. 33-57.

Hakimi, S. L. & Amin, A. T. (1974). Characterization of Connection Assignment of Diagnosable Systems, *IEEE Transaction on Computers*, Vol.23, No.1, pp. 86-88.

Kohda, T. (1994). A Simple Discriminator for Identifying Faults in Highly Structured Diagnosable Systems, *Journal of Circuits, Systems, and Computers*, Vol. 4, No. 3, pp. 255-277.

Kohda, T.; Yoshida, K.; Sujaku,Y., et al. (1997). Decentralized Self-Diagnosis in Multi-Agent Systems, *Proceeding of the 6th Multi-Agent and Cooperative Computing Workshop*, Kobe, Japan.

Preparata, P.; Metze, G. & Chien, R. T. (1967). On the Connection Assignment Problem of Diagnosable Systems, *IEEE Transaction on Electronic Computers,* Vol. 16, No. 6, pp. 848-854.

Weiss, G. (1999). *Multiagent Systems - A Modern Approach to Distributed Artificial Intelligence,* The MIT Press.

11

Evolution of Adaptive Behavior toward Environmental Change in Multi-Agent Systems

Atsuko Mutoh, Hideki Hashizume, Shohei Kato and Hidenori Itoh
Nagoya Institute of Technology
Japan

1. Introduction

An evolution-based approach to ecological modeling and simulation-based analysis of multiagent behaviors are important means to understand the origin and evolutionary process of a real creature. This is because a simulation enables us to experiment with a virtual world rapidly and repeatedly. However, a real creature is too complex to program on computers. This naturally demands that we grasp the essence of the real creature, simplify it, and program it as an agent (Todd & Wilson, 1993). In this approach, even if an agent that has only a simple mechanism initially, it can evolve and obtain complex behaviors through the process of evolution (Langton, 1986). This kind of synthetic method gives us a possible answer as to why or how the real creature obtains complex behaviors. Many studies have reported on the biology and behavior of real creatures with this approach. For example, from the aspect of animal behaviors, foodforaging (Koza et al., 1992) and herding (Oboshi et al., 2003; Werner & Dyer, 1993) are well-researched. Other examples are studies of specific creatures, such as egrets (Toquenaga et al., 1994), magicicadas (Marco Remondino, 2006), and the monarch butterfly (Hashizume et al., 2008; Sawada et al., 2002; 2004).

The monarch butterfly (*Danaus plexippus L., Nymphalidae, Lepidoptera*) is a good target for study. It has an interesting habit. The monarch butterfly is a migratory butterfly that requires three to five generations per annual migration. We will describe its habit in detail below (The University of Kansas Entomology Program, 2008).

The monarch butterfly mainly lives in North and Central America. As winter ends and spring begins, spring populations of the monarch butterfly in Mexico prepare for migration. And they start to migrate north. The migrating females lay eggs and repeat alternation of generations. In the beginning of summer, they reach the southern part of Canada. Fall populations which are born at the beginning of fall are known to be biologically and behaviorally different from spring populations. Temperature and day length influence their eggs. Fall populations migrate south back to Mexico only one generation. This travel is more than 3500 km. But it takes them only 75 days to travel using air current. It means that the butterfly flies 50 km per day. They return to Mexico again in a single generation. And the monarch butterfly repeats their migration.

The butterfly migrates as described, and its migration is different from that of a bird. We stated before that the monarch butterfly requires three to five generations per annual migration. This means that the migration cannot be taught by parents. Stated differently, genes teach the migration to the butterfly. Many researches and experiments (Alerstam et al., 2003; Etheredge et al., 1999; Perez et al., 1997; Schmidt-Koenig, 1985; Walker, 2001) have been

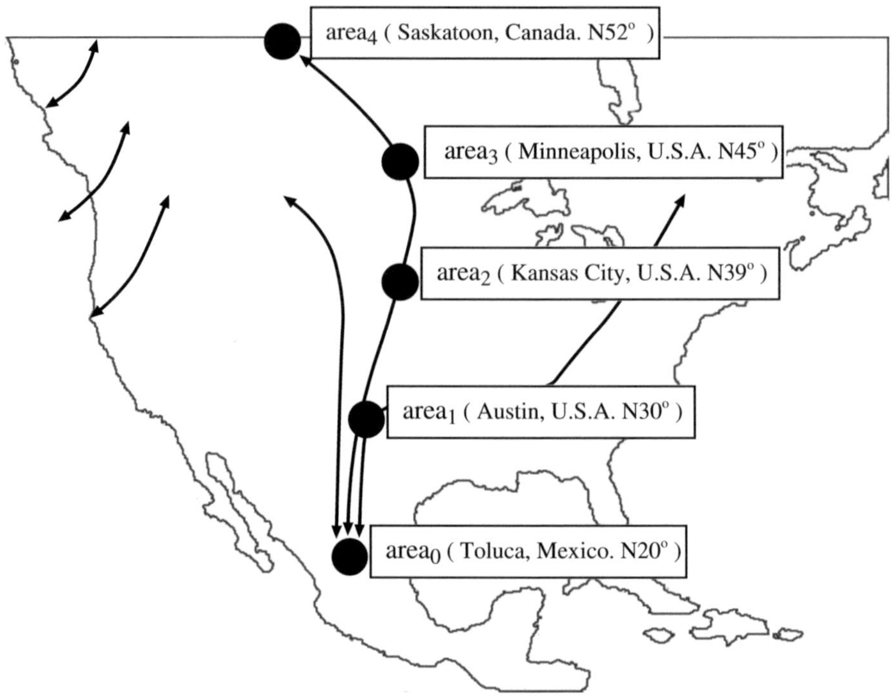

Fig. 1. Spring and fall migrations of the monarch butterfly in North and Central America (revised, from (Brower & Malcolm, 1991)), and 5 areas model

conducted on the proximate factors why the monarch butterfly migrates, and we know that the butterfly migrates by the combination of all the different physiological functions. However, evolutionary factors of its migration have yet to be determined. In other words, we do not know the catalyst for the monarch butterfly to start migration, and it has not been clear what processes the butterfly has gone through until it acquired the current migration style. For answering the question, we frame the hypothesis that environmental change of temperature is a trigger for the butterfly to acquire the migration behavior. It is believed that one of the selection pressures that has driven this species' evolution was the gradual rise in air temperature after the ice age. A non-migratory butterfly had slowly evolved and adapted to the environmental changes and then became a migratory butterfly over time.

In this paper, we model areas from the habitat where the monarch butterfly lives, and design agents based on the monarch butterfly. The agent has genes expressing both physical features and action decision ability. This paper attempts to investigate what adaptive behaviors the agents obtain under the dynamic environment and to assess the validity the model to compare the agent's behavior with the monarch butterfly's behavior.

The paper is organized as follows. Second section gives a definition of the ecosystem consisting of areas, plants, and agents. Third section executes the simulation using the eco-system and describes our observation about the result. Fourth section concludes the paper and lastly gives future extensions.

2. Ecosystem

The ecosystem we designed consists of areas, plants, and agents. Each agent conducts one action per area per day, which we define as unit time. We define one year as a number of fixed days, *DAY*.

2.1 Area

2.1.1 Definition

An area consists of a two-dimensional 50×50 grid of square locations. The ecosystem has five areas. Five areas are $area_0$, $area_1$, ... , $area_4$, located south to north modeled after North and Central America (Fig. 1).
The area has plants, agents, and temperature as an environmental parameter. We express $area_i$ (i : identifier) as

$$area_i(\boldsymbol{Agent_i}, \boldsymbol{Plant_i}, tmpr_i). \tag{1}$$

$\boldsymbol{Agent_i}$ is a set of agents, $\boldsymbol{Plant_i}$ is a set of plants (we will describe the agents and plants later), and $tmpr_i$ is the temperature.

2.1.2 Seasonal temperature change

The temperature, $tmpr_i$, changes periodically for short-term like seasonal change. We call it short-term change. For a short-term change, we use real temperature data from Central and North America. Figure 1 shows the real temperature data, but it is an average of the monthly data. We wanted averaged daily data, so we approximated the real temperature data into an approximate average daily data using a sin function (Figure 2). The temperature: $tmpr_i(d)$ in $area_i$ for day d is determined by

$$tmpr_i(d) = \alpha_i \sin(2\pi d/DAY) + \beta_i, \tag{2}$$

where α_i and β_i are constant numbers in each area.

2.1.3 Air current

The ecosystem has an air current from $area_4$ to $area_0$. The air current helps the agent which moves in the same direction[1]. Hence, if the agent starts migration south from $area_1$, $area_2$, $area_3$, or $area_4$, the agent can directory land on $area_0$ (we will see the agent and its actions later).

2.2 Plant

2.2.1 Definition

A plant p_j (j : identifier) is expressed by

$$p_j(age_j), \tag{3}$$

where age_j is the number of days for which the plant has existed. The plant is the energy source for the agent.

---

[1] Fall populations of the monarch butterfly are said to glide and be carried by an air current during fall migrations(Gibo & Pallett, 1979).

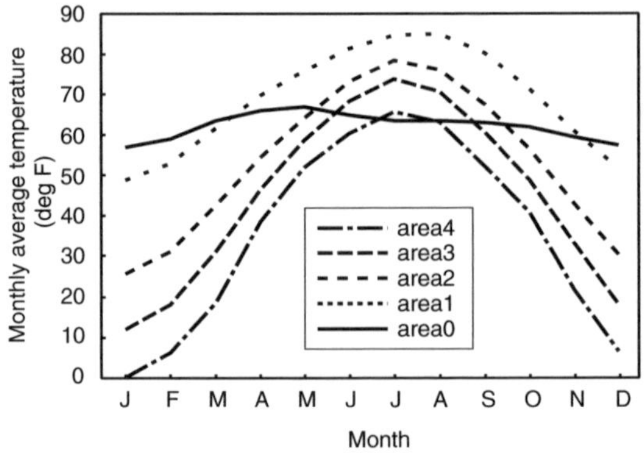

Fig. 2. Real temperature data (National Oceanic and Atmospheric Administration, 2008).

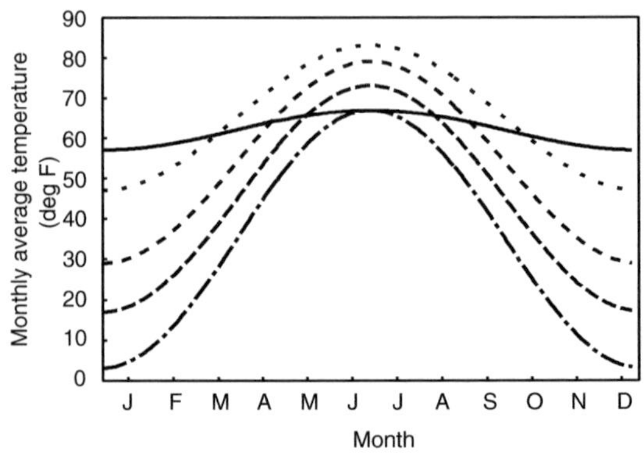

Fig. 3. Approximate temperature data.

2.2.2 Appearance & Disapperance

The birth number of plants: N_i^{plant} in $area_i$ is determined by

$$N_i^{plant} = M_i^{plant} \times (1 - \Delta suit\_tmpr^{plant} / S_t), \tag{4}$$

$$\Delta suit\_tmpr^{plant} = |tmpr_i(d) - suit\_tmpr^{plant}|, \tag{5}$$

where M_i^{plant} is the maximum birth number of plants in $area_i$ in one day, S_t is a constant, and $suit\_tmpr^{plant}$ is the most suitable temperature for the plant. As you know from Eq 4, the temperature in the focused area determines the birth number of plants. In our simulation the upper limit of the birth number in each area is different. The birth number in $area_0$ is smaller than the others [2]. After the birth number is determined, each plant is set in a random grid.

[2] It is because the shortage of food or milkweed in the southern area is thought to have caused the migration of the Monarch butterfly.

If the plant suffers either of the following conditions, it is removed from the simulation. T_d^{plant} is the maximum lifetime of plants.

$$\text{"}An\ agent\ eats\ the\ plant\text{"} \quad \text{or} \quad age_j > T_d^{plant} \tag{6}$$

2.3 Agent

2.3.1 Definition

Agent a_j (j is identifier) is expressed by

$$a_j((ea_j, st\_table_j), (age_j, in_j)), \tag{7}$$

where ea_j is the environmental adaptation scale, st_table_j is the action decision table, age_j is the number of days the agent has existed, and in_j is the energy level.
The first two elements, ea_j and st_table_j, are inherited. It should be noted that ea_j and st_table_j are encoded into different genes. However, the last two elements, age_j and in_j, are not inherited. age_j and in_j are initialized when the agent is born.

2.3.2 Environmental adaptation scale

The environmental adaptation scale (EA), ea_j is an integer fulfilling $0 \leq ea_j \leq M_{ea}$ where M_{ea} is the maximum number of EA. ea_j is calculated by

$$ea_j = \text{count}(bitset_{ea_j}), \tag{8}$$

where $bitset_{ea_j}$ is an array of bits representing the EA, and count is the function that returns the number of bits that are set to 1 in the array. We use the EA to represent the physical features of the agent, for example, "thickness of the exoskeleton." In other words, if the EA is large, it means that the agent can stand a large temperature variation, and it also means that the agent is heavy and spends a lot of energy for actions. If the EA is small, it conversely means that the agent cannot stand a large temperature variation and nevertheless the agent is light.
We use the EA to implement for the agent a sensory system that enables it to feel temperature.

2.3.3 Sense

Agent, a_j, senses the information shown in Table 1. The information is about the internal information of its own energy level, in_j, and about external information, ex_j. The internal information is on whether the agent has the energy level in the condition of "$in_j > I_e$." I_e is a certain energy level. The external information is on "finding plants?", "finding other agents?", and "how does the agent feel about the temperature?"
To sense all of this information, the agent has visibility around constant grids to find other agents and plants and has a temperature sensor. Therefore, the agent can feel whether $tmpr$ is "hot," "cold," or "suitable." To implement this sensor, the agent has a range of temperatures named $suit\_tmpr_j$[3] given by

$$S_b - K_s \times \frac{ea_j}{M_{ea}} \leq suit\_tmpr_j \leq S_b + K_s \times \frac{ea_j}{M_{ea}}, \tag{9}$$

where S_b and K_s are constant values to construct $suit\_tmpr_j$. If $tmpr$ is within the range of $suit\_tmpr_j$, the agent feels the area is "Suitable." If $tmpr$ exceeds the maximum temperature

[3] $suit\_tmpr_j$ takes the value within a certain finite range because ea_j is also finite. Therefore, the agent cannot have a perfect $suit\_tmpr_j$ that covers all temperatures.

of $suit\_tmpr_j$, it feels the area is "Hot." Also, if $tmpr$ is below the minimum temperature of $suit\_tmpr_j$, it feels the area is "Cold."

2.3.4 Action

Five actions ($\in ACT$: Table 2): "eat", "reproduce", "migrate north", "migrate south", and "do-nothing" can be performed by the agent. We explain them below.
The first action is "eat." The agent can eat a plant to absorb energy if the agent is next to the plant. Otherwise, if the agent finds a plant within its range of vision, it moves toward the plant. We categorize this action as "eat." Incidentally, if the agent cannot find any plants, the agent changes the action from "eat" to "do-nothing" (we will see "do-nothing" later.).
The second action is "reproduce." The agent can make an offspring if it is next to another agent (we will also see the reproduction process later.). Otherwise, if the agent finds another agent within its range of vision, the agent moves toward it. We categorize this action as "reproduce." If the agent cannot find any agents, the agent changes the action from "reproduce" to "do-nothing."
The third action is "migrate north." When the agent selects the "migrate north" action, the agent migrates to the northern areas. If the agent is in $area_i$, it migrates to $area_{i+1}$. Note that the agent in $area_4$ cannot migrate northward. Hence, in this case the agent changes the action from "migrate north" to "do-nothing."
The forth action is "migrate south." "migrate south" is almost the same as "migrate north" except for the direction. When the agent selects the "migrate south" action, the agent migrates to the southern areas. If the agent is in $area_i$, it migrates to $area_0$. Note that the agent in $area_0$ cannot migrate southward. The action is changed from "migrate south" to "do-nothing."
The fifth action is "do-nothing." The agent which selects "do-nothing" does not move and stays the same grid for one day. We allow the agent to select "do-nothing." In addition to this, if the agent fails in the previous four actions, the agent must perform "do-nothing."

Info	Statement	Decision
in_j	Enough energy?	X_0 = Yes/No
ex_j	Find plants?	X_1 = Yes/No
	Find other agents?	X_2 = Yes/No
	Temperature?	X_3 = Hot/Cold/Suitable

Table 1. Sensory information.

Action	(Abbr.)	Detail
eat	(E)	Eat a plant or approach it
reproduce	(R)	Reproduce a new agent or approach another agent
migrate north	(Mn)	Migrate to northern area
migrate south	(Ms)	Migrate to southern area
do-nothing	(N)	Do not move

Table 2. A set of ACT.

2.3.5 Action decision table

The agent, a_j, decides which action, act, performs by

$$act = st\_table_j(X_0, X_1, X_2, X_3), \tag{10}$$

where st_table_j is the action decision table, and $X\_$ is a sensory information. st_table_j combines a condition alternative table with an action table. The former table is a common table for all agents and it has 24 columns. Conversely, each agent does not have the same action table, because the table is expressed by gene. st_table_j has four entries. As you see from Table 1, $X\_$ has a decision for each statement. A set of $X\_$ determines agent's action. Table 3 provides a concrete example of the action decision table.

		1	2	3	4	5	···	24
Sensory Information	X_0	Y	Y	Y	Y	Y	···	N
	X_1	Y	Y	Y	Y	Y	···	N
	X_2	Y	Y	Y	N	N	···	N
	X_3	H	C	S	H	C	···	S
Actions	E				√		···	
	R			√			···	
	Mn	√					···	
	Ms		√				···	
	N					√	···	√

Table 3. An example of action decision table. The agent performs a checked action corresponding with a set of alternatives of sensory information. Key: Y=Yes, N=No, H=Hot, C=Cold, S=Suitable.

2.3.6 Energy level update

After the action, the energy level is updated by

$$in_j \leftarrow in_j + \mathrm{f}(act, ea_j, suit\_diff), \tag{11}$$

where function f is the update function of the energy level. $suit\_diff$ is the difference in temperature between $tmpr$ and the edge of $suit\_tmpr_j$ is given by

$$suit\_diff = \begin{cases} tmpr - \max(suit\_tmpr_j), & \text{"Hot"} \\ \min(suit\_tmpr_j) - tmpr, & \text{"Cold"} \\ 0, \quad \text{"Suitable"} \end{cases}, \tag{12}$$

where function max returns the maximum temperature within the range of $suit\_tmpr_j$, and function min returns the minimum temperature within the range of $suit\_tmpr_j$. If the agent with ea_j performs act in the condition of $suit\_diff$, the function outputs the amount of change in the energy level. We later explain in detail which action increases and decreases the energy level.

We categorize the actions into three groups according to the way of decreasing the energy, (a) decreasing in a certain amount of energy: "reproduce" provided that the agent succeeds in making its offspring, (b) decreasing in proportion to ea_j: "migrate north/south", and (c) decreasing in proportion to $suit\_diff$: moving by "eat", moving by "reproduce", or "do-nothing" actions.

However, the only one action that the agent can actually increase its energy level is to perform "eat" action when it encounters a plant.

Symbol	Value	Description
$DAY(1year)$	300	Number of days of 1 year.
SW	10	Amplitude of the temperature caused by short-term change.
$av\_tmpr_i(0)$	10,20,30,40,50	Average yearly temperature in year 0.
M_{ea}	30	Maximum number of EA.
I_e	100	Threshold in which an agent senses it has enough energy.
S_b	50	Constant value to construct $suit\_tmpr_j$.
K_s	15	Constant value to determine the width of $suit\_tmpr_j$.
I_f	100	Energy level which a newborn agent has.
T_D	100	Agent's maximum lifetime.

Table 4. Parameters Setting.

2.3.7 Reproduction

Two agents, a_{p1}, a_{p2}, reproduce and leave offspring agent, a_j, with

$$a_j((ea_j, st\_table_j), (age_j, in_j)), \tag{13}$$

$$\begin{aligned} ea_j &= \mathrm{mu}_{\mathrm{ea}}(\mathrm{cr}_{\mathrm{ea}}(ea_{p1}, ea_{p2})), \\ st\_table_j &= \mathrm{mu}_{\mathrm{st}}(\mathrm{cr}_{\mathrm{st}}(st\_table_{p1}, st\_table_{p2})), \\ age_j &= 0, \\ in_j &= I_f, \end{aligned}$$

where $\mathrm{cr}_{\mathrm{ea}}$ and $\mathrm{cr}_{\mathrm{st}}$ are the crossover functions for $ea\_$ and $st\_table\_$, respectively. $\mathrm{mu}_{\mathrm{ea}}$ and $\mathrm{mu}_{\mathrm{st}}$ are the mutation functions for $ea\_$ and $st\_table\_$, respectively. Note that age_j is initialized by 0, and that in_j is also initialized by I_f which is the initial energy level.
We detail each function. $\mathrm{cr}_{\mathrm{ea}}$ is the function which cross over parent agent's environmental adaptation scales. This function performs uniform crossover for $bitset_{ea\_}$. Meanwhile, $\mathrm{cr}_{\mathrm{st}}$ performs one-point crossover for action table. $\mathrm{mu}_{\mathrm{ea}}$ and $\mathrm{mu}_{\mathrm{st}}$ give mutation to each element to increase biological diversity. $\mathrm{mu}_{\mathrm{ea}}$ makes one of the bits in $bitset_{ea\_}$ flipped. $a\mathrm{mu}_{\mathrm{st}}$ changes one of the columns into the others.

2.3.8 Death

cIf the agent suffers either of the following conditions, it dies and is removed from the simulation.

$$in_j < 0, \tag{14}$$

$$age_j > T_D, \tag{15}$$

where T_D is the maximum lifetime. The first condition is "starvation," and the second is "death because of old age."

3. Experiment

In this section, we present the details of an experiment carried out using our defined ecosystem. The purpose of this experiment is to observe how the agents evolve and what adaptive behaviors the agents obtain in an environment that has short-term change and is locally bias of food distribution. The parameter setting is listed in Table 4.

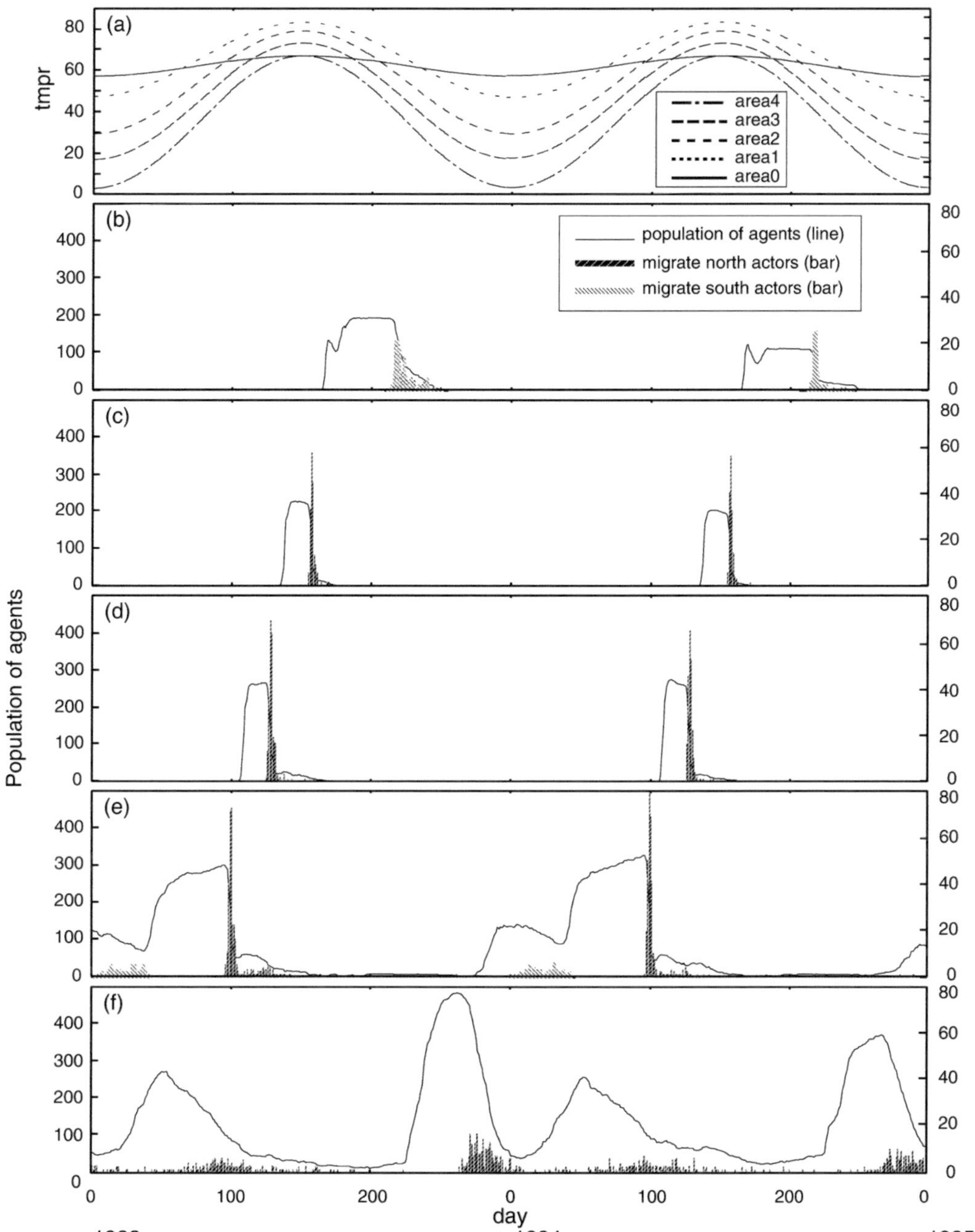

Fig. 4. (a) Temperature for 2 years. (b) Population of agents and number of migrate actors which behave "migrate north/south" in $area_4$. (c) is in $area_3$. (d) is in $area_2$. (e) is in $area_1$. (f) is in $area_0$.

The results are shown in Figure 4. We executed a simulation using our defined ecosystem for a period of 2000 years. It is difficult to describe all the results for the entire period. So in Figure 4, we extracted 2 years from the 2000 years, and now are providing a detailed analysis. Figures 4(b)-(f) show the population changes and the number of migrate actors. As is evident from these figures, the agents obtained three emergent behaviors and adapted to the environment.

3.1 Stay in $area_0$

Figure 4(f) shows that some agents stayed in $area_0$ throughout the year. This means that a certain number of agents did not move to other areas, but remained in $area_0$. From the aspect of temperature, $area_0$ is the most suitable area. However, $area_0$ had a food shortage problem. So, other behaviors were observed.

3.2 Migration between $area_0$ and $area_1$

We focus on Figures 4(e) and (f) in this subsection. We confirmed the agents moved to $area_1$ from $area_0$ by selecting the "migrate north" action between year 1983 day 260 and year 1984 day 10. Then, between year 1984 day 0 and year 1984 day 40, some agents selected and executed a "migrate south" action and went back to $area_0$. These agents migrated between $area_0$ and $area_1$ for only 40-80 days. We can easily assume one reason for the agents to behave like this, a food shortage problem in $area_0$. Around year 1983 day 270, $area_0$ held the biggest number of agents. This caused a food shortage. The number of plants in $area_0$ decreased to 9 (in this 2 year period, the maximum number of plants in $area_0$ was 93.). When $area_0$ reached this condition, the agents selected to go to $area_1$. Stated another way, the action decision table of the agents evolved to selecting "migrate north" when the agent could not find any plants. However, it was not necessarily the best behavior from the aspect of temperature. The movement north around year 1983 day 260 - year 1984 day 10 meant that the agent left the most suitable area based on temperature. $area_1$ was a little colder at this time. Therefore, the agents soon returned to $area_0$.

3.3 Migration between $area_0$ and $area_4$

As in Figures 4(b) - (f), this migration behavior can be confirmed. First, we talk about the northward migration. A small number of the agents moved to $area_1$ from $area_0$ between year 1983 day 260 and year 1984 day 10. The number of agents in $area_1$ increased and around year 1984 day 100 moved to $area_2$. Moving to $area_3$ from $area_2$ was around year 1984 day 130, and moving to $area_4$ from $area_3$ was around year 1984 day 160. The agents stayed in $area_4$ for 60 days and then started back to $area_0$. This was around year 1984 day 220. As stated above, the agents established a migration behavior between $area_0$ and $area_4$. The reason why the agents migrated over the areas is attributed to the agents' adaptation to both short-term change and a food shortage.

3.4 Patterns of cross-generational migration

We have other results that helped us determine when the migration began and how many agents migrated. Before showing these results we will define the four migration behaviors that our ecosystem can achieve: migration between $area_0$ and $area_1$, migration between $area_0$ and $area_2$, migration between $area_0$ and $area_3$, and migration between $area_0$ and $area_4$. Figure 5 presents the results. It shows the development of migratory agents for a 2000 year period. Each migratory agent increased year by year. At the end of the experiment, all migration behaviors became apparent. Fig. 6 shows the more detail description of migration between $area_0$ and $area_3$ and between $area_0$ and $area_4$ in year 2000. We add some analysis to the

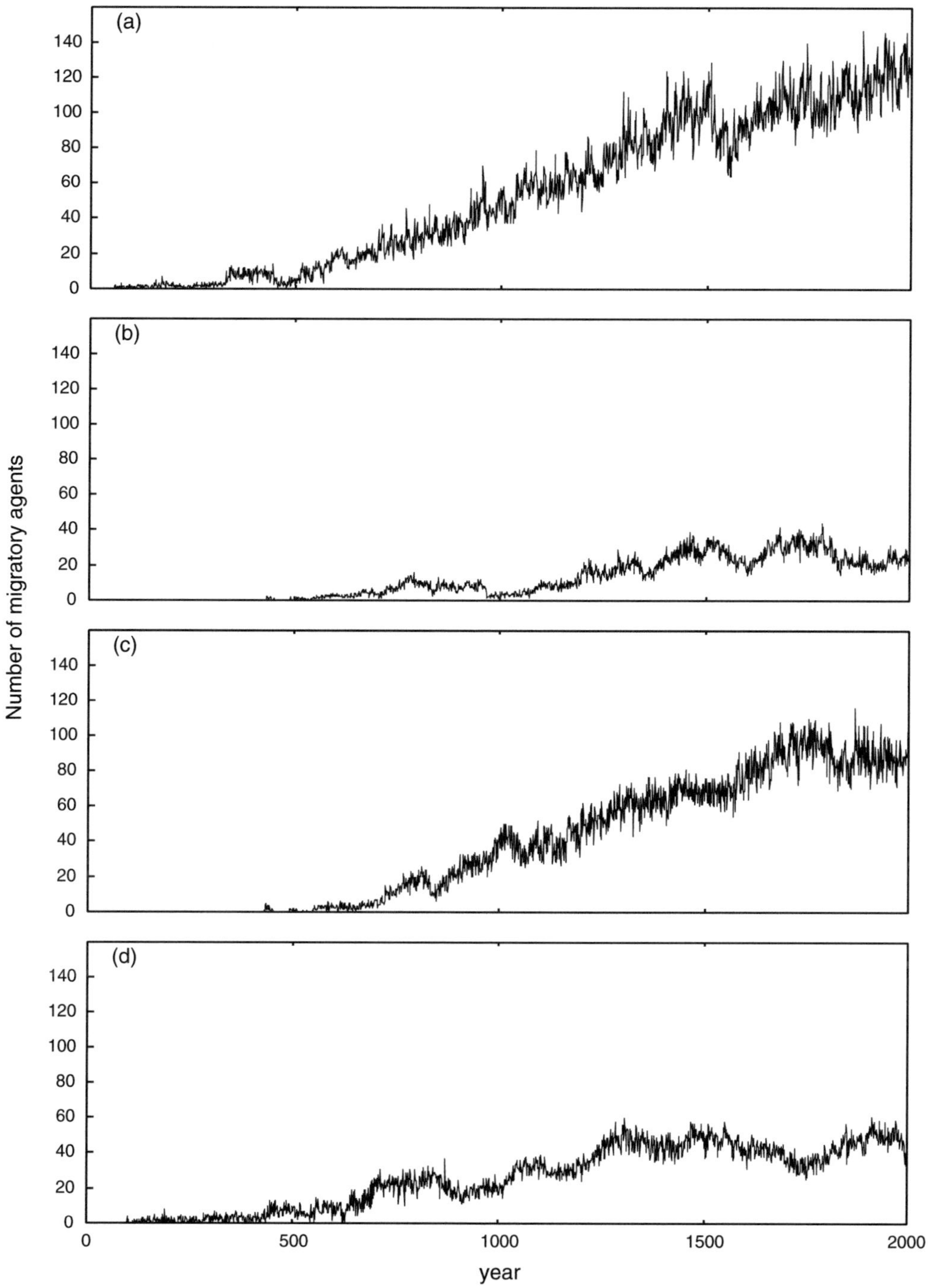

Fig. 5. (a) Number of migratory agents between $area_0$ and $area_1$. (b) is between $area_0$ and $area_2$, (c) is between $area_0$ and $area_3$, (d) is between $area_0$ and $area4$. All points are average of 50 trials.

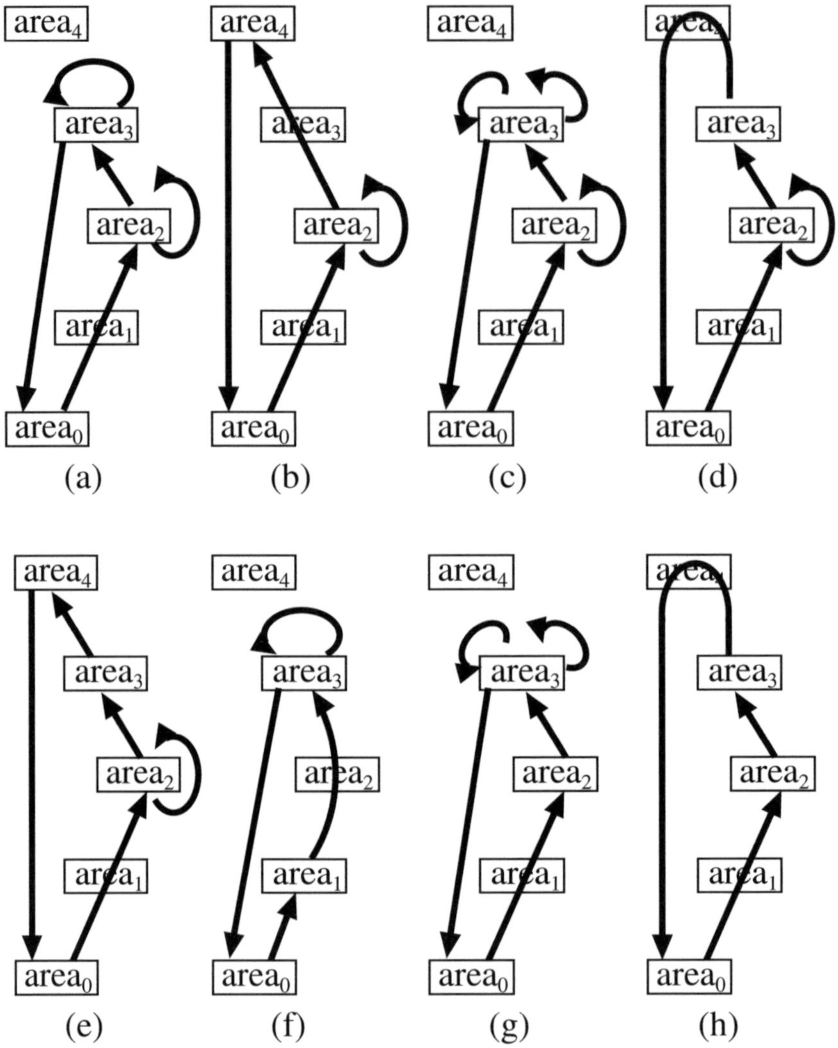

Fig. 6. Patterns of cross-generational migration in year 2000. One arrow is the length that one agent moves for its life. For example, migration of (a) takes five generations per annual migration. Each percentage of total is followings: (a) 25.8%, (b) 14.9%, (c) 11.6%, (d) 11.5%, (e) 8.4%, (f) 6.0%, (g) 5.0%, and (h) 4.0%.

figure. From the figure, we can understand how far one agent moved and where the agent reproduced. One line is the route which the agent moved for its life. We focus on Fig. 6 (a) as an instance. This migration took 5 generations per annual migration. The first generation was born in $area_0$ and it moved to $area_2$ through $area_1$ and then this generation made its offspring in $area_2$. The second generation did not move over areas but stayed in $area_2$ and it made the third generation. The third generation left for $area_3$ and made the forth generation. The forth generation stayed in $area_3$. The fifth generation moved back to $area_0$ from $area_3$. This is the detail analysis for Fig. 6 (a). And we focus on the common phenomenon in Fig. 6. The behavior until the second generation was quite same. The first generation moved to $area_2$

from $area_0$ through $area_1$ and the second generation stayed in $area_2$ and it made offspring there. The possible reason of this phenomenon is the temperature in $area_0$ and $area_1$. At this time (year 2000), the temperature in $area_0$ and $area_1$ were so high that it was not suitable for many agents to behave "reproduce" action because it needed a lot of energy. So many agents moved to $area_2$ at a first move and executed "reproduce" action.
It is difficult for us to compare the result with the monarch butterfly's migration. Because no one knows the precise migration patterns when and where the monarch butterfly alternates its generation. However, from the aspect which the monarch butterfly takes some generations per annual migration, the simulation gave us the same emergent behaviors.

4. Conclusion

In this paper, an artificial ecosystem for migratory agents was described. Firstly, we constructed an ecosystem consisting of five areas, plants and agents. Each area has two kinds of dynamic changes in temperatures: long-term and short-term changes. Each agent living in the area has two genetic components: an environmental adaptation scale and an action decision table. The environmental adaptation scale enables the agents to have a temperature sensor. Secondly, we conducted the experiment with this ecosystem. The result showed that the agents obtained migration behavior similar to that of the monarch butterfly.
In this paper, it is particularly worth noting that we tried to realize a real creature on the computer with as simple mechanisms as possible. On the environment we focused on only temperature from an endless number of environmental parameters. Also on the monarch butterfly, we focused on only two elements from various kinds of parameters such as physical features, sensors, and so on. This policy relates to the policy which we stated in introduction.
For future works, firstly, the research is needed additional experiment. We confirmed that the agents acquired migration behavior under our proposed model. To construct the model, we defined four elements: short-term change and long-term change for dynamic environment, and environmental adaptation scale and action decision table for agents. We need additional experiment to understand which elements are indispensable. Secondly, we need more rigorous evaluation of the stability of migration behavior. In case of many times migrations by one agent, we can determine that the agent behaves stably and adaptively to the environment. However, if the migration takes some generations like our simulation, we cannot clearly state whether the agents are always stable. Lotka-Volterra (Lotka, 1925; Volterra, 1928) equation modeling the relationship between predator and prey is famous and it can provide rigorous evaluation of balance of the relationship. Our model and results of experiment also need this kind of mathematical evaluation.

5. References

Alerstam, T., Hedenstrom, A. & Akesson, S. (2003). Long-distance migration: evolution and determinants, *Oikos* 103(2): 247–260.

Brower, L. & Malcolm, S. (1991). Animal Migrations: Endangered Phenomena 1, *Integrative and Comparative Biology* 31(1): 265–276.

Etheredge, J. A., Perez, S. M., Taylor, O. R. & Jander, R. (1999). Monarch butterflies (danaus plexippus l.) use a magnetic compass for navigation, *Proceedings of the National Academy of Sciences of the United States of America* 96(24): 13845–13846.

Gibo, D. L. & Pallett, M. J. (1979). Soaring flight of monarch butterflies, danaus plexippus (lepidoptera: Danaidae) during the late summer migration in southern ontario, *Canadian Journal of Zoology* 57(7): 1393–1401.

Hashizume, H., Mutoh, A., Kato, S., Itoh, H. & Kunitachi, T. (2008). Multi-agent simulations of adaptive behavior with temperature-sensing agents, *IEEE SMC International Conference on Distributed Human-Machine Systems* pp. 109–114.

Koza, J. R., Roughgarden, J. & Rice, J. P. (1992). Evolution of food-foraging strategies for the caribbean anolis lizard using genetic programming, *Adaptive Behavior* 1(2): 171–199.

Langton, C. G. (1986). Studying artificial life with cellular automata, *Physica. D* 2: 135–149.

Lotka, A. J. (1925). *Elements of Physical Biology*, Williams.

Marco Remondino, A. C. (2006). An evolutionary selection model based on a biological phenomenon: The periodical magicicadas, *From Animals to Animats 9, Lecture Notes in Computer Science* 4095: 485–497.

National Oceanic and Atmospheric Administration (2008). National Weather Service, *http://www.nws.noaa.gov/* .

Oboshi, T., Kato, S., Mutoh, A. & Itoh, H. (2003). Collective or scattering: Evolving schooling behaviors to escape from predator, *Proceedings of the 8th International Conference on the Simulation and Synthesis of Living Systems: Artificial Life VIII* pp. 386–389.

Perez, S., Taylor, O. & Jander, R. (1997). A sun compass in monarch butterflies, *Nature* 387(6628): 29–29.

Sawada, T., Mutoh, A., Kato, S. & Itoh, H. (2002). A model of biological differentiation in adaptiogenesis to the environment, *Proceedings of the 8th International Conference on the Simulation and Synthesis of Living Systems: Artificial Life VIII* pp. 93–96.

Sawada, T., Mutoh, A., Kato, S. & Itoh, H. (2004). A model of artificial life adapting to the global environmental chnage and its analysis, *The 18th Annual Conference of Japanese Society for Artificial Intelligence* .

Schmidt-Koenig, K. (1985). Migration strategies of monarch butterflies., *Contributions in Marine Science[CONTRIB. MAR. SCI.].* 68.

The University of Kansas Entomology Program (2008). Monarch watch, *http://monarchwatch.org/* .

Todd, P. & Wilson, S. (1993). Environment structure and adaptive behavior from the ground up, *From Animals to Animats 2: Proceedings of the 2nd International Conference on Simulation of Adaptive Behavior* pp. 11–20.

Toquenaga, Y., Kajitani, I. & Hoshino, T. (1994). Egrets of a feather flock together, *Proceedings of the 4th International Workshop on the Synthesis and Simulation of Living Systems: Artificial Life IV* 1(4): 391–411.

Volterra, V. (1928). Variations and fluctuations of the number of individuals in animal species living together, *ICES Journal of Marine Science* 3(1): 3–51.

Walker, T. J. (2001). Butterfly migrations in florida: Seasonal patterns and long-term changes, *Environmental Entomology* 30(6): 1052–1060.

Werner, G. M. & Dyer, M. G. (1993). Evolution of herding behavior in artificial animals, *From Animals to Animats 2: Proceedings of the 2nd International Conference on Simulation of Adaptive Behavior* pp. 393–399.

12

Evolutionary Adaptive Behavior in Noisy Multi-Agent System

Takamasa Iio, Ivan Tanev, Katsunori Shimohara and Mitsunori Miki
Doshisha University
Japan

1. Introduction

Multi-agent systems have become more and more important in many aspects of computer science such as distributed artificial intelligence, distributed computing systems, robotics, artificial life, etc. Based on the belief that any complex system is more than the sum of its individual elements (Holand, 1999, Morgan, 1923, Morowitz, 2002), multi-agent systems introduce the issue of the emergence of behavior through interactions between agents (Forrest, 1991). Accordingly, a coordinated behavior needed to archive complex tasks might emerge in multi-agent systems from relatively simple defined interactions between agents. An agent is a virtual entity that can act, perceive the proximity of its environment and communicate with others; it is autonomous and has the ability to achieve its goals. Multi-agent systems contain a world (environment), entities (agents), relations between the entities, a way the world is perceived by the entities, a set of operations that can be performed by the entities and changes in the world as a result of these actions.

The main application areas of multi-agent systems are problem solving, simulation, collective robotics, software engineering, and construction of synthetic worlds (Ferber, 1999). Considering the latter application area and focusing on the autonomy of agents and the interactions that link them together (Parunak, Van, Brueckner, Fleischer & Odell, 2002), the following important issues can be raised: What is the minimum amount of perception information needed by agents in order to perceive the world? How can agents cooperate? What are the methods, and what are the lower bounds of communications, required for them to coordinate their actions? What architecture should they feature so that they can achieve their goals? What approaches can be applied to automatically construct their functionality, with the quality of such a design being competitive with human-handcrafted design? These issues are of special interest, since the aim is to create multi-agent systems, which are scalable, robust, flexible, and able to adapt to changes automatically. These features of multi-agent systems are believed to be particularly important in real world applications where the approaches to construct synthetic worlds can be viewed as practical methods, techniques towards creating complex "situation-aware" multi-computer, multi-vehicle, or multi-robot systems based on the concepts of agents, communication, cooperation and coordination of actions.

The purpose of our research is an automatic design of the coordinated behavior among agents. Particularly, we are interested in the robustness of the coordinated behavior to some uncertainty derived from a mechanical or electrical noise of real-world applications. In this document we intend to highlight the following issues:

- Applying the genetic programming paradigm for evolving the coordinated behavior among agents, which interact with each other according to implicit interaction in an ideal noiseless environment,
- Testing the capability of the above behavior in a noisy environment, and
- Evolving the behavior again in two different environments; noiseless environment and noisy environment, for a comparative investigation of the robustness of the two types of evolved behavior.

We employ the predator prey pursuit problem (Benda, 1986) to verify the hypothesis of emergence of surrounding behavior in multi-agent systems from simply defined interactions between the agents. The noisy environment is implemented as the perceptual noise of predator agents; that is to say, in noisy environment the predator agents get uncertain perception information with some noise.

The remaining of the document is organized as follows. Section 2 introduces an instance of the general, well defined yet difficult to solve predator-prey pursuit problem as the task which we use in this work. Section 3 elaborates on the strongly typed genetic programming, employed as an algorithmic paradigm to evolve the functionality of agents. Section 4 explains the model of the perceptual noise of the predator agents. In Section 5, the comparative empirical results of evolution of surrounding behavior in a noiseless environment, execution of the surrounding behavior in a noisy environment and re-evolution of the surrounding behavior in each of the noiseless and the noisy environment are presented. Our conclusions are drawn in Section 6.

2. Configuration of a multi-agent system

2.1 Instance of Predator prey pursuit problem

In order to investigate relationships between a coordinated behavior among agents and uncertainty of their perception, we address predator prey pursuit problem (Benda, 1986), which is a game that some predator agents chase and catch a prey agent on a two dimensional field. The problem is general, well-defined and well-studied in multi-agent systems yet difficult to solve because the predator agents cannot capture the prey agent without a harmonious teamwork.

In our work, there are four predator agents and a prey agent on a two dimensional torus field. Considering a more realistic instance of the problem than the previous works (Haynes & Sen, 1996, Haynes, Wainwright, Sen & Schoenefeld, 1997, Luke & Spector, 1996), the field is a simulated continuous torus instead of coarse grid. The snapshot of our software is shown in Figure 1. All agents have moving and perceptual abilities. Their moving abilities are also continuous; they can turn to any angle from their current heading and can run with speed equal to 0, 0.25, 0.5, 0.75 and 1.0 of their maximum speed. We introduce a proximity perception model in that the predator agents can see the prey agent and only the closest predator agent, only when these agents are within the limited range of visibility of their simulated sensors. The prey employs random wandering if there is no predator in sight and an a priori handcrafted optimal escaping strategy as soon as predator(s) become "visible." In order to make a situation where the predator agents cannot capture the prey unless they collaborate with each other, we made the maximum speed of the predator agents lower than

that of the prey agent but the range of visibility of the predator agents wider than that of the prey to allow the predators to stalk the prey.
The situation requires a relatively complex behavior that the predator agents surround the prey agent on all sides in the world, and the behavior should be emerged from simple, local, implicit and proximity-defined interactions between the predator agents.

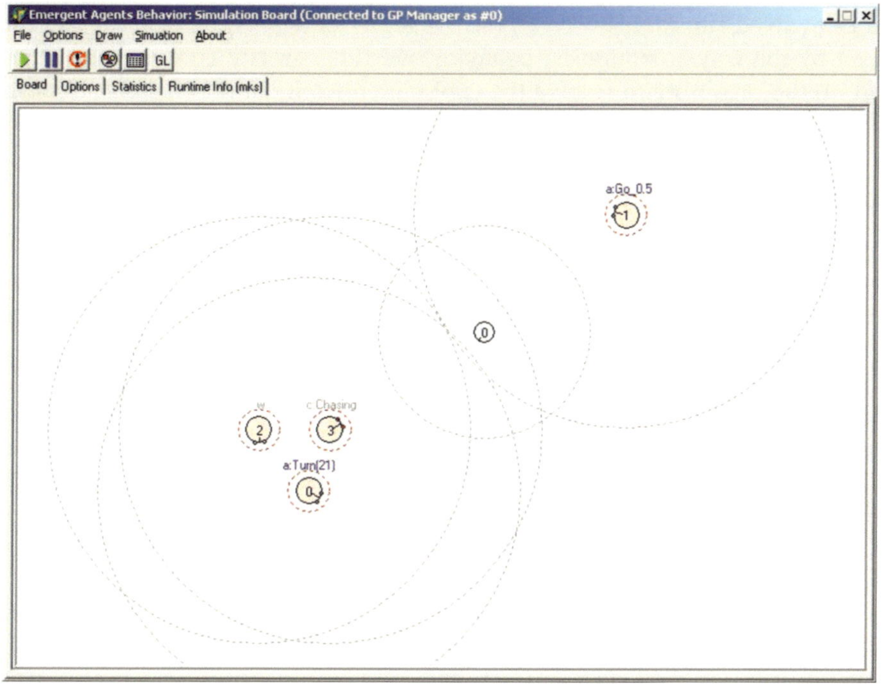

Fig. 1. A snapshot of the instance of predator prey pursuit problem.

2.2 Architecture of the agents

We adopted a subsumption architecture (Brooks, 1986) as the architecture of the predator agents; it was comprised of functional modules separated in three levels: wandering, greedy chase and surrounding (Figure 2(a)). Wandering module makes the predator agents walk

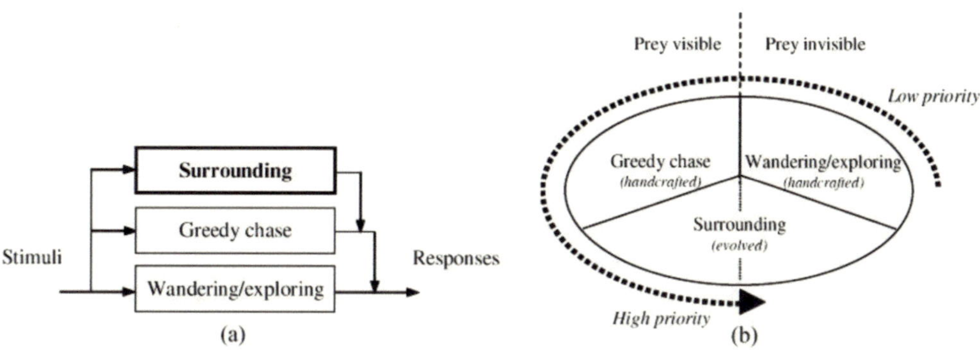

Fig. 2. Subsumption architecture of the agents: functional structure (a) and states (b).

around randomly when other agents are not within their sight, and greedy chase module makes them chase the prey agent while it is within their sight. These modules are handcrafted. Surrounding module makes the predator agents run evolved behavior program when another predator agent is in their sight. The program is designed automatically via simulated evolution. The highest priority module is surrounding, the next is greedy chase, and the lowest priority is wandering. The priority allows the following two things to be evolved simultaneously; (i) the capability of agents to resolve social dilemmas, determined by the way surrounding behavior overrides greedy chase when the prey is in sight, and (ii) the capability to resolve the exploration-exploitation dilemma, determined by the ability of surrounding behavior to override wandering when the prey is invisible.

3. Genetic programming to automatically design surrounding behavior

We employ genetic programming to automatically design surrounding behavior represented as a set of stimulus-response rules of the predator agents. Genetic programming is a domain-independent problem solving approach in which a population of computer programs (individuals' genotypes, in this case surrounding behavior programs) is evolved to solve problems (Koza, 1992).

The simulated evolution in genetic programming is based on the Darwinian principle of reproduction and survival of the fittest. The fitness of each individual is based on the quality with which the phenotype of the simulated indivdual is performing in a given environment; that is to say, predator agents that can capture the prey agent successfully and quickly have a higher fitness value, and their surrounding behavior program are more likely to remain in the next generation.

In the remaining of this section, we elaborate strongly-typed genetic programming for limiting the search space of genetic programming and the major attributes of genetic programming; function and terminal set, genetic representation, genetic operations and fitness evaluation.

3.1 Strongly-typed genetic programming with exception handling

Genetic programming can automatically evolve a set of stimulus-response rules of arbitrary complexity without the need to a priori specify the extent of such complexity; however, that might often cause an enormous computational effort needed to discover a huge search space while looking for potential solutions to the problem. In that respect the introduction of "pruning algorithms" is a significant towards an efficient search for a solution in huge and multidimensional search spaces (Morowitz, 2002). We impose a restriction on the syntax of evolved genetic programs based on some a priori known semantics. The approach is known as strongly typed genetic programming and its advantage over canonical GP in achieving better computational effort is well proven (Montana, 1995).

Considering the sample rule shown in Figure 3, which express a reactive behavior that if each predator agent gets the stimulus of its own speed being less than 20 mm/s, it turns to the bearing of the peer agent (i.e. the closest predator agent that is visible) plus 10 degrees, it is noticeable that both the return values of functions and their operands are associated with data types such as Boolean (the return value of Boolean expression (Speed < 20)), speed (e.g. variable Speed and constant 20), and angle of visibility (bearing) (e.g. variable Peer a and constant 10). An eventual arbitrary creation or modification of a genetic program semantically would make little sense: indeed, it is unfeasible to maintain Boolean expressions comparing operands of different data types, because they have different physical units.

Moreover, since we introduce sensor range limits, there is a clear possibility of maintaining phenotypically inactive, genotypically neutral code in genetic programs; for example, if a Boolean expression, that compares a perception variable of a certain data type with a constant value beyond that data type's limits (e.g. Peer d > 1000, if that sensors' range is only 400) evaluates always as a constant True or False. Analogically, the semantics of action Turn( ) imply a parameter of data type angle. And allowing only addition and subtraction as arithmetic operations implies that each operand involved in the expression that defines the parameter (the resulting turning angle) should have the same data type angle. Addressing these concerns, the grammar of strongly-typed genetic programming establishes generic data types of visible angle, distance, speed, and Boolean with corresponding allowed ranges of values for their respective instances (variables and ephemeral constants). In addition, it stipulates the data type of the results of arithmetic and logical expressions, and the allowed data type of operands (perception variables and ephemeral constants) involved in these expressions.

We would like to emphasize that proposed approach is not based on domain-specific knowledge, and therefore the proposed strongly-typed genetic programming cannot be considered a "stronger" approach compromising the domain-neutrality of the very GP paradigm itself. The limitations imposed on the syntax of genetic programs are solely based (i) on the natural presumption that the predator agents are fully aware of their physically reasonable limits of their perception- and moving abilities; and (ii) on the common rule in strongly-typed 3G algorithmic languages that all the operands in addition, subtraction and comparison operations should have the same data types. These limitations do not incorporate a priori obtained knowledge, specific for the domain nor the external world where the agents are situated.

```
IF (Speed<20) THEN Turn(Peer_a+10)
```

Fig. 3. Sample stimulus-response rule.

3.1.1 Function set and terminal set

Genetic programs can be represented as parsing trees whose nodes are functions, variables or constants. The nodes that have sub-trees are non-terminals; they represent functions to which the sub-trees represent the arguments. Variables and constants are terminals; they take no arguments and they always are leaves in the parsing trees.

The set of those terminals includes the perceptions (stimuli) and actions (responses) the predator agents are able to perform as summarized in Table 1.

The function set comprises the arithmetic and logical operators, and the IF-THEN function which establish the relationship between current perceptions and corresponding actions. The terminal set comprises the sensory abilities, state variable, ephemeral constants and moving abilities. The sensory abilities and state variable are variable numbers; these numbers can be renewed by the perceptions of each predator agents, while the ephemeral constants and moving abilities are constant numbers. The detail of those sets is described in Table 1.

Category	Designation	Explanation
Function set	IF-THEN IF-THEN-NA, LE, GE, WI, EQ, NE, + , −	IF-THEN IF-THEN with exception handling ≤ , ≥ , Within, = , Not = , + , -
Terminal set		
Sensory abilities	Prey_d, Peer_d	Distance to the prey and to the closest agent, mm.
	Prey_a, Peer_a	Bearing of the prey and of the closest agent, degrees
	PreyVisible, PeerVisible	True if prey/agent is "visible," false otherwise
State variable	Speed	Speed of the agent, mm/s
Ephemeral constants	Integer	
Moving abilities	Turn(a)	Turns relatively to a degrees (a > 0: clockwise)
	Stop, Go_1.0	Sets speed to 0, or to maximum, respectively
	Go_0.25, Go_0.5, Go_0.75	Sets speed to 25%, 50%, 75% of maximum

Table 1. Function set and terminal set of strongly-typed genetic programming.

3.1.2 Representation of genotype

Inspired by its flexibility, and the recently emerged widespread adoption of document object model (DOM) and extensible mark-up language (XML), we represent evolved genotypes of simulated the predator agents as DOM-parse trees featuring equivalent flat XML-text in a way as first implemented in [DOM/XML]. Our additional motivation stems from the fact that despite the recently reported use of DOM/XML for representing computer architectures, source code, and agents' communication languages, we are not aware of any attempts to employ XML technology for representing evolvable structures such as genetic programs in a generic, standard, and portable way. Our approach implies that the genetic operations are performed on DOM-parse trees using off-the shelf, platform- and language neutral DOM-parsers. The corresponding XML-text representation (rather than S-expression) is used as a flat file format, feasible for migration of genetic programs among the computational nodes in an eventual distributed implementation of the genetic programming. A fragment of XML representing of the above sample stimulus-response rule (refer to Figure 3) is shown in Figure 4. The benefits of using DOM/XML-based representations of genetic programs, as documented in (Tanev, 2003) can be briefly summarized as follows:

i. XML tags offer a generic support for maintaining data types in genetic programming (strongly typed genetic programming);
ii. W3C-standard XML schemas offer a generic way to represent the grammar of genetic programming;
iii. Fast prototyping of genetic programming by using the standard built-in API of DOM-parsers for maintaining and manipulating genetic programs;

iv. OS neutrality of parsers;
v. Algorithmic language neutrality of DOM-parsers;
vi. Inherent Web-compliance of an eventual parallel distributed implementation of genetic programming.

```
<IF-THEN-NA>
   <COND-THEN-NA>
     <COND_TDistance>
       <VAR_TDistance>Peer_d</VAR_TDistance >
       <OPER TDistance>LE</OPER_TDistance >
       <CONST TDistance>20</CONST_TDistance >
     </COND_TDistance >
   </COND-THEN-NA>
   <THEN> ... </THEN>
   <NA>    ... </NA>
</IF-THEN-NA>
```

Fig. 4. Fragment of XML representation of sample stimulus-response rule.

3.1.3 Genetic operations

Binary tournament selection is employed; a robust, commonly used selection mechanism, which has proved to be efficient and simple to code. Crossover operation is defined in a strongly typed way in that only the nodes (and corresponding sub-trees) of the same data type (i.e. labelled with the same tag) from parents can be swapped. Sub-tree mutation is also allowed in a strongly typed way in that syntactically correct sub-tree replaces a random node in a genetic program. The routine refers to the type of node it is going to currently alter and applies a randomly chosen rule from the set of applicable rules as defined in the grammar of strongly-typed genetic programming. The transposition mutation also operates on a single genetic program by swapping two random nodes having the same data type.

3.1.4 Breeding strategy

We adopted a homogeneous breeding strategy in which the performance of a single genetic program cloned to all the predator agents is evaluated. Anticipating that the symmetrical nature of a world populated with identical predator agents is unlikely to promote any specialization in their behavior, we consider the features of such a homogeneous multi-agent society as (i) adequate to the world and (ii) consistent with our previously declared intention to create a robust and scalable multi-agent system.

3.1.5 Fitness functions

The fitness F measured for the trial starting with a particular initial situation is evaluated as the length of the radius vector of the derived agents' behavior in the virtual energy-distance-time space as:

$$F = \sqrt{dE_A^{\ 2} + D_A^{\ 2} + T} + K_c \times C \tag{1}$$

where dE_A is the average energy consumption during the trial, D_A is the average distance to the prey by the end of the trial, and T is the elapsed time of the trial. C is the complexity of the agents' genetic representation in tree nodes, and K_C (equal to 0.1) is the scaling coefficient of the penalty imposed for complex genetic representations of the agents. Actually, T is an especially prime term in Eq.1, and therefore we may regard the fitness function as the function of the time needed for the predators to capture the prey. The trial is limited to 300s of "real" time or to the time the prey is captured; and with a sampling rate of 500ms it is simulated with up to 600 time steps. Smaller fitness values correspond to better performing predator agents.

The selection pressure, which favours more parsimonious agents' representations, is introduced as a measure to reduce the bloat in GP. The bloat (or the uncontrolled growth of genotypic representations during an evolutionary run) drastically reduces the computational performance of the implementation. The quantities dE_A and D_A are averaged over all predator agents. The energy consumption estimation dE for each predator agent takes into account both the basal metabolic rate and the energy consumption for motion as follows:

$$dE = E_{BMR} \times T + E_M \times D \tag{2}$$

where E_{BMR} is the basal metabolic rate, equal to 0.05 units per second, and E_M is the energy consumption for moving activities equal to 0.01 units per mm traversed during the trial. The trial is limited to 300 s of "real" time or to the time the prey is captured; and with a sampling rate of 500 ms it is simulated with up to 600 time steps. Smaller fitness values correspond to better performing predator agents. Notice that the agents are explicitly rewarded for capturing the prey (for minimizing the elapsed time of the trial) rather than for demonstrating surrounding behavior, which might eventually be needed to capture the prey. Surrounding, being discovered through simulated evolution, should emerge from the simply defined perception and moving abilities of the agents.

In order to obtain more general solutions to the problem the fitness of each genetic program is evaluated as an average of the fitness measured over 10 different initial situations. However, based on empirically proven data that in the initial stages of evolution agents are hardly able to successfully resolve more than a few (out of 10) initial situations, in order to enhance the computational performance of strongly-typed genetic programming, we applied an evaluation of the fitness function (Miller & Goldberg, 1995). The number of initial situations used to evaluate genetic programs in a population gradually increases with the evolution of the population. Starting from 4 for the first generation of each run, the number of situations is revised (until it reaches the value of 10 initial situations) on completion of each generation and it is set to exceed 2 the number of situations successfully solved by the best-of-generation genetic program. Given that with additional initial situation(s) they have to resolve, the agents would perform either better or, more likely worse, the fitness of the best-of-current generation could be occasionally somewhat worse than fitness of the best genetic program of the previous generation. Therefore, it is reasonable to anticipate non-monotonous fitness convergence characteristics of strongly-typed genetic programming.

4. Perceptual noise model

Since the purpose of our work is to investigate the relationship between the robustness of evolved surrounding behavior and the uncertainty of the predator agents, we introduce a perceptual noise model to their sensory abilities; distance to the prey and to the closest agent (i.e. Prey_d and Peer_d) and bearing of the prey and of the closest agent (i.e. Prey_a and Peer_a). In our model the perceptual noise term is added to the variable of sensory abilities of the predator agents as follows:

$$Peer\_d_{noise} = Peer\_d \pm Random\left(Peer\_d \times n\right) \tag{3}$$

$$Peer\_a_{noise} = Peer\_a \pm Random\left(Peer\_d \times n\right) \tag{4}$$

where $Peer\_d_{noise}$ and $Peer\_a_{noise}$ represent perceived distance and angle to the closest predator agent in its sight, and *Peer_d* and *Peer_a* mean exact distance and angle between these agents. In distance and angle to the prey, $Peer\_d_{noise}$, *Peer_d*, $Peer\_a_{noise}$ and *Peer_a* are replaced to $Pray\_d_{noise}$, *Pray_d*, *Pray_a* and $Prey\_a_{noise}$ respectively.

The second term *n* of each expression represents perceptual noise levels; the addition of the term makes the perception of predator agents uncertain. The noise increases in proportional to the distance between agents (i.e. *Peer_d* and *Prey_d*). In the other words, the further the peer predator agent and the prey agent are from a certain predator agent, more ambiguous the distance and the bearing from itself to the peer predator agent are; of course they are invisible if they move outside of its sight. This model that the location of a far-away object is perceived uncertainly is simple and natural. The perceptual noise reflects simple and usual supposition that it is hard to identify the exact location of a far-away object. The perceptual model of the predator agents is visualized in Figure 5.

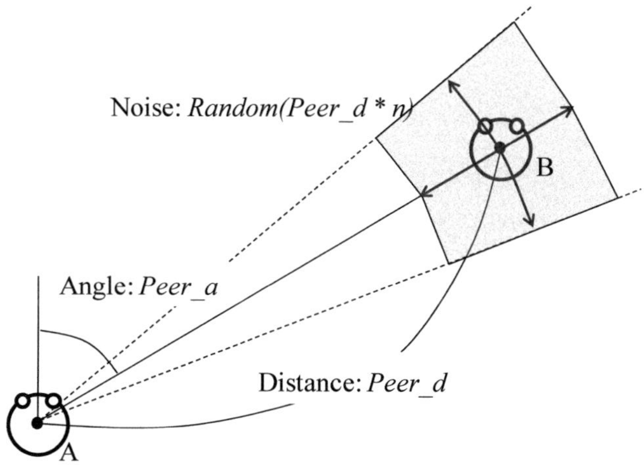

Fig. 5. Perceptual noise model in the predator prey pursuit problem.

Figure 5 illustrates a situation in which the predator agent A perceives a location of the peer predator agent B. If the agent A has a noiseless sensor, it can perceive the exact location information. However, because of the perceptual noise the predator agent A cannot precisely determine the exact location of the peer predator agent B. Therefore, the predator agent A randomly perceives that the peer predator agent B is located somewhere in the gray zone in Figure 3. For example if the noise level is 2.0%, the second term N of the formula takes the value under plus or minus 8; therefore, if the distance between these agents is 400mm (Peer_d = 400) and the angle between them is 30 degree (Peer_a = 30), the distance that the predator agent perceives results in the value from 392mm through 408mm, and also the angle results in the value from 22 degree through 38 degree. The perceptual noise model make the communication of predator agents instable, and therefore, it might result in inadequate surrounding behavior.

5. Empirical results and discussion

5.1 Evolution of the surrounding behavior of the predator agent

The values of parameters of strongly-typed genetic programming used in our simulation are summarized as follows: Population size was 600, Selection ration was 10%, Elitism was 1%, Mutation ratio was 2% and Trial interval was 600 steps. The fitness value of 300, employed as a termination criterion roughly corresponds to a successful team of predator agents that capture the prey by the middle of the trial of 600 steps.

The result, shown in Figure 6(a) indicates typical fitness convergence characteristic. Note that smaller fitness values correspond to better performing predator agents, since the fitness value is strongly affected by elapsed time of the trial as mentioned above (see Section 3.1.5). We consider these empirical results as an evidence of the very feasibility of applying a genetic programming paradigm for automatic design of autonomous agents capable of accomplishing complex tasks through local, implicit and proximity-defined interactions.

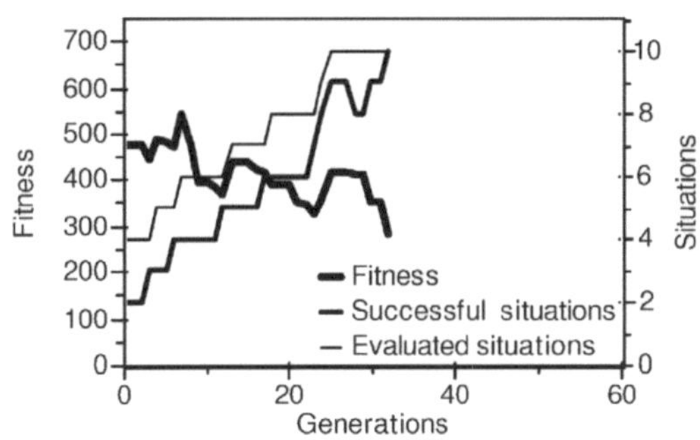

(a)

```
1.  Program Main;
2.  type TDistance =     0..400;
3.       TVisAngle = -180..180;
4.       TSpeed    =     0..22;
5.  var  Peer_d, Prey_d              : TDistance;
6.       Peer_a, Prey_a              : TVisAngle;
7.       Speed                       : TSpeed;
8.       PreyVisible, PeerVisible : Boolean;
9.  Procedure GP;
10. begin
11.   try if (Prey_a >= -49) then begin
12.     Turn(-22+Prey_a-Peer_a+Prey_a);
13.     if (Speed <= 16) then  begin
14.         Turn(-Peer_a-Prey_a-22);
15.     end;
16.   end;
17.   except begin Null; end;
18. end;
19. begin //-- main program --
20.   GP;
21. end.
```

(b)

Fig. 6. Typical fitness convergence characteristic (a) and human-readable representation of sample best-of-run genetic program (b).

A human-readable representation of a sample best-of-run genetic program is shown in Figure 6(b). Figure 7 illustrates the execution of Turn(- 22 + Prey a - Peer a + Prey a) which is the most often executed command of the evolved solution (Figure 6(b), Line 12). The sensory feedback involved in computing the turning angles implies that agents orient themselves towards the directions which ensure that the perception variables Prey_a and Peer_a comply with the equation "- 22 + Prey_a – Peer_a + Prey_a = 0." Moving in these directions tends to separate the closest agents away and yields a characteristic chase of the

prey from the two opposite sides of the world when only two agents are involved. When more than two agents simultaneously execute the same command (a situation which is not elaborated in the figure) their team perform a surrounding approach to the prey.
The traces of the entities in the world for one of the 10 initial situations are shown in Figure 8. Agents employ a basic model of implicit interactions—only the distance and the bearing of the closest agent (and the prey) are perceived. The prey is captured in 118 simulated time steps (top). Large white and small black circles denote the predator agents in their initial and final position, respectively. The small white circle indicates the prey, initially situated in the center of the world. The numbers in rectangles show the timestamp information. The emergence of the following behavioral traits of predator agents is noticeable (each agent is governed by the sample best-of-run genetic program):

- Switch from greedy chase into surrounding approach (Agent #2, time step 65);
- Zigzag movement, which results in a lower chasing speed indicating "intention" to trap the prey (Agent #1, following time step 40), and
- Surrounding approach (agents #0, #2 and #3) at the final stages of the trial.

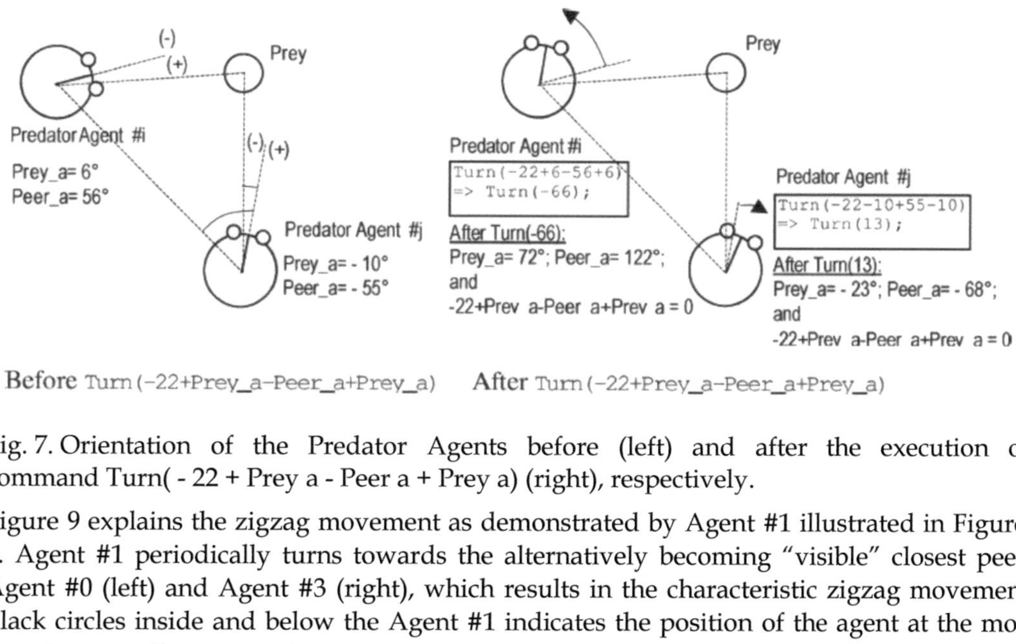

Fig. 7. Orientation of the Predator Agents before (left) and after the execution of command Turn(- 22 + Prey a - Peer a + Prey a) (right), respectively.

Figure 9 explains the zigzag movement as demonstrated by Agent #1 illustrated in Figures 8. Agent #1 periodically turns towards the alternatively becoming "visible" closest peers Agent #0 (left) and Agent #3 (right), which results in the characteristic zigzag movement. Black circles inside and below the Agent #1 indicates the position of the agent at the most recent consecutive moments.
Although such basic model offers the benefits of simplicity and scalability, the following issues related to the feasibility of applying the basic model in real-world applications remain still open: How much does the perceptual noise affect the evolved surrounding behavior? Can the predator agents capture the prey well even in noisy environment? Taking into consideration that the real-world applications indeed suffer from some mechanical and electrical noises, our model should involve some kind of countermeasures against these noises. Does the model acquire the robustness to the noises via the evolutionary approach? We focus our attention on the evolution of the surrounding behavior in a noisy multi-agent system.

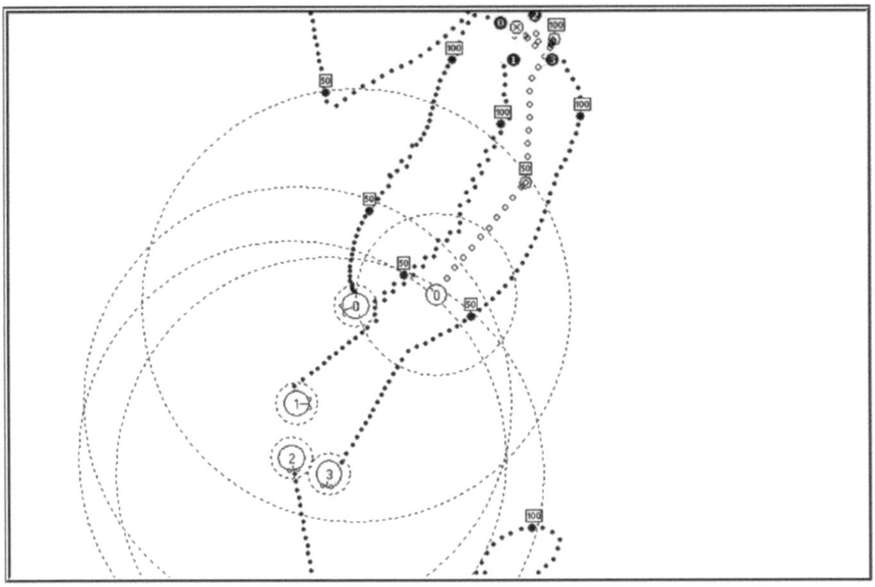

Fig. 8. Traces of the entities with predator agents governed by the sample best-of-run genetic program.

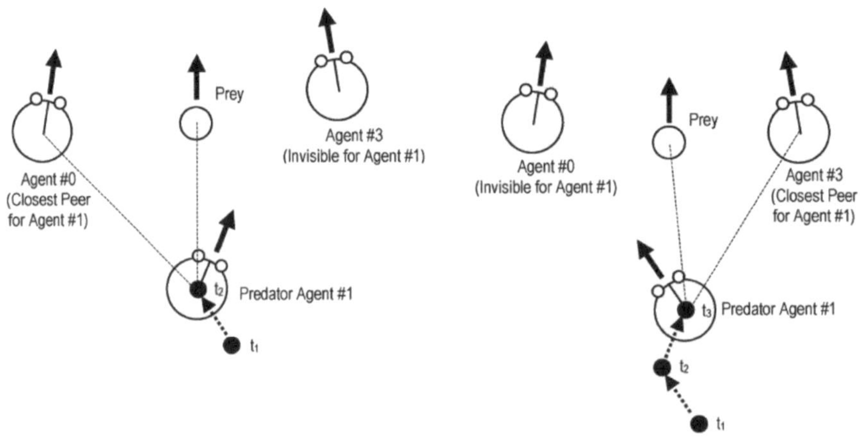

Fig. 9. Explanation of the zigzag movement, which results in a lower chasing speed of the predator Agent#1 as illustrated in Figure 8.

5.2 Evolution in noisy multi-agent system

Since the predator agents with perceptual noise cannot perceive the exact location information of other agents, they might not be cooperated well each other; that is to say, their coordinated surrounding behavior would be poor. The quantitative effect of the perceptual noise on the coordinated surrounding behavior is still unknown. Therefore, we investigate the relationship between the fitness of the predator agents and the perceptual noise levels, and moreover we attempt to verify the supposition that the robustness of the predator agents behavior is related to an environment in which the evolutionary process by genetic programming runs.

5.2.1 The evolved surrounding behavior of the predator agents suffering from the perceptual noise

We evolved a surrounding behavior of predator agents with noiseless perception, and then evaluated the evolved surrounding behavior to the predator agents suffering from the perceptual noise, in order to investigate how much the surrounding behavior evolved in noiseless environment is affected by the perceptual noise. The levels of perceptual noise were between 0% and 3.0% in incremental of 0.5%. The fitness of the evolved surrounding behavior was different with every evaluation because of the randomness of perceptual noise. We conducted the evaluation 50 times. Figure 10 shows the average of the results.

The obtained results indicate that the fitness was worse almost linearly with the increase of perceptual noise levels, and also the success situations, which is the average number of (total 10) initial situations in which the predator agents successfully captured the prey, decreased with the increase of perceptual noise levels.

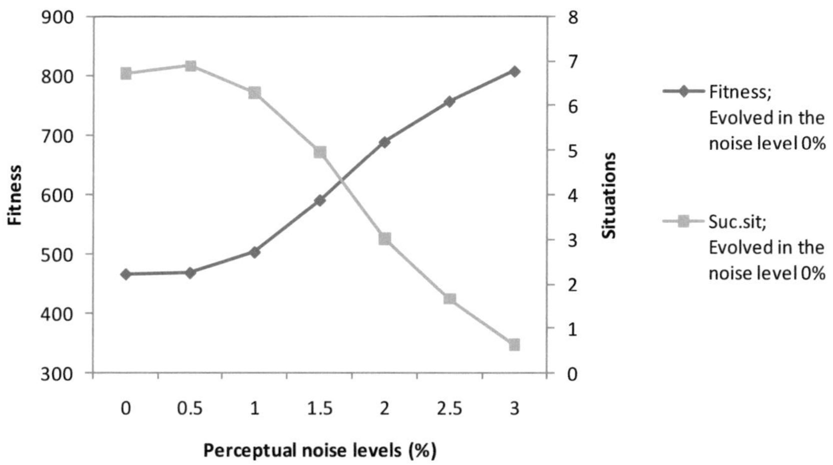

Fig. 10. Changes in the fitness and the success situations of the surrounding behavior in each noisy environment. Note that the surrounding behavior has been already evolved in noiseless environment.

This detrimental effect observed in the behavior of predator agents was most pronounced at the final stages of each trial as shown in Figure 11. The predator agents closed in on the prey at least to some extent but when they eventually enclose the pray, their erratic moving derived from perceptual noise made capturing the pray difficult.

5.2.2 Incremental evolution of the surrounding behavior in noisy environment

The surrounding behavior evolved in noiseless environment through genetic programming did not worked well in each noisy environment. Taking into account that genetic programming is a technique to automatically design agents' behavior without providing explicit domain-specific knowledge about how to achieve a task (Angleine, 1994), we might develop more robust surrounding behavior to noisy environment; in other words, the surrounding behavior involving the solution to uncertainty in noisy environment might be acquired through the interaction between genetic programming and noisy environment without incorporating the explicit knowledge of perceptual noise into the predator agents.

Fig. 11. Typical failure of the evolved surrounding behavior in noisy environment.

In order to investigate the above assumption, we evolved again the evolved behavior in noisy environment with noise rate of 0% and 2%, respectively. The initial population includes some of the best-of-run behavior program evolved in noiseless environment, because the randomly created initial population can hardly adapt in complicated and uncertain noisy environment.

As Figure 12 shows, the results verify that both the fitness and the success situations of the re-evolved surrounding behavior in noisy environment were better than those of the re-evolved in noiseless environment. The behavior evolved in the noise level 2% features a moderate degradation when applied in environments with up to the perceptual noise level 1.5%, and eventually, both the fitness and capture rate converge at similar value of the noise level 2.5%. The shape of graph shows that while the fitness of the surrounding behavior re-evolved in noiseless environment (i.e. the perceptual noise level 0%) seems linear with respect to the perceptual noise level, that of the surrounding behavior program evolved in noisy environment (i.e. the perceptual noise level 2%) seems to draw a sigmoid curve. This indicates that the fitness tend to keep well until a certain threshold (in the behavior evolved in the perceptual noise level 2%, the threshold is 1.5%), hence, the surrounding behavior is more robust on a specific noise level range.

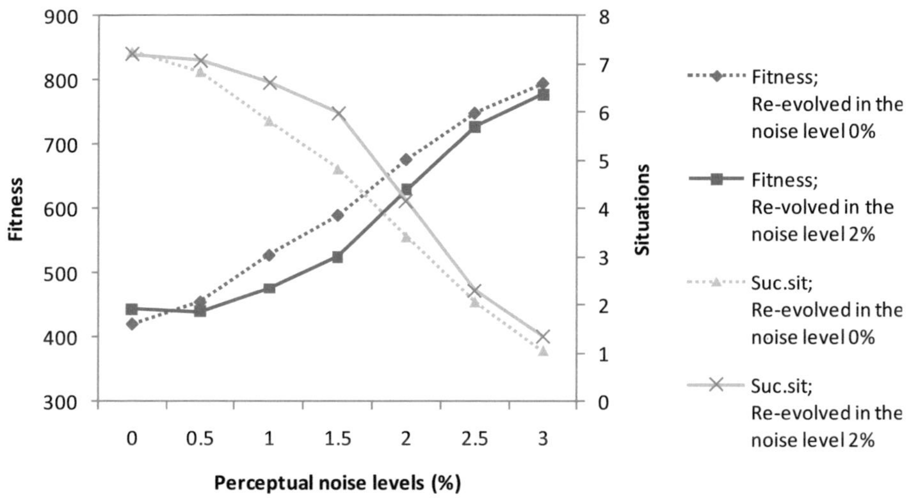

Fig. 12. Changes in the fitness and the success situations of the re-evolved surrounding behavior with the perceptual noise 0% and 2%.

Through the evolution in noisy environment, we could generate a behavior whose fitness is stable until a certain threshold. It seems to be natural conclusion, but what improves the robustness of the behavior? We suppose one reason is that the behavior program obtained a specialized structure to be robust to the perceptual noise. Figure 13 show a comparison of the genetic programs evolved in noiseless environment and in noisy environment.

Unfortunately, we were unable to discover such a structure in a program because the logic of automatically evolved code is hardly understandable by human. However, some interesting points can be discussed as follows: The instruction Turn() is present the program evolved in noisy environment (Figure 8, left) not that often compared to the program evolved in noiseless environment (Figure 8, right); and the variables for perceptual

```
Procedure GP;
begin

  if (PeerVisible)
   then
    begin
     try if (Prey_d <= 389)
      then
       begin
        try if (Peer_a within 135)
         then
          begin
           Turn(-Peer_a-9+Prey_a);
           Go_1.0;
           Go_1.0;
           Exit;
          end;
         except
          begin
           Go_0.25;
          end;
       end;
      except
       begin
        Go_0.75;
        Turn(-5-5-36);
        Turn(-Peer_a-9+Prey_a);
        try if (Peer_a within 135)
         then
          begin
           Turn(-Peer_a-9+Prey_a);
           Exit;
           Go_1.0;
           Exit;
          end;
         except
          begin
           Go_0.25;
           Turn(-9-Prey_a-36);
          end;
       end;
    end;
end;
```

```
Procedure GP;
begin

  if (PeerVisible)
   then
    begin
     try if (Prey_d <= 389)
      then
       begin
        try if (Prey_d <= 389)
         then
          begin
           try if (Prey_d <= 389)
            then
             begin
              try if (Prey_d <= 389)
               then
                begin
                 Turn(-Peer_a-9-5);
                 Go_1.0;
                 Go_1.0;
                 Exit;
                end;
               except
                begin
                 Go_1.0;
                 Turn(-5-9-5);
                 Go_1.0;
                 Exit;
                end;
             end;
            except
             begin
              Go_0.75;
             end;
          end;
         except
          begin
           Go_0.25;
          end;
       end;
      except
       begin
        Go_0.75;
       end;
    end;
end;
```

Fig. 13. The comparison of genetic programs evolved in noiseless (left) and noisy (right) environments, respectively.

information (i.e. Peer_a, Peer_d, Prey_a and Prey_d) rarely appear in the left-, conversely to the right program shown in Figure 8. In our mode, such variables are perturbed directly by the perceptual noise. Consequently, in the case of high noise level, it is considered that a program involving many such variables is more difficult. As a result, a program evolved in noisy environment might be evolved to limit the reliance on such variables.

6. Conclusion

We presented the result of our work on the use of genetic programming for evolving surrounding behavior of agents situated in inherently cooperative environment. We use the predator-prey pursuit problem to verify our hypothesis that relatively complex surrounding behavior may emerge from simple, implicit, locally defined, and therefore - scalable interactions between the predator agents. Proposing perceptual noise model of the predator agents we investigated the relationship between the evolved surrounding behavior and the perceptual noise. We demonstrated that relatively complex, surrounding behavior emerges even from the simple, basic model of implicit, proximity defined interactions among the agents. We observed the relatively simple motion of the predator agents in the direction away from the closest predator agents yields emergent collective behavioral traits of predator agents such as (i) a characteristics zigzag movement, which results in a lower chasing speed indicating "intention" to trap the prey, and ultimately, (ii) a surrounding of the prey. Although the above surrounding behavior was performed efficiently in noiseless environment, the performance of it was worse as the perceptual noise level increased. We evolved the behavior again in each of two different environment; noiseless environment and noisy environment, and compared the performance of these types of behavior. The behavior evolved in noisy environment get better performance than that evolved in noiseless environment.

In the future we are planning to incorporate evolvable rather than handcrafted escaping strategy of the prey as used in our current approach. We are also interested in enhancing the currently used perception and communication models into a model, which allows for predator agents to analyze the effects of their own actions on the reaction of the other agents in the world. We are planning to investigate both the survival value of such reflection and the robustness of the team of predator agents.

7. References

Angeline, P. J. (1994). Genetic programming and emergent intelligence, In: *Advances in Genetic Programming*, Kinnear, K. E. Jr. (Ed.), pp. 75-98, MIT Press, 0-262-11188-8, Cambridge, MA, USA

Benda, M.; Jagannathan, B. & Dodhiawala, R. (1986). On optimal cooperation of knowledge sources," In: *Technical Report BCS-G2010-28*, Boeing AI Center, Boeing Computer Services, Bellevue,WA.

Brooks, R. A. (1986). A robust layered control system for a mobile robot, *IEEE Journal of Robotics and Automation*, Vol. 2, No. 1, pp. 14-23, 0882-4967.

Ferber, J. (1999). *Multi-Agent Systems: An Introduction to Distributed Artificial Intelligence*, Addison-Wesley Longman: Harlow, 0201360489,

Forrest, S. (1991). Emergent computation: Self-organising, collective, and cooperative phenomena in natural and artificial computing networks, In: *Emergent Computation*, Forrest, S. (Ed.), pp. 1-11, MIT Press, 0-262-56057-7, Cambridge, MA, USA.

Haynes, T. & Sen, S. (1996). Evolving Behavioral Strategies in Predators and Prey, *Adaptation and leaning in multiagent systems*, pp. 113-126, Springer Verlag.

Haynes, T.; Wainwright, R.; Sen, S. & Schoenefeld, D. (1997). Strongly Typed Genetic Programming in Evolving Cooperation Strategies, *Proceedings of the 6th International Conference on Genetic Algorithms*, pp. 271-278, Morgan Kaufmann Publishers, Inc.

Holand, J. H. (1999). *Emergence: From Chaos to Order*, Perseus Books, 0738201421, Cambridge, 1999.

Koza, J. R. (1992). *Genetic Programming: On the Programming of Computers by Means of Natural Selection*, MIT Press, 0262111705, Cambridge, MA, USA.

Luke, S. & Spector L. (1996). Evolving Teamwork and Coordination with Genetic Programming, In Genetic Programming 1996: Proceedings of the First Annual Conference. Koza, J. et al (Ed.), pp. 141-149. MIT Press, 10884750, Cambridge, MA, USA.

Miller, B. L. & Goldberg, D. E. (1995). Genetic Algorithms, Tournament Selection, and the Effects of Noise, *Complex Systems*, Vol. 9, pp. 193-212, .

Montana, D. (1995). Strongly typed genetic programming, *Evolutionary Computation*, Vol. 3, No. 2 , pp. 199-230, MIT Press, 1063-6560.

Morgan, C. (1923). *Emergent Evolution*, Henry Holt and Co, 0404604684.

Morowitz, H. J. (2002) *The Emergence of Everything: How the World Became Complex*, Oxford University Press, 019513513X , New York, USA.

Parunak, H.; Van, D.; Brueckner, S.; Fleischer, M. & Odell, J. (2002) Co-X: Defining what agents do together, *Proceedings of the AAMAS 2002 Workshop on Teamwork and Coalition Formation*, Shehory, O.; Ioerger, T. R.; Vassileva, J. & Yen, J. (Eds.), pp. 62-69.

Tanev, I. (2003). DOM/XML-based portable genetic representation of morphology, behavior and communication abilities of evolvable agents, *Proceedings of the 8th International Symposium on Artificial Life and Robotics*, pp. 185-188.

13

Data Mining for Decision Making in Multi-Agent Systems

Hani K. Mahdi, Hoda K. Mohamed and Sally S. Attia
Computer and Systems Engineering Department,
Faculty of Engineering, Ain Shams University, Cairo
Egypt

1. Introduction

The intelligent agent paradigm has generated such a remarkable interest in many application domains over the last two decades. It is growing to be a continuously evolving and expanding area. Agents, Software Agents or Intelligent Agents are intelligent in the sense that they are adaptive, independent, and possess reasoning capability. They can plan and execute tasks in cooperation with other agents in order to satisfy their goals. A Multi-Agent System (MAS) is defined as a loosely coupled network of problem solvers that work together to solve problems that are beyond the individual capabilities or knowledge of each problem solver (Agent). The increasing interest in MAS research is due to significant advantages inherent in such systems, including their ability to solve problems that may be too large for a centralized single agent, provide enhanced speed and reliability, and tolerate uncertain data and knowledge. Some of the key research issues related to problem-solving activities of agents in a multi-agent system MAS are in the areas of coordination, negotiation, and communication.

With advances in Web technologies, collaborative applications are now server based and the user interface is typically a Web browser. Thus, a collaborative application can be a Web-based solution that runs on a local server that allows people communicate and work together, share information and documents, and talk in real-time over the Internet. Recently, much research has been conducted in distributed artificial intelligence and collaborative applications. Several interesting methodologies and systems have been developed in areas such as distributed multi-agent systems for decision support, web search and information retrieval, information systems modeling, and supply chain management.

This chapter considers applying different data mining techniques for the decision making process in a Multi-Agent System for Collaborative E-learning (MASCE). The dynamism in e-learning can be made more powerful with the help of intelligent agents. Intelligent agents - the so called e-assistants or helper programs - can reside inside a computer and make the learning in e-learning occur dynamically to suit the need of the user. They can track the user's likes and dislikes in different areas, the level of knowledge and the learning style and accordingly recommend the best matching helpers for collaboration.

A previous research outlined the development and the implementation processes of a Multi-Agent System for Collaborative E-learning (MASCE) which is designed to be used to assist the teaching and learning processes. This system considers the blended learning environment as a supplement to the face-to-face lecture. The goal is to incorporate the intelligence of the multi-agent system in a way that enables it to actively and intelligently support the educational processes, where multiple agents can interact to exchange information so that students may collaborate on how best to gain knowledge.

In this chapter we are going to outline the application of different data mining techniques to discover important information previously unknown from the large database tables obtained from MASCE. The use of data mining facilitates the decision making process. As the world grows in complexity, overwhelming us with the data it generates, data mining becomes our only hope for explaining the patterns that underlie it. Intelligently analyzed data is a valuable resource. It can lead to new insights and, in commercial settings, to competitive advantages.

Data mining is defined as the process of discovering patterns in data. The process must be automatic or (more usually) semiautomatic. The patterns discovered must be meaningful in that they lead to some advantage. The data is invariably present in substantial quantities. Useful patterns allow us to make nontrivial predictions on new data. In other words, they help to explain something about the data.

First, we are going to apply Rough Sets techniques to the decision tables in order to obtain decision rules that can be used to classify new unseen cases. Second, Decision Tree algorithms such as ID3 will be applied to the same decision tables to obtain decision trees that can be used in classification of new objects. Third, a hybrid data mining algorithm combining rough sets and decision trees is applied and the results are compared with the previous two techniques to determine which is most suitable for decision making in this particular application of multi-agent systems.

2. Multi-agent systems and their applications

Agents and Multi-Agent Systems (MAS) have emerged as a powerful technology to cope with the increasing complexity of a variety of Information Technology scenarios. We are not going to explain the full details of the agents because these are covered in other chapters. We are only going to provide a basic overview.

2.1 Multi-agent overview

The most widely accepted definition for the "agent" term is that "an agent acts on behalf of someone else, after having been authorized". This definition can be applied to software agents, which are instantiated and act instead of a user or a software program that controls them. The difficulty in defining an agent arises from the fact that the various aspects of agency are weighted differently, with respect to the application domain at hand. Wooldridge & Jennings have succeeded in combining general agent features into the following generic abstract definition integrating all the characteristics into the notion of an agent: "An agent is an autonomous software entity that -functioning continuously - carries out a set of goal-oriented tasks on behalf of another entity, either human or software system. This software entity is able to perceive its environment through sensors and act upon it through effectors, and in doing so, employ some knowledge or representation of the user's preferences" (Wooldridge, 1999).

An agent may have, depending on the domain it is situated in, some or all of the properties listed below (Symeonidis & Mitkas, 2005):

- Autonomy (considered a must-have feature by many researchers in the field of agents)
- Interactivity: Reactivity or Pro-activeness
- Adaptability
- Sociability
- Cooperativity
- Competitiveness
- Mobility
- Learning

In this chapter, we are going to concentrate on the "***learning***" feature which means that an agent should be able to learn (get trained) through its reactions and its interaction with the environment. This is one of the most fundamental features that agents should have. We are going to use different data mining techniques to extract decision rules which can help agents make intelligent decisions. The more efficient the training process, the more intelligent the agents.

(Nwana, 1995) classified agents with respect to the following dimensions:

- Mobility that differentiates agents into static or mobile.
- The *logic paradigm* they employ, which classifies them as either *deliberative* or *reactive.*

The fundamental characteristics that describe the agent are: *autonomy*, *cooperativity* and *learning*. Based on these axes, agents can be classified as collaborative agents, collaborative learning agents, interface agents and truly smart agents as shown in Figure 1. The combination of two or more of the above approaches classifies agents as hybrid, leading to mobile deliberative collaborative agents, static reactive collaborative agents, static deliberative interface agents, mobile reactive interface agents, etc.

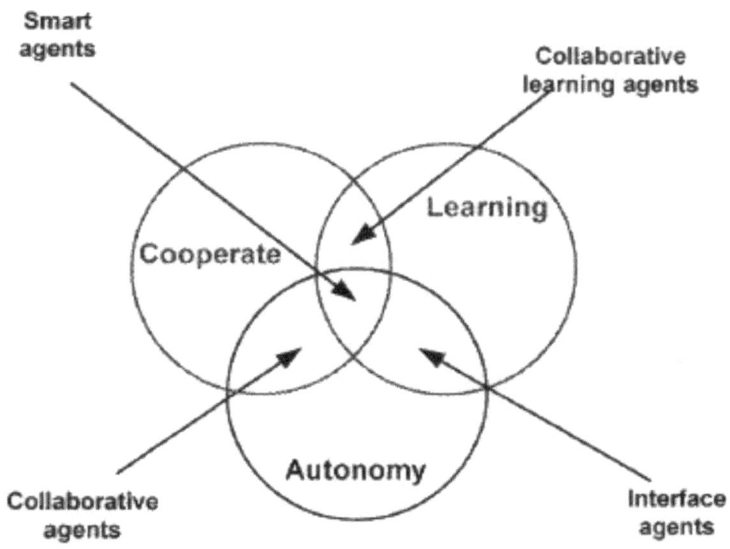

Fig. 1. The Nwana agent classification, according to their fundamental characteristics (Nwana, 1995)

A multi-agent system is one that consists of a number of agents, which interact with one-another. In the most general case, agents will be acting on behalf of users with different goals and motivations. To successfully interact, they will require the ability to cooperate, coordinate, and negotiate with each other, much as people do (Wooldridge, 2002). Several architectural styles have been used in the development of multi-agent systems (Buse and Wu, 2007; Sellers and Giorgini, 2005).

In order for MAS to solve common problems coherently, the agents must communicate amongst themselves, coordinate their activities, and negotiate once they find themselves in conflict. Agents communicate via messages, which can be of two types: assertions and queries.

MAS architectures exploit the coupling of the agent effectiveness, acting within a distributed environment, with the advantages of a strict and successfully coordinated framework, as far as communication and agent collaboration is concerned. MAS complexity is mainly dependent on the number of agents that participate in it. One could, therefore, argue that the simplest form of MAS consists of a single agent, while more elaborate MAS structures may comprise a substantial number of cooperating agents, or even smaller MAS (Symeonidis & Mitkas, 2005).

2.2 Multi-agent systems applications

The following issues differentiate between the rationale for MAS and single-agent systems (Agent Working Group, 2000):

- A single agent that handles a large amount of tasks lacks performance, reliability, and maintainability. On the other hand, MAS provide modularity, flexibility, modifiability, and extensibility, due to their distributed nature.
- A single agent cannot obtain (and provide to humans) extensive and specialized knowledge. MAS, composed of multiple distributed processes can access more knowledge resources, exploiting concurrent execution.
- Applications requiring distributed computing are better supported by MAS than by a single (often static) agent.
- Intelligence, as described by neuroscientists of the human mind, can be approached by a multi-processing system, rather than serial computing. Such a multi-processing computational system can only be implemented as a wide distributed environment where many agents act. Thus, MAS appear as the optimal solution for implementing.

It becomes evident that the choice between MAS or single-agent architecture must be guided by the application needs. If we decide, for example, to implement a system notifying us whenever we have an incoming e-mail, then a static single-agent implementation seems sufficient. On the other hand, if we are to implement a large-scale electronic marketplace, where many agents take part in electronic auctions to buy or sell goods, MAS architecture will be more suitable.

Multi-agent systems and e-learning

Dynamism in e-learning can be made more powerful with the help of intelligent agents. In e-learning, Intelligent Agents help make the learning in e-learning happen dynamically to suit the need of the user (Chen and Chiu, 2005; Shang et al. 2001). They can collect information about the user's likes and dislikes while using the system, the level of knowledge and accordingly recommend the best matching helpers for collaboration.

E-learning has become one of the most popular teaching methods in recent years. At the same time, in the computational intelligence field, the Intelligent Agent paradigm gained a tremendous interest in many application domains over the last two decades. Current research in this area has approached integrating agents into educational systems. That is why we thought of building a Multi-Agent System for Collaborative E-learning (MASCE) as will be shown in details in the next section.

3. Proposed Multi-Agent System for Collaborative E-Learning (MASCE)

MASCE is to assist teaching and learning process and also to encourage collaborative learning among peers. This system shall be used in a blended learning environment as a supplement to the face-to-face lecture where students can use the system in the lab or from home after attending the traditional lecture in the faculty. The objective is to incorporate the intelligence of the multi-agents system in a way that enables it to actively and intelligently support the educational processes, where multiple agents can interact to exchange information so that students may collaborate on how best to gain knowledge (Mahdi and Attia, 2008).

The proposed MAS system considers two types of users; namely students and instructors. Each of these users has a corresponding agent. These are Student Agent and Instructor Agent. The Student Agent runs on the student's computer. Thus, each student is equipped with a Student Agent, which helps the learning process of the student. It manages the student's personal profile and also tracks the student actions during learning process and updates his profile accordingly. On the other hand, the Instructor Agent provides teaching materials, assesses the progress and participation of different students through quizzes, and manages the progress of the course.

The innovation in the proposed system is the introduction of the Assistant Agent which is initialized as soon as any of the users starts to use the system. The Assistant Agent runs on the system's server. It plays a centric role in the proposed system. It has a collaboration mechanism which will be used for "match-making" and "community-building" to help increase collaboration between peers in a certain course. It also gives hints to the instructor of the course to help in the teaching process such as statistics of the results of quizzes and summaries of students' profiles to help in the final grading. It acts a mediator (facilitator) between Student Agents and Instructor Agent of a specific course. After receiving the preferences (goals) of the instructor and the students, it will run autonomously and self-dependently. All the Assistant Agents of different courses are under the control of the Assistant Manager Agent. Thus the proposed MAS consist of three types of agents.

a. Student Agent

Each student has the corresponding Student Manager Agent that helps the learning process of the student. It acquires the student's preferences and profile. During the learning process, as the student enrolls in new courses, a dedicated student agent for each course is created. It tracks the student actions in that course. Accordingly, the tracking mechanism updates the student's profile and preferences. All the student agents of different courses of the same student are under the control of the Student Manager Agent as shown in Figure 2.

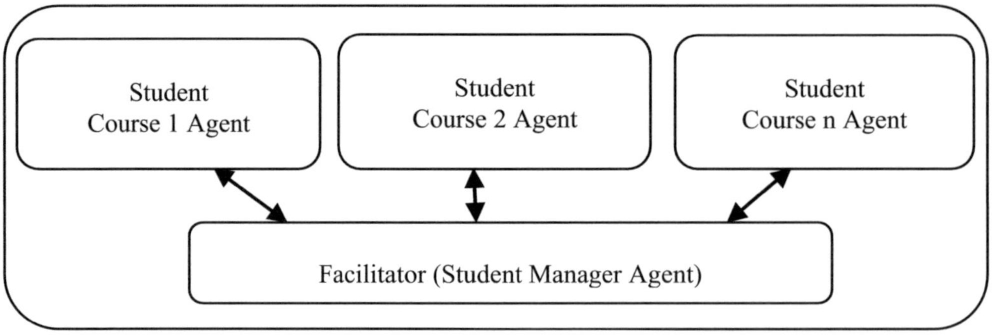

Fig. 2. Student Agent

b. Instructor Agent

The Instructor Manager Agent or simply the Assistant Agent assists the teaching process while interacting with the instructor. It is assigned for each instructor. For each course that is taught by the instructor a dedicated instructor agent is created. It provides teaching materials when requested by Assistant agent for distributing to students' agents, assesses the progress and participation of different students through quizzes, and manages the progress of the course. All the instructor agents of different courses of the same instructor are under the control of the Instructor Manager Agent as shown in Figure 3.

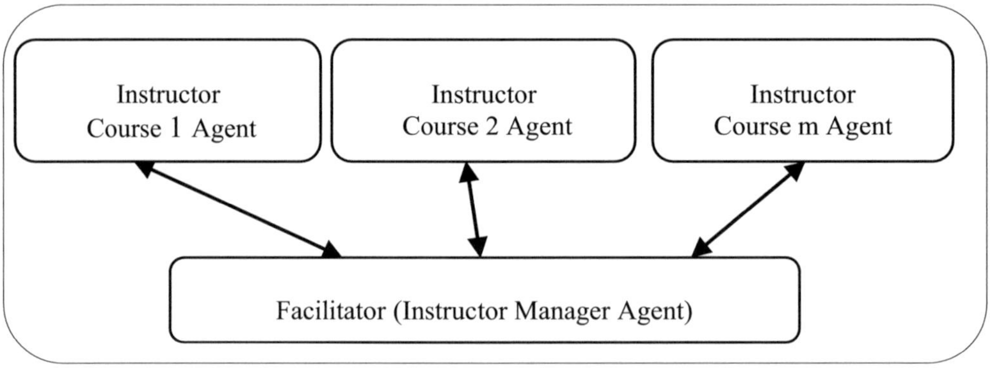

Fig. 3. Instructor Agent

c. Assistant Agent

The innovation in the proposed system is the introduction of the Assistant Agent shown in Figure 3which is initialized as soon as any of the users starts to use the system. The Assistant Manager Agent or simply the Assistant Agent plays a centric role in the proposed system. For each course, a dedicated Assistant Course Agent is created. It has a collaboration mechanism which will be used for "match-making" and "community-building" to help increase collaboration between peers in a certain course. It also gives hints to the instructor of the course to help in the teaching process such as statistics of the results of quizzes and summaries of students' profiles to help in the final grading. It acts a mediator (facilitator) between Student Agents and Instructor Agent of a specific course. After receiving the preferences (goals) of the instructor and the students, it will run autonomously and self-dependently. All the Assistant Agents of different courses are under the control of the Assistant Manager Agent as shown in Figure 4.

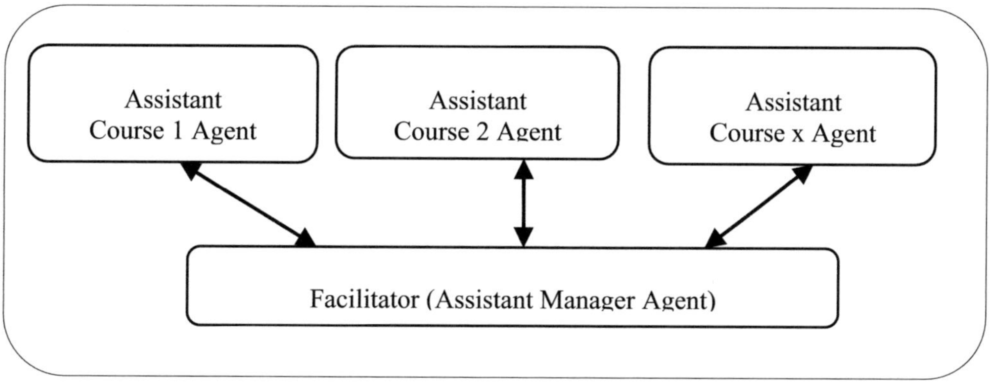

Fig. 4. Assistant Agent

The analysis and design phase of MASCE is done using Beliefs, Desires, Intentions-Agent Based Software Development (BDI-ASPD) (Jo et al., 2004). We find desires first from the system requirements and then find its intention and corresponding belief. This idea comes from the natural approach we usually do in the real world. An agent's beliefs are a set of data describing the state of the environment. They are the knowledge that intentions use to fulfill their goals (desires).

The course material is going to be structured in a hierarchical form where the course is divided into chapters and each chapter is divided into sections which in turn are divided into subsections and so on until we reach the leaves (concepts which cannot be divided any further). For each of these leaves the following will be provided:

1. Teaching materials
2. Quizzes to test student's knowledge level
3. Students' notes (blogs)
4. Discussion forums
5. Questions asked by students requiring help

The student can review all the teaching materials provided and add notes to his blogs if he wants to. He will take quizzes after each module to test his understanding (knowledge level) in that part so as to update his profile. If the student asks a question in a particular section, the Assistant Agent (Match Maker) will try to find the best potential helper for that question who is currently available online, willing and able to provide help. The Assistant Agent uses the students' models in that match making process.

Some of the parameters which are going to be used to in the model are static, they are collected from the student himself through a questionnaire given to the student when he first uses the system including:

1. Help willingness
2. Initial availability
3. Preferences such as cognitive style Maximum numbers of concurrent discussions,
4. Initial belief of the student knowledge level through a simple quiz given to the student to classify him as either: novice, beginner, intermediate or advanced.
5. Weighted importance of various attributes: such as if he requires help quickly from any available willing helper, or he would rather wait to be matched with the helper with the best knowledge level in the concept he is asking about.

Some of these parameters are dynamic; they are updated dynamically as the student interacts with the system and more new information is collected. Old information may be outdated or even wrong. For example, after each help session between two students, an evaluation form is presented to each of them to evaluate his colleague. These peer evaluations along with the collected information about student by the tracking system such as rate of his responses, are all used to update the helpfulness parameter. The actions (parameters) that the tracking system will monitor and that will be collected, modeled and analyzed are:

1. Actual Availability
2. Frequency of logging to the system (number of times in one week period for example)
3. Banned topics or users
4. Preferred users
5. Quizzes taken to update student's knowledge level
6. Downloaded teaching materials
7. Blogs visited and notes added by the student to his blog
8. Number of postings on the forums
9. Frequency and type of questions asked to instructor or peers (not content-based)
10. Number of help requests accepted or rejected
11. Peer evaluation

Whenever a student has a question or a problem in a particular part of the course, he notifies his personal student agent. Interacting with the student personal agent in this manner also helps make users aware of the extent of the effort directed towards locating a suitable helper for them. Users tell their agents any important information that should be considered – e.g. that they know little about a particular topic, and that someone who would help on this topic should be someone who has been voted a good helper by others in the past. Sometimes it might be the case that the learner has a straightforward question, and that speed of response is more important, than depth of knowledge in a topic. This information is then conveyed by the personal student agent to the Assistant Agent (Match Maker) who tries to find the best potential helper who is currently ready or available (online), able (has a good knowledge level of that part) and willing to help. This helps fulfilling the first goal of MASCE.

The assistant agent also groups students together according to their similar preferences and complementing abilities into "buddies groups" to solve group projects or assignments. Thus a community of learners may be built up. So in addition to the one-to-one relationships that grow through the use of MASCE, learners can be arranged into groups with similar concerns who support each other on specific issues. This might be a problem solving session with one or more learners assisting each other with similar problems, or it might be a longer term study group where each member contributes to mutual understanding of the subject matter in some way. Interaction at the one-to-one and the group level is designed to bring learners closer together, and contribute to the evolution of a community of learners anxious to support each other in their learning. Thus the second goal of MASCE which is the promotion of collaboration and knowledge sharing can be fulfilled.

Using this principle of the ready, willing and able helper greatly increases the likelihood of benefit among participants: helpers are dedicated, and are not receiving help requests for which they have too little time or knowledge; the helpee is more likely to receive the kind of help they require, and will perceive the positive attitude of the helper. In return, the helpee may be more enthusiastic to assist the helper should an occasion arise where he is in a position to do so (students can add others to a 'friends list', indicating to their agent their particular willingness to help that person in the future). Thus the kind of community of learners that is built in MASCE is designed to benefit everybody which is the third goal of MASCE (Mahdi and Attia, 2008 a).

4. Data mining techniques used in MASCE

Data mining refers to the analysis of the large quantities of data that are stored in computers. Data mining is about solving problems by analyzing data already present in databases. Data mining is defined as the process of discovering patterns in data. The process must be automatic or (more usually) semiautomatic. The patterns discovered must be meaningful in that they lead to some advantage (Chakrabarti et al., 2009).

Data mining tasks can be categorized into: summarization, classification, clustering, association, and trend analysis. Classification is a method of predicting the decisions for the new cases, based on their conditional features using a model learned from the already known attributes. It has been commonly studied by many data mining researches. Rule Based Classification (RBC) system is a part of classification which represents knowledge via a set of propositional rules. Rule-based data mining algorithms have a number of desirable properties. Rule sets are relatively easy for people to understand. RBC is widely used in the real world applications because of the easy interpretability of the extracted rules (Qin, 2009). We will be focusing our research on classification task and more specifically on rule based classification. Modeling in RBC starts with the process of extracting a set of rules from data source that identifies key relationship between the attribute and class label. Then, the obtained rules are tested with unseen data. Rough Classifier (RC) and Decision Tree Classifier (DTC) are categorized as RBC. Both techniques apply different approach to perform classification but produce same structure of output with good classification results (Mohsin & Abd Wahab, 2008).

4.1 Three levels of knowledge diffusion for MAS

Following the above perspective, data mining techniques can be applied in three alternative manners, leading to three different types of knowledge, which, in turn, correspond to three distinct ways of knowledge diffusion to the MAS architecture (Symeonidis & Mitkas, 2005):

- Data mining on the application level of MAS

Data mining is performed on available application data, in order to discover useful rules and/or associations and/or patterns. The extracted knowledge is related to the scope of the end-user application and not its internal architecture. In this case, the technology coupling issue is viewed macroscopically, where the knowledge models extracted are intended to improve the efficiency of the MAS.

- Data mining on the behavior level of MAS

In this case, data mining is performed on log files containing agent behavior data (i.e., actions taken, messages exchanged, decisions made). The goal is to better predict future agent behaviors by eliminating unnecessary or redundant agent activity. The extracted knowledge may result in more efficient agent actions. In this case, the coupling issue is viewed microscopically, where the knowledge models extracted are intended to improve the performance of an agent engaged in a MAS (i.e., to improve the internal MAS action flow).

- Data mining on evolutionary agent communities

At this level, we perform evolutionary data mining techniques on agent communities, in order to study agent societal issues. This approach tries to achieve the satisfaction of the goals of an agent community, which evolves and learns through interaction. In this case, coupling is considered at a higher level of abstraction, where the main focus is on the formulation of the problem that the agent community has to deal with and the way the extracted knowledge is diffused to the agent community.

4.2 Rough sets mining in MASCE

Rough set theory has proved to be useful in Data Mining (DM) and Knowledge Discovery (KD). It constitutes a sound basis for data mining applications. The theory offers mathematical tools to discover hidden patterns in data. It identifies partial or total dependencies in databases, eliminates redundant data and gives an approach to solve some challenges as null values, missing data, dynamic data and others.

In the past decade there has been done a substantial progress in developing rough set methods for DM and KD. In particular, new methods for extracting patterns from data, decomposition of decision tables as well as new methodology for data mining in multi-agent systems have been developed.

Rough set theory was introduced by Pawlak in 1982. Since then, it has often proved to be an excellent mathematical tool for the analysis of a vague description of objects. The adjective vague (referring to the quality of information) is concerned with inconsistency or ambiguity. Rough sets can be applied on information represented in the form of a table called information system. It is composed of a 4-tuple as follows: $S = < U, Q, V, f >$ where U is the closed universe, a finite set of N objects $\{x_1, x_2, \ldots x_N\}$, Q is a finite set of n attributes $\{q_1, q_2, \ldots q_n\}$, the attributes in Q are further classified into disjoint condition attributes C and decision attributes D, $Q = C \cup D$. Such information systems are called decision tables, $V = \cup_{q \in Q} V_q$ where V_q is a domain (value) of the attribute q, $f = U \times Q \rightarrow V$ is the information function such that $f(x, q) \in V_q$ for every $q \in Q$, $x \in U$ (Cios et al., 1998).

The rough set philosophy is based on the assumption that with every object of the universe U there is associated a certain amount of information (data, knowledge). This information can be expressed by means of a number of attributes. The attributes describe the object. Attributes with preference-ordered domains are called criteria because they involve an evaluation such as: bad, medium, good.

Objects which have the same description are said to be indiscernible (similar) with respect to the available information. The indiscernibility relation thus generated constitutes the mathematical basis of rough set theory. It induces a partition of the universe into blocks of indiscernible objects, called elementary sets, which can be used to build knowledge about a real or abstract world. The use of the indiscernibility relation results in information granulation.

Any subset X of the universe may be expressed in terms of these blocks either precisely (as a union of elementary sets) or approximately. In the latter case, the subset X may be characterized by two ordinary sets, called the lower and upper approximations. A rough set is defined by means of these two approximations, which coincide in the case of an ordinary set. The lower approximation of X is composed of all the elementary sets included in X (whose elements, therefore, certainly belong to X), while the upper approximation of X consists of all the elementary sets which have a non-empty intersection with X (whose elements, therefore, may belong to X).

The difference between the upper and lower approximation constitutes the boundary region of the rough set, whose elements cannot be characterized with certainty as belonging or not to X (by using the available information). The information about objects from the boundary region is, therefore, inconsistent or ambiguous. The cardinality of the boundary region states, moreover, the extent to which it is possible to express X in exact terms, on the basis of the available information. For this reason, this cardinality may be used as a measure of vagueness of the information about X (Cios et al., 1998).

We say that two objects of an information system are indiscernible if for a subset of the attributes A, they have the same value for each attribute: $IND(A) = \{(x, y) \in U \times U: \text{for all } a \in A, f(x, a) = f(y, a)\}$. The indiscernibility relation IND(A) splits the universe U into a family of equivalence classes $\{X_1, X_2, X_3, \ldots X_r\}$ and is denoted by A*. Objects belonging to the same equivalence class X_i are indiscernible. The equivalence classes X_i's are called A-elementary sets. $Des_A(X)$ denotes the description of A-elementary set $X \in A^*$: $Des_A(X) = \{(a = b): f(x, a) = b, \forall x \in X, a \in A\}$.

A given subset of attributes $A \in Q$ determines the approximation space AS = (U, IND (A)) in S. For a given $A \in Q$ and a concept $X \in U$, the A-lower approximation $\underline{A}X$ of set X is the union of all those elementary sets each of which is fully contained by X i.e. $\underline{A}X$ contains all objects that can be classified as certainly belonging to the concept X (based on knowledge from A). $\underline{A}X$ is also called the A-positive region $POS_A(X)$ of X in S.

$$\underline{A}X = \{x \in U: [x]_A \subseteq X\} = \{Y \in A^*: Y \subseteq X\} \tag{1}$$

The A-upper approximations of set X is $\bar{A}X$ is the union of those elementary sets each of which has non-empty intersection with X i.e. it contains all objects that cannot be classified as not belonging to the concept X (based on knowledge from A).

$$\bar{A}X = \{x \in U: [x]_A \cap X \neq \Phi\} = \cup\{Y \in A^*: Y \cap X \neq \Phi\} \tag{2}$$

For given information system some attributes may be redundant (superfluous) with respect to a specific classification A*. Using the dependency properties of attributes, we can find a reduced set of the attributes without loss of classification power.

For an information system S, with $A \subseteq Q$ an attribute $a \in A$ is called dispensable if IND(A) = IND(A–{a}), otherwise a parameter a is indispensable. Absence of dispensable attributes does not reduce the classificatory power while the indispensable attributes carry the essential information about objects and cannot be removed without changing the classificatory power. The set of all indispensable attributes is called a core of A = Core (A). It may be an empty set. (from master thesis)

A proper subset $E \subset A$ that preserves the classification generated by A is called a reduct of A, RED(A) if E is orthogonal (cannot be further reduced) and if E preserves classification as A i.e. E is a minimal set of attributes that discerns all objects in S that are discernable by A. More than one reduct of A can be identified forming a family of reducts $RED^F(A)$, their intersection forms core of A i.e. $Core(A) = \cap RED^F(A)$ (Cios et al., 1998).

One of the important applications of rough sets is the generation of decision rules for a given information system for classification of known objects, or prediction of classes for new objects. One can find the rules classifying objects through different methods. The mostly adopted algorithm for extracting rules extracts rules using the intersections between classifications and partitions: Let decision table $DT = \langle U, C \cup D, V, f \rangle$ where C represents the set of condition attributes, D represents the set of decision attributes, $C^* = \{X_1, X_2, \ldots, X_r\}$ represents the condition classification of U and $D^* = \{Y_1, Y_2, .., Y_m\}$ represents the decision classification of U. The decision rules are logically described as follows: If (conditions) then (decisions). The decision rule which is called τij can be extracted as follows:

$$\tau_{ij} = Des_C(X_i) \Rightarrow Des_D(Y_j) \text{ such that } X_i \cap Y_j \neq \Phi \text{ for } X_i \in C^* \text{ and } Y_j \in D^* \quad (3)$$

A rule is said to be deterministic if $X_i \subseteq Y_j$ i.e. $X_i \cap Y_j = X_i$, otherwise a rule is non deterministic. The set of all decision rules $\{\tau_{ij}\}$ for all classes $Y_j \in D^*$ is called the decision algorithm of the information system S (Slowinski, et al. 2005; Komorowski, et al. 1998).

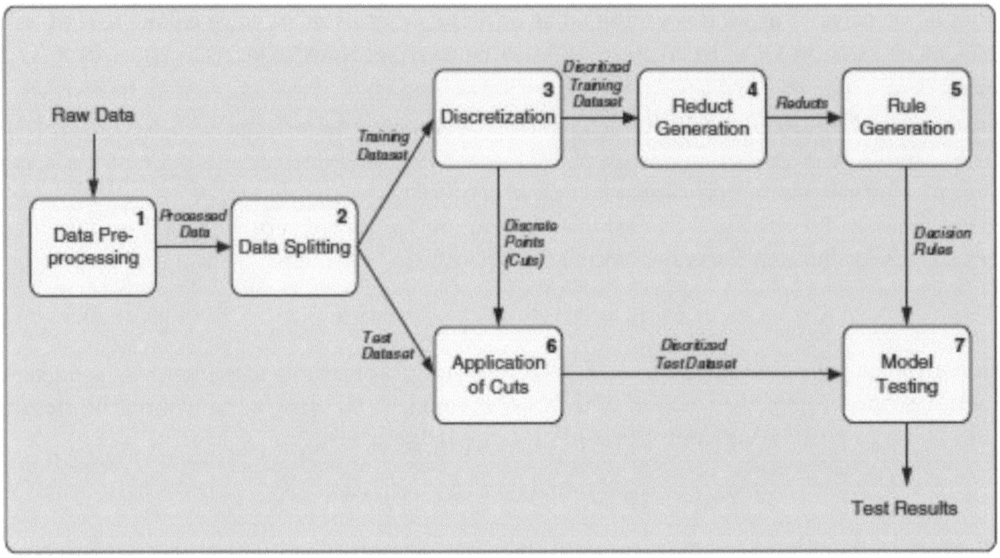

Fig. 5. Process map and the main steps of the rough sets analysis (Olson & Delen, 2008)

The rough sets algorithm implemented in MASCE can be summarized as follows:

This algorithm takes as input a decision table $S = (U, C \cup D, V, f)$ and produces as output the set of decision rules $\{\tau_{ij}\}$ (Attia at al., 2004).

Step 1: Vertical reduction: The vote value is calculated for all the tuples (similar tuples are collapsed into one and their number is added to the vote). Then tuples, with vote values less than the noise filter threshold, are removed from the database table.

Step 2: Horizontal reduction: Attributes reduction is made by calculating the best reduct RED as follows, let all attributes be called AR and the user preferred attributes if any be UA.

Begin

2.1. Construct the modified discernibility matrix M(C):

Each entry m_{ij} contains the condition attributes whose values are not identical on both x_i and x_j where x_i, x_j belong to different classes of IND(D) i.e. they represent different decision concepts. M(C) is a diagonal symmetric matrix.

$m_{ij} = 0$ if $x_i, x_j \in$ same IND(D)

$= \{c \in C: f(c, x_i) \neq f(c, x_j)\}$ if $x_i, x_j \in$ different IND(D)

2.2. Find the CORE from discernibility matrix:

For any $c \in C$, $c \in$ CORE(C) if and only if there exists i, j, $1 \leq j < i \leq N$ such that $m_{ij} = \{c\}$. Note that a core may be empty

2.3. Determine the attribute set UA which user prefers to emphasize. If UA is empty that means that the user does not have preference for any attribute.
2.4. Let RED = CORE $\cup$ UA
2.5. AR = AR - RED
2.6. Find attribute a in AR which has the maximum SGF(a, RED, D)
2.7 RED = RED $\cup$ $\{a_i\}$, AR = AR – $\{a_i\}$ (i =1, 2,...m)
2.8 If k(RED, D) = 1, then stop, otherwise go to step 2.6

/*End of Step 2 */

Step 3: Generate the reduced relation by removing those attributes which are not in the best reduct RED.

Step 4: Combine similar tuples in the reduced relation.

Step 5(a): Transform tuples in the reduced relation into decision rules for each class in D.

Step 5(b): For the same class in the reduced table, two tuples can be combined if the values of the condition attributes differ in only one attribute, thus obtaining a more general set of decision rules.

Or instead of steps 5(a) and 5(b) we can use the following alternative method for generation of decision rules:

Step 6(a): Extract the decision rule which is called τij as follows: $\tau_{ij} = Des_C(X_i) \Rightarrow Des_D(Y_j)$ such that $X_i \cap Y_j \neq \Phi$ for $X_i \in C^*$ and $Y_j \in D^*$.

Step 6(b): Call A rule (deterministic) if $X_i \subseteq Y_j$ i.e. $X_i \cap Y_j = X_i$, otherwise a rule is non-deterministic. The set of all decision rules $\{\tau_{ij}\}$ for all classes $Y_j \in D^*$ is called the decision algorithm of the information system S.

/* End of the algorithm*/

The significance of an individual attribute {a} added to the set A with respect to the dependency between A and D (Decision set) is represented by significant factor SGF, given by:

$$SGF(a, A, D) = k(A+\{a\}, D) - k(A, D) \text{ where } k(A, D) = card(POS_A(D)) / card(U) \quad (4)$$

Complexity of the chosen algorithm

This algorithm can learn a set of decision rules from databases efficiently and effectively. A basic role is played by the reduct and the core. Intuitively, a reduct of the relation is its essential part, which defines all basic concepts occurring in the considered data, whereas core is its most important role. Reducing a relation consists of removing irrelevant or superfluous attributes in such a way that the set of elementary categories in the relation is preserved. This procedure eliminates all unnecessary data from the relation, preserving only useful data. Thus concise, accurate decision rules are derived from the reduced relation.

Suppose there are N tuples in the database which is relevant to the learning task and A attributes for each tuple. The time complexity for the worst case is analyzed as follows. During reduction, to construct the discernibility matrix, it takes O(N×N) steps. To search core attributes in the discernibility matrix costs O(N×N) steps. The best reduct or user minimal attribute subset can be found in A × O(N×N) steps. Since A is usually much less than N, the worst case in the reduction process is O(N×N).

In this research work, we introduce the idea of using Rough Sets as a data mining technique to find the candidate helpers for collaboration with peers. In our case, the condition attributes C are the parameters of the student model explained in Section 3 such as quiz results, peer evaluation, skill level and number of help sessions ignored. The decision parameter D is whether the student is a candidate helper or not. Each of the family of equivalence classes X_1, X_2,....X_r describes a group of students having the same values for different parameters in their models and thus can be candidate helpers for each other. They can be matched together in a one-to-one help session where each of the helper and the helpee profits the other (Mahdi & Attia, 2008 b).

4.3 Decision trees mining in MASCE

Decision tree induction is a well-known discipline in Machine Learning presented by Quinlan in 1986 (Quinlan, 1986). The basic algorithm for decision tree induction is a greedy algorithm that constructs decision trees in a top-down recursive divide-and-conquer manner. In the process of constructing a tree, the criteria of selecting test attributes influences the classification accuracy of the tree. Presently, there are many criteria for choosing the test attribute in building decision tree, such as ID3 (Quinlan, 1986) and C4.5 (Quinlan, 1993) which use an entropy-based measure known as information gain as a heuristic for selecting the attribute.

Decision trees represent a supervised approach to classification. A decision tree is a simple structure where non terminal nodes (internal) represent tests on one or more attributes and terminal (leaf) nodes reflect decision outcomes. The ordinary tree consists of one root, branches, nodes (places where branches are divided) and leaves. In the same way the decision tree consists of nodes which stand for circles, the branches stand for segments connecting the nodes. A decision tree is usually drawn from left to right or beginning from the root downwards, so it is easier to draw it. The first node is a root. The end of the chain "root - branch - node-...- node" is called "leaf". From each internal node (i.e. not a leaf) may grow out two or more branches. Each node corresponds with a certain characteristic and the branches correspond with a range of values. These ranges of values must give a partition of the set of values of the given characteristic (Quinaln, 1986).

Constructing decision tress

The problem of constructing a decision tree can be expressed recursively. First, select an attribute to place at the root node and make one branch for each possible value. This splits up the example set into subsets. If at any time all instances at a node have the same classification, stop developing that part of the tree. The only thing left to decide is how to determine which attribute to split on. There are a number of possibilities for each split. Which is the best choice? The number of yes and no classes are shown at the leaves. Any leaf with only one class—yes or no—will not have to be split further, and the recursive process down that branch will terminate (Witten & Frank, 2005).

Because we seek small trees, we would like this to happen as soon as possible. If we had a measure of the purity of each node, we could choose the attribute that produces the purest child nodes. The measure of purity that we will use is called the information and is measured in units called bits. Associated with a node of the tree, it represents the expected amount of information that would be needed to specify whether a new instance should be classified yes or no, given that the example reached that node.

ID3

One of the oldest decision tree algorithms is ID3. It was designed for when there are many attributes and the training set contains many objects, but where a reasonably good decision

tree is required without much computation. The basic structure of ID3 is iterative. ID3 adopted an information based method that depends on two assumptions. Let C contain p objects of class P and n of class N. The assumptions are:
(1) Any correct decision tree for C will classify objects in the same proportion as their representation in C. An arbitrary object will be determined to belong to class P with probability p/(p + n) and to class N with probability n/ (p + n).
(2) When a decision tree is used to classify an object, it returns a class. A decision tree can thus be regarded as a source of a decision 'P' or 'N', with the expected information needed to generate this decision given by

$$I(p,n) = -\frac{p}{p+n}\log_2\frac{p}{p+n} - \frac{n}{p+n}\log_2\frac{n}{p+n} \tag{5}$$

If attribute A with values [A_1, A_2 . . . . A_v] is used for the root of the decision tree; it will partition C into [C_1, C_2 . . . . C_v] where C_i contains those objects in C that have value A_i of A. Let C_i contain p_i objects of class P and n_i of class N. The expected information required for the subtree for C_i is I(p_i, n_i). The expected information required for the tree with A as root is then obtained as the weighted average:

$$E(A) = \sum_{i=1}^{v}\frac{p_i + n_i}{p+n}I(p_i, n_i) \tag{6}$$

where the weight for the ith branch is the proportion of the objects in C that belong to C_i. The information gained by branching on A is therefore:

$$\text{gain}(A) = I(p, n) - E(A) \tag{7}$$

A good rule of thumb would seem to be to choose that attribute to branch on which gains the most information. ID3 examines all candidate attributes and chooses A to maximize gain(A), forms the tree as above, and then uses the same process recursively to form decision trees (Witten & Frank, 2005).

Complexity of ID3 Algorithm

At each non-leaf node of the decision tree, the gain of each untested attribute A must be determined. This gain in turn depends on the values p_i and n_i for each value A_i of A, so every object in C must be examined to determine its class and its value of A. Consequently, the computational complexity of the procedure at each such node is $O(|C|.|A|)$, where $|A|$ is the number of attributes above. ID3's total computational requirement per iteration is thus proportional to the product of the size of the training set, the number of attributes and the number of non-leaf nodes in the decision tree. The same relationship appears to extend to the entire induction process. No exponential growth in time or space has been observed as the dimensions of the induction task increase, so the technique can be applied to large tasks (Zhao & Zhang, 2008).
The main problem of ID3 is that a sub-tree may repeat several times in a decision tree, and that an attribute may be used for several times in some certain paths of the tree ,which degrades the efficiency of classification. Missing values pose an obvious problem. It is not clear which branch should be taken when a node tests an attribute whose value is missing. Sometimes, missing value is treated as an attribute value in its own right. If this is not the

case, missing values should be treated in a special way rather than being considered as just another possible value that the attribute might take. A simple solution is to record the number of elements in the training set that go down each branch and to use the most popular branch if the value for a test instance is missing.

4.4 Integrated Rough Sets and Entropy (RSE) algorithm in MASCE

Rough Set Entropy (RSE) algorithm for combining Rough Sets and Entropy heuristics is used to induce classification rules. This algorithm is based on Information gain and equivalence relation. It is applied to discrete-valued attributes. We divide the algorithm into three stages (Yang et al., 2003):

(1) First, we select a condition attribute based on information gain; let us call the selected condition attribute c.

(2) Second, use the concepts of rough sets to build equivalence classes. For our knowledge representation system J = (U, C $\cup$ D), subset P={c, d} $\subseteq$ C $\cup$ D (c is the selected condition attribute in step (1), d is the decision attribute) determines an equivalence relation in U: IND(P)={(u, w) $\in$ U x U: q(u) = q(w) for every q$\in$ P} where the number of U/IND(P) is no more than k x m (k is the number of values of c, m is the number of values of d).

(3) Finally, classification rules can be extracted from equivalence classes, for each equivalence class, we get classification IF-THEN rule by extracting attribute values which are identical for all the samples in the equivalence class, we use the condition attribute values as the rule antecedent and use the class label (decision) attribute value as the rule consequent.

Complexity of the Integrated RSE Technique

Comparing RSE with traditional Rough Sets, RSE is simpler because we do not need to build discernibility matrix, nor reduct calculations which can be very time consuming instead of large number of attributes and samples. If we use the RSE, we only need selecting a condition attribute once at the root node, so its time complexity is O(A*N), then it uses rough set theory to establish the equivalence classes then extract classification rules (Yang et al., 2003).

Suppose that the total number of training sample is n, the number of condition attributes is a. If we use ID3 algorithm to get a decision tree, at the worst case, the maximal length from the root node to each leaf node is a, so the total node number of decision tree is less than A*N. At the root node, ID3 algorithm requires analyzing each sample for each condition attribute is O(A*N). For the other nodes, the time complexity is less than root node, so the worst complexity is O(A * N * A *N) i.e. $O(A^2 * N^2)$.

5. Results and analysis

Whenever the student using the system needs help in a certain topic in a certain course, he can either choose among three different machine learning techniques so that MASCE can help him to find the candidate helpers: rough sets, decision trees or an integrated approach Rough Sets Entropy (RSE) combining both rough sets and decision trees. These different classifiers are applied every 12 hours on the decision table - a snapshot of it is shown in Table 1-after it has been updated with students' data collected during the last 12 hours such that the extracted decision rules are always up to date. The decision attribute is Decision with binary values {Yes, No}.

ID	topic	is online	willing to help	maximum concurrent discussions	is preferred agent	is banned agent	is banned topic	quiz result	help evaluation	help ignore	decision
1	Word	Y	N	N	N	Y	N	F	VG	P	N
2	Presentation	Y	N	N	N	Y	N	F	F	P	N
3	XML	Y	Y	Y	N	Y	N	G	F	P	N
4	Power Point	Y	Y	N	N	Y	N	F	E	F	N
5	HTML	N	Y	N	N	Y	N	VG	F	E	N
6	Java	Y	N	Y	Y	Y	Y	G	F	P	N
7	Java Script	Y	N	N	Y	Y	Y	F	P	F	N
8	Power Point	Y	Y	N	Y	N	N	VG	F	VG	N
9	Power Point	N	N	N	N	N	Y	P	P	P	N
10	PDF	Y	Y	Y	N	Y	Y	F	F	F	N
11	PDF	Y	Y	Y	N	N	Y	F	G	E	N
12	UML	N	Y	Y	Y	Y	N	VG	E	P	N
13	PDF	N	Y	N	Y	N	Y	G	F	P	N
14	Java	Y	Y	Y	N	N	Y	F	P	Et	N
15	UML	N	Y	Y	Y	Y	N	F	G	P	N
16	Programming	Y	Y	N	N	Y	N	F	P	F	N
17	Programming	N	Y	Y	N	N	N	F	G	P	Y
18	Java	N	Y	N	Y	N	N	VG	E	P	N
19	Oracle	N	N	Y	N	N	Y	E	VG	VG	N
20	Power Point	N	Y	Y	N	N	Y	G	VG	E	N

E = Excellent, VG = Very Good, G= Good, F=Fair, P = Poor

Table 1. Snapshot (only 20 records) of MASCE Decision Table (100 records) filled with random data

The major criticism of rough sets is that it requires all of the variables to be in nominal format. Rough sets cannot work with numerical continuous valued variables. In order to use such variables, one should perform discretization. Discretization, is a process of converting continuous numerical variables into range labels. We had to assign range labels for some of the condition attributes which have numerical continuous values such as: quiz results, help evaluation and help ignore. The condition attributes of the decision table after discretization are as follows:

- Topic, with possible values {Java, Oracle, Java Script, HTML, UML, PowerPoint, Presentation, PDF, Programming, Documentation and Word}
- Willing to help, with binary values {Yes, No} but filled according to the assumption the 75% of the students are willing to help while only 25% are not willing to help. This assumption agrees with data obtained when trying system with real users
- Help ignore, with possible values {Poor, Fair, Good, Very Good, Excellent} following a normal distribution with mean 25 and standard deviation 10 for those who are willing to help but ignoring help requests.
- Maximum concurrent discussions, with binary values {Yes, No}
- Is preferred agent, with binary values {Yes, No}
- Is banned agent, with binary values {Yes, No}
- Is banned topic, with binary values {Yes, No}
- Quiz results, with possible values {Poor, Fair, Good, Very Good, Excellent} according to normal distribution with mean 65 and standard deviation 15.

Help evaluation, with possible values {Poor, Fair, Good, Very Good, Excellent} with normal distribution dependent on the result of the quiz-result, i.e. mean of this normal distribution is the result of the quiz-results according to the assumption that high quiz results implies higher probability of good peer evaluation.

5.1 Results of Rough Sets classifier

Applying Rough Sets Algorithm to MASCE decision table to determine whether a student is a good candidate for help or not. We first tried the Rough Sets Classifier on MASCE decision table consisting of 100 records filled with random data as shown in Table 1. Applying RS algorithm for finding best reduct, it was found to be: best reduct = {willing to help, maximum concurrent discussions, is banned user, is banned topic}. Using these attributes to build decision rules used for classification new unseen cases asking for candidate helpers, we obtained the following decision rules:

willing to help	maximum concurrent discussions	is banned agent	is banned topic	decisi on	vot e	count of attributes
Y	Y	N	N	Y	10	4
Y	Y		Y	N	9	4
N		Y	Y	N	7	4
Y	N	N	Y	N	7	4
	N	N	N	N	8	4
N	N	N		N	3	4
Y	Y	Y	N	N	11	4
N		N	Y	N	3	4
Y	N	Y	Y	N	6	4

Table 2. Extracted Decision Rules from Rough Sets Classifier

5.2 Results of Decision Trees (ID3) classifier

Choosing to apply decision trees as the machine learning technique on the same decision table to find candidate helpers, we obtained the following decision tree as shown in Table 3.

willing to help	maximum concurrent discussions	is banned agent	quiz result	topic	decision	vote	count of attributes
		Y			N	56	1
Y	Y	N		Documentation	Y	2	4
N	Y	N		Documentation	N	1	4
	N	N		Documentation	N	4	3
Y		N		HTML	Y	2	3
N		N		HTML	N	1	3
Y		N		Java	Y	1	3
N		N		Java	N	1	3
		N	Very Good	Java Script	N	1	3
		N	Poor	Java Script	Y	1	3
		N	Fair	Java Script	N	3	3
		N	Excellent	Java Script	N	1	3
	Y	N		Oracle	Y	2	3
	N	N		Oracle	N	2	3
		N		PDF	N	3	2
		N		Power Point	N	3	2
		N		Presentation	N	2	2
		N		Programming	N	3	2
		N		UML	N	4	2
		N		Word	N	2	2
	Y	N		XML	Y	2	3
	N	N		XML	N	2	3

Table 3. Extracted Decision Rules from Decision Trees Classifier

5.3 Results of Integrated Rough Sets Entropy (RSE) classifier

Choosing to apply an integrated approach (Rough Sets Entropy) to the same decision table for finding the candidate helpers, we obtained the root node for the decision tree as (is banned agent). Using this root node and following the RSE algorithm we obtained the following decision rules shown in Table 4.

willing to help	maximum concurrent discussions	is banned agent	is banned topic	decision	vote	count of attributes
		Y		N	55	1
Y	Y	N	N	Y	10	4
		N		N	44	1

Table 4. Extracted Decision Rules from the Integrated Rough Sets Entropy

5.4 Evaluating deducerd ules

We often need to compare a number of different learning methods on the same problem to see which one is the best to use. It seems simple: estimate the error (using different estimation procedures that will be explained shortly), perhaps repeated several times, and choose the scheme whose estimate is smaller. This is quite sufficient in many practical applications: if one method has a lower estimated error than another on a particular dataset, the best we can do is to use the former method's model. However, it may be that the difference is simply caused by estimation error, and in some circumstances it is important to determine whether one scheme is really better than another on a particular problem. This is a standard challenge for machine learning researchers. If a new learning algorithm is proposed for a certain problem, it must be shown that it improves on the state of the art for the problem at hand and demonstrate that the observed improvement is not just a chance effect in the estimation process.

It is important that the testing data that will be used was not used in any way to create the classifier. As we did in our research, we tried out several learning schemes on the training data and then we want to evaluate them to see which one works best. Other measurements are: the time taken during mining, the complexity of algorithm, and the coverage of the rules. The performance of a classification system cannot be based only on the higher accuracy but the quality of knowledge such as minimum number of rules, rule length, and rule strength also need to be assessed. A good rule set must has a minimum number of rules and each rule should be short as possible. Moreover, an ideal model should be able to produces fewer rule with shorter rule and classify new data with good accuracy.

A comparative study is carried out for the three used classifiers: Rough Set Classifier (RC), Decision Tree Classifier (DTC) and the integrated RSE in terms of accuracy, rule number, rule length and rule coverage. Integrated Rough Sets and Entropy classifier (RSE) outperformed both Rough Sets (RS) classifier and Decision Tree Classifier (ID3) since it performs smaller number of simpler, shorter rules (less number of attributes) as well as a higher coverage.

5.5 Predicting performance

Repeated cross-validation

The question of predicting performance based on limited data is an interesting, and still controversial, one. There are different techniques but the repeated cross-validation is probably the evaluation method of choice in most practical limited-data situations.

The standard way of predicting the error rate of a learning technique given a single, fixed sample of data is to use stratified n-fold cross-validation. The data is divided randomly into n parts in which the class is represented in approximately the same proportions as in the full dataset. Each part is held out in turn and the learning scheme trained on the remaining nine-tenths; then its error rate is calculated on the holdout (test) set. Thus the learning procedure is executed a total of n times on different training sets (each of which have a lot in common). Finally, the n error estimates are averaged to yield an overall error estimate. Tests have also shown that the use of stratification improves results slightly. Thus the standard evaluation technique in situations where only limited data is available is stratified n-fold cross-validation (Witten & Frank, 2005).

Different n-fold cross-validation experiments with the same learning method and dataset often produce different results, because of the effect of random variation in choosing the folds themselves. Stratification reduces the variation, but it certainly does not eliminate it entirely. When seeking an accurate error estimate, it is standard procedure to repeat the cross-validation process 10 times and average the results. This involves invoking the learning algorithm n*n times on datasets. Obtaining a good measure of performance is a computation-intensive undertaking (Witten & Frank 2005).

Leave-One-Out

Leave-one-out cross-validation is simply n-fold cross-validation, where n is the number of instances in the dataset. Each instance in turn is left out, and the learning method is trained on all the remaining instances. It is judged by its correctness on the remaining instance, one or zero for success or failure, respectively. The results of all n judgments, one for each member of the dataset, are averaged, and that average represents the final error estimate. This procedure is an attractive one for two reasons. First, the greatest possible amount of data is used for training in each case, which increases the chance that the classifier is an accurate one. Second, the procedure is deterministic: no random sampling is involved. There is no point in repeating it 10 times, or repeating it at all: the same result will be obtained each time.

On the other hand, its disadvantage is the high computational cost, because the entire learning procedure must be executed n times and this is usually quite infeasible for large datasets. Another disadvantage is that it cannot be stratified, worse than that, it guarantees a non-stratified sample.

Bootstrapping

An alternative, called **Bootstrapping**, involves sampling with replacement to choose elements of the training and test sets. Starting with n training examples, first sample n times, **with replacement**, to give another set (a bag, actually) of n examples. There will nearly always be duplicates in the training set; use the elements not in the training set as a test set. Compute error = 0.632 * test-error + 0.368 * training-error. Repeat steps 1-3 and output average accuracy. These coefficients come from the probability that a particular example will not be picked in n tries is as follows:

$$\left(1-\frac{1}{n}\right)^{n} \cong e^{-1} = 0.386 \tag{8}$$

thus the test set will contain roughly 36.8% of the examples; the training set 63.2% on the average.

Cost of evaluation

In the two-class case with classes yes and no, a single prediction has the four different possible outcomes TP, TN, FP and FN. The True Positives (TP) and True Negatives (TN) are correct classifications. A False Positive (FP) occurs when the outcome is incorrectly predicted as yes (or positive) when it is actually no (negative). A False Negative (FN) occurs when the outcome is incorrectly predicted as negative when it is actually positive (Witten & Frank, 2005).

Confusion matrix

In a multiclass prediction, the result on a test set is often displayed as a two dimensional confusion matrix with a row and column for each class. Each matrix element shows the number of test examples for which the actual class is the row and the predicted class is the column. Good results correspond to large numbers down the main diagonal and small, ideally zero, off-diagonal elements.

	Predicted +	Predicted -
Actual +	True Positives (TP)	False Negatives (FN)
Actual -	False Positives (FP)	True Negatives (TN)

Table 5. Confusion Matrix Parameters

The performance measures can consist of any or all of the following properties of this matrix (Witten & Frank, 2005):

Property	Formula	Interpretation
Accuracy	(TP+TN)/(TP+TN+FP+FN)	Proportion of classifications that were correct
Sensitivity	TP/(TP+FN)	Proportion of actual positives that were predicted that way
Specificity	TN/(TN+FP)	Proportion of actual negatives that were predicted that way
Positive Predictivity	TP/(TP+FP)	Proportion of predicted positives that really were
Negative Predictivity	TN/(TN+FN)	Proportion of predicted negatives that really were

Table 6. Different Performance Measures

We chose to use *Leave-One-Out* technique for testing. As was mentioned earlier, Leave-One-Out is most suitable for small size datasets. Each instance of the dataset is left out, and the learning method is trained on all the remaining instances. It is judged by its correctness on the remaining instance, one or zero for success or failure, respectively. The results of all n judgments, one for each record of the dataset, are averaged, and that average represents the final accuracy estimate.

Confusion matrix using rough sets classifier

	Predicted +	Predicted -
Actual +	TP = 10.0	FN = 0.0
Actual -	FP = 17.0	TN = 73.0

Table 7. Confusion Matrix using Rough Sets Classifier

Confusion matrix using decision trees classifier

	Predicted +	Predicted -
Actual +	TP = 8.0	FN = 2.0
Actual -	FP = 10.0	TN = 80.0

Table 8. Confusion Matrix using Decision Trees Classifier

Confusion matrix using integrated rough sets and entropy classifier

	Predicted +	Predicted -
Actual +	TP = 0.0	FN = 10.0
Actual -	FP = 0.0	TN = 90.0

Table 9. Confusion Matrix using Integrated Rough Sets and Entropy

Comparison of performance measures for three classifiers

Property	Rough Sets	Decision Tree	Rough Sets & Decision Tree
Accuracy	0.83	0.88	0.90
Sensitivity	1.00	0.80	0.00
Specificity	0.82	0.88	1.00
Positive Predictivity	0.37	0.44	Not a Number (as both TP and FP = 0)
Negative Predictivity	1.00	0.98	0.90

Table 10. Comparison of Performance Measures for Three Classifiers

Analyzing the previous data it can be shown that regarding *Accuracy* (Proportion of classifications that were correct) RSE classifier (with 90% accuracy) outperformed both RS classifier (with 83% accuracy) and DT classifier (with 88% accuracy). Also, regarding

Specificity (proportion of actual negatives that were predicted that way), RSE classifier (with 100% specificity) outperformed both RS classifier (82% specificity) and DT classifier with (88% specificity).

On the other hand, regarding *Sensitivity* (i.e. proportion of actual positives that were predicted that way) RSE scored 0 as it was not able to predict any actual positives, while RS classifier had sensitivity of 100% followed by DT classifier with 80% sensitivity.

6. Conclusions and future work

The use of Data Mining techniques in a Multi-Agent System for Collaborative E-Learning (MASE) is introduced. A comparative study is carried out for the three used classifiers: Rough Set Classifier (RC), Decision Tree Classifier (DTC) and the integrated RSE Classifier in terms of accuracy, sensitivity and specificity.

Regarding accuracy & specificity measures, the Integrated Rough Sets and Entropy (RSE) Classifier outperformed the two other techniques.

Quality of the knowledge extracted is also compared in terms of rule number, rule length and rule coverage. Integrated Rough Sets and Entropy classifier (RSE) outperformed both Rough sets (RS) classifier and Decision Tree Classifier (ID3) since it performs smaller number of simpler, shorter rules (less number of attributes) as well as a higher coverage.

Comparison of the two techniques, Rough sets and ID3, in general terms is very difficult. These two methods use different classification criteria. Rough sets is typically based on relations between condition and decision attributes, concepts of positive and boundary region, core and reducts. On the other hand, decision trees (ID3) uses entropy (Information gain) for the classification process. Another difference is the way to represent the derived knowledge. Rough sets uses information tables where as ID3 uses decision trees. Certain kinds of problems are best represented by tables, others by trees while some need a totally different type of data structures. When the sample size is small or when the underlying distribution of data deviates significantly from multivariate normal distribution, rough sets may perform better than decision trees since there is no assumption on the data size and the distribution. Rough sets may also perform better when the data is imprecise, incomplete. To summarize, there is no best approach for all problems. That is why instead of a single method, a hybrid approach benefiting from the combined strengths of both rough sets and decision trees is used and which gave good accuracy and fewer, simpler, shorter rules with high coverage. So according to these experiments, the integrated RSE approach is the most suitable (among the three techniques investigated) for application in our system MASCE.

We find that the decision rules constructed by the integrated method are much simpler in structure (less number of rules and shorter rules) than the constructed decision rules extracted by the other two classifiers. Since the complexity of this algorithm is much less, the computation time is much less. Furthermore, they have higher classification accuracy. All this indicators lead to the conclusion that the integrated rough sets and entropy approach is the most suitable one among the implemented three machine learning techniques to be used in data mining in Multi-Agent System for Collaborative E-learning (MASCE).

We are thus providing an online web mining opposite to the offline web mining which is an aftermath analysis that could give some hints on how an on-line course is effectively used and how its structure could be improved. We are presenting in this research an integrated web mining where the patterns automatically discovered are used to assist learners in their on-line learning. In other words, mined patterns are used on-the-fly by the system to improve the application or its functions. We claim that this is quite a promising approach that successfully combines machine learning techniques with agent technology in e-learning systems in order to provide higher quality services towards the end users of e-learning systems (both students and instructors).

This study showed that advanced data mining methods could successfully be used to help decision making in multi-agent systems with a relatively high degree of accuracy. However, in the context of predictive accuracy, one should be aware of several issues that delimit the applicability and predictive accuracy of data mining models: (i) the nature of the data (including the richness, correctness, completeness and representation of the data itself), (ii) the data mining methods (including their capabilities and limitations to handle different types and combination of data) and (iii) the application domain (including understandability and availability of related factors needed to develop accurate predictive models).

The models (extracted decision rules in our case) are only as good and as predictive as the data used to build them. One of the key determinants of predictive accuracy is the amount and quality of the data used for a study. Although all of the models built in this study provided an acceptable level of prediction accuracy based on variables at hand, their performance levels could be improved by including more relevant variables.

It is recommended that more (and relevant) variables be added to the model when possible to increase the accuracy levels. It is also recommended to test the three classifiers using different techniques other than Leave-One-Out such as Bootstrapping and n-fold cross validation and comparing the results with those obtained here as a future work to this research. Different data mining techniques can also be tested and their results compared with the three classifiers studied in this research.

7. References

Agent Working Group (2000). *Agent Technology, Green Paper*, Technical report, version 1.0, Object Management Group, available at: http://www.jamesodell.com/ec2000-08-01.pdf, last accessed 12/12/2010

Attia, S. S., Mahdi H. K. and Mohammad, H. K. (2004). Data Mining in Intelligent Tutoring Systems using Rough Sets, *Proceedings of the 2004 International Conference on Electrical, Electronic and Computer Engineering (ICEEC'04)*, Cairo, Egypt

Buse. D. P. and Wu, Q. H. (2007). *IP Network-based Multi-Agent Systems for Industrial Automation*, Springer-Verlag, London

Chakrabarti, S., Cox, E., Frank E. et al. (2009). *Data Mining: Know It All*, Morgan Kaufmann Publishers, Burlington, MA

Chen, S. Y., Chiu, M. L. (2005). *Building an Agent-Based System for E-Learning in Digital Design, Computer-Aided Design Applications*, Vol. 2

Cios, K. J., Pedrycz W. and Swiniarski, R. W. (1998), *Data Mining Methods for Knowledge Discovery*, Kluwer Academic Publishers

Jo, Ch., Chen, G., Choi, J. (2004). A New Approach to the BDI Agent-Based Modeling, *Proceedings of the 2004 ACM Symposium on Applied Computing*

Komorowski, Pawlak, Z., Polkowski, L. and Skowron, A. (1998). Rough Sets: A Tutorial, in *Rough-Fuzzy Hybridization: A New Method for Decision Making*, Pal S. K. and Skowron, A. (Ed.), Springer-Verlag

Mahdi, H. K., Attia, S. S. (2008 a). Prioritizing of MAS Architectures for Developing Collaborative E-Learning, *Proceedings of the International Conference on Technology Communication and Education*, Kuwait

Mahdi, H. K., Attia, S. S. (2008 b). Small Dataset Size Clustering in MASCE, *Proceedings of the 2008 International Conference on Frontiers in Education: Computer Science and Computer Engineering*, Las Vegas, Nevada, USA

Mohsin, M., Abd Wahab, M. (2008). Comparing the Knowledge Quality in Rough Classifier and Decision Tree Classifier in Information Technology, In *International Symposium on Information Technology 2008*, Kuala Lumpur, Malaysia

Nwana, H. S. (1995). Software agents: An overview, Knowledge Engineering Review, 11(2):205-244

Olson D. L., Delen D. (2008). *Advanced Data Mining Techniques*, Springer-Verlag, Berlin, Heidelberg

Qin, B., Xia, Y., Prabhaka, S., Tu, Y. (2009). A Rule-Based Classification Algorithm for Uncertain Data, in *IEEE International Conference on Data Engineering*.

Quinlan, R. (1986). Induction of Decision Trees, *Machine Learning*, Vol. 1, No. 1, Kluwer Academic Publishers, Boston, 1986

Quinlan, R. (1993). *C4.5: Programs for Machine Learning*, Morgan Kaufmann Publishers

Sellers, B. H. and Giorgini, P. (2005). *Agent-Oriented Methodologies*, Idea Group Inc.

Shang, Y., Shi, H. and Chen, S. (2001). An Intelligent Distributed Environment for Active Learning, *ACM Journal of Educational Resources in Computing*, Vol. 1, No. 2

Slowinski, R., Greco, S., Matarazzo, B. (2005). Rough Set Based Decision Support, in *Search Methodologies Introductory Tutorials in Optimization and Decision Support Techniques*, Burke, E. K., Kendall, G., (Ed.), Springer

Symeonidis, A. L., Mitkas P. A. (2005). *Agent Intelligence through Data Mining*, Springer Science + Business Media, Inc, USA

Wooldridge, M. (1999). Intelligent agents, In *Multi-Agent Systems: A Modern Approach to Distributed Artificial Intelligence*, Weiss & Gerhard, (Ed.), The MIT Press, Cambridge, MA, USA

Wooldridge, M. (2002). *Introduction to Multi-Agent Systems*, John Wiley & Sons, first edition

Witten, I. H., Frank, E. (2005). *Data Mining: Practical Machine Learning Tools and Techniques*, 2nd Edition, Morgan-Kaufmann, CA, USA

Yang, J., Wang, H., Hu, S. and Hu Z. (2003). A New Classification Algorithm based on Rough Set and Entropy, *Proceedings of the Second International Conference on Machine Learning and Cybernetics*, November 2003

Zhao Y. and Zhang Y. (2008). Comparison of Decision Tree Methods for Finding Active Objects, *Advances in Space Research*, Vol. 41, No. 12

Part 3

Multi-Agent Systems Simulation

14

Decision Support based on Multi-Agent Simulation Algorithms with Resource Conversion Processes Apparatus Application

Konstantin Aksyonov, Eugene Bykov,
Leonid Dorosinskiy, Elena Smoliy and Olga Aksyonova
Ural Federal University
Russian Federation

1. Introduction

The chapter focuses on one of possible approaches to decision support problem, which is based on multi-agent simulation modelling. Most decision support cases generally consist of a set of available alternatives definition, estimation and selection of the best one. When choosing a solution one needs to consider a large number of conflicting objectives and, thus, to estimate possible solutions on multiple criteria.

Multiple objectives become now one of decision support problem regular features, which brings to that decision making people need to estimate multiple forces, influences, interests and consequences that may result from a decision.

We can name increase in performance and reliability, decrease in cost and risk, estimate of system sensitiveness to factor change, structure optimization and much more among the problems of existing organizational technical systems operation and the new ones design. Difficulties in understanding the cause-and-effect dependencies of a complex system lead to ineffective system organization, errors in its design, large costs of error correction. Today modelling becomes the only practically effective tool of an optimal or acceptable decision search in a complex system, the tool for responsible decision making.

Use of situational models in process control facilitates efficiency and taken decisions quality growth, decision taking time decrease, resource consumption rationalization. Dynamic situations modelling systems design is one of perspective directions of decision support systems development. Currently multi-agent systems area is under major research; one of its features is agent collaborations interaction, such agents identify decision making people. An important area of multi-agent technologies application is simulation. Multi-agent systems engineering approaches can be distinguished into two types:

1. Based on object-oriented methods and technologies and
2. Use of traditional knowledge engineering methods.

Object-oriented method extensions and multi-agent systems engineering technologies are developed in methodologies of first type. Certain CASE (Computer-Aided Software Engineering) tools support information systems development based on object-oriented methods (All Fusion, Rational Rose). Object oriented agent behaviour definition language UML-RT is utilized in multi-agent simulation system AnyLogic. Methodologies of second type are built on basis of traditional knowledge engineering methods extension. An actual task is development of dynamic situations modelling system, based on object-oriented technologies.

The main idea of the chapter is situational, multi-agent, simulation and expert modelling methods and tools integration in order to increase the decision support effectiveness in situational control of resource conversion.

2. Multi-agent resource conversion processes in organizational-technical systems

Analysis of various resource conversion processes (RCP), including industrial, organizational-technical, business-processes, etc., reveals their following features.

1. Objects of organizational-technical systems have complicated structure and behaviour algorithms, rely on multiple parameters, which obviously results in their models complexity; this requires complicated hierarchical modular patterns definition at model design stage, as well as intrasystem processes definition utilization (Sovetov & Yakovlev, 2001).
2. Process may be represented accurately within elemental resource conversion operations at lowermost decomposition levels (Aksyonov & Goncharova, 2006).
3. Information flows parameters estimation, defined normalized data structures setting for decision support might be complicated enough in organizational-technical systems. Such systems are characterized with probabilistic behaviour, caused by multiple objective and subjective factors impact, high unsteadiness of information sources and targets, frequent changes in documents provision nomenclature and form, weak routes and information processing methods formalization within an organization, lack of qualified professionals in IT area. All this results in intellectual decision support system requirement, which is able to undertake all formalized functions of executives and provide considerable support in hardly-formalizable tasks. Organizational tasks in many cases have no precise solution algorithms, but are solved within the scope of certain scenarios, generally known by executives, but varying in every specific situation. Such scenarios can hardly be defined with algorithmic models; knowledge representation might be more adequate, as long as it allows behaviour rules modification and provides logical output based on knowledge base contents (Shvetsov, 2004).

In this research, we will define the resource conversion process (RCP) as the process of an input conversion (resources necessary for process execution) into output (products – outcomes of process execution). The main objects of discrete Multi-agent RCP are presented on Fig. 1: operations (*Op*), resources (*Res*), control commands (*U*), conversion devices (*Mech*), processes (*PR*), sources (*Sender*) and resource receivers (*Receiver*), junctions (*Junction*), parameters (*P*), agents (*Agent*). Process parameters are set by the object characteristics function. Relations between resources and conversion device are set by link object (*Relation*). The agents existence resumes availability of the situations (Situation) and decisions (action plan) (*Decision*).

Agents control the RCP objects. There is a model of the decision-making person for every agent. An agent (software or hardware entity) is defined as an autonomous artificial object, demonstrating active motivated behaviour and capable of interaction with other objects in dynamic virtual environment. In every point of system time a modelled agent performs the following operations: environment (current system state) analysis; state diagnosis; knowledge base access (knowledge base (KB) and data base (DB) interaction); decision-making. Thus the functions of analysis, situations structuring and abstraction, as well as resource conversion process control commands generation are performed by agents (Fig. 2).

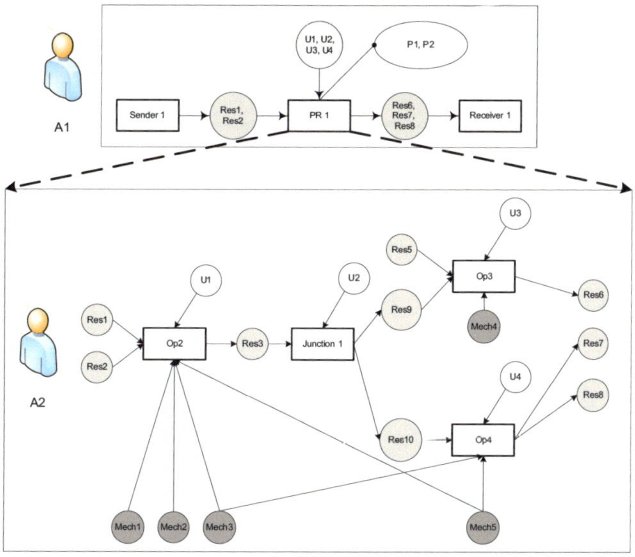

Fig. 1. Hierarchical multi-agent RCP

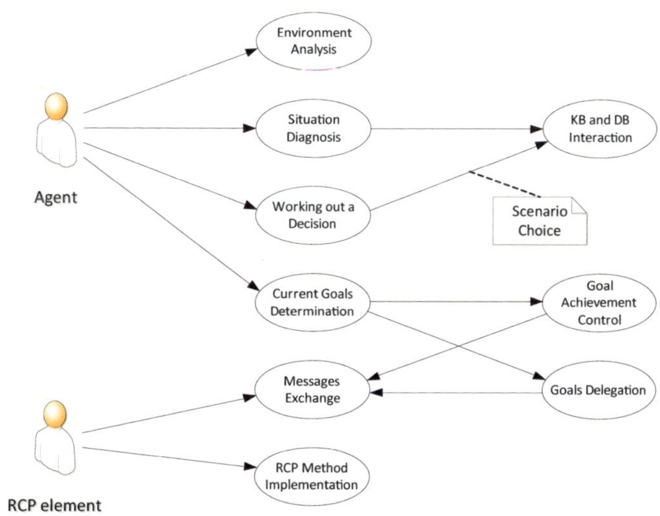

Fig. 2. Use-case diagram determines relations between agents and RCP elements

More detailed information about multi-agent resource conversion processes apparatus is presented in (Aksyonov et al., 2008a).

Current state of multi-agent resource conversion processes dynamic situations modelling systems is defined in next section.

3. Current state of dynamic situations modelling systems

Dynamic situations modelling systems area state analysis reveals unavailability of resource conversion processes oriented systems. Nearest functionality analogues include simulation and expert modelling tools, particularly real-time expert system G2 (G), multi-agent simulation system AnyLogic (L), business-processes modelling system ARIS (T), simulation system Arena (A). Results of these tools comparative analysis are presented in Table 1.

Comparison criteria	T	G	L	A
Subject area conceptual model design	○	○	○	○
RCP description language	●	●	●	●
Systems goals definition:				
- Graphical	●	●	○	○
- Balanced scorecard based	●	○	○	○
- Hierarchical process model	●	●	●	●
Commands description language	○	●	○	○
Use of natural language for model definition	○	●	○	○
Multi-agent modelling availability				
- "Agent" element	○	○	●	○
- Agents behaviour models	○	○	●	○
- Agent's knowledge base support	○	○	○	○
- Message exchange language	○	○	○	○
Simulation modelling	●	●	●	●
Expert modelling	○	●	○	○
Situational modelling	○	●	○	○
Object-oriented approach				
- Use of UML language	●	○	○	○
- Object-oriented programming	○	●	●	○
- Object-oriented simulation	○	●	●	○
- Subject area conceptual model and object-oriented simulation integration	○	○	○	○
Retail price, ths $	50	70	8	4

Table 1. Modelling tools comparison

As we can see, all current systems lack support of some features that might be useful in effective simulation. For example, problem domain conceptual model design and agent-based approach implementation is limited. Another disadvantage of two most powerful systems, ARIS ToolSet and G2, is a very high retail price, which might stop a potential customer. Also systems such as AnyLogic and G2 require programming skills from users. So, from a non-programming user's point of view, no system has convenient multi-agent resource conversion process definition aids. Again, AnyLogic and G2 make use of high-level programming language, which results in these products being highly functional.

Simulation, situational modelling and expert systems are used in modelling, analysis and synthesis of organizational-technical systems and business processes. Multi-agent resource conversion processes theory (Aksyonov & Goncharova, 2006) may be used for organizational-technical systems definition from decision support point of view, a dynamic component of business processes, expert systems, situational modelling and multi-agent systems. Decision support system development requires selection or development of mathematical apparatus.

4. Hierarchical models of control systems

Conceptual analysis or knowledge structuring phase is usually bottleneck in intelligent systems design lifecycle. Structuring methodology is close to large-scale systems (Gig, 1981) or complex systems theory (Courtois, 1985), where engineering process is traditionally emphasized (Bertalanffy, 1950; Bouling, 1956). A major contribution to this theory was made by object-oriented analysis classics (Buch et al., 1993). System analysis is closely interwoven with system theory and includes a set of complicated systems (technical, economical, ecological, etc.) oriented research and modelling methods (Chastikov et al., 2003).

Hierarchical approach (Mesarovich & Takahara, 1978) is traditionally used as a methodological approach for formal system definition decomposition into tiers (or blocks/modules) in complex systems engineering and structuring methods. Top hierarchy tiers are populated with the least detailed views, reflecting only the most common features and characteristics of designed system. Detail level increases on lower hierarchy tiers, while the system is no longer regarded as a whole, but in separate blocks (Chastikov et al., 2003).

Each tier introduces own views on the system and its elements. K-th tier element is considered a system for (k-1)-th tier. Tier-to-tier advancement is severely directional and is defined by engineering strategy - deductive descending «top-down» or inductive ascending «bottom-up» (Chastikov et al., 2003).

In relation to processes formalization deductive descending engineering strategy is used in IDEF0, IDEF3, DFD, EPC notations, as well as in dynamic processes hierarchical models design (aggregates, Petri nets, extended Petri nets). Inductive ascending strategy is used in high-level integration system graphs.

High-level integration system graphs (Avramchuk et al., 1988) are used for multi-agent resource conversion processes hierarchical structure definition (Aksyonov & Goncharova, 2006). An example of such hierarchy is presented on Fig. 3.

From dynamic simulation point of view, only those elements are simulated which were not decomposed at system analysis phase. When using system graphs apparatus all data required for simulation is obtained on first step of dynamic system model design (0-level integration).

5. Object-structural approach to control systems models design

Object-structural approach, offered by T. A. Gavrilova (Gavrilova, 1989), allowed consolidation of these two, traditionally anticipated, engineering strategies. Strategies synthesis, as well as introduction of iterative returns to previous decomposition tiers, allowed a dual concept, offering wide capabilities at knowledge structuring phase to analysts, together for subject area conceptual and functional structure definition.

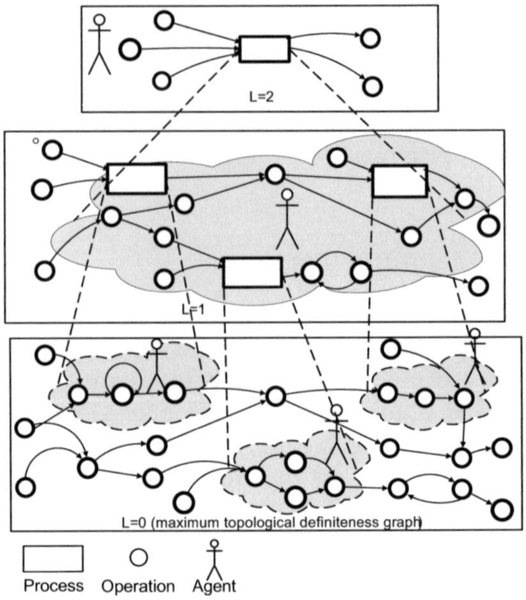

Fig. 3. Multi-agent resource conversion processes hierarchical structure

Fig. 4 illustrates this concept applied to functional structure engineering of an expert system for assistance in multi-service network (further referenced as MSN) development.

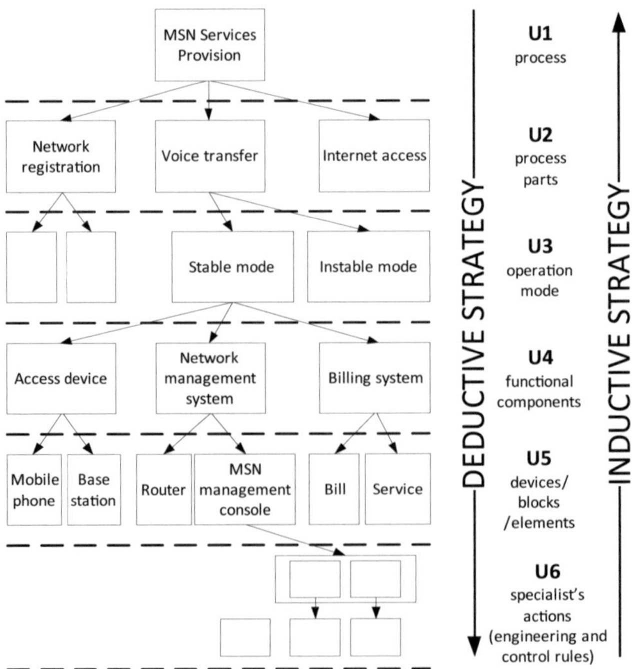

Fig. 4. Dual engineering strategy

6. Knowledge representation model

One of the most important problems in intelligent systems engineering is selection and design of subject area knowledge representation models, that allow the easiest native transition from nonformalized knowledge and views to formal models and knowledge base. Knowledge elicitation and acquisition process might be very complicated in intelligent systems engineering.

Knowledge structuralization complexity is revealed in requirement for subject area model, that allows the most adequate transition to technical implementation with least effort (Shvetsov, 2004).

Subject area conceptual model needs subject area structure to be defined, available objects and subjects behaviour determined, logical interaction models designed. Minsky defined a frame as a structure for stereotyped (standard) situations representation (Minsky, 1975). This structure is filled with various information: defining objects and events expected in certain situations as well as providing guidelines on use of information, contained in a frame. Main idea is to concentrate all knowledge, related to specific objects or events class, in a common data structure, but not to distribute it between a multitude of small structures like logical formulae and productive rules. Such knowledge is either concentrated within the structure itself or available from the structure (e.g. stored within a related structure) (Jackson, 1998).

Each frame is associated with various information (including procedures), e.g. information defining frame use, expected results of frame execution, directions for actions when expectations are not fulfilled, etc.

Frame-based approach reveals the following advantages: frame concept is natively integrated with subject area conceptual modelling; frame structures are easily defined within object-oriented design; inheritance capabilities are effectively supported; subject area hierarchical representation is provided. Thus, frame-based approach selection might be a reason for object-oriented approach and object programming languages application in dynamic situations modelling system development. Such approach minimizes costs for software development as well.

Analysis of Shvetsov's object-oriented design and programming-related research reveals three main model classes, implementing class-based representation formalism: semantic networks and frames-based models; database theory and semantic data patterns-based models; abstract data types-based models. Frame-based languages extend semantic and object-oriented data models capabilities, which substantiates their application and further research in this area.

This research makes use of frame approach, based on frame-like structures association with J.F.Sowa's conceptual graphs constructions (Sowa, 2000), in order to design subject area conceptual model and achieve software development costs reduction. Active and passive frames distinction and agent behaviour consideration are among approach advantages.

Basic frame-concept (FC) construction is presented on Fig. 5 (left) *Frame name* is a unique identifier, used within subject area conceptual model.

Frame-concept level application information contains informal verbal definition of available frame-concept application situations, behaviour scenarios, selection features, etc. Dynamic subject area components and agents behaviour is defined in behaviour scenarios structure, containing scenario selection block that allows current frame alternative behaviour options generation.

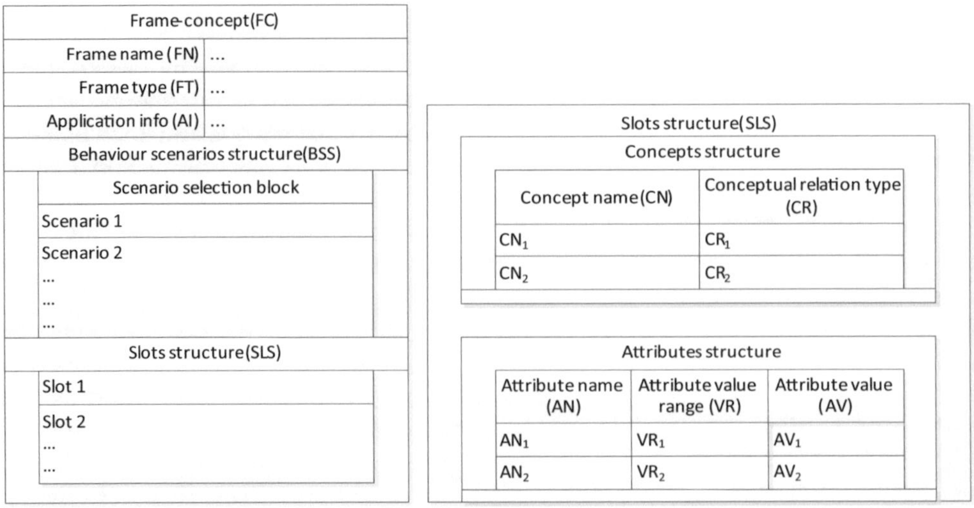

Fig. 5. Frame-concept (left) and slots (right) structure

Slots structure consists of two structures: concepts structure and attributes structure (Fig. 5, right). Concepts structure contains list of frame-concepts, in some way embedded into or descendent from current frame-concept; relation type is indicated in «conceptual relation» field, being relation of specific concept (SC) SCi to current frame-concept FC, SCi is i-th frame-concept name. Frame-concepts are combined into conceptual graphs structures to form subject area logical organization.

Conceptual graph is a bipartite graph with two types of nodes: concept nodes or conceptual nodes and conceptual relations nodes. Thus, frame-semantic knowledge representation is used.

Frame-concept model is defined in the following way:

$$
\begin{aligned}
&FC = \langle FN, FT, AI, BSS, SLS \rangle \\
&SLS = \langle CS, AS \rangle \\
&CS = \{(CN_1, CR_1), (CN_2, CR_2), \ldots, (CN_n, CR_n)\} \\
&AS = \{(AN_1, VR_1, AV_1), (AN_2, VR_2, AV_2), \ldots, (AN_m, VR_m, AV_m)\}
\end{aligned}
\tag{1}
$$

- where FC - frame-concept, FN - frame name, FT - frame type, AI - application information, BSS - behaviour scenario structure, SLS - slots structure, CS - concepts structure, AS - attributes structure, CN_n - concept name, CR_n - conceptual relation, AN_m - attribute name, VR_m - attribute available values range, AV_m - attribute value.

Thus, frame-concept and conceptual graph-based approach to subject area definition allows frame-semantic knowledge representation model use.

Multi-agent resource conversion processes architecture design is described in next sections.

7. Multi-agent resource conversion process model

Multi-agent resource conversion process model was developed on the basis of several approaches integration: simulation and situational modelling, expert and multi-agent systems, object-oriented approach.

The resource conversion processes simulation core is built on the widespread mathematical schemas of dynamic processes description (Petri nets, queuing systems, and system dynamics models). However, it is difficult enough to present all the features of the RCP with the help of specified models (Aksyonov & Klebanov, 2008). This was the reason for further RCP model extension.

Simulation engine algorithm of agent-containing model (Fig. 6) consists of the following main stages: current point of system time identification $SysTime = \min_{j \in RULE} T_j$; agent actions processing (state diagnosis, control commands generation); conversion rules queue generation; conversion rules execution and operation memory state (i.e. resources and mechanisms values) modification. Simulator makes use of expert system unit for situations diagnosis and control commands generation (Aksyonov et al., 2008a).

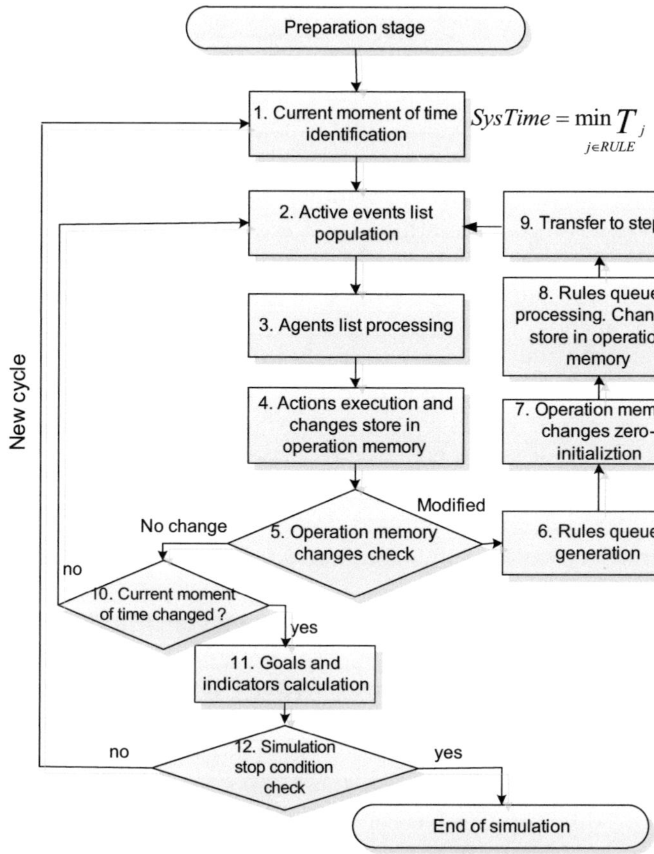

Fig. 6. Simulation algorithm

Each agent possesses its knowledge base, set of goals that are needed for behaviour configuration setting, and priority that defines agent order in control gaining queue.

Generally in case of any corresponding to agent's activity situation an agent tries to find a decision (action scenario) in the knowledge base or work it out itself; makes a decision; controls goals achievement; delegates the goals to its own or another agent's RCP objects; exchanges messages with others.

Multi-agent resource conversion process agent may have hybrid nature and contain two components:

- Intelligent (production rules and/or frame-based expert system access)
- Reactive (agent activity is defined on UML activity diagram)

Right selection and implementation of multi-agent architecture is a key factor in multi-agent object oriented decision support system design.

8. Multi-agent RCP extension with InteRRaP architecture

Two main agent architecture classes are distinguished. They are:

1. **Deliberative** agent architecture (Wooldridge, 2005), based on artificial intelligence principles and methods, i.e. knowledge-based systems;
2. **Reactive** architecture, based on system reaction to external environment events.

All currently existing architectures cannot be defined as purely behavioural or purely knowledge-based. Any designed architecture is hybrid, offering features of both types.

Multi-agent resource conversion process architecture is based on InteRRaP (Muller & Pischel, 1993; Aksyonov et al., 2009a) architecture, as the most appropriate for subject area. InteRRaP architecture represents an aggregate of vertically ordered levels, relating to common management structure and using common knowledge base. Architecture consists of blocks: external environment interface, reactive sub-system, planning sub-system, cooperation with other agents, and hierarchical knowledge base. External environment interface defines agent capabilities in external environment objects and events perception, influenceability, and means of communication. Reactive sub-system utilizes agent capabilities in reactive behaviour, as well as partly utilizes agent knowledge of procedural kind. It is based on «behaviour fragment» concept as reaction draft in some standard situation. Planning sub-system contains planning mechanism that provides agent local plans capability (not related to co-operative behaviour). Cooperation sub-system is responsible for building co-operative behaviour plans, focusing on certain joint goals, or fulfilment of obligations for other agents, as well as implementation of agreements.

In accordance with InteRRaP architecture common concept, multi-agent RCP agent model is represented in four levels:

1. **External environment** model corresponds to the following MRCP elements: convertors, resources, tools, parameters, goals. External environment performs the following actions: generates tasks, transfers messages between agents, processes agent commands (performs resource conversion), alters current state of external environment (transfers situation S_n into state S_{n+1}).
2. **External environment interface** and reactive behaviour components are implemented in form of agent production rules base and inference machine (simulation algorithm).
3. **Reactive behaviour** components performs the following actions: receives tasks from external environment, places tasks in goal stack, collates goal stack in accordance with adopted goal ranging strategy, selects top goal from stack, searches knowledge base. If appropriate rule is located, component transfers control to corresponding resource convertor from external environment. Otherwise, component queries local planning sub-system.
4. **Local planning** level purpose is effective search for solutions in complex situations (e.g. when goal achievement requires several steps or several ways for goal achievement are

available). Local planning component is based on frame expert system. Frame-concept and conceptual-graph based approach is utilized for knowledge formalization.

Subject area conceptual model and agent local planning knowledge base design is based on UML class diagram extension. Semantically this notion may be interpreted as definition of full decision search graph, containing all available goal achievement ways (pre-defined by experts). Current knowledge base inference machine is implemented in decision search diagram, based on UML sequence diagram. Each decision represents agent activity plan. Each plan consists of a set of rules from reactive component knowledge base. Based on located decision, current agent plan is updated. Examination of all available options, contained in knowledge base, generates agent plans library.

If an agent, when processing task or message received from external environment, is unable to locate appropriate rule in its knowledge base (e.g., select an option from several ones), the reactive behaviour component queries plans library, indicating goal (i.e. task to execute, or external environment state to bring into). Planning sub-system searches plans library, selects appropriate plan and places first rule of selected plan into reactive component goals stack.

9. Intelligent agent operation algorithm

Special-purpose object-oriented language RADL (Reticular Agent Definition Language) in form of **When-If-Then** construction implemented in agents and multi-agent systems engineering system *Agent Builder* (Reticular Systems, Inc.) (Andreichikov & Andreichikova, 2004) is used as a basis for agent behaviour rules. Mental model includes intentions, desires, obligations and capabilities as well as agent behaviour rules definition. Specific intelligent actions are calculated on the basis of this model. Rule constituents perform the following functions: **When<...>** contains new messages, received from other agents; **If<...>** compares current mental model with rule application conditions; **Then<...>** defines actions, associated with current events, mental model and environment state.

Considering that agent mental model is represented with goal-setting model and **When** function is immediately incorporated into algorithm, the following agent behaviour rules structure will be used in resource conversion processes subject area:

- **Name** <Rule Name>
- **If** <Message Conditions, RCP Conditions, G_Ag Conditions>
- **Then** <G_Ag Changes, Message Actions, Private Actions>

- where *Message Conditions* - message related conditions; *RCP Conditions* - resource conversion process related conditions; *G_Ag Conditions* - goal realted conditions; *G_Ag Changes* - agent current goals modifying actions; *Message Actions* - message generation actions; *Private Actions* - convertors and resource related actions (activity plan), targeting set goals achievement.

Rules parts may be represented in form of first-order predicates. We assume that n-ary predicate on A set is a n-ary function, certain on A set, with the values from *{true, false}* set. An aggregate of sets with elements from A $(a_1, a_2, ..., a_n)$, resulting in $P(a_1\ a_2, ..., a_n)=true$ is a n-ary relation, corresponding to P predicate. On the contraty, any n-ary R relation on A set corresponds to P predicate $P(x_1, x_2, ..., x_n)$

$$P(a_1, a_2, ..., a_n) = \begin{cases} \text{true, if } (a_1, a_2, ..., a_n) \in \mathrm{R}, \\ \text{false, if } (a_1, a_2, ..., a_n) \notin \mathrm{R}. \end{cases} \quad (2)$$

Then part includes actions and action plans, i.e. either a set of serial-parallel operations, bound to time, or a **Decision**.
Next section presents development principles and technical decisions of designed object-oriented multi-agent resource conversion processes based decision support system, relying on above-stated multi-agent resource conversion process model and multi-agent architecture.

10. Multi-agent systems simulation and engineering systems integration

Object-oriented decision support system BPsim.DSS ("Business Processes Simulation - Decision Support System") is implemented on basis of dynamic situations modelling system BPsim.MAS ("Multi-Agent Simulation"), software engineering system BPsim.SD ("Software Designer") and technical economical engineering system BPsim.MSN ("Multi-Service Network") integration.
The following program packages are being used during multi-agent resource conversion processes subject area business process modelling and software design (www.bpsim.ru), offering a comprehensive solution for business modelling and techno-economic engineering problems, which in turn considerably simplifies and speeds analysts' work:

- *BPsim.MAS* - multi-agent dynamic situations modelling system (Aksyonov et al., 2008a). BPsim.MAS offers the following functionality:
  a. Multi-agent resource conversion process model design;
  b. Dynamic simulation;
  c. Experiment results analysis;
  d. Model- and results-based reporting;
  e. Experiment data export to Microsoft Office family products.
- *BPsim.SD* - Software Developer CASE tool
  BPsim.SD offers automation on the following phases of software development:
  a. DFD diagrams design is not automated. As in every CASE tool a DFD diagram needs to be designed manually;
  b. Use-case diagrams design is fully automated, use-case diagrams are achieved by a transition from a DFD diagram. This process lets us keep our business objects;
  c. Classes diagram design is partially automated. The core classes' frames are generated automatically, that greatly simplifies work on the final class diagram. Benefit is estimated in 10-15%;
  d. Sequence diagram design is semi-automatic.
  e. Database structure generation is automated.
  BPsim.SD offers an opportunity of forms design. This allows the end-user place the controls on the form as he wants them to be positioned. Some of the controls can be associated with data on the phase of GUI design before passing the project to the developers. After this phase a developer receives GUI forms in an appropriate format, i.e. the forms are saved in a software development file format (Aksyonov et al., 2008b).
- *BPsim.MSN* - techno-economic engineering intellectual system (Aksyonov et al., 2009b) automates the following functions:
  a. Subject area conceptual model engineering;
  b. Filling the knowledge base data;
  c. Decision search diagrams design, setting up dialog-based expert system;
  d. Decision search.

- *BPsim Wizard Technology* – a framework of intelligent software assistants for step-by-step model definition. A wizard is a dialog-based program assistant targeting information integration and conversion from one system (BPsim.DSS / BPsim.MAS / BPsim.SD) to another. BPsim Wizard Technology performs the following functions:
  a. Transfers information between simulation, decision support and software engineering modules in the framework of a single complex problem;
  b. Simplifies a non-programming user experience when getting started with BPsim products family;
  c. Validates data on various stages of simulation model design, subject area conceptual model and information system engineering.

Various tools and methods use on all stages of organizational technical systems analysis and synthesis and their support by BPsim products is presented in Table 2.

No	Stage	Tool	Support in BPsim
1.	Processes definition	IDEF0 notation	SD, MSN
		DFD notation	SD, MSN
		UML use-case diagram	SD, MSN
		Multi-agent resource conversion processes notation	MAS
2.	Software engineering	DFD use-case, class, sequence diagrams	SD, MSN
3.	Knowledge formalization	Semantic networks	MSN
		Frames	MSN
		Production rules	MAS
4.	Decision support	Simulation	MAS
		Multi-agent simulation	MAS
		Situational control	MAS, MSN
		Dialog-based expert systems	MSN

Table 2. Methods used in BPsim products

Recently a model and algorithm that are based on transition from multi-agent resource conversion process model to information system model and represented with frame-based semantic network have been developed. A choice of frame-based semantic network as a knowledge representation model facilitates further technical implementation of transition algorithms, since the frame concept can easily be combined with object-oriented design. The transition is implemented on the basis of a dialog-based expert system.

A data processing function, unidirectional or bidirectional, confirms to any converter while automating enterprise processes. The functions include generation, reception, transmission, modification, deletion, etc.

Information system engineering problem domain conceptual model allows the demonstration of the structure of the information system and interconnections between its components. First level of semantic network comprises nodes corresponding to information system database and software. Further these nodes are decomposed up to user interface variables and objects and database tables and stored procedures.

Much more information of real life is required for information system engineering. This must be taken into consideration in data analysis, when data is structured according to certain rules. Each node of resource conversion process semantic network can be represented with corresponding class that possesses its properties and methods for the engineering method implementation.

Fig. 7 demonstrates transition algorithm from resource conversion process problem domain "Resource" object to problem domain elements presented in a form of decisions search visual diagram, built on sequence diagram with integrated dialog-based expert systems apparatus.

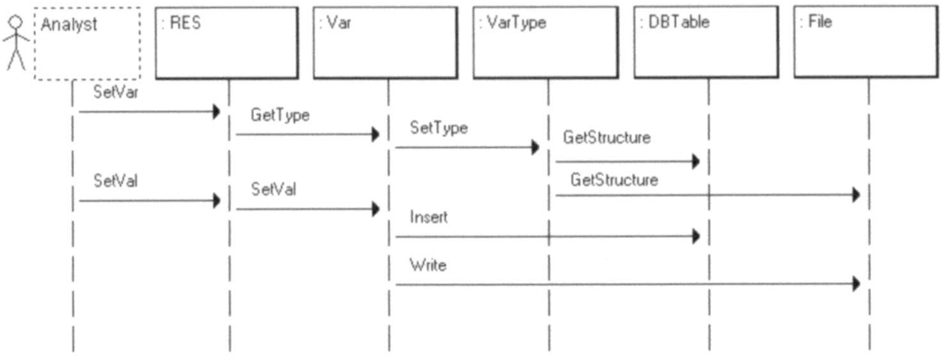

Fig. 7. "Resource design" decision search diagram

BPsim.DSS agent model is represented with four levels in compliance with InteRRaP architecture general concept. External interface and reactive behaviour components together with external environment model are implemented in BPsim.MAS tool. Local planning component is based on BPsim.MSN expert system module. Expert system shell visual output mechanism builder is based on decision search diagrams (UML sequence diagram extension) and presented on Fig. 8. Cooperation level is based on both modules.

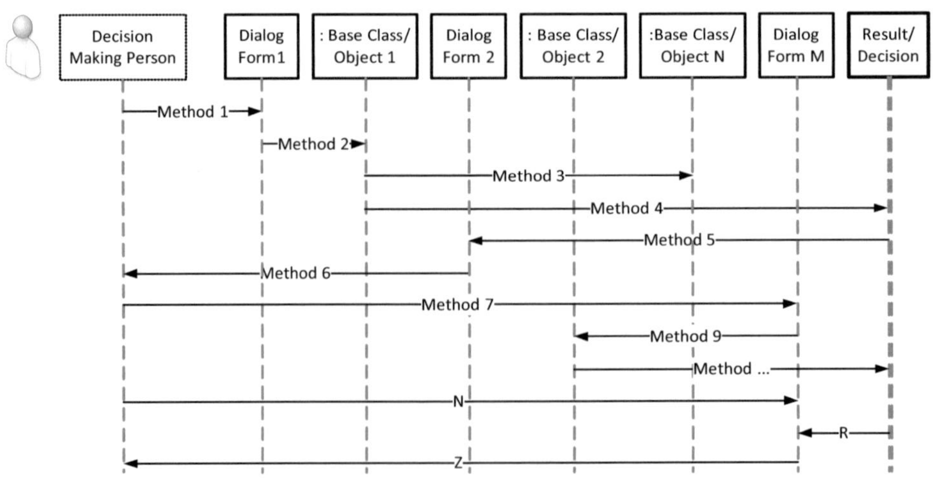

Fig. 8. General decision search diagram in decision support system BPsim.DSS

An example, illustrating decision search diagram workflow, is presented on Fig. 9. For simplification the dialog form classes are not shown on the diagram. The example illustrates work of expert system for real estate agency. The figure shows available house/apartment search in the database on the basis of user set criteria. The search is run in form of decision search diagram.

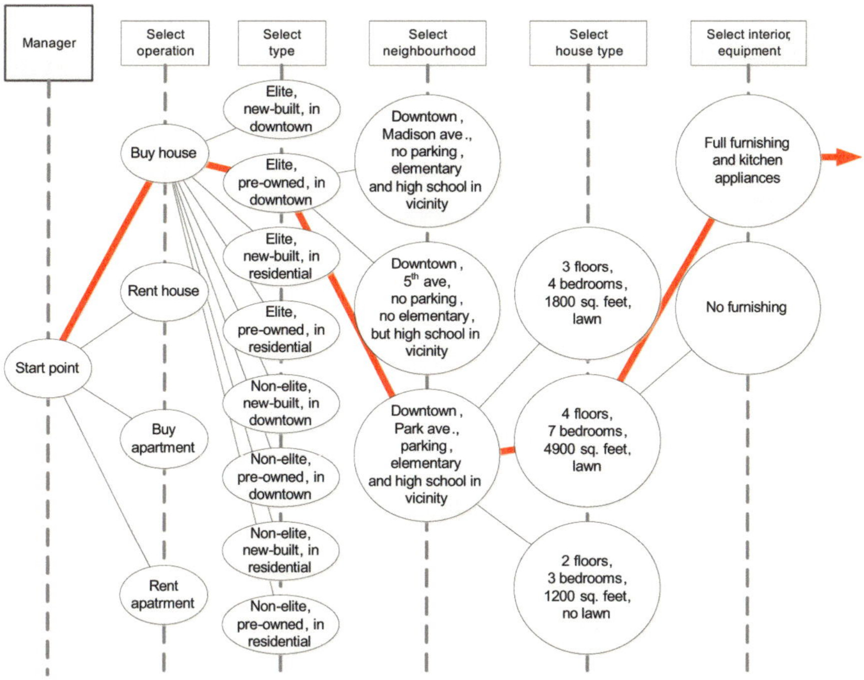

Fig. 9. Decision search tree for decision search diagram

Scheme, presented on Fig. 10, shows interaction of separate units during agent activity within BPsim.MAS and BPsim.MSN integrated scope. Basic principles and separate agent activity stages were mentioned above in section, devoted to InteRRaP architecture conceptual model.

Object-oriented decision support system BPsim.DSS allows the following features implementation:

1. Subject area conceptual model definition
2. Multi-agent resource conversion process dynamic model design
3. Dynamic simulation
4. Experiment results analysis
5. Reporting on models and experiment results
6. Data export to MS Excel and MS Project

Decision support system visual output mechanism builder, based on decision search diagrams (Fig. 8), as well represents agent knowledge base, based on frame-concepts. So, agent knowledge base may be defined in two ways: productive (see Fig. 12 later on) and frame-concept - based (see Fig. 15 later on).

There are several examples demonstrating BPsim.DSS system application. They are presented in the next section.

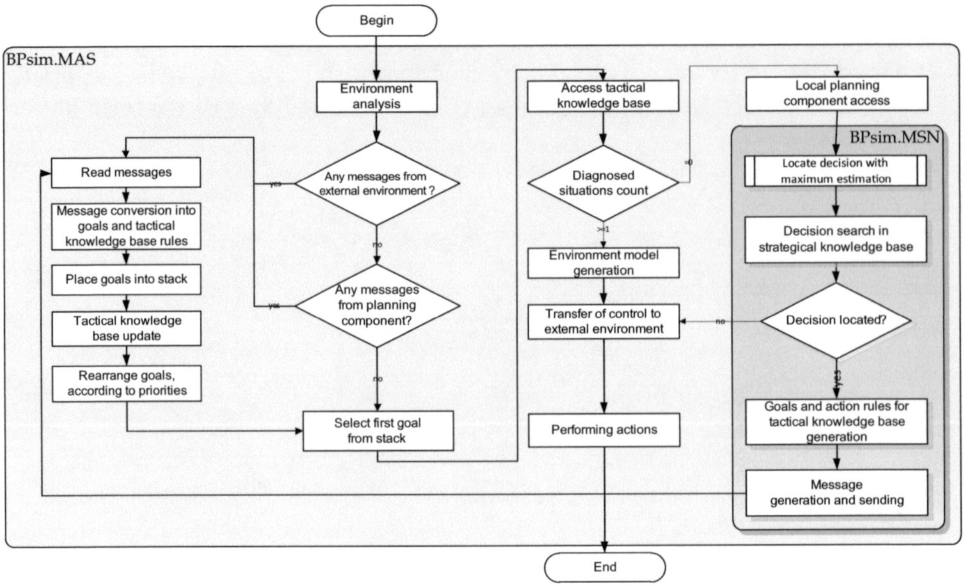

Fig. 10. Intellectual agent activity algorithm

11. BPsim.DSS system application

11.1 BPsim.DSS application to IT projects management

Decision support system BPsim.DSS was used on various stages of Ural State Technical University Common Information System (CIS) development and deployment, starting with educational process analysis stage, performing re-engineering, and ending with separate CIS units deployment efficiency estimation.

Model of an agent (decision making person), controlling software development process in Ural State Technical University, was developed in decision support system BPsim.DSS. Model consists of simulation model "Educational process software development" and decision support models, including the main model "CIS implementation options selection". Model knowledge base contains information on networking, hardware and software, information systems, IT-projects, teams of IT-specialists.

Expert system module is used for project alternatives and effective alternative search algorithms knowledge base development. Simulation model is used for separate project stages monitoring, detection of errors and conflicts, occurred on initial planning stage, solution of vis major, that happens during development project control and CIS deployment. Simulation model is based on Spiral model of software lifecycle and is designed in BPsim.DSS.

Currently AS-TO-BE model data is implemented in CIS program modules and deployed in Ural State Technical University. Due to "Contingent traffic" process improvement and automation dean's office employees work efficiency was raised by 27%, student desk employees work efficiency was raised by 229%. Deployment economical effect is estimated by about 25 thousand euro per calendar year. Economical effect is achieved in shortening and automation of unnecessary document processing stages, information double input prevention and employee load decrease.

Table 2 presents effiency of BPsim use compared to the use of an average CASE tool. Data is based on the CIS development, during which the following diagrams were designed in order to build the final product: 25 DFD diagrams, 14 use-case diagrams, 1 classes diagram and 18 sequence diagrams. Table makes use of experimental statistical data, acquired during development of other projects, which include average times of a certain diagram type design time. Thus, an average time of a single use-case diagram design is 40 minutes, for classes diagram it is also 40 minutes and 90 minutes for a single sequence diagram.

Stage	Average CASE tool	BPsim	Efficiency	Number of diagrams	Benefit, min
DFD diagrams design	Varies, manual	Varies, manual	-	25	-
Use-case diagrams design	40 mins per diagram, manual	5 mins per diagram, automated	35 mins per diagram	14	490
Classes diagram design	40 mins, manual	6 mins, base classes automation	34 mins	1	34
Sequence diagrams design	90 mins, manual	50 mins, semi-automatic	40 mins per diagram	18	720
Database structure generation	5 mins, automated	5 mins, automated	-	N/A	-
GUI design	N/A	Forms designer	+	N/A	N/A

Table 3. Estimation of BPsim efficiency

11.2 BPsim.DSS application for industrial enterprise marketing strategy development on the basis of competing agents model

BPsim.DSS was used for multi-agent dynamic model development of Urals Industrial Group, CJSC (further referenced as UIG), plastic window frames construction, installation and maintenance enterprise. The main reason for modelling is UIG behaviour algorithm and pricing strategy development, targeting share of the market growth and transition to higher technological level, increasing enterprise competitiveness. One more reason for simulation is search for optimal market share (or production volume). The general UIG business process is presented on Fig. 11.

Model makes use of the following parameters:

- enterprises (share of product market; sales volume; premises price per square meter; processes timing data);
- competitive environment (number of competitors on market, share of the market, strife intensity, competitors prices, reaction on time and price, estimated competitiveness rate, elasticity of demand on price, demand seasonality, market capacity).

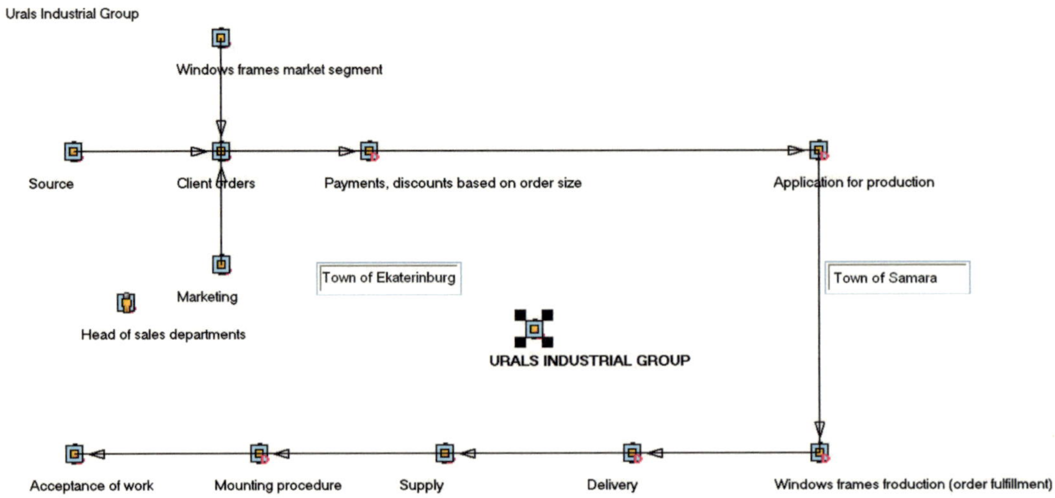

Fig. 11. UIG general business process, presented in BPsim.MAS

The model considers manufacture, sale, installation, servicing processes of the enterprise. Fragment of the model together with single agent's knowledge base in If-Then form is presented on Fig. 12.

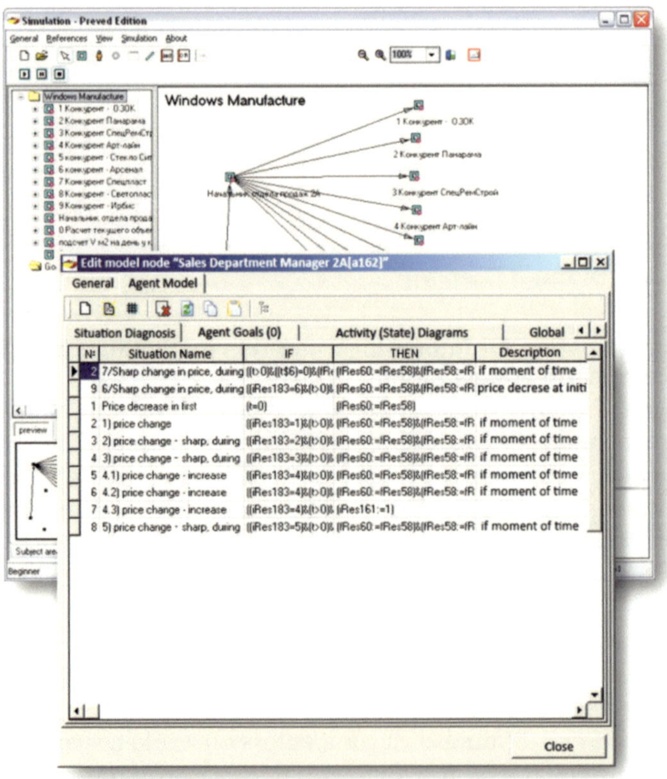

Fig. 12. UIG frames manufacturing process and agent's knowledge base

Deployment in Urals Industrial Group focused on effective pricing strategy search, considering passive and active competitors behaviour. A number of experiments considering various agents-competitors behaviour sets (active/passive) were run. Fig. 13 presents the output data, which are various strategies, resulting in two small competitors' displacement from the market.

After a series of experiments a pricing policy, resulting in share of the market growth from 6.6% to 20-22%, was determined. Limiting to current problem the optimal values of processes characteristics were calculated. The projected saving rate from the modelling results implementation is estimated by €1.9 million per year. In addition, optimal values for the number of distribution points and mounting units depending on seasonal demand and applied to the current pricing strategy were calculated in the framework of the current project.

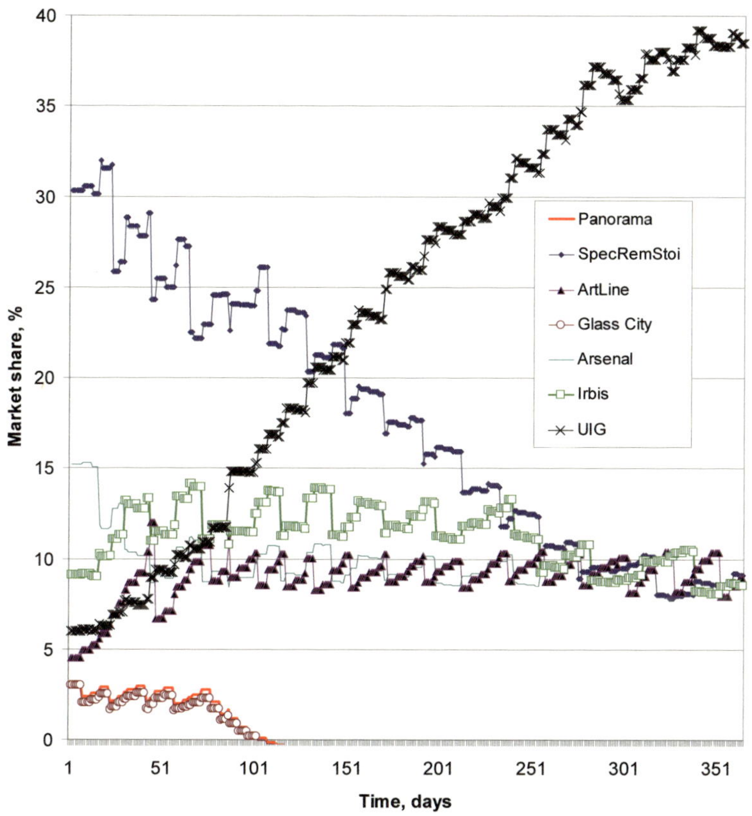

Fig. 13. Competitors displacement from market (competitors' passive behaviour)

11.3 BPsim.DSS application to multi-service telecommunication networks technical economical engineering

Another application of BPsim.DSS included multi-service telecommunication network models design and telecommunication services area business processes dynamic simulation (Fig. 14).

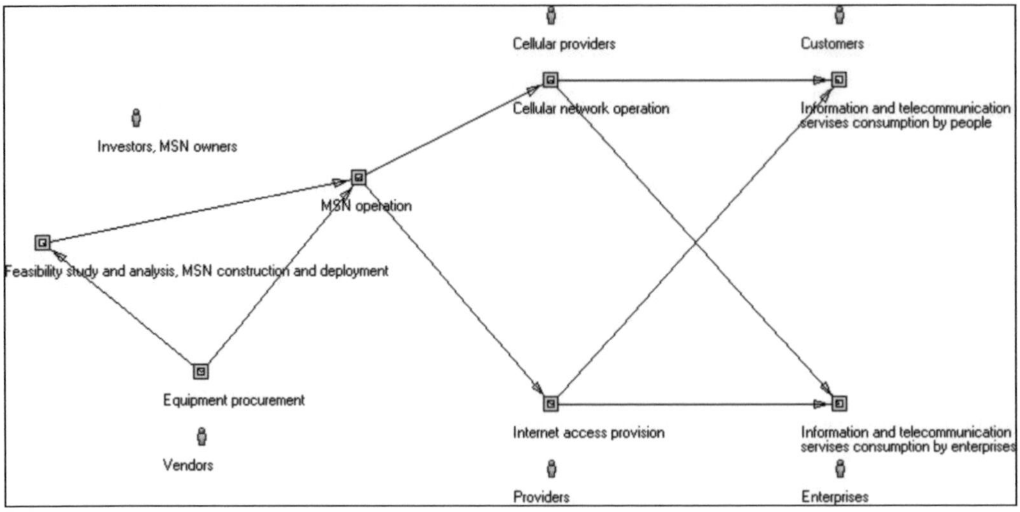

Fig. 14. Telecommunication technologies-based services market main processes and players

Currently leading Russian region cellular carriers engineers polling revealed, that carriers' development departments use their own experimental knowledge base when engineering data-communication networks, while data-communication implementation engineering solutions are foisted by hardware vendors. No operator either makes use of data-communication networks automated design aids, or models various designed/existing network behaviour situations when developing new regions, introducing new services or modifying data-communication network topology.

Development of automated design and modelling methods and aids requires large quantity of primary data for qualitative MSN technical and economical engineering, which includes: telecommunication hardware and technologies types and parameters; engineers, economists, project managers, marketers, and lawyers' level of knowledge.

Decision support systems fit most for MSN technical and economical engineering problem solution. Decision support systems can make use of simulation, expert and situational modelling (Aksyonov & Goncharova, 2006). Decision support systems development and deployment within cellular communication operators is a pressing and needed problem.

The following mathematical methods are used in MSN and business processes modelling, analysis and synthesis tasks: teletraffic theory may be used on all MSN levels except services level; simulation, situational and expert modelling methods are used for business processes analysis and synthesis tasks. Expert and situational modelling methods, neural networks, multi-agent and evolutionary modelling methods can be used in RCP formalization.

Multi-agent resource conversion processes theory is applied for MSN definition from decision support point of view.

Frame-concept and conceptual graphs based approach, offered by A. N. Shvetsov and implemented in form of «Frame systems constructor» expert system shell (FSC), is used as a means of knowledge formalization. A frame-based semantic network, representing feasible relations between frame-concepts, is defined in form of extended UML classes diagram, at the stage of system analysis.

UML sequence diagram is used for visual FSC output mechanism builder implementation (Fig. 15). This approach allows visual (in form of flowchart) problem solution flow definition, when solution turns into a sequence of procedure (method/daemon) calls from one frame to another. Hereby, this approach allowed visual object-oriented ontology and knowledge-based output mechanism constructor implementation in form of decision search diagrams. Fig. 16 illustrates a fragment of decision search process in form of decision search diagram, with a fragment of MSN simulation model on background.

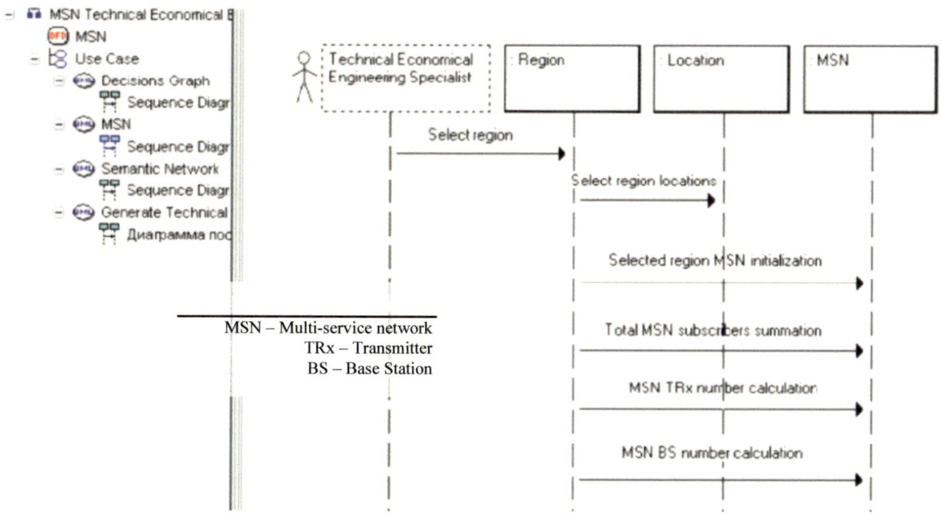

Fig. 15. Visual FSC output mechanism builder

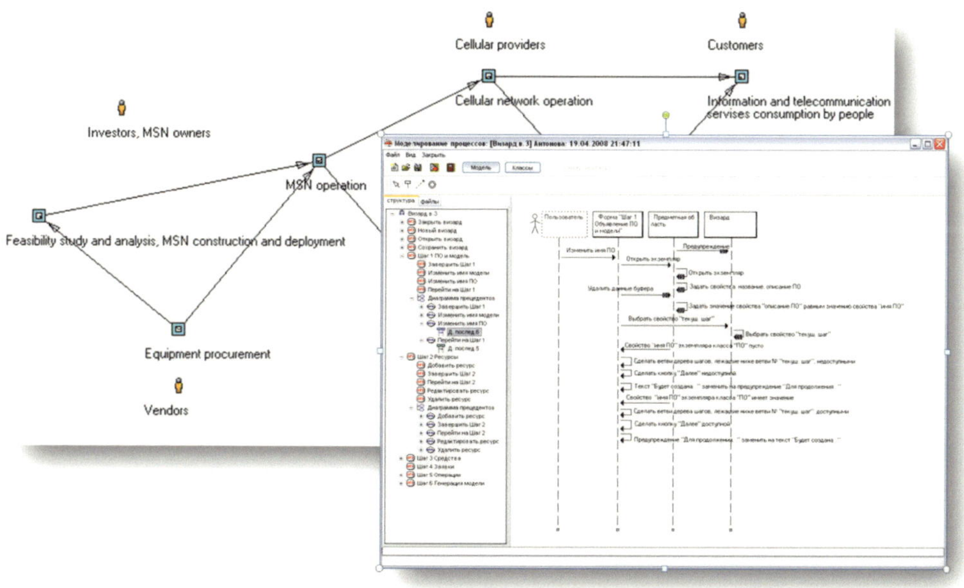

Fig. 16. MSN model and decision search process

BPsim.DSS was applied for MSN technical economical engineering in Ural region, covering metropolis Ekaterinburg, Russia, and satellites. Designed model is shown on Fig. 17.

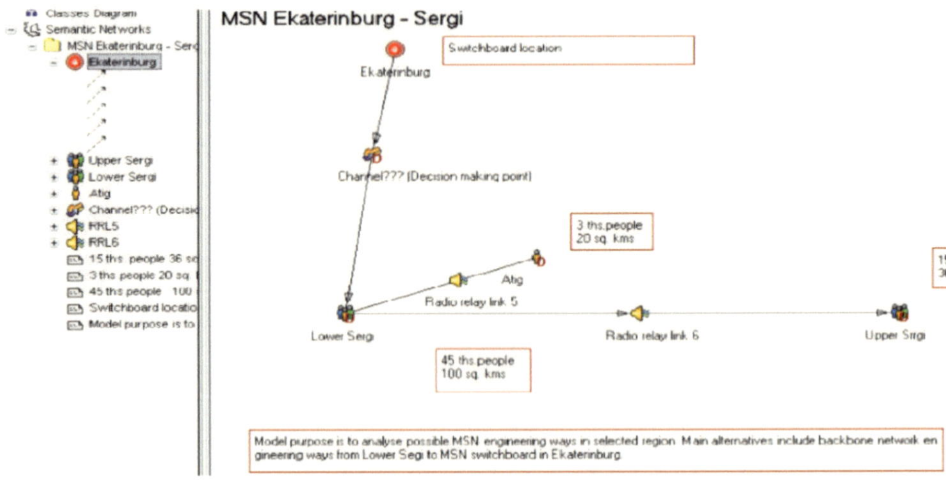

Fig. 17. MSN Ekaterinburg – Sergi model view

This constructor, provided that being filled with MSN subject area knowledge and technical and economical engineering rules, represents an intelligent MSN automated engineering system.

Graphical implementation of the model is presented on Fig. 18. Model allows switching on and off Base Stations (Access network elements) and Transport Networks, as well as changing elements parameters and allowing to select from options of renting or constructing a specific element.

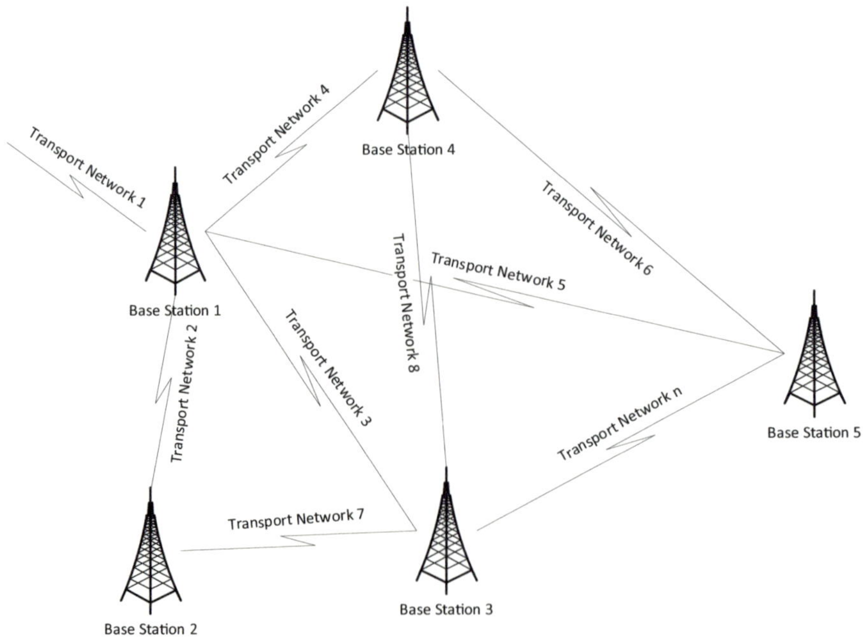

Fig. 18. Modelled MSN graphical model

The model is designed with a main purpose of MSN technical economical engineering with a centre in the metropolis and covering surrounding towns. Main goal is to estimate available MSN deployment options for provision of cellular and data transfer services.
Synthesized model allows estimation of main investment indicators (IRR, EBI, Payback Period), that are required for substantiated decision making in MSN engineering.
Live, one of the experiments that performed best, was implemented and performance indicators were measured after a certain while of performance. The real indicators were close to ones estimated with aid of decision support system BPsim.DSS.
Transition from engineering to simulation modelling is implemented by semantic match making between FSC and multi-agent RCP elements. BPsim.DSS system from the object-structure analysis (OSA) (Gavrilova, 1989) point of view is presented in Table 4.

Stratum	Knowledge type	Stratum levels *[BPsim.DSS functionality]*
s_1	WHAT FOR-knowledge	Strategic analysis: system purpose and functions *[Mission, vision, strategies, goals, indicators]*
s_2	WHO-knowledge	Organizational analysis: system project team *[Experts, analysts, decision-making people (agents)]*
s_3	WHAT-knowledge	Conceptual analysis: main concepts, conceptual structure *[FSC (hardware, technologies, MSN, services, processes, etc.)]*
s_4	HOW-knowledge	Functional analysis: hypotheses and decision-making models *[Agents' behavioural models (scenarios)]*
s_5	WHERE-knowledge	Tridimensional analysis: environment, hardware, telecommunications *[Geographic information system (regional geographic characteristics)]*
s_6	WHEN-knowledge	Time analysis: time parameters and limitations *[Simulation modelling (limitations in payback period, MSN deployment period, etc.)]*
s_7	WHY-knowledge	Causal analysis: system explanation system engineering *[Expert systems, knowledge and agent-rules bases, output mechanizm]*
s_8	HOW MUCH-knowledge	Economic analysis: resources, expenses, profits, payback *[Solution (MSN technical and economical project)]*

Table 4. Engineering and simulation system BPsim.DSS from OSA point of view

11.4 BPsim.DSS application to subaru auto dealer logistical processes simulation

Finally, BPsim.DSS was applied to Subaru auto dealer sale process. Simulation result analysis helped this process be optimized, i.e. certain initial parameters being modified, resulting in effective logistics and warehouse processes. Initial data for simulation included sales statistics for each model, average retail pricing and dealer price markup, together with sales statistics depending on initial car location (at warehouse on location, at official Subary representative's warehouse in Moscow, at Japanese warehouse ready for delivery),

including number of contracts and average delivery time from the order date. The main purpose was to estimate the necessary number of cars of each model at the warehouses on location and in Moscow, in order to achieve sales results of 20 to 40 cars per month.
Another model for Subaru auto included simulation of car repair process. The model considered main repair process stages, resulting in effective search of repair strategy.
Model was designed to examine, analyse and improve repair department activity of two dealers in Siberian region of Russia, and was based on the statistical data from the dealers. The model can be used by other enterprises, provided that it is adapted accordingly.

12. Conclusion

In this chapter we have presented the following keynote features.
Some popular dynamic situations modelling systems including AnyLogic, ARIS, G2, Arena were compared. This comparison revealed the necessity of a new system development, for it to be focused on multi-agent resource conversion processes. Among the disadvantages of the named systems we can name an incomplete set of features for dynamic situations modelling system; no support for subject area conceptual model engineering and multi-agent models, containing intelligent agents, design; incomplete multi-agent resource conversion processes problem orientation; programming user orientation; high retail price.
Multi-agent resource conversion process situational mathematical model requirements were designed. The model must provide the following functions: dynamic resource conversion processes modelling; definition of intelligent agent communities, controlling the resource conversion process; situational approach application.
System development required multi-agent resource conversion process model definition. The following features of the model were designed:

- Multi-agent resource conversion process main objects;
- Graphical notation;
- System graphs apparatus was applied to hierarchical process structure definition;
- Frame-semantic representation, based on frame-concepts and semantic graphs, was selected for knowledge representation model, which allowed subject area conceptual model definition;
- InteRRaP hybrid architecture was selected as a basis of multi-agent system;
- Multi-agent resource conversion process output mechanism, rule types, intelligent agent activity algorithm and situational simulation modelling algorithm were designed.

Based on the model and multi-agent resource conversion process system analysis, a software family of BPsim products was developed. It offers the full list of functional features, required from a problem-oriented dynamic simulation modelling systems and implements the following specific features:

- Subject area conceptual model definition;
- Multi-agent models definition, including both reactive and intelligent agents;
- Multi-agent resource conversion processes problem orientation;
- Balanced scorecard methodology integration;
- Significantly lower retail price.

Simulation, expert, situational and multi-agent modelling integration with object-oriented approach allowed implementation of new object-oriented multi-agent resource conversion processes simulation and decision support method, reflected in development of object-oriented decision support system BPsim.DSS, deployed at companies in Ural region of Russia.

The mathematical model is based on discrete resource conversion process model. Within its framework the problem of transition between the knowledge representation, conceptual model and their technical implementation on relational database level, was solved. This approach allows Transact-SQL language to be used for subject area models design, data and knowledge input, logical output mechanism implementation.

13. Acknowledgment

This work was supported by the State Contract No. 02.740.11.0512.

14. References

Aksyonov K.A., Sholina I.I. & Sufrygina E.M. (2009a). Multi-agent resource conversion process object-oriented simulation and decision support system development and application, *Scientific and technical bulletin*, Vol. 3 (80), Informatics. Telecommunication. Control, St.Petersburg, pp.87-96.

Aksyonov K.A., Smoliy E.F., Popov M.V. & Dorosinskiy L.G. (2009b). Development of decision support system «BPsim3»: Multi-service telecommu-nication networks design and modelling application, *Proceedings of 10th Inter-national PhD Workshop on Systems and Control*, September 22-26, 2009, Hluboka nad Vltavou, Czech Republic, pp. 112-117

Aksyonov K.A., Bykov E. A., Smoliy E. F. & Khrenov A. A. (2008a). Industrial enterprises business processes simulateon with BPsim.MAS, *Proceedings of the 2008 Winter Simulation Conference*, Pages 1669-1677

Aksyonov K.A., Spitsina I.A. & Goncharova N.V. (2008b). Enterprise information systems engineering method based on semantic models of multi-agent resource conversion processes and software, *Proceedings of 2008 IADIS International Conference on Intelligent Systems and Agents, part of Multi Conference on Computer Science and Information Systems (MCCSIS)*, July 22-27, 2008, Amsterdam, Netherlands, pp. 225-227.

Aksyonov K.A. & Klebanov B.I. (2008). *Resource conversion processes simulation*, USTU, Ekaterinburg

Aksyonov, K.A. & Goncharova N.V. (2006). *Multi-agent resource conversion processes dynamic simulation*, Ekaterinburg, USTU

Andreichikov A.V. & O.N.Andreichikova (2004). *Intelligent information systems*, Moscow: Finance and statistics.

Avramchuk E.F., Vavilov A.A. & S.V.Emelianov (1988). *Technology of system simulation*, Moscow: Machine construction industry; Berlin: Techniques

Bertalanffy L. (1950). An Outline of General Systems Theory, *British Journal of the Philosophy of Science*, Vol. 1, pp. 134-164

Bouling K.L. (1956). General Systems Theory, *The Skeleton of Science. Management Science*, № 2, pp. 197-208

Buch G., Rambo D. & A. Jacobson (1993). *UML Language. User Manual*, Moscow: DMK

Chastikov A. P., Gavrilova T. A. & Belov D. L. (2003). *Expert systems development. CLIPS environment*, St. Petersburg

Courtois P. (1985). On Time and Space Decomposition of Complex Structures, *Communications of the ACM*, Vol. 28, № 6., pp. 596-610
Gavrilova T.A. (1989). *Training expert system developers team*, Kishinev, pp. 59-62
Gig J. van (1981). *Applied General Systems Theory*, Mir, Moscow
Jackson P. (1998). *Introduction to expert systems. 3rd Edition*. Addison Wesley
Mesarovich M. & Takahara Ya. (1978). *Common system theory: mathematical basics*, Moscow, Mir
Minsky M. (1975). *A framework for representing knowledge in the psychology of computer vision*, P.H.Winston (ed.), McGraw-Hill
Muller J.P. & M.Pischel (1993). *The Agent Architecture InteRRaP: Concept and Application*, German Research Centre for Artificial Intelligence (DFKI)
Shvetsov, A.N. (2004). *Corporate intellectual decision support systems design models and methods*, DPhil research paper, St.Petersburg, Russia
Sovetov B.Y. & Yakovlev S.A. (2001). *Systems modelling*, Moscow, High School
Sowa J.F. (2000). *Knowledge representation: Logical, Philosophical, and Computational Foundations*, Pacific Grove, CA: Brooks/Cole Publishing Co.
Wooldridge M. (1995). Intelligent Agent: Theory and Practice, *Knowledge Engineering Review*, Vol. 10 (2).

15

Agent-based Simulation Analysis for Effectiveness of Financing Public Goods with Lotteries

Ichiro Nishizaki, Tomohiko Sasaki and Tomohiro Hayashida
Hiroshima University
Japan

1. Introduction

In this chapter, we present the result of agent-based simulations to examine the effectiveness of financing public goods. Morgan (2000) develops a mathematical equilibrium model of lotteries for financing public goods. Moreover, Morgan and Sefton (2000) conduct experiments with human subjects and focus on the following three points. First, when it is efficient to provide a positive amount of public goods, the provision of the public goods through the lottery mechanism is more than the provision through the voluntary contribution mechanism. Second, the provision of the public goods increases with the size of the lottery prize. Third, wagers of the lottery mechanism vary with the return from the public goods. On the whole the results of the experiments support the above three predictions from the mathematical equilibrium model.

Simulation analysis is advantageous for implementing a model of a certain social system and examining the effectiveness of the social system, and from this viewpoint we employ simulation analysis in order to show the effectiveness of lotteries for financing and to examine the validity of the mathematical equilibrium model and the experiments with human subjects. While mathematical models are based on optimization such as maximization of the individual payoff or utility, our agent-based simulation model is based on adaptive behaviors of agents, that is, agents evaluate results of their decisions and revise policies to select one among multiple alternatives as actual decision makers do so. From this sense we can expect a reasonable interpretation of the gaps between the results of the mathematical equilibrium model and the experiments with human subjects.

As concerns approaches based on adaptive behavior models, Holland and Miller (1991) interpret most of economic systems as complex adaptive systems, and point out that simulations using artificial societies with adaptive agents is effective for analysis of such economic systems. Axelrod (1997) insists on the need for simulation analysis in social sciences, and states that purposes of the simulation analysis include prediction, performance, training, entertainment, education, proof and discovery.

In the literature, some successful attempts of agent-based simulations are reported. For the iterated prisoner's dilemma game, Axelrod (1987) examine the effectiveness of strategies generated in an artificial society system, in which agents endowed with strategies are adaptively evolved by using a genetic algorithm.

Dorsey et al. (1994) employ an artificial decision mechanism using neural networks to imitate decision making of auctioneers, and compare the behavior of artificial agents with that of real auctioneers which often deviates from Nash equilibria. To estimate bid functions of bidders, i.e., to establish appropriate weights of a neural network for determining bids, they employ a genetic adaptive neural network algorithm based on genetic algorithms instead of the error back propagation algorithm which is a commonly used method. The objective of their study is to identify the optimal bid function given the bids of the experimental subjects, and then they explore neural networks as an aid in evaluating economic data.

Andreoni and Miller (1995) use genetic algorithms to model decision making in auctions. As in Dorsey et al. (1994), they also compare the decisions of artificial adaptive agents with the experimental data by human subjects, and find that the two types of decisions by the artificial agents and the human subjects resemble each other. Erev and Rapoport (1998) investigate a market entry game by using an adaptive learning model based on reinforcement learning proposed by Roth and Erev (1995). Rapoport et al. (2002) also deal with market entry games, and compare the decisions observed in experiments with human subjects with the actions of artificial adaptive agents with a learning mechanism using reinforcement learning, and analyze behavioral patterns in the aggregate level of the experimental data.

Leshno et al. (2002) consider equilibrium problems in market entry games through agent-based simulations with agents' decision mechanism based on neural networks, and the neural networks are trained not by some teacher signals but by outcomes of games. They compare the results of the simulations with the experimental data by human subjects shown in Sundali et a. (1995), and find some similarities between phenomena of the simulations and the experiments. Nishizaki et al. (2005) investigate the effectiveness of a socio-economic system for preserving global commons by simulation analysis. Moreover, using an agent-based simulation model, Nishizaki et al. (2009) examine the behavior of agents with respect to the social norm by varying values of some parameters. A number of attempts have been made for performing multi-agent based simulations and developing the related techniques underlying ideas from distributed artificial intelligence and multi-agent systems (BanerjeSen, 2002; Chellapilla and Fogel, 1999; Conte et al., 1997; Downing et al., 2001; Epstein and Axtell, 1996; Moss and Davidsson, 2001; Niv et al., 2002; Parsons et al., 2002; Sichman et al., 2003).

By the above mentioned researches and the related articles, the effectiveness of simulation analysis with artificial adaptive agents has been recognized. In this chapter, to examine the effectiveness of lotteries for financing public goods, we give results of the agent-based simulations with decision and learning mechanism based on neural networks and genetic algorithms by extensively varying values of the parameters of the mathematical equilibrium model (Morgan, 2000) which is also the basis of the experiments with human subjects by Morgan and Sefton (2000). In particular, it should be noted that, in our system, a genetic algorithm is used not to establish appropriate weights of a neural network such as Leshno et al. (2002) but to develop agents with good performance, as used in Nishizaki et al. (2009).

In the simulations, we deal with three parameters: the exogenous contribution which becomes the prize in the lottery game and utilizes for funding the public goods directly in the voluntary contribution game, the marginal per capita return of the public good provision, and the group size which is the number of players in the games. Furthermore, providing a simple learning mechanism and a more elaborate one, we examine which of agent behaviors with those two learning mechanisms approaches closer to the prediction of the mathematical equilibrium model.

In section 2, we briefly review the mathematical equilibrium model by Morgan (2000) and the experiment with human subjects by Morgan and Sefton (2000). In section 3, we describe agent-based simulation model with learning mechanisms based on neural networks and genetic algorithms. We give the results of the simulations in section 4, and analyze sensitivity with respect to parameters of our model in section 5. Finally, in section 6 we make some concluding remarks.

2. A mathematical equilibrium model and experiments for financing public goods by lotteries

A mathematical equilibrium model for financing public goods by lotteries is developed by Morgan (2000). Let the set of players be denoted by $N = \{1, \ldots, n\}$, where a player is a contributor in a voluntary contribution game or a bettor in a lottery game. In general, player i has the following payoff function:

$$U_i = w_i + h_i(G), \tag{1}$$

where w_i is the wealth of player i and $G \in \mathbb{R}_+$ denotes the level of the public goods provided; $\mathbb{R}_+$ is the set of non-negative real numbers; player i has a diminishing marginal payoff from the provision of the public goods, i.e., the payoff $h_i(G)$ from the provision G of the public goods is characterized by $h_i'(\cdot) > 0$ and $h_i''(\cdot) < 0$; and U_i is assumed to be quasi-linear.
For a voluntary contribution game, player i chooses $x_i \in [0, w_i]$ so as to maximize the payoff

$$U_i = w_i - x_i + h_i(x(N)), \tag{2}$$

where x_i is the amount of wealth contributed by player i, and $x(N) \equiv \sum_{i \in N} x_i$ denotes the total contribution of all the players.
For a lottery game, player i chooses a wager $x_i \in [0, w_i]$ so as to maximize the expected payoff

$$U_i = w_i - x_i + \frac{x_i}{x(N)} R + h_i(x(N) - R), \tag{3}$$

where R is a prize of some fixed amount.
The results of the mathematical equilibrium model by Morgan (2000) are summarized as follows.

1. Voluntary contributions underprovide the public goods relative to first-best levels.
2. The lottery with a fixed prize has a unique equilibrium.
3. The lottery with a fixed prize provides more of the public goods than the voluntary contributions.

In the experiment by Morgan and Sefton (2000), a linear-homogeneous version of the above-mentioned model by Morgan (2000) is dealt with. For the voluntary contribution game, each player has the same endowment e, and an exogenous contribution R is used to fund the public goods together with the total contribution of all the players. Thus, the payoff of player i is represented by

$$U_i = e - x_i + \beta(x(N) + R), \tag{4}$$

where β is the constant marginal per capita return of the provision of the public goods, and player i chooses a contribution $x_i \in [0, e]$ so as to maximize the payoff (4).
Assuming $\beta < 1$, for all i, the predicted equilibrium contribution of the voluntary contribution game is

$$x_i^{VC} = 0. \tag{5}$$

For the lottery game, the whole sum of wagers is assigned to the public good provision, and the exogenous contribution R is used to fund a prize. Therefore, the expected payoff of player i is represented by

$$U_i = e - x_i + R\frac{x_i}{x(N)} + \beta x(N). \tag{6}$$

Player i chooses a wager $x_i \in [0, e]$ so as to maximize the payoff (6). Then, the predicted equilibrium contribution of the lottery game is

$$x_i^L = \frac{R(n-1)}{n^2(1-\beta)}. \tag{7}$$

In the experiment, the payoff (4) is given to a subject in the voluntary contribution game or the payoff (6) in the lottery game. The primary parameters of the experiment are given as: the number of players $n = 4$, the initial endowment $e = 20$, the exogenous contribution $R = 8$, and the marginal per capita return $\beta = 0.75$. The game is iterated 20 times each treatment. The results are summarized as follows.

1. In the voluntary contribution game, the average contribution in the initial round was about 10.5, it decreased as rounds proceeded, and finally it became 8.075 in the final 20th round. The final average contribution 8.075 was considerably larger than the equilibrium contribution $x_i^{VC} = 0$.
2. In the lottery game, the average wager in the initial round was about 10, it was almost changeless as rounds proceeded, and finally it became 10.35 in the final 20th round. The final average wager 10.35 was larger than the equilibrium wager $x_i^L = \frac{8(4-1)}{4^2(1-0.75)} = 6$ and the final average contribution of 8.075 in the voluntary contribution game of the experiment.
3. In the treatment of the lottery game with the exogenous contribution $R = 16$ which was twice as large as that of the baseline treatment, the average wager in the initial round was about 13, it was almost changeless as rounds proceeded, and finally it became 13.825 in the final 20th round. This result implies that large prize lotteries will be more successful fund-raising devices than smaller scale endeavors.
4. In the treatment of the lottery game without the marginal per capita return, i.e., $\beta = 0$, the average wager in the initial round was about 8, it extremely decreased as rounds proceeded, and finally it became 2.425 in the final 20th round. This result implies that wagers are substantially reduced when the link between the public good provision and the lottery proceeds is broken.

3. A simulation model

In most of mathematical models, it is assumed that players are rational and then they maximize their payoffs. Such optimization approaches are not always appropriate for analyzing human behaviors and social phenomena. Models based on adaptive behavior can be alternatives to the optimization models, and it is natural that behaviors of agents in simulation models are described by using adaptive behavioral rules. In particular, we employ a learning model of agents taking account of not only a payoff of self but also those of the others from a viewpoint that observation of other players' actions and payoffs may affect learning of agents (Duffy and Feltovich, 1999).

To examine the influence of learning mechanisms on the performance of agents, we employ an agent model with a decision and learning mechanism based on neural networks (e.g. Hassoun (1995)) and genetic algorithms (e.g. Goldberg (1989)), and this choice enables us to provide two grades of learning mechanisms: one is a simple learning mechanism based only on genetic algorithms, and the other is a more elaborate one based on both genetic algorithms and the error back propagation algorithm.

An agent corresponds to a neural network which is characterized by synaptic weights between two nodes in the neural network, a threshold which is a parameter for an output of a node, and a learning rate concerned with learning by error-correction. Because a structure of neural networks is determined by the number of layers and the number of nodes in each layer, an agent is prescribed by the fixed number of parameters of the neural network. By forming a chromosome consisting of these parameters characterizing an agent, each of the artificial agents is evaluated through the fitness computed from the payoff obtained by playing the voluntary contribution or the lottery game, and they evolve in our artificial genetic system. From this sense, in our simulation model, a player of the game is referred to as an artificial autonomous agent. The structures of a neural network and a chromosome in the genetic algorithm are depicted in Fig. 1.

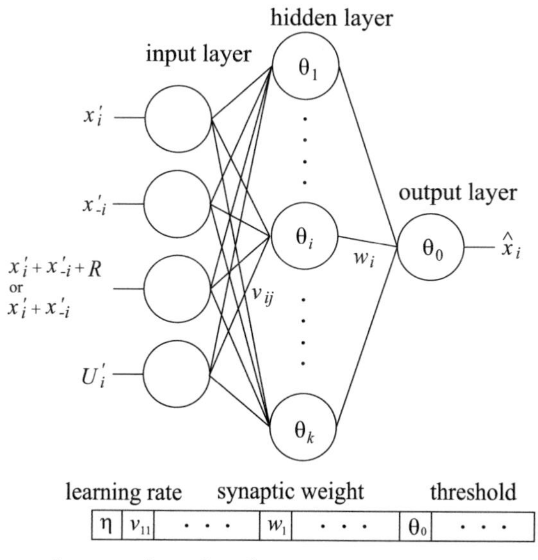

Fig. 1. Structures of a neural network and a chromosome in the genetic algorithm

We design a simulation model related to the experiment by Morgan and Sefton (2000) to compare with their results. In our simulation model, the population of agents is divided into a certain number of groups, and each group has the same number of agents. Each agent in a group determines the amount of contribution or wager by an output of the neural network and plays the voluntary contribution or the lottery games. In the voluntary contribution game, an agent obtains a payoff defined by (4). In the lottery game, an agent obtains the following payoff:

$$U_i = \begin{cases} e - x_i + R + \beta x(N) & \text{if winning} \\ e - x_i + \beta x(N) & \text{otherwise.} \end{cases} \tag{8}$$

The payoff (8) differs from (6) of the mathematical model in the third term, which is an expected payoff $R\frac{x_i}{x(N)}$.

We provide two learning mechanisms for artificial autonomous agents in our simulation system. One is a simple learning mechanism based only on genetic algorithms, and in this mechanism agents evolve, that is, the synaptic weights and the thresholds are revised through the fitness which is computed by payoffs obtained in the games. The other is a learning mechanism based on both the genetic algorithm and the error back propagation algorithm, and in addition to learning by the genetic algorithm, after finishing games, the parameters of the neural network for the agent are revised by the error back propagation algorithm with teacher signals (target outputs) obtained by computing optimal contributions or wagers for the given contributions or wagers of the other agents. For convenience of reference, let the simple learning mechanism and the more complicated one be denoted by GA and GABP, respectively. By providing the two learning mechanisms, we can verify whether actions of agents with more elaborate learning mechanism are closer to the predictions of the mathematical equilibrium model.

The flows of simulations with GA and GABP are shown in Fig. 2, and they are summarized as follows.

Step 1 (Generating the initial population) Let the number of agents in a group and the number of groups in the population of the simulations be n and 10, respectively. Then, the initial population of $10n$ agents is formed.

Step 2 (Dividing the population into groups) From the population, n agents are randomly chosen and then one group is formed, and this procedure is repeated 10 times. Eventually, 10 groups are made in all.

Step 3 (Playing games) For each group, the voluntary contribution game or the lottery game is played by n agents.

The voluntary contribution game.

Step 3-1-VC (Determining the amount of a contribution) The contribution x_i' of agent i, the sum x_{-i}' of the contributions of the other agents, the total fund $x_i' + x_{-i}' + R$ for the public goods, and the payoff U_i' of agent i in the previous generation are input values to a neural network for agent i, and they are normalized into $[0, 1]$. Let $\hat{x}_i$ be an output of the neural network. In particular, for the first generation, the input values are randomly determined from $[0, 1]$. The contribution of agent i of the present generation is determined as $x_i = \lfloor (e+1)\hat{x}_i \rfloor$, where $\lfloor \cdot \rfloor$ denotes rounding off fractions.

Step 3-2-VC (Informing about the contributions of the others) Agent i is informed about the sum x_{-i} of the contributions of the other agents in the present generation.

Step 3-3-VC (Computing the payoff) The payoff U_i of agent i is calculated by (4).

The lottery game.

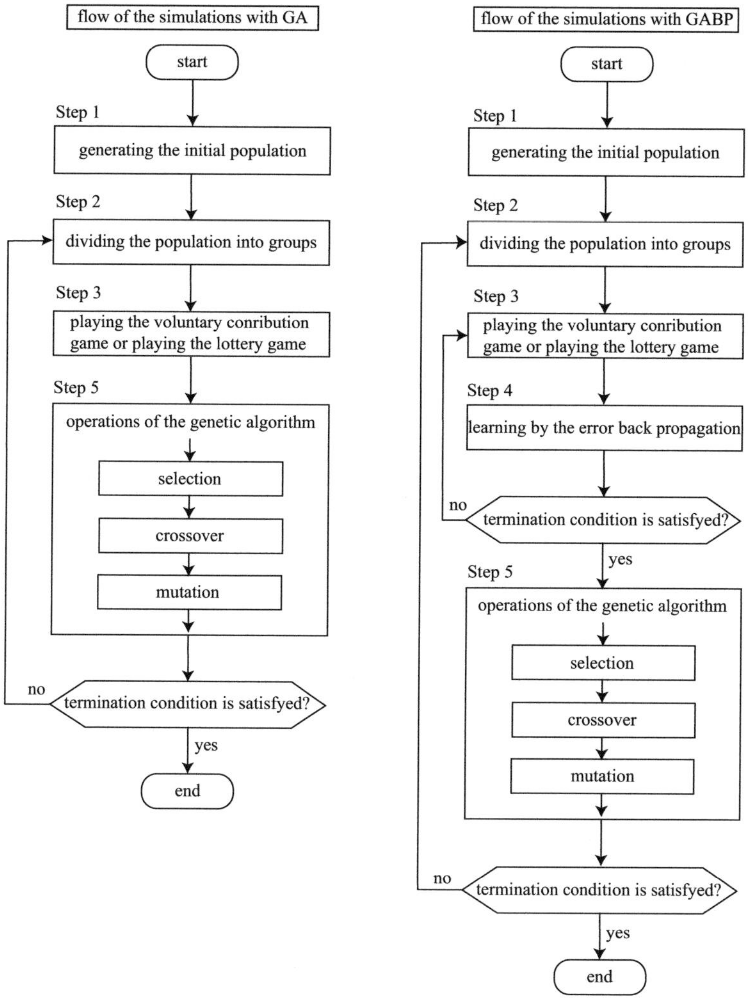

Fig. 2. Flowcharts of simulations with GA and GABP

Step 3-1-L (Determining the amount of a wager) The wager x_i' of agent i, the sum x_{-i}' of the wagers of the other agents, the total fund $x_i' + x_{-i}'$ for the public goods, and the payoff U_i' of agent i in the previous generation are input values to the neural network for agent i, and they are normalized into $[0,1]$. Let $\hat{x}_i$ be an output of the neural network. In particular, for the first generation, input values are randomly determined from $[0,1]$. The wager of agent i is determined as $x_i = \lfloor (e+1)\hat{x}_i \rfloor$.

Step 3-2-L (Drawing lotteries) After wagers of all the agents are determined, winners are selected by a roulette wheel in which agent i draws a winning with the probability $p_i = x_i / \sum_{j=1}^{n} x_j$.

Step 3-3-L (Informing about the contributions of the others) Agent i is informed about the result of the lottery and the sum x_{-i} of the wagers of the other agents in the present generation.

Step 3-4-L (Computing the payoff) The payoff U_i of agent i is calculated by (8).

Step 4 (Learning by the error back propagation algorithm) *This step is executed only for GABP.* The synaptic weights of the neural network for agent i are revised by teacher signals obtained by computing the optimal wagers for the given wagers of the other agents in the error back propagation algorithm. For agent i, the wagers of self and the sums of the wagers of the other agents for the last k games are recorded and they are used as training data. If the round number does not reach the given maximal round, return to Step 3.

Step 5 (Performing genetic operations) The following genetic operations are performed to each of the chromosomes for all the agents, and then the population of the next generation is formed.

Step 5-1 (Reproduction) The fitness f_i of each agent is obtained by appropriately scaling the payoff x_i obtained in the present generation. As a reproduction operator, the elitist roulette wheel selection is adopted. The elitist roulette wheel selection is a combination of the elitism and the roulette wheel selection. The elitist means that a chromosome with the largest fitness is preserved into the next generation. By a roulette wheel with slots sized by the probability $p_i^{selection} = f_i / \{\sum_{i=1}^{10n} f_i\}$, each chromosome is selected into the next generation.

Step 5-2 (Crossover) A single-point crossover operator is applied to any pair of chromosomes with the probability of crossover p^c. Namely, a point of crossing over on the chromosomes is randomly selected and then two new chromosomes are created by swapping subchromosomes which are the right-hand side parts of the selected point of crossing over on the original chromosomes. The operation of crossover is depicted in Fig. 3.

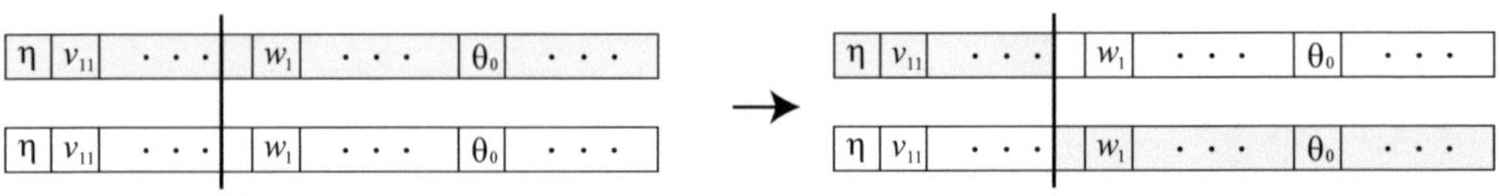

Fig. 3. The operation of crossover

Step 5-2 (Mutation) With the given small probability of mutation p^m, each gene, which represents a synaptic weight, a threshold or a learning rate, in a chromosome is randomly changed. The selected gene is replaced by a random number in $[-1, 1]$ for a synaptic weight, or in $[0, 1]$ for a threshold and a learning rate.

If the number of generations does not reach the given final generation, return to Step 2.

4. The results of the simulations

4.1 Treatments of the simulations

In the simulations, the voluntary contribution and the lottery games are played by agents, and there are three important parameters in the model: the exogenous contribution R which is used to fund the public goods or a prize, the marginal per capita return β of the public good provision, and the group size n which is the number of agents in a group. Then, we conduct the three simulations: the exogenous contribution simulation, the marginal per capita return simulation, and the group size simulation. Furthermore, providing two learning mechanisms, GA and GABP, we verify whether actions of agents with more elaborate learning mechanism are closer to the predictions of the mathematical equilibrium model. Each simulation consists of four treatments, and all of the simulations are summarized in Table 1.

simulations	voluntary contribution		lottery	
	GA	GABP	GA	GABP
exogenous contribution R	R-VC-GA	R-VC-GABP	R-L-GA	R-L-GABP
marginal per capita return β	β-VC-GA	β-VC-GABP	β-L-GA	β-L-GABP
group size n	n-VC-GA	n-VC-GABP	n-L-GA	n-L-GABP

Table 1. Treatments of the simulations

The general settings of the simulations and the parameters of the neural networks and the genetic algorithm are given as follows.

1. The initial endowment is usually set at $e = 20$, and only for the case where the equilibrium wager is larger than 20, it is set at $e = 40$.
2. Let n denote a group size, and because 10 groups are provided for each treatment, the population size of each generation becomes $10n$.
3. Each treatment of the simulations shown in Table 1 is performed 10 runs.
4. There are 6 units in the hidden layer of the neural networks.
5. Each of the output functions of units in the hidden and the output layers is a logistic function $f(x) = 1/\{1 + \exp(-x)\}$.
6. For the GABP treatments, the game is repeated 10 rounds in each generation.
7. After finishing the game in each round, the error back propagation algorithm is performed using 10 sets of the training data. To do so, each agent records the results of the games, i.e., x_i and x_{-i}, for the last 10 games.
8. Each of the initial values of synaptic weights and thresholds is set at 1 so that a contribution or a wager in the first generation becomes the maximal values, i.e., 20 or 40, and the initial value of the learning rate is set at a random number in $[0, 1]$.
9. For simulations with GABP, the fitness is computed by using the payoff only at the first round in each generation in order to exclude the effect of learning by the error back propagation algorithm.
10. The probabilities of crossover and mutation are specified at $p_c = 0.6$ and $p_m = 0.01$, respectively.
11. When a certain gene is selected for mutation, the gene is replaced by a random number in $[-1, 1]$ if it is for a synaptic weight, and the gene is replaced by a random number in $[0, 1]$ if it is for a threshold or a learning rate.
12. The simulations last until generation 1000 which is the final generation for treatments with the group size $n = 2, 4, 10$, or until generation 2000 which is the final generation for treatments with $n = 50, 100$.

4.2 The exogenous contribution simulation

In the exogenous contribution simulation, the group size and the marginal per capita return are fixed at $n = 4$ and $\beta = 0.75$, respectively, related to the experiment by Morgan and Sefton, and each treatment consists of four cases with $R = 2, 4, 8, 16$. Each of the treatments is repeated 10 times, and then numerical data given in the tables and the figures of this section are averages of the 10 runs.

4.2.1 The voluntary contribution games: R-VC-GA and R-VC-GABP

The result of the voluntary contribution games is summarized in Table 2 where the average contributions of the last 100 generations in the GA treatments are shown in the fourth column of GA, the average contributions of the 10 rounds in the final generation in the GABP treatment are shown in the third column of GABP, and the result of the experiment by Morgan and Sefton is also given in the rightmost column. As seen in the table, the average contributions of both the GA and the GABP treatments are close to the equilibrium of zero, and the contributions of the GABP treatments are closer to the equilibrium than those of the GA treatments. Thus, the result supports the predictions of the mathematical equilibrium model that the equilibria are zero regardless of the value of R, and it is found that the actions of agents with more elaborate learning mechanism are closer to the predictions of the mathematical equilibrium model.

R	equilibrium	GABP	GA	experiment with human subjects
2	0	0.033	0.220	—
4	0	0.022	0.199	—
8	0	0.023	0.175	$10.5 \rightarrow 8.075$
16	0	0.031	0.228	—

Table 2. The voluntary contribution games: treatments R-VC-GA and R-VC-GABP

Transitions of contributions of the GA treatments are depicted in Fig. 4. The left graph with the full length of the 1000 generations shows the whole transitions of the GA treatments, and the right graph with the initial 150 generations is given to see changes in the early generations. Moreover, the equilibrium of contribution given by (5) is shown at the both sides of the vertical axis. As seen in Fig. 4 and Table 2, the average contributions of all the treatments with $R = 2, 4, 8, 16$ approach 0.2 up to around generation 200, and for the pace of convergence of the average contributions, an obvious difference among the four treatments is not found.

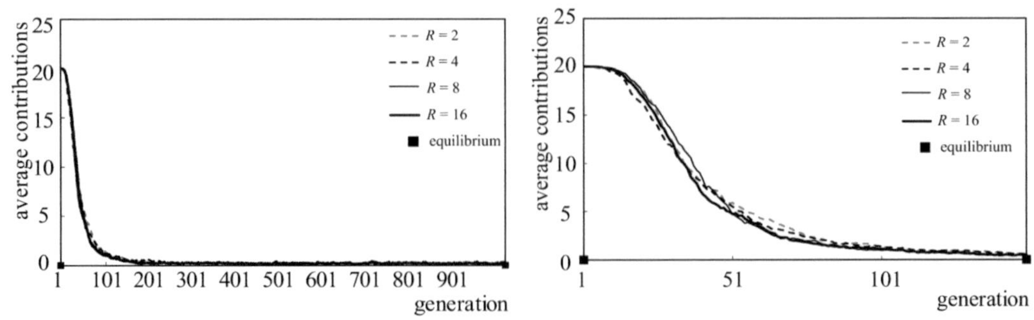

Fig. 4. Transitions of treatments R-VC-GA

Transitions of contributions of the GABP treatments are depicted in Figure 5. The left graph with the full length of the 1000 generations also shows the whole transitions of the GABP treatments, and the right graph tracing transitions of the 10 rounds in the final generation is given to show the effect of learning by the error back propagation algorithm. As seen in Fig. 5 and Table 2, the average contributions of all the treatments with $R = 2, 4, 8, 16$ approach zero up to about generation 200, and for convergence of the sequence, an obvious difference among the four treatments is not also found. By the learning by the error back propagation algorithm, average contributions approach almost zero at the fourth round in all the four treatments.

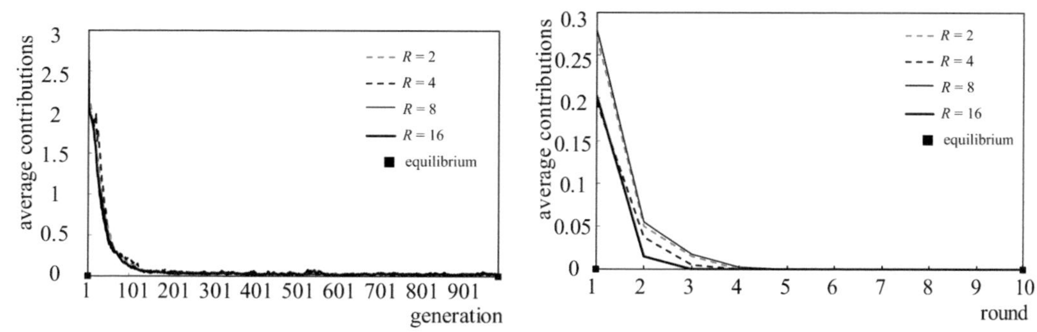

Fig. 5. Transitions of treatments R-VC-GABP

We compare the result of the voluntary contribution games in the exogenous contribution simulation with the corresponding result of the experiment by Morgan and Sefton. In the experiment, the voluntary contribution game with $R = 8$ is played. The average contribution at the initial round of the game is about 10.5, it decreases as the round proceeds, and it finally becomes 8.075 at the final 20th round of the game. This contribution is considerably larger than the equilibrium of zero, but the contribution slightly decreases as subjects gain experiences. For the result of the simulation, the average contributions decrease from 20 to almost zero until around generation 200 in the both GA and GABP treatments.

We summarize the result of the voluntary contribution games as follows. The contributions of both the simulation and the experiment decrease as the learning develops. While the contribution of the experiment is larger than the equilibrium, that of the simulation approaches the values of the equilibrium. Because the repetition of the game in the simulation is vary large compared with that of the experiment, it suggests that human subjects with rich experience of the game may make contributions close to the values of the equilibrium. The contributions of the experiment correspond to those of the simulation from generation 39 to generation 43. Although this correspondence depends on the initial arrangement of the simulation, in general it would be expected to exist some correspondence between the result of the experiment and a part of the whole transition of the simulation with a larger process of the learning.

4.2.2 The lottery games: R-L-GA and R-L-GABP

The result of the lottery games is summarized in Table 3. The equilibria of wagers shown in the second column of the table is calculated by (7), and they increase with growing the exogenous contribution R, i.e., the size of the prize. As seen in the table, the average wagers of both the GA and the GABP treatments are close to the values of the equilibria, and the wagers of the GABP treatments are closer to the values of the equilibria than those of the GA treatments. Thus, the result supports the predictions of the mathematical equilibrium model that the equilibria of wagers increase as the value of R becomes larger, and it is found that actions of agents with more elaborate learning mechanism are closer to the predictions of the mathematical equilibrium model.

R	equilibrium	GABP	GA	experiment with human subjects
2	1.5	1.471	2.222	—
4	3	2.975	3.735	—
8	6	5.954	5.868	$10 \rightarrow 10.35$
16	12	11.835	10.560	$13 \rightarrow 13.825$

Table 3. The lottery games: treatments R-L-GA and R-L-GABP

Transitions of wagers of the GA treatments are depicted in Fig. 6, which is in a form similar to Fig. 4 of the voluntary contribution games. As seen in Fig. 6 and Table 3, the differences among the average wagers of the treatments can be seen from around generation 40, and the average contributions of the treatments with $R = 2, 4, 8, 16$ converge at about 2.2, 3.7, 5.9, 10.6, respectively, after around generation 150. Compared with the equilibria of wagers, the average wagers of the treatments with $R = 2, 4$ are slightly larger than the values of the equilibria, and those of the treatments with $R = 8, 16$ are slightly smaller than the values of the equilibria. For convergence of the sequences, an obvious difference among the four treatments is not found.

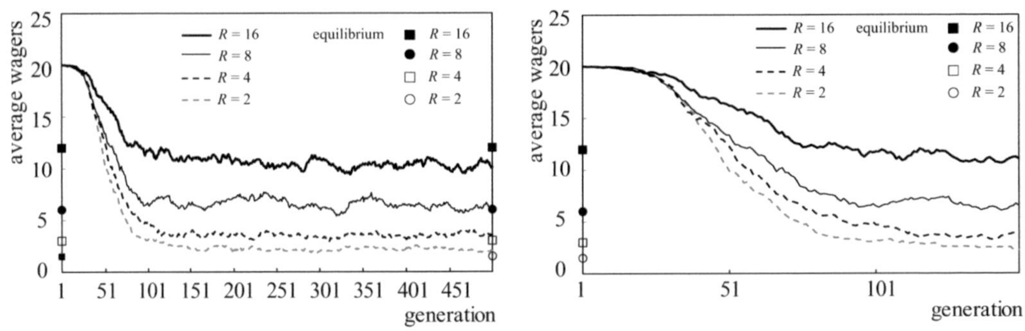

Fig. 6. Transitions of treatments R-L-GA

Transitions of wagers of the GABP treatments are depicted in Fig. 7, which is also in a form similar to Fig. 5 of the voluntary contribution games. After around generation 70, each of the average wagers clearly converges at the corresponding equilibrium. Compared with the GA treatments, the transitions of the GABP treatments converge at the equilibria more exactly and earlier, and variances of the wagers are obviously smaller than those of the GA treatments. By the learning of the error back propagation algorithm, the average wagers of the treatments with $R = 2, 4, 8$ converge almost at the equilibria after the third round, and even for the treatment with $R = 16$, although there exists an oscillation around the equilibrium, the average wagers after the sixth round stably converge at the equilibrium.

To examine the relation between the average wagers of the simulations and the equilibria of the mathematical model, we perform additional treatments with R = 1.4, 2.7, 5.4, 6.7, 9.4, 10.7, 13.4 in addition to the original treatments with $R = 2, 4, 8, 16$. In Fig. 8, given the

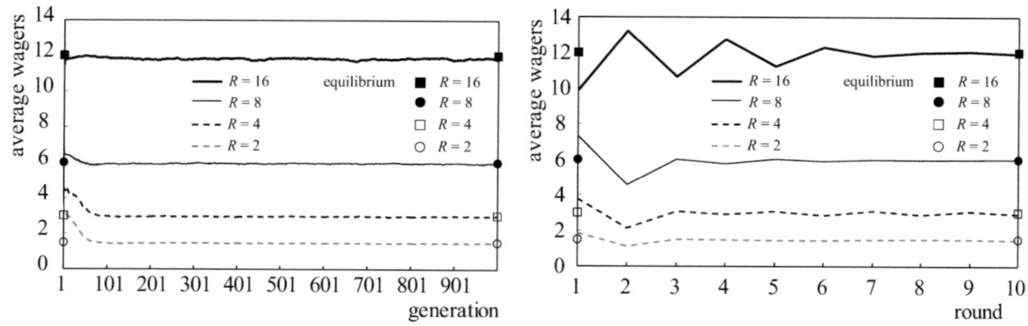

Fig. 7. Transitions of treatments *R*-L-GABP

equilibria in the horizontal axis, we show the differences between the average wagers of the simulations and the equilibria in the vertical axis. An seen in the left graph of Fig. 8 for the GA treatments, the average wagers of the simulations are higher than the values of the corresponding equilibria in the games whose equilibrium values are smaller than 6, and the average wagers of the simulations are lower than the values of the equilibria in the games whose equilibrium values are larger than 8. In contrast, for the GABP treatments, the average wagers of the simulation are close to the equilibria regardless of the sizes of the equilibria. As we described in the previous section, the learning mechanism of GABP is complicated and requires a heavy load of computation. Because in the learning of the experimental subjects or ordinary people, complicated computations are not performed generally from the viewpoint of bounded rationality, it is supposed that the learning of the experimental subjects might be closer to the learning mechanism of GA rather than that of GABP. This suggestion might give some reason for the fact that the average wagers by human subjects shown in Table 3 from the experiments by Morgan and Sefton (2000) are larger than the value of the equilibria.

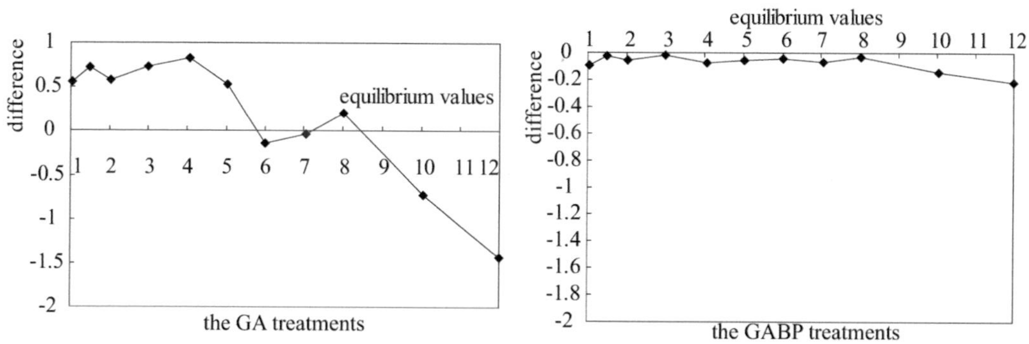

Fig. 8. Differences between the wagers of the simulation and the equilibria

We compare the result of the lottery games in the exogenous contribution simulation with the corresponding result of the experiment by Morgan and Sefton. In the experiment, by comparing two lottery games with $R = 8, 16$, they examine how the size of the prize influences the wagers of the experimental subjects. The average wager at the initial round of the game in the treatment with $R = 8$ is about 10, the round goes on but it rarely changes, and it finally becomes 10.35 at the 20th round of the game. The average wager at the initial round of the game in the treatment with $R = 16$ is about 13, it is almost changeless even though the round proceeds, and it finally becomes 13.825 at the 20th round of the game. Although the change by acquiring experience is not found in each of the treatments with $R = 8, 16$, the experiment supports the equilibrium prediction that the wagers increase as the value of R becomes larger. For the corresponding results of the simulation, in the GA treatment with $R = 8$, the average wager starts at 20, it decreases as the generation goes on, and after around generation 150 it converges at almost 6. In the GA treatment with $R = 16$, after around generation 150, the average wager finally oscillates in the interval between 10 and 11. In the GABP treatments, the average wagers converge sooner and closer to the equilibria than those in the GA treatments. In particular, the wagers of the human subjects in the experiments $R = 8$ and $R = 16$ correspond to parts of the transition of the wagers of the simulation. Namely, for the treatment with $R = 8$, the transition of wagers from 10 to 10.35 in the experiment corresponds to the transition from a wager at generation 68 to a wager at generation 70 in the simulation, and for the treatment with $R = 16$, the transition from 13 to 13.825 in the experiment corresponds to the transition from a wager at generation 69 to a wager at generation 73 in the simulation. Finally, as seen in Table 3, Figs. 6 and 7, the results of the simulation including the results of the treatments not only with $R = 8, 16$ but also with $R = 2, 4$ more clearly support the equilibrium prediction that the wagers increase as the value of R grows larger.

4.2.3 Summary of the exogenous contribution simulation

To conclude this subsection, we summarize the results of the simulation for the exogenous contribution R.

- Although it can be found that there exists a clear difference between the equilibrium values of the mathematical model and the average contributions of the experiment with human subjects in the voluntary contribution games, in the simulation, we observe that the average contributions of the simulation are sufficiently close to the value of the equilibria with the passage of time or with enough learning of agents.
- While the result of the experiment by Morgan and Sefton supports the equilibrium prediction that the wagers increase as the value of R grows larger, the result of the simulation supports it more obviously.
- In both of the voluntary contribution games and the lottery games, the contributions and the wagers of the GABP treatments are close to the equilibrium values of the mathematical model, compared with the GA treatments. Thus, it is found that the actions of agents with more elaborate learning mechanism are closer to the predictions of the mathematical equilibrium model.
- From comparing Tables 2 and 3, we observe that the lottery mechanism provides more of the public goods than the voluntary contributions mechanism.

4.3 The marginal per capita return simulation

In the marginal per capita return simulation, the exogenous contribution and the group size are fixed at $R = 8$ and $n = 4$, respectively, as in the experiment by Morgan and Sefton, and each treatment consists of five cases with $\beta = 0.00, 0.25, 0.50, 0.75, 0.95$.

4.3.1 The voluntary contribution games: β-VC-GA and β-VC-GABP

The result of the voluntary contribution games is summarized in Table 4 which is similar to that of the exogenous contribution simulation. As seen in the table, although the average contributions of the GA and the GABP treatments with $\beta = 0.95$ slightly deviate from the equilibrium contribution of zero, the average contributions of the other treatments are very close to the equilibrium of zero. Because a gap between a marginal payoff from the private good and a marginal return from the public good provision decreases as the value of β approaches one, particularly in the GA treatment with $\beta = 0.95$, it becomes difficult for agents to discriminate between a payoff from the private goods and a return from the public good provision, and therefore it seems that the average contribution slightly deviates from the equilibrium of zero. Thus, the result of the simulation supports the predictions of the mathematical equilibrium model that the equilibrium contributions are zero if $\beta < 1$ and β is not close to 1. Moreover, the contributions of the GABP treatments are closer to zero than those of the GA treatments, and then it follows that the actions of agents with more elaborate learning mechanism are closer to the predictions of the mathematical equilibrium model.

β	equilibrium	GABP	GA	experiment with human subjects
0.00	0	0.009	0.061	—
0.25	0	0.010	0.065	—
0.50	0	0.011	0.091	—
0.75	0	0.023	0.175	$10.5 \rightarrow 8.075$
0.95	0	0.237	1.751	—

Table 4. The voluntary contribution games: treatments β-VC-GA and β-VC-GABP

Transitions of contributions of the GA treatments are shown in Fig. 9. Because the result of the treatment with $\beta = 0$ almost overlaps with that of $\beta = 0.25$, the transition of the treatment with $\beta = 0$ is omitted from the figure. As seen in Fig. 9 and Table 4, the average contributions of all the treatments with $\beta = 0.00, 0.25, 0.50, 0.75$ approach about zero up to around generation 100, and for convergence of the sequences, the smaller the value of β is, the sooner the average contribution approaches zero. In the treatment with $\beta = 0.95$, although the average contribution slightly deviates from the equilibrium of zero, it becomes below 2.0 after around generation 400.

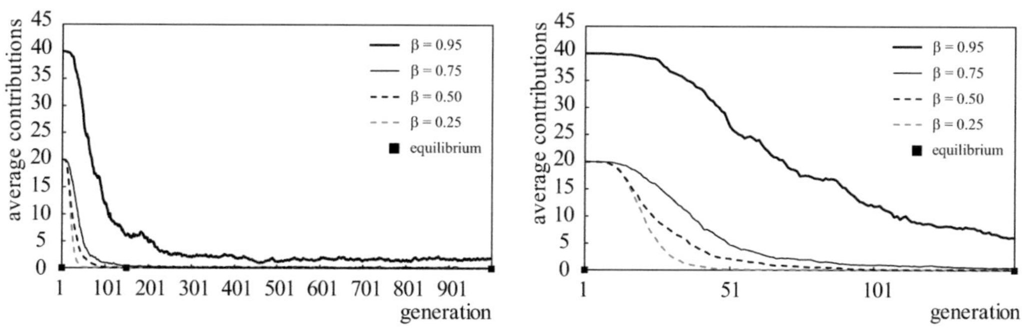

Fig. 9. Transitions of treatments β-VC-GA

Transitions of contributions of the GABP treatments are shown in Fig. 10. While the transitions of the average contributions shown in Fig. 10 is similar to those of Figure 9, the finally converging contributions of the GABP treatments are smaller than those of the GA treatments as seen Table 4. As seen in the right graph of Fig. 10, the average contributions of the first round in the final generation are already close to zero for the treatments with $\beta = 0, 0.25, 0.50, 0.75$, and even for the treatment with $\beta = 0.95$, after the third round the average contribution almost converges at zero by the learning by the error back propagation algorithm.

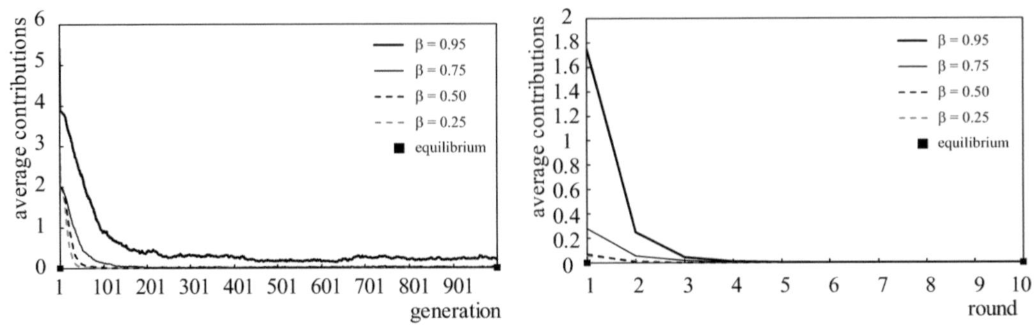

Fig. 10. Transitions of treatments β-VC-GABP

For the treatments with respect to the marginal per capita return in the experiment by Morgan and Sefton, they conduct only the treatment with $\beta = 0.75$. As for the case with $\beta = 0.75$, in the exogenous contribution simulation we already gave the description about the comparison between the results of the simulation and the experiment for this case.

4.3.2 The lottery games: β-L-GA and β-L-GABP

The result of the lottery games is summarized in Table 5. The equilibria of wagers shown in the second column of the table is calculated by (7), and they increase with the marginal per capita return β. As seen in the table, almost all the average wagers of the GA and the GABP treatments are close to the equilibrium wagers except for the GA treatment with $\beta = 0.95$, and the average wagers of the GABP treatments are closer to the equilibria than those of the GA treatments. For the GA treatment with $\beta = 0.95$, from the same reason as that of the voluntary contribution games, it becomes difficult for agents to discriminate between a payoff from the private goods and a return from the public good provision, and therefore it seems that the average wager deviates from the equilibrium of 30. Thus, the result of the simulation almost supports the predictions of the mathematical equilibrium model that the equilibrium wagers increase as the value of β becomes larger, and it is also found that the actions of agents with more elaborate learning mechanism are closer to the predictions of the mathematical equilibrium model.

β	equilibrium	GABP	GA	experiment with human subjects
0.00	1.5	1.46	1.58	$8 \rightarrow 2.425$
0.25	2	1.95	2.09	—
0.50	3	2.97	4.01	—
0.75	6	5.95	5.87	$10 \rightarrow 10.35$
0.95	30	28.46	13.00	—

Table 5. The lottery games: treatments β-L-GA and β-L-GABP

Transitions of wagers of the GA treatments are depicted in Fig. 11. As seen in Fig. 11 and Table 5, the differences among the average wagers of the treatments can be seen from around generation 20, each of the average wagers of all the treatments converges after around generation 100, and the average wagers increase as the value of β becomes larger. Only for the treatment with $\beta = 0.95$, the average wager deviates from the equilibrium, and for the other treatments, the average wagers converge almost at the equilibria. The average wagers of the treatments with $\beta = 0.00, 0.25, 0.50, 0.75$ are almost the same as or slightly larger than the values of the equilibria, and that of the treatment with $\beta = 0.95$ is smaller than the value of the equilibrium. For speed of the convergence of the sequences, an obvious difference among them is not found.

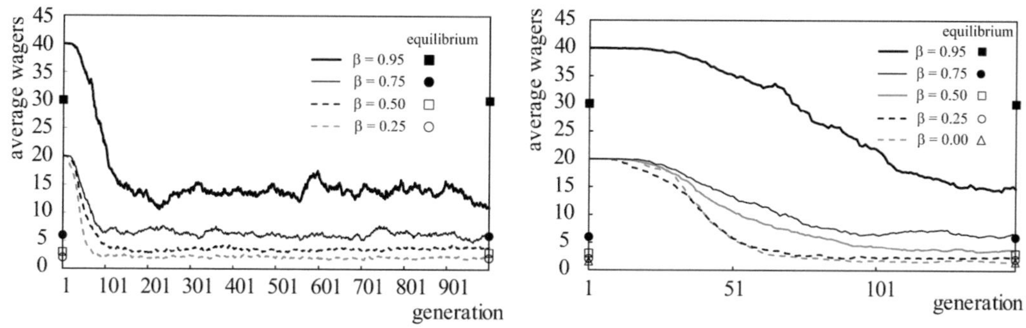

Fig. 11. Transitions of treatments β-L-GA

Transitions of wagers of the GABP treatments are depicted in Fig. 12. After around generation 70, each of the average wagers clearly converges at the corresponding equilibrium except for the treatment with $\beta = 0.95$. Compared with the GA treatments, the transitions of the GABP treatments converge at the equilibria more exactly and earlier, and variances of the wagers are obviously smaller than those of the GA treatments. Although the average wager of the treatment with $\beta = 0.95$ slightly deviates from the equilibrium, it is fairly close to the equilibrium, compared with that of the GA treatment. By the learning of the error back propagation algorithm, the wagers of the treatments with $\beta = 0, 0.25, 0.50, 0.75$ converge almost at the corresponding equilibria after the third round, and even for the treatment with $\beta = 0.95$, although there exists an oscillation around the equilibrium, the wagers after the seventh round stably converge at the equilibrium.

The relation between the average wagers of the simulations and the equilibria from the mathematical model are shown in Fig. 13. To examine the relation, we perform the another nine treatments with $\beta = 0.6250, 0.7000, 0.7300, 0.7860, 0.8125, 0.8500, 0.9000, 0.9250, 0.9400$ in addition to the original treatments with $\beta = 0.00, 0.25, 0.50, 0.75, 0.95$. An seen in the left graph of Fig. 13 for the GA treatments, the average wagers of the simulations are close to the values of the equilibria in the games such that the equilibria are smaller than 10. When larger than 10, the difference between the average wagers of the simulation and the equilibria of the mathematical model increases with the value of the equilibrium. In contrast, for the GABP treatments, the wagers of the simulation are close to the equilibria regardless of the sizes of the equilibria. The result of the GA treatments whose learning mechanism is simpler than that of GABP is consistent with the result of the experiment by Morgan and Sefton (2000) that the wager of 2.425 in the treatment with $\beta = 0.00$ is relatively close to the equilibrium of 1.5 and

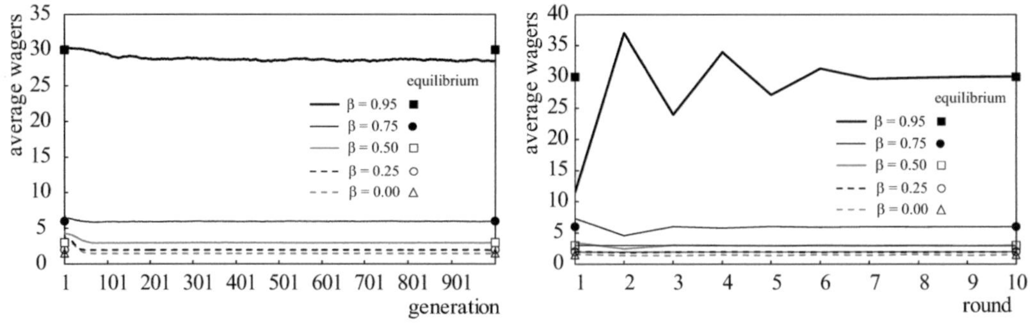

Fig. 12. Transitions of treatments β-L-GABP

the wager of 10.35 in the treatment with $\beta = 0.75$ is considerably larger than the equilibrium of 6, as seen Table 5.

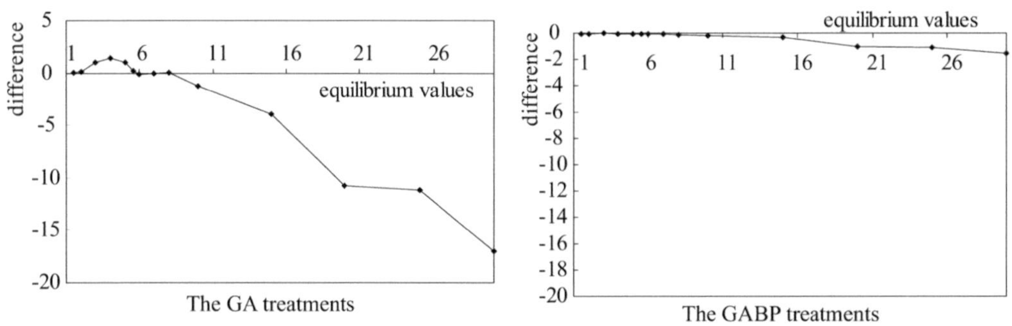

Fig. 13. Differences between the wagers of the simulation and the equilibria

We compare the result of the lottery games in the marginal per capita return simulation with the corresponding result of the experiment by Morgan and Sefton. In the experiment, by comparing two lottery games with $\beta = 0.0$ and $\beta = 0.75$, they examine how the size of the marginal per capita return influences the wagers of the experimental subjects. The average wager at the initial round of the game in the treatment with $\beta = 0.0$ is about 8, it decreases as the round goes on, and it finally becomes 2.425 at the 20th round of the game. The average wager at the initial round of the game in the treatment with $\beta = 0.75$ is about 10, it remains almost the same even though the round goes on, and it finally becomes 10.35. The change of wagers by acquiring experience can be found only in the treatments with $\beta = 0.0$, and the experiment supports the equilibrium prediction that the wagers increase with the marginal per capita return β.

For the corresponding results of the simulation, in the GA treatment with $\beta = 0.0$, the average wager starts at 20, it decreases as the generation goes on, and after around generation 50 it converges at about 1.5. In the GA treatment with $\beta = 0.75$, after around generation 100, the average wager finally converges at almost 6. In the GABP treatments, the average wagers converge sooner and closer to the equilibria than those of the GA treatments. In particular, the transitions of wagers of the human subjects in the experiments $\beta = 0.0$ and $\beta = 0.75$ correspond to parts of the transitions of wagers in the simulation. Namely, for the treatment with $\beta = 0.0$, the transition of wagers from 8 to 2.425 in the experiment corresponds to the transition from a wager at generation 44 to a wager at generation 73 in the simulation, and for the treatment with $\beta = 0.75$, the transition from 10 to 10.35 in the experiment corresponds to the transition from a wager at generation 66 to a wager at generation 71 in the simulation. Finally, as seen in Table 5, Figs. 11 and 12, the results of the simulation including the results of the treatments not only with $\beta = 0.00, 0.75$ but also with $\beta = 0.25, 0.50, 0.95$ more clearly support the equilibrium prediction that the wagers increase as the value of β grows larger.

4.3.3 Summary of the marginal per capita return simulation

To conclude this subsection, we summarize the results of the simulation for the marginal per capita return β.

- Although the average contribution and wager of the treatments with $\beta = 0.75$ in the experiment with human subjects differ from the equilibria of the mathematical model, in the simulation, we observe that the average contribution and wager of the simulation are sufficiently close to the values of the equilibria with the passage of time or with enough learning of agents.
- While the result of the experiment by Morgan and Sefton supports the equilibrium prediction that the wagers increase with the marginal per capita return β, the result of the simulation supports it more obviously.
- In both of the voluntary contribution games and the lottery games, the contributions and the wagers of the GABP treatments are closer to the values of the equilibria in the mathematical model than those of the GA treatments. Thus, it is found that the actions of agents with more elaborate learning mechanism are closer to the predictions of the mathematical equilibrium model.
- From comparing Tables 4 and 5, we observe that the lottery mechanism provides more of the public goods than the voluntary contributions mechanism does.
- As the marginal per capita return β approaches one, i.e., $\beta \to 1$, in particular for the lottery game, the average wager in the simulation deviates from the equilibria because it becomes difficult for agents to discriminate between a payoff from the private goods and a return from the public good provision.

4.4 The group size simulation

In the group size simulation, the exogenous contribution and the marginal per capita return are fixed at $R = 8$ and $\beta = 0.75$, respectively, and each treatment consists of five cases with $n = 2, 4, 10, 50, 100$.

4.4.1 The voluntary contribution games: n-VC-GA and n-VC-GABP

The result of the voluntary contribution games is summarized in Table 6. Because any treatment with respect to the group size n is not conducted in the experiment by Morgan and Sefton, the result from the experiment is not shown in the table.

As seen in the table, for all of the GABP treatments and the GA treatments with $n = 2, 4, 10$, the average contributions are very close to the equilibrium of zero, and the contributions of the GABP treatments are closer to zero than those of the GA treatments. The average contributions of the GA treatments with large group sizes such as $n = 50, 100$ slightly deviate from the equilibrium contribution. It is supposed that the reason is because the amount of the public good provision is extremely enlarged as the group size n becomes larger. Namely, the increase of the public good provision makes the payoff from the private goods relatively smaller, and then because the effect of increasing the payoff by maximizing the private goods is reduced, it seems that the average contributions slightly deviate from the equilibrium.

n	equilibrium	GABP	GA
2	0	0.01	0.33
4	0	0.02	0.18
10	0	0.04	0.36
50	0	0.16	1.64
100	0	0.28	2.20

Table 6. The voluntary contribution games: treatments n-VC-GA and n-VC-GABP

Transitions of contributions of the GA treatments are shown in Fig. 14, where the results of the treatments with $n = 2, 4, 10$ and $n = 50, 100$ are separately depicted in the left and the right graphs, respectively, because the maximal generations of them are not the same, and to see changes in the early generations the lower graph is also provided. As seen in Fig. 14 and Table 6, the average contributions of the treatments with $n = 2, 4, 10$ approach almost zero up to around generation 200. For the treatments with $n = 50, 100$, the average contributions become below 1.8 and 2.6, respectively, after around generation 300, and they finally converge not at zero which is the values of the equilibria but at about 1.6 and 2.2, respectively. By convergence of the sequences, we do not observe an obvious difference among the treatments with $n = 2, 4, 10$, but the convergences of the treatments with $n = 2, 4, 10$ are earlier than those of the treatments with $n = 50, 100$.

Transitions of contributions of the GABP treatments are shown in Fig. 15, where the left and the right graphs are for the treatments with $n = 2, 4, 10$ and with $n = 50, 100$, respectively, and the lower graph is provided for seeing the effect of learning by the error back propagation algorithm. The average contributions of the treatments with $n = 2, 4, 10$ approach almost zero up to around generation 200, and even for the treatments with $n = 50, 100$, the average contributions converge below 0.3 after around generation 200. By the learning by the error back propagation algorithm, the average contributions approach zero for all of the treatments at the third round. In particular, for the treatments with $n = 50, 100$, although the average contributions in the early rounds are larger than 1.0, it is observed that they quickly converge at zero by the learning by the error back propagation algorithm.

4.4.2 The lottery games: n-L-GA and n-L-GABP

The result of the lottery games is summarized in Table 7. The equilibria of wagers shown in the second column of the table is calculated by (7), and they decrease as the group size n becomes larger. As seen in the table, for all of the GABP treatments and the GA treatments with $n = 2, 4, 10$, the average wagers of the simulation are close to the values of the equilibria in the mathematical model, and the wagers of the GABP treatments are closer to the values of the equilibria than those of the GA treatments. The results of the GA and GABP treatments where the group size n does not exceed 50 support the predictions of the mathematical equilibrium model that the equilibrium wagers decrease as the value of n becomes larger. Conversely, however, the average wagers of the treatments with $n = 100$ are larger than those of the

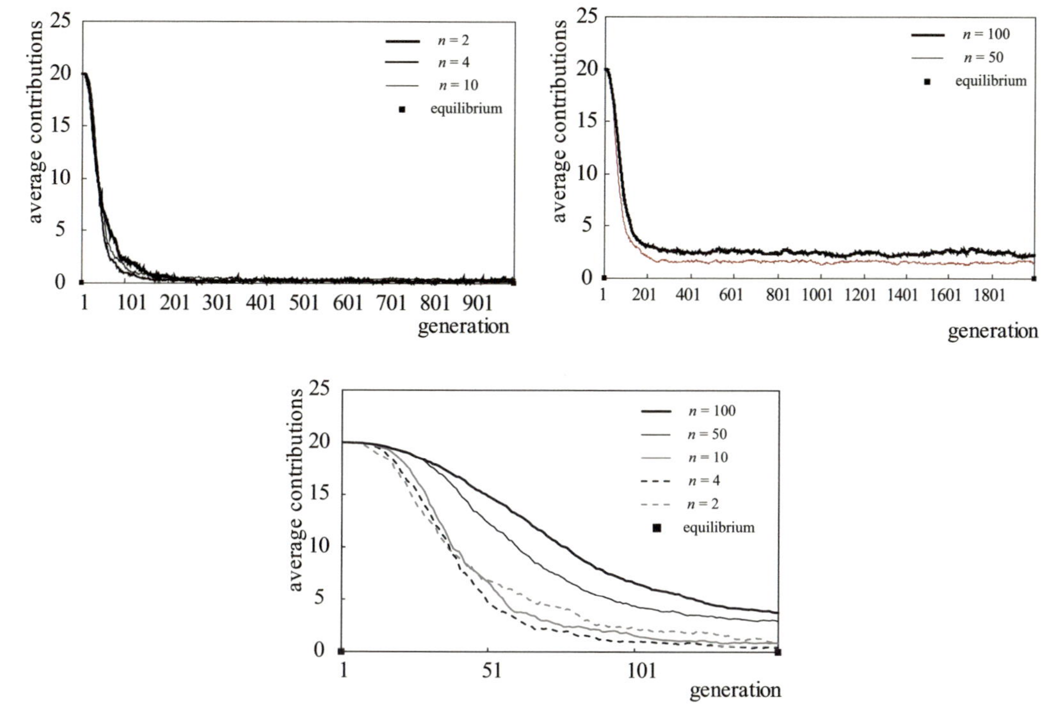

Fig. 14. Transitions of treatments n-VC-GA

treatments with $n = 50$; and besides, the average wagers of the treatments with $n = 50, 100$ deviate from the equilibria. We think that the reason of the deviation is the same as that of the voluntary contribution games in the simulation with respect to the group size as mentioned in the previous subsection.

n	equilibrium	GABP	GA
2	8	7.86	6.70
4	6	5.95	5.87
10	2.88	3.12	3.80
50	0.63	2.27	2.96
100	0.32	2.69	3.24

Table 7. The lottery games: treatments n-L-GA and n-L-GABP

Transitions of wagers of the GA treatments are depicted in Fig. 16. As seen in Fig. 16 and Table 7, although the transitions of the treatments with $n = 2, 4, 10$ slightly oscillate after around generation 200, they are not way from the corresponding equilibria. For the treatments with $n = 50, 100$, however, the average wagers converge at about 3 and they do not approach to the corresponding equilibria of 0.63 and 0.32 anymore.

Transitions of wagers of the GABP treatments are depicted in Fig. 17. It is found that after around generation 100, each of the average wagers of the treatments with $n = 2, 4, 10$ exactly converges at the corresponding equilibrium. Contrastively, the average wagers of the treatments with $n = 50, 100$ converge at about 2.5 which is larger than the values of

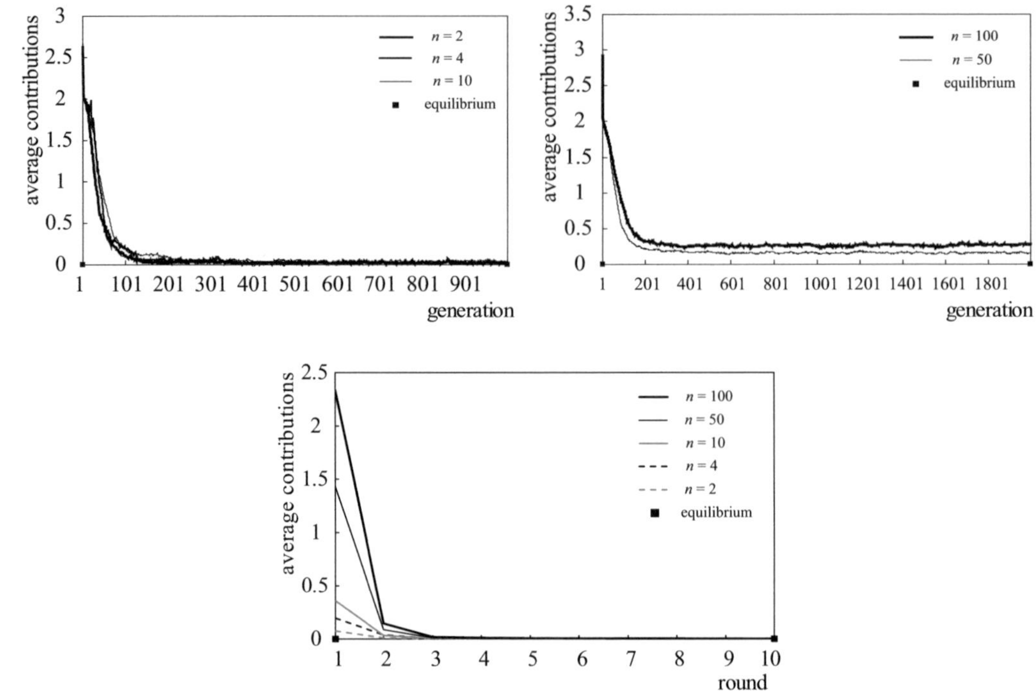

Fig. 15. Transitions of treatments n-VC-GABP

the corresponding equilibria. Comparing with the results of the GA treatments shown in Fig. 16, transitions of the GABP treatments converge at the equilibria more exactly and earlier, and variances of the wagers are obviously smaller than those of the GA treatments. As seen in the lower graph in Fig. 17, by the learning of the error back propagation algorithm, the average wagers of the treatments with $n = 2, 4$ converge almost at the equilibria after the third round, and for the treatment with $n = 10$, although there exists an oscillation around the equilibrium, the wagers after the ninth round converge at the equilibrium. For the treatments with $n = 50, 100$, however, the average wagers violently oscillate around about 3, which is larger than the values of the equilibria.

When the utility functions (4) and (6) are employed, one finds that the enlargement of the public good provision incurred by increase in the group size n makes the payoff from the private goods relatively smaller than the return of the public good provision. Thus, it is difficult for us to analyze the influence of the group size by using the simulation model with utility functions of agents (4) and (6). To relax this difficulty, we provide the following utility function diminishing return of the public good provision

$$U_i = e - x_i + R\frac{x_i}{x(N)} + \beta\alpha \log(x(N)), \tag{9}$$

where a parameter α is specified as follows. The parameter α is determined so that, at equilibrium, in case of $n = 4$, $R = 8$, and $\beta = 0.75$, the third term of (6) representing the

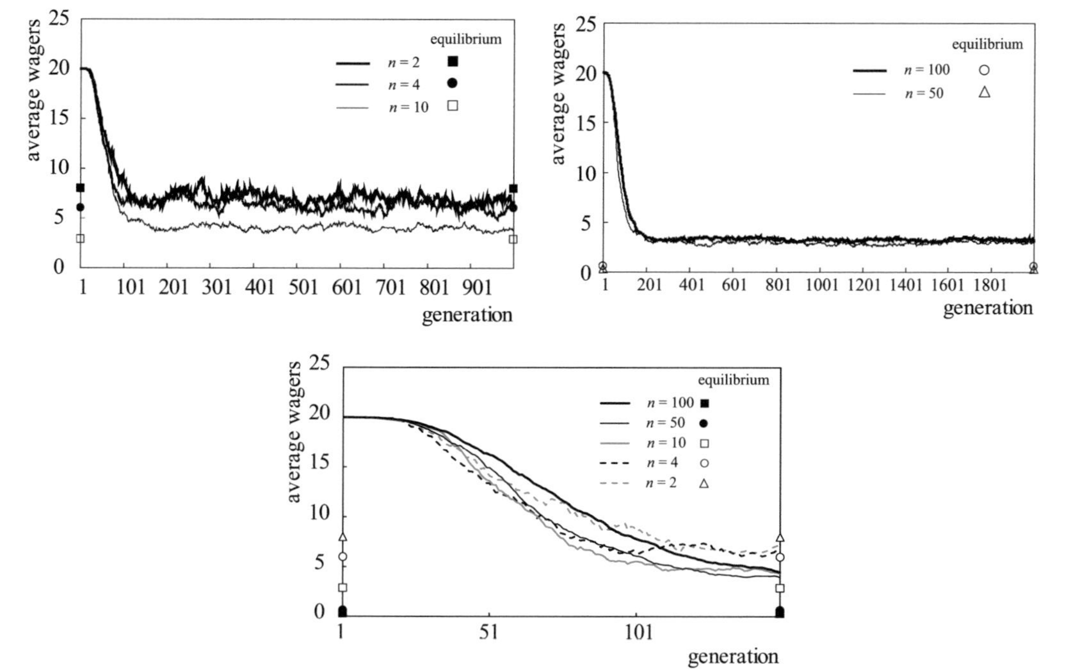

Fig. 16. Transitions of treatments n-L-GA

public good provision is equal to that of (9). To be more precise, assuming

$$0.75 \cdot 4 \cdot 6 \approx 0.75\alpha \log(4 \cdot 6),$$

we set $\alpha = 4$. We perform another simulation with the GABP treatments with $n = 50, 100$. The result of the simulation is given in Table 8, and it should be noted that the equilibria are not the same as those of Table 7 because of the different utility function (9).

n	equilibrium	GABP
50	0.374	1.02
100	0.109	1.01

Table 8. The lottery games: treatment n-L-GABP with the revised utility function

Comparing the results shown in Tables 7 and 8, the average wagers of the treatment with the revised utility function (9) are closer to the equilibria than those of the treatments with the original utility function (6). Although the average wagers in the original simulation shown in Table 7 increase when the group size increases from $n = 50$ to $n = 100$ and this phenomenon is against the predictions of the mathematical equilibrium model that the wagers decrease as the value of n becomes larger, the average wagers of the simulation with the revised utility function shown in Table 8 slightly decrease. Thus, it is found that if a utility function can be specified appropriately, it is possible to obtain results of the simulation supporting the predictions of the mathematical equilibrium model that the wagers decrease as the group size n becomes larger.

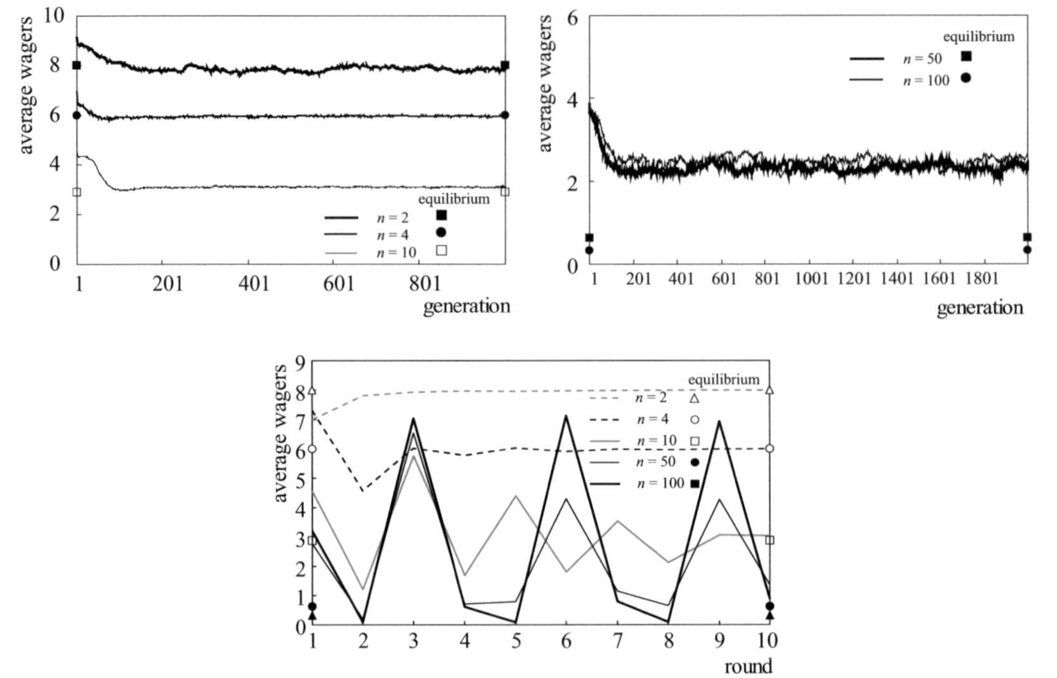

Fig. 17. Transitions of treatments n-L-GABP

4.4.3 Summary of the group size simulation

To conclude this subsection, we summarize the results of the simulation for the group size n.

- We obtain the results that the average contributions and wagers of the simulations are close to the corresponding equilibria expect for the treatments of the lottery games with $n = 50, 100$. For the lottery games, the result of the treatments with group sizes smaller than 50 supports the equilibrium prediction that the wagers decrease as the group size n becomes larger.

- For the lottery games, the result of the treatments with large group sizes such as $n = 100$ in the simulation with the original setting is not consistent with the predictions of the mathematical equilibrium model. However, if a utility function can be specified appropriately for the treatments with large group sizes, we show that it is possible to obtain results of the simulation which support the predictions of the mathematical equilibrium model.

- In both of the voluntary contribution games and the lottery games, the contributions and the wagers of the GABP treatments are closer to the values of the equilibria in the mathematical model than those of the GA treatments. Thus, it is found that the actions of agents with more elaborate learning mechanism are closer to the predictions of the mathematical equilibrium model.

- Comparing Tables 6 and 7, we observe that the lottery mechanism provides more of the public goods than the voluntary contribution mechanism.

5. Sensitivity analysis

In our simulation model, we employ the agent-based simulation model in which artificial adaptive agents have a mechanism of decisions and learning based on neural networks and genetic algorithms. Because the structure and the performance of the simulation model depend on the parameters of neural networks and genetic algorithms, it is important to verify whether or not the specified parameters are appropriate. In this section, we analyze the sensitivity on the parameters of the number of units in the hidden layer of the neural networks, the number of learning data in the error back propagation algorithm, the probabilities of crossover and mutation in the genetic algorithm. In practice, after we have evaluated the results of the sensitivity analysis shown in the following, we determine the values of these parameters which are used in the simulations shown in the previous section. For the sensitivity analysis, the treatments described in the following subsections are performed. Each treatment of the simulations is repeated 10 times, and numerical data given in the tables in the following subsections are averages of the 10 runs in the same way as the simulations shown in the previous section.

5.1 The number of units in the hidden layer of the neural networks

The number of units in the hidden layer of the neural networks is set at 6 in the simulations shown in the previous section. In this setting we show the effectiveness of lotteries for financing, and examine the validity of the mathematical equilibrium model and the experiments with human subjects. In this subsection, by varying the number of units in the hidden layer, we examine appropriate values of the parameter. To do so, we carry out simulations where the number of units is 2, 4, 6, or 8, and values of the other parameters of the neural networks and the genetic algorithms are the same as those of the simulations in the previous section. We provide two treatments where the exogenous contribution is set at $R = 2, 8, 16$, fixing the marginal per capita return and the group size at $\beta = 0.75$ and $n = 4$; and the marginal per capita return is set at $\beta = 0.00, 0.50, 0.75$, fixing the exogenous contribution and the group size at $R = 8$ and $n = 4$. Because the number of units in the hidden layer is a parameter for the neural networks, we perform the treatments with the learning mechanism of GABP, and both the voluntary contribution game and the lottery game are played. The average contributions and wagers of the simulation for sensitivity analysis is given in Tables 9 and 10.

the number of units	voluntary contribution			lottery		
	$R=2$	$R=8$	$R=16$	$R=2$	$R=8$	$R=16$
2	0.20	0.19	0.18	**1.48**	**5.97**	11.73
4	0.05	0.05	0.04	1.46	5.92	**11.85**
6	**0.03**	**0.04**	**0.02**	**1.48**	**5.95**	**11.78**
8	**0.02**	**0.01**	**0.02**	1.46	5.90	11.77
equilibrium	0.00	0.00	0.00	1.50	6.00	12.00

Table 9. Sensitivity analysis for the number of units in the hidden layer: the exogenous contribution R

In the tables, the contribution or the wager which is the closest to the values of the corresponding equilibrium is highlighted by underlined and boldfaced numbers, and the contribution or the wager which is the second closest is highlighted by boldfaced numbers.

the number of units	voluntary contribution			lottery		
	$\beta = 0.00$	$\beta = 0.50$	$\beta = 0.75$	$\beta = 0.00$	$\beta = 0.50$	$\beta = 0.75$
2	0.15	0.13	0.19	1.45	**2.99**	**5.96**
4	**0.01**	0.02	**0.04**	1.44	2.62	5.09
6	**0.01**	**0.01**	**0.04**	**1.46**	**2.97**	**5.95**
8	**0.01**	**0.01**	**0.04**	**1.46**	2.78	4.86
equilibrium	0.00	0.00	0.00	1.50	3.00	6.00

Table 10. Sensitivity analysis for the number of units in the hidden layer: the marginal per capita return β

As seen in Tables 9 and 10, the contributions or the wagers of the case where the number of units is 6 are the first or the second closest to the values of the equilibria, and therefore we conclude that it is appropriate to provide 6 units in the hidden layer of the neural networks.

5.2 The number of learning data in the error back propagation algorithm

The number of learning data in the error back propagation algorithm is set at 10 in the simulations shown in the previous section. In this subsection, by varying the number of learning data, we examine appropriate values of the parameter. To do so, we carry out simulations where the number of learning data is 3, 5, or 10, and values of the other parameters of the neural networks and the genetic algorithms are the same as those of the simulations in the previous section.

We provide two treatments which are the same as the treatments of the simulation for the sensitivity analysis withe respect to the number of units in the hidden layer of the neural networks. Because the number of learning data is a parameter for the neural networks, we perform the treatments with the learning mechanism of GABP. The result of the simulation for sensitivity analysis is shown in Tables 11 and 12.

the number of learning data	voluntary contribution			lottery		
	$R = 2$	$R = 8$	$R = 16$	$R = 2$	$R = 8$	$R = 16$
3	0.04	**0.02**	**0.03**	**1.45**	5.87	11.75
5	**0.02**	**0.02**	**0.03**	1.44	**5.93**	**11.78**
10	**0.03**	0.04	**0.02**	**1.48**	**5.95**	**11.78**
equilibrium	0.00	0.00	0.00	1.50	6.00	12.00

Table 11. Sensitivity analysis for the number of learning data: the exogenous contribution R

the number of learning data	voluntary contribution			lottery		
	$\beta = 0.00$	$\beta = 0.50$	$\beta = 0.75$	$\beta = 0.00$	$\beta = 0.50$	$\beta = 0.75$
3	**0.01**	0.02	**0.04**	1.47	**2.97**	5.92
5	**0.01**	**0.01**	**0.04**	**1.46**	**2.98**	**5.93**
10	**0.01**	**0.01**	**0.04**	**1.46**	**2.97**	**5.95**
equilibrium	0.00	0.00	0.00	1.50	3.00	6.00

Table 12. Sensitivity analysis for the number of learning data: the marginal per capita return β

As seen in Tables 11 and 12, the contributions or the wagers of the case where the number of learning data is 10 are the first or the second closest to the values of the equilibria as well as the case with learning data of 5, and therefore we think that it is appropriate to provide 10 sets of learning data for the error back propagation algorithm in the simulation.

5.3 The probability of crossover in the genetic algorithm

The probability of crossover in the genetic algorithm is set at 0.6 in the simulations shown in the previous section. In this subsection, by varying the probability of crossover, we examine appropriate values of the parameter. To do so, we carry out simulations where the probability of crossover is 0.5, 0.6, or 0.7, and values of the other parameters of the neural networks and the genetic algorithms are the same as those of the simulations in the previous section.
We provide two treatments similarly, and because the probability of crossover is a parameter for the genetic algorithm, we perform the treatments with the learning mechanism of GA. The result of the simulation for sensitivity analysis is shown in Tables 13 and 14.

the probability of crossover	voluntary contribution			lottery		
	$R = 2$	$R = 8$	$R = 16$	$R = 2$	$R = 8$	$R = 16$
0.5	0.24	0.25	0.26	**1.94**	**6.39**	**10.28**
0.6	**0.22**	**0.18**	**0.23**	2.22	**5.87**	**10.56**
0.7	**0.22**	**0.23**	**0.22**	**2.18**	7.36	9.42
equilibrium	0.00	0.00	0.00	1.50	6.00	12.00

Table 13. Sensitivity analysis for the probability of crossover in the genetic algorithm: the exogenous contribution R

the probability of crossover	voluntary contribution			lottery		
	$\beta = 0.00$	$\beta = 0.50$	$\beta = 0.75$	$\beta = 0.00$	$\beta = 0.50$	$\beta = 0.75$
0.5	0.07	**0.09**	0.22	1.74	**3.28**	**6.60**
0.6	**0.06**	**0.09**	**0.18**	**1.58**	4.01	**5.87**
0.7	**0.06**	**0.09**	**0.17**	**1.69**	**3.44**	7.39
equilibrium	0.00	0.00	0.00	1.50	3.00	6.00

Table 14. Sensitivity analysis for the probability of crossover in the genetic algorithm: the marginal per capita return β

As seen in Tables 13 and 14, the contributions or the wagers of the case where the probability of crossover is 0.6 are the first or the second closest to the values of the equilibria, and therefore the probability 0.6 is appropriate as the crossover probability in the genetic algorithm.

5.4 The probability of mutation in the genetic algorithm

The probability of mutation in the genetic algorithm is set at 0.01 in the simulations shown in the previous section. In this subsection, by varying the probability of mutation, we examine appropriate values of the parameter. To do so, we carry out simulations where the probability of mutation is 0.01, 0.03, or 0.05, and values of the other parameters of the neural networks and the genetic algorithms are the same as those of the simulations in the previous section.
We provide two treatments similarly, and because the probability of mutation is a parameter for the genetic algorithm, we perform the treatments with the learning mechanism of GA. The result of the simulation for sensitivity analysis is shown in Tables 15 and 16.

the probability of mutation	voluntary contribution			lottery		
	$R = 2$	$R = 8$	$R = 16$	$R = 2$	$R = 8$	$R = 16$
0.01	**0.22**	**0.18**	**0.23**	**2.22**	**5.87**	**10.56**
0.03	**1.89**	**1.47**	**1.55**	**2.93**	**7.52**	**10.63**
0.05	3.06	3.09	3.05	4.18	7.65	10.50
equilibrium	0.00	0.00	0.00	1.50	6.00	12.00

Table 15. Sensitivity analysis for the probability of mutation in the genetic algorithm: the exogenous contribution R

the probability of mutation	voluntary contribution			lottery		
	$\beta = 0.00$	$\beta = 0.50$	$\beta = 0.75$	$\beta = 0.00$	$\beta = 0.50$	$\beta = 0.75$
0.01	**0.06**	**0.09**	**0.18**	**1.58**	**4.01**	**5.87**
0.03	**0.26**	**0.48**	**1.75**	**2.13**	**4.62**	**7.33**
0.05	0.62	1.33	3.03	2.75	5.31	7.54
equilibrium	0.00	0.00	0.00	1.50	3.00	6.00

Table 16. Sensitivity analysis for the probability of mutation in the genetic algorithm: the marginal per capita return β

As seen in Tables 15 and 16, the contributions or the wagers of the case where the probability of mutation is 0.01 are almost the closest to the equilibria, and therefore the probability 0.01 is appropriate as the mutation probability in the genetic algorithm.

6. Conclusions

In this chapter, we have presented an agent-based simulation model in which artificial adaptive agents have a mechanism of decisions and learning based on neural networks and genetic algorithms. By the simulations, we have shown the effectiveness of lotteries for financing, and have examined the validity of the mathematical equilibrium model and the experiments with human subjects in detail.

Dealing with three parameters: the exogenous contribution, the marginal per capita return, and the group size, we have performed simulations and examined the effectiveness of the lottery mechanism compared with the voluntary contribution mechanism. From the result of the simulations, we have observed that the transitions of the average contributions and wagers approach almost the corresponding the predictions of the mathematical equilibrium model, and the actions of agents with more elaborate learning mechanism are closer to the values of the equilibria. Moreover, from the simulation, it is also found that the lottery mechanism provides more of the public goods than the voluntary contribution mechanism does. Thus, the results of the simulation support the equilibrium prediction more obviously compared with the experiments with human subjects, and with the results of the simulations, we have given some interpretation on the differences between the equilibrium of the mathematical model and the result of the experiments with human subjects.

7. References

Andreoni, J. and Miller, J.H. (1995). "Auctions with artificial adaptive agents," *Games and Economic Behavior* 10, 39–64.

Arbib, M.A. (ed), (1987). *The Handbook of Brain Theory and Neural Networks*, The MIT Press, Cambridge.
Axelrod, R. (1987). "The evolution of strategies in the iterated prisoner's dilemma," *Genetic Algorithms and Simulated Annealing*, L. Davis, (ed.), Pitman, London, 32–41.
Axelrod, R. (1997). "Advancing the art of simulation in the social sciences," *Simulating Social Phenomena*, R. Conte, R. Hegselmann and R. Terna (eds), Springer-Verlag, 21–40.
Banerje, B. and Sen, S. (2002). "Selecting parters," *Game Theory and Decision Theory in Agent-Based Systems*, S. Parsons, P. Gmytrasiewicz and M. Wooldridge (eds), Kluwer Academic Publishers, Boston/Dordrecht/London, 27–42.
Chellapilla, K. and Fogel, D.B. (1999). "Evolving neural networks to play checkers without expert knowledge," *IEEE Transactions on Neural Networks* 10, 1382–1391.
Conte, R., Hegselmann, R. and Terna, R. (eds), (1997). *Simulating Social Phenomena*, Springer-Verlag.
Dorsey, R.E., Johnson, J.D. and Van Boening, M.V. (1994). "The use of artificial neural networks for estimation of decision surfaces in first price sealed bid auctions," *New Directions in Computational Economics*, W.W. Cooper and A.B. Whinston (eds.), Kluwer, 19–40.
Downing, T.E., Moss, S. and Pahl-Wostl, C. (2001). "Understanding climate policy using participatory agent-based social simulation," *Multi-Agent Based Simulation*, S. Moss and P. Davidsson (eds.), Springer-Verlag, Berlin, 198–213.
Duffy, J. and Feltovich, N. (1999). "Does observation of others affect learning in strategic environments? An experimental study," *International Journal of Game Theory* 28, 131–152.
Epstein, J.M. and Axtell, R. (1996). *Glowing Artificial Societies*, Brookings Institution Press, Washington D.C.
Erev, I. and Rapoport, A. (1998). "Coordination, "magic," and reinforcement learning in a market entry game," *Games and Economic Behavior* 23, 146–175.
Goldberg, D.E. (1989). *Genetic Algorithms in Search, Optimization, and Machine Learning*, Addison Wesley, Massachusetts.
Hassoun, M.H. (1995). *Fundamentals of Artificial Neural Networks*, The MIT Press, Cambridge.
Holland, J.H. and Miller, J.H. (1991). "Adaptive intelligent agents in economic theory," *American Economic Review* 81, 365–370.
Leshno, M., Moller, D. and Ein-Dor, P. (2002). "Neural nets in a group decision process," *International Journal of Game Theory* 31, 447–467.
Morgan, J. (2000). "Financing public goods by means of lotteries," *Review of Economic Studies* 67, 761–784.
Morgan, J. and Sefton, M. (2000). "Funding public goods with lotteries: experimental evidence," *Review of Economic Studies* 67, 785–810.
Moss, S. and Davidsson, P. (eds.), (2001). *Multi-Agent-Based Simulation*, Springer-Verlag.
Nishizaki, I., Katagiri, H. and Oyama, T. (2009). "Simulation analysis using multi-agent systems for social norms," *Computational Economics* 34, 37–65.
Nishizaki, I., Ueda, Y. and Sasaki, T. (2005). "Lotteries as a means of financing for preservation of the global commons and agent-based simulation analysis," *Applied Artificial Intelligence* 19, 721–741.
Niv, Y., Joel, D., Meilijson, I. and Ruppin, E. (2002). "Evolution of reinforcement learning in foraging bees: a simple explanation for risk averse behavior," *Neurocomputing* 44-46, 951–956.

Parsons, S., Gmytrasiewicz, P. and Wooldridge, M. (eds), (2002). *Game Theory and Decision Theory in Agent-Based Systems*, Kluwer Academic Publishers.

Rapoport, A., Seale, D.A. and Winter, E. (2002). "Coordination and Learning Behavior in Large Groups with Asymmetric Players," *Games and Economic Behavior* 39, 111–136.

Roth, A.E. and Erev, I. (1995). "Learning in extensive form games: experimental data and simple dynamic models in the intermediate term," *Games and economic behavior* 8, 163–212.

Sichman, J.S., Bousquet, F. and Davidsson, P. (eds.), (2003). *Multi-Agent-Based Simulation II*, Springer-Verlag.

Sundali, J.A., Rapoport, A. and Seale, D.A. (1995). "Coordination in market entry games with symmetric players," *Organizational Behavior and Human Decision Processes* 64, 203–218.

Part 4

Case Studies

16

Integrating RFID in MAS through "Sleeping" Agents: a Case Study

Vincenzo Di Lecce[1], Alberto Amato and Marco Calabrese
D.I.A.S.S., Politecnico di Bari, Taranto
Italy

1. Introduction

Intelligent Agent technology is an important, exciting and relatively new paradigm in software design. The term intelligent agent is now used as an umbrella term representing a wide range of software with different characteristics and abilities [1]. This fact led to many definitions of intelligent agent, but the authors agree with the definition proposed by Wooldridge and Jennings [2] stating that an intelligent agent is a problem solving entity characterized by the following properties:

- autonomy, the agent does the major part of its tasks without user intervention
- social ability, the agent is able to communicate with other agents (or human beings) to solve a given problem. This property has an enormous importance because it requires that the agent is able to understand a language, to know when and with who this should communicate and so on.
- Proactiveness, the agent takes the initiative to act on the surrounding environment when appropriate
- Responsiveness, the agent is aware of the surrounding environment and can react to its variations.

The natural evolution of the intelligent agent technology is the Multi Agent System (MAS) technology [3].Systems of this kind are composed of a set of intelligent agents interacting and collaborating each other to solve complex problems that are beyond the individual capability or knowledge of each agent.

There are many applications of MAS in various problems. For example MAS technology was used in [4] to increase the reliable of a distributed sensor network, in [5] this technology was used for databases integration, in [6] as decision support system for an intelligent transport system, in [7] a MAS that implements mine detection, obstacle avoidance and route planning was proposed.

In this work the authors will show the advantages that MAS technology can obtain combining the autonomy and proactivity of the intelligent agents and the intrinsic mobility of the RFID devices.

---

[1] Corresponding author

RFID is a generic technology concept that refers to the use of radio waves to identify objects. RFID is a non-contact interrogation method for identification of objects. An RFID system essentially consists of three parts:

1. RFID tag itself that is a device of various shapes (the shape varies according to the application in which the tag will be used) composed of memory unit and an antenna that is used to communicate with the remote reader device. The dimension of this memory is continuously increasing and today there are some RFID tags with various kilobyte of memory.
2. the RFID transponder is a device supplying and communicating with the tag by means of a radio wave. There are various types of RFID reader varying in resolution, reading distance, etc.
3. a backend information management system that is the system that use the data stored in each RFID to accomplish the various tasks (supply chain management, factory automation, etc.).

In this work the authors propose to use the high memory capacity RFID for introducing the new concept of "sleeping agent". In order to show the suitability of this concept in real world applications, the authors propose as case study a model of clinical risk management system based on a MAS employing sleeping agents.

The remaining part of this work is organized as follows: in section II there is a brief related works overview, in section III the RFID technology is introduced while in section IV the sleeping agent is presented. The analyzed case study is described in section V while the proposed MAS is presented in VI. Finally conclusions and remarks are proposed in section VII.

2. Related works

Due to the flexible and dynamic characters of intelligent agents, they are being used widely as an interface system between user and information retrieval systems for whatever application.

An example of this kind of applications can be an expert system developed for the user assistance to a better understanding of scientific data retrieved from environmental monitoring systems (these collected data are actually translated by expert chemists or biologists) [4].

In practical application, each agent is defined as a software entity, that is capable of flexible autonomous action in order to meet its design objective [8]. A multi agent system can be defined as an organization composed of autonomous and proactive agents that interact with each other to achieve common or private goals [9 - 10].

According with Qiao and Zhu [11], in conceptual schemes of each agent it is possible to recognize five components:

- Perception, a channel for an agent to receive information from the external world.
- Effector, an interface for an agent in order to modify or influence the state of MAS.
- Communication, a mechanism for an agent to exchange communication with other members of the agent society.
- Objectives, list of roles that an agent can play
- Knowledge processor, a knowledge base system that stores and processes the necessary knowledge for an agent so that this one can play the role the MAS has assigned to it.

To create a structured, flexible, and scalable MAS we can layer different functions and components needed to solve the problem [12]. A good abstraction can be achieved and a large class of different problems solved by using a layered approach.
Each layer represents a single functionality in order to minimize the interlayer communications and localize (by one or more agents) the activity. The number of agents performing functions in each layer is defined according to the goals that layer must satisfy.
There are many applications where the MAS systems are successfully used. In [13] the authors propose a MAS to implement mine detection, obstacle avoidance and route planning with a group of autonomous agents with coordination capabilities. [14] presents multi agent system approach and software prototype aimed at the air traffic control in airport airspace.
Since one of the most important characteristic of the intelligent agents is their ability to communicate among them to reach a common goal, there are interesting works on the negotiation policies that agents can have. An interesting example of these works is [15].

3. RFID technology and applications

RFID is one of the most successful pervasive computing technologies. Born as a replacement for traditional barcode, nowadays its wireless identification capability is changing heavily many human activities such has health centers, logistic and production chain, etc.
Each RFID tag contains a unique identifier, so, if a RFID is attached to an item, reading its presence is equal to reading the presence of that item. From this point of view they are not too different from the barcode. The real advantages of the RFID become clearer considering their reader devices. A RFID reader is able to read simultaneously more than one RFID also through physical barriers and from a distance [16]. This fact makes these devices interesting for many applications. For example, in the fields of physical distribution, the technology to recognize multiple items in a cardboard box or a shopping basket at a time attracts attention.
RFID tags are classified into two types. One is the passive type that is battery-less, and the other is an active type that has its own battery. The passive type tags are cheap and have long lifetime. For this reason, they can be used in several places.
The main limit of this kind of RFID devices is their small amount of memory (typically 96 bits). This quantity is enough to store an electronic product code but it needs the connection to a local or remote database to obtain additional information about a specific tagged item. This requires a network infrastructure that guarantees secure, reliable and speedy access to a central database where the additional data are stored. In [16] there is an interesting analysis of the security issues concerning this kind of applications.
Nowadays RFID tags with high quantity of memory are becoming ever more popular. These devices become the keys of new kind of applications storing all the data on a given item locally in its RFID. For example, the Boeing has announced its intention to use high memory RFID to track the maintenance and repair history of parts for its upcoming Dreamliner 787 family of airplanes [17].
In this work the authors propose to use this kind of RFID to store the agent code.

4. The sleeping agent

The sleeping agent is an intelligent agent embedded in a tag RFID with high memory capacity. Its main task is to interact with other agents to satisfy its goals or to cooperate to reach a global goal. These objectives are defined according to the specific application domain in which they are used.

They are defined "sleeping" because they are not ever running processes in the system on which the MAS is running. Normally, they are stored in an RFID in wait state (sleeping) and are loaded/awoken into the main system when the MAS needs their activities. At this time, the sleeping agent performs its task and, if it is required by the application, it is stored again in its RFID with an updated state.

Considering that RFID tags are devices used to identify an object in a contact less way, one of their primary application field is the logistic.

The main innovation of the sleeping agent relies on the fact that it makes each object, identified by a RFID, an active entity. It can interact with the surrounding environment exploiting all the characteristics of an intelligent agent.

Since the sleeping agent is not an ever running process in the system, its use allows for implementing model of systems composed of several entities whose activities are asynchronous. Two interesting examples of such systems are the following:

- distributed supply chain simulations: in this application each item can be represented by a sleeping agent doing its work when needed (e.g. in correspondence of some transport node). Using an agent rather than a simple identifier introduces into the system a high level of flexibility. Indeed, with this approach, thanks to the sleeping agent, each item can interact with the supply chain to optimize it.
- health care centers: in this application, there is the need to identify reliably each patient. A RFID with a sleeping agent is given to each patient (e.g. using a wristband). The sleeping agent becomes a kind of patient's avatar representing he/she in each interaction with the health center services (diagnoses, medical doctor, etc.). In the long period in which the patient stays in bed without having other services by the health care center, the sleeping agent stays in the RFID without overloading the computer system where the MAS is running.

These two examples are fields in which the classical RFID technology is reaching good results in terms of performance and spreading. For this reason in this work a MAS modeling a health care system using the sleeping agent is presented.

5. Case study

Healthcare systems represent an interesting testbed for the integration of MAS with RFID technologies. Furthermore, the employment of sleeping agents is particularly suited for this framework since it allows for reengineering healthcare systems efficiently as it will be shown hereinafter.

In the latest years, healthcare has become one of the most important sectors of interest for the Information and Communication Technology (ICT) market. This occurs because the same nature of the "clinical practice" is mainly focused on the information management and analysis. On the other hand, the exponential growth of the technological ability to acquire biological data in digital format, which can be extended to extract useful information for diagnostic and therapeutic aspects, plays an important role in this slow but substantial transformation. Two visible examples of this change are the major spread of personal computers within hospitals and the enormous amount of messages sent using the internal network of healthcare facilities to exchange information among the various operators.

A critical challenge is then how to globally publish, in a semantic integrated view, information coming from geographically distributed information sources such as databases, programs, etc. In the Italian context for example, many medical databases/archives are owned by the Public Administration, and they are often managed at a regional or at a provincial level. Two noteworthy examples of such databases are the INAIL 's and the INPS 's archives where most of the citizen heath related data are stored.

Focusing the attention on patient care, the clinical risk management represents an important aspect. The clinical risk management refers to the procedures for avoiding risks associated with direct patient care in order to minimize errors in the clinical practice and improve the quality of the service offered. It is the analysis about the probability of a patient being victim of an adverse event or inconvenience resulted, although involuntary, from improper medical care provided during the period of hospitalization.

The safety of the patient can be assured only by designing secure organizational systems and perhaps more importantly, by establishing and implementing procedures to reduce all high-risk situations in clinical settings. Indeed, according to a recent survey by National Institute of Health, the first cause of accident risk is just the lack of proper procedures, followed by a poor work organization and only at the end the causes are linked to logistical situations and inadequate structures. Referring to the first type of clinical risk, the most frequent mistakes are: incorrect diagnoses (medical error), the prescription of inappropriate therapy (for pharmacological principle, unfitting care for specific subjects, wrong dosage) or inaccurate interventions. The common denominator of all these clinical acts is the traceability of patient and all cares connected to this one [18].Another important aspect concerns the process phase standardization that could provide a quality system for obtaining secure patient data (UNI EN ISO 9000:2000).

Traceability systems in the hospital context are generally:

- Traceability system of wards (including also emergency ward)
- Traceability system of pharmaceuticals: from the delivery of the drug produced by the manufacturer to the administration of the single dose
- Traceability system of medical devices
- Traceability system of blood bags
- Traceability system of implantable device

Numerous experiments carried out in the early nineties have implemented traceability systems in view of technological supports in use. Current tendency is to focus, in particular, on the management of patients' physical paths (patient flow). A more rational management of the physical patient flow could solve the typical hospital problems such as: delays, long waiting times, queues, erased interventions, patients placed in inappropriate care setting, nursing staff under stress, waste and high costs etc.

From a technological point of view, hospital information systems (like many distributed complex systems) are committed to face with the following problems:

- data redundancy
- legacy systems
- unstructured data
- security
- traceability

Data redundancy concerns the possibility of conflicting information due to data replication across multiple locations, while legacy systems take into account the pre-existing technology already in use. Unstructured data require of course a special assessment since they cannot be processed in their natural form.

To overcome the aforementioned criticalities and to face with the strict requirements regarding efficient traceability a re-engineering effort is due in the traditional healthcare system. Two models regarding patient identification and assistance during the hospital stay can be compared. In particular, these two representative models characterize respectively traditional (generally barcode-enhanced) systems and those based on RFID technology [19,20]. The main difference is that the barcode model considers hospital as an organization structured in functional blocks, while the RFID (re-engineered) model considers the patient at the center of the clinical process. This difference reflects the operating principle: it will be passive in the case of optical systems and active for Radio Frequency Systems. This difference of course impacts also on the hospital organization in relation to the quality of health services for the patient.

The presence of separate functional areas that are typical of barcode system, draws attention to the problem of risks associated with information duplication. Indeed, in these systems the uniqueness of the chosen communication channel (i.e. "medical record" in the system database) determines that the contact among different information flows can occur only after or before the processes have been developed by each functional unit.

Contrarily, at the base of the re-engineering process a new patient-centred data model is requested. The model is basically characterized by the disappearance of the medical record concept, seen as an instrument for getting information about activities produced by the system in relation to the patient, to whom it is associated, Therefore the concept of "health condition" replaces the medical record and refers to the patient condition in a specific moment. Since the health condition is linked by a univocal relationship to the patient that it describes, it is clear that there is a direct relationship with the activities related to: physical examinations made by the medical staff; drug management (prescription, administration) made by the pharmaceutical staff and performance of other hospital operations for monitoring patient health condition (analysis and investigations) together with other correlated actions.

A patient-centred model is then able to intercept all important entities characterizing hospitalization but from a different view RFID model introduces simplification without introducing any substantial approximation of the modelled reality.

Furthermore, in a traditional system, asynchronism of communication can lead to lack of communication phenomena, which can be associated to the delta time characterizing the accesses for reading or writing the medical record. The presence of a single communication node determines a possible break thus leading inevitably to the collapse of the whole macro system with all the relative risks connected to this. Contrariwise, in an interconnected model, similar to that using RFID technology, it is ensured that the temporary absence of information flow does not inhibit data exchange to all other entities of the system, which can continue to operate even under reduced conditions.

The application of RFID model can be considered as useful also for the optimization introduced in operation traceability. On the other hand, a system producing a single intra-hospital communication output and characterized by sequential writing access, can easily suffer from the possibility of being improperly altered, differently from what actually occurs if the exchange of data and information among the operators takes place in real-time.

In conclusion, the use of RFID technology produces several advantages to health care processes with only a slight reengineering of specific structures. A more rational use of hospital information systems allows for a better organization of clinical data. Moreover, it is noteworthy to remember the launch of RFID and Wi-Fi compliant transponders on the market. These allows for unifying access points, thus simplifying them, (from a specialized portal to a pervasive wiring) and obtaining, through triangulation techniques and/or the power density calculation, the precise location of monitored entities.

It is well known that the process for examining the clinical risk must start from the identification of risks analytically, and therefore define the potential risks according to predetermined international grading scale in order to organize and implement the risk reduction project. A possible solution for reducing the incidence of errors related to "mistaken identity" seems to be the use of identification wristbands with advanced RFID or barcode systems at the time of admission to hospital. Of course, this solution cannot be considered as the only or essential strategic element in the clinical risk management for the patient safety.

6. Proposed multi-agent system architecture

As seen in the previous paragraph, RFID can be used to improve many aspects of clinical risk management. The main advantage of the RFID based model compared to the one based on barcode is that the former sees the patient as the centre of the clinical process with clear advantage in terms of optimization of clinical risk and resource.

The authors propose a multi-layer MAS architecture as shown in figure 1. In each layer there are agents that have same features and common goals, but they are able to satisfy their own scope with different approaches and with different results. The designed layers are:

- User area: In this area there is an instance of sleeping agent for each patient in the clinical setting. This sleeping agent is stored in the RFID that the patient receives when he/she comes into a health centre. It is possible to consider this agent as an avatar of the patient in the proposed model of health centre. The main task of this agent is to interact with all the other agents into the system to satisfy the patient necessity. This agent is defined "sleeping" because it is not permanently allocated in the main system, where the clinical model is running. Indeed, this agent is loaded into the system only when the patient needs some services (he/she goes into a certain ward, he/she receives some pills, etc.). When the patient necessity has been satisfied the sleeping agent can return back into the RFID with its new updated state or it can stay in running state to accomplish other tasks. In this way, it is possible to save a big amount of system resources in terms of memory and processing time. It should be highlighted that the couple RFID-sleeping agent is the point of contact between the real world health centre and the MAS based clinic model and it is absolutely transparent for the patient.
- Interface area is designed to allow for the communication between the agents in the user area and those in the brokerage area. In this area various problems about systems compatibility and security are faced.
- Brokerage area: In this area there are two classes of agents: broker agent and coach agent. The broker agent receives the service requests from the upper layer and it analyzes a local database in which services offered by MAS (that are the same that in the real world the health center offers) are stored. Starting by one query, it produces as many messages as the request needs. The language, that Broker uses to communicate, is

generated using understandable and common language for all agents. The Coach is a complementary agent of the Broker, because it is able to assemble the information contained in the messages sent by the lower level as response to a broker query. At the end of the process the Coach sends a message to the Interface that translates the answer in a language understandable by the sleeping agent and/or the user.

- Analysis area: in this area all the services provided by the clinic: medical doctor, analysis devices, etc are modeled as "service agents".
- Knowledge area: In this area there are all the information sources present into the health centre (e.g. databases used by the medical doctor to store information about patient, connections to other regional or national databases, etc.).

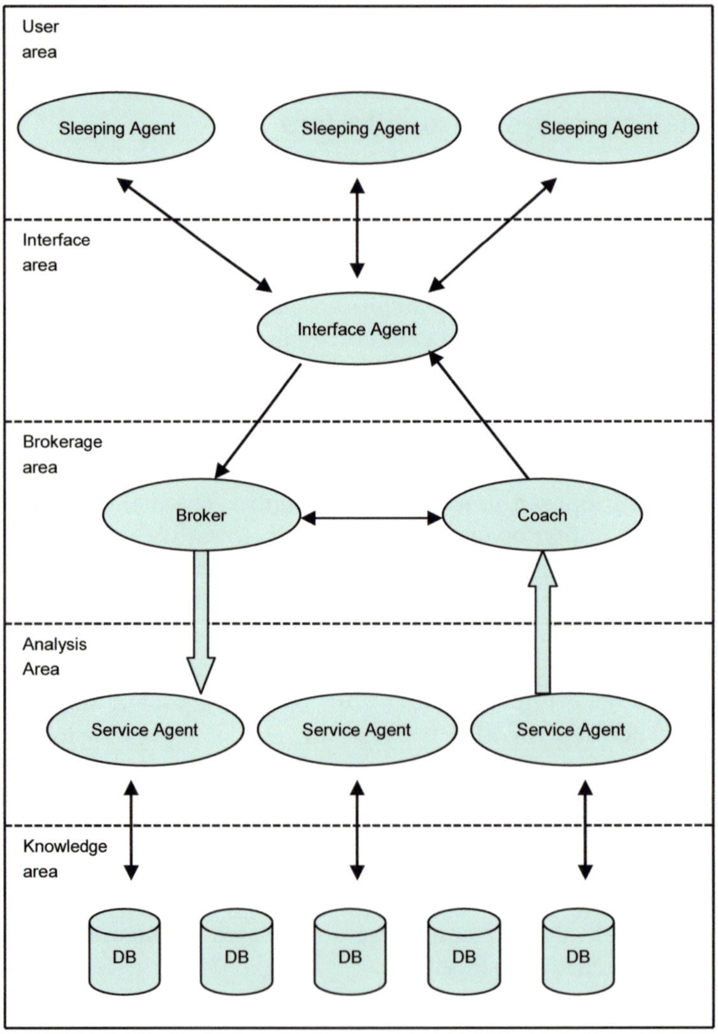

Fig. 1. A schematic overview of the proposed MAS

The adoption of an agent with standard characteristics would require the allocation of computational resources always associated to it. The introduction of sleeping agent represents a possible problem solution. This agent frees its allocated resources when the patient is in standby (namely the patient does not interact with healthcare system i.e. when he/she stays in his/her room). This statement introduces an important advantage to the system: it reduces the computational cost since it is based on a distributed asynchronous communication model. The interaction between patient and health care center are handled in automatic by the sleeping agent in a transparent way for the user.

On the other hand, a RFID becomes patient ownership in the proposed system. The sleeping agent is stored in the RFID memory, letting the patient transport information about himself/herself across the healthcare centers. This represents the second advantage introduced by the proposed system: i.e. proactive event-driven solution to patient data flow. This approach improves also the security of the data management system. Indeed, the sleeping agent can handle also the private key of an asymmetric cryptography system. Data are stored in the database using the cryptography and they can be read only with the physic presence of the patient.

7. Conclusions

In this work the authors propose a new kind of intelligent agent based on the new finding in RFID technology. The sleeping agent can be used to implement MAS systems to solve various problems. As case study the authors proposed a MAS modeling a health care center. In this model the sleeping agent is resident on a patient's RFID wristband. This kind of agent is the virtualization of a single patient in the healthcare system and plays the role of a proactive user for the clinical information system. The sleeping agent memorized on a RFID is a convenient solution to the problem of patient identification and traceability that allows for several benefits in terms of data integration, computational effort, asynchronous communication, privacy and so on.

8. References

[1] Nwana, H.S., Software Agents: An Overview, *Knowledge Engineering Review*, Vol. 11, No. 3, pp 1-40, Sep. 1996. http://www.cs.umbc.edu/agents/introduction/ao

[2]Wooldridge, J., and N. R. Jennings, Intelligent Agents: Theory and Practice, *The Knowledge Engineering Review*, 1995, 10 (2), pp 115-152.

[3] Francesco Amigoni, Arnaldo Brandolini, Gabriele D'Antona, Roberto Ottoboni, and Marco Somalvico, Artificial Intelligence in Science of Measurements: From Measurement Instruments to Perceptive Agencies, *IEEE Transactions On Instrumentation And Measurement*, vol. 52, no. 3, june 2003 pp. 716-723

[4] A. Amato, V. Di Lecce, C. Pasquale, V. Piuri, Web Agents in an Environmental Monitoring System, CIMSA 2005 - *IEEE International Conference on Computational Intelligence for Measurement Systems and Giardini Naxos*, Italy, pp. 262-265, July 20-22, 2005.

[5] V. Di Lecce, A. Amato, M. Calabrese, Data Integration in Distributed Medical Information Systems, CCECE 2008, *Proceedings of IEEE 21st Canadian Conference on Electrical and Computer Engineering*, Niagara Falls, Canada, pp. 1497 - 1502, May 4-7 2008. (ISSN: 0840-7789 ISBN: 978-1-4244-1642-4)

[6] Vincenzo Di Lecce, Alberto Amato:Multi Agent Negotiation for a Decision Support System in Route Planning. *International Conference on Computational Intelligence for Modelling, Control and Automation* CIMCA '08 - Vienna

[7] Kashif Zafar, Shahzad Badar Qazi, A. Rauf Baig Mine Detection and Route Planning in Military Warfare using Multi Agent System, *Proceedings of the 30th Annual International Computer Software and Applications Conference* (COMPSAC'06)

[8] N. R. Jennings and M. Wooldridge. Applying Agent Technology In *Journal of Applied Artificial Intelligence special issue on Intelligent Agents and Multi-Agent Systems*, 1995

[9] Sikora R., Shaw M.J., Coordination Mechanisms for Multi-Agent Manufacturing Systems: Applications to Integrated Manufacturing Scheduling, *IEEE Trans. Syst., Man and Cyber.*, Vol. 44/2, 1997

[10] Wiendahl H.-P., Ahrens V., Agent-Based Control of Self-Organized Production Systems, *Annals of the CIRP*, Vol. 46/1, 1997

[11] Qiao B., Zhu J. Agent-Based Intelligent Manufacturing System for the 21st Century, *Proc. International Forum for Graduates and Young Researchers at Expo 2000* Hannover, Hannover, Germany, 2000

[12] V. Di Lecce, C. Pasquale, V. Piuri, A Basic Ontology for Multy Agent System Communication in an Environmental Monitoring System, IEEE/CIMSA 2004 – *Proceedings of International Symposium on Computational Intelliginece for Measurement Systems and Applications*, Boston, MA, USA, pp. 45-50, July 14-16, 2004.

[13] Kashif Zafar, Shahzad Badar Qazi, A. Rauf Baig, Mine Detection and Route Planning in Military Warfare using Multi Agent System, in *Proceedings of the 30th Annual International Computer Software and Applications Conference* (COMPSAC'06) 0-7695-2655-1/06

[14] Vladimir Gorodetsky, Oleg Karsaev, Vladimir Kupin, Vladimir Samoilov, Agent-Based Air Traffic Control in Airport Airspace, in *2007 IEEE/WIC/ACM International Conference on Intelligent Agent Technology*, pp. 81-84.

[15] Jana Dospisil, Tony Polgar, Constraint agents can negotiate, International Conference on EUROCON'2001, *Trends in Communications*, Volume 1, 4-7 July 2001 Page(s):140 - 144 vol.1

[16] Melanie R. Rieback, Bruno Crispo, Andrew S. Tanenbaum, Is Your Cat Infected with a Computer Virus?, in *Proceedings of the Fourth Annual IEEE International Conference on Pervasive Computing and Communications* (PERCOM'06)

[17] http://www.rfidjournal.com/article/articleview/3850/1/1/

[18] Bates D., Cohen M., Leape L., Overhage M., Shabot M., Sheridan T., Reducing the Frequency of Errors in Medicine Using Information Technology, *Journal of the American Medical Informatics Association*, Vol. 8, Num. 4, Harvard Medical School, Boston, MA, USA, 2001

[19] White Paper Automatic identification of medical devices. Final version ECRI. August, 2005

[20] Young D., Pittsburgh hospital combines RFID, bar codes to improve safety, *American Journal of Health-System Pharmacy*. 63(24):2431-2432, 2006

17

A Multi-Agent Approach to Electric Power Systems

Nikolai I. Voropai, Irina N. Kolosok, Lyudmila V. Massel,
Denis A. Fartyshev, Alexei S. Paltsev and Daniil A. Panasetsky
Energy Systems Institute
Russia

1. Introduction

Electric power systems are rather complicated objects for modeling, investigation and control because of many elements and complex structure. Comprehensive multi-functional software is necessary to study multi-dimensional systems of the kind. The problems of current state estimation should be solved for monitoring of electric power system operation conditions.

Emergency control actions are required to improve stability of electric power systems. A multi-agent approach can be used to solve such complex problems of electric power systems.

The chapter deals with the following important areas of modeling, investigation and control of large electric power systems:

- Effective construction of comprehensive software by using the multi-agent approach;
- Decomposition of state estimation problem for large electric power system by using phasor measurement units and the multi-agent approach;
- Multi-agent approach to coordination of emergency control devices against voltage collapse.

The effectiveness of multi-agent approach for solving the above problems is illustrated by test examples.

2. Effective construction of comprehensive software by using the multi-agent approach

2.1 Methodical approach to multi-agent software development

Traditionally, there are active complex research of energy systems (electrical power system, natural gas industry, mineral oil providing system, carbon providing system, heat supply system), Fuel Energy Complex (FEC) and energy security problem of Russia in Melentiev Energy Systems Institute of Siberian Branch of the Russian Academy of Sciences (ESI SB RAS). Results of researching the branch energy systems often are input data for FEC research. And results of researching the developing trends of FEC must be taken into account while analyzing developing process of the branch energy systems.

It is necessary to co-ordinate input and output information to get grounded conclusions and recommendations whish are prepared for outer organizations. That is why we must create integrated informational and computational environment for investigating i.e. IT-infrastructure (infrastructure based Informational Technologies) of research activities. IT-specialists of the Institute have proposed the project of creating such IT-infrastructure taking into consideration the specificity of power engineering researches and up-to-date tendencies in the development of Informational Technologies (Massel et al., 2008).

We interpret **IT-infrastructure** as a combination of Hardware, Software, Dataware and Telecommunication for supporting research activities; technologies of their making and using; both inner and outer standards for making informational and program products in the field of energy researches, exchange of them and outsourcing at the informational market. On the one hand, IT-infrastructure is integrated informational and computational environment for energy researches implementation. On the other hand, it creates preconditions for stage-by-stage transition to the creation of distributed data bases and program complexes; distribution and parallelization computations; outsourcing on the base science intensive informational and computational products (creation of Web-services).

There is an active work that deals with method of software that supports energy research to become intelligent.

One of possible way is to integrate multi-agent technologies, ontologies and service-oriented architecture as a platform for intelligent software development for energy research. Using the multi-agent systems conception based on Service-Oriented Architecture (SOA) implementation, where the problem of knowledge representation solved with a help of ontologies had been proposed by authors. Such knowledge representation gets additional advantage when designing software with Model-Driven Architecture (this approach is developed and used in ESI SB RAS).

Conception of creating programs, which can exist autonomously and interact with each other in independently manner perfectly combines with technical abilities which SOA gives.

Usage of software agents, particularly, intelligent software agents, is good, because experts could delegate their authorities for solving complex tasks to such agents. Intelligence is a feature of software agents that contains in their ability to knowledge processing. One of the modern technologies of knowledge representation is using ontologies. At first time, SOA had been used to create applications in commercial area and later it becomes more popular in scientific research and other subject areas.

Implementation of IT Infrastructure of science research in ESI SB RAS created the necessary prerequisites for using such modern and available technologies as Web-services. One of the main ideas of ES problem research support is increasing the intelligent and adaptation level of software tools (Massel et al., 2009). Using the Web-services technology per se can't influence increasing the intelligent level of software tools for supporting research. Therefore, using the multi-agent technologies, which were conceived from intersection of systems theory and artificial intelligence and became popular nowadays had been proposed by authors (Fartyshev et al., 2009).

The original author's methodical approach to multi-agent software complexes development for energy research includes:

- the method of designing and implementing the multi-agent software complex which can be used for the new generation software for energy research support;
- by using Service-Oriented Architecture of multi-agent software it is possible to consider the agents as the Web-services, application is built from;
- data models and algorithm of data processing are the base of universal software components which can be used while multi-agent software constructing.

The author's method is a direction which combines agency conception and object-oriented approach to software development. Following this direction it is possible to implement the multi-agent software complex. The method consists of the following generic stages:

1. Formulating purposes of the development.
2. Formalizing the use cases of multi-agent software.
3. Defining the agents structure and their main and auxiliary functions.
4. Defining the type and main properties of agents environment.
5. Specification the agents structure and distribution the functions among agents. Choosing the agents architecture.
6. Defining base interactions (relations) among agents.
7. Defining possible agents actions (operations).
8. Designing and implementing multi-agent software complex architecture.
9. Testing implemented multi-agent software.
10. Integrating the multi-agent software into the IT-infrastructure of energy research.

Service-Oriented Architecture is one of the key concepts in the whole implementation plan of multi-agent software complex. Considering separate agents in the view of Web-services gives certain advantages like using mutual assistance, parallelism, high degree of reusing and so on. Multi-agent software complex is implemented in distributed client-server architecture where the application server is the central component (Fig. 1).

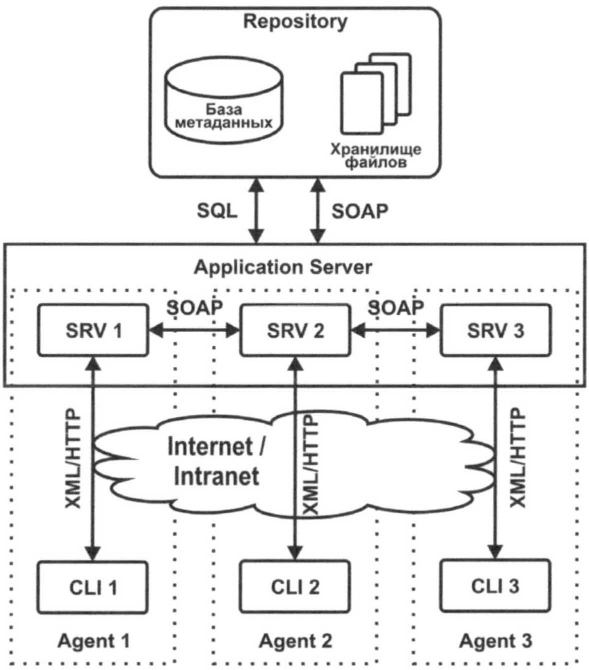

Fig. 1. Architecture of multi-agent software

Thus, agent is a certain application consists of client (service consumer) and server (service provider) at the physical implementation view point.

The main task of the agent client part is providing the user-friendly interface which is used to access the agent's features mainly implemented in its server part. Agents can work with data and knowledge by connecting the Repository through the Simple Object Access Protocol (SOAP) or by using the Structured Query Language (SQL). Agents can connect to each other also by using the SOAP. However, there can be used other similar to SOAP technologies that could transmit XML data through the Hyper-Text Transfer Protocol (HTTP), for instance XML-Remote Procedure Call (XML-RPC), to provide the agents interconnection.

There is need to use all three components of SOA: service provider, service consumer and register of services in implementation of the multi-agent software complex based on SOA. Register of services is the component that cares about service publication and providing the links to the services that are already registered in it. Register is used for service discovery and publication accordingly by service consumers and service providers. The existing Repository of IT-infrastructure of science research (Massel et al., 2008) is used in service register role.

The universal system components compound the base of multi-agent software complex are the following:

- the new standard for storing and representing the information models of FEC, that are one of the key elements in ES problem research;
- service for uploading and downloading information models of FEC into the Repository of IT-infrastructure;
- agents messaging services;
- agents integration services;

Developed method and architecture were used to design and implement multi-agent software INTEC-M for energy security problem research.

2.2 Multi-agent software INTEC-M

Design and implementation of the multi-agent software INTEC-M for supporting the ES problem research were done based on author's method and in accordance with developed architecture.

There is distribution of functions between different agents in the idea of INTEC-M software implementation. Such software is a compound of mentioned above system components and specific intellectual and traditional agents for specific solving of certain subject area problem.

The common scheme of agents working process in accordance with computational experiment in researching the developing trends of FEC considering energy safety requirements is shown at Fig.2.

Every implemented agent solves the certain task that corresponds to the certain stage of computational experiment. One of the main advantages of proposed approach is independence of hard-coded sequence of computational experiment stage that is accomplished by such agent's properties as autonomy and mobility.

The main purpose of *Agent of extraordinary situations modeling* is fusion of human-readable wordings of extraordinary situations scenarios with its digital interpretation in model. The agent gives a researcher an opportunity to store, classify, configure and apply different types of extraordinary situations in the computational experiment process.

Agent of development scenarios of FEC modeling is a software tool allowing a researcher to form the FEC development variants tree which is the main base during the computational experiment process.

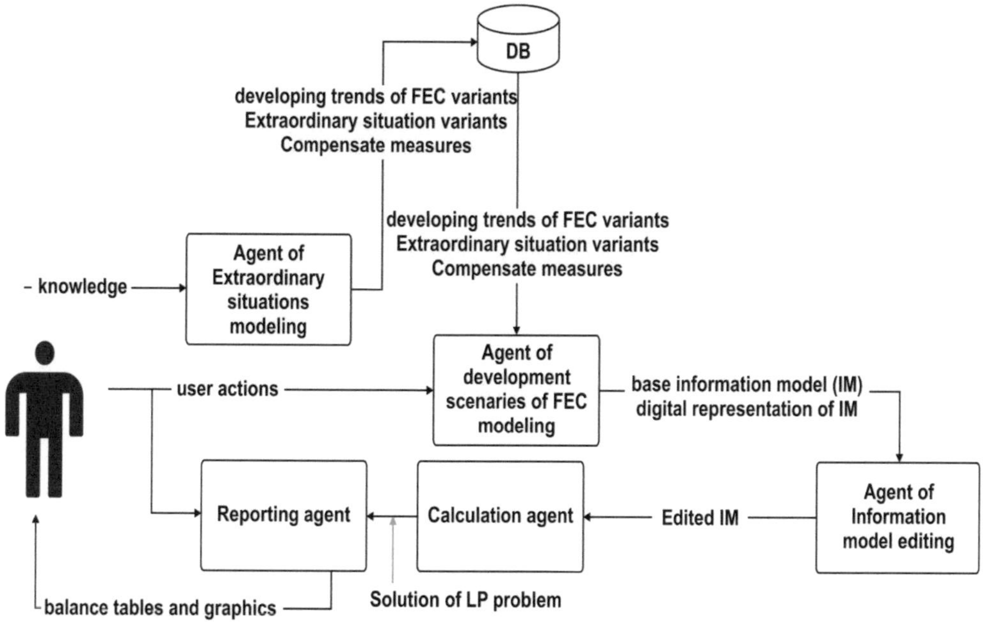

Fig. 2. The common scheme of agents working process

Agent of FEC information models editing gives a researcher accessible and effective software tools for working with FEC information models including its creation from the beginning.

Calculation agent is an open source software tool (lp_solve) for solving Mixed Integer Linear Programming (MILP) problems implemented by third-party. It was included in INTEC-M software, because the common linear programming problem is traditionally solved in FEC development trends research considering energy safety requirements.

The main purpose of reporting agent is to create and then analyze different table reports and its graphic representations of computational experiment results. The agent gives an opportunity to a visual comparing of summary and detailed computational experiment data.

Agents get the additional property of mobility which is valued agents property in multi-agent systems by using such modern and standardized technologies as Java and XML.

The main advantages of INTEC-M software are the following:

- The uniform ideology and technology of development;
- Adaptive to changing behavior of computational experiment scheme;
- Cross-platform;
- Trends to parallel data processing;
- IT-infrastructure integration.

The joint computational experiment of evaluation of possible deficits fuel and energy resources and measures for its to compensate in extraordinary situations was processed. As the extraordinary situation it was taken cold winter in Central Federal District of Russia.

Effectiveness of using implemented INTEC-M software for ES problem research of Russia and its regions is implied in useful, psychologically comfortable work that improved by many experts.

3. Decomposition of state estimation problem for large electric power system by using phasor measurement units and the multi-agent approach

3.1 Decomposition of state estimation problem

State estimation of electric power systems (EPS) is an important procedure that allows on-line calculation of state variables for a current scheme of electric network on the basis of teleinformation. The obtained calculated model of power system is then used to solve various technological problems to effectively control electric power system.

The calculations for a large system encounter the problems related to the inhomogeneity of calculated schemes, large volumes of various data to be processed and the requirement for high speed software. Besides, the need for online state estimation of such systems increases the burden on the available computing resources in the EPS Control Center. The distributed data processing at decomposition of the state estimation problem is an effective method of solving these problems.

Until recently state estimation in Electric Power Systems was mainly based on the SCADA (Supervisory Control and Data Acquisition) measurements: voltage magnitudes, branch power flow, nodal power injections and, occasionally, current magnitudes. The advent of WAMS (Wide-Area Measurement System) that contains phasor measurement units (PMU) as the main measurement equipment makes it possible to synchronously and accurately control the EPS state and essentially improve the results of state estimation. The use of PMU measurements offers new possibilities in decomposition of the state estimation problem.

The distributed approach to state estimation applies *decomposition* and *aggregation* procedures. The SE procedure thereby consists of the following stages:

1. Division of the calculated scheme into subsystems by one or another method at the decomposition stage.
2. State estimation for each subsystem.
3. Solution of the coordination problem consisting in calculation of the boundary variables and check of the boundary conditions. If the conditions are not met, the subsystems are recalculated with new values of boundary variables.
4. Formation of the general solution for the whole scheme by combination of solutions for individual subsystems and solution of the coordination problem at the aggregation stage.

In large-scale interconnections that consist of EPSs operating in parallel and have no single control center, the aggregation stage may be neglected. The calculation terminates by solving the coordination problem at the solution coordination center, resulting in the estimated state obtained for each subsystem that is balanced in the boundary regions with the states of neighboring subsystems.

Flow chart of distributed state estimation is shown in Fig.3.

Decomposition of the state estimation problem proposed by authors is based on structural (by subsystems) and functional (by the problems solved) decomposition. The structural decomposition is made by dividing the calculated scheme into subsystems by one or another method. The functional decomposition is made in accordance with the problems solved within the SE procedure. The main of them are: analysis of network topology (formation of current calculated scheme); analysis of observability; analysis of bad data; calculation of estimates and calculation of steady state with regard to the estimates obtained.

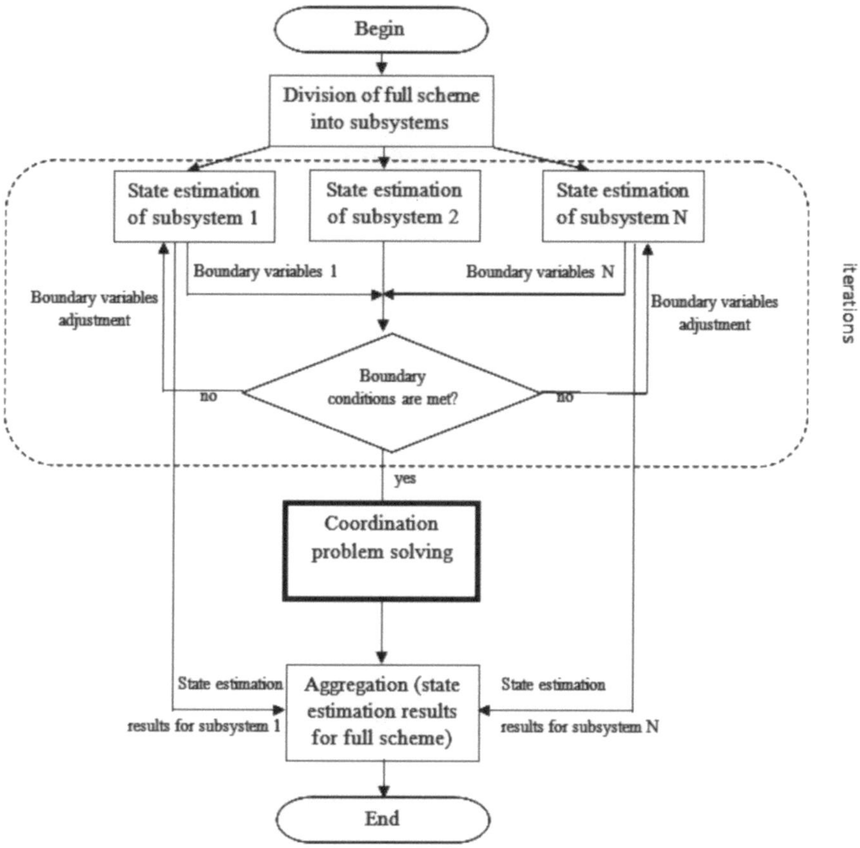

Fig. 3. Flow chart of distributed state estimation

3.2 Algorithms of the calculated scheme division into subsystems

The calculated scheme can be divided into subsystems by the following techniques: decomposition utilizing geographical characteristics, decomposition by boundary nodes, by tie-lines, based on the structure of gain matrix, by Danzig-Wolf decomposition algorithm and others.

The main algorithms of state estimation problem decomposition suggest dividing the calculated scheme into subsystems whose boundaries are either nodes or branches.

As boundary conditions at decomposition with boundary nodes the equality of voltage magnitudes and phases at these nodes for the *i, j, …, k*-th subsystems should be met (Gamm, 1983):

$$U_i = U_j = \ldots = U_k ; \tag{1}$$

$$\delta_i = \delta_j = \ldots = \delta_k ; \tag{2}$$

Besides the boundary balance relationships should be met. For example for boundary node *l*, common for the *i, j, …, k*-th subsystems

$$P_l + \sum_{s=i,j,\dots,k} \sum_{m\in\omega_s} P_{lm}(U_l,\delta_l,U_m,\delta_m) = 0\,; \tag{3}$$

$$Q_l + \sum_{s=i,j,\dots,k} \sum_{m\in\omega_s} Q_{lm}(U_l,\delta_l,U_m,\delta_m) = 0\,, \tag{4}$$

where ω_s - a set of nodes of the *s*-th subsystem, that are adjacent to the *l*-th node.
As boundary conditions at decomposition with boundary branches the relationships for active (5) and a reactive (6) power flows should be observed:

$$P_{ij}(X_i,X_j) = -P_{ji}(X_i,X_j) - \Delta P_{ij}(X_i,X_j)\,, \tag{5}$$

$$Q_{ij}(X_i,X_j) = -Q_{ji}(X_i,X_j) - \Delta Q_{ij}(X_i,X_j) + Q_{gij}(X_i,X_j)\,, \tag{6}$$

where P_{ij} and Q_{ij} - power flows from *i-th* subsystem to *j-th* subsystem, $\Delta P_{ij}(X_i,X_j)$, $\Delta Q_{ij}(X_i,X_j)$, $Q_{gij}(X_i,X_j)$ - aggregate losses of active and reactive power and aggregate power of section links, X_i, X_j - state vectors for *i-th* and *j-th* subsystems.
For boundary branch *m-l*

$$U_m^2 - (U_l - \frac{P_{ml}r_{ml} + Q_{ml}x_{ml}}{U_m})^2 - (\frac{P_{ml}x_{ml} - Q_{ml}r_{ml}}{U_m})^2 = 0\,, \tag{7}$$

$$\delta_m - \delta_l - \mathrm{arctg}\frac{P_{ml}x_{ml} - Q_{ml}r_{ml}}{P_{ml}r_{ml} + Q_{ml}x_{ml}} = 0\,. \tag{8}$$

Decomposition of calculated scheme with boundary branches is more often used.

3.3 PMU measurements usage for the solution of decomposition of state estimation problem

For decomposition of power system state estimation problem it is necessary to maintain accurate values of voltage magnitudes and phases at boundary nodes of subsystems for iteration-free solution of coordination problem. A simple but not an optimal solution is placement of PMUs at all boundary nodes. Based on the measurements to be received from the placed PMUs the voltage magnitude and phase at a neighbor node can be calculated using the electrical circuit equations. The phasor voltage measurement obtained by the equations further will be named as "calculated" PMU.
The study shows that the accuracy of parameters of the "calculated" PMU practically equals the accuracy of measurements of the physical PMU (Kolosok et al., 2009). With an optimal combination of physical and "calculated" PMU at all boundary nodes of subsystems it is possible to determine voltage magnitudes and phases required to coordinate the solutions obtained for individual subsystems.
In order to minimize the number of PMUs authors analyze not only the list of boundary nodes but the list of internal branches within subsystems that are incident to these nodes as well. The boundary nodes may happen to belong to one and the same subsystem and bound one and the same branch. Then it is enough to place a physical PMU at one end of the branch and a "calculated" PMU at the other.

Installation of PMU in boundary nodes allows to fix boundary variables U and δ on the values metered with high accuracy. In this case:

- boundary conditions (1), (2) are fulfilled automatically, and
- solution of a coordination problem consists in calculation of node injections in boundary nodes on (3), (4), using estimations of branch power flows, received from results of separate subsystems.

Thus state estimation of separate subsystems can be calculated in parallel, independently from each other, accomplishment of iterative calculations on subsystems is not required.

When decomposition of calculated scheme into subsystems with boundary branches PMU is installed in one of nodes of a boundary branch then a "calculated" PMU can be received on other end of a branch. In this case:

- the combination of measurements from physical and "calculated" PMU in an incident node provide accomplishment of boundary conditions (7), (8) in boundary branches,
- as PMU, installed in a node, allows to receive or calculate measurements (pseudo-measurements) of power flows of all branches departing from a node the boundary conditions (5), (6) also will be fulfilled.

In this case SE of separate subsystems also can be calculated independently from each other, accomplishment of iterative calculations on subsystems is not required.

For coordination of phase angles of the voltages received from local state estimation only one PMU measurement of phase angle is enough in each subsystem. Such node is appointed for subsystems reference node. PMU measurements coordinate results of state estimation of separate subsystems. In one arbitrary selected subsystem the reference node with a zero angle is traditionally set. Actually, the zero value of an angle of a reference node does not correspond with the PMU metered angles of other nodes. Therefore it is necessary to install PMU device in a reference node or to appoint the node with PMU as a reference.

Bad data detection in telemetry, or validation of measurements, is one of the most important problems in EPS state estimation. In this work bad data detection is based on the test equation method. This method makes it possible to carry out validation of information prior to solving the SE problem. Solving the problem of state estimation for EPS with low redundancy of measurements we face the problem of validating the critical measurements and critical sets. It is impossible to detect uniquely gross errors in these measurements. One of possible approaches for solution of this problem is the use of PMU measurements. Optimal placement of PMU increases the redundancy of SCADA measurements and eliminates critical measurements and critical sets, i.e. allows detection of all bad data in measurements.

Accurately synchronized measurements provided by PMU placed near boundary nodes essentially increase the redundancy of measurements and efficiency of methods for detection of bad data in boundary regions.

3.4 A two-stage algorithm for decomposition of the calculated scheme into subsystems in state estimation

The idea of decomposing the state estimation problem with PMU placement at boundary nodes is rather attractive. In reality, however, due to high cost of PMUs they can only be used when the number of boundary nodes is small.

To calculate large inhomogeneous schemes the authors propose a method of dividing the calculated scheme with respect to voltage levels (Gamm et al., 2007 (a)). This method decreases essentially a negative impact of inhomogeneity of calculated scheme and telemetric information in calculation of subsystems of one voltage class but for the complex scheme inevitably leads to a large number of boundary nodes. Therefore, the paper proposes a two-stage algorithm to decompose the calculated scheme into subsystems that combines the positive features of both approaches.

At the first stage the scheme is divided into rather large areas with minimum number of intersystem ties and boundary nodes. This decomposition can be made on the basis of administrative division, for example, the entire scheme of Russia's Unified Energy System is decomposed into regional power subsystems of large regions in the country that operate in parallel or it can be decomposed artificially into separate areas by special algorithms (Gamm & Grishin, 1995). PMUs are placed at the boundary nodes of the areas. Highly accurate measurements obtained from PMU make it possible to register the values of magnitudes and phases of nodal voltages at the boundary nodes and make calculations for the areas in parallel.

At the second stage the calculated scheme of each area in turn is divided into subsystems that correspond to the levels of nodal voltages. The calculations start with the subsystem of the highest voltage level (750-500 kV). Normally this part of the scheme is well provided with highly accurate telemetry and contains a basic node. Then the calculations are made successively for the rest of the subsystems. The subsystems are ranked by voltage levels (220 kV, 110 kV, etc.). Every time the node bordering the subsystem of higher voltage level is chosen as a basic one. After calculations of lower voltage levels of large areas the coordination problem is solved, which include calculation of node injections in boundary nodes or calculation of power flows in boundary branches.

The functional decomposition of the state estimation problem is performed in accordance with the problems solved within the state estimation procedure. The main of them are: analysis of network topology; analysis of observability; analysis of bad data; calculation of estimates and steady state by the estimates obtained.

The current calculated scheme is formed for the entire scheme. Bad data analysis and calculation of estimates and steady state are performed by the test equation technique for each subsystem of a certain voltage class before solving the state estimation problem (Gamm et al., 2007 (b)).

State estimation is made according to two criteria: the method of weighted least squares and the robust criterion that allows the estimates to be obtained and bad data to be suppressed simultaneously.

Control is transferred to one or another state estimation program depending on operation of the bad data detection program. In case of bad data detection or their absence the program for calculation of estimates operates on the basis of the least squares method. However, if it is impossible to detect erroneous measurements and, hence, identify bad data the program operates according to the robust criterion. State estimation is made starting at the upper level of the structural decomposition.

3.5 Full algorithm

The full algorithm for solving the state estimation problem based on structural and functional decomposition is as follows.

1. The complete calculated scheme of EPS is decomposed into rather large areas. Phasor measurement units are placed at the boundary nodes of subsystems. PMU device is placed in the basic node of full scheme.

1A. PMU devices are placed in the boundary (not transit) nodes of subsystems. In the subsystems that have no basic node of the complete scheme one of the boundary nodes with PMU of the highest voltage class is chosen as a basic one. Measurements of nodal injections at boundary nodes are excluded from the vector of measurements.

1B. If the boundary nodes of two or more subsystems are transit, the decomposition with boundary nodes is used. PMU is installed in one of nodes of a boundary branch then a "calculated" PMU can be received on other end of a branch. While calculating the first subsystem the measurements of node injections of second subsystems are excluded from the vector of measurements, and vice-versa.

2. At the second stage of decomposition the calculated scheme of each area is divided into subsystems that correspond to the levels of nodal voltages. The boundaries of the subsystems are the nodes adjacent to the nodes of the voltage class of this subsystem. For example for the 750-500 kV voltage class subsystem the nodes with the voltage of 220 kV are boundary nodes and vice-versa.
3. The calculation starts with the subsystem of the highest voltage level (750-500 kV) for each subsystem. Normally this part of the scheme is well provided with highly accurate measurements and contains a basic node. The state estimation algorithm for subsystems with boundary nodes is as follows:
   3.1. For each subsystem that contains boundary nodes the problem of bad data detection is solved by the test equation technique.
   3.2. In case of bad data detection or their absence the state estimation is made according to least squares method.
   3.3. In the event that erroneous measurements cannot be detected and hence it is impossible to detect bad data, the state estimation is made according to the robust criterion (bad data suppression).
4. The rest of the subsystems in the scheme are successively calculated. They are ranked by voltage level (220 kV, 110 kV, etc.). Every time the node bordering the subsystem of higher voltage level is chosen as a basic node. The estimates of the boundary variables of the state vector that are obtained at the upper level of decomposition are registered.
5. The injections at boundary nodes between the subsystems of different voltage class are calculated.
6. After all subsystems of the first level of decomposition have been calculated similar problem is solved for the boundary nodes with PMU, if these nodes are transit, power flows in the boundary branches are calculated.
7. Due to obtain general solution for full scheme the results received from subsystems and results of coordination problem solution are aggregated.

3.6 Multi-agent approach

The multi-agent approach to the power system state estimation is based on the structural and functional decomposition of state estimation problem described earlier.

For each agent the subsystem of a certain voltage class is used as an object to be modeled. To implement the algorithm of state estimation by the test equation technique a multi-agent system (MAS) has been developed (Fig.4).

Functionality of agents:

- MAS_0– a common MAS, that contains all subsystems and all agents.

- A_{DE} – a decomposition agent, that makes decomposition of the calculated scheme into subsystems by voltage level;
- A_{AG} – an aggregation agent, that aggregates data received by coordination agent from subsystems, and forms the full scheme regime;
- MAS_I , *i*=1,…,*n* – a MAS's, that contain subsystems of first decomposition level;
- MAS_{IJ} – an agent of *i*-th subsystem of the *j*-th voltage level (Fig.5) that transfers the values of voltages and phase angles at its boundary nodes to a lower level. It contains a local multi-agent system that consists of three agents:
- A_{BD} – an agent of bad data that detects bad data and, depending on results of its operation, starts either agent A_{SQ} or agent A_R;
- A_{SQ} – an agent of state estimation by the least squares method, started by the agent A_{BD} if bad data are found or there are no bad data;
- A_R – an agent of state estimation in accordance with the robust criterion. It is started by the agent A_{BD} if it is impossible to identify bad data;
- A_K – coordination agent that coordinates calculations in big subsystems, and calculates boundary variables (active and reactive powers in boundary nodes and power flows in boundary branches);
- A_k – coordination agent for voltage level areas, that calculates active and reactive powers in boundary nodes of these areas;

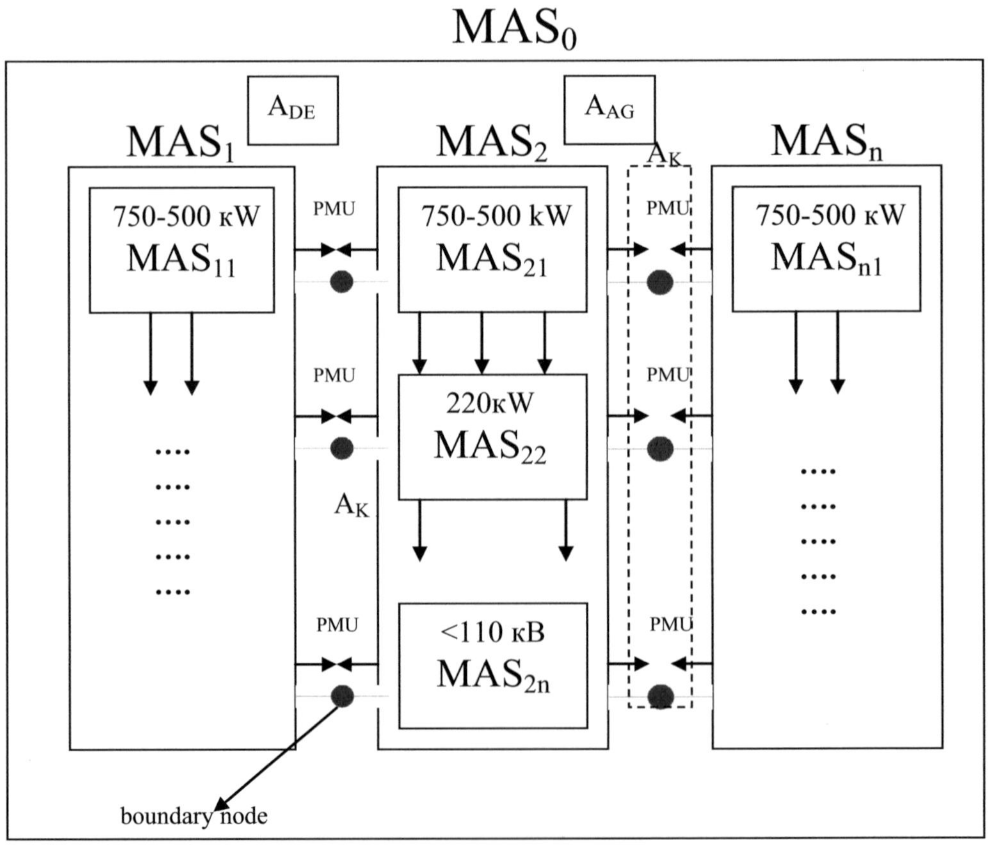

Fig. 4. Architecture of multi-agent system

Agents A_K and A_k may be mobile agents, and can move between subsystems, collecting data for further calculations.

Usage of multi-agent approach to distributed state estimation allows following advantages:

1. To organize a flexible choice of a method of solving different problems of state estimation for each subsystem;
2. To coordinate and quickly exchange data between tasks which are solved in different levels and distributed territorially (mobile agents).

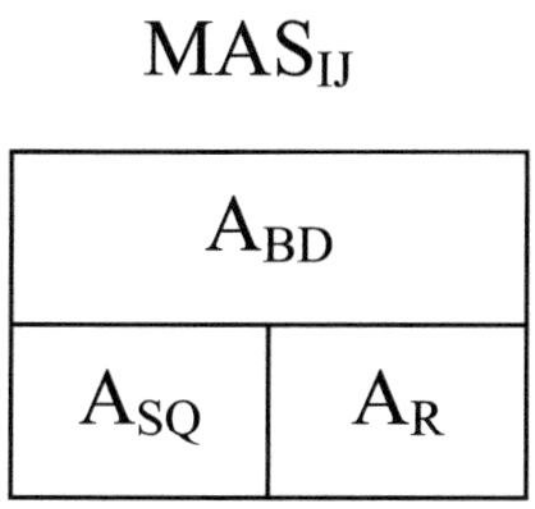

Fig. 5. Structure of agent of i-th subsystem of the j-th voltage level

3.7 Case study

In order to test the efficiency of the suggested decomposition algorithm of state estimation the calculations of a real scheme consisting of 107 nodes and 175 branches were made (Fig.6). The calculations were based on real measurements. The efficiency of the algorithm was assessed by comparing the results of calculations made for subsystems to the results of the calculation made for the entire scheme.

At the first stage the genetic algorithm was used to divide the entire scheme into two subsystems containing 55 and 52 nodes with 6 boundary nodes in which the PMU data (measurements of magnitudes and phases of nodal voltages) were modeled. The calculations of these subsystems were carried out in parallel which reduced the time of solving the SE problem almost twice: from 0.49 s to 0.27 s.

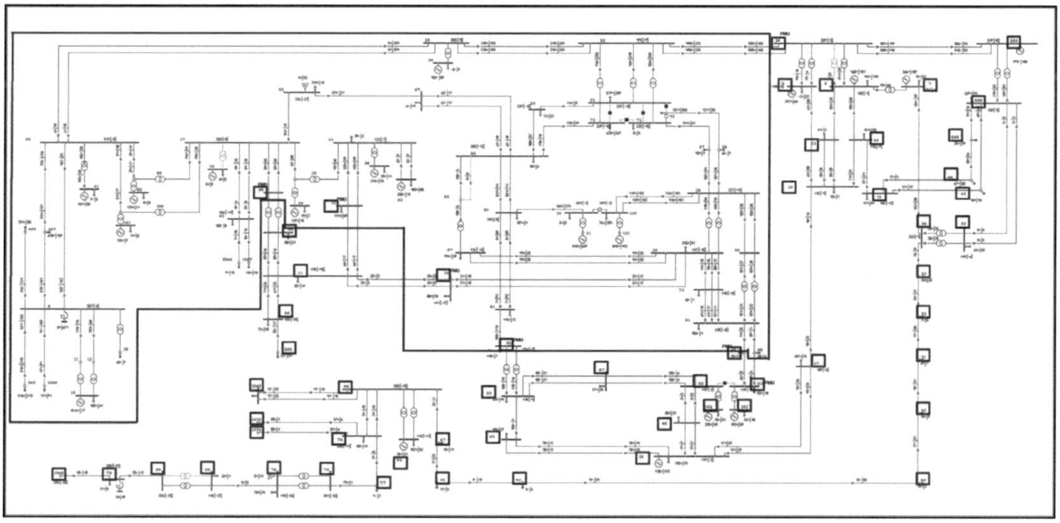

Fig. 6. EPS scheme fragment

At the second stage of decomposition each of the subsystems in turn was decomposed into three areas corresponding to the voltage levels of 500 kV, 220 kV, 110 kV and lower. The calculation of these areas according to the above algorithm was made successively, therefore the full time of solution could increase. However, owing to the improved convergence of the iteration processes in the calculation of areas of the same voltage class the total time of the calculation for all the three areas practically did not change.

More efficient operation of bad data detection algorithm and application of the robust criterion of state estimation for two of six areas improved considerably the results of state estimation: the value of the state estimation objective function at the point of solution decreased almost by a factor of 6 and the estimates at boundary nodes were noticeably improved.

Decomposition by voltage levels and usage of PMU measurements in boundary nodes allow to considerably improve the effectiveness of bad data detection methods. Table 1 shows the comparison of calculation results in voltage level areas with calculation results by full subsystem. Apparently from the table, while calculations are made by subsystems and PMU devices are used, number of critical measurements and groups of the doubtful data is essentially reduced.

	500 kV area	220 kV area	110 kV area	Full subsystem
Number of nodes	5	25	30	55
Number of branches	7	24	44	80
Measurements	31	98	133	265
Not observable nodes by δ / U	no/no	4/0	5/1	9/1
Redundancy	3,44	2	2,06	2,43
Unchecked data without PMU	2	23	17	35
Unchecked data with PMU	2	7	13	24
Doubtful data groups without PMU	0	0	4	6
Doubtful data groups with PMU	0	0	4	5

Table 1. Comparison of calculation results in voltage level areas with calculation results by full subsystem

4. A multi-agent approach to coordination of emergency control devices against voltage collapse

4.1 Emergency control problem

Power Industry spends a lot of money to protect a power system against different severe disturbances. Nevertheless, large interconnected Power Systems throughout the world are frequently subjected to widespread blackouts which interrupt millions of consumers and cost billions of dollars.

Analysis of the recent blackouts showed, that the most severe interruptions occurred in highly loaded interconnected power systems due to EHV line disruption followed by multiple contingencies.

These accidents highlighted the deficiency of the existing protection systems that cannot maintain the integrity of the transmission grid during multiple contingencies (Lachs, 2002).

Power system behavior in an emergency state is characterized by complex interaction between discrete and continuous control devices. Continuous control devices are automatic voltage regulators, turbine governors, FACTS devices, etc. Discrete control devices are different protection relays, under load tap changers, etc. Currently both continuous and discrete control devices substantially use local signals only and do not coordinate their actions with each other. Absence of coordination between discrete and continuous control devices is the shortcoming of the existing protection system and may lead to blackout.

The paper presents a control system based on the multi-agent approach. The control system provides coordination of different discrete and continuous control devices to prevent voltage collapse of the power system during the post-disturbance period.

4.2 Voltage instability mechanism

To understand the importance of the discrete and continuous control devices coordination, one should understand the mechanism of voltage instability that may occur any time after the first severe contingency and lead to blackout.

Existing practice shows that if protection system works correctly, most power systems have sufficient stability to withstand the first heavy disturbance in EHV transmission system. The post-disturbance phase represents a deceptively calm period that lasts several minutes with a normal level of frequency and then voltage collapse that lasts seconds (Lachs, 1992).

The first heavy disturbance leads to increase in the reactive power losses and reactive power output of rotating units in the vicinity of the affected region. So, the first disturbance effects influence only the affected region, being initially a local problem. But sometime after, the lack of reactive power in the affected region might increase considerably, leading to voltage collapse in the neighboring regions and even in the whole system. This happens because if the disturbance is not dealt with timely, the after-effects spread out through the EHV transmission network and actuate different control devices such as automatic voltage regulators, automatic transformer tap changers, current protection relays, etc. These control devices act at the different speed, respond to changes in the immediate vicinity and act without coordination with one another. Their actions in response to the post-disturbance conditions are actually the main cause of power system breakdown; consequently, the timely control of the discrete and continuous control devices under the post-disturbance conditions is the only means to prevent voltage collapse of the whole system. Undoubtedly, the absence of different control actions coordination during the post-disturbance period can cause different types of instability. But first of all, one should cope with voltage instability because it was the main cause of the recent blackouts. New system protection system philosophy has to be proposed to prevent voltage instability during the post-disturbance period.

4.3 System protection philosophy

A new system protection philosophy is needed to control the post-disturbance phenomenon. A new protection system must detect the critical situation and coordinate the work of control devices to exclude any possibility of voltage instability. So, how can the new protection system identify the critical situation and what kind of control actions should the system use to control the capacity of available reactive power resources?

A. Parameters-Indicators

The main symptoms that precede the voltage collapse are considerable reduction of transmission voltage levels and increase of reactive power outputs on rotating units (Makarov et al., 2005; Taylor & Erickson, 1997). Reduction of voltages and increase of rotating unit excitation were proposed in different papers to indicate the proximity to voltage collapse. Thus, these two criteria may be used to detect the critical situation appearance and activate protection system.

B. Control Actions

Power industry has already used the philosophy of load shedding by selecting non-essential load to prevent frequency reduction. The analysis of recent blackouts showed that the rapid load shedding is usually the only way to prevent the collapse of the whole system. On the one hand, load shedding should be as fast as possible, on the other hand, it should be optimal. The optimal load shedding scheme can be realized by using different optimization procedures, but it is hard to solve optimization problem for any possible situation in advance, because the number of situations is too big. This means that some optimization computations should be made during the post-disturbance period. In spite of the fact that there is a number of optimization techniques that can be used to calculate emergency control actions quickly, the amount of input data required to solve the problem is usually too big. The state estimation alone can take from tens of seconds to minutes. However, load shedding under the post-disturbance conditions has to work faster. Hence, load shedding procedure has to use less complex methods to control post-disturbance phenomenon. The following simple countermeasures to control post-disturbance phenomenon were proposed in (Lachs, 1992):

- Countermeasure 1. Fast tap changing on transmission substation transformers.
- Countermeasure 2. Raising terminal voltage on selected synchronous condensers and hydro generators.
- Countermeasure 3. Fast tap changing on selected generator transformers.
- Countermeasure 4. Strategic load shedding at selected transmission substations only if voltage levels and reactive outputs do not meet the requirements, or some transmission lines are overloaded.
- Countermeasure 5. Re-arranging generator MW outputs. Connecting part of the disconnected load.

Countermeasures 1 - 3 have approximately the same execution time and their main purposes are to impede the sharp increase of series reactive power losses, to increase transmission line charging and to inhibit tap changing on subtransmission and distribution transformers. Load is shed (Countermeasure 4) only after countermeasures 1 - 3. This will decrease the amount of the load to be shed. Countermeasure 5 considers an optimization procedure. The optimization procedure takes much more time in comparison with countermeasures 1 - 4 and provides post-emergency operation optimization.

Thereby, countermeasures 1 - 4 provide fast control of the post-disturbance phenomenon to avoid voltage collapse and countermeasure 5 provides long-time-period post-emergency operation optimization.

The proposed control principles can be applied to various parts of the grid that work independently.

Briefly, the control actions aim to control the capacity of the available reactive power resources and do not let reactive power demand of the affected region increase beyond their sustainable capacity to exclude the possibility of voltage instability.

The proposed control system can be built by using distributed intelligence principles. The distributed intelligence is taken to mean the multi-agent system (Panasetsky & Voropai, 2009).

4.4 Multi-agent control system structure

Current overload of the network elements in postdisturbance period is a serious problem, which can lead to cascade line tripping. However, the proposed MAS does not solve the problem of the current overload, except current overload problem of the generator excitation system, which directly influences the reactive power output of generator. The proposed multi-agent control system provides reactive power control to prevent generator tripping and preserve load bus voltages within the normal range. Current and ohm relays coordination problem is the further work goal.

A power system presented in Fig.7 is used to illustrate the main principles of the proposed multi-agent approach.

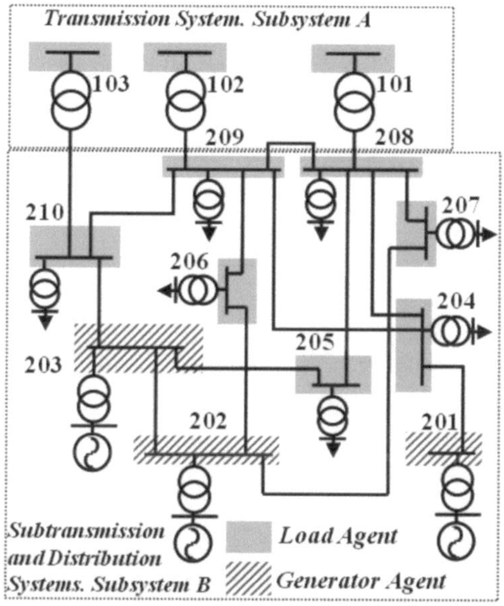

Fig. 7. A part of the modified IEEE One Area RTS-96 system

This power system is a part of the modified 24 bus IEEE One Area RTS-96 system. It is divided into two subsystems - Subsystem A and Subsystem B that correspond to transmission and subtransmission plus distribution systems respectively.

The proposed MAS consists of two types of agents: Load Agents and Generator Agents (see. Fig.7). Any agent at any time has the following set of local data:

- Local state variables (primary and secondary voltages, power flows, etc.).
- Operating characteristics of the local equipment (generator terminal voltage, tap range of the tap changer, excitation current of the generator, etc.).

Any agent has two goals:

- Local goal. It consists in maintaining local state variables and equipment operating characteristics within the normal range.
- Global goal. It consists in voltage collapse prevention.

To make different parts of the proposed MAS system work independently, each agent must know only about the limited number of agents, which influence his activity most. For instance, Load Agents, installed at Bus101 – Bus103 in Subsystem A must know much about the agents in Subsystem B, because all these agents can influence them. On the other hand, in spite of the fact that agents in Subsystem B could know much about one another, they must know only about three agents in Subsystem A: Load Agents, installed at Bus101 – Bus103, because these three agents can only influence them. In this case, subtransmission system produces minimal influence on transmission system.

A. MAS Ontology

Agents communicate with each other, by using some communication language. According to FIPA standards, messages exchanged by agents have a number of fields and in particular: sender, receiver, communicative intention (also called "performative"), content, language, ontology and some fields used for control. Ontology is the vocabulary of symbols and their meanings. For the effective communication, both the sender and the receiver must ascribe the same meaning to symbols. Ontology can include different elements such as agent actions, terms, concepts, etc. Agent actions indicate actions that can be performed by some agents. Terms are expressions identifying entities (abstract or concrete) that "exist" in the world. For voltage control purposes, the following simple Voltage Control Ontology can be proposed:

Agent actions of the Voltage Control Ontology:

- Increase Reactive Power.
- Stop Reactive Power Increase.
- Start Load Shedding.

Terms of the Voltage Control Ontology:

- Owner.
- Voltage Rate.

The Voltage Control Ontology usage principles will be given in the next sections.

B. Generator Agent

Generator Agent obtains local information about excitation current of the generator, primary and secondary voltages at the generating substation, active power flows and transformer tap ranges. If excitation current goes beyond of its normal range, Generator Agent tries to decrease it to exclude the possibility of the generator tripping. Generator Agent sends messages to other agents that can decrease the shortage of the reactive power in the affected region. The sent messages apply FIPA Request Interaction Protocol and include Increase Reactive Power action of the Voltage Control Ontology. The sequence diagram for the Request Interaction protocol used by the Generator Agent is depicted in Fig.8.

Before sending a message, Generator Agent could use a rule set to identify whether receiver is able to help him. In our research, we used the following simple rule: Generator Agent do not send Request message to another agent if electric coupling between them has become too weak. For instance, if Bus202 – Bus203 active power flow is equal to zero, Generator Agent at Bus 203 does not send Request message to Generator Agent at Bus 202.

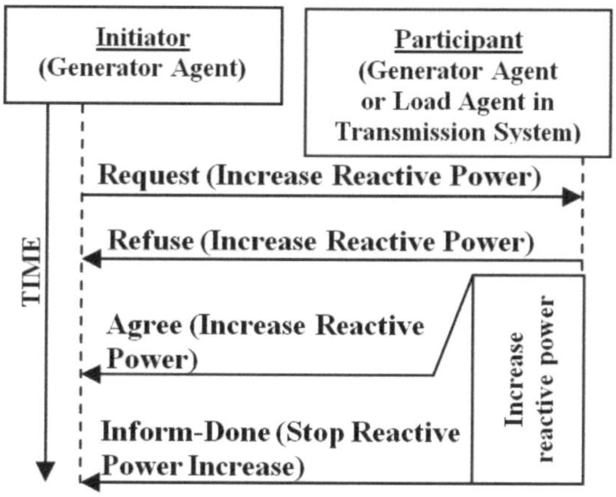

Fig. 8. Request Interaction protocol used by Generator Agent

In response to his request, Generator Agent can receive either Refuse or Agree message. Agree message means that Request Interaction protocol participant starts to increase reactive power. Sometime later, Generator Agent will receive Inform-Done message with Stop Reactive Power Increase action, which means that the participant stopped increasing reactive power (see Fig.8). Thus, Generator Agent always knows when reactive power increase in his subsystem is stopped. If reactive power increasing is stopped, but Generator Agent is still overexcited, it starts Load Shedding procedure.

FIPA Contract Net Interaction Protocol is used in Load Shedding procedure. In this protocol, the initiator wishes to optimize some function that characterizes the Load Shedding Procedure. We use minimal voltage rate function, but of course, it could be function, which includes some economic aspects. Generator Agent sends n Call for Proposal messages to Load Agents and solicits from them m proposals and k refuses (see Fig.9). The proposals contain voltage rates at primary buses of the Load Agents. After that, Generator Agent accepts j proposals and sends j Accept-Proposal messages to those Load Agents which have the lowest voltage rates at their primary buses. When Load Agent receives Accept-Proposal message it starts to shed the load until its primary voltage will not increase up to the specified value.

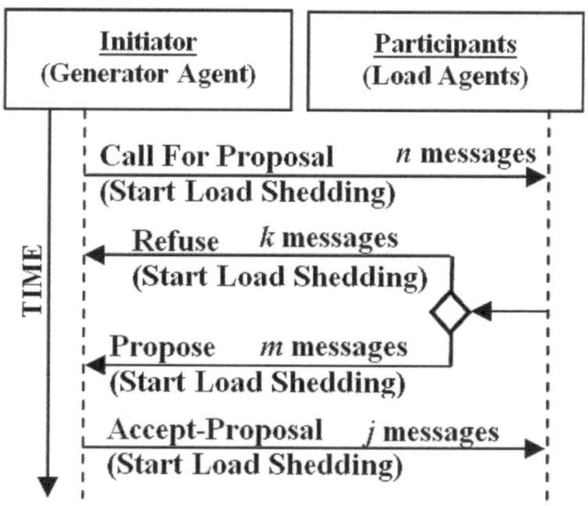

Fig. 9. Contract-Net Interaction protocol used by Generator Agent

C. Load Agent

Load Agent obtains local information about primary and secondary voltages at the substation, transformer tap ranges and active power flows. Load Bus agent takes part in Load Shedding procedure (see Fig.9). It also can shed the load independently in case of critical voltage drop. If it is installed at transmission system substation, Load Agent can take part in reactive power regulation (see Fig.8). In this case, Load Agent changes transmission transformer tap ratio until primary voltage will not decrease or secondary voltage will not increase up to specified values. Changing transmission transformer tap ratio, Load Bus agent must coordinate its actions with generators in transmission system.

Now consider situation when Generator Agent receives Request message. First, it analyzes operating characteristics of the generator and if they are within the normal range it starts to increase reactive power output according to the algorithm, presented in Fig.10.

Where $U_{GEN\ SV}$ – generator secondary voltage, $U_{GEN\ TV}$ – generator terminal voltage, I_F – excitation current, $I_{F\ MAX}$ – the highest possible excitation current.

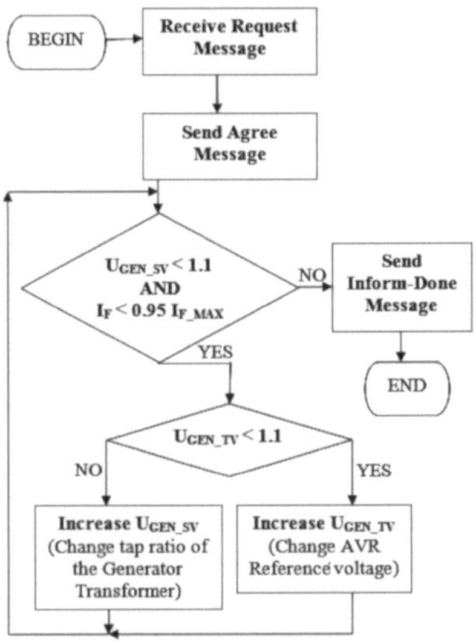

Fig. 10. Reactive power output increasing algorithm of Generator Agent

4.5 Multi-agent control system implementation

The success of multi-agent system mainly depends on the availability of appropriate technology (development tools, programming languages) that allows its implementation. Any kind of programming language could be used for MAS realization, but object-oriented languages are more suitable, because the concept of agent is close to the concept of object.

The computer model of the proposed MAS for power system voltage stability control was implemented in JADE. JADE has become a firm favorite with researchers in power engineering in recent years. JADE implements a famous object-oriented language Java (Bellifemine et al., 2000). Agents, developed for the JADE platform consist of three basic layers: a message handling layer; a behavioral layer; a functional layer. Message handling layer is responsible for the sending and receiving of messages from other agents. The behavioral layer provides control of when an agent has to implement some task. The functional layer embodies the action the agent can perform.

Necessary power flows and time domain simulations were carried out in Matlab/PSAT environment. Java capabilities of the JADE environment were used to implement communication between Matlab/PSAT and JADE, Fig.11.
To provide communication between Matlab and JADE, Box Agents are used. Box Agents are Java objects that contain different data structures. During Time Domain Simulation, information about power system operating conditions at each integration step passes from Matlab environment to JADE by means of Box Agents. After that, agents inside JADE environment process this information, produce control actions if needed, put information about control actions inside Box Agents and pass Box Agents back to Matlab environment.

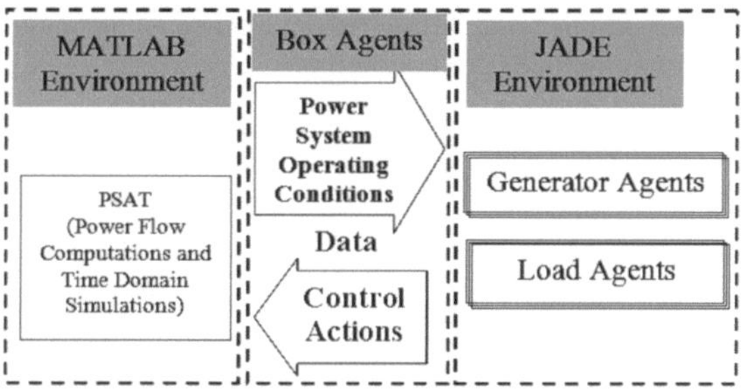

Fig. 11. MAS implementation

Thus, there is no need to use computer hard disc during the simulation, all computations are performed inside the main memory and simulation process is faster. The proposed MAS software realization allows one to use complex Matlab/PSAT routines and to model complex behavior of the agents.

4.6 Case study

A. The Test System

Modified IEEE One Area RTS-96 system is used as a case study. Initially this test power system contained 24 buses and had no dynamic elements. During modification, the following changes in the test system structure were made:

- To explore the influence of the ULTCs actions during low voltage conditions, transformers equipped with ULTCs were installed between subtransmission system and distribution system loads.
- Each load was modeled as 50% constant impedance and 50% constant current for both active and reactive components.
- Each generator was modeled by six order dynamic model and was equipped with Type I Turbine Governor (TG) and Type II Automatic Voltage Regulator (AVR).
- Three machines connected to Bus201 - Bus203 in subtransmission system (see Fig.6) were equipped with over excitation limiters (OXLs).

After modification, IEEE One Area RTS-96 system contains 42 buses. Parameters of the unmodified 24-bus test system can be found in PSAT test folder. For better understanding of the transient process, agents were installed only at the buses depicted in Fig.7.

B. Disturbance

To test the proposed MAS for an extreme contingency, the following sequence of disturbances is examined:

- 2 seconds after the simulation starts. Loss of the generator connected to the Bus 201.

- 40 seconds after the simulation starts. Loss of Bus208 - Bus207 line.

C. Preliminary remarks to the simulation process

During the simulation process, two types of automatic systems are considered:

- Automatic system based on conventional principles
- Automatic system based on multi-agent principles.

Both automatic systems do not provide for decentralized Under Voltage Load Shedding (UVLS) scheme. Undoubtedly, decentralized ULVS scheme is an effective means of preventing voltage collapse and it should be provided for both conventional and multi-agent automatic systems. However, the main purpose of the simulation is to demonstrate the MAS advantages in relation to reactive power sources coordination for the purpose of generator tripping prevention. It should also be mentioned, that the proposed centralized multi-agent ULVS scheme (see Fig.9) differs from conventional centralized ULVS scheme, because it is actuated without time delay in case when there is no available reactive power in a subsystem.

D. Dynamic simulation for automatic system based on conventional principles

Conventional automatic system includes the following set of the decentralized devices:

- TG and AVR at each generator.
- OXLs at the generators, connected to Bus201 - Bus203. OXLs maximum field currents for generators connected to Bus202 and Bus203 are 3 and 2.5 respectively. OXLs maximum voltage output signal is 0.1.
- ULTCs are installed at the subtransmission substations Bus204 - Bus210. ULTC time delay for the first tap movement is 20 seconds. ULTC time delay for subsequent tap movements is 5 seconds. ULTC tap range is ±12 steps.

Voltage reductions at load substations during the simulation are shown in Fig.12. The change of rotor currents during simulation is represented in Fig.13. The change in AVR reference voltages during simulation is given in Fig.14.

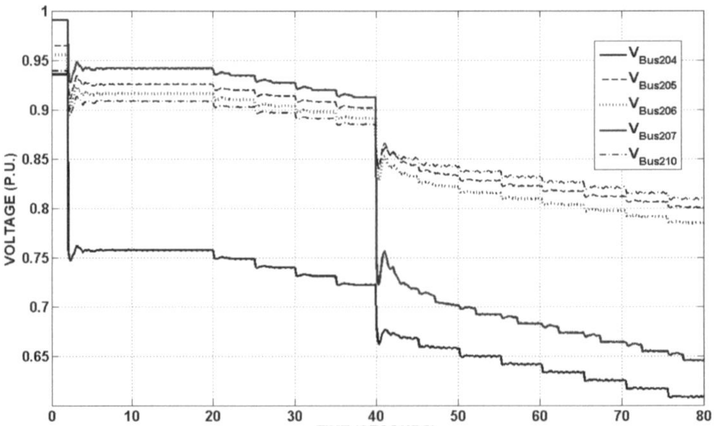

Fig. 12. Changes in HV substation voltage level

After the first disturbance, rotor current of the generator, connected to Bus203, reaches its thermal limit, and AVR reference voltage of the generator starts to decrease. 20 seconds after the first disturbance, ULTCs on all transformers at the affected subtransmission substations starts to work. This leads to further decrease of generator 203 AVR reference voltage.

Compensating reactive power shortage, generator 202 increases its excitation current. After the second disturbance, rotor current of generator 202 reaches its thermal limit and rotor current of generator 203 exceeds its thermal limit. AVR reference voltages of both generators continue to decrease and after a while, this will lead to generator 203 tripping and to the voltage collapse.

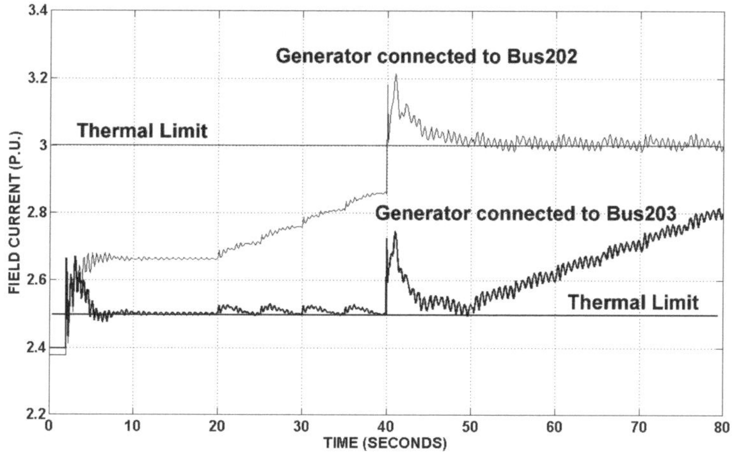

Fig. 13. Rotor current change

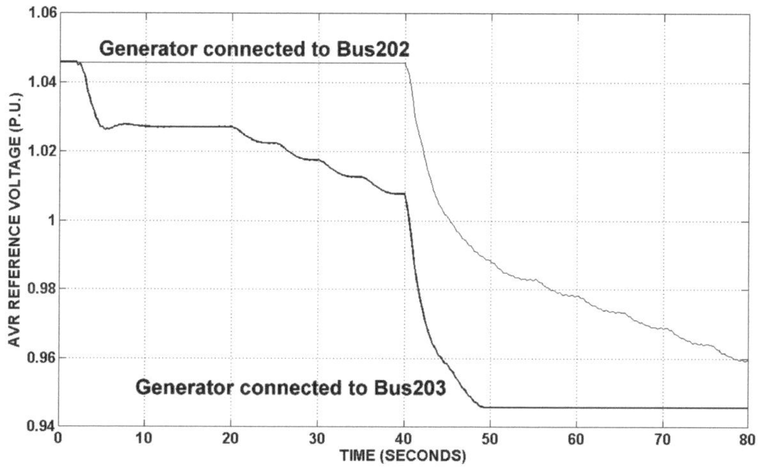

Fig. 14. AVR reference voltage change

E. Dynamic simulation for automatic system based on multi-agent principles

In addition to the set of local devices, represented for conventional automatic system, multi-agent automatic system also includes ULTCs for transmission transformers at Bus101 - Bus103. Trying to exclude generator tripping, multi-agent automatic system coordinates the work of local devices. Voltage reductions at load substations during the simulation are shown in Fig.15.

After the first disturbance, rotor current of the generator, connected to Bus203, reaches its thermal limit and the generator sends request message to generator 202 and to the transmission transformers, connected to Bus101 - Bus103. Transmission transformers at Bus101 - Bus103 as well as generator 202 are trying to decrease reactive power shortage of the subsystem. Their joint actions decrease generator 203 excitation current. Excitation current becomes lower than its thermal limit, and generator 203 AVR reference voltage starts to increase. After the second disturbance, rotor currents of both generators reach their thermal limits and generators send request messages to each other and to transmission transformers at Bus101 - Bus103, but in this case, the generators receive refuse messages and immediately start load shedding procedure. Thus, during the transient process, rotor currents of the generators remain within the normal range. This fact excludes the possibility of the generator tripping.

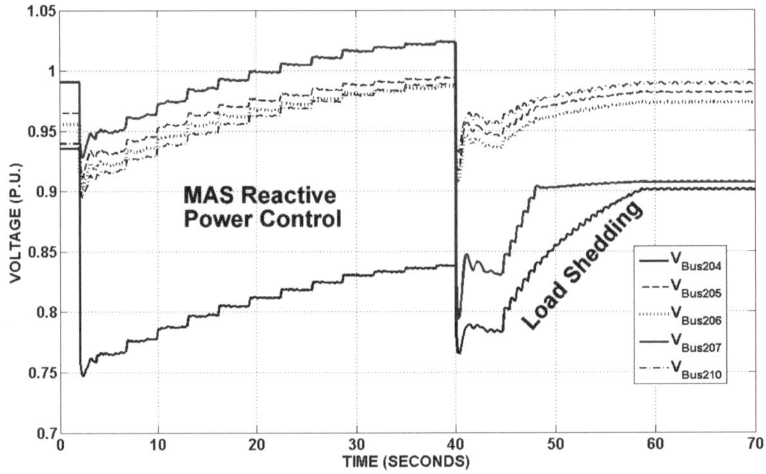

Fig. 15. Changes in HV substation voltage level

The change of rotor currents during simulation is presented in Fig.16.

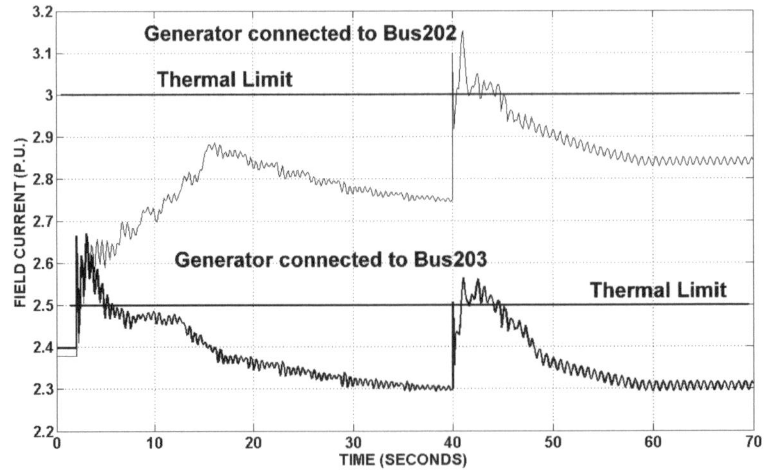

Fig. 16. Rotor current change

The change in AVR reference voltages during simulation is given in Fig.17.

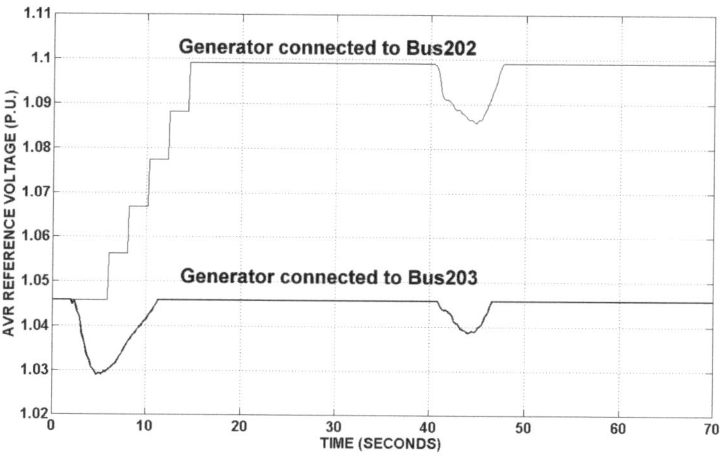

Fig. 17. AVR reference voltage change

5. Conclusions

In this chapter authors have given the examples of multi-agent approach usage in three different energy problems. This approach has shown good results in solving of these problems, despite its relative novelty. Efficiency of multi-agent approach to energy problems has been proved by numerical simulations. Plans of future investigations include development and improvement of described methods and realization of these methods in practical applications.

6. References

F. Bellifemine, G. Caire, T. Trucco, G. Rimassa. (2000). JADE Programmer's Guide, CSELT & University of Parma. Available: http://www.jade.tilab.com/doc.

Fartyshev D.A., Arshinsky V.L., Massel A.G. (2009). Multi-agent software for energy safety problem research. *Proceedings on XIV Baikal conference,* Irkutsk.- pp. 283-289 (in Russian).

Gamm A.Z. (1983). Decomposition algorithms for solution of power system state estimation problem, *Electronnoye modelirovanie,* 1983, No.3, pp.63-68 (in Russian).

Gamm A.Z., Grishin Y.A. (1995). Distributed information processing in automated power system control systems. *Proc. of V Int. Workshop "Distributed information processing",* Novosibirsk, Russia, pp. 243-247 (in Russian).

Gamm A.Z., Kolosok I.N., Paltsev A.S. (2007). Methods for decomposition of EPS state estimation problem when solving it on the basis of multi-agent technologies. *Scientific Proceedings of Riga Technical University "Power and Electrical Engineering",* Riga, Latvia, pp.205-214.

Gamm A.Z., Grishin Y.A., Glazunova A.M., Kolosok I.N., Korkina E.S. (2007). New EPS state estimation algorithms based on the technique of test equations and PMU measurements. *Proc. of the IEEE International Conference "PowerTech'2007",* Lausanne, Switzerland, 7p.

Kolosok I.N., Korkina E.S., Paltsev A.S. (2009). Decomposition of power system state estimation problem with the use of PMU data for large dimension schemes. *Proc. of the International Workshop "Liberalization and Modernization of Power Systems: Coordinated Monitoring and Control towards Smart Grids"*, Irkutsk, Russia: SEI, pp.28-35.

Lachs W.R. (2002). Controlling Grid Integrity After Power System Emergencies, *IEEE Trans. Power Syst.*, Vol.17, No.2, pp.445-450.

Lachs W.R. (1992). Voltage Instability in Interconnected Power Systems: a Simulation Approach, *IEEE Trans. Power Syst.*, Vol.7, No.2, pp.753-761.

Makarov Yu.V., Reshetov V.I., Stroev V.A., Voropai N.I. (2005). Blackout prevention in the United States, Europe and Russia. *Proc. of the IEEE*, Vol.93, No.11, pp.1942-1955.

Massel L.V., Kopaygorodsky A.N., Chernousov A.V. (2008). IT-infrastructure of research activities realized for the power engineering system researches. *Proc.of X International Conference "Computer Science and Information Technologies"*, Turkey.– p.106–111.

Massel L.V., Fartyshev D.A., Arshinsky V.L. (2009). Intellectual information technologies in energy safety problem research. *Proceedings of the 11th International Workshop on Computer Science and Information Technologies* (CSIT'2009), Greece, 2009.– Vol. 1.– P. 25–28.

Panasetsky D.A., Voropai N.I. (2009). A multi-agent approach to coordination of different emergency control devices against voltage collapse. *Proc. of IEEE International Conference "PowerTech 2009"*, Bucharest, Romania, 7p.

Taylor C., Erickson D. (1997). Recording and analyzing the July 2 cascading outage, *Comput. Applicat. Power Syst.*, Vol.10, No.1.

18

Multi-Agent Systems and Blood Cell Formation

Bessonov Nikolai[1], Demin Ivan[2], Kurbatova Polina[2],
Pujo-Menjouet Laurent[2] and Volpert Vitaly[2]
[1]*Institute of Mechanical Engineering Problems, 199178 Saint Petersburg*
[2]*Université de Lyon, Université Lyon1, CNRS UMR 5208 Institut Camille Jordan*
F - 69200 Villeurbanne Cedex,
[1]*Russia*
[2]*France*

1. Introduction

The objective of this chapter is to give an insight of the mathematical modelling of hematopoiesis using multi-agent systems. Several questions may arise then: what is hematopoiesis and why is it interesting to study this problem from a mathematical point of view? Has the multi-agent system approach been the only attempt done until now? What does it bring more than other techniques? What were the results obtained? What is there left to do?

We hope that the following will give the reader all the answers to these questions. And even more, we would be delighted if after reading it, you would like to know more on this subject and try to work on it to contribute to the understanding of this complex field.

Let us start with the biological background in order to get a clear idea of the problem behind the model.

1.1 Hematopoiesis: what is it?

Hematopoiesis (from the ancient Greek meaning to make (ποιεῖν) blood (αἷμα)) is the scientific name used to describe the blood cell formation.

1.2 Where does it occur?

It appears in the yolk sac or blood islands during early embryogenesis. Then, with the development of the individual, it reaches the spleen, liver and lymph nodes to eventually settle down in the medulla, also known as bone marrow once this latter has been completely formed. This process takes place in the femur, tibia or any other long bones for children to finally moves to the pelvis, cranium, vertebrae and sternum in the adult bodies.

1.3 How does it work?

There are two main branches in hematopoiesis: myeloid and lymphoid (see Fig. 1). These two branches originate from the same cell type: the hematopoietic stem cells (HSC). The lymphoid branch gives birth to the T and B cells, antibodies and memory cells. Maturation, activation and some of proliferation of these latter are developed mostly into secondary

lymphoid organs such as the spleen, thymus and lymph nodes. This is the reason why we shall not be focused on this branch. We might mention it from time to time though during this chapter when we would like to describe hematopoiesis in its whole.
Consequently, our main attention will be given to the myeloid branch. Three blood cell types arise from this branch through three cell lineages: red blood cells (erythrocytes), white blood cells and platelets (megakaryocytes) (see Fig. 1). Their daily production is fairly high: each second for instance, the body produces 2 millions of erythrocytes, also 2 millions of platelets and 700,000 granulocytes. Their lifetime differs from one type to another (120 days for erythrocytes, about 7 to 10 for the thrombocytes, and 6 to 14 hours only for the granulocytes (the shortest lifetime of these cell types).

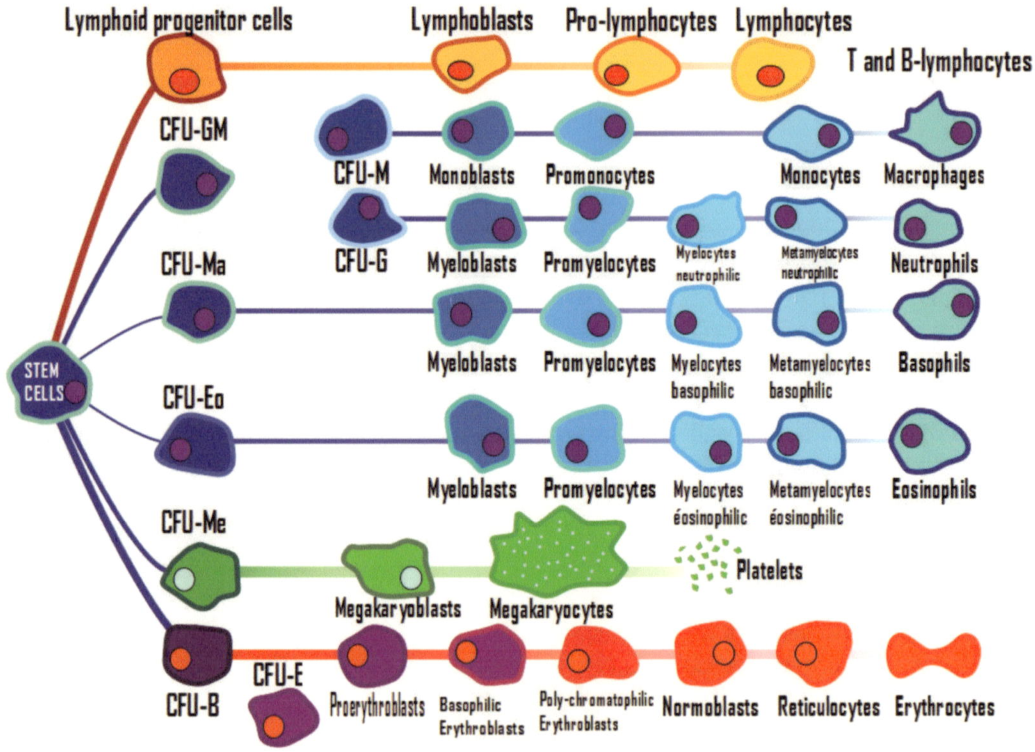

Fig. 1. Illustration of hematopoiesis: all blood cells originate from the stem cell compartment on the left and are released in the blood stream on the right. The lymphoid branch, on top, releases T and B-lymphocytes. The myeloid branch consists of the red lineage (bottom), white lineage in blue and platelets in green.

1.4 The myeloid branch: an insight

Let us have a closer look at the myeloid branch. But before doing this, it seems important to remind that all cells in each lineage originate from the HSC. These particular cells are able to self-renew. Their lifetime and number are still unknown, even if some attempts were done to predict their number in the body (Dingli et al., 2007a, b). Besides self-renewing, each stem cell can differentiate to a more mature cell, also called progenitor cells or it can die by apoptosis (natural cell death). HSC when differentiating give birth to early progenitor cells, too immature to belong to the myeloid or lymphoid branch. It might indeed be possible for them to move from one lineage to another one with no major difficulty. It is also possible for progenitor cells to self-renew under specific circumstances such as anemia, blood transfusion or any case of strong stress related to a loss of blood (see section 3.1.3). In normal cases progenitor cells are more incline to differentiate or die. It is only after few divisions that a cell reaches one of the three specific lineages and should not change its fate. These lineages are:

-the red blood cell lineage: progenitors are called CFU-B and CFU-E (where CFU stands for Colony Forming Units), their maturation evolves through different stages of precursor cells called erythroblast to finally become reticulocytes and eventually reach the blood stream under the form of erythrocytes, ready to transport oxygen.

-the megakaryocytic lineage: progenitors are called CFU-Me, and after having differentiated into megakaryoblasts, they become mature megakaryocytes. These cell types are really large (about 40 to 100 μm when the other blood cell sizes range between 1.5 to 24 μm). The megakaryocytes then split into hundreds of parts and give birth to platelets ready to reach the blood stream.

It is interesting to note that in the early stage of development, the young erythrocytes and megakaryocytes have a common root, the bipotential primitive megakaryocyte-erythroid precursor (MEP), located right after the stem cell compartment and right before the CFU-B and CFU-Me branches.

-the white blood cell lineage: the progenitors are located into three subgroups, CFU-GM (that gives also two other subgroups the CFU-M and CFU-G), CFU-Ma and CFU-Eo, who, after several differentiations and having proceeded through different stages (the "blast" precursors ones), respectively give birth to four white cell types: the macrophages, neutrophils, basophils and eosinophils, all of them ready to protect our body.

1.5 How do these processes regulate?

This is one of the key and challenging questions of this chapter. It is well known now that each lineage has at least one hormone regulating each lineage production. Indeed, several regulation factors are involved in the blood system to keep it in homeostasis. These controls are quite complex and many molecules and kinetic cascades are required. In this paragraph we describe only the main stimulating factor corresponding to each lineage. We refer the reader to more biologically detailed publications to get a better idea of all the chemical reactions and feedbacks implicated.

For the red blood cell lineage, this stimulating hormone is called erythropoietin (EPO). When produced in high quantity by the kidneys, it prevents the erythrocyte population from being lost by apoptosis. A large quantity of progenitor and precursor cells can then differentiate and a large quantity of erythrocytes would rapidly reach the blood stream. This happens in cases of important blood loss, anemia or any other stress erythropoiesis.

For platelets, the regulating factor is called thrombopoietin (TPO) and seems to target the differentiation of megakaryocytic. It is produced in the liver.

For the white cell population, the hormone is called granulocyte colony-stimulating factor (G-CSF). This molecule seems to stimulate survival, proliferation and maturation of the white cell progenitors and precursors. It is mainly produced by endothelium and macrophages and is overproduced in case of pathologies like neutropenia. See Fig. 2 for an overview of these different stimulating factors in the myeloid branch.

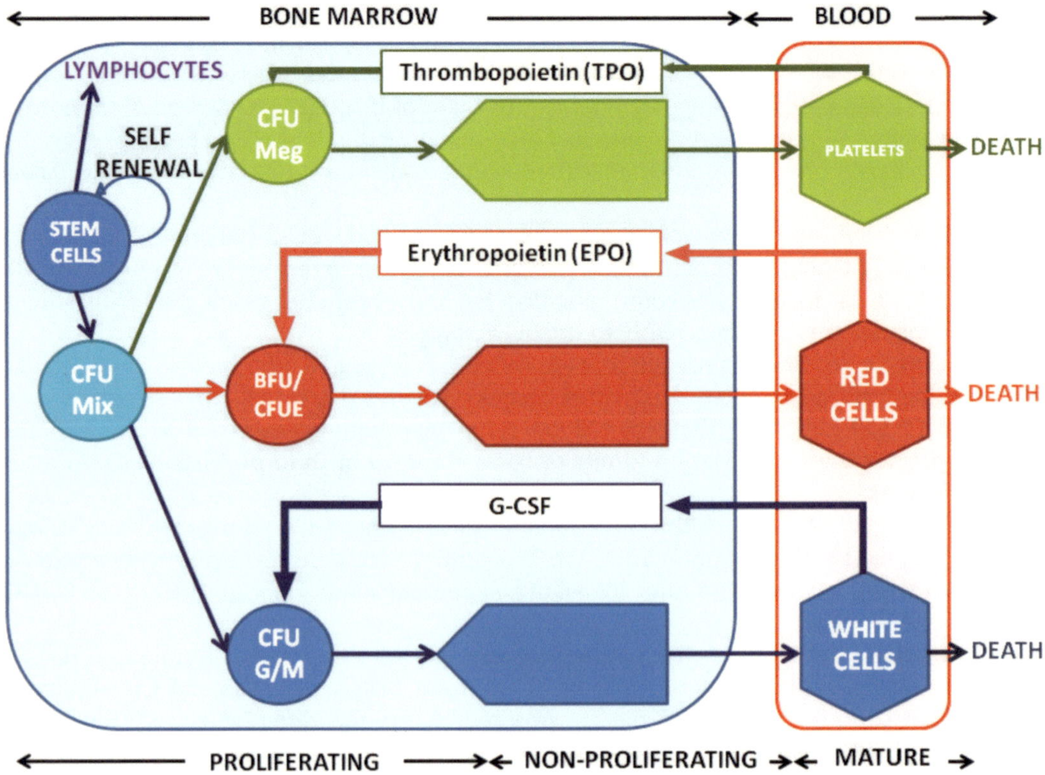

Fig. 2. Illustration of the differentiation pathways in the myeloid giving a representation of control of the platelet (in green), red blood cell (in red) and granulocyte or monocyte (G/M) (including neutrophils, basophils and eosinophils) production (in blue). The control loops, respectively mediated by thrombopoietin (TPO), erythropoietin (EPO) and the granulocyte colony stimulating factors (G-CSF) are indicated.

2. Objective of the chapter: what is the problem about?

Even if the regulating hormones presented in the previous paragraph are widely investigated in the biologist community, several questions and important issues remain open: how, for instance does thrombopoietin exactly act on the megakaryocytic lineage? Does it act on the apoptosis rate also, like EPO on erythrocytes or does it act only on the differentiation rate? What about G-CSF? Moreover, is spatial distribution of the cell in the bone marrow important or not in homeostasis? Do cells communicate between each other? If yes, how do they proceed? How do some diseases spread in the blood system, while some others do not? Is it possible for anyone to develop leukemia without knowing it, and to recover without any cure? How do stem cells and progenitor cells choose their lineage? Is this due to the environment of the cell, that is some external information or does it come from some stochasticity, some random noise inside the cell itself that leads its decision to prefer one lineage rather than another one?

Some of these questions have been tackled for almost 50 years now from a mathematical point of view, with different models and techniques. Some researchers used non linear

partial differential equations with delay or not, some studied several systems of ordinary differential equations, linear or not, stochastic differential equations, etc. However, among all the existing models, and to the best of our knowledge, very few attempts were made to take the bone marrow structure and cell interaction into account.
The objective of this chapter is to try to answer some of the previous questions by the use of multi-agent systems and taking the bone marrow structure and space competition between cells into consideration. Before this, it seems necessary to justify the reason why the approach of the problem with the use of multi-agent system would be a good technique in comparison with other models. This is the reason why, in the next section we set up the state of the art, reminding some of the previous models and results obtained in the past decades. Then, we introduce different multi-agent approaches used to model hematopoiesis. In section 4, we give some of our contributions to this field and eventually conclude with what we believe was successful, what needs to be improved and the work planned for future investigations.

3. State of the art: different approach to model hematopoiesis

3.1 Deterministic models:

3.1.1 The first models

Deterministic models are considered to be the first models describing cell cycle. In 1959, Lajtah et al. were the first to introduce a cell cycle model with a resting phase. Then, in the early 1970's, Burns and Tannock (1970) as well as Smith and Martin (1973) carried on Lajtah's work using a two phase model: the proliferating phase and the resting phase. This study was then generalized by Mackey in the late 1970's and applied to the study of hematopoietic stem cell. All these models consist in systems of ordinary differential equations, linear or not. In 1976, Wazewska-Czyzewska and Lasota (1976) proposed a similar model but they introduced a discrete model and applied it to erythrocyte production.

3.1.2 Development of the models: going to more realistic and complex models

Each model afterward was more or less built from the first ones, with significant improvement, adding nonlinearity, delay. Several systems of partial differential equations arose then from that time; some were structured in age, size or maturity, sometimes two of them at the same time, sometimes with discrete delays, other times with distributed delays. They have been used to describe different parts of hematopoiesis: it could have been the stem cell compartment only, the red blood cell lineage, the myeloid lineage, with feedback or not regulating the production. The objective of each model was to understand the possible dysfunction of the system leading to diseases like anemia, leukemia, neutropenia or thrombocytopenia. Some of these diseases are chronic (this will be developed below) and oscillations of the size of cell populations could occur: this is the case for chronic myelogenous leukemia, cyclic neutropenia or cyclic thrombocytopenia. Incorporating one or several feedback loops on one or more lineages in the model was then necessary to simulate a possible regulation of the blood cell in the bone marrow.

3.1.3 Some success stories

All these deterministic models combined with the study of the influence of different parameters allowed the authors of these researches to obtain accurate results and even predictions in rather good agreement with the experiments.

It has been proven for instance by Crauste et al. (2008) that EPO was not the only growth factor involved in the recovery of red blood cell homeostasis in case of stress erythropoiesis (anemia, important blood loss, blood transfusion, etc.). It was indeed shown mathematically that some glucocorticoids were necessary to explain the rapid recovery of normal red blood cell levels in mice suffering from severe loss of erythrocytes. It is indeed believed that glucocorticoids encourage progenitor cells to self-renew which does not happen or rarely in non pathological cases. In the same paper, the authors predicted also the fact that after such a pathological event, new born cells, too rapidly put in the blood stream were too weak to get a longer lifetime than usual. Consequently, the death rate of such cells was shown to be higher than the average normal erythrocytes.

Another prediction was made in a cyclic neutropenia model (Colijn et al., 2005a, b). The authors forecast that the G-CSF treatment (stimulating factor for the white cell lineage) would decrease the rate of apoptosis among neutrophil precursors back to normal levels while the differentiation rates for the neutrophil lineage would rise. It has also been assumed that apoptosis rate of the proliferating stem cells should be amplified for treated cyclical neutropenia (CN). Foley et al. in 2006 and Colijn et al. in 2005 (a, b) suggested then that it would be possible to get the same therapy effect with less G-CSF as usually used by changing the timing and duration of the treatment. This was obtained by combining the existing models on hematopoiesis with a model of G-CSF pharmacokinetics and changing the time interval between treatments and taking the time in the cycle into account.

Other approaches allowed nice discoveries: it was, for instance, possible to explain how such a short cycle of about 24 to 48 hours for blood cells could induce the oscillations of about 40 up to 80 days in the whole blood system in case of chronic myelogenous leukemia (CML). This work has been investigated by Pujo-Menjouet et al. (2005) and Adimy et al. (2007). The authors used different deterministic models and found two groups of parameters able to change either the period of the oscillations or their amplitude. These two groups were:

- the parameters involved in cell loss (apoptosis and differentiation) able to change the periods of the population dynamics, and
- the parameters involved in the cell cycle regulation (duration of the proliferating phase, and reentry rate of the resting cells into proliferation) able to change the amplitude of the cell population.

Many other results were achieved with deterministic models and one of the latest models try to include treatment strategies using not only the stimulating factors such as EPO or G-CSF as mentioned above but also some drug associated to chemotherapy such as Imatinib to treat certain types of leukemia (Michor et al. (2007a, b)).

However, it seems important to note that something quite relevant is missing in all the models cited in this section. Not a single model here takes the bone structure into account. Moreover, there are three big issues that should be incorporated in the studies: how to cell communicate between each other and get the information from the environment? How do they decide which lineage should be chosen when they are still immature enough to decide and be able to change from one branch to another one (like the MEP presented in section 1.4)? Finally, what could be said about the niches (places seeded by stem cells to give birth to different colonies of all blood cell types)? Is the number of cells in this niche large enough to consider continuous deterministic models, or is it possible to describe these niches with other discrete and stochastic models taking space competition into account?

The last question would be answered yes. Under the assumption that a study is mainly focused on very few niches at the same time in a tiny part of the medulla; a discrete and stochastic approach would make sense.
This is what is developed in the next paragraph.

3.2 A different approach: the multi-agent models

Before the introduction of the multi-agent models, it appears necessary to have an insight of what has been done in term of stochastic models. They have been used to describe the mechanism of cell proliferation determined with a certain probability, and not by previous deterministic mechanisms. It is also important to remind one of the rare existing models with reaction diffusion taking the spatial structure of the bone marrow into account. This will help to justify the use of our software based on the multi-agent systems taking the medulla structure into account.

3.2.1 Stochastic models

In every deterministic model, any cell fate such as differentiation, apoptosis or self-renewal is predicted by specific processes well defined, like a good engine that self-regulates. In case of deregulation, the whole mechanism reacts and tries to reach back its non pathological equilibrium, also called homeostasis. Sometimes things do not occur in this way, and other equilibria can be reached, changing the population fate and subsequently the whole system.
However, in vivo, the cell decisions may not originate from well determined laws, and the parameters involved in the problem can exhibit great sensitivities to tiny changes. These small variations could appear in the inside of the cell (intrinsic) as well as its external environment (extrinsic). This problem has been investigated in the study of stem cells in the late 1990's and year 2000's with the work of Abkowitz (1996, 2000), Dingli, (2006, 2007a, b), Newton (1995), Roeder and Loeffler (2002, 2006b). The authors used discrete models where decisions ruling the cell future could be made following stochastic processes.
Some studies have shown the high sensitivity of stability of the HSC system to perturbation and death rates but not to proliferation rates (Lei and Mackey, 2007). The influence of extrinsic fluctuation has been modelled by Gillespie (1992) and Shahrezael (2008). Concerning the intrinsic perturbation, the influence of intern information and variation inside the cell nucleus leading to a drastic change of its fate is still in discussion amongst biologists. It is currently being investigated by mathematicians who would like to understand the influence of these changes to the lineage choice of a progenitor cells due to the different changes occurring randomly in the nucleus (variation during transcription of a gene, translation or mRNA, etc.). Sensitivity to such modifications would decrease as cells increase their maturity. In other words, it would be more difficult for a precursor cell to change its lineage, while, an immature cell, let say a MEP progenitor could be easily influenced to become either a megakaryocyte or an erythrocyte. This decision could occur as explained above at the molecular level, when stochasticity would have a greater influence. Thus multi-scale models would be necessary. This has been already proposed by Crauste et al. in 2010.
All these works are of great interest, but still, one important thing is missing in the models: space. Consequently, cell competition for space, their communication depending on their position, and of course the bone marrow structure should be taken into account. However, one deterministic approach exists and is briefly explained in the next paragraph.

3.2.2 Spatial models

In 2005, Bessonov et al. proposed a spatial model in order to describe the influence of the medullar stroma. Indeed, in these compact areas, spatial position and competition are important. This is even more a crucial matter in case for instance of acute leukemia. When this pathology develops in the bone marrow, immature cells, mostly white cells, overtake the space dedicated to more mature cells. These latter are pushed out from the marrow directly to the blood stream without completing their maturation process. The whole system is rapidly invaded by immature cells unable to satisfy the function requested. Furthermore, they stop the development of cells from other lineages which causes anemia due to a lack of erythrocytes and hemorrhages because of a lack of platelets. The approach introduced by Bessonov et al. in 2005 consists in a simplified continuous model describing cell movement in the stroma. It is built with reaction-diffusion systems of partial differential equations with convection. The role of cell diffusion was used to illustrate a random motion in the stroma, mechanical pressure between cells was set up explain the space competition in the marrow and Darcy law in porous medium allowed the authors to simulate the medullar stroma. Existence of a diffusion threshold for leukemic cells was proven, below which the healthy state loses its stability and let the leukemic cells overtake the system. Their simulations showed also the action of chemotherapy on the proliferation velocity of the cells.

3.2.3 Multi-agent models: a compromise

There exist two ways to combine spatial models with stochasticity. One way could be to include some stochasticity in the continuous reaction-diffusion system of partial differential equations. The second way would be to consider discrete multi-agent models. To the best of our knowledge, the first way has not been tackled yet. This is the reason why we focus our attention here on the second approach: the multi-agent models.

The main objective of the use of the multi-agent systems applied to hematopoiesis is to simulate cells as individual capable of self-renewal, apoptosis or differentiation in a closed space representing a part of the bone marrow. The first models appeared in 2006 with Pimentel 2006 who introduced a simple interface based on the early 1978's Mackey model on hematopoiesis. In 2008, D'Inverno et al. worked on a multi-agent model simulating stem cells but the problem was more adapted for the intestinal crypt cells.

Ramas at the same period developed a software package named Netlogo (http://ccl.northwestern.edu/netlogo/), a "programmable modeling environment for simulating natural and social phenomena", with one application to the blood cell formation. However, Netlogo's aim is not to model hematopoiesis only. Thus, many specificities related to the bone marrow do not appear. This is the reason why in 2006, Bessonov et al. created a new multi-agent based software dedicated only to the cell interaction in the bone marrow. This work integrated complex processes that have not been taken into account by the previous studies, such as cell communication, size difference, cell differentiation, space competition, pathological and non pathological cell mutations, spread of diseases like leukemia and the bone marrow niche.

All the details of this new interface are developed in the next section.

4. A specific multi-agent model adapted to hematopoiesis

How is it possible to model hematopoiesis in the bone marrow in a realistic way using at the same time the space structure and the cell population dynamics? The aim of this section is to present an attempt to answer this question by the use of the multi-agent systems. It has been introduced by Bessonov et al. for the first time in 2006. An improved version of the software was given in Bessonov et al. in 2009 and new perspective applications are introduced at the end of this section.

4.1 The software basis

Before showing simulations of the software we propose the basic assumptions made to obtain a clear, realistic and understandable approach of the problem. It appears necessary thus for a start to expose the way the cell cycle was modeled. Then it seems interesting to get an insight of how the bone marrow structure could be described and how the space competition could be simulated.

4.1.1 Modeling the cell cycle

In the software it was necessary to depict precisely the different cell fates. We assume here that cells are small disks having three possibilities: self renew (a capacity mostly authorized for stem cells, but this can be applied to any other cell types, such as progenitors, precursors or mutated cells), differentiate or die by apoptosis (natural death).

4.1.1.1 The division process

Before dividing, a cell will grow to get enough room for its two daughter cells. Note that we assume here that a mother cell will give birth to two daughter cells. But this is not exclusive. It is possible in the software to let a cell be able to divide into more than two cells: this could be used to get a faster result in the simulations. A stem cell could for instance give birth to 4 cells, one would be another stem cell, and the other three cells would correspond to the progenitors of the three lineages of the myeloid branch (see Fig. 3). Each cell can be given a specific color depending on its type: yellow for instance for stem cells, red for the red

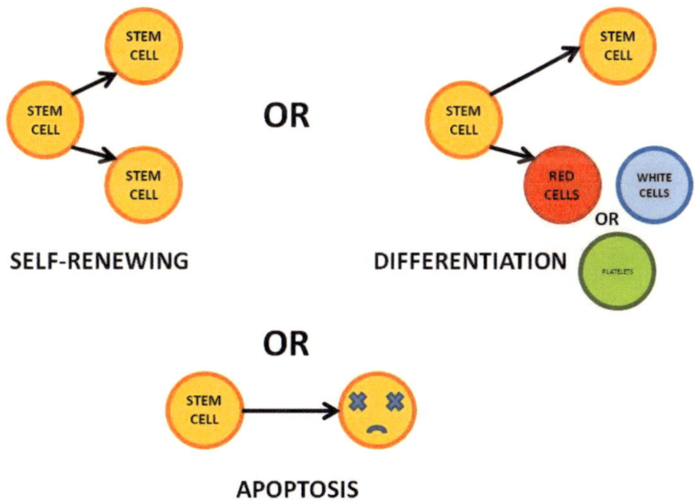

Fig. 3. Different stem cell fates taken into account by the software. A stem cell in yellow can either give birth to two daughter cells with exactly the same structure as their mother, or give birth to one stem cell and one differentiated progenitor (red cell, white cell or platelet), or die by apoptosis.

lineage, green for platelets and blue for the white lineage. This depends totally on the user's decision. Each lineage can be simulated at the same time or not. One can focus only on one branch, each one having a specific property or not: the size of the white cells or erythrocytes decreases as their maturity increases but this is exactly the opposite for megakaryocytes for instance. The size of each cell type can be determined by the user just by changing the radius of the disks illustrating the cells.

4.1.1.2 Stochasticity in proliferation

A cell can die by apoptosis at any time. The proliferation duration can be constant and defined by the user for each cell type, but it can be determined and occur within a time distribution: a constant time plus or minus a range whose value is defined by the user. This is one of the various specificities of this software. It is also possible to decide what could be the probability for a stem cell for instance to give birth to a red white or platelet progenitor. This ability of the software seems quite important for hematologists in the sense that almost 45 % of the blood consists of red blood cells that is about 99% of the hematocrit (portion of cells in the blood, the other portion consist of plasma, that is the remaining 55% of blood). The rest of the hematocrit is composed of white cells for 0.2%, and megakaryocytes between 0.6 to 1%. Thus, it seems realistic to assume that a stem cell has more chances to give birth to a red blood cell rather than a cell from another lineage. The software offers this possibility by choosing different probability for a cell to give birth to a certain cell type. This possibility includes also the probability to die. Thus, even apoptosis can be given a random rate that can be determined by the user (see Fig. 4). This is also relevant in the sense that apoptosis is rather important in the erythrocyte lineage, and this rate can be reduced under the influence of EPO. The influence of EPO and other simulating factors will be described later on.

4.1.2 The bone marrow structure

The bone marrow is set up as a simple rectangle in the software. Any time that a cell is pushed away from the rectangle border, it is assumed to reach the blood stream. The size of the rectangle can be chosen easily by the users, and modified anytime. Moreover, in order to be more realistic, it is possible to introduce fixed segments of different size anywhere in the rectangle to simulate the porosity of the bone marrow. These segments cannot be crossed by the cells and they are considered as walls necessary to bypass for the cells. The user can place the segments in different ways: they can be put like a bottle neck to force the cells to use only one way out to the blood stream, they can be in 3 of the 4 borders of the rectangle to give only one possible side for cells to reach the stream, they can also represent different niches where stem cells could develop colonies forming grapes of new born cells. Viscosity of the blood cells in the bone marrow can also be decided by changing a parameter value in the run window of the software.

When dividing, each cell giving birth to two or more daughter cells pushes away the other individuals. Space competition is then described. Consequently, if one cell type divides more rapidly than others, the bone marrow would swiftly be full of this type of cells and offspring, the other cells would be pushed away out in the bone marrow, or would have no room to develop their lineage. This phenomenon can occur for instance in case of acute myeloid leukemia described in the next section. It seems more realistic for stem cells to be fixed in a niche and the more a cell is mature, the more its ability to get detached from the colony would be important. This has not yet been taken into account in the software, but it is under current investigation. For the moment, all the cells have the same ability to move out from the bone marrow walls.

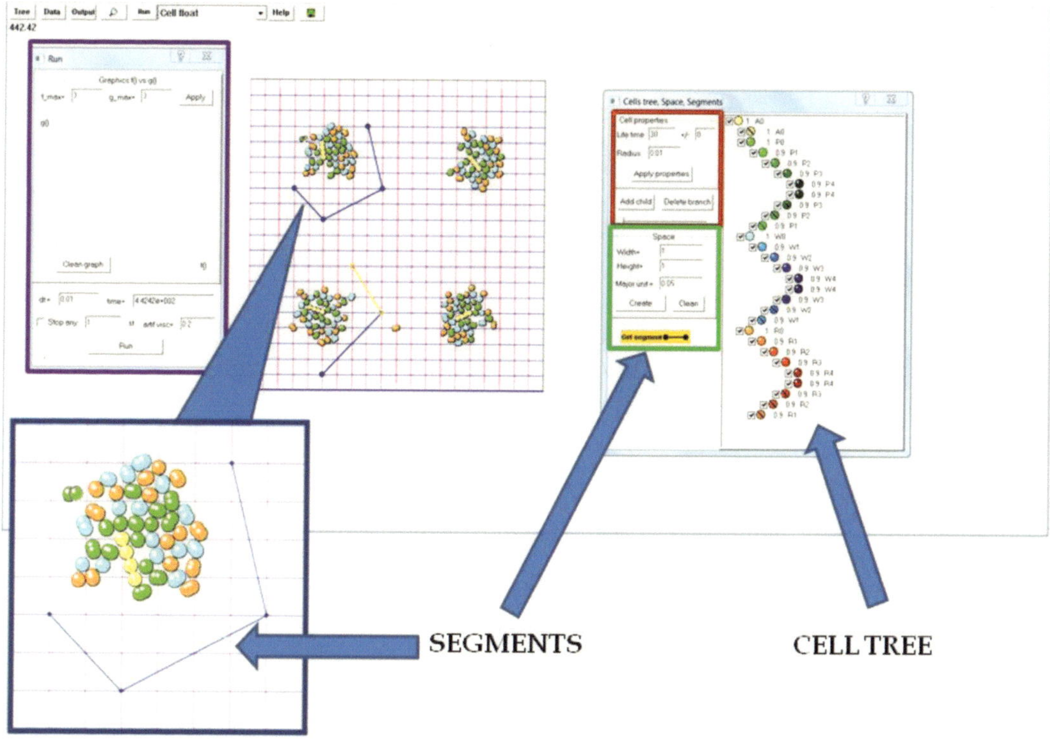

Fig. 4. Presentation of the different windows given by the software. The top left window represent the running application with different parameters such as viscosity. The left window gives the illustration of the tree consisting of all the cells and offspring, each differentiation probability are set up in this tree, each colour represents a cell type, the red frame corresponds to some of cell properties such as the life time, size (radius), etc. The green frame deals with the space property (size of the domain, and addition of segments). The small disks in the grids represent the different cells dividing, differentiating and dying with a focus on one part of the simulation at the bottom left of the figure.

4.2 Normal and pathological hematopoiesis

After setting up all the adjustments for the specific problem chosen by the user: number of cell lineages, cell fate, different probabilities (differentiation rates, apoptosis rates, etc.), size, bone marrow structure... It is possible to simulate normal and pathological hematopoiesis.

4.2.1 Normal hematopoiesis

To get an accurate model of normal hematopoiesis it is important to collect as many information about the different parameters as possible. This is the reason why it is necessary to exchange many discussions with hematologists. One attempt has been made, taking each size of cell type into account, with different proliferating times, apoptosis probabilities and different niches. The result has been plotted. However, many parameters need to be set up properly in good agreement with the experimental observations. This is under current investigation (see Fig. 5).

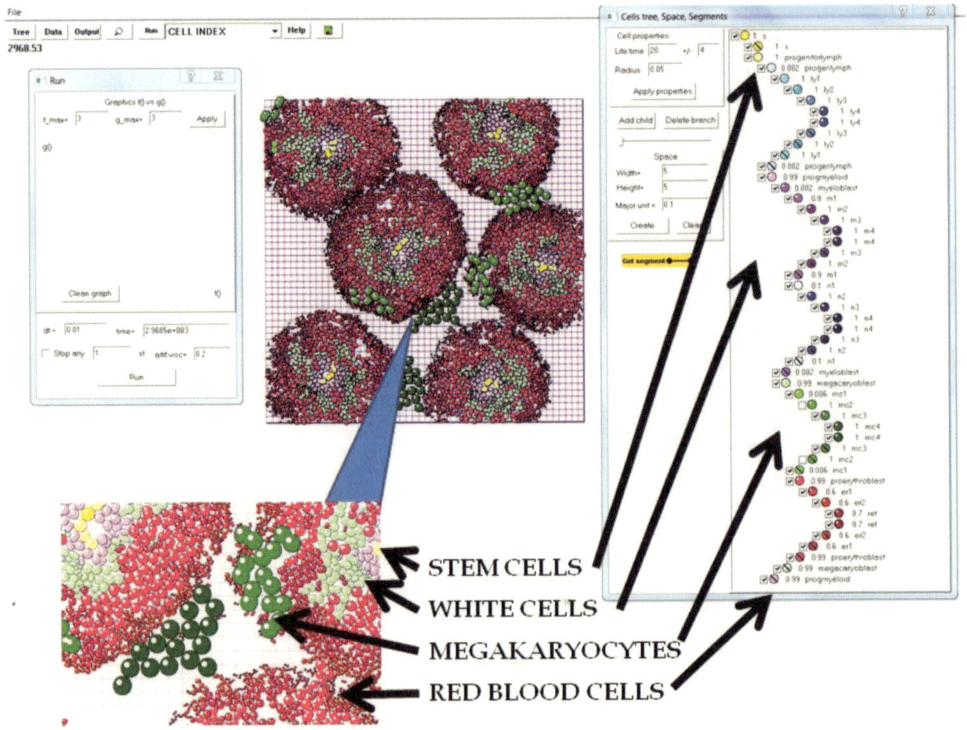

Fig. 5. Attempt of the simulation of a full normal hematopoiesis in one tiny part of the bone marrow. Each cell type has been determined with its size, colour, differentiation properties, etc. It is then possible to identify the dynamics for each lineage. One can observe the different colonies formed after the seeding of six hematopoietic stem cells.

4.2.2 Pathological hematopoiesis: an application to leukemia

Different pathologies could be simulated: stress erythropoiesis such as anemia, thrombocytopenia or leukemia amongst the most known possible diseases. We decide here to present only some results related to leukemia. We were interested in the different possibilities for leukemia to spread in the bone marrow. It is indeed known that some leukemia can be removed from the body without even the individual to be aware of suffering from the disease. However, in some cases, the pathology can settle down and spread until all the malignant cells fulfill the bone marrow. It can also be possible to get chronic symptoms of the disease. In other words, pathological cells and non pathological cell population would oscillate which could correspond to chronic myeloid leukemia cases.

Everything starts with a single cell that mutates. Settlement of the disease depends on different factors. Here are some of the main explanations of the pathological dynamics. The software allows the user to choose any cell to be a mutant cell. It can be a stem cell as well as any other cell. This cell can have the same properties as a normal cell but it can also have the ability to divide faster than the other, with a proliferation time much shorter than an average cell, or a division rate much more important. This cell can also differentiate and keep mutating to obtain more aggressive malignant cells. Here are three examples of the spread of the disease in the bone marrow.

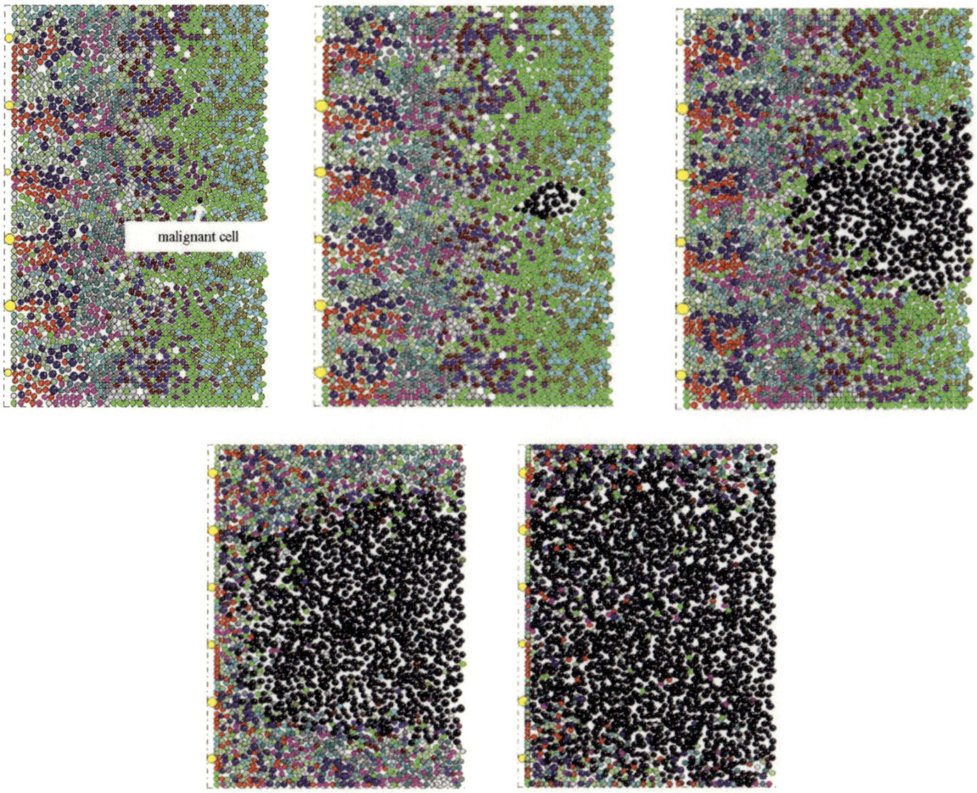

Fig. 6. Illustration of the spread of a disease. A malignant cell is placed in the bone marrow during normal hematopoiesis (top left) and develops to eventually invade the whole domain. This could correspond to a case of acute leukemia (illustration taken from Bessonov et al. 2006).

4.2.2.1 Acute leukemia

In this example, we consider a malignant cell that mutates. The cell chosen is not a stem cell. This choice was made in order to show that the disease can spread and settle down the marrow even if it is not a stem cell. It all depends on the properties given on the mutant cell. In this case, the pathological cells proliferate more rapidly than the average cells. At the early stage of the disease, it seems that leukemic cells will not stay in the marrow. But rapidly, they start to wash out the non pathological cells from the bone marrow and spread all around the place to eventually occupy almost all the medullar medium (see Fig. 6). It is important at this point to note that production of normal cells does not decrease in presence of the pathology. The only event occurring here is the strong local pressure that pushes other cells out to the blood systems. As a consequence, a large number of immature cells invade the blood stream which gives the onset of the symptoms. The proliferation time is of great importance in the spread velocity of the disease. It has been illustrated in Fig. 7. For a long proliferation time, malignant cells remain localized in a small region and do not seem to spread in the whole system. On the contrary, for a short proliferation time the disease would easily spread out and invade the bone marrow. A combination of different parameters would then allow the system to reach different equilibria depending on the threshold reached. A mathematical analysis corresponding to the simulation has not yet been done but should be investigated in the future showing a great range of dynamics. It is interesting for instance to note that if the density of stem cells is increased, and the same values for parameters are kept, then leukemia in these specific simulations has less chances to develop. Furthermore, if a mutation is given to a mature cell, this cell will have more difficulties to multiply and let the disease spread, and vice versa. Each choice could be driven by a specific type of leukemia one wants to model.

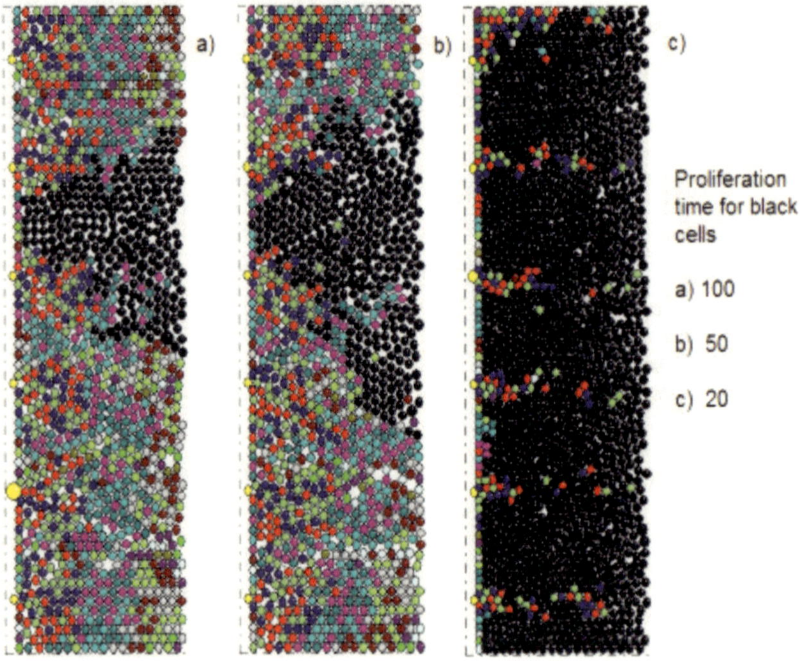

Fig. 7. Comparison between three simulations with different proliferation times for leukemic cells. The first one is modelled with a proliferation time of 100 time unit, the second 50, and the third 20 (illustration taken from Bessonov et al. 2006).

4.2.2.2 Chronic myelogenous leukemia (CML)

Chronic myelogenous leukemia occurs when concentration of cells of all types oscillate periodically. This kind of behavior has been observed in the 1970's and studied in the late 1990's and beginning of the 2000's (see section 3.1.3). It is possible, using a specific choice of parameters to obtain such oscillations with the Bessonov's software. Moreover, this application is able to get an output of the cell population leaving the bone marrow. Each cell type can be counted and put in a specific file. This file can be analyzed by any mathematical software able to analyze sets of data. The result we obtain with the example shown here seems qualitatively equivalent to the clinical data obtained in the 1970's (see Fig. 8). Getting quantitative results would be quite interesting for the biologist community in the sense that it would be then possible to replicate quite accurately the experimental or clinical data. This is still under investigation.

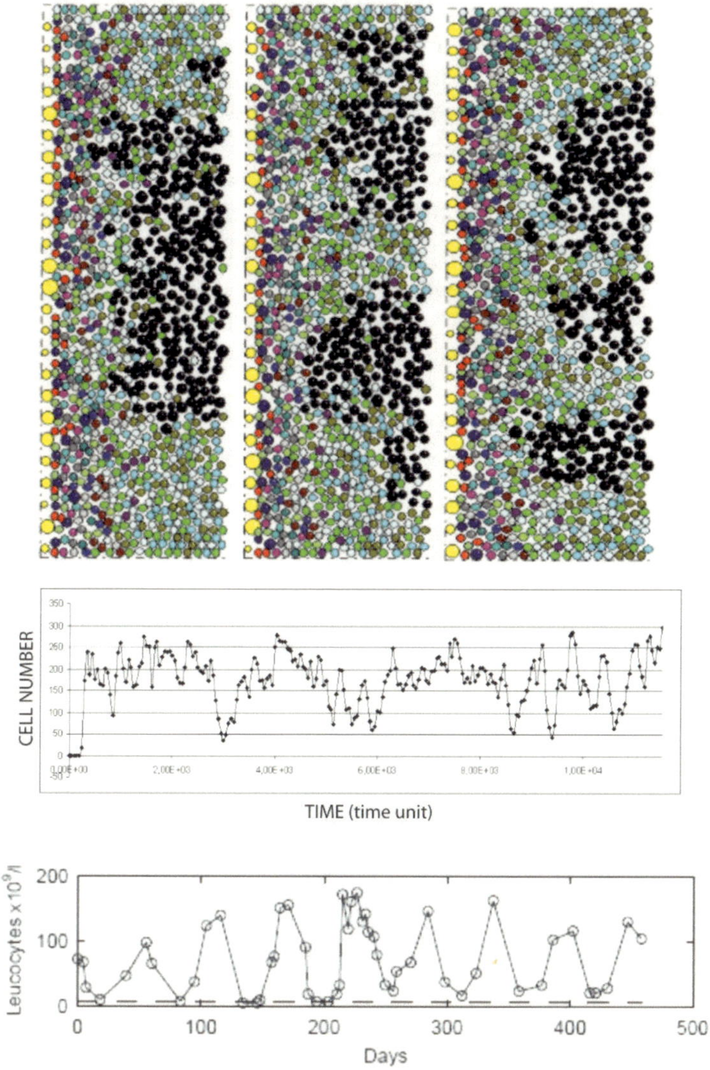

Fig. 8. Simulation of a pathological case. The black cells are malignant cells. The cell distributions are taken at three different times. The black cells form one, two or three domains almost periodically as shown in the time series right below the figure. It is possible to show that the concentrations of all cell types oscillate in time too (not shown here). The time series of the malignant cell population in the bone marrow could correspond to a CML case as illustrated by a time series of a leukocyte population in the bone marrow taken from a patient having CML (Fortin et al. 1999) (illustration taken from Bessonov et al. 2006).

4.2.2.3 A case where the disease fades out

Let us consider a case where the disease seems to spread in the bone marrow but eventually is being washed out and the systems returns to normal. In this example, the first generations of mutant cells can self-renew, and also differentiate to more aggressive cells. The last generations of mutant cells cannot self-renew. In this case, a simple simulation can exhibit a rapid increase of the pathology in the bone marrow. But after a certain period of time, the malignant cell population is washed out from the bone marrow and is replaced by normal cells (see Fig. 9). A question may arise then from this point: how is it possible for a population of mutant cells able to develop rapidly to disappear from the space representing the bone marrow here? The answer could enlightened by a simple focus of the individual level. In the simulation proposed here, all the stem cells are attached to the left wall of the domain, which is not the case for all the other cells. Thus, each cell except the stem cells is either condemned to die by apoptosis, differentiate, self-renew or leave the blood stream after a certain period of time. This is also the case for the cells defined as mutant cells in the example here. They are also part of the dynamics rules of the software. They can self-renew or differentiate but do not increase their number. It may thus be impossible for these cells to overcome their loss and eventually, they are pushed out of the bone marrow by the younger generations of healthy cells. In some cases however, self-renewing mutant cells can divide with a rate large enough to spread out and settle down in the medulla.

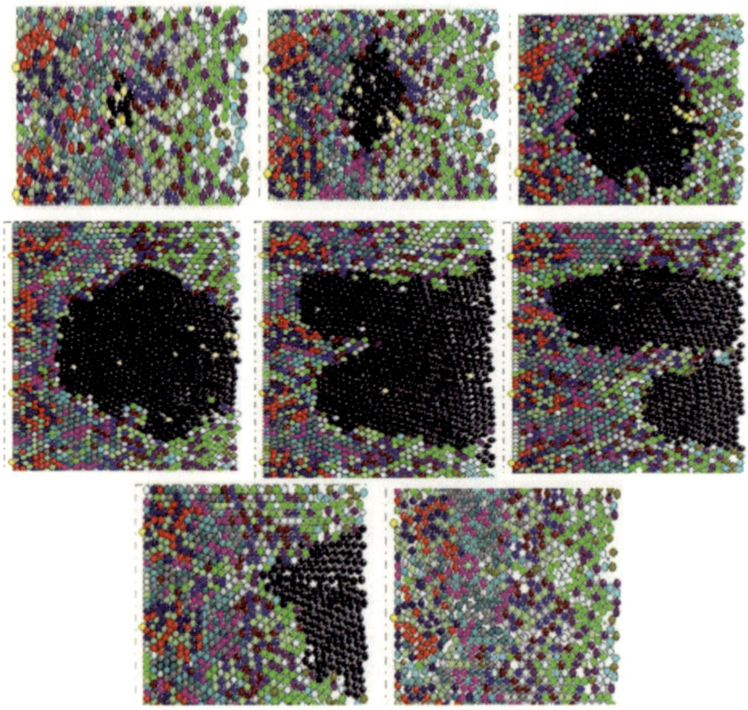

Fig. 9. Evolution of the disease spread: malignant (black) cell population grows from a malignant focus but not for a long time but eventually get washed out by the healthy cells. The disease free steady state is then stable in this example. This could correspond to what happens frequently in everyone's body (illustration taken from Bessonov et al. 2006).

In the next section, we go further into the cell environment, by taking the cell communication into account. Thus, not only space competition in the bone marrow plays a role for the development of different cells, but also the influence of the environment and the communication between cells in one neighborhood via some exchange of molecules.

4.3 Cell communication

Cell communication corresponds to another application of the Bessonov's software. In this section, we give an overview of the possibilities given by this application and the influence of different parameters on the cell population dynamics.

4.3.1 How does cell communication is taken into account in the software?

4.3.1.1 A simple example

It is known now that cell differentiation, self-renewal and apoptosis properties can be ruled by complex dynamics of molecules produced inside and outside each cells. For instance, it has been discovered that the stimulation hormones like EPO (see 1.5) would decrease the apoptosis rate in the red blood cell lineage. On the other hand, cell differentiation and the choice of one of the lineages can be regulated by a system of transcription factors. Some mathematical models have been attempted to tackle this problem (Roeder 2006, Crauste 2010). In Huang et al. (2007), the authors developed a model of binary cell fate decisions combining stochastic and deterministic instructions. In our work, we decided to give the possibility for the user to add this ability of cell differentiation through communication with the environment to the existing other applications provided by our software and described above. As mentioned by Roeder et al. (2006a) lineage specification is "a competition process between different interacting lineages propensities".
Even if our software allows the user to simulate several cell lineage specifications and communication with as many stimulating factors as wanted, we believe that a description of the application use with the simplest model of only two subpopulations would be more understandable.

4.3.1.2 An exchange of information

Let us then start with one population of undifferentiated cells denoted by A. These cells can divide, giving two daughter cells. One of the daughter cell would be exactly of the same type of its mother (self-renewing), and the other would be of either type G or type F. Two possible lineages are then given to the undifferentiated cells. The color given to the A-type cell would be white, if would be blue for the G-type and red for the F-type (see Fig. 10). Each cell denoted i- not even a cell type but really each individual - is characterized by two functions: fi and gi depending on time the time t, which could correspond for instance to a certain amount of two types of molecules. We assume in this simulation that every new born cell is undifferentiated, that is white. In other word, every time that a stem cell divides, it gives rise to two white cells. These cells are prescribed by the same initial amount of molecules, *i.e.* f0, g0. This content changes with time with a rate defined by two differential equation describing the evolution of fi and gi with respect to time:

$$\frac{dfi}{dt}=a(Fi-fi),\ \text{and}\ \frac{dgi}{dt}=a(Gi-gi), \qquad (1)$$

where a is a constant, and the Fi and Gi can be chosen to satisfy the so-called "average rule", that is

$$Fi=\sum_{j\neq i} fj/N,\ \text{and}\ Gi=\sum_{j\neq i} gj/N, \qquad (2)$$

where N is the sum of the number N of neighbor cells, which is defined automatically in the software code. The other possibility to define Fi and Gi is to follow the "max rule", that is the cell content fi will evolve depending on the influence of its neighbor having the greatest amount of F-type molecule and likewise for gi. In other words,

$$Fi=\max_{j\neq i} fi \text{ and } Gi=\max_{j\neq i} gi. \quad (3)$$

From a biological point of view, this means that each individual releases the molecules of F or G-type with a rate proportional to their concentration, and similarly, it receives the molecules from its neighboring cells with a rate proportional to their concentrations.

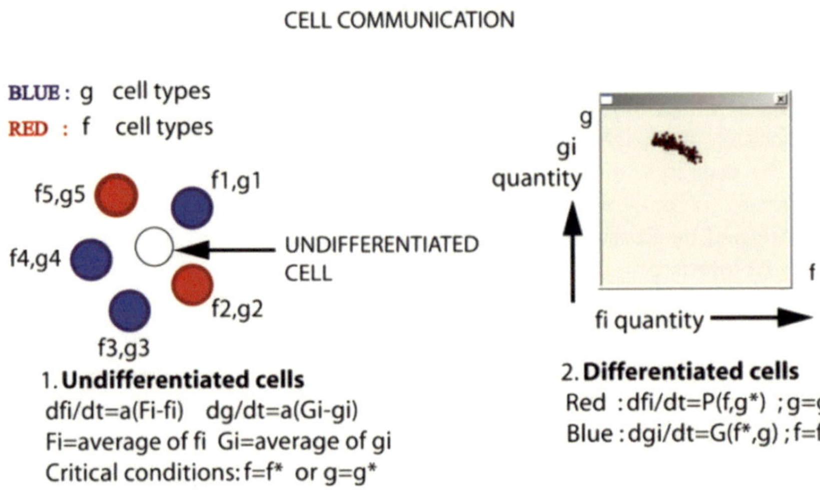

Fig. 10. Cell communication: each cell denoted "i" at a time t is characterized by two parameters, fi(t) and gi(t). Under specific conditions the neighboring cells can influence the undifferentiated (white) ones. This influence depends on the number of each cell type around. After a certain time, the simulation is stopped, the software counts the number of each cell type (f and g) and plot their distribution in the f − g plane (illustration taken from Bessonov et al. 2006).

4.3.1.3 Choice of one lineage and evolution of the cell content

Different rules are set up for an undifferentiated cell to remain white or to choose a lineage. A new born cell stays white as long as $fi^2(t)+gi^2(t) \leq \sigma$, where σ is a given parameter set up by the user. This means that a cell needs a specific threshold of molecule concentration to be differentiated taking the color of the greater concentration between fi and gi to become red or blue.

When a cell has "chosen" its lineage, its content can evolve depending on the following rules:

$$\frac{dfi}{dt}=P(fi,gi), \; gi=gi^{*}=\text{constant} \quad (4)$$

for red cells, and

$$\frac{dgi}{dt}=Q(fi,gi),\ fi=fi^*=constant \quad (5)$$

for blue cells, where fi* and gi* stand for the concentration of molecules of F and G-type at the moment when differentiation has been decided. In other words, if a cell is of type F, the amount of "F-molecules" would change depending on the defined function P but the "G-molecule" content will remain constant and vice versa with function Q. This property gives the specific shape of the figures representing the simulations on the cell type evolution with a blank squared shape on the upper right part of the plot (see Fig. 11). The function P and Q are defined to be quadratic functions as follows

$$P(f,g)=a_1+a_2f+a_3f^2+a_4fg+a_5g, \quad (6)$$

and

$$Q(f,g)=b_1+b_2g+b_3g^2+b_4fg+a_5f, \quad (7)$$

where ai and bi, i=1,...,5 are some constants defined by the user. The quadratic form of P and Q was chosen for simplicity, but can be modified anytime by the user.

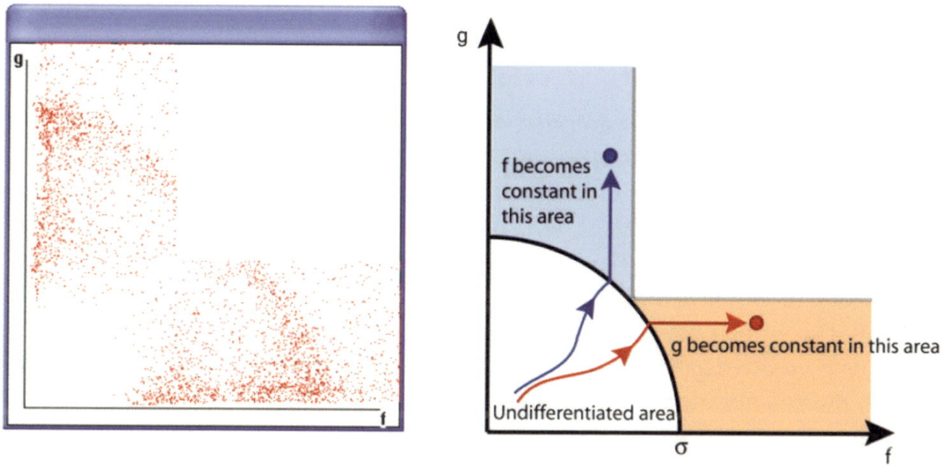

Fig. 11. Cell position in the f–g plane. A white cell remains undifferentiated as long as $fi^2(t)+gi^2(t) \leq \sigma$ (inside the disk (figure in the left)), where σ is a given parameter. If the concentrations of f and g become sufficiently high (greater than σ), the cell chooses its type. Once the differentiation occurs and the cell chooses its type, further evolution of f and g becomes different. For red cells df i/dt =P(fi,gi), gi = g*i (it remains constant), for blue cells dgi/dt = Q(fi,gi), fi=f*i (it remains constant). In other words, after differentiation, the value of f in red cells increases and the value of g remains constant; for blue cells g increases and f remains constant which gives the specific shape of the f – g graph (right) (illustration taken from Bessonov et al. 2009).

In each figure it is then possible to represent the cell of all types with undifferentiated cells on the quarter of disk on the bottom left angle with radius equal to σ (corresponding to the distance between the origin of the axis and the bottom left part of the blank squared shape.

Everything above this disk, between the y-axis and the blank squared shape would correspond of cells of blue G-type and the higher the cell is located the more mature it is. On the other hand, all cells on the right side after the disk and below the blank squared shape are the red F-type cells. And thus, the choice of the lineage can be well defined depending on the zone a cell can be plot. Consequently, if all cells remain within the disk, this means that all cells remain undifferentiated; this could correspond to a case of acute leukemia. They can also be located in one or two lineages, or the three depending on the sets of parameters chosen. This will be developed in the next paragraph.
Furthermore, cell generations can be observed by the "circular stripes" appearing in the simulations. This is correlated to the ratio of the proliferation time between the stem cells and the first daughters. Let us see some examples in the next paragraph.

4.3.2 Examples of cell communication and differentiation

We remind the reader here the starting bases of the cell communication application. At the beginning of the simulation, only undifferentiated cells are produced by the stem cells. Once the whole domain has been filled up with all the white cells, the process stops and each cell is prescribed randomly one of the two (red or blue) types with some value fi and gi. The application starts again and then, all new born undifferentiated cells are obliged to choose one of the types depending on their environment and the parameters set up as explained in the previous paragraph. Some structures can appear. This process starts with a random distribution of the cells, but specific structures can appear depending on the different sets of parameters.
The application can give different outputs: the number of cells of each type can appear in a specific file as explain in a previous section. In other words, after a certain time τ_i, which represents the moment when the ith cell leaves the bone marrow. The cell is then registered into the file with its fi and gi content, which determines its type depending on the level of red or blue molecule inside. To be more convenient, the software plots directly all these cells on the (f,g)-plane. In other words, it $(f(\tau_i),g(\tau_i))$ plots corresponding to each cell leaving the bone marrow. The graph obtains represent then the population of blood cells released in the system. Let us give three examples corresponding to the influence of the main parameters: starting with the proliferation time, then the cell size, and finally a combination of the cell communication parameters with the self-renewal processes.

4.3.2.1 Cell communication and the proliferation time parameter

In this example, let us assume that cell of the second generation cannot differentiate anymore. This may represent a simplified case of normal hematopoiesis. Almost no undifferentiated cells are found in the bone marrow, and a great proportion of cells clearly belong to one of the two types and increasing the proliferation time would improve the cell differentiation process. It is possible to give a biological explanation behind these simulations. It is indeed, easy to understand that in the case of non pathological hematopoiesis, a cell being given more time to mature will leave the bone marrow with a more complete functional material than cells having little time to fulfill the maturation process. It has been shown for instance that in case of stress erythropoiesis (like anemia or blood loss), cell proliferation is accelerated due to the combination of self-renewal process of progenitors, but also the apoptosis rate decreases in the bone marrow, due to the effect of EPO, but once in the blood stream, cell death is greater than normal due to the fact that they have not completed their formation and are released in the stream with a weaker structure. Moreover, changing the distribution of time (the +/- time column) would imply a change in the sharpness of cell generation plots in the sense that the zones representing each generation does not show clear borders when the distribution of time is increased ((see Fig. 12). This makes sense since the cell proliferation occurs more randomly in time. The process tends to be then more stochastic.

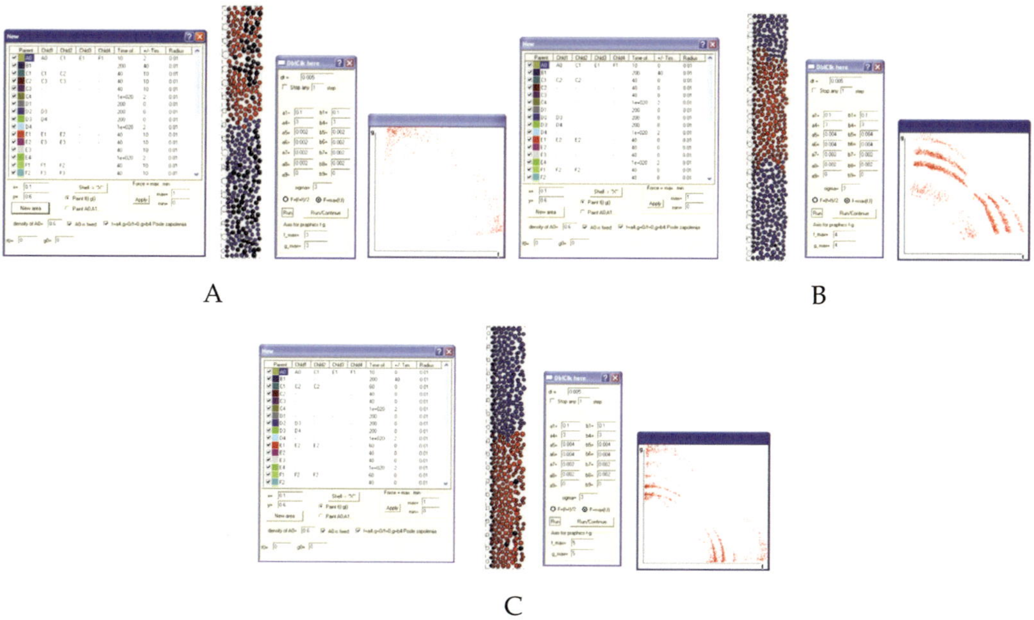

Fig. 12. Changes in cell proliferation time. A. In this simulation, the proliferation time is not exact but distributed. Thus in the plot on the f -g plane one can observe a less structured differentiated cell distribution. B. In this simulation, the cell lineages have been modified: no offspring for several cell generations. In the plot on the f -g plane one can observe then a well defined structure of all the cell generations depending on their maturity level as well as their differentiation profile. This could correspond to a non pathological case. C. Changes in cell proliferation time that gives a simulation where almost no cells are undifferentiated and cell generations are well separated (illustration taken from Bessonov et al. 2009).

4.3.2.2 Cell communication and the cell size parameter

As explained in the paragraph 4.1.1.1., the cell size decreases in correlation with their maturity except for the megakaryocytic lineage. Thus, it appears necessary to consider the influence of the cell size parameter in our application. When comparing the simulations with the size decrease taken into account, one can see that no undifferentiated cells can be found in the blood stream. All of them remain in the bone marrow (in the non pathological case considered here). On the other hand, the cell generations are clearly defined. This result was expected since, with increasing maturity, the cells get smaller, they need less space in the bone marrow, and so they can stay longer than the one whose size has not changed, and thus can gain more differentiation molecules (red or blue). And thus, the f and g colonies appear much more distinct than a simple simulation where no evolution of size is taken into account (see Fig. 13).

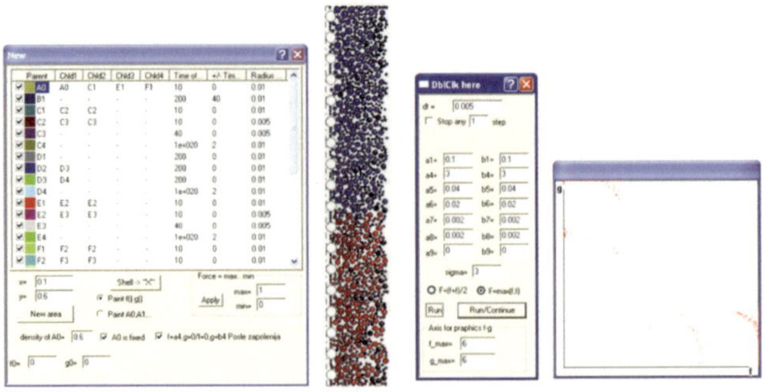

Fig. 13. Changes in cell radius in order to get smaller size as maturity increases, gives clear and definite compartments of cell generations (illustration taken from Bessonov et al. 2009).

4.3.2.3 Cell communication and the self-renewal process

Let us assume that the system is under a stress erythropoiesis such as a severe anemia or blood loss. Then it has been shown that progenitor cells and sometimes precursor cells can self-renew under stimulating glucocorticoids. What is expected with this change in the parameter set up is an increase of undifferentiated. The population is indeed forced to increase and to give rapidly efficient cells to be released in the blood stream. This process could also be pushed to and extreme case, where most of the cells leaving the bone marrow could be undifferentiated. This would then correspond to cases of acute leukemia, where it is not possible for cells to differentiate, and thus malignant cells would only self-renew with almost no differentiation. The system, after a certain time would then be filled with undifferentiated cells only (see Fig. 14).

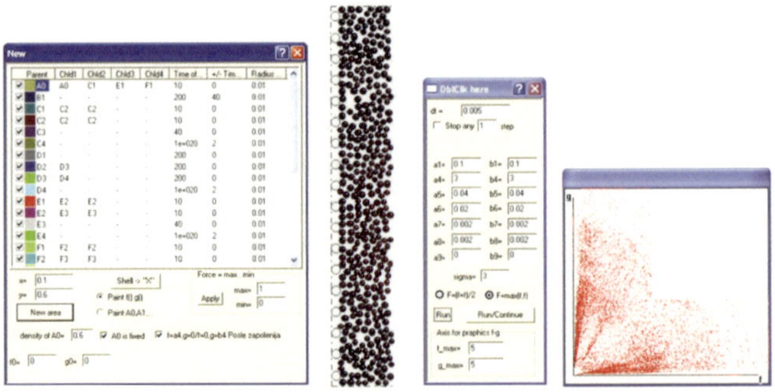

Fig. 14. Adding self-renewal ability in progenitors leads to a nice illustration of what could occur in case of severe bleeding or anemia, and action of the glucocorticoids on cell differentiation (illustration taken from Bessonov et al. 2009).

4.4 Niches and colonies in the bone marrow

In this section, the mechanical interaction and the cell displacement are the same as in the previous software interface. However, instead of imposing self-renewal, differentiation and apoptosis like it is in the previous model (even if it is a stochastic process in the software, it is set up by the user through different parameter choices), these properties are ruled out by intrinsic and extrinsic regulation with no user implication.

4.4.1 Hybrid models

Hereafter we propose a new approach of mechanical interactions between cells both from intrinsic and extrinsic regions. In order to do so, we focus our attention on intra-cellular regulation, described by ordinary differential equations, and on extra-cellular regulation, described by partial differential equations.

We restrict ourselves here to the simplest model where cells are represented as elastic balls. In other words, we consider two elastic balls with their centres at the points x1 and x2, and with the radii, respectively given by r1 and r2. If the distance d12 between the centres is less than the sum of the radii, r1 + r2, then there is a repulsive force between them, denoted by f12 depending on the distance d12. Moreover, if a particle with the centre at xi is surrounded by several other particles with their centres at the points xj, j=1,..., k, then we consider the pair wise forces fij assuming that they are independent of each other. This assumption corresponds to small deformation of the particles. Hence, we find the total force Fi acting on the i-th particle from all other particles, $Fi=\sum_{j^1 i} fij$. The motion of the particles can now be described as the motion of their centers. By Newton's second law

$$m\ddot{x}i+\mu m\dot{x}i-\sum_{j^1 i} f(dij)=0, \quad (8)$$

where m is the mass of the particle, the second term in the left-hand side describes the friction by the surrounding medium. Dissipative forces can also be written in a different form. This is related to dissipative particle dynamics (Karttumen, 2004). Intra-cellular regulatory networks for the i-th cell are described by a system of ordinary differential equations

$$\frac{dui}{dt}=F(ui,ue), \quad (9)$$

where ui is a vector of intra-cellular concentrations, ue is a vector of extra-cellular concentrations, F is the vector of reaction rates which should be specified for each particular application. Evolution of the concentrations of the species in the extra-cellular matrix is described by the diffusion equation

$$\frac{\partial ue}{dt}=D\Delta ue+G(ue,c), \quad (10)$$

where c is the local cell density, G is the rate of consumption or production of these substances by cells. These species can be either nutrients coming from outside and consumed by cells or some other bio-chemical products consumed or produced by cells. In particular, these can be hormones or other signalling molecules that can influence intra-cellular regulatory networks. In some cases, convective motion of the medium should be taken into account.

4.4.2 1-D model example

We begin with the 1D model example where cells can move along the line. The coordinates x i in equation (1.1) are real numbers. Each cell can divide or die by apoptosis. After division a cell gives birth to two daughter cells identical to itself (this is the case of self-renewal division, there is no differentiation taken into account in this example). We suppose that cell division and death are influenced by some bio-chemical substances produced by the cells themselves.

We consider the case where there are two such substances, whose concentrations are denoted by ue and ve and satisfy the following system of equations:

$$\begin{cases} \dfrac{due}{dt} = d1\dfrac{\partial^2 ue}{\partial x^2}+b1c-q1ue, \\ \dfrac{dve}{dt} = d2\dfrac{\partial^2 ve}{\partial x^2}+b2c-q2ve. \end{cases} \tag{11}$$

These equations describe the evolution of the extracellular concentrations ue and ve with their diffusion, production terms proportional to the concentration of cells c and with the degradation terms. We note that cells are considered here as point sources with a given rate of production of u and v. The cell concentration is understood as a number of such sources in a unit volume. In numerical simulations, where cells have a finite size, we consider them as distributed sources and specify the production rate for each node of the numerical mesh. Intra-cellular concentrations ui and vi in the i-th cell are described by the equations:

$$\begin{cases} \dfrac{dui}{dt} = k1^{(1)}ue(x,t)-k2^{(1)}ui(t)+H1, \\ \dfrac{dvi}{dt} = k1^{(2)}ve(x,t)-k2^{(2)}vi(t)+H2. \end{cases} \tag{12}$$

Here and in what follows we write equations for intra-cellular concentrations neglecting the change of the cell volume. This approximation is justified since the volume changes only twice before cell division and this change is relatively slow. The first term in the right-hand side of the first equation shows that the intra-cellular concentration ui grows proportionally to the value of the extra-cellular concentration ue (x, t) at the space point x where the cell is located. It is similar for the second equation. These equations contain degradation terms and constant production terms, H 1 and H 2. When a new cell appears, concentrations ui and vi are set to zero.

If the concentration ui reaches some critical value uc, then the cell divides. If vi reaches vc, the cell dies. Consider first the case where

$$k1^{(1)} = k1^{(2)} = k2^{(1)} = k2^{(2)} = 0. \tag{13}$$

Then ui and vi are linear functions of time which reach their critical values at some times $t=\tau u$ and $t = \tau v$,

respectively. If $\tau u < \tau v$, then all cells will divide with a given frequency, if the inequality is opposite, then all cells will die.

Next, consider the case where $k1^{(1)}$ is different from zero (see Bessonov, 2010 for other examples). If it is positive, then cells stimulate proliferation of the surrounding cells, if it is negative, they suppress it. Both cases can be observed experimentally. We restrict ourselves here by the example of negative $k1^{(1)}$. All other coefficients remain equal to zero. Therefore, cells have a fixed life time τv. If they do not divide during this time, they die.

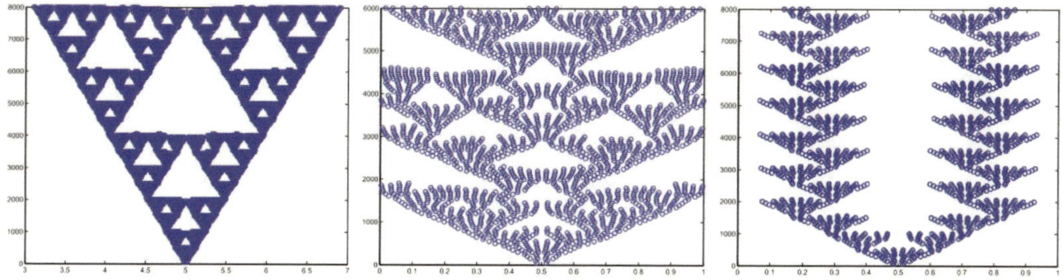

Fig. 15. Dynamics of cell population in the case where cells either self-renew or die by apoptosis. Cells are shown with blue dots. Horizontal axis shows cell position, vertical axis shows time.

We carry out the 1D simulation where cells can move along the straight line. Initially, there are two cells in the middle of the interval. Figure 15 shows the evolution of this population in time. For each moment of time (vertical axis) we have the positions of cells (horizontal axis) indicated with blue points.

The evolution of the cell population in Figure 15 (left) can be characterized by two main properties. First of all, it expands to the left and to the right with approximately constant speed. Second, the total population consists of relatively small sub-populations. Each of them starts from a small number of cells. Usually, these are two cells at the right and at the left of the previous sub-population. During some time, the sub-population grows, reaches certain size and disappears giving birth to new sub-populations.

This behavior can be explained as follows. The characteristic time of cell division is less than the one of cell death. When the sub-population is small, the quantity of u e is also small, and its influence on cell division is not significant. When the sub-population becomes larger, cell division is slowed down because of growth of ue. As a result the sub-population disappears. The outer cells can survive because the level of u e there is less.

The geometrical pattern of cell distribution for these values of parameters reminds Serpinsky carpet (Figure 15, left), an example of fractal sets. The pattern of cell distribution depends on the parameters. Other examples are shown in Figure 15 (middle and right).

The simulations presented here do not use the extra-cellular variable ve. Instead of the variable ue, which decelerates cell proliferation, we can consider ve assuming that it accelerates cell apoptosis. In this case, qualitative behavior of cell population is similar.

4.4.3 Erythropoiesis modeling

We consider two types of erythroid cells, progenitors and reticulocytes. Erythroid progenitor fate (differentiation, self-renewal, death by apoptosis) is supposed to be regulated by intra-cellular mechanisms (protein competition) and extra-cellular substances. The main external source of control in what follows will be Fas-ligand, a membrane protein produced by reticulocytes that activates the intra-cellular protein Fas. Other extra-cellular substances include EPO and glucocorticoids, among others. We will restrict our model to the influence of EPO, and even though we do not detail this action in the following, the level of EPO can be considered either constant or proportional to mature erythrocyte quantity. Fas-ligand will act on progenitor differentiation and apoptosis, whereas EPO will inhibit progenitor apoptosis and increase self-renewal.

We assume intracellular regulation of erythroid progenitors is determined by two proteins, ERK and Fas (Crauste, 2010), although several other proteins may play a role in this regulation. A simplified model is given by the system of two ordinary differential equations (Crauste, 2010)

$$\frac{dE}{dt}=\left(\alpha\left(EPO\right)+\beta E^{k}\right)\left(1-E\right)-aE-bEF, \tag{14}$$

$$\frac{dF}{dt}=\gamma\left(F_{L}\right)\left(1-F\right)-cEF-dF, \tag{15}$$

where E and F are intra-cellular concentrations of ERK and Fas, a, b, c, d are some non-negative parameters, α is a function of erythropoietin (EP O) and γ is a function of Fas-ligand, whose concentration is denoted by F L . For fixed values of EP O and F L , (14)-(15) is a closed system of ordinary differential equations. It can have from one to three stationary points. Its detailed analysis is presented in (Crauste, 2010).

The concentration of Fas-ligand is described by the diffusion equation

$$\frac{dF_{L}}{dt}=d\Delta F_{L}+W-\sigma F_{L}, \tag{16}$$

where W is a source term proportional to the concentration of reticulocytes. Though Fas-ligand is considered as a surface protein, and its interaction with erythroid progenitor basically occurs when they are in physical contact with reticulocytes, we model it as if it could diffuse in the extracellular matrix. If the diffusion coeffcient is suffciently small, it is located in a small vicinity of reticulocytes. Therefore, Fas-ligand influences erythroid progenitors when they are suffciently close to reticulocytes.

Let us summarize the model. System (14)-(15) is considered inside each erythroid progenitor with its proper initial condition (see below) and with the value of F L which can depend on its spatial location and on time. Erythroid progenitors can proliferate or die by apoptosis. Apoptosis occurs if the intracellular Fas concentration reaches some critical value F c. In this case, the cell is removed from the computational domain.

If the cell does not die by apoptosis, then it proliferates, that is it divides at the end of cell cycle. Cell cycle is composed of two parts: G0/G1 phases and S/G2/M phases. The duration of the G0/G1 phase is chosen randomly from 0 to some maximal value τ max with the typical values 6 − 12 hours, the duration of the remaining part of cell cycle is fixed, usually 12 hours.

Cell proliferation can result in self-renewal or differentiation. In the first case, the two daughter cells are also erythroid progenitors. For each of them we consider intracellular regulation with system (14)-(15). The values of ERK and Fas in the newly born cells can either be some given parameters or equal half those of the mother cell. In the case of differentiation, the two daughter cells become reticulocytes. The choice between self-renewal and differentiation is determined by the values of ERK in the process of cell cycle. Once it reaches a critical value Ec , the cell self-renews. Otherwise, it differentiates. These assumptions are in agreement with actual biological understanding of these processes. We do not consider intracellular regulation for reticulocytes. Once they appeared, they remain in the computational domain one cell cycle more in order to become mature erythrocytes. Then they are removed. This corresponds to the fact that erythrocytes leave the bone marrow to enter blood flow. Reticulocytes produce Fas-ligand with a constant rate. Fas-ligand influences intracellular regulation of erythroid progenitors through equation (15). It increases Fas production rate resulting in apoptosis of the progenitors if Fas concentration is sufficiently high or in their differentiation for intermediate values of F L . For greater values of Fas-ligand, trajectories of system (14)-(15) move towards greater values of F and to smaller values of E. Hence, the critical value of ERK may not be reached and the cell will differentiate.

Let us finally recall that proliferation and apoptosis change cell spatial distribution. New cells, when they appear, push each other creating cell displacement (see Fig. 16).

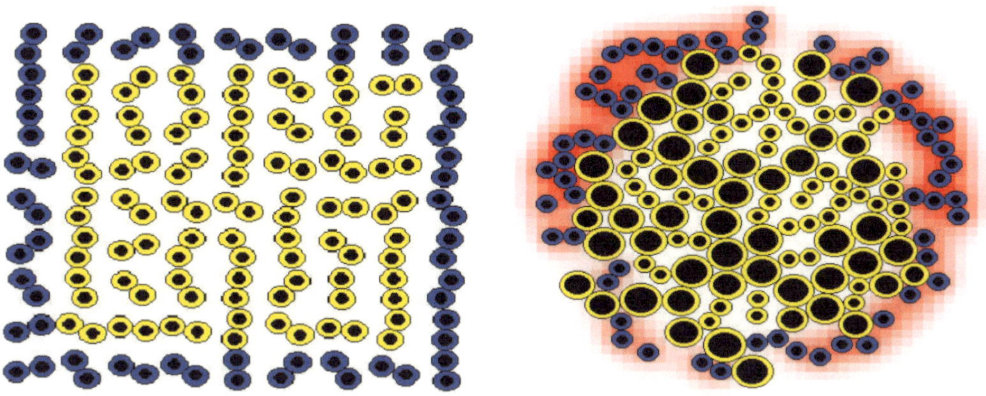

Fig. 16. Modelling of erythroblastic islands: initial cell distribution (left) and a stable island (right). Yellow cells in the center are erythroid progenitors, blue cells at the border are reticulocytes producing Fas-ligand (in red).

5. Conclusion

In this chapter, our goal was to give an insight of the different attempts to model the blood cell formation: several purely deterministic, some purely stochastic, few taking the space structure of the bone marrow and thus space competition into account. It appeared important to us to develop a compromising model where stochasticity is mixed with the medulla structure. This approach using the multi-agent systems seems to us a good way to describe different mechanism related to the normal and pathological hematopoiesis. We have shown that with our software it was possible to get a rich variety of behaviors. Our simulations found some interest in the community of biologists and clinicians. However, even if we obtained some relevant results none of them where quantitatively compared with experimental data. This is part of the perspective work taken in consideration. Another objective would be to consider the stimulation factors more explicitly by closing with the use of different feedbacks.

6. References

Abkowitz, J. L., Golinelli, D., Harrison, D. E., Guttorp, P. (2000). In vivo kinetics of murine hemopoietic stem cells, *Blood,* 96, 3399-3405.

Abkowitz, J. L., Golinelli, D., Harrison, D. E., Guttorp, P. (1996). Evidence that hematopoiesis may be stochastic in vivo,, *Nat. Med.,* 2, 190-197.

Adimy, M. and Crauste, F. (2007). Modelling and asymptotic stability of a growth factor-dependent stem cells dynamics model with distributed delay, *Discrete and Continuous Dynamical Systems Series B,* 8(1); 19-38.

Bessonov, N., Ducrot, A. and Volpert, V. (2005). Modeling of leukemia development in the bone marrow, *Pro. of the annual Symposium on Mathematics applied in Biology and Biophysics;* Tom XLVIII, Vol. 2 : 79-88.

Bessonov, N., Pujo-Menjouet, L. & Volpert, V. (2006), Cell modelling of hematopoiesis, *Math. Model. Nat. Phenom.,* 1, No. 2, 81–103

Bessonov, N., Demin, I., Pujo-Menjouet, L., & Volpert, V. (2009), A multi-agent model describing self-renewal of differentiation effects on the blood cell population, *Mathematical and Computer Modelling,* 49, 2116–2127

Bessonov, N., Kurbatova, P. & Volpert, V. (2010), Particle dynamics modelling of cell populations, *Prooceedings of the conference JANO, Mohamadia 2008, Math. Model. Nat. Phenom.,* 5, No. 7, 42–47

Bessonov, N., Kurbatova, P. &Volpert, V. (2010) Dynamics of growing cell populations, *CRM, preprint num. 931 for Mathematical Biology,* February 2010

Burns F.J. & Tannock I.F. (1970) On the existence of a G0-phase in the cell cycle, *Cell Tissue Kinet,* 19 : 321-34.

Colijn, C. and Mackey, M.C. (2005a). A mathematical model of hematopoiesis: Cyclical neutropenia", part I, *J.Theor. Biol.* 237, 117–132.

Colijn, C. and Mackey, M.C. (2005b). A mathematical model of hematopoiesis: Cyclical neutropenia", part II, *J. Theor. Biol.* 237; 133–146.

Crauste, F., Pujo-Menjouet L., Genieys S., Molina C. & Gandrillon O. (2008) Adding Self-Renewal in Committed Erythroid Progenitors Improves the Biological Relevance of a Mathematical Model of Erythropoiesis, *Journal of Theoretical Biology,* vol. 250(2), p. 322-338.

Crauste, F., Demin, I. , Gandrillon, O. & Volpert, V. (2010) Mathematical study of feedback control roles and relevance in stress erythropoiesis, *J. Theo. Biol.,* 263, 303–316

Dingli, D. and Michor, F. (2006). Successful therapy must eradicate cancer stem cells, *Stem Cells,* 12, 2603-10. Epub 2006 Aug 24.

Dingli, D., Traulsen, A. & Pacheco, J.M. (2007a) Stochastic dynamics of hematopoietic tumor stem cells, *Cell Cycle,* 6 : 461-6

Dingli, D. & Pacheco, J.M. (2007b) Ontogenic growth of the haemopoietic stem cell pool in humans, *Proc R Sci B,* 274 :2497-501

D'Inverno, M. and Saunders, R. (2008). Agent-based modelling of stem cell self- organisation in a niche, In : Lecture Notes in Computer Science. Berlin/Heidelberg : *Springer,* (volume 3464/2005)

Foley, C., Bernard, S. and Mackey, M.C. (2006). Cost-effective G-CSF therapy strategies for cyclical neutropenia: Mathematical modelling based hypotheses, *J. Theor. Biol.*, 238; 754-763.

Fortin, P. and Mackey, M.C. (1999). Periodic chronic myelogenous leukemia: Spectral analysis of blood cell counts and etiological implications, *Brit. J. Haematol.*, 104 ; 336–345.

Gillespie, D. T. (1992). Markov Processes: An Introduction for Physical Scientists, *Academic Press*, San Diego, CA.

Huang, S., Guo, Y.-P. May, G., and Enver, T. (2007). Bifurcation dynamics in lineage-commitment in bipotent progenitor cells, *Dev. biol.* 305, 695-713.

Karttunen, M., Vattulainen, I., Lukkarinen (2004), A., *A novel methods in soft matter simulations*, Springer, Berlin,

Lajtha L.G. (1959). On DNA labeling in the study of the dynamics of bone marrow cell populations, Stohlman Jr. F, ed. The Kinetics of Cellular Proliferation. *New York : Grune and Stratton*; 173-82

Lei, J. and Mackey, M. C. (2007). Stochastic differential delay equation, moment stability, and application to hematopoietic stem cell regulation system, *SIAM J. Appl. Math.* 67, 387-407.

Michor F. (2007a). Reply: The long-term response to Imatinib treatment of CML, *Br. J. Cancer* 96, 679-680.

Michor, F. (2007b). Quantitative approaches to analyzing imatinib-treated chronic myeloid leukemia, *Trends Pharmacol Sci.*; (5):197-9. Epub 2007 Apr 6.

Newton, M. A., Guttorp, P., Catlin, S., Assuncao, R. and Abkowitz, J. L. (1995). Stochastic modeling of early hematopoiesis, *J. Amer. Stat. Assoc.* 432, 1146-1155.

Pimentel, J. (2006). Agent Based Model for the Production Mechanism and Control of Blood Cells in the Human Body, *Proceedings of The National Conference On Undergraduate Research (NCUR), The University of North Carolina at Asheville, North Carolina.*

Pujo-Menjouet, L., Bernard, S. and Mackey, M.C. (2005). Long period oscillations in a G0-model of hematopoietic stem cells, *SIAM JAppl Dynam Syst*; 4 : 312-32.

Roeder, I. and Loeffler, M. (2002). A novel dynamic model of hematopoietic stem cell organization based on the concept of within-tissue plasticity, *Exp. Hematol.* 30, 853-861.

Roeder I. and Glauche, I. (2006a). Towards an understanding of lineage specification in hematopoietic stem cells: A mathematical model for the interaction of transcription factors GATA-1 and PU.1., *J. Theor. Biol.* 241, 852-865,doi:10.1016/j.jtbi.2006.01.021.

Roeder, I., Horn, M., Glauche, I., Hochhaus, A., Mueller, M.C. and Loeffler M. (2006b). Dynamic modeling of imatinib-treated chronic myeloid leukemia: functional insights and clinical implications, *Nat Med.*, 1181-4. Epub 2006 Oct 1.

Shahrezael, V., Ollivier J. F. and Swain, P. S. (2008). Colored extrinsic fluctuations and stochastic gene expression, *Mol. Syst. Biol.* 4, 1-9.

Smith, J.A. & Martin, L. (1973). Do cells cycle?, *Proc. Natl. Acad. Sci. USA*, 70; 1263-1267.

Wazewska-Czyzewska, M. and Lasota A. (1976). Mathematical problems of the dynamics of a system of red blood cells, *Mat. Stos.* (3) 6; 23-40.

19

Identification of Relevant Genes with a Multi-Agent System using Gene Expression Data

Edna Márquez[1], Jesús Savage[1], Christian Lemaitre[2],
Jaime Berumen[3], Ana Espinosa[3] and Ron Leder[1]
[1]*Universidad Nacional Autónoma de México, Cd. Universitaria, Coyoacán, México D.F.*
[2]*Universidad Autónoma Metropolitana,*
[3]*Hospital General de México, Unidad de Medicina Genómica*
México

1. Introduction

In recent years, technology for information extraction from gene activity in cells, has made an important breakthrough with the DNA microarrays. With this technology it is possible for researchers to know which genes are active in a particular cell in particular situation. The comparison of gene expression patterns (which genes are active) of two cells of the same type, one normal and the other belonging to a tumor, can be of great help in understanding what are the genes that might be involved in the tumor formation.

Microarray technology is a high throughput information extraction technology; with a single microarray it is possible to extract, at once, information about the expression of thousand of genes. A typical experiment might involve the study of several microarrays and the comparison of the information extracted from them with standardized microarray gene expression databases.

From a computing point of view, microarray technology, opens interesting research issues at different levels, like data analysis and statistical information processing, information standardization, and automation of the whole information processes involved in each experiment.

This chapter addresses this latter issue. We present a multi-agent platform automating information processing of experimental microarray samples and its comparison with publicly accessible microarray databases.

A complete system for gene expression analysis can be based on different agents to solve parts of the problem, and due the diversity of paths that knowledge discovery could find, a system based on coordinated multiple agents can improve performance.

Here we describe a multi-agent system that was used for gene expression analysis in samples of cervical cancer for obtaining specific knowledge about the genetic basis of the cancer. Cervical cancer is one of the most common in Females. Its incidence in Mexico (50 per 100,000 inhabitants per year) is among the highest in the world (Lazcano-Ponce, 2009).

Section 2 presents an introduction to microarray for gene expression analysis; in section 3 there is information about multi-agent system technology related with gene expression analysis; in section 4 we discuss the architecture of a multi-agent system proposed, in section 5 we present the outcome reached and finally the conclusions.

2. Background gene expression analysis with microarrays technology

Microarrays are a molecular biology technique that appeared in 90's which display the expression of thousands of genes in a matrix.
One kind of probes that can be used for the design of microarrays is transcriptome others can detect loss or gain of genes and other mutations can be detected in DNA. The difference between each of them is the type of DNA that is fixed on the plates of the microarray.

2.1 Microarrays that detect changes in gene expression

When one wants to determine a change in the level of expression of a gene, this may be detected by expression analysis of microarray called chips or biochips. The DNA to be studied is immobilized by hybridization of mRNA, a known gene product by cDNA. This comes from healthy tissue cells (control) and patients (study samples). If a gene is over expressed in a certain disease, a greater amount of cDNA hybridizes at a point (spot) representing the affected gene and therefore the fluorescence intensities are dissimilar between the study group and the control group. Once characterized the genes involved in certain diseases, the cDNA of human cells may be hybridized to determine whether the person has the pattern of gene expression related to disease and to optimize diagnosis and treatment.
The chips of gene expression can also be used to determine changes in the expression over time, such as during the cell cycle. This represents an important tool in cancer research, that could identify new cancer markers for diagnostic purposes.

2.2 Microarray data analysis

The true potential of microarrays is realized when they are used for global approaches to gene expression patterns. There have been large-scale analyses of gene expression changes in bacteria, yeast and in animals to identify genes with similar expression pattern. To this end we have developed computer programs that may interest the researcher because they facilitate this type of global analysis. In this type of analysis one first identifies genes with significant changes during the experiment.. This is achieved by filtration of genes and identification of active genes. After obtaining purified data on a reduced number of genes grouping or clustering methods are applied. Several methods have been described (hierarchical clustering, self-organizing maps, k-means), each with tradeoffs.
Currently we recommend using more than one technique for each data set. The idea of identifying clusters or partitions of genes is that genes that have expression patterns contain near the same regulatory mechanisms, and eventually could create maps for precise control of transcription.
Microarray analysis provides quantitative information about the complete transcription profile of cells that could facilitate drug and therapeutics development, disease diagnosis, and better understanding basic cell biology. One of the challenges in microarray analysis, especially in cancerous gene expression profiles, is to identify genes or groups of genes that are highly expressed in tumor cells but not in normal cells and vice versa.

After reading the microarrays and creating the numerical matrix with gene expression intensities the analysis process continues with data normalization, filtering of genes and clustering samples and/or genes.

2.3 Normalization of data

The signal obtained from microarrays must be standardized or normalized because its difference expressed in the genes among the samples could differ a lot, so that data from different microarrays can be reliably compared. These methods are applied in the pre-processing of datasets.
The normalization is applied to expression data to adjust the individual hybridization intensities of genes in the microarrays.
The oligonucleotide microarrays are normalized using the two algorithms more reported, Affymetrix Microarray Suite (MAS) and Robust Multichip Average (RMA) (Irizarry, 2003), which remove the variation in overall chip intensities.
And finally in the preprocessing phase the transformation of level expression of genes to an equal rank in all chips permits a continuous spectrum of values. Generally the Log2 transformation is used with the clustering methods.

2.4 Statistical analysis

In order to reduce the initial amount of genes included in the microarray analysis it is recommended by specialists to use statistical methods, like T-test and significant analysis of microarrays (SAM) (Tusher, 2001). With these statistical tests experimental results are compared to standard samples for differences in gene expression according their signal values in nature (molecular biology).
With SAM differentially expressed genes are chosen using the false discovered rate (FDR), which represents the ratio of false positives to all positives according to a determined threshold.. The T-test uses the p-value of the fold change value (FC) that express the difference of genes between two groups of samples. In the case of SAM this value is expressed with delta value (Δ-value). The amount of filtered genes depends on the chosen threshold for those parameters. Also, the FC and d-value could show if the differentially expressed genes are up or down regulated.
When there are two experimental conditions, the most basic statistical test used for the two-sample comparision are differential expression tests within genes like SAM and T-test.

2.5 Genes differentially expressed

A key goal of microarray experiments is to identify genes that are differentially expressed while keeping the probability of false discoveries acceptably low. From a statistical perspective, it involves minimizing false negatives or maximizing power of the statistical test (sensitivity), and minimizing false positives (specificity). Microarray data are often assessed as fold-changes between experimental conditions. While this scale has interpretive value, inference based solely on fold-change is misleading because error variability for each gene is heterogeneous under different biological conditions and intensity ranges.
The main application of biochips is the comparison between genes expressed in diseased tissue and normal tissue to find those genes that change significantly their level of expression and thus related to the disease.

This finding could help to identify genes or groups of genes as targets for potential therapeutic intervention or prevention of diseases, like a cancer or diabetes.

The expression level could increase, this case exists when the gene is up regulated, or decrease, gene is down regulated, in the experiment. With this information researchers create sets of genes in order to find the minimal number of marker genes identifying potential points for therapeutic intervention, understanding tumor behavior and for facilitating drug development.

2.6 Machine learning and gene expression analysis

Machine learning is a computer area with a very important application in Bioinformatics. It has methods for knowledge discovery of molecular biology to identify genes or to find gene patterns.

Some reasons to apply machine learning in Bioinformatics are (Bergeron, 2003):

- New experimental approaches based on biochips, which can obtain huge genetic data from individual genomes (mutations, polymorphisms) or cellular approaches (gene expression).
- The huge volume of data generated by various genome projects (human and other organisms).
- Universal access to databases of biological information.

Machine learning approaches perform well in domains with a large amount of data, this is the situation in gene expression analysis. There are two types of learning: supervised learning, where the learner has some prior knowledge of the data and the output has been given a priori to the learner, and unsupervised learning, where no prior information of the output is given to the learner.

Machine learning supervised and unsupervised methods have been used in applications of gene expression analysis like Gepas (www.gepas.org), Dchip (sites.google.com/sites/dchipsoft/), Weka (www.cs.waikato.ac.nz/weka), and works like (Tamayo, 1999; Dembelé , 2003, Wang 2003; Márquez 2008)

3. Gene expression analysis through agents technology

3.1 Microarrays and multi-agent systems

The use of microarrays in genetic studies is a very dynamic field, new applications, new procedures and new microarrays with more gene capacity are appearing all the time. These are not the only changes in this field. A whole area of active research and new findings is emerging, related to the generation and management of all the related data, as well as the statistical studies of it, including machine learning techniques for better test selection procedures.

Such an information-intensive, dynamic field demands a flexible approach for information system design. It is clear that a traditional approach of solving the basic information processing issues of one particular application as a single fixed process will not survive long due to rapidly changing procedures and related technology. This rapid change introduces extra complexity to the information processing involved in the general problem of the information exploitation of microarray applications.

Now, agent technology offers an advantageous alternate option for building software in bioinformatics. The complexity of required systems offers an advantage to an architecture that can distribute tasks to specialized agents. Recently, there has been some agent-based systems to tackle the complexity of bioinformatics systems (Karasavvas, 2004; Keele, 2005; Lam, 2006; Luck, 2005; Merelli, 2005; Moreau, 2003; Štiglic, 2004).

We distinguish the following basic processes in the microarray analyisis system, that would be better handled by specialized agents:

1. Pre-processing, application of a set of techniques and methods of analysis prior to data mining, to work with different algorithms whose nature will be assessed at processing time.
2. Mining, in this step there is advantage to using different machine learning algorithms for finding patterns and relationships of genes and tumors.
3. Representation, a simple representation of the information and findings with diagrams, graphs and tables to make the results easy to understand.
4. Interaction with external databases, , the use of databases that exist on the Internet, as well as for the handling of knowledge generated and control their access.

3.2 Current situation

Today, the process of gene expression analysis to identify genes involved in diseases. It is in many cases quite troublesome for researchers since they need to go through different tricky stages of the process: a) There is no single package solution; they need to use several software programs to complete the analysis. This implies the user must provide the data format required by the program and the user must understand the software performance, this is not easy; b) the user must have some experience or he must make many experiments with the parameters of the programs to solve his problems, and make many experiments and, c) with the result of their experiments they must search information for characterization of genes using external databases. The previous process is more difficult if you consider that the researchers, in most cases, are biologists or medical scientists with only basic knowledge in computer systems and they have to do almost manually. With a view toward helping or solving those problems we present a multi-agent system.

The aim of our research is to automate the whole gene expression analysis process. To do that we organize our system architecture in a 2-layer structure. The upper layer is where the different agents interact. Each agent is a specialist in a well-defined component of the process and has the skills to se different types of mathematical and computing tools. The lower layer corresponds to the specific tools needed in each component of the process. The general strategy to solve a specific type of gene expression analysis is defined at the upper layer where multi-agent technology can look for the best procedure through the multi-agent interaction protocols facilities. The decisions of which specific tools need to be used for each task are taken by each agent who is a problem solver specialist.

Our multi-agent system has been developed as a bioinformatics tool to help researchers in two main tasks, 1) gene selection through an expression analysis process, and 2) tumor classification. This tool must be conceived as part of the toolset available to the human researchers in order to assist them during the diagnosis process.

4. Multi-agent system for gene expression analysis (MAS-GEN)

In order to accomplish the process of gene expression analysis using a multi-agent system architecture, we identify four operational agents coordinated and organized by one

manager. The gene identification process can be distributed among a few operational agents, each one in charge of a specific subprocess. And some tasks can be solve in parallel. We decompose the gene specification process in the following subprocesses: preprocessing data, gene identification, tumor classification and use of external databases, as showing in figure 1. Each subprocess is assigned to a specialized agent to carry out the current tasks and to make the right decisions that allow reliable and useful knowledge.
The MAS-GEN system is in fact a new layer inserted between the user and the specialized problem solving toolsets used currently in the semiautomatic setting. The multi-agent system for gene expression analysis involves the completion of different tasks that can be distributed among autonomous agents.
In addition to the four operational agents, a manager agent is in charge of the coordination and the planning of the overall process and mediates the communication between the agents. These agents are rule based problem solving systems programmed in Clips, a well-known expert system shell.

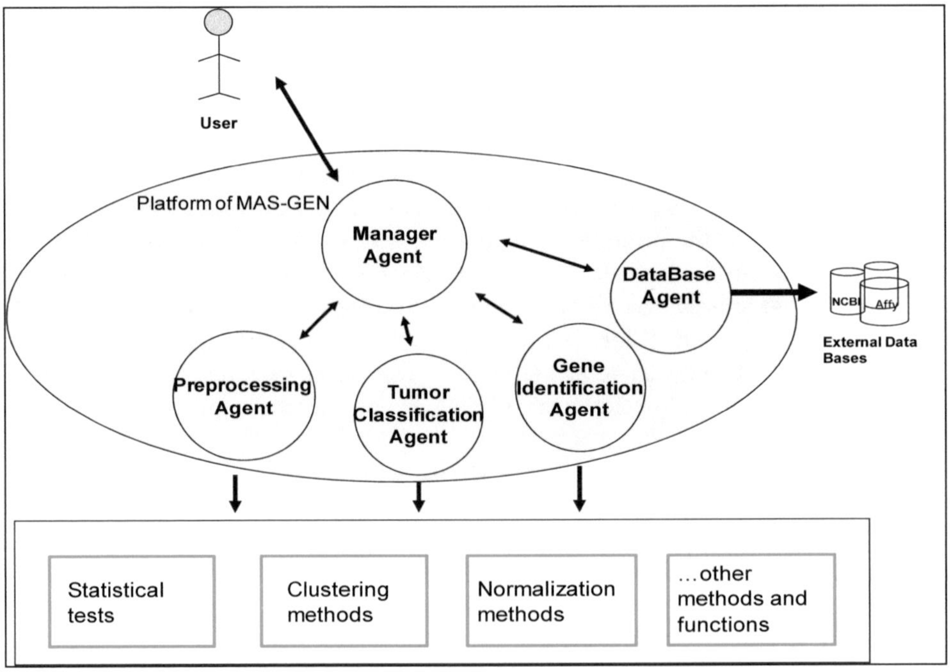

Fig. 1. MAS-GEN architecture for gene expression analysis. The platform of agents includes four operational agents and one manager agent. The specialized methods for solving their task are independent of agents. The external databases are used through database agent

Our agent platform has been tested for gene expression analysis using microarray samples of tumor cells of cervical cancer. However, its architecture is flexible enough to incorporate other functions or procedures to work with other type of diseases and other Affymetrix GeneChips. This is due to its layer architecture that separates the agent's process logic from its toolset layer where can coexist different concurrent tools in such different programming languages such as Java, C or R. This layer independence allows our platform to incorporate or modify new functions for the processing, analysis and data presentation tasks, causing no problem in performance.

4.1 Platform of agents

4.1.1 Preprocessing agent

The preprocessing agent get the data of intensity of expressed genes, it could use functions already implemented in the R language for microarray of Affymetyrix by Bioconductor (http://www.bioconductor.org/). Intensities may come from a single microarray or several at once, according to the user request. This agent must normalize the data, the algorithm RMA (Robust Multi-Averaging) (Irizarry, 2003), or MAS (Normalization of Affymetrix), (http://www.affymetrix.com/support/technical/manual/) which are currently the most widely used directly on data from Affymetrix microarrays and/or apply log or log2 on data already read. According to the task to be executed with the data, identification of genes or the classification of tumors, this agent decides what must be the data format in the matrix. The normalized data are assigned to an expression matrix. If the expression data of one gene in the matrix are incomplete the agent obtains the values or removes the raw data to avoid noise in data.

4.1.2 Gene identification agent

The gene identification agent's goal is to extract a list with the most important genes and reducing the initial amount of genes. If the agent has enough data it will apply the most used statistical filters, t-test and SAM (significant analysis of microarrays) (Tusher, 2001). Through the filters the agent reduces the number of genes from thousands to hundreds or less. According to the user request, the agent obtained the final list with the most relevant genes. The agent uses clustering methods to create the lists of genes, from the formated data that it gets from pre-processing agent. It could interact with the classification agent to test the capacity of lists of genes to classify the samples, controls and cases, and with the agent of external data bases to characterize the genes. With the knowledge provided by the others agents this agent decide what genes could be more important in the experiment.

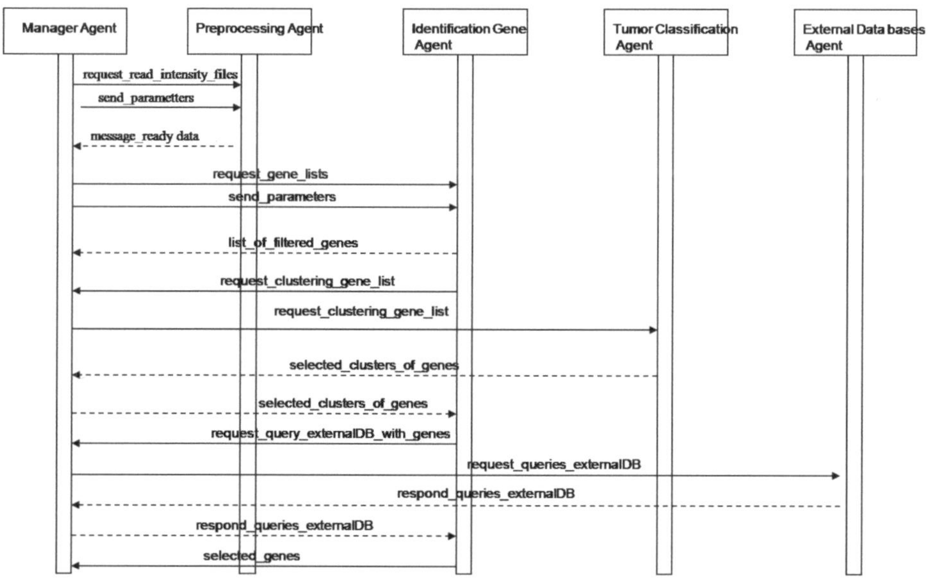

Fig. 2. An example of the sequence of messages to identification of genes. The agents send and receive messages with the manager agent when other requires something to another agent

4.1.3 Tumor classification agent

The goal of this agent is grouping the microarray samples, i.e. control and cases, as well as the identification of cancer type and tumor variants. For creation of groups in the samples, the agent uses machine learning, clustering methods like self-organizing maps (SOM) (Tamayo. 1999), vector quantization (VQ) , fuzzy k-means (c-means) (Dembelé , 2003; Wang 2003) and principal component analysis (PCA) (Price, 2006).

If the request for classification of samples comes from the gene identification agent, the tumor classification agent must review if the list of selected genes could classify in control and cases the samples. In this case the agent uses clustering methods and should select the lists of genes with less misclassification samples.

If the request of classification samples is the main goal of the user of MAS-GEN, the agent must find the clusters with the patters of samples, which could represent variants of cancer type. Once one has groups of tumors, another task of this agent should be to indicate what kind of tumor represents a new sample, which helps to determine accurate treatment.

4.1.4 Database agent

The goal of this agent is gathering knowledge about the identified genes. There are several databases that give access to genomical information through the Internet that will help in the characterization of genes to identify the relation between a gene and diseases. This agent will execute the queries to the external databases, and will standardize the results.

With the knowledge of the genes that this agent gets, the gene identification agent should verify the relevance of the genes, i.e. in a biological process, in a biological function, about the disease of the study

4.1.5 Manager agent

The manager agent coordinates all activities of the multi-agent system. It does the planning for the overall solution and distributes tasks among all agents, according to their specialization. The communication that is required between the agents is through this agent, since it is responsible for sending and receiving messages among the agents, the other agents can not interchange messages directly. Each operational agent only has permissions to send and receive messages with the manager agent, they can not access directly any other agents in the system.

At the request of the user the manager agent plans the general task that each must do. The manager agent organizes and coordinates the cooperation of all agents.

The other agents plan and execute their tasks in an autonomous fashion. The manager agent waits for queries or results of other agents and the user.

We had decided on a centralized architecture for MAS-GEN due to the small number of processes that may be involved all our agents; rather than an architecture where different actors could negotiate among themselves solutions.

4.1.6 Agent ontology

The agents have an ontology about their domain, they need to use the same language to interchange knowledge about genes, diseases or genomic words. The ontology defines the structure of messages that indicate the request to another agent and the answer, also defines the concepts about the problem domain.

For the database agent the ontology is very important because it has to communicate via Web to genomical databases and gets the knowledge about genes, searches and gathers relevant information to make decisions by other agent like the gene identification agent. Actually most genes do not have a unique name or identification, according to the database then it is important to have an ontology to find information in different sources in the Internet.

Example of ontology:

Concept Gene:

Their attributes or fields of its structures are: ID, symbol, source_information, chromosome, pahways, disease relation and more.

4.2 Responsibilities of the agents

The reponsibilities assigned to each agent of MAS-GEN are in table 1.

Agent	Responsibilities
Preprocessing Agent	Read data files Data normalization Statistical tests Data format Local planning Send/receive messages
Gene Identification Agent	Create lists of genes Filter of genes Clustering of genes Request information of genes Characterization of genes Send/receive messages
Tumor Classification Agent	Find patterns of samples Clustering of samples Evaluate clusters of genes Classification of new samples Local planning Send/receive messages
External Data Base Agent	Communicate with external databases of genes Get information of genes from databases of genes Local planning Send/receive messages
Manager Agent	Coordinate other agents Global planning Communication with the user Show the results Send/receive messages

Table 1. Responsibilities of agents in MAS-GEN

5. A case study

5.1 Data set

The multi-agent system for gene expression analysis has been used to help identification of relevant genes related to cervical cancer.

Data of gene expression was generated using the Affymetrix HGFocus GenChip of mRNA that contains ~8600 genes. The sample taken from 41 Mexican women with diagnostic of cervical cancer and from 12 controls (from women without cervical cancer). All tumors correspond to Human Papillomavirus 16 (HPV16) infection that represents the most important risk factor for the development of cervical cancer and are linked to a high incidence of cervical cancer in Mexico and HPV16 is the most frequently detected (50%) worldwide (Sanjosé, 2007).

The experiments to identify the involved genes in the process of cervical cancer using the multi-agent system, requires the cooperation of all agents of the system. In the sequential graph of figure 2. there are interchange requests among the operational agents via manager agent. MAS-GEN can perform various experiments with the data with minimal user intervention.

The manager agent does the overall planning with different configurations of methods or tasks to be executed by operational agents. That is the overall planning is composed of sub-plans in which combines the types of normalization of data, statistical tests for filtering, clustering methods to group genes, and/or samples and databases for characterization of genes.

The user can obtain results with different lists of genes found as relevant by all these sub-plans. MAS-GEN helps to identify the genes that occurred more relevance easily.

This does not mean that the user can not interact in the process. The user could also select the processes that are considered appropriate for analysing gene expression. Also MAS-GEN can help those researchers unexperted.

Here are some results obtained for gene expression analysis using data from samples of cervical cancer with MAS-GEN.

5.2 Results

In figure 3 there are some tables that present to the user the results of gene expression analysis with MAS-GEN. The presentation of results is through the manager agent, according the information could use tables and charts.

The results presented in tables seen as 3a, show the clusters created with a selected list of genes. The gene identification agent selects the lists of genes and checks on collaboration with the tumor classification agent the capacity of genes to divide the samples in the basic groups: control and cases. In 3a, there are 3 tables of this way, one for each cluster method: SOM, VQ and c-means. In this case can see VQ and c-means are the better methods to classify the samples with fewer mistakes.

In 3b, we reduced the number of dimenssions of the samples, to 2dim, in order to create a graphic to visualize the separation of samples. We used the 2 principal components generated by PCA method. In the graphic it is clear the separation between this 2 basic kinds of samples:tumor and controls.

The table 3c shows the user see the results given by the SAM statistical method, to find the differentially expressed genes.

Finally, the system can create graphics like boxplot and histogram to see the distribution of data and also a specific normality graph.

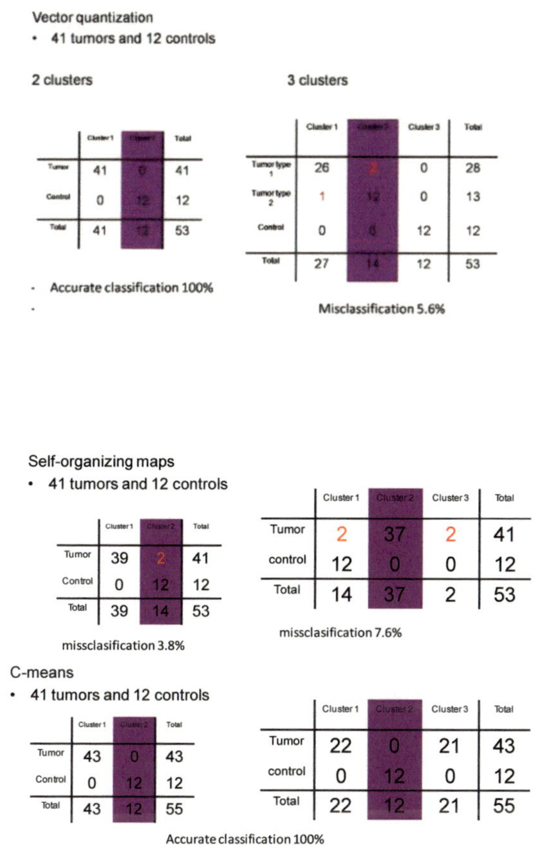

a) Sample classification with VQ, SOM and C-means clustering

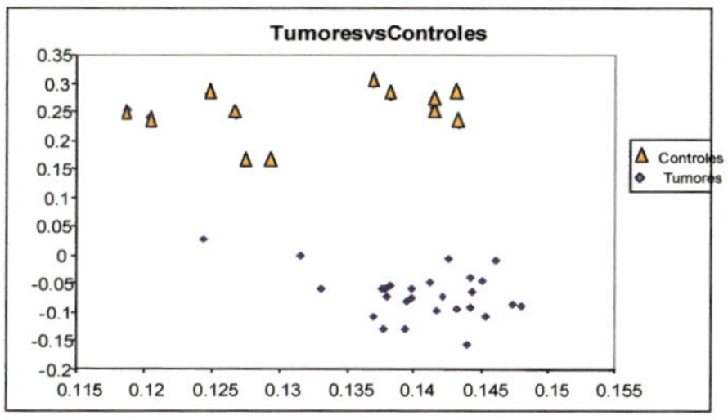

b) Sample classification with PCA

Genes	dvalue
Gene 1	22.2062528
Gene 2	21.7209105
Gene 3	20.0554556
Gene 4	18.315625
Gene 5	17.9860076
Gene 6	17.4859484
Gene 7	17.0050989
Gene 8	16.6034879
Gene 9	16.3210851
Gene 10	16.2168375

c) List of 10 better genes filtered with SAM

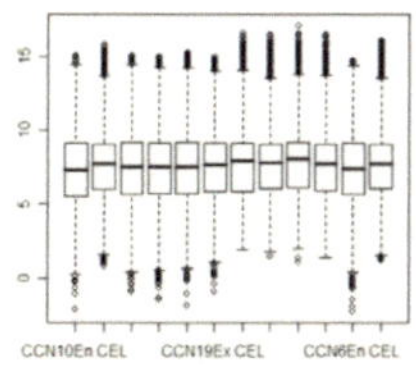

d) Box-plots of controls

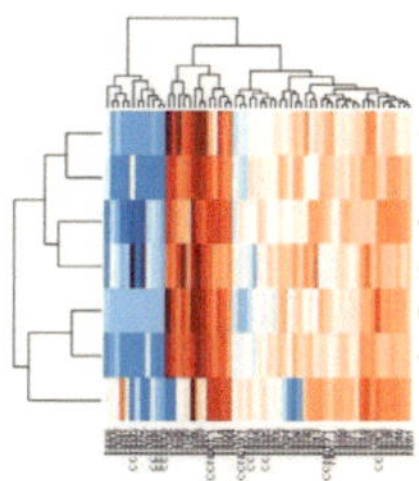

e) dendogram of genes

Fig. 3. Examples of result presentation to user from MAS-GEN

Another clustering method, the hierarchical dendogram to join up samples or genes.

The user could see the results of the better lists of genes, with the information about the capacity of sample classification, characterization of genes with queries of DB agent. The knowledge given by MAS-GEN allows to the user to support the decision of selected genes.

6. Acknowledgments

This work was supported by PAPIIT-DGAPA UNAM under Grant IN-107609, by IIMAS-UNAM and Hospital General de México.

7. Conclusions

The multi-agent system is a tool that helps biologists and medical teams responsible for the analysis of gene expression to better understand the genetic details of disease. MAS-GEN provides a comprehensive and flexible tool for performing various procedures instead of using several different software applications representing an investment of users time and adaptation of their data to those applications. In addition, with MAS the decision-making and analysis flows in an automated fashion via the manager agent.

Distributing the analysis into pre-processing methods, data filtering, machine learning, and presentation and display of results provide a versatile system that can be conveniently adapted to the rapidly changing area of genomic bioinformatics. The modular architecture of independent multi-agent software allows for straight forward implementation of procedural changes without troublesome dependency-related software conflicts. This flexibility also insures that software development effort will not become obsolete.

The analysis of gene expression is feasible through a multi-agent collaboration with the operational agents specializing in distributed tasks of data preprocessing, gene identification, classification of tumors, and database management. A single management agent assigns tasks and controls data flow, simplying the human interaction with the system. Some of the operational agent work can be executed in parallel because the agents have sufficient independence.

This system further facilitates and simplifies the completion of the analysis of gene expression because it automates the steps the researcher performs for the complete task of identification of genes and classification of samples. Transparent to the user are the tasks to be performed and the decisions taken to find genes that may differ in certain samples or to create pools of data to be used later. Having already defined filter parameters and types of tests to apply, the user only has to provide the files containing the microarray data obtained from the Affymetrix platform and identify the samples as cases or controls. The system uses the knowledge from expert analyses of gene expression so that others can perform these tasks at the same level of expertise..

With this type of multi-agent system for the analysis of gene expression it is like using a single software tool to complete the expert analysis of genes without user intervention. The system will make decisions in a similar way as do the genomics specialists.

The implementation of the agents using Java and CLIPS gives flexibility to their development and provides simplicity compared with existing software tools that require deployment of more staff to administer the system. MAS-GEN offers an effective expert and simplified solution that focuses only on administering the single managing agent for complete gene expression analysis.

8. References

Bergeron B., *Bioinformatics Computing*, Prentice Hall, USA, 2002

Dembelé, D., et al., Fuzzy C-means method for clustering microarray data, *Bioinformatics* 2003, 973-980

Eisen M, et al., Cluster analysis and display of genome-wide expression patterns, *Proc Natl Acad Sci U S A*. 1998, 14863-8.

Price A., et al., Principal components analysis corrects for stratification in genome-wide association studies, *Nature at Genet*. 2006, 904-9.

Irizarry R. et al.: Exploration, normalization, and summaries of high density oligonucleotide array probe level data. *Biostat.*, 2003.

Jennings N. An Agent-Based Approach for Building Complex Software Systems. *Communications of the ACM*, Vol 44, No4, 2001.

Karasavvas, K., Burger, A., Baldock, R., A multi-agent bioinformatics integration systems with adjustable autonomy, *Journal of Biomedical Informatics*, No. 37, 205-219, 2004.

Keele, J., Software agents in molecular computational bioloy. *Briefing in Bioinformatics*, vol. 6, n.4, 370-379, 2005

Lam, H., Vazquez, M., Junega, B., Gene expression analysis in multi-agent environment, *International Transactions on Systems Science and Applications*, Vol 1, 2006.

Lazcano-Ponce E, *Innovation in cervical cancer prevention and control in Mexico.* Arch Med Res. 2009 Aug; 40(6):486-92. Review

Luck, M., Merelli, E., Agents in bioinformatic, *Knowledge Engineering Review*, Vol. 20, Num. 2 117-125, Cambridge University Press, 2005.

Márquez E., Savage J., Espinosa A., Berumen J., Lemaitre C., Gene expression analysis for tumor classification using vector quantization, *Third IAPR International Conference on Pattern Recognition in Bioinformatics* (PRIB 2008)

Merelli, E.,. Validating MAS models with mutations. In *Proceedings of the First International Workshop on Multi-agent systems for Medicine, Computational biology and Bioinformatics*. AAMAS, 2005.

Moreau, L., Miles, S., Goble, C., On the use of agents in bioinformatics grid, *3rd International Symposium on Cluster Computing and the Grid*, 2003.

Quackenbush,J., *Computational analysis of microarray data, McMillan magazines, review*, junio 2001, 418-427

Štiglic, G, Kokol, P, Using Multi-Agent System for Gene Expression Classification, *Proceedings of the 26th Annual International Conference of the IEEE EMBS*, 2952-2955, 2004.

Tamayo, P., et al., Interpreting patterns of gene expression with self-organizing maps: methods and application to hematopoietic differentiation, *Proc Natl Acad Sci*, Vol. 96, No. 6, 1999, pp. 2907-2912.

Tusher V., et al., Significance analysis of microarrays applied to the ionizing radiation response. *Proc Natl Acad Sci U S A* 2001, 5116-5121

Wang, J. et al., Tumor classification and marker gene prediction by feature selection and fuzzy c-means clustering using microarray data, *BMC Bioinformatics*, 2003

20

Collecting and Classifying Large Scale Data to Build an Adaptive and Collective Memory: a Case Study in e-Health for a Pro-active Management

Singer Nicolas, Trouilhet Sylvie, Rammal Ali and Pécatte Jean-Marie
Information Systems and Health Team
University of Toulouse, CUFR Champollion, IRIT
Avenue Pompidou 81100 Castres
France

1. Introduction

E pluribus unum... this could be the motto of our research. Indeed, if similar applications cooperated, they would all benefit and develop their knowledge. For example, when searching for information on the Web, it would be useful to find a user who had similar concerns and communicate with them via a social network. This concern has led to collaborative web tools such as Mawa (Singer & *al*, 2005). This web assistant can help a user by gathering documents in relation to user's own interests.

However in several domains, collective tools don't yet exist. There are three main reasons for this:

- Firstly, information is highly distributed and grows in a wide environment; therefore a suitable tool must take this large scale into account,
- Secondly, information changes; new data occurs and some data can become obsolete; no centralized entity can support this scalability,
- And finally, the privacy of data must sometimes be respected, making some data incomplete or anonymous.

In such situations, the adoption of a multi-agent architecture is a suitable choice because it can support the distributed nature of input data and the need for scalability. Multi-agent technology allows the development of large scale systems which can be automatically deployed in an open environment. It has proved its adequacy in many health problems that require coordination of a lot of entities and information (Moreno & Nealon, 2003), (Isern & *al*, 2010). It can also be helpful in widespread applications such as smart monitoring for physical infrastructures. Indeed, today precise knowledge about the current condition of the infrastructure is not available. This is not due to a lack of measurements but rather to a lack of an integrated interpretation of the available information. As wrote Florian Fuchs, "what is missing today, however, is the intelligence for making use of the available data"(Fuchs & *al*, 2010).

Large scale and dynamic applications require protocols for task repartition and really cooperative resolution. We propose a multi-agent model which collects and synthesizes data

with respect to these constraints. It uses a distributed unsupervised classification. Furthermore, employing the multi-agent paradigm, it addresses privacy by keeping information local to agents, while aggregated data is distributed between agent groups.
A system based on this model is composed of agents, each having as a task to classify a subset of data, eventually incomplete. They communicate with each other to aggregate partial results and constitute a distributed global classification which can be considered as a macroscopic view. Such a system can be deployed in an open environment because new agents can be automatically created.
This chapter is divided into three sections. In the first, we present the context: how to find similarities in a dynamic environment, between user-centric applications with privacy problem and incomplete data. We also describe related works in multi-agent classification. Our multi-agent model is described in section 3. Section 4 presents an experiment in a home care application. We talk about the results and we explain the benefits of such an application.

2. Multi-agent classification

2.1 Relevance of distributed classification

The problem of classification consists in placing objects, each having a set of attributes, into clusters. The clustering method uses some distance measure between attributes. Clustering is usually studied as a centralized problem. But in situations described in the introduction, classical methods cannot be implemented:

- In some cases, the available classes cannot be anticipatively identified. Moreover, data are dynamic; some objects can disappear or new can appear. Thus, supervised classification is not relevant; the classification method must be adaptive.
- Many applications have a vertical distribution or a horizontal one. A distribution is vertical when the distribution is about the attributes of objects. Some attributes of an object can be unknown by a classifier. A distribution is horizontal when the distribution is about the objects. Each group needs a distinct classifier, and several classifiers are also necessary. So they have to exchange their results.
- In an open and large environment, the use of a single classifier may delay the process. In this context, it becomes necessary to think about hybrid methods able to review classes set while running and eventually to modify them by introducing some new classes or deleting obsolete ones. Furthermore, classification should stay as accurate as possible, even if some attributes are not available.

The dynamic clustering has been introduced some years ago (Lecoeuche & Lurette, 2003). It supports the problem of non-stationary data: processing such data type means having evolving classes. In addition, systems using different classifiers can offer complementary information about patterns to be classified. They are usually based on neural network architectures. They do not consider both vertical and horizontal distribution of large object sets.
Some previous studies on clustering have proposed a multi-agent system as a basis of a decentralized approach. We consider four previous works on multi-agent classification. SAMARAH uses an unsupervised collaborative multi-strategy method to enhance classification. NeurAge tackles the problem of vertical distribution. In the work done by S. Mukhopadhyay, acquaintance lists allow the system to choose the most relevant agents for a

given service. And finally, the research by Quteishat is about negotiation between classifier agents. We underline how our method is positioned compared to them.

2.2 Related works, similarities and originality

SAMARAH is a multi-agent hybrid learning system that uses a collaborative multi-strategical clustering (Gançarski & Wemmert, 2007). It is based on the idea that the information offered by different classifiers about objects is complementary. And thus the combination of different classification methods may increase their efficiency and accuracy. The system integrates different kinds of unsupervised classification methods and gives a set of classes as result. Finally, by combining the agents' answers, a common result is produced representing a consensus among the information obtained by each agent. To solve a local conflict, two agents can use some operators like split, merge or reclassify. This method of combination of classifiers enables many classification methods to collaborate (Forestier & *al*, 2008).

With its collaborative algorithm, this approach is close to ours: the agents work together in a cooperative way through a mutual refinement of their respective partitions. But the aim is different: SAMARAH allows one to carry out classification of complex objects with a lot of attributes (like heterogeneous images) to improve classification (like scene understanding). Objects are complex but agents must know all the attributes of each object.

NeurAge, and its successor ClassAge, are multi-classifiers systems, composed of several neural agents having the same goal (Santana & *al*, 2006). When a pattern is shown to the system, all agents produce their outputs. Then, they communicate among themselves in order to reach a common result. They use a confidence based negotiation method in several rounds. For all attributes, agents calculate the training mean: an agent A checks the information given by another agent B for a test pattern. After checking, the confidence degree of A toward B can be decreased. So, the attacked agent B can quit the round. The agent with the highest confidence degree is said to be the most suitable one to classify the test pattern. This method uses a vertical data distribution in which each agent has to classify an unknown pattern based on a subset of the attributes. In the experimental work, the system is composed of five agents. The NeurAge system was extended, allowing the use of non neural agents. The features of both systems are the same (Canuto & *al*, 2008).

A distributed method is proposed, but two main differences exist between the NeurAge/ClassAge approach and ours. NeurAge/ClassAge is not suitable in an open environment where the number of classes can evolve. The problem solving is not collective because one classifier is chosen to correctly classify the input pattern.

In (Peng & *al*, 2001), authors explain the rational for using multi-agent classifier system for text documents and compare the single-agent classifier approach with a multi-agent classifier one in terms of computation time and quality of classification. Their method relies upon the creation of an interconnected environment of agents. In this environment, all agents compute a classification of their own documents and send these documents to other agents if their classification is unsuccessful (that is if the agent's thesaurus does not match any words of the document). Acquaintance lists are dynamically adapted and allow the system to choose the most relevant agent for a given service. The time tests show that the multi-agent classification is relevant in the case of a big thesaurus. This method is also much more flexible in allowing a new thesaurus to be smoothly introduced in the system. Finally fault tolerance and privacy (of the thesaurus) are better implemented (Mukhopadhyay & *al*,

2003). As in Neurage, the classification is not truly collective. Each agent makes its own complete classification and the best one is chosen.
Quteishat and his team have developed a Multi-Agent Classifier system based on the Trust-Negotiation-Communication model (Quteishat & al, 2010). The proposed TNC-based MAC system consists of an ensemble of neural network-based classifiers. The agents are organized hierarchically: parent agent, team managers and team member. Agents use a negotiation method to assign a class to an input sample. Each agent within the team gives a prediction of the output class and a trust value. Then, the team manager selects the prediction with the highest trust value and gives its prediction to the parent agent. Each prediction has a trust value, a reputation value, and a confidence factor. The parent agent makes a final decision and assigns a predicted output class for the input sample. In the experiment, there are two agent teams: the first is the Fuzzy Min-Max agent team and the second is the Fuzzy ARTMAP agent team (Quteishat & al, 2009).
If we compare TNC-based MAC system and ours, both use a similar protocol; agents are grouped and use a multi-stage cooperation (intra group and inter group). So with a growing number of teams, the system can be spread in a wide application. It also has the ability to add new classes online. But, the developed auction method does not permit a collective decision making. Indeed, only a response is chosen by the centralizer agent.

	Samarah	**NeurAge**	**Mukhopadhyay's system**	**TNC-based MAC system**
Type of distribution	no data distribution	vertical distribution	distribution of the thesaurus	no data distribution
Classification method	unsupervised classification method	multi-layer perceptron and radial basis functions	unsupervised clustering algorithm with a learning stage	supervised classification network
Agent's skills	K-means algorithm	distribution of the methods: each agent has a given method	all agent have the same skill, they are identical except for the thesaurus	incremental learning method such as FMM
Type of cooperation	collective answer	negotiation between agents	answer of the most competent	auction method for negotiation
Type of application	image interpretation	generic system	text classification	industrial applications (power generation plant)
Dynamics in an open environment	yes	no	yes (reconfiguration of acquaintances)	yes

Table 1. Related studies, comparative analyse

Table 1 gives a synthetic view of these systems. We retained six features we consider important and which are as below for our system:

Type of distribution	**Classification method**	**Agent's skills**
vertical and/or horizontal with overlaps	unsupervised classification	any classification method
Type of cooperation	**Type of application**	**Dynamics in an open environment**
collective answer	e-health (but can be applied in other domain)	yes (adding online new agent and new class)

The aim of our study is not to propose a more efficient method or to improve the performance of existing ones. We rather adapt classical classifiers to increase the number of situations in which they can be relevant and propose a fault-tolerant and flexible model. So we use a collaborative society of agents that use existing algorithms to calculate partial classifications (method based on the K-nearest neighbours, decision trees, ISODATA clustering…) and that cooperate to combine these individual results.

Our system must have two essential characteristics. The first is the dynamic evolution of classifications - if needed, new objects can be added at any moment, and the system is able to reconfigure its classes and generate new classification patterns. The second is that the system is generic with respect to attributes and thus is able to function on any type of application having strongly distributed entries. We introduce below a classification actually multi-agent because the classification result is not the work of a simple entity (or agent), but really a collective work.

3. A multi-agent model for collecting and classifying large scale data

The model we have developed is composed of three elements: the agents, objects and attributes. An agent is itself composed of knowledge, behaviour and communication skills. The knowledge is a sub-set of objects i.e. evolutionary and distributed data. Each object is described with a non-exhaustive list of attributes.

The agent's skill is a classical classification method. It allows the construction of local partitions. To share its local results, an agent uses a restricted cooperation protocol. A pre-treatment of input data is needed before starting the classification. Indeed, this phase depends on the application domain. A "distributor" agent computes the most adequate settings and sets the weights of attributes. Figure 1 presents this agent-based architecture.

3.1 A multi-agent classification in three stages

Let $A_1, \ldots, A_n$ be agents of the system,$P_1, \ldots, P_m$ be objects to classify, and $X_1, \ldots, X_r$ be numerical attributes of the objects. Each attribute X_j has a weight W_j. Our classification method is composed of three stages.

The first step is the construction of clusters by applying a local classification: A classification agent Ai knows the values of a subset of attributes concerning several objects. By using the unsupervised classification algorithm ISODATA it builds clusters. Each cluster is characterized by a mid-vector calculated by ISODATA. The ISODATA algorithm is similar to the kmeans algorithm, but it allows a dynamic number of clusters while the k-means assumes that the number of clusters is known *a priori* (for a description of the ISODATA algorithm, see (Memarsadeghi & *al*, 2006)).

The second step is the call for participation and the acquaintance group constitution. It aims to form groups of agents to generalize the classification. To constitute groups:

1. A_i sends its attributes to other agents;
2. A_i receives the attributes of other agents;
3. For each other agent, A_i calculates the sum of the weights of common attributes (calling S_1), and the sum of the weights of non-common attributes (calling S_2);
4. If $S_1 >= S_2$, A_i responds to the agent concerned and they become member of the same group;
5. The agents of a group are those that achieved correspondence in the previous step.

The third and last step is the generalization of the classification. The agents of a group compute a new classification using the method described in the next section.

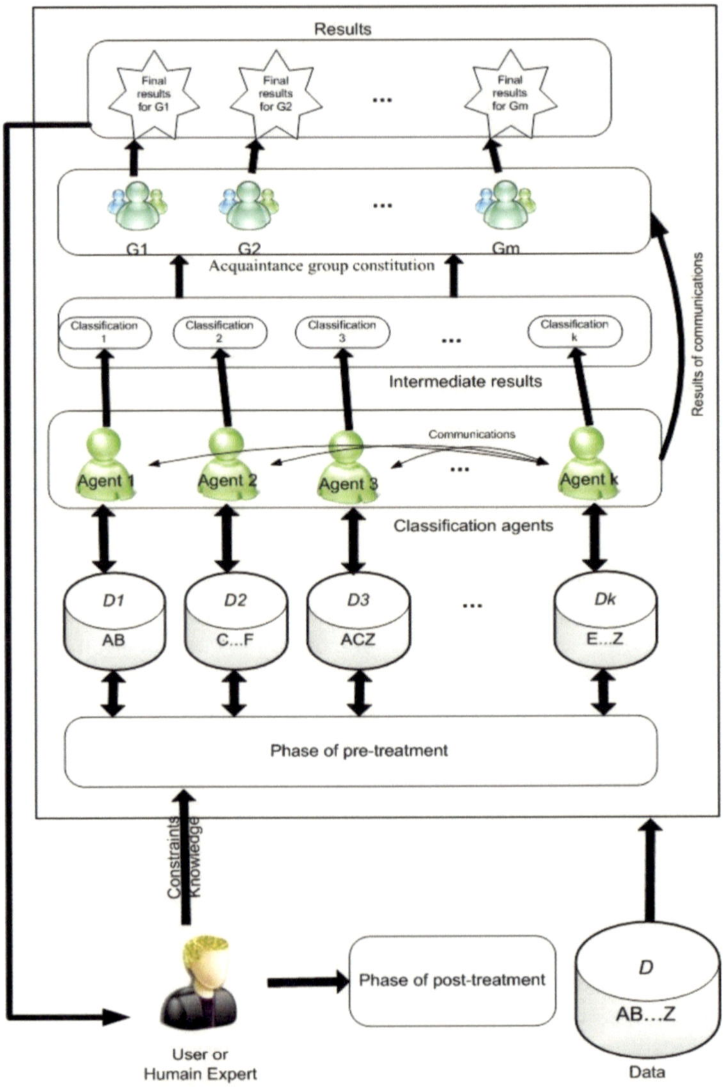

Fig. 1. The multi-agent architecture

3.2 Clustering with undefined values

In this section, we tackle the problem of clustering a set of points in multidimensional space where some coordinates (dimensions) are undefined. It can happen for example if some points have a missing coordinate because of the input method, or if the points have different dimensions (that is we try to classify a point in a *k1*-dimensional space with a point in a *k2*-dimensional space, with *k1* different from *k2*). Traditional clustering methods, like k-means or ISODATA, need all coordinates to properly run. Measuring distances between points and calculating mid-vector values are at the heart of these classical algorithms. We propose to adapt the way these algorithms compute their values to handle the case where some data is undefined. We call it "heterogeneous clustering".

More formally, given a set of points (x_1, x_2, ..., x_n), where each observation is a *d*-dimensional real vector, clustering these points aims to partition the n points into k sets ($k < n$) $S = \{S_1, S_2, \ldots, S_k\}$ with some objectives to achieve, like for example minimizing the sum of distances between points inside the same set. We focus here on two well-known clustering algorithms: k-mean and ISODATA. These two algorithms heavily rely on vector Euclidian length and distance computing. For example here is an overview of the four steps of the k-mean algorithm:

Step 1. Begin with a decision on the value of k = number of clusters

Step 2. Put any initial partition that classifies the data into k clusters.

Step 3. Take each point in sequence and **compute its distance from the centroid** of each of the clusters. If a point is not currently in the cluster with the closest centroid, switch this point to that cluster and **update the centroid** of the cluster gaining the new point and the cluster losing the point.

Step 4. Repeat step 3 until convergence is achieved, that is until a pass through the points causes no new assignments.

The two main operations of this algorithm are the computing of the distance between a point and his centroid and updating the centroid in computing the average value of each coordinate of the points belonging to it.

Let $x_i = (x_{i1}, x_{i2}, \ldots, x_{id})$ be a point treated as a vector in a real d-dimensional space. We call x_{in} the nth coordinate of x_i. The distance between two points x_i and x_j is traditionally defined as:

$$d(x_i, x_j) = \sqrt{\sum_{k=1}^{d} (x_{ik} - x_{jk})^2}$$

Of course this distance cannot be compute if one of the x_{ik} or x_{jk} is unknown. We propose to adapt the calculation method to handle the case where x_i and x_j have some undefined coordinates.

Let c_i be the set of defined coordinates of x_i and let c_j be the set of defined coordinates of x_j. We defined the new distance as

$$d(x_i, x_j) = \sqrt{\sum_{k \in c_i \cap c_j} (x_{ik} - x_{jk})^2}$$

That is, the new distance takes only into account the common coordinates of x_i and x_j. If the set of common coordinates is empty, the distance is undefined. For this reason, we state that

points must at least share one common defined coordinate. Namely, one coordinate i exists, where x_i is known for all points. If this is not the case, clustering cannot be done.
To compute the centroid vector V of a set of n points S, traditional algorithms used the following calculation:

$$V_i = \frac{1}{n}\sqrt{\sum_{x \in S} x_i} \quad \text{where } i \text{ is the } i^{th} \text{ coordinate of vector } V.$$

To adapt to the fact that some x_i are unknown we change this calculation in the following way: let n' be the number of points where the coordinate i is defined, and be S' the set of this points. The new i^{th} coordinate of the centroid vector is computed with:

$$V_i = \frac{1}{n'}\sqrt{\sum_{x \in S'} x_i}$$

That is to calculate the ith coordinate of the centroid vector, we average the ith coordinates of all points where this coordinate is known. If the S' set is empty, the ith coordinate of the vector is undefined. Because we have stated that points must share one known coordinate in common, we are sure that at least one coordinate of the centroid vector is defined.
To resume, when a calculation needs to be made on an undefined coordinate, the corresponding point is neutralized. In a distance operation, this means that the distance to this point coordinate counts as zero. In a statistical operation (like computing an average) this means that this point does not count in the number of samples.
At first it seems that these new calculation methods will lead to weird or inconsistent results. But in a context where some coordinates are somehow linked to others and where the set of defined coordinates is bigger that the undefined one, our method makes it possible to force a clustering that will have be impossible with the traditional clustering algorithms, and that leads to informative results as shown in the experimentation section.
However, we can illustrate how our modifications impact clustering on the simple example below.
We consider a data set composed of two points P_1 and P_2 defined in a three dimensional space and two points P_3 and P_4 defined in a two dimensional space. The coordinates of these points are: P_1 {0, 1, 1}, P_2 {0, 3, 1}, P_3 {0, undef, 1} and P_4 {0, undef, 5}.
We can see that the second coordinate of points P3 and P4 is undefined, and that coordinates one and three are defined for all points (so our constraint of at least one defined coordinate for all points is verified). If we cluster this four points with the k-mean algorithm (run several times to avoid the local optimum problem) and a number of cluster parameter of two we obtain:

Cluster 1 mid-vector {0, 2, 1}	**Cluster 2** mid-vector {0, undef, 4}
P_1 [0, 1, 1], P_2 [0, 3, 1], P_3 [0, undef,1]	P_4 [0, undef, 4]

The second coordinate of Cluster 2 mid-vector is undefined because it contains only one point where the same coordinate is undefined. All coordinates of cluster 1 mid-vector are defined because the three points it contains defined at least one time each coordinate.

If we applied our calculation method to the ISODATA algorithm with a min distance between clusters of 1, a max distance in clusters of 0.3 and a max number of clusters of 4, we obtain:

Cluster 1 mid-vector {0, 1, 1}	**Cluster 2** mid-vector {0, undef, 4}	**Cluster 3** mid-vector {0, 3, 1}
P_1 [0, 1, 1], P_3 [0, undef,1]	P_4 [0, undef, 4]	P_2 [0, 3, 1]

We don't have tried yet to extend our method to other clustering algorithms because the ISODATA and k-mean satisfy our needs in this applicative context. However there is no reason why our methodology could not be applied to other type of clustering algorithms, as long as they are approximation for the k-center problems, k-median problems or k-means problems.

3.3 Step by step example

Points/ Attributes	P_1	P_2	P_3	P_4	P_5	P_6	P_7	P_8	P_9	P_{10}
X_1	1	2	6	2	6	-	3	-	7	-
X_2	2	2	5	3	4	7	-	5	-	1
X_3	3	1	4	4	1	-	5	-	4	-
X_4	-	5	-	4	-	1	3	7	3	7
X_5	4	-	5	-	7	2	6	5	2	5
X_6	-	3	-	7	-	3	7	1	1	3

Table 2. A set of ten points with some known and unknown attributes

Thereafter we apply our proposal on an example with 4 agents, 10 points and 6 attributes. We consider that after the phase of pre-treatment, agent A_1 knows the values of attributes X_1, X_2 and X_3 for points P_1, P_2, P_3, P_4, and P_5. Agent A_2 knows the values of attributes X_4, X_5, and X_6 for points P_6, P_7, P_8, P_9, and P_{10}. Agent A_3 knows the values of attributes X_1, X_3, and X_5 for points P_1, P_3, P_5, P_7, and P_9. Finally agent A_4 knows the values of attributes X_2, X_4, and X_6 for points P_2, P_4, P_6, P_8, and P_{10}. To clarify the example, we state that the weight of each attribute is one (Table 2).

By applying a local classification method (in our case ISODATA) each agent builds its partition. Each class is characterized by a mid-vector calculated by ISODATA. The result of the local classification is:

Agent A_1:
C_1={P_3}, mid-vector {X_1=6; X_2=5; X_3= 4}
C_2={P_1, P_2} ,mid-vector {X_1=1.5; X_2=2; X_3=2}
C_3={P_4} ,mid-vector {X_1=2; X_2=3; X_3=4}
C_4={P_5} ,mid-vector {X_1=6; X_2=4; X_3=1}

Agent A_2:
C_1={P_8} ,mid-vector {X_4=7; X_5=5; X_6=1}
C_2={P_{10}} ,mid-vector {X_4=7; X_5=5; X_6=3}
C_3={P_7} ,mid-vector {X_4=3; X_5=6; X_6=7}
C_4={P_6, P_9} ,mid-vector {X_4=2; X_5=2; X_6=2}

Agent A_3:
C_1={P_3, P_9}, mid-vector {X_1=6.5; X_3=4; X_5=5}
C_2={P_1}, mid-vector {X_1=1; X_3=3; X_5=4}
C_3={P_5}, mid-vector {X_1=6; X_3=1; X_5=7}
C_4={P_7}, mid-vector {X_1=3; X_3=5; X_5=6}

Agent A_4:
C_1={P_4}, mid-vector {X_2=3; X_4=4; X_6=7}
C_2={P_2, P_{10}}, mid-vector {X_2=1.5; X_4=6; X_6= 3}
C_3={P_8}, mid-vector {X_2=7; X_4=5; X_6=1}
C_4={P_6}, mid-vector {X_2=7; X_4=1; X_6=3}

According to the call for participation algorithm described in section 3.1, we compute that there are two groups of agents. The first group contains A_1 and A_3 (they share the X_1 and X_2 attributes), and the second group contains A_2 and A_4 (they share the X_4 and X_6 attributes). By applying the method described in 3.2, each group of agents computes a new classification:

Group A_1, A_3:
C_1 = {P_1, P_2, P_4} with mid-vector {X_1 =1.67; X_2 = 2.33; X_3 = 2.67; X_5=4}
C_2 = {P_3, P_7} with mid-vector {X_1 = 4.5; X_2 = 5; X_3 = 4.5; X_5=5.5}
C_3= {P_5} with mid-vector {X_1 = 6; X_2 = 4; X_3 = 1; X_5=7}
C_4= {P_9} with mid-vector {X_1 = 6; X_2 = undef; X_3 = 4; X_5=2}

Group A_2, A_4:
C_1 = {P_8} with mid-vector {X_2 =5; X_4 = 7; X_5 = 5; X_6=1}
C_2 = {P_4, P_7} with mid-vector {X_2 = 3; X_4 = 3.5; X_5 = 6; X_6=7}
C_3= {P_2, P_{10}} with mid-vector {X_2 = 1.5; X_4 = 6; X_5 = 5; X_6=3}
C_4= {P_6, P_9} with mid-vector {X_2 = 7; X_4 = 2; X_5 = 2; X_6=2}

Finally, group A_1, A_3 and group A_2, A_4 form a new group because they share the X_2 and X_5 attributes, and the final classification compute by this new group is:
C_1 = {P_4} with mid-vector {X_1=2; X_2 =3; X_3=4; X_4 = 4; X_5=undef; X_6=7}
C_2 = {P_7} with mid-vector {X_1=3; X_2=undef; X_3=5; X_4=3; X_5=6; X_6=7}
C_3= {P_3, P_5, P_8, P_9} with mid-vector {X_1=6.33; X_2=4.67; X_3=3; X_4=5; X_5=4.75; X_6=1}
C_4= {P_1, P_2, P_6, P_{10}} with mid-vector {X_1=1.5; X_2=3; X_3=2; X_4=4.33, X_5=3.67; X_6=3}

4. Experimentation in e-health for a pro-active management

We applied the multi-agent model in an e-health application. We aim to help professional home care teams by increasing the number of elderly people looked after in their home with an adaptive and non-intrusive remote assistance. Thanks to our multi-agent approach, home monitoring is tackled in a collective and cooperative way. This application differs from other home care systems because it is centered on groups instead on individuals (Singer & *al*, 2010).

Patterns are used to estimate the state of elderly people, to link them to their community, and to try to forecast the evolution of their activity.

The global classification can be seen as a super classification where people are gathered into new clusters. The meaning of a cluster is obtained by comparing the state of people that belong to it. For example, as seen later in our experimentation, four classes emerge which one is the class of healthy people. Another interest is in the reduction of the number of sensors to install. If we find that two risks are inter related, then measuring the first is sufficient to anticipate the second. This reduction is beneficial to the private life of the person and is a way to cut down monitoring costs.

4.1 Meta monitoring application

The system is based on a variety of sensors carried by monitored people or installed in their homes. Those sensors are presence and movement sensors or medical measuring apparatus. Information coming from sensors is transformed into indicators. These Indicators are physiological data (blood pressure) or data about daily activities and positions (sleeping time). Their abstraction from raw data requires a software layer.

For our experimentation we have chosen to consider ten indicators over ten people. See Table 3 for the meaning of the indicators and Table 4 for their values for each people concerned by the experimentation. Let's note that values will be normalized between zero and one before clustering. Table 4 also indicates some characteristics of these people. Some are nocturnally overactive, others suffer from apathy during daytime, and one person has disorientation problems that lead to wandering behaviors. Other people are considered as "normal". If all goes well, our system will underline this classification throw his clustering method. To clarify the results, we state that the weight of each attribute is 1 (each attribute is equally important).

I_1	Corporal temperature (in Celsius)
I_2	Systolic blood pressure (in mmHg)
I_3	Sleeping time (in minutes)
I_4	Number of times the person gets out of bed in the night
I_5	Number of times the person goes to the toilet in a day
I_6	Time spent in the kitchen (in minutes)
I_7	Time spent in the living room (in minutes)
I_8	Number of times the person gets outdoor
I_9	Longest immobility daytime
I_{10}	Eating disorders (true or false)

Table 3. Indicators

Indicators are collected by data-processing agents constituting the system. Because several people living in different houses must be surveyed, a given indicator will not be systematically collected by the same agent. Similarly, two agents monitoring two different people can collect some indicators for the first and others for the second. There can also be some overlaps in the vertical and horizontal distributions. For example, two agents can collect the number of times the same person goes to the toilet. To sum up, an agent collects one or several indicators with the aim to detect and evaluate global risk patterns for one or several people.

In this experimentation, three agents Ai are used to collect the indicators of ten people P_i. Data are horizontally (indicators) and vertically (people) distributed. Agent A_1 collects indicators from number one to eight about people from number one to four. Agent A_2 is affected to people numbered five to seven and collects indicators numbered one to three and six to ten, and agent A_3 takes care of people numbered five to eight and collects indicators numbered three to ten. See Table 5 for an overview of this repartition.

The local, partial classification of each agent gives the results of Table 6. We used the ISODATA algorithm with parameters set as:

- Max number of clusters: 4
- Min number of points in a cluster: 1
- Max number of iteration: 10
- Max distance in a cluster : 0,3
- Min distance between two clusters : 1

Agent A_1 finds two clusters with P_4 isolated. Agent A_2 finds two clusters with P_5 isolated. Agent A_3 finds two clusters with P_8 isolated.

	P_1	P_2	P_3	P_4	P_5	P_6	P_7	P_8	P_9	P_{10}
	Nocturnally overactive			Daytime underactive		Normal people		Wand-ering	Normal people	
I_1	37,5	38	37	37,5	40	37,5	37	37,5	37	37
I_2	190	180	170	110	100	150	150	190	145	140
I_3	240	180	240	780	720	420	420	480	480	420
I_4	10	11	9	1	2	0	1	1	1	2
I_5	8	7	8	6	5	4	3	4	5	4
I_6	180	190	160	30	15	120	90	240	100	120
I_7	180	200	180	360	300	180	120	240	120	180
I_8	1	0	2	0	0	2	2	6	1	2
I_9	120	90	120	360	330	90	120	15	90	120
I_{10}	0	0	0	1	1	0	0	1	0	0

Table 4. Indicator values of ten people

Agents then use the restricted cooperation protocol described in section 3 (call for participation / acquaintance group constitution / heterogeneous classification). A consequence of our distribution is that the second step of our algorithm results in a single group containing all agents. Indeed each agent shares with another agent one commonly defined coordinate.

The unified classification is computed in merging the data of all agents and using the method described in section 3.1. Table 7 gives the result of this clustering.

A_1	P_1	P_2	P_3	P_4
I_1	37,5	38	37	37,5
I_2	190	180	170	110
I_3	240	180	240	780
I_4	10	11	9	1
I_5	8	7	8	6
I_6	180	190	160	30
I_7	180	200	180	360
I_8	1	0	2	0

A_2	P_5	P_6	P_7
I_1	40	37,5	37
I_2	100	150	150
I_3	720	420	420
I_6	15	120	90
I_7	300	180	120
I_8	0	2	2
I_9	330	90	120
I_{10}	1	0	0

A_3	P_8	P_9	P_{10}
I_3	480	480	420
I_4	1	1	2
I_5	4	5	4
I_6	240	100	120
I_7	240	120	180
I_8	6	1	2
I_9	15	90	120
I_{10}	1	0	0

Table 5. Agent repartition

	Agent A_1							
	I_1	I_2	I_3	I_4	I_5	I_6	I_7	I_8
C_1 (P_1,P_2,P_3)	0,17	0,89	0,07	0,91	0,93	0,72	0,28	0,17
C_2 (P_4)	0,17	0,11	1	0,09	0,60	0,07	1	0

	Agent A_2							
	I_1	I_2	I_3	I_6	I_7	I_8	I_9	I_{10}
C_1 (P_6,P_7)	0,08	0,56	0,40	0,40	0,13	0,33	0,26	0
C_2 (P_5)	1	0	0,90	0	0,75	0	0,91	1

	Agent A_3							
	I_3	I_4	I_5	I_6	I_7	I_8	I_9	I_{10}
C_1 (P_9,P_{10})	0,45	0,14	0,30	0,42	0,13	0,25	0,26	0
C_2 (P_8)	0,50	0,09	0,20	0,47	0,25	0,33	0,30	0

Table 6. Clustering results of each agent

	I_1	I_2	I_3	I_4	I_5	I_6	I_7	I_8	I_9	I_{10}
C_1 (P_4, P_5)	0,58	0,06	0,95	0,09	0,60	0,03	0,88	0	0,91	1
C_2 (P_1, P_2, P_3)	0,17	0,89	0,07	0,91	0,93	0,72	0,28	0,17	undef	undef
C_2 (P_6, P_7, P_9,P_{10})	0,08	0,56	0,43	0,14	0,30	0,41	0,13	0,29	0,26	0
C_2 (P_8)	undef	undef	0,50	0,09	0,20	1	0,50	1	0	1

Table 7. Final result of the multi-agent clustering

4.2 Analysis of results and discussion

One way to evaluate the efficiency of our system is to compare its results with a centralized clustering where all data are defined. If we apply the ISODATA algorithm to cluster our ten people monitored with the ten indicators known, we obtain the results of Table 8.

	I_1	I_2	I_3	I_4	I_5	I_6	I_7	I_8	I_9	I_{10}
C_1 (P_4, P_5)	0,58	0,06	0,95	0,14	0,50	0,03	0,88	0	0,96	1
C_2 (P_1, P_2, P_3)	0,17	0,89	0,07	0,91	0,93	0,72	0,28	0,17	0,28	0
C_2 (P_6, P_7, P_9,P_{10})	0,04	0,51	0,43	0,09	0,20	0,41	0,13	0,29	0,26	0
C_2 (P_8)	0,17	1	0,50	0,09	0,20	1	0,50	1	0	1

Table 8. ISODATA algorithm results when all information is available

Results are very good and we can see, in comparing Table 7 and Table 8, that our system underlines the same four classes of people as the centralized ISODATA method. Consequently, we can say that, on this experimentation, the needed approximations of our method don't alter the quality of the clustering. One reason the results are so good, is

because some indicators are linked to others. For example, the indicator "longest immobility time" is influenced by the "time spent in the living room" one. When the first is missing, clustering can still give the same result because of the second presence.
Another way to evaluate our system is to compare its results to the case where only known indicators about people would be used to do the clustering. In this experimentation it means that the global clustering made by our three agents would only take into account the common indicators of all agents, that is I_3, I_6, I_7 and I_8. ISODATA applied to such a case leads to the clustering of Table 9.
Results are much degraded. We obtain two classes where only P_4 and P_5 are correctly cluster together, all other persons being in the same class. Such a poor clustering highlights the quality of our method that, despite the missing of some information, gives as good results as methods where all information is known.

	I_3	I_6	I_7	I_8
C_1 (P_4, P_5)	0,95	0,03	0,88	0
C_2 (P_1, P_2, P_3,P_6, P_7, P_8,P_9,P_{10})	0,30	0,60	0,23	0,33

Table 9. Clustering results on the subset of common indicators between agents

The last way to evaluate our system results is to compare clusters to the pathology of monitored people. Not surprisingly, all initially spotted classes emerge. Overactive people are clustered with other overactive people, normal people with normal people and so on. The only quality of our system for this last point is to confirm the relevance of the chosen indicators to characterize these pathology and behaviors.
To conclude, the example shows that multi-agent classification can be a good replacement when a centralized approach is not possible.

5. Summary and future study

In some contexts where information is highly distributed with privacy and real life constraints, traditional classification methods do not work. As presented in section 2, multi-agent systems provide solutions to handle classification in such contexts. We believe that these systems constitute an essential approach to efficiently classifying large and distributed information volumes in many practical domains.
As presented in section 3, the originality of our system is its ability to take into account heterogeneous data with missing indicators. This property is very interesting in applications where the reliability of input data is not guaranteed. For example, section 4 illustrates the use of our method in a home care application. We have shown that results can be as good as classical methods as long as some indicators are inter-related.
For future studies and projects, other potential use in the e-health field could be:

- To collect global and anonymous statistical data about old people taken care of in their own homes.
- To monitor specialized alarms depending on the detected event. Once the classification is set up and a person's status is known, decisions can be taken to personalize the monitoring of the individual - activated sensors, generated alarms and danger zones.
- The remote monitoring of people suffering from chronic health problems. This would be useful for people suffering from cardiac and pulmonary illnesses, asthma or

Alzheimer's. The possibility of having a global vision of several monitored people can bring richer and more relevant information on the follow-up. The classification of elderly people and their case history would allow new people entering the system to get a better service; in particular, it would make it possible to generate more appropriate alerts according to the risks.

Future studies will also try to better highlight the differences between centralized and multi-agent classification methods. More tests will have to be done to measure system performances and quality of results.

6. References

Canuto A., Santana L. E., Abreua M. & Xavier Jr J. (2008). An analysis of data distribution in the ClassAge system: An agent-based system for classification tasks, *Neurocomputing*, Volume 71, Issues 16-18, pp. 3319-3325

Forestier G., Wemmert C. & Gançarski P. (2008), Multi-source Images Analysis Using Collaborative Clustering, *EURASIP Journal on Advances in Signal Processing, Special issue on Machine Learning in Image Processing*, p. 11, Hindawi

Fuchs Florian, Berger Michael & Linnhoff-Popien Claudia (2010). Smart Monitoring for Physical Infrastructures, *Handbook of Ambient Intelligence and Smart Environments*, Part V, 583-607, DOI: 10.1007/978-0-387-93808-0_22

Gançarski, P. & Wemmert C. (2007). Collaborative Multi-step Mono-level Multi-strategy Classification, *Journal on Multimedia Tools and Applications*, Vol. 35, No. 1, pp. 1—27, Springer Ed., ISSN: 1380-7501

Isern D., David Sánchez D., Moreno A. (2010) Agents applied in health care: A review, *International Journal of Medical Informatics*, Volume 79, Issue 3, March 2010, pp. 145-166

Lecoeuche S. & Lurette C. (2003) Auto-adaptive and Dynamical clustering Neural Network, *ICANN'03 proceedings*, pp 350—358, Springer

Memarsadeghi N., Mount D.M., Netanyahu N. S. & LeMoigne, J. (2006) A Fast Implementation of the ISODATA Clustering Algorithm, *International Journal of Computational Geometry and Applications.*

Moreno A. & Nealon J. (2003) *Application of Software Agent Technology in the Health Care Domaine*, Birkhauser Verlag Editors

Mukhopadhyay, S., Peng, S., Raje, R., Palakal, M. and Mostafa, J. (2003), Multi-agent information classification using dynamic acquaintance lists. *Journal of the American Society for Information Science and Technology*, 54: 966–975. doi: 10.1002/asi.10292

Peng, S., Mukhopadhyay, S., Raje, R., Palakal, M. & Mostafa J. (2001). A comparison between single-agent and multi-agent classification of documents, *Proceedings of 15th International Parallel and Distributed Processing Symposium*, pp. 935-944, ISBN: 0-7695-0990-8, San Francisco

Quteishat A., Peng Lim C., Tweedale J. & Jain L. C. (2009) A Multi-Agent Classifier System Based on the Trust-Negotiation-Communication Model, *Advances in Soft Computing*, Volume 52, Applications of Soft Computing, pp. 97-106

Quteishat A., Peng Lim C., Saleh J. M., Tweedale J. & Jain L. C. (2010) A neural network-based multi-agent classifier system with a Bayesian formalism for trust measurement, *Soft Computing - A Fusion of Foundations, Methodologies and Applications*

Santana, L.; Canuto, A. & Abreu M. (2006). Analyzing the Performance of an Agent-based Neural System for Classification Tasks Using Data Distribution among the Agents, *Proceedings of International Joint Conference on Neural Networks*, pp. 2951-2958, ISBN: 0-7803-9490-9, Vancouver

Singer N., Pecatte J.-M., Trouilhet S., (2005), The multi-agent cooperative navigation system Mawa: a model of dynamic knowledge specialization for a user-centric analyse of the Web, *International Conference on Computational Intelligence for Modelling, Control and Automation and International Conference on Intelligent Agents, Web Technologies and Internet Commerce* Vol-2, pp.289-294

Singer N., Trouilhet S., Rammal R. & Pecatte J.-M. (2010) Distributed Classification: Architecture and Cooperation Protocol in a Multi-agent System for E-Health, *Agent and Multi-Agent Systems: Technologies and Applications*, Lecture Notes in Computer Science, Volume 6070/2010, 341-350, DOI: 10.1007/978-3-642-13480-7_36

21

Developing a Multi-agent Software to Support the Creation of Dynamic Virtual Organizations aimed at Preventing Child Abuse Cases

Pedro Sanz Angulo and Juan José de Benito Martín
University of Valladolid
Spain

1. Introduction[1]

Child abuse is a serious and worldwide problem that our society must try to completely eradicate. This goal, undoubtedly ambitious, requires an intensive work in the education of every individual and, of course, in the recognition of the children's rights.

Although in recent years significant progresses have been made in this sense, we must do everything in our power to adequately protect children, responding promptly and in a personalized way to each abuse situation. For this purpose, we must employ all the available resources and, furthermore, search for new solutions and tools.

In order to provide an adequate response, all those stakeholders (both entities and people) that are involved in the prevention, detection and intervention activities should work together creating collaborative networks in which they provide what they really do best, i.e., their core business.

However, network collaboration must face numerous challenges in order to become an effective instrument. Every abuse case is unique, so networks must involve different components in each new situation, and even these components can change during the performance: it is necessary, therefore, a dynamic and flexible networking model that allows the continuous evolution of resources and services, as well as the incorporation of new ones.

These inter-collaborative problems in child abuse domain are difficult to solve without considering the new organizational models and, of course, the Information and Communication Technologies that make them possible. In this way, the *Dynamic Virtual Organization* (DVO) is probably the best organizational response to the problem.

In a DVO a set of business partners come together dynamically, on demand, and in accordance with the requirements of a specific problem, disappearing when those needs have been met. DVOs are rapid creation and fast dissolution organizations, constructed *ad hoc* the opportunity of collaboration.

---

[1] This work is derived from the participation of the authors in a research project financed by the autonomous government of Castile and León (Spain), with reference number VA009A09, entitled "Information and Communication Technologies in the Creation of Organizational Networks: Application to the Field of Child Abuse Prevention."

But the effective creation of a Dynamic VO only is possible in the context of the *Virtual Organization Breeding Environments* (VBE). The VBEs are clubs of organizations prepared to work in long term relations and from which temporary coalitions emerge able to respond dynamically to the different business opportunities.
Based on these ideas and concepts, our work is currently focused both on the definition of a VO Breeding Environment for our community (Castile and León - Spain) and on the development of a multi-agent expert system able to support the partner selection process in an agile and efficient way.
The introduction of the VBE concept in conjunction with the use of software agents whose behaviour is guided by expert system modules is a novelty in the field of child abuse prevention. This combination will allow us optimizing the use of resources and it also will facilitate the communication between institutions and professionals, making possible a more agile response of the DVOs.
According to these ideas, the present document aims at justifying the use of DVO-VBE concepts for the child abuse problem and, secondly, at presenting the tool we are developing for the selection of partners in these scenarios, the VCAP (*Virtual Child Abuse Prevention*) platform.
About the first part, we present the problem of child abuse, its typologies and the different kinds of prevention, in order to establish the context of our job. We also present some initiatives, both domestic and international, that consider networking as the best way to prevent the child maltreatment. In addition, we analyze the DVO and VBE concepts and discuss their correspondence with the networking model in the child abuse domain.
With regard to the implementation of the multi-agent VCAP platform in which we are currently working, first we describe the partner selection model that we are using, which has been defined based on the study of the different existing approaches associated to the selection of partners. From this model, and following the methodology proposed for JADE platform, we describe the main elements and artefacts defined during the analysis and design of our platform. Finally, we present the multi-agent expert software we are developing, the different tools we are employing and its capabilities.
All this work would not be possible without our previous experience in the development of the DVEBreeder tool (Sanz & de Benito, 2009), a multi-agent expert system which has been designed to support the selection of partners in Dynamic Virtual Enterprise context. In particular, this tool allows to select the best combination of partners for the installation of photovoltaic solar panels.

2. Child abuse problem and networking

The United Nations Convention on the Rights of the Child 1989 defines child abuse as (United Nations, 1989) "all forms of physical or mental violence, injury or abuse, neglect or negligent treatment, maltreatment or exploitation, including sexual abuse, while in the care of parent(s), legal guardian(s) or any other person who has the care of the child." In short, we can say that there is child abuse if children's rights are not respected and there is not a response to their needs (Sanz et al., 2008); we cannot forget that abuse is, primarily, the lack of good treatment.
There is a great variety of abuse types depending on its forms (physical, sexual, psychological, neglect, etc.), the place, the involved actors, the degree of intensity, and so on. Each abuse situation is unique and requires, of course, a different approach, so an

appropriate response must be designed to each particular case. In this sense, prevention is the best possible approximation to the problem.
Prevention may take place at three different levels: primary, secondary and tertiary.

a. *Primary prevention* aims to decrease the incidence or onset of abuse cases, through the child advocacy and a special attention to their needs. It is applied to the general population, to make the community becomes aware about the problem and acquires positive habits and behaviours that prevent the appearance of the child abuse.
b. *Secondary prevention* focuses, in turn, on the concept of risk. This prevention is addressed to social groups, families or individuals classified as "high risk" to avoid those situations that end up in abuse.
c. Finally, *tertiary prevention* tries to reduce the duration and severity of the consequences of the problem; namely, it aims at decreasing the stage of rehabilitation or cure. It also requires the intervention in the context, family, etc., to prevent its recurrence.

As we will see later, our work can be perfectly included in the latter two levels of prevention, and especially in the tertiary one.
With regard to the roles of the different actors involved in the situation of maltreatment, it is necessary to establish a typology since obviously the institutional respond designed to punish the abuser has to be different to the necessary answer to attend or to cure the victim. From a systemic consideration, the number of stakeholders includes the aggressors, either adult or minor, the direct victims and those minors who are involved in an indirect way, in a situation of observation, being passive subjects.
Obviously, all citizens have, or can have some type of connection with the child maltreatment and this one can take place in different contexts although it tends to concentrate at school, at home and in the street (Lila et al., 2008).

2.1 Networking in the child abuse domain

Both in the Spanish Public Administration and in most of the governments of the western countries, the institutional answer to the child abuse is characterized by a frequent interaction between organizational systems, but also by the difficulty to coordinate all their functions. This difficulty is mainly due to the own nature of the problem of child abuse, which includes phenomena and situations as diverse and has such unique characteristics that make difficult to develop an integrated action.
Networking is, clearly, the best way to create a collaborative workspace where to achieve the pursued goals. It is based on the communication of the different agents and institutions, so an optimum exchange of information, both qualitative and quantitative, must exist between them.
The originators of the sociotherapeutic networking were Speck and Attneave (1974). They created therapeutic teams to intervene in families in crisis, in the United States, in order to break destructive patterns of family relationships and provide support for alternative options. Several years later, in the eighties, Elkaim (1989) carried out the first practice at European level in deprived areas of Belgium. Since then, the networking experiences have evolved and multiplied.
In our country, Spain, we find the networking pilot program of Burlada (Pamplona). Its promoters recognize that one of the challenges of any network program is (De Miguel & Fernández, 2002) to provide a process able to organize the different institutional levels and professional resources, in order to ensure the creativity and competence of each one of these instances.

These and other works, experiences and projects emphasize the need of networking as a means to achieve the ultimate goal of prevention and resolution of child abuse, establishing guidelines and procedures that normally are constructed *ad hoc*. However, they do not possess software tools capable of solving the different problems of such relationships, e.g. the need for a rapid intervention.

Our job will serve, precisely, to overcome this deficiency. We pursue the interconnection, in a quick and efficient way, of those professionals and institutions that must be part of the answer. Starting from a simple notification in the system, a dynamic consortium will be configured in order to respond to the specific abuse case in a personalized way and with a little human intervention.

3. The organizational basis of our work

There are a lot of similarities between the networking that a child abuse situation requires and the networking of a dynamic virtual organization. Below, we will summarize the more interesting ideas to understand our work, although previously it is necessary to describe this paradigm as well as the VO Breeding Environments concept.

3.1 The dynamic virtual organization

In order to survive in the present context, companies must be able to constantly meet their customers' needs, while improving productive efficiency and adapting continuously to a global, competitive and dynamic environment.

However, added value creation for customers has become an increasingly complex process which requires the mix of different kinds of resources and expertise that companies do not necessarily have (Beer et al., 1990). Companies are forced to cooperate, sometimes even with their direct competitors, what has led to the introduction of multiple organizational concepts based on collaboration. In this sense, the paradigm of Virtual Enterprise (VE) represents one of the most relevant examples of collaborative networks.

A Virtual Enterprise is an organizational model that allows a number of organizations, institutions or individuals (legally independent and geographically dispersed) to develop a cooperation environment aimed at achieving a specific objective (Sanz & de Benito, 2009). This environment allows the manufacture of products or the provision of services of higher quality and tailored to the needs of the market, incurring in a lower cost, a risk-sharing and in a reduction of the time to market, resulting in a better response to the customer requirements. In short, the goal is to create a *best-of-everything* organization (Adams et al., 2001) through the coalition of the complementary strengths of each member.

There are a lot of benefits associated to this business model: a faster access to new markets and new business opportunities; partners can overcome challenges, achieve business goals, access to resources (skills, materials, know-how, expertise,...), etc., which usually are outside the scope of a single firm; increases the utilization of assets; improves customer service and product quality; reduces risks, costs, etc.; allows to achieve economies of scale; SMEs achieve international presence; etc.

However, although a company can be capable of supplying a quality product with reduced costs, it does not mean it has the ability to adapt efficiently to those changes in customers` demand. This ability, known as agility, is really provided by the dynamic models of VE (DVE, *Dynamic Virtual Enterprise*), also known as *Agile Virtual Enterprises* (AVE).

The same idea is also very appealing in other non-business oriented contexts (Camarinha-Matos & Afsarmanesh, 2006), what leads us towards the paradigm of *Dynamic Virtual Organization* (DVO), a most suitable concept for our current work and which encompasses the former.

In a Dynamic Virtual Organization a set of business partners come together dynamically, on demand, and in accordance with the requirements and needs (Ouzounis, 2001) of the problem, disappearing when those needs have been met. DVOs are rapid creation and fast dissolution organizations (Browne & Zhang, 1999), constructed *ad hoc* the opportunity of collaboration.

A Dynamic VO often evolves through four stages (Camarinha-Matos, 2003): creation, operation, evolution and dissolution. To summarize, the phase of creation includes identifying the business opportunity, the selection of partners, the design of the company and its constitution. After that, the DVO reaches the operation stage which covers all activities of the current mission (Do et al., 2000). During this phase the structure of the DVO can need to be changed and a phase of reconfiguration will begin (Dang, 2004). In any case, when DVO is considered no longer effective it is dissolved.

As shown in Fig. 1., both in the phases of creation and reconfiguration, the key element is the search, identification and selection of partners (Camarinha-Matos & Afsarmanesh, 2001; Petersen, 2003; Fischer et al., 2004; etc.). This task is complex and it is determined by the negotiation needs. It consumes, in addition, large amounts of time and resources which translates into a loss of flexibility.

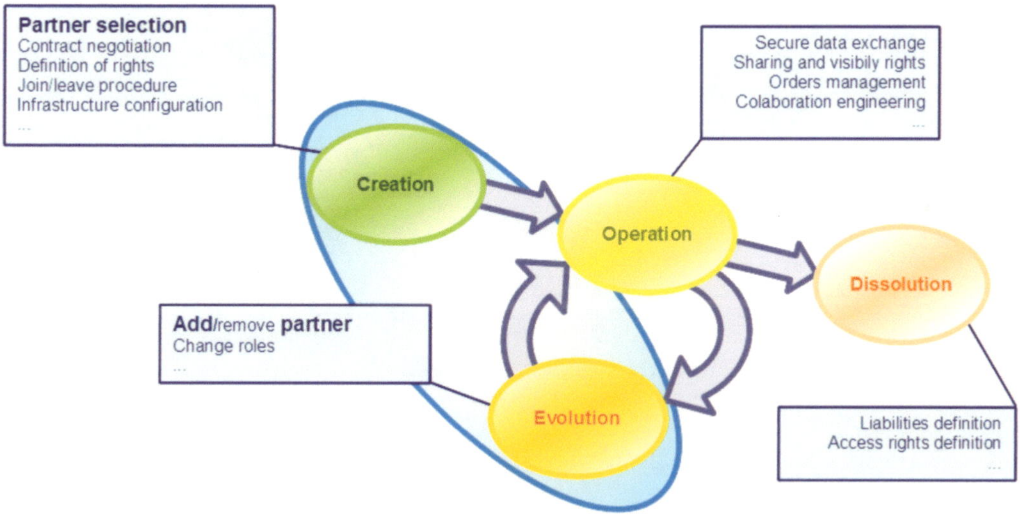

Fig. 1. The life cycle of a DVO and the scope of the partner selection process in it. Adapted from (Camarinha-Matos, 2003)

3.2 The DVO in the context of the virtual organization breeding environments

As mentioned before, the creation of a DVO whenever a new collaboration opportunity emerges requires large amounts of time and resources, causing a reduction of the agility associated with this business model. The effectiveness of the process depends largely on the availability of adequate information about potential partners, their level of preparedness to engage in a Dynamic VO, the existence of trust, etc.

Most of all these problems have an easy solution when long term collaborations are considered. This is the reason why different authors have begun to consider that the formation of such organizations has to take place in the context of *Virtual Organization Breeding Environments* (Afsarmanesh & Camarinha-Matos, 2005), *pool communities* (Do et al., 2000), *virtual industrial parks* (Nayak, 2001), *virtual industry clusters* (Siqueira & Bremer, 2001; Rabelo et al., 2000), etc.,

The VO Breeding Environments, like the other equivalent concepts, are composed of organizations that are prepared to collaborate in long term relations (Camarinha-Matos et al., 2005). When a collaboration opportunity is identified, a subset of the VBE members can be rapidly selected to form a virtual organization. VBEs emerge as an evolution of *clusters* and *industrial districts* (Bremer et al., 1999; Mejía y Molina, 2002).

Fig. 2 shows how the creation of VO Breeding Environments and the genesis of Dynamic Virtual Organizations are different processes that are triggered by very different reasons.

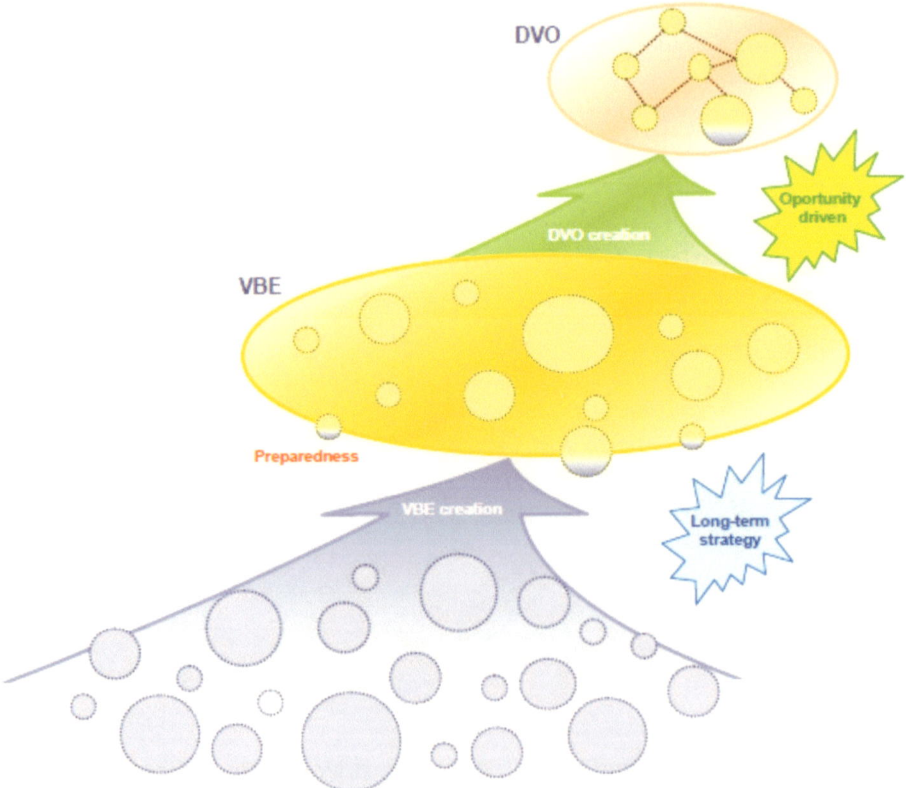

Fig. 2. Creation of DVOs in the VBE context. Adapted from (Camarinha-Matos et al., 2005)

A VBE is created as a long term association and its members are recruited from the *"open universe"* of organizations according to the criteria defined by the VBE administrators. By contrast, a VO is a temporary organization triggered by a specific collaboration opportunity, and its partners are primarily selected from the VBE members.

The VBEs simplify the configuration and establishment of DVOs since they solve, or reduce, many of the obstacles associated with the temporality of such organizations, contributing, thus, to their creation in a more efficient way. Partners of the DVO can, this way, benefit fully from unexpected changes in their context, providing an agile response to the problems or the opportunities. These entities are, in short, prepared to operate in an agile way following the definition provided by Goranson (1999).

The introduction of VBEs to solve the selection of partners' problem is an important organizational innovation. However, to make this concept operational and to ensure that the DVO really reacts swiftly and appropriately to the changes in demand, new tools and innovations of technological nature are required. After all, the concept of DVO absolutely depends on innovation to achieve its full potential and the agility that characterizes it.

3.3 Equivalence between DVO and networking in child abuse domain

As can be easily intuited, there are several similarities between networking that a child abuse situation requires and the collaborative networking of the DVOs.

We can start, for example, talking about the VO Breeding Environment. In the child abuse domain it is obvious that the VBE would be constituted by any entity or person involved in the solution: schools, social services, health centres, youth services, law enforcement agencies, state security bodies, and so on. All of them bring to the partnership their core business, what they do best, so the VBE contains all necessary processes that the abuse situation requires. In addition, these entities are required to share certain culture of work, ICT infrastructure, etc., to achieve the highest possible performance.

After identifying a new case of abuse (either in the school, or in a health centre, or through a complaint at the police station or in the child line, etc.), it is the time to go to the breeding environment and select the set of institutions and/or persons that are the best prepared to respond to the particular problem.

The union of the selected entities configures, ultimately, the DVO responsible for providing the personalized answer to the child abuse situation. Naturally, different DVOs can arise from the breeding environment to provide this response, although the selection of the best one depends both on the requirements and needs of the particular situation of abuse and on the features and capacities of the partners.

After the selection process, partners need to work together and coordinate their actions in order to find an efficient and agile solution to the problem. This operation phase lasts until an adequate response to the initial problem has been provided. That moment coincides, precisely, with the dissolution of the DVO.

In addition, whenever it is necessary, more partners can be searched, or even their number can be reduced, the roles or the structure can change, etc., according to the evolution of the abuse case. In short, during the operation of the DVO an evolution-reconfiguration phase can take place.

Finally, we must also notice that those entities which form part of a particular dynamic virtual organization can be simultaneously partners of another consortium created in response to a different abuse case.

4. The VCAP multi-agent expert platform

Our fundamental objective is to enhance and develop a networking model through the creation of DVOs capable of facing child abuse problems in an agile and efficient way. For

this purpose, it is necessary to align the VBE and DVO concepts to the child abuse domain and provide efficient tools to support its formation and operation.
In this paper we propose a multi-agent approach to support the selection process in this context. This technology provides several advantages over other proposed methods, especially for its ability to manage complex and distributed problems. But in addition, our agents have an intelligent behaviour through a rule-based Expert System (ES) implemented in their decision module.
Through this platform the best combination of partners is defined dynamically, in real time, based on the system state, the predefined objectives and the features both of the problem and of the stakeholders. The identification and assignment of partners emerge from the interaction between agents, through different negotiation mechanisms. In this sense, we can introduce the Virtual Child Abuse Prevention (VCAP) concept.

4.1 The selection model

From the review of the multiple R&D projects and studies related to the identification and selection of partners in virtual organizations, the coexistence of two opposing positions can be easily observed.
A common solution is to follow a *top-down* approach, known as *planning* approach, where the planner designs the network and selects the partners that best fit his plan (Camarinha-Matos & Afsarmanesh, 2006). The opposite alternative is based on the use of a *bottom-up* (competition or emerging) approach; in this case, the client or broker announces the collaboration opportunity, waits till some consortia are formed spontaneously (by the initiative of some members), analyzes the received bids and selects the most appropriate according to his needs.
Intermediate solutions can be defined between these two extreme alternatives. Thus, for example, we found what we call *hierarchical* approach, where the broker or coordinator only defines the highest level business processes (abstract definition) and selects the appropriate partners for each one of them. Each one of these new members of the Dynamic VO is responsible for refining the design in accordance with its local capacities, so planning and detail are alternating in the process.
The planning approach is the most used solution in the research literature (Rocha & Oliveira, 1999; Petersen, 2003; etc.), including its hierarchical variant (Ouzounis, 2001), since it is easier to implement and allows greater control over the resulting DVO. The button-up approach (Rabelo et al., 2000), in turn, leads to forms of Dynamic VOs more efficient and agile, but its control is often far more complex.
Based on the study of the different approaches, we have created a generic and simple model with a multi-approach orientation which pools the advantages of the existing solutions and mitigates their weaknesses, making possible the formation of dynamic virtual organizations in a more effective and efficient way.
To achieve this goal, each involved actor in the selection process can select the service providers in two different ways (see Fig. 3).
First, when an entity needs a service it can ask the VBE for the list of suppliers and selects one through a negotiation process that takes into account multiple criteria, both objective and subjective. On the other hand, it can also post its needs and expect the formation of DVOs (or sub-DVOs) and then selects one. In both cases, the formation of the resulting DVO is transparent with respect to the entity that is requesting the service.

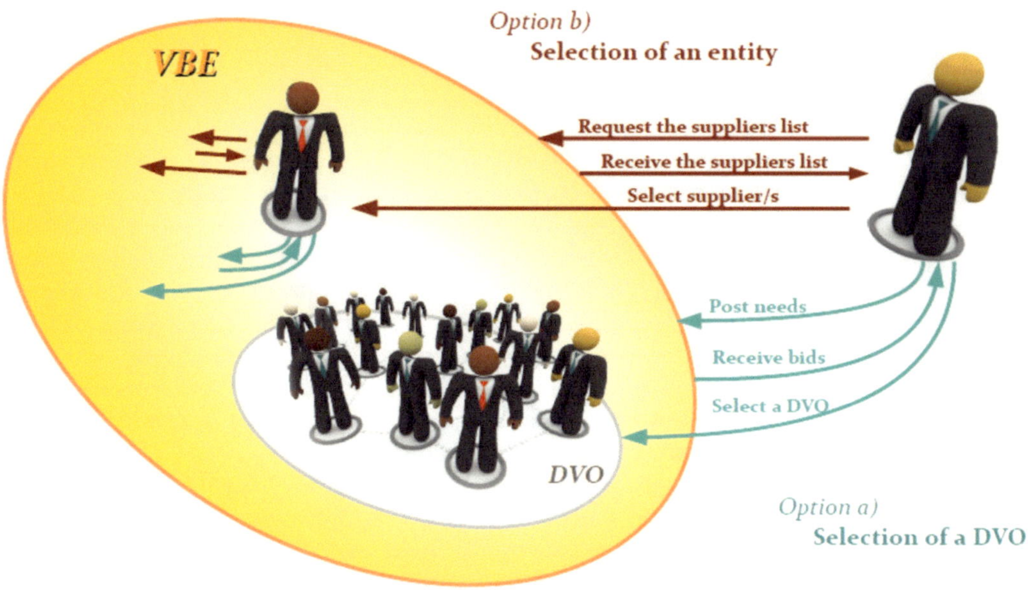

Fig. 3. Our model for the partner selection process

Allowing this simple choice our model makes possible the formation of DVOs that fit the different models and planning structures found in the literature and, in addition, any other possible combination, as can be seen in Fig. 4.

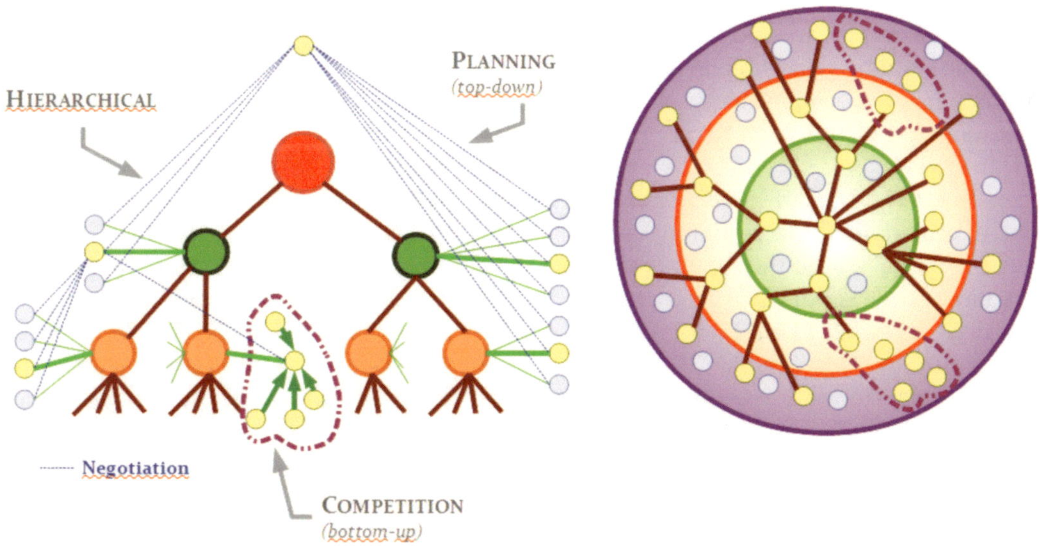

Fig. 4. A possible example of DVO created from our selection model

This model constitutes the selection conceptual basis for the VCAP multiagent platform. In the development of this platform we are following an iterative process of planning, analysis, design, construction, testing and validation. The following describes the most important aspects of this process.

4.2 Planning

Planning is the early stage of the software development cycle, where it is decided which technology-tool combination is the most appropriate solution for the problem.

As we know, the selection of partners is a key activity in the success of any collaborative network, particularly in the dynamic ones. This is, undoubtedly, a complex problem with no easy solution because involves a lot of elements, variables and factors of both objective and subjective nature. To address the resolution of this problem, over recent years different approaches have been used (computational automation - integer programming, AHP, etc. - Web services, multi-agent technology, etc.) what has led to a variety of solutions and R & D projects aimed at providing both the technological bases and the operating practices necessary to support the selection process in this kind of consortia.

Among the different existing solutions, the multi-agent technology highlights significantly. In fact, there are many features in the domain of DVOs that make these organizational models an appropriate application area for *Multi-Agent Systems* (MAS), as evidenced by several authors (Ambroszkiewicz et al., 1998; Camarinha-Matos and Afsarmanesh, 2001; Dignum & Dignum, 2002; Petersen, 2003; etc.).

These features have led to the emergence of multiple and diverse software solutions that use this technology to carry out the selection of partners in virtual organizations. However, the developed systems have a high degree of automation based primarily on quantitative issues, what prevents reflecting the full reality of companies and their decision-making mechanisms. Therefore, these systems do not lead to a fully realistic and satisfactory solution.

In order to provide an adequate solution to the problem that concerns us, it is first necessary to examine and understand how organizations make decisions, particularly those decisions aimed at building partnerships with other entities in order to resolve a case of child abuse. In this sense, we can see that such decisions are not made based on complex mathematical functions or statistical hypotheses; rather, they often rely on their "experience", "knowledge" and "intuition".

Therefore, to give an effective response, software agents should behave, think and act like a human expert in the considered domain would do, but how can we do this? For this purpose we have used the *Expert Systems* (ES). By definition, an expert system is a computer program that simulates the thought process (learning, memorization, reasoning, communication, etc.) of a human expert to solve complex decision problems in a specific domain. By this way, ES can (Castillo & Alvarez, 1991) store data and knowledge, draw logical conclusions, make decisions, communicate with human experts, explain their decisions, etc., and, as a consequence of all above, take actions.

Thanks to these systems, and in particular to a rule-based ES, we obtain agents with a rational behavior based on the knowledge and expertise of human experts in the child abuse area. Thus, without resorting to complex mathematical procedures, the agents are able to make the best decisions based on the needs of the problem and on the structured knowledge that has been supplied to them.

The introduction of the expert system is a clear innovation, from the technological point of view, over other existing multi-agent solutions.

After justifying the technology to use, the next step is to select the development tools and methodologies to employ in the building of the software application. In particular, we have analyzed and compared the major multi-agent standards, platforms and development methodologies. Similarly, we have analyzed the different tools for the building of the expert system, taking into account previous decisions related to the MAS. It should be noted that in the choice of these tools we have tried to make use of free software or, alternatively, software under the Academic Free License.

FIPA (*IEEE Foundation for Intelligent Physical Agents*) is, without any doubt, the multi-agent standard which has currently been accepted by a larger number of developers, since it incorporates all aspects of this paradigm described so far by both the research community and the industry. For this reason, in this work we have followed the FIPA specifications and JADE (*Java Agent Development Environment*) as the implementation tool. Jade is a fairly commonly used development environment, not only for its strict conformity with the standard, but also by other qualities such as flexibility, good management of both the platform and the message exchange, code extensibility, easiness of both debugging and development of distributed applications on different machines, extensive documentation, etc. It is also written in Java, it is free software and the user group is very active.

In short, we believe that the selection of FIPA and Jade is a fairly accurate solution, given the nature of our problem and the wide acceptance of both the standard and the tool. This election, however, significantly constrains the choice of the development methodology, because since 2006 there is a methodology (Nikraz et al., 2006) explicitly defined to address the analysis and design of Jade-based applications, which we have followed.

Another key element in the MAS building, especially to achieve efficient information exchange between agents, are the ontologies. An ontology is simply a model of the real world, and for the specific case of an agent, an ontology defines its environment. In this work we have chosen to follow the methodology proposed by Noy and McGuinness (2001), which faces the ontology construction from an iterative approach in which the ontology has to be assessed and streamlined to throughout its life cycle. As ontology development tool we have chosen Protégé, a Java-based graphical tool developed by the Stanford University.

Finally, we have addressed the issues associated with the construction of the expert system with which we are going to build the decision module of the most of the agents of our multi-agent platform. In the market there are a lot of programming languages (LISP, Prolog, OPS5 ...), shells (EMYCIN, Crystal, Leonardo, XiPlus, Exsys, VP-Expert ...) and development environments (CLIPS, JESS, KEE, ART, Egeria , Kappa, etc.) which can be used for this purpose. In our case, and based on both our objectives and decisions summarized in the preceding paragraphs, we have finally decided to use JESS (*Java Expert System Shell*). Jess is a development environment with the same functionality, and even higher, than CLIPS but also it is based on Java what allows an easy integration with the Jade platform.

4.3 Analysis and design of the VCAP multi-agent expert system

The analysis of the platform has been made following the steps defined by the Jade methodology. Thus, we have identified the different types of users, agents and external resources in the system, along with their responsibilities and the acquaintance relationships that exist between them.

One of the major artefacts defined in this stage is the agent diagram. Fig. 5 shows the agent diagram for our platform.
In this diagram four types of elements can be distinguished:

- First, we identify the *users*, those individuals who must interact with the system: these elements are represented in the diagram by the UML actor symbol. In our case, we identify two different actors: the administrator of the platform and those entities that form part of the breeding environment. It should be noted that the same entity can have multiple roles in the platform: for example, VBE member-manager, VBE member-client (when a member of the breeding environment needs a service that other member from the own environment provides), or even client-VBE partner-manager.

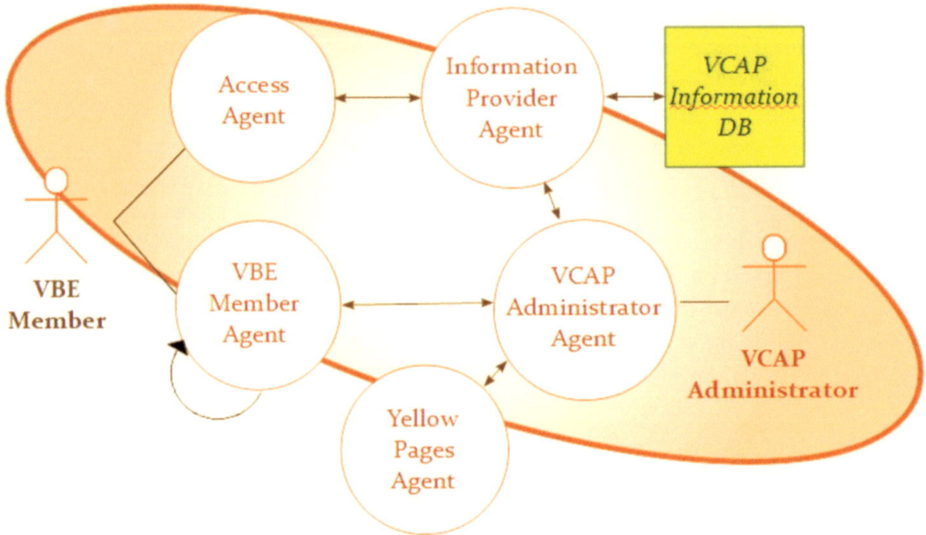

Fig. 5. Agent diagram for the VCAP platform

- In addition to humans, we also find those external systems that must interact with the system under development, i.e., the *resources*, which are represented in the diagram by rectangles. As can be seen, and contrary to what happens in UML case diagrams, the agent diagram provides an explicit distinction between humans and resources: this is due to that the interaction with people through a user interface presents some additional problems with respect to the interaction with an external system. In our case, external resources are simple data bases that have been built as valid XML documents.
- The *agents* that will form the multi-agent platform are represented by circles. In the picture we can appreciate that an agent has been added for each user (the *VBE Member Agent* and the *Administrator Agent*) and for every resource (the *Information Provider Agent*, which allows accessing to the information about the platform and its operational). Furthermore, an *Access Agent* has been added, whose sole function is to verify that the user-agent who wants to connect to the platform really belongs to it, and the *Yellow Pages Agent*, defined to identify the agents based on the services they provide. Although the yellow pages mechanism can be fully distributed across all

agents in the system, we have decided to adopt a centralized approach that maps completely to the *Directory Facilitator* (DF) agent provided by Jade, in order to save work in the successive phases of the development process.

- Finally, *relations* are represented in the diagram by arrows, which join the instances of the above items: this way we specify that such elements must interact in some way while the system is operational. Although most of the relationships shown in the figure are fairly obvious, it is necessary to comment on a couple of them. On the one hand, we see that the yellow pages agent is only related to the administrator agent: although this behavior may be more inefficient, this decision is quite deliberate because, by allowing that only the administrator agent can carry out both the registration and the search of services, we improve the security and robustness of the system. On the other hand, when the customer is internal (i.e., an entity belonging to the breeding environment), relations-negotiations will occur between the VBE members agents, although with different roles.

Another interesting artifact generated during the analysis is the agent deployment diagram, which indicates how agents are going to be physically deployed between the different hosts/devices. The deployment diagram for our scenario is shown in Fig. 7.

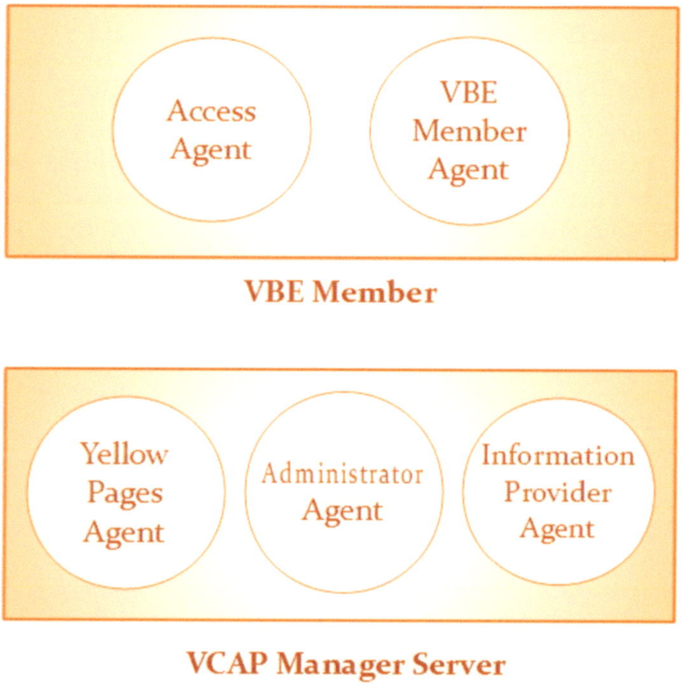

Fig. 7. Agent deployment diagram for our scenario

During the design stage, and prior to the implementation, we are working in the definition of different elements as the interactions between agents and the interaction protocols, message template (see Fig. 8), the description of the services to be registered/searched in the yellow pages agent, the agent-resource and agent-user interactions, the internal agent behaviors, the content language, the ontologies, etc.

With regard to the yellow pages mechanism, which is maintained by the DF agent of Jade, VBE member agents can register the services they provide in the yellow pages catalog, while others can search for the services they need to carry out their activities in such catalog. In addition, the same agent can register one or more services and, simultaneously, can require any other ones from the other agents.
In the design phase we have also addressed the interaction with the external resources. In our case, we have considered only tree active resources, which are the XML documents that contain information about both the business process, and the activities that comprise it, and VBE members, including their behavior during their membership to the breeding environment.

```
MessageTemplate registroDeProcesos =
    MessageTemplate.and (
        AchieveREResponder.createMessageTemplate
            (FIPANames.InteractionProtocol.FIPA_REQUEST),
        MessageTemplate.and (
            MessageTemplate.MatchPerformative (ACLMessage.REQUEST),
            MessageTemplate.MatchConversationId (
                "registrar-proceso-de-negocio")));
```

Fig. 8. Example of a message template for a FIPA-REQUEST interaction

For these situations, the JADE methodology proposes to employ a transducer approach: this way we avoid embedding code to access data within those agents that need to consult the file with the information. For this reason, we are using two classes that contain the necessary methods to access and manage the information through DOM code. Thus, we get the information provider agent does not include inside the code, resulting in different advantages for the future: modularity, easy modification, reuse, etc.
Another issue to consider is the agent-user interactions. In our scenario we can easily identify three agents that need to interact with the users of the system (those that have an acquaintance relationship with an actor element in the agent diagram), namely the VBE-member agent, the administrator agent and the access agent. Although there are several ways to get the human-software interactions, we have considered using *Graphical User Interfaces* (GUI) which are by far the most common type of interface. Specifically, and given the current requirements of the application, we have only considered necessary to create local Swing-based GUI.
However, there is an interaction problem between agents and graphic elements, since these entities work in different threads. Although Jade has some ways to tackle this problem, we are using the `jade.core.GuiAgent` class, built specifically for this purpose.
In the design stage we are currently defining the ontologies of the system. In particular, we are working in the main ontology, i.e., the ontology associated with the child abuse domain: actors, types, business processes and their main characteristics, etc. We have also defined an ontology for the management of the platform, which considers the information about users, their characteristics, their relations, the last operational, etc.
Based on all these considerations, and bearing in mind the notion of container that Jade incorporates, we get the architecture that is depicted in Fig. 9.

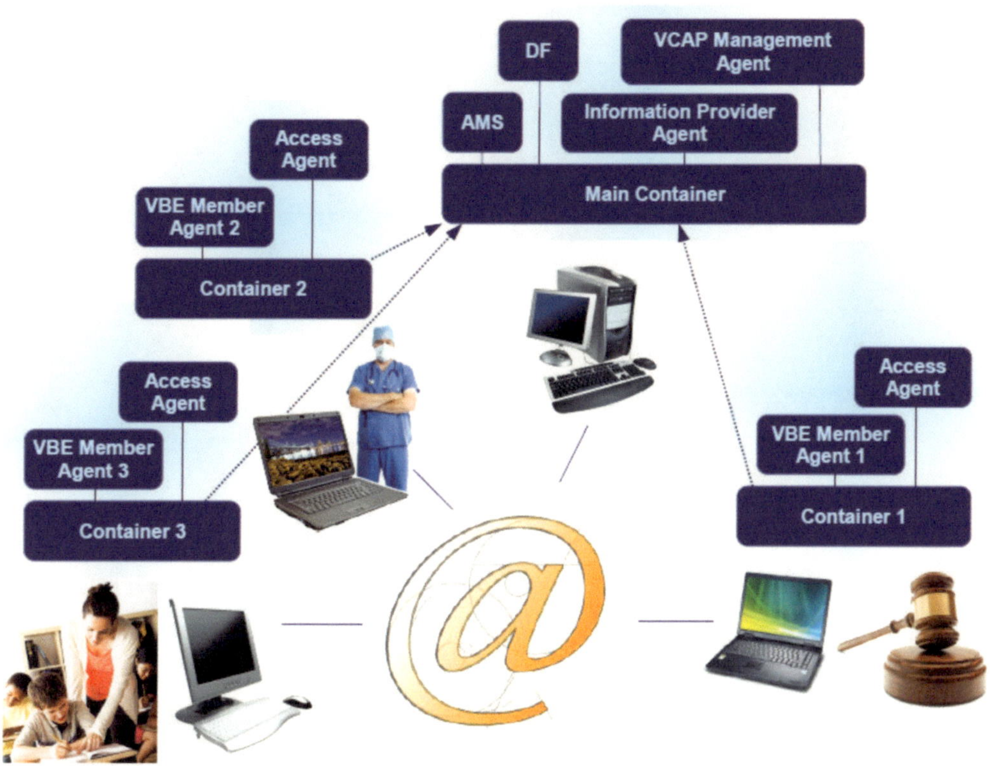

Fig. 9. Distributed structure of the VCAP platform

As seen in this figure, there is a main container on the manager server in which the VCAP Administrator Agent resides, in addition to the Information Provider Agent, the Yellow Pages Agent (where the Resource Agents register their services) and the rest of agents that Jade incorporates for the platform management.

Also, there are multiple remote containers: specifically, so many remote containers as institutions and professionals the breeding environment has. In each of these containers we can identify the VBE Member Agent (associated to the different actors involved in the solution) and an Access Agent for security issues.

We have considered that all of these entities can provide their core business and, at the same time, be the promoters of the DVO formation process. It is also possible that a third entity or person starts the process, but for now we consider that the system is open only to the VBE members. Perhaps in the future the platform can be opened to everyone, but to do that previously it is necessary to solve some security problems.

The union of these remote containers with the main container results into the distributed agent platform shown in the Fig. 9.

4.4 Current development of the VCAP platform

The current development of the VCAP platform is possible thanks to our experience in the creation of the DVEBreeder tool (see Fig. 10), a multi-agent expert platform developed to support the selection of partners in the enterprise domain (Sanz & de Benito, 2009).

Fig. 10. Some snapshots of the GUIs of the DVEBreeder platform

To address the construction of the platform, we have used the tools and *plug-ins* that appear graphically represented in Fig. 11.

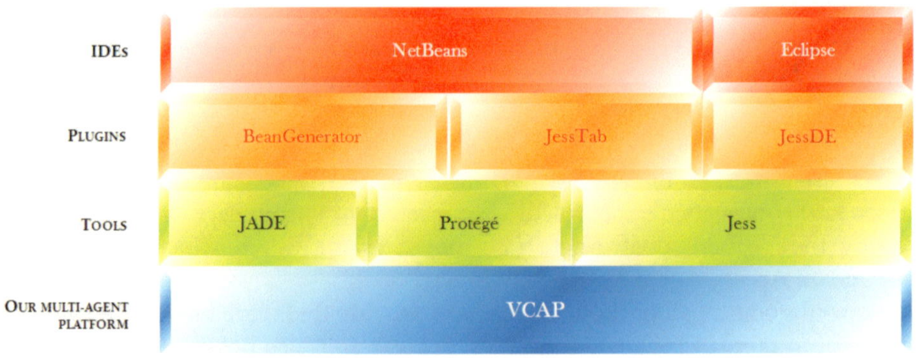

Fig. 11. Overview of the software tools used in the implementation

The VCAP platform inherits most of the features of its predecessor: the integration of multi-agent and expert system technologies; the identification of the intelligent agents is made through an multi-approach model that takes into account the VBE concept; the negotiation between autonomous agents is based on the knowledge embodied in their decision modules; the communication between agents is quite simple thanks to the platform used in the MAS development (Jade); the behaviour of the agents is quite similar to the behaviour that a human expert can have thanks to JESS (see Fig. 12), the rule-based expert system; it is flexible, dynamic and scalable; it is FIPA-compliant agent platform; the interface is intuitive and the code reuse is simple thanks to its open structure, etc.

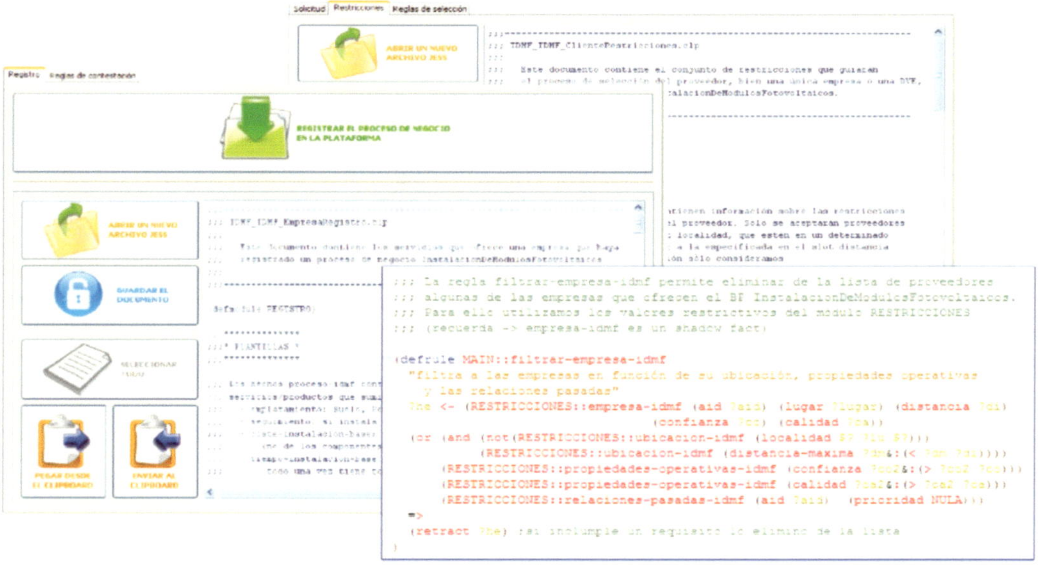

Fig. 12. Example both of a Jess rule and of the GUIs where the decision modules of agents can be modified

Finally, Fig. 13 shows a summary of the platform performance in the application domain.

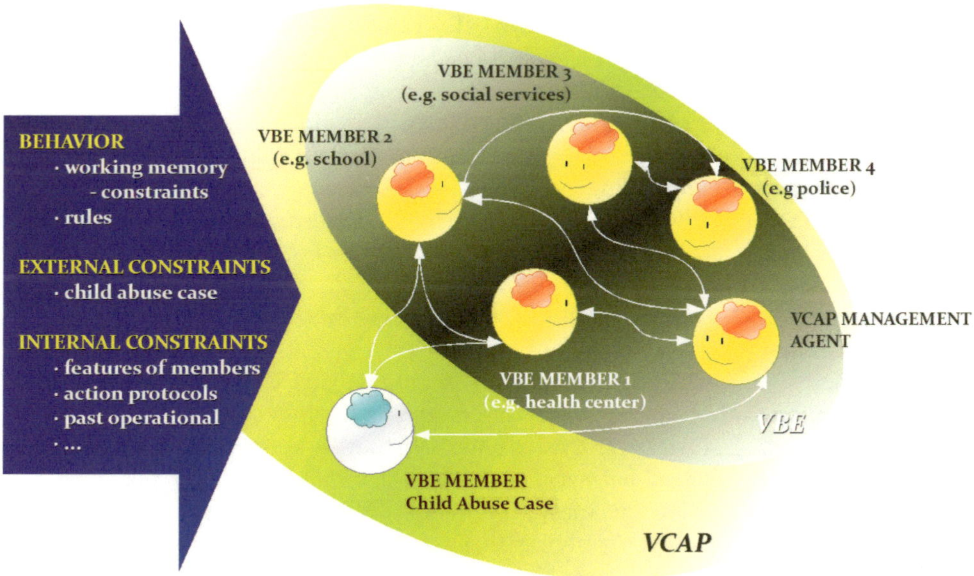

Fig. 13. Simplified scheme of the VCAP platform performance

5. Conclusions

In this article we have tried to justify the utilization of the DVO paradigm and the VBE concept as a valid way to create collaborative networking in the child abuse domain. Based on both concepts, we have also presented our current work oriented towards the creation of a multi-agent expert system able to select and join those entities/persons that can provide the best response for a particular child maltreatment case; in other words, we offer a tool for the creation of DVOs that emerge from the VBE context.

After having done the planning and the analysis, we are currently working in the design and implementation phases. To do this, we are defining some elements of the platform as e.g. the application domain ontology, the service descriptions, the agent decision modules, etc. Others, such as the agent interactions, the message templates, the interaction protocols or the ontologies for the management of the platform, are very similar to those established in the DVEBreeder platform, a tool created for the business domain, what undoubtedly will greatly facilitate the final implementation of the platform.

In summary, we believe that the VCAP software will be an innovative tool able to solve the Child Abuse Prevention problem in an agile and efficient way.

6. Acknowledgments

We would like to express our gratitude to the managers and members of REA, the Association for the Children and Youth Advocacy of Castile and León, and in particular to Ms Mª Elena Villa Ceinos.

7. References

Adams W.M.; Wallas, R.M. & Sengupta, A. (2001). Collaborative Commerce: The Agile Virtual Enterprise Model. In: Nirmal, P., Judith, M.R. (eds.): *Pushing the Digital Frontier: Insights into the Changing Lands of E-Business*. Penn State eBusiness Research Center, pp. 242-262.

Afsarmanesh, H. & Camarinha-Matos, L.M. (2005). A Framework for Management of Virtual Organization Breeding Environments. *Collaborative Networks and their Breeding Environments*, Springer, Boston, pp. 35-48.

Ambroszkiewicz, S.; Cetnarowicz, K. & Radko, B. (1998). Enterprise Formation Mechanisms based on Mobile Agents. *Proceedings of Workshop on Intelligent Agents in Information and Process Management, KI'98*, pp. 23-34

Beer, M.; Eisenstat, R.A. & Spector, B. (1990). Why Change Programs don't Produce Change. *Harvard Business Review*, 68 (6), pp. 158-166

Bremer, C.; Mundim, A.; Michilini, F.; Siqueira, J. & Ortega, L. (1999). A Brazilian Case of VE Coordination. In *Networking Industrial Enterprises*, Springer, pp. 377-386

Browne, J. & Zhang, J. (1999). Extended and Virtual Enterprises - Similarities and Differences. *International Journal of Agile Management Systems*, 1 (1), pp. 30-36

Camarinha-Matos, L.M. & Afsarmanesh, H. (2001). Virtual Enterprise Modeling and Support Infrastructures: Applying Multi-Agent System approaches. *Multi-Agent Systems and Applications, Lecture Notes in Artificial Intelligence*, pp. 335-364

Camarinha-Matos, L.M. & Afsarmanesh, H. (2003). Elements of a Base VE Infrastructure. *Journal of Computers in Industry*, vol. 51, nº 2, pp. 139-163

Camarinha-Matos, L.M. & Afsarmanesh, H. (2006). Creation of virtual organizations in a breeding environment. In *Proceedings of INCOM'06*, St. Etienne, France

Camarinha-Matos, L.M. (2003). Infrastructures for Virtual Organizations - Where We Are. Emerging Technologies and Factory Automation, 2003. *Proceedings of ETFA '03.* IEEE Conference, vol. 2, pp. 405- 414

Camarinha-Matos, L.M.; Silveri, I.; Afsarmanesh, H.; Oliveira, A.I. (2005). Towards a Framework for Creation of Dynamic Virtual Organizations. *Collaborative Networks and their Breeding Environments* (PRO-VE'05), Springer, pp. 69-81.

Castillo, E. & Alvarez. E. (1991). *Expert systems. Uncertainty and Learning.* Elsevier Applied Science and Computational Mechanics Publications, London and New York

Dang, V.D., (2004). *Coalition Formation and Operation in Virtual Organisations.* PhD, School of Electronics and Computer Science, University of Southampton

De Miguel, M. & Fernández, M. (2002). Detección precoz del maltrato infantil. Programa piloto de trabajo en red. *Anales del Sistema Sanitario de Navarra,* 25(2), pp. 25-34

Dignum, V. & Dignum, F. (2002). Towards an Agent-Based Infrastructure to Support Virtual Organisations. In Camarinha-Matos, L.M. (ed.), *Collaborative Business Ecosystems and Virtual Enterprises,* Kluwer Academic Publishers, pp. 363-370

Do, V.T.; Halatchev, M. & Neumann, D. (2000). A Contextbased Approach to Support Virtual Enterprises. *Proceedings of the 33rd Hawaii International Conference on System Sciences,* vol. 1, nº 4-7.

Elkaïm, M. (1989). *Las prácticas de la terapia de red.* Barcelona: Gedisa

Fischer, M.; Jähna, H. & Teich, T. (2004). Optimizing the Selection of Partners in Production Networks. *Robotics and Computer-Integrated Manufacturing,* 20, pp. 593-601

Goranson, H.T. (1999). *The Agile Virtual Enterprise: Cases, Metrics, Tools.* Quorum Books

Lila, M.; Herrero, J. & Gracia, E. (2008). Multiple victimization of Spanish adolescents: A multilevel análisis, *Adolescence,* 43, pp. 333-350

Mejia, R. & Molina, A. (2002). Virtual Enterprise Broker: Processes, Methods and Tools. In *Collaborative Business Ecosystems and Virtual Enterprises,* Springer, pp. 81-90

Nayak, N.; Chao, T.; Li, J.; Mihaeli, J.; Das, R.; Derebail, A. & Hoo, J.S. (2001). Role of Technology in Enabling Dynamic Virtual Enterprises. *Proceedings of the International Workshop on Open Enterprise Solutions: Systems, Experiences and Organizations,* Rome, Italy

Nikraz, M.; Caire, G. and Bahri, P.A. (2006). A Methodology for the Analysis and Design of Multi-Agent Systems Using JADE. *International Journal of Computer Systems Science and Engineering,* 21(2)

Noy, N.F. & McGuinness, D.L. (2001). *Ontology Development 101: a Guide to Creating your First Ontology.* Stanford Knowledge Systems Laboratory Technical Report KSL-01-05 and Stanford Medical Informatics Technical Report SMI-2001-0880.

Ouzounis, E. K. (2001). An *Agent-Based Platform for the Management of Dynamic Virtual Enterprises.* PhD thesis. University of Berlin.

Petersen, S.A. (2003). *An Agent-based Approach to Support the Formation of Virtual Enterprises.* Ph.D thesis. Norwegian University of Science & Technology.

Rabelo, R.; Camarinha-Matos, L.M. & Vallejos, R. (2000). Agent-based Brokerage for Virtual Enterprise Creation in the Moulds Industry. In *E-business and Virtual Enterprises,* Kluwer Academic Publishers, pp.281-290

Rocha, A. & Oliveira, E. (1999). An electronic market architecture for the formation of virtual enterprises. In *Infrastructures for Virtual Enterprises,* Kluwer, 153, pp. 421 - 432

Sanz, P. & De Benito, J.J. (2009). Design and Implementation of a Multi-agent Framework for the Selection of Partners in Dynamic VEs. *Leveraging Knowledge for Innovation in Collaborative Networks*, Springer, pp. 341–348.

Sanz, P.; Villa, M.E.; Manso, M.A. & De Benito, J.J. (2008). Aplicación de la Tecnología Multiagente y los Sistemas Expertos al trabajo en Red para la Prevención del Maltrato Infantil. *Proceedings of the IX Congreso Estatal de Infancia Maltratada.* Valladolid. Spain

Siqueira, J. E. M. & Bremer, C. F. (2000). Action research: The formation of a manufacturing virtual industry cluster. *E-Business and Virtual Enterprises: Managing Business-to-Business Cooperation*, Kluwer Academic Publishers, pp. 261– 68

Speck, R. & Attneave, C. (1974). *Redes Familiares.* Amorrortu Editores, Buenos Aires

United Nations - Office of the High Commissioner of Human Rights (1989). *Convention on the Rights of the Child*, resolution 44/25 of 20 November 1989. Last visit in February 2010. Available at http://www2.ohchr.org/english/law/crc.htm

22

Obtaining Knowledge of Genes' Behavior in Genetic Regulatory System by Utilizing Multiagent Collaborative Computation

Adang Suwandi Ahmad[1] and Arwin Datumaya Wahyudi Sumari[2]
[1]*School of Electrical Engineering and Informatics, Institut Teknologi Bandung, Achmad Bakrie Building, 2nd Floor, Jl. Ganeca 10, Bandung, 40132,*
[2]*Department of Electronics, Indonesian Air Force Academy, Jl. Laksda Adisutjipto, Yogyakarta, 55002*
Indonesia

1. Introduction

All living organisms are built from millions of cells that work together in a very systematic manner. The trait of each organism is determined by the cells. The function of a living cell is performed by a sequence of well-coordinated activities by a large number of genes. The gene itself is a sequence of Deoxyribonucleic Acid (DNA). The products of a cell are made by the proteins synthesized in accordance with the instructions contained in the DNA (Willett, 2006) since it encodes all the information required for the development and functioning of an organism (Emmert-Streib & Dehmer, 2008).

The expression of a gene is a biological process which a DNA sequence is translated to become a protein. The protein is an important molecule for determining the structure, mortality, metabolism, signaling, reproduction, etc. of a cell. Some genes influence how other gene or genes are expressed. Modifying genes may change the affect of other genes. The expression of a gene or genes is regulated by a mechanism called Genetic Regulatory System (GRS). The GRS' task is to control whether genes are active or inhibit.

Of ways for understanding and analyzing the behavior of GRS is by using microarray data. Microarray is sets of miniaturized reaction areas that may also be used to test the binding of DNA fragment (Reece, 2004). and it exploits the preferential binding of complementary nucleic acid sequences to simultaneously measure expression levels of thousands of genes (Dill, Liu, & Grodzinski, 2009). By having knowledge regarding the influence of a gene or genes to the others in microarray data, we can make estimations of the genes behavior in GRS in order to obtain better products in the future. According to (Ewens & Grant, 2005), there are three basic questions that can be answered by using microarray data:

a. What genes are expressed in a given sample?
b. Which genes are differentially expressed between different samples?
c. How can one find different classes, or clusters, of genes which are expressed in a correlated fashion across a set of samples? How can one find different classes of samples based on their gene expression behavior?

In this paper we address the utilization of Multiagent Collaborative Computation (MCC) to model the genes' interactions in GRS to address questions (a) and (b). Simply, each gene will be represented by an agent that performs internal activities and performs communications with other genes as occurred in biological genes. On each interaction time, we can have knowledge regarding individual gene expressiveness and all genes behavior. The process in obtaining this knowledge will be carried out by Knowledge-Growing System (KGS) based on Observation Multi-time Arwin-Adang-Aciek-Sembiring (OMA3S) information-inferencing fusion and the results will be compared to the MCC results. The comparison has also been done to ensure the accuracy of the KGS-based MCC results. In our research, we use data of yeast cycle database taken from [6] as the case study. The rest of the paper is structured as follows. The concept of MCC and a review of the state-of-the-art of GRS research will be delivered in Section 2. In Section 3, we present the concept of KGS as well as OMA3S method that is used as its knowledge-growing mechanism. The utilization of MCC to GRS as well as the knowledge production by KGS will be delivered in Section 4. Finally, the paper is concluded in Section 5 with some concluding remarks.

2. State-of-the-art of genetic regulatory system research and the concept of multiagent collaborative computation

2.1 State-of-the-art on genetic regulatory system research

The research, studies, and experiments on GRS have been done widely all over the world. These efforts are aimed to one objective, namely how to obtain the most suitable model in order to present the mechanism occurs in GRS. In these endeavors, there are two approaches that have been carried out as studied comprehensively by (Ahmad & Sumari, 2009a) as follows.

In the first approach the GRS mechanism is directly modeled by utilizing available methods such as Dynamic Bayesian Network (DBN) based on knowledge growing, weight matrices, petri nets, artificial gnome model, Neural Network (NN) or its combination with fuzzy technique such as Evolving Connectionist System (ECOS), piece-wise linear, Boolean, and power graph analysis.

The second one is to model the GRS by inferring its structure utilizing techniques such as best-fit extension problem, linear programming combined with supervised learning framework, DBN, evolutionary computation, graph and Linearized Additive Model (LAM), steady-state gene expression, Dynamic Differential BN (DDBN), combination of DBN with Reversible Jump Markov chain Monte Carlo (RJMCC) or with Greedy search algorithm and Markov Chain Monte Carlo (MCMC), Bayesian and MCMC, iterative algorithm based on epistemic approach of conjecture and refutation, NN, and combination of clustering techniques with NNs.

At the time of the writing of this paper, we have not found literatures that study methods in obtaining knowledge regarding the behavior of genes in GRS in order to estimate their expression in the future especially that utilizes multiagent approach. This is the primary matter that will be discussed in this paper. Our hypothesis is by accurately estimating the GRS behavior in the future we can carry out anticipation actions in order to prevent the negative expression of genes that can cause negative effects to living organisms.

2.2 Multiagent collaborative computation

MCC is a new paradigm in MultiAgent System (MAS). It is the emulation of how human beings work in collaborative manner in solving problems or finding solutions of given problems or in achieving a common or joint goal or objective, by sharing resources they have for the successfulness of their work. Working in collaborative manner does not need leader. What it needs is a divider agent for dividing the work or task to be solved or given into subworks or subtasks, and distributes them to some collaborative agents, and a fusion agent that is tasked to fuse the results from collaborative agents to obtain a comprehensive result or joint goal. By doing it, the subworks can be processed in parallel manner to achieve the subgoals, and therefore it can save the processing time. Before we go deeper into MCC, we start this section with the reintroduction of the concept of agent and the concept of collaborative computation as well as its merit.

a. The Concept of Agent (Ahmad & Sumari, 2008)

There have been many literatures that study agent, but in this section we view an agent from a comprehensive perspective. In real life, agent is defined as a thing that causes a significant effect on a situation. In order to give this effect, agent must have capabilities. "Capability" in this circumstance is the ability to manage when the tasks will be carried out, knows where to move, knows how to do the tasks, knows the success level of the tasks being carried out, and the consequences of the tasks being done. The essential thing that enables the agent in performing its activities is the brain, a place where the information processing is carried out. This is the most grandeur that is not possessed by other living things.

In accomplishing the assigned tasks, the agent always senses its surrounding environment to get as much as information that can affect its activities. The gathered information is processed in its brain, combining it with the existing information, making inferencing on the fused information, performing information-inferencing fusion, and making the best decision for actions to be done in anticipating the environment dynamics. The relation of an agent with its surrounding environment as well as its information processing mechanism is simply depicted in Fig. 1.

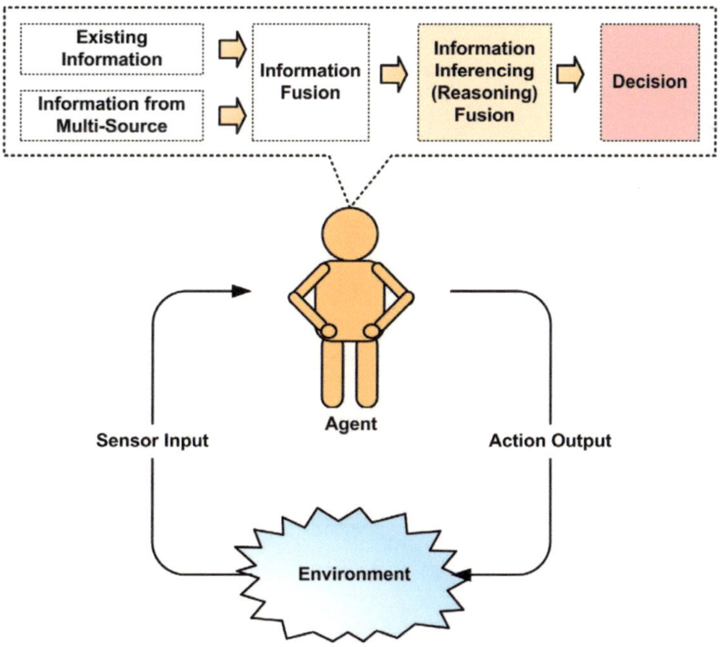

Fig. 1. The concept of agent along with its information-inferencing fusion capability

In many literatures, agent is stated must have an intelligent characteristic. However, because there is no uniform definition of what agent is, one common consensus is taken that the autonomy or we call this as self-governing, as its the essential characteristic. Self-governing means the agent has capability to instruct itself to accomplish the tasks and do self-evaluation to value the success rate of the assigned tasks accomplishment for future enhancement.

b. The Concept of Collaborative Computation

Collaboration is taken from the Latin word "collaborare" meaning "to work together", while "collaborative" is an adjective form of "collaboration". So, collaboration is defined as to work with another or others on a joint project or in deeper definition is a process in which

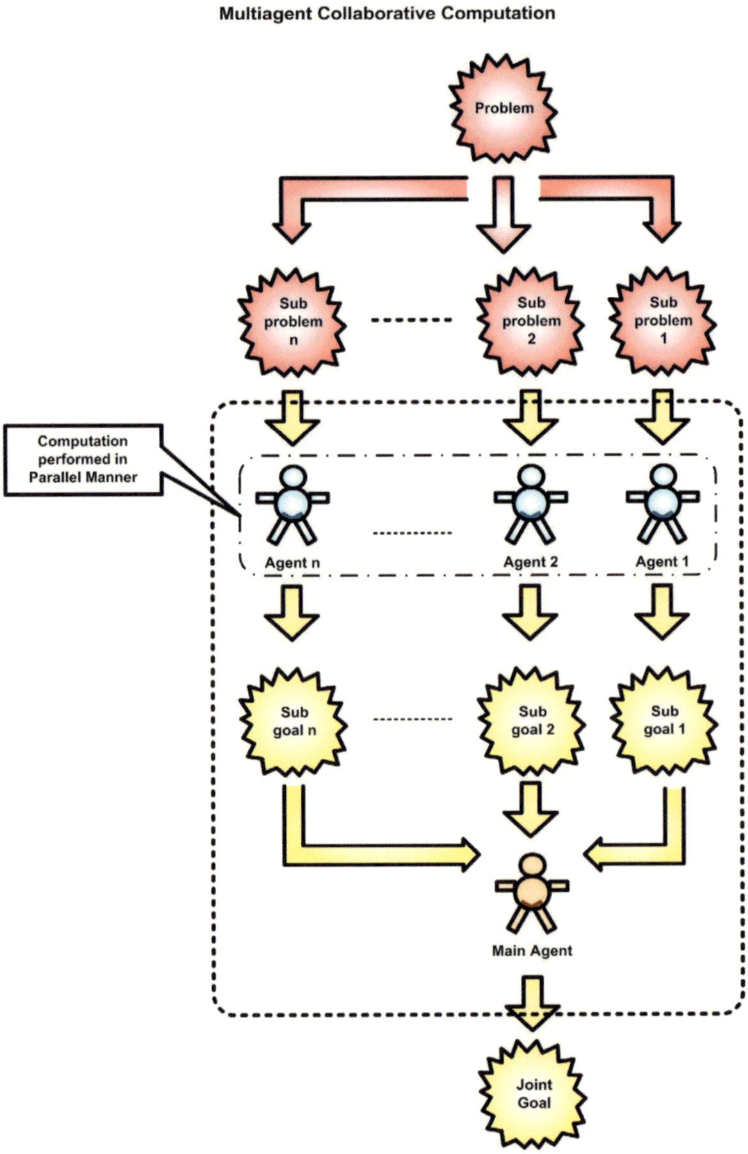

Fig. 2. The concept of collaborative computation in a group of agents (Sumari & Ahmad, 2009)

entities share information, resources and responsibilities to jointly plan, implement, and evaluate a program of activities to achieve a common goal (Camarinha-Matos & Afsarmanesh, 2008).

In collaborative scheme, a group of entities enhance the capabilities of each other that implies in sharing risks, resources, responsibilities, and reward. Collaboration involves mutual engagement of participants to solve a problem together, which implies mutual trust and thus takes time, effort, and dedication. On the other side, "computation" is defined as a calculation involving numbers or quantities. By employing computational approach, we can manipulate a large database to solve problems at hand very fast. The consequence is faster, more complete, and more accurate results than that can be achieved by conventional approach.

By combining the two definitions previously explained, we define "collaborative computation" as a calculation on quantities done by a group of agent or multiagent that works together to achieve common or joint goals (Ahmad, Sumari, & Zubir, 2009) as depicted in Fig. 2. In an MCC scheme, each agent in the collaborative framework performs its own tasks to achieve its own goals. The goals achieved by each agent actually are partial parts of joint goal, which is the combination of partial goals. In simple word, the system is given a problem along with the goal that has to be achieved. The problem is then divided into several sub-problems that have to be solved by the agents. In achieving the sub-goals, the agents perform computation in parallel. The achieved sub-goals are then combined to become a single comprehensive goal that is called as joint goal (Sumari & Ahmad, 2009).

c. The Merits of Multiagent Collaborative Computation Approach (Sumari, 2010)

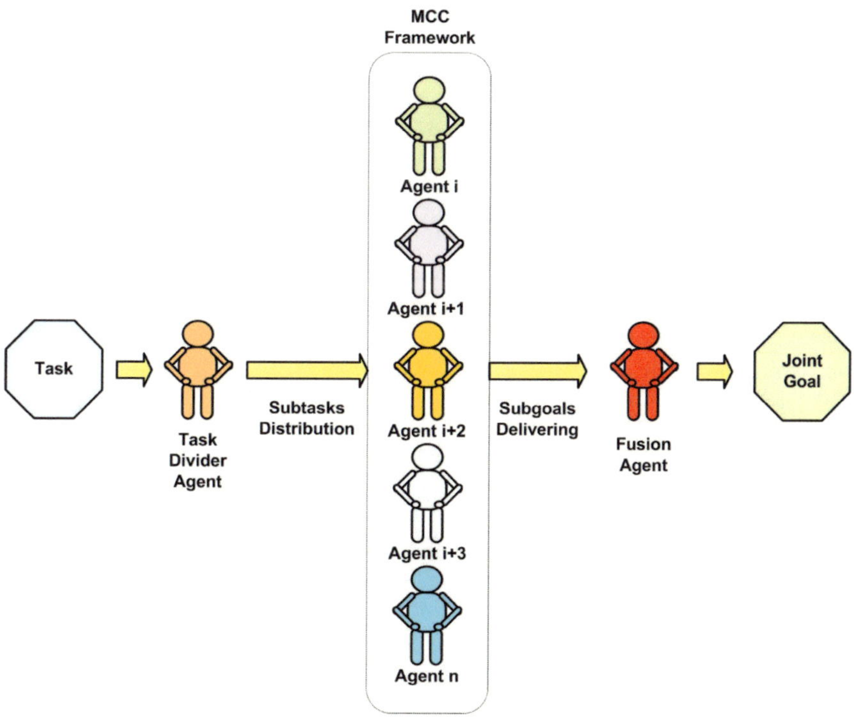

Fig. 3. The concept of MCC (Sumari, 2010)

GRS is a very complex structure that regulates millions of genes in living organism's body. We believe that multiagent approach is suitable to model the genes' interactions in GRS with some strong reasons. MAS is aimed to cope with large-scale, realistic, and complex problems that cannot be handled by single agent in order to find a solution of global problems or to regulate or control complex systems. In MCC framework, the given task will be divided into subtasks according to each agent specific task. By performing this, the information processing can be done in simultaneous manner by all agents so that the processing time can be reduced to minimum.

Assume that we have n agents in MCC framework. Given a task that a single agent can process it in t time. If the task is divided into n subtasks and distributed them to n agents, theoretically, the result of the process can be obtained in t/n time with total $t/n+\tau$ where τ is the time reserved for dividing the task and fusing or combining the subgoals into a joint goal or the ultimate result. Therefore, by utilizing MCC the information-processing time can be reduced from t to $t/n+\tau$, or $(t/n+\tau) < t$. This mechanism is illustrated in Fig. 3.

3. Knowledge-growing system and OMA3S information-inferencing fusion method

3.1 What is knowledge-growing? (Sumari et.al, 2010a)

It is not easy to find any literature that defines or describes what the term "Knowledge-Growing" is. The only research that used this term was for industrial application, that is, examined how the knowledge growing old in human brain and used the analogy of it for building a reconfiguration system for car application. It concentrated on the optimization of knowledge retrieval rather than emulating the way of human brain grows the knowledge over time, and used actuality measurement to measure the knowledge that is very often used to solve an actual problem.

Up to the writing of this paper, there is no research that examines and develops an intelligent method for an intelligent system that emulates the mechanism how the human brain grows the knowledge from time to time. Our approach in developing KGS was started from our observation to an intelligence characteristic displayed by human brain in performing such matter by fusing information perceived by human sensory organs and deliveres it to the brain. This approach is discussed in detail in (Ahmad & Sumari, 2008). The original concept of information fusion, even though it also adopted the mechanism occurs in living things' brain, it is just defined how to fuse the information for making estimation regarding a phenomenon, see (Hall & Llinas, 2001) for the detail.

3.2 The concept of KGS

Essentially, KGS is a system that is capable of growing its knowledge along with the accretion of information it receives as the time passes (Ahmad & Sumari, 2009b). The concept of KGS emerges from the observation of the mechanism occurs in human brain when performing information-inferencing fusion to obtain new knowledge. In order to have a more depth understanding on this mechanism, we developed a model of Human Inference System (HIS) as the basis for our model of KGS as depicted in Fig. 4. The general formula to obtain the number of inferencing is presented in (1).

$$\lambda = \left(2^{\delta} - \delta\right) - 1 \tag{1}$$

with λ is the number of inferencing from fused information and δ is the number of information sources or sensors.

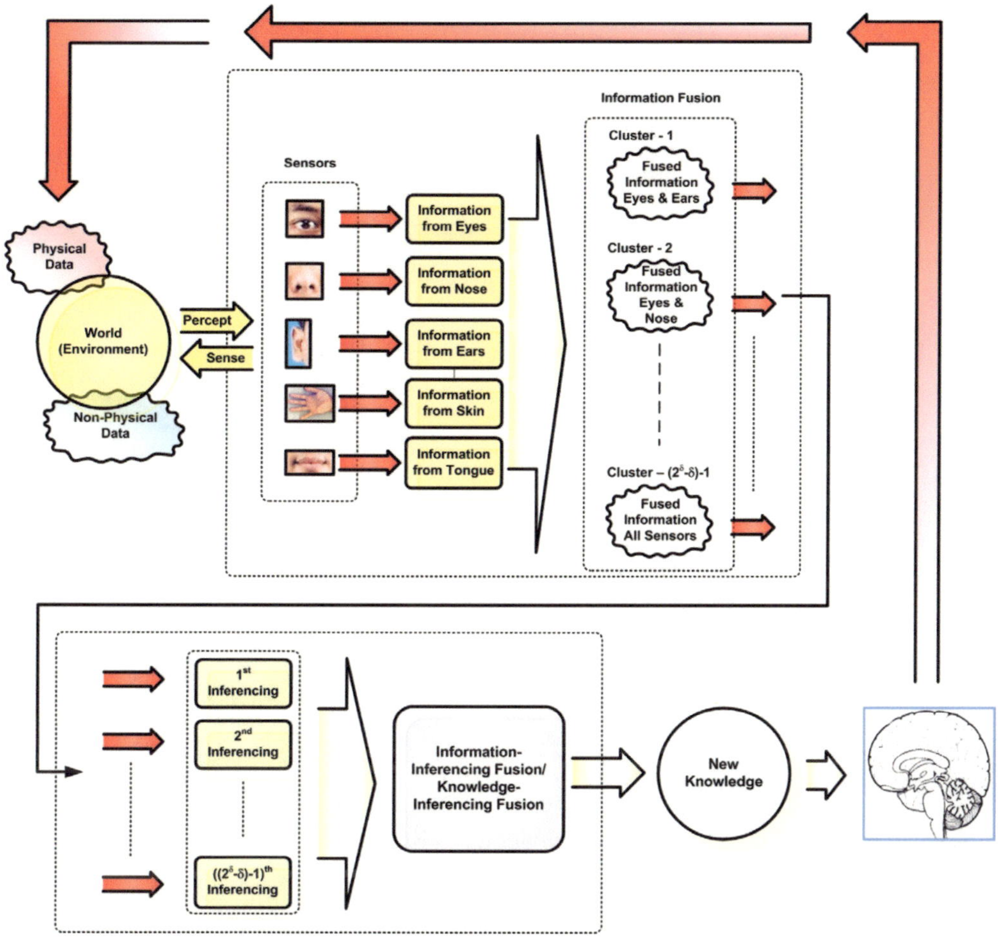

Fig. 4. A simplified illustration of human inference system (Sumari et.al, 2010b)

3.3 Knowledge growing mechanism

As we can see in Fig. 4, the process in obtaining new knowledge from the gathered-and-delivered information of a phenomenon observed by the sensory organs will have to get through a five-step process, i.e. information fusion, information inferencing, information-inferencing fusion, knowledge inferencing, and knowledge-inferencing fusion. Based on the HIS model, we developed the mechanism that will be occurred in our model of KGS as depicted in Fig. 5.

New knowledge in this scheme is called as information with Degree of Certainty (DoC) whcih is introduced by (Sumari et.al, 2009b), that is, a value that determines the certainty of the new knowledge regarding the observed phenomenon is considered accurate. Term "γ" is the representation of the time needed to obtain the new knowledge. The DoC is obtained by applying A3S (Arwin-Adang-Aciek-Sembiring) method (Ahmad & Sumari, 2008).

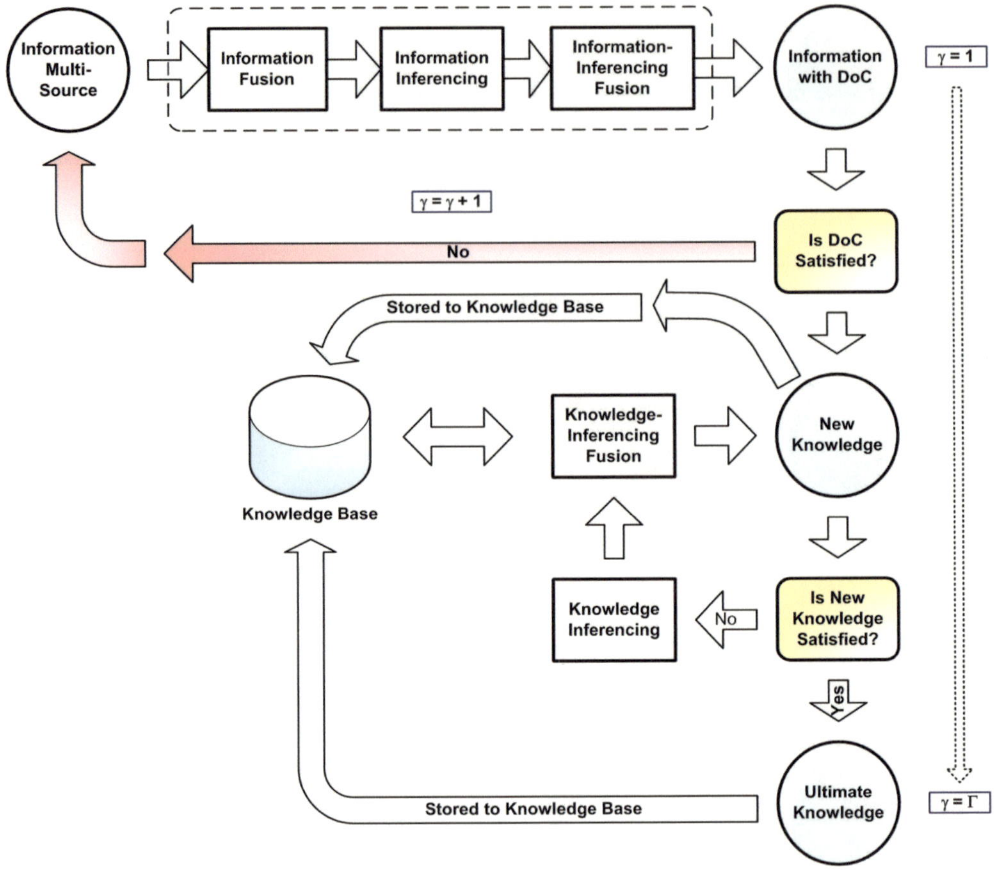

Fig. 5. The mechanism of growing the knowledge in KGS as the representation of Fig. 4 (Sumari et.al, 2009a)

3.4 OMA3S information-inferencing fusion method

To grow the knowledge, the requisites that have to be fulfilled are there has to be a knowledge base and fusion mechanism. The fusion will be applied to the received information with the existing or prior information/knowledge. The knowledge is the result of the combination between the new information and the existing one which is called as after-processed information or posterior information. The mature technique for this situation is Bayes Inference Method (BIM) (Hall, 1992), a special case of probability theory.

For performing the information-inferencing fusion, we have developed a method called A3S information-inferencing fusion which is aimed to improve BIM for managing multi-hypothesis multi-indication problems (Ahmad & Sumari, 2008). The A3S version which involves the time parameter in the computation is called OMA3S (Sumari et.al, 2009c). The detail how this method works is illustrated in Table I followed by its paired equations given in (2) and (3).

$$P\left(\psi_1^j\right)=\frac{\sum_{i=1}^{\delta} P\left(\upsilon_i^j\right)}{\delta} \tag{2}$$

$$P(\psi)_{estimate}=\odot\left[P\left(\psi_1^j\right)\right] \tag{3}$$

with $P\left(\psi_1^j\right)$ is New-Knowledge Probability Distribution (NKPD), $P\left(\upsilon_i^j\right)$ is information j from sensor i, while $i=1,...,\delta$ is the number of sensor and $j=1,...,\lambda$ is the number of fused information. The $P\left(\psi_1^j\right)$ and $\psi_1^j \in \Psi$ is the representation of "fused information" of the information delivered from multi-sensor. The word "estimated" means the selected fused information is the most likely inferencing/knowledge from all available inferencing/knowledge given information from multi-sensor. $P(\psi)_{estimate}$ is the largest value of $P\left(\psi_1^j\right)$ that is called as DoC and $\odot[...]=\max_{j=1,...,m}[...]$. Term $P\left(\psi_1^j\right)$ defines NKPD at $\gamma=1$.

Information from -th Sensor	Probability Distribution of Information from i^{th} Sensor and Probability Distribution of jth Fused Information						
	1	2	3	...	j	...	λ
1	$P\left(\upsilon_i^1\right)$	$P\left(\upsilon_i^2\right)$	$P\left(\upsilon_1^3\right)$	...	$P\left(\upsilon_1^j\right)$	...	$P\left(\upsilon_1^\lambda\right)$
...	...	...	...	...	...	...	...
i	0	0	$P\left(\upsilon_i^3\right)$	...	$P\left(\upsilon_i^j\right)$	...	$P\left(\upsilon_i^\lambda\right)$
...	...	...	...	...	...	...	...
δ	0	0	0	...	0	...	$P\left(\upsilon_\delta^\lambda\right)$
ψ (DoC)	$P\left(\psi_1^1\right)$	$P\left(\psi_1^2\right)$	$P\left(\psi_1^3\right)$	...	$P\left(\psi_1^j\right)$	...	$P\left(\psi_1^\lambda\right)$

Table 1. The illustration of the computation mechanism of A3S information-inferencing method

Next observations on the same phenomenon will result in new NKPD at next time series and these NKPD will form NKPD over Time (NKPDT) as presented in (4) and (5).

$$P\left(\theta_j\right)=\frac{\sum_{\gamma=1}^{\Gamma} P\left(\phi_\gamma^j\right)}{\Gamma} \tag{4}$$

$$P(\theta)_{estimate}=\odot\left[P\left(\theta_j\right)\right] \tag{5}$$

with $P\left(\theta_t^j\right)$ is NKPDT, $P\left(\psi_t^j\right)$ is information j observed at observation time γ, while $\gamma=1,...,\Gamma$ is the number of observation time and $j=1,...,\lambda$ is the number of fused information. The $P\left(\theta_j\right)$ and $\theta_j \in \Theta$ is the representation of "knowledge" of the information delivered from multi-sensor at observation time γ. $P(\theta)_{estimate}$ is the value of DoC of $P\left(\theta_j\right)$ or the ultimate knowledge after a certain observation time.

3.5 Measuring KGS-based MCC's degree of certainty

The KGS-based MCC's certainty of the phenomenon it observes is measured by using DoC in (6)

$$DoC = \left| P(\theta)_{estimate} - \phi_1^j \right| \tag{6}$$

where $j = 1,...,\lambda$ and ϕ_1^j is the knowledge in term of probability value of the j best hypothesis at observation time γ_1.

4. The utilization of KGS-based MCC to GRS

4.1 GRS database

In this research we use five kinds of yeast25 database as presented in Table 2.

Database	Type	Number of Gene	Time Sequence (t)
Yeast25	Alpha	25	18
	Cdc15	25	24
	Cdc28	25	17
	Cho	25	17
	Elu	25	18

Table 2. Yeast25 database for validating KGS-based MCC

As previously mentioned in earlier section, the genes regulated by GRS will be represented by agents that will be working together in MCC paradigm. The experiments and the results delivered in this section are taken from (Sumari, 2010). We use data from (Zubir, 2009) namely yeast25-cho database as presented in Table 2. In this database, there are 25 genes from ACE2 to SIC1 as listed in column 1 with an interaction time interval from t-1 to t-17 or 17t times as shown in line 1. In order to give a view on the challenge in obtaining the knowledge regarding what genes are expressed in a given sample as well their behavior in a certain interaction time, the complexity of the data given in Table 3 is depicted in Fig. 6 and Fig. 7. The expressiveness of individual genes in 17t of interaction time is presented in Fig. 6, while the genes behavior in 17t of interaction time is presented in Fig. 7. The challenge in this case is to obtain knowledge from this phenomenon to answer the questions raised in Section 1.

Gene/Time	t1	t2	t3	t4	t5	t6	t7	t8	t9
ACE2	148	113	144	209	319	360	434	411	462
ASH1	380	256	201	256	320	327	245	366	795
FKH1	52	64	67	167	330	348	227	177	167
MBP1	360	326	321	425	502	484	487	410	401
MCM1	1350	1815	2095	1835	1907	1861	1734	1991	1446
NDD1	210	150	312	409	394	413	322	292	234
STB1	78	123	226	145	54	53	47	11	75
SWI4	87	115	183	104	79	77	71	88	101
SWI5	121	167	272	268	323	540	634	591	606
SWI6	421	520	699	846	869	853	740	721	558
ALG7	97	70	156	168	153	137	164	112	124

CDC20	93	235	325	208	108	168	158	124	145
CDC21	17	59	106	93	57	37	18	18	19
CDC5	86	106	89	154	219	367	549	602	480
CDC6	554	471	967	930	936	876	809	831	864
CLB2	92	158	122	145	259	348	489	554	422
CLB5	562	785	1756	949	659	612	467	563	455
CLN1	149	1045	1344	1305	998	1013	717	571	323
CLN2	445	1620	2485	1303	916	808	738	636	303
CTS1	552	1080	447	258	287	466	435	299	217
EGT2	989	1244	732	786	1083	1284	816	678	1293
FAR1	235	263	160	165	303	468	429	880	903
HTA1	905	810	1490	1594	2037	999	1178	976	843
PCL2	153	510	620	260	224	235	157	130	238
SIC1	352	295	355	308	361	356	294	212	541

Table 3a. Genes' names and their interaction values over time for yeast25-cho from t1 to t9 (continued to Table 3b)

Gene/Time	t10	t11	t12	t13	t14	t15	t16	t17
ACE2	398	226	187	325	433	343	466	344
ASH1	1862	1180	640	544	388	327	517	959
FKH1	91	74	118	172	194	163	144	106
MBP1	277	341	364	507	467	484	473	382
MCM1	2227	1945	1334	1179	1830	1506	1517	1440
NDD1	198	215	319	365	333	246	250	238
STB1	120	140	129	98	66	45	75	44
SWI4	191	172	134	111	74	43	70	83
SWI5	540	463	357	449	937	743	1024	659
SWI6	651	758	641	741	887	885	744	692
ALG7	124	151	170	202	186	172	155	70
CDC20	160	172	166	175	111	113	112	112
CDC21	28	82	90	89	36	19	12	15
CDC5	238	219	202	324	326	435	496	471
CDC6	1149	902	689	859	799	832	707	921
CLB2	236	185	151	218	267	365	350	365
CLB5	1207	1325	643	647	657	509	464	508
CLN1	1152	1870	1388	989	1074	769	614	601
CLN2	791	1288	1624	1035	839	687	868	433
CTS1	1161	1840	1181	830	979	828	507	553
EGT2	4297	3430	3240	1598	1355	1044	2123	1813
FAR1	1794	1437	725	535	570	621	739	1194
HTA1	1934	1815	1998	1103	1888	2346	1708	1580
PCL2	428	659	409	284	276	178	203	211
SIC1	1286	813	595	490	398	400	389	692

Table 3b. Genes' names and their interaction values over time for yeast25-cho from t10 to t17

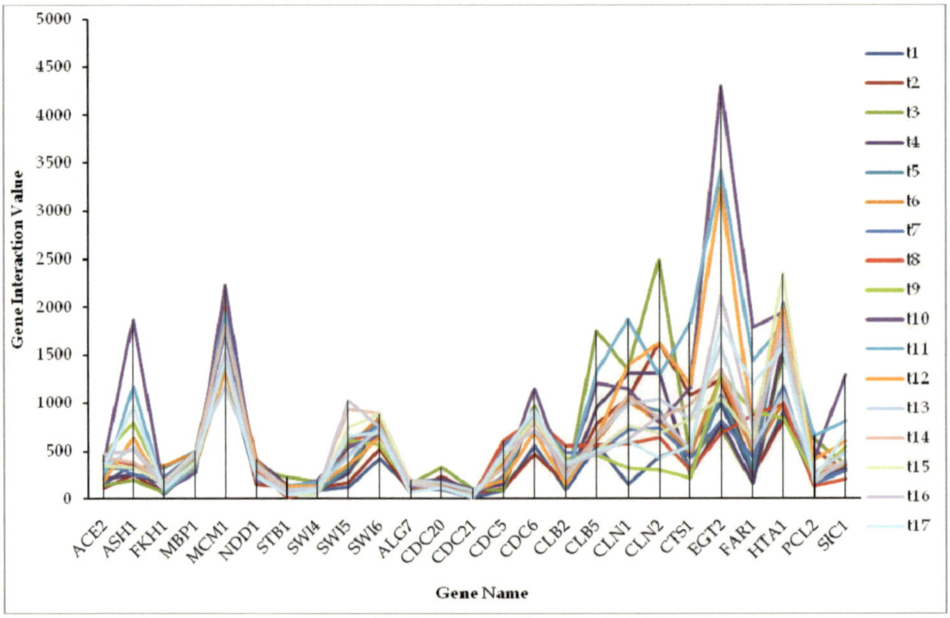

Fig. 6. The expressiveness of individual genes in 17t of interaction time (Sumari, 2010)

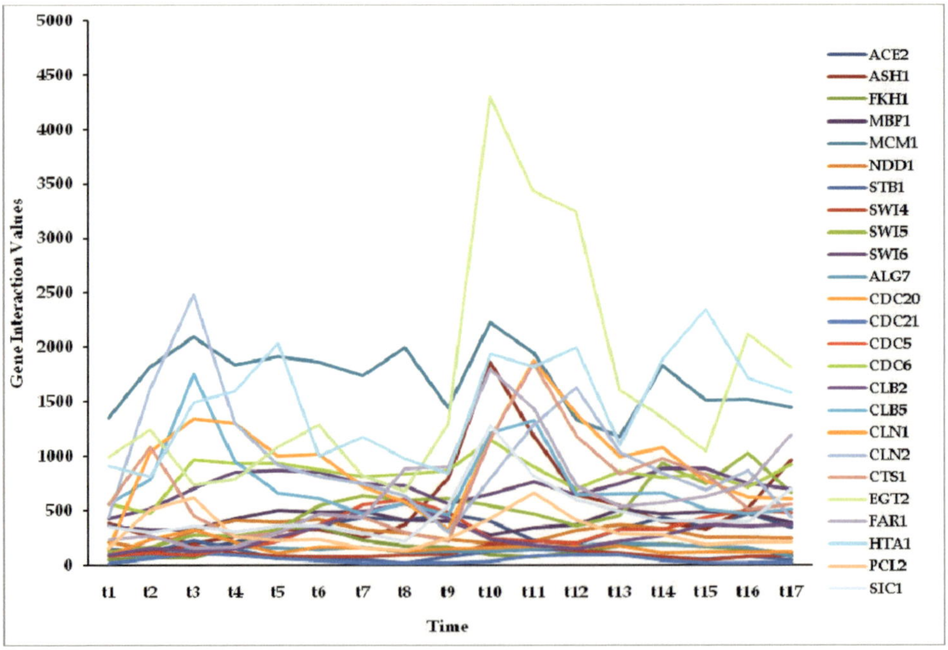

Fig. 7. The genes behavior in 17t of interaction time (Sumari, 2010)

4.2 The KGS-based MCC's task and objective

In this situation the task of KGS-based MCC is to carry out computation to obtain values of genes behavior in a unity and individual genes expressiveness in an interval of interaction time. Its objective is to obtain DoCs based on those obtained values to show genes behavior in a comprehensive manner and to find out the most expressive genes, that is, the most probable genes that give big influence to the product of their interaction. Therefore, for this purpose we create a strategy as follows.

- First, represent the genes into agents in multiagent system and construct the MCC framework for it.
- Second, represent the genes' interaction values into two-value state namely active and inhibit, where an active gene will be assigned binary value '1' and binary value '0' if it is inhibited or not active.
- Third, observe the genes' interaction state in time-by-time manner and put arcs on the genes which relate to each other as the representation of the existence of communication amongst agents. In this case only the active ones. Carry out this procedure until the last t in time series. During the interaction time, agents apply OMA3S method to obtain knowledge in collaborative manner. The result will be system's knowledge at certain interaction time t.
- Fourth, obtain the inferencing of the KGS-based MCC behavior as the representation of genes behavior in biological GRS. This inferencing will become the ultimate knowledge obtained by the system.

a. The Representation of Genes into MCC Structure

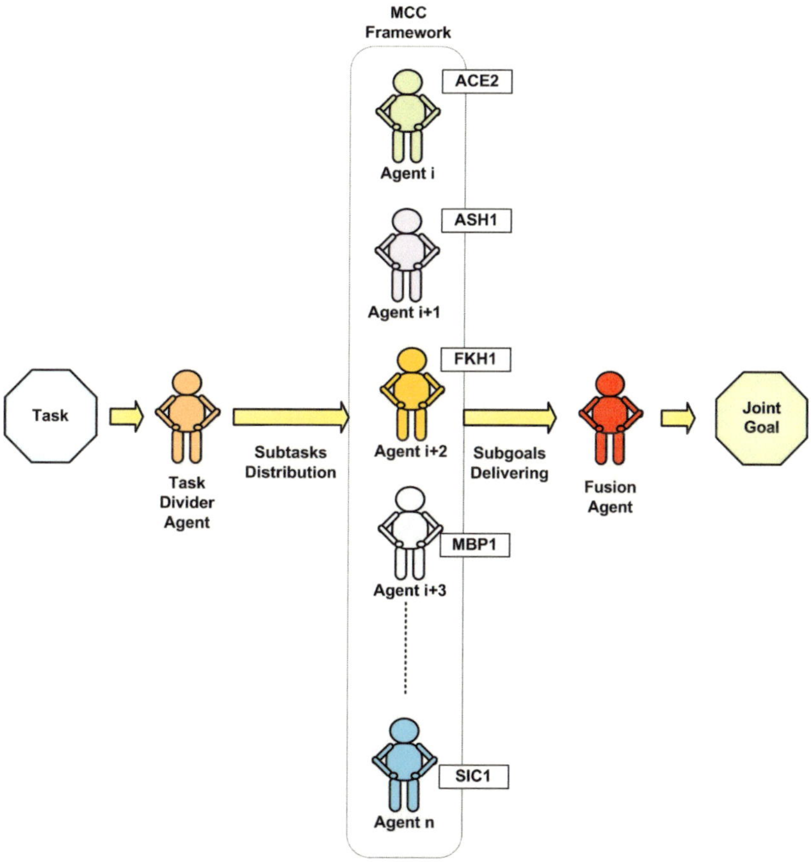

Fig. 8. The representation of genes of yeast25-cho by means agents in MCC structure

We assume that the task divider agent is already done its task and produces Table 2. Refer to Figure 3 in Section 2.2 we can simply convert the genes of yeas25-cho into agents in MCC structure as follows. The first and the last genes in the list namely gene ACE2 and gene SIC1 are represented by agent $\boldsymbol{i}$ and agent $\boldsymbol{n}$ where $\boldsymbol{i = 1,\dots,n}$ and $\boldsymbol{n}$ = 25. The structure of the MCC is depicted in Fig. 8.

b. The Representation of Genes' Interaction Values into Two-Value State

The simplest means to represent the existence of the interaction among genes is by representing them with value '1' for 'active' interaction and '0' for 'inhibit' interaction as alsi done by (Pasanen and Vihinen, 2005). This is what is called as Boolean representation of genes interaction in GRS. We realize that each gene has its own highest and lowest value that cannot be treated identically one to another. In order to minimize the chances of error in collaborative computation process, we use the threshold-value equation as presented in (7).

$$\phi_\tau^i = \begin{cases} 1, & if\ \psi_\tau^i < \dfrac{\sum_{i=1}^{\lambda} \psi_\tau^i}{\lambda} \\ 0, & if\ \psi_\tau^i \geq \dfrac{\sum_{i=1}^{\lambda} \psi_\tau^i}{\lambda} \end{cases} \tag{7}$$

with $\phi_\tau^i \in \Pi$ is a binary-sequence which represents a set of interaction value at observation time *t*, ψ_τ^i is the interaction value of agent *j* at observation time *t*, and τ is the number of interaction sequence *t* when the observation is carried out. The parameter *t* in this case is dimensionless. The application of (7) to the data given in Table 3 is presented in Table 4.

Gene/Time	t1	t2	t3	t4	t5	t6	t7	t8	t9
ACE2	1	1	1	1	0	0	0	0	0
ASH1	1	1	1	1	1	1	1	1	0
FKH1	1	1	1	0	0	0	0	0	0
MBP1	1	1	1	0	0	0	0	1	1
MCM1	1	0	0	0	0	0	0	0	1
NDD1	1	1	0	0	0	0	0	0	1
STB1	1	0	0	0	1	1	1	1	1
SWI4	1	0	0	1	1	1	1	1	1
SWI5	1	1	1	1	1	0	0	0	0
SWI6	1	1	1	0	0	0	0	0	1
ALG7	1	1	0	0	0	1	0	1	1
CDC20	1	0	0	0	1	0	0	1	1
CDC21	1	0	0	0	0	1	1	1	1
CDC5	1	1	1	1	1	0	0	0	0
CDC6	1	1	0	0	0	0	1	0	0
CLB2	1	1	1	1	1	0	0	0	0

CLB5	1	0	0	0	1	1	1	1	1
CLN1	1	0	0	0	0	0	1	1	1
CLN2	1	0	0	0	1	1	1	1	1
CTS1	1	0	1	1	1	1	1	1	1
EGT2	1	1	1	1	1	1	1	1	1
FAR1	1	1	1	1	1	1	1	0	0
HTA1	1	1	0	0	0	1	1	1	1
PCL2	1	0	0	1	1	1	1	1	1
SIC1	1	1	1	1	1	1	1	1	0

Table 4a. The conversion results of genes interaction values from Table 2a (continued to Table 4b)

Gene/Time	t10	t11	t12	t13	t14	t15	t16	t17
ACE2	0	1	1	0	0	0	0	0
ASH1	0	0	0	1	1	1	1	0
FKH1	1	1	1	0	0	0	1	1
MBP1	1	1	1	0	0	0	0	1
MCM1	0	0	1	1	0	1	1	1
NDD1	1	1	0	0	0	1	1	1
STB1	0	0	0	0	1	1	1	1
SWI4	0	0	0	0	1	1	1	1
SWI5	0	1	1	1	0	0	0	0
SWI6	1	0	1	0	0	0	0	1
ALG7	1	0	0	0	0	0	0	1
CDC20	0	0	0	0	1	1	1	1
CDC21	1	0	0	0	1	1	1	1
CDC5	1	1	1	0	0	0	0	0
CDC6	0	0	1	0	1	0	1	0
CLB2	1	1	1	1	1	0	0	0
CLB5	0	0	1	1	1	1	1	1
CLN1	0	0	0	0	0	1	1	1
CLN2	1	0	0	0	1	1	1	1
CTS1	0	0	0	0	0	0	1	1
EGT2	0	0	0	1	1	1	0	0
FAR1	0	0	0	1	1	1	0	0
HTA1	0	0	0	1	0	0	0	0
PCL2	0	0	0	1	1	1	1	1
SIC1	0	0	0	0	1	1	1	0

Table 4b. The conversion results of genes interaction values from Table 2b

c. The Observation to Agents Interaction and Obtaining Knowledge from It
Some influence graphs will be presented to show the interaction amongst KGS-based MMC agents in GRS, and knowledge that is acquired by all agents collaboratively at t_1, t_6 and after t_6, at t_{17} and after t_{17}. The expressiveness of single agents and their behaviour at a certain time and at a certain time interval such as from t_1 to t_6 are depicted in Fig. 9 to Fig. 15, while for all 17t of interaction time is presented in Fig. 16.

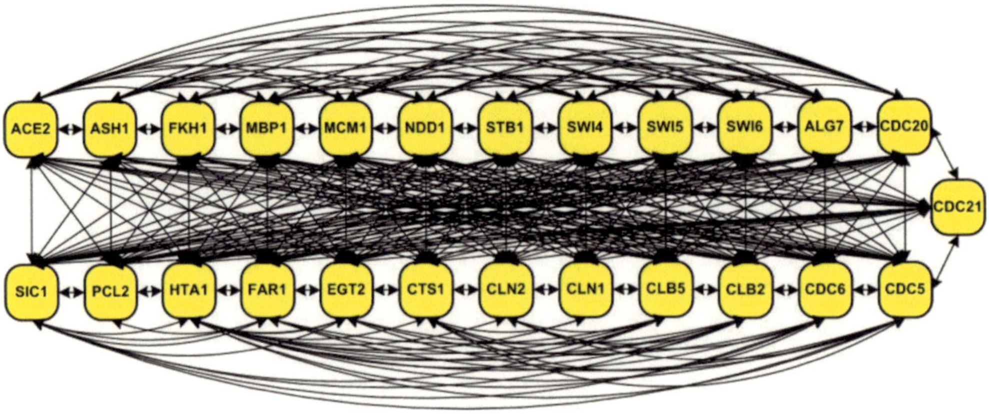

Fig. 9. Influence graph of KGS-based MCC behaviour at t_1. Yellow colour represents the active agents during the interaction at that time

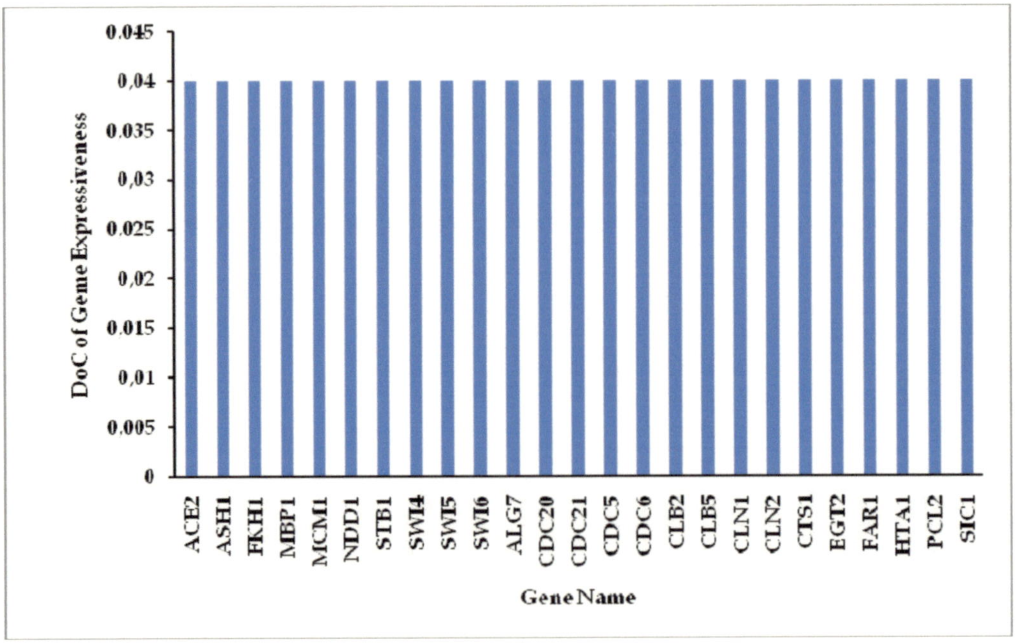

Fig. 10. Knowledge acquired by agents at t_1.

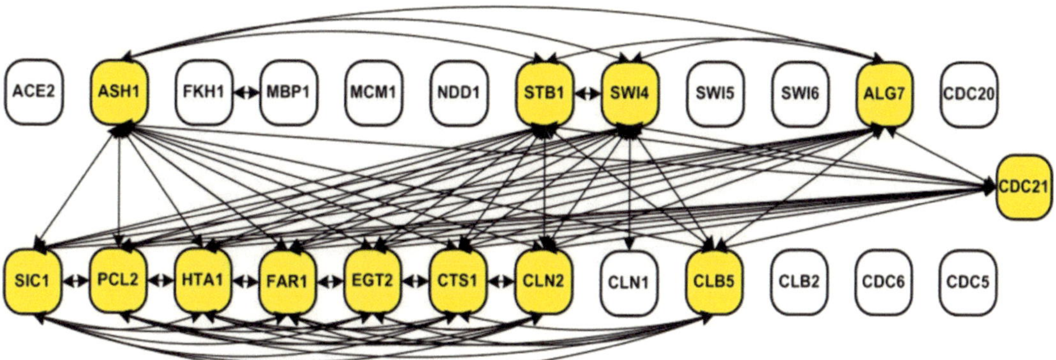

Fig. 11. Influence graph of KGS-based MCC behaviour at t_6

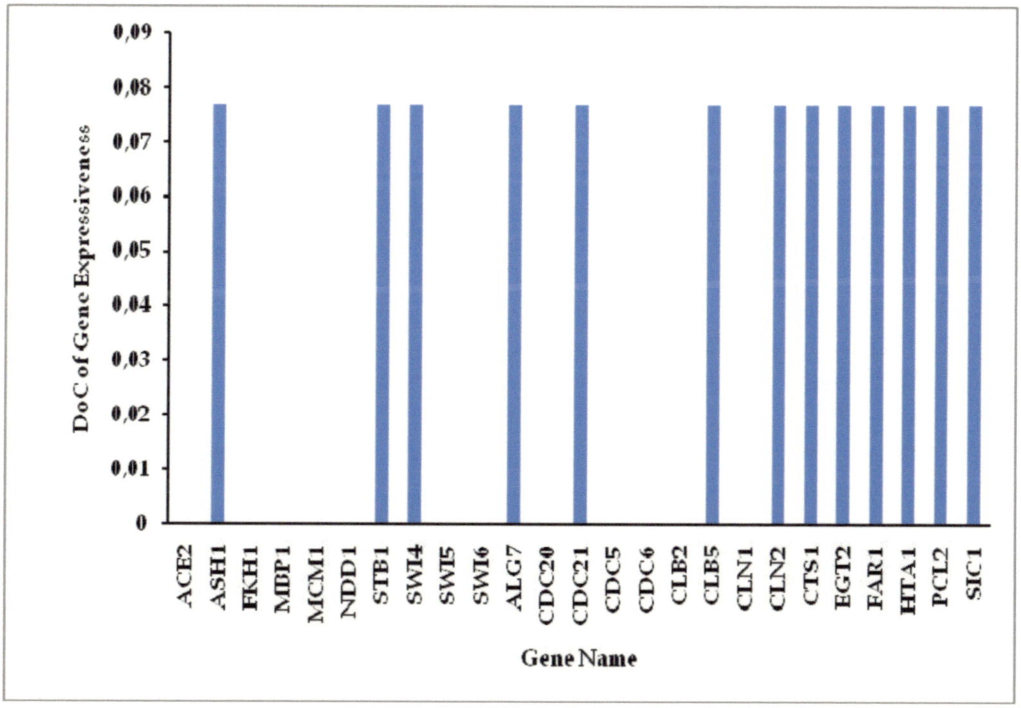

Fig. 12. Knowledge acquired by agents at t_6

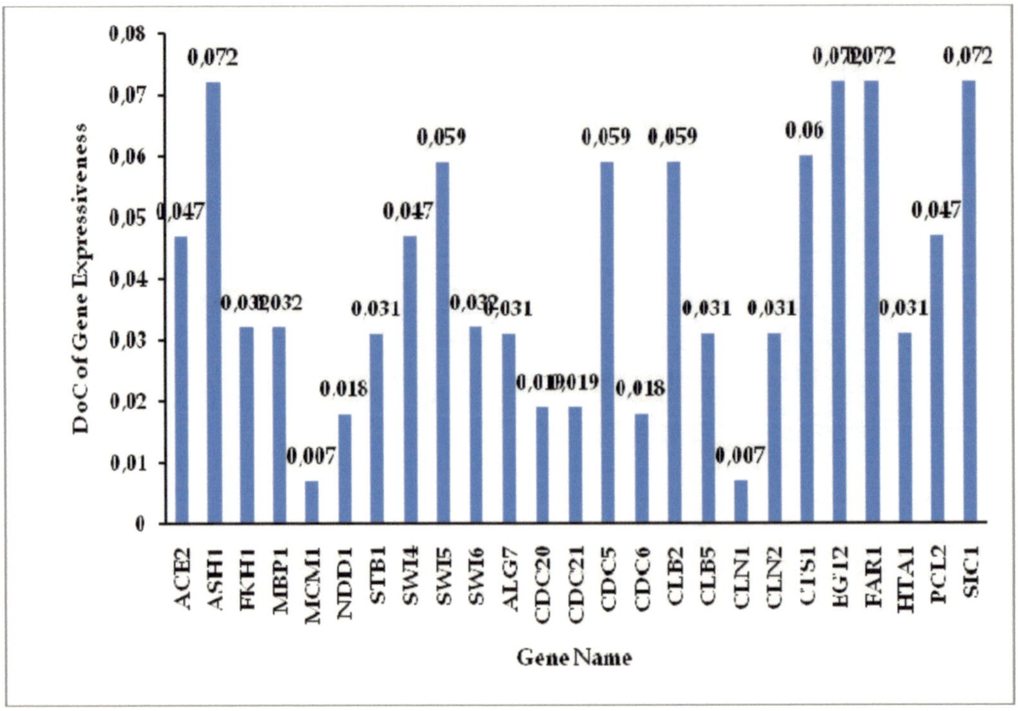

Fig. 13. Knowledge acquired by agents after 6t of interaction time

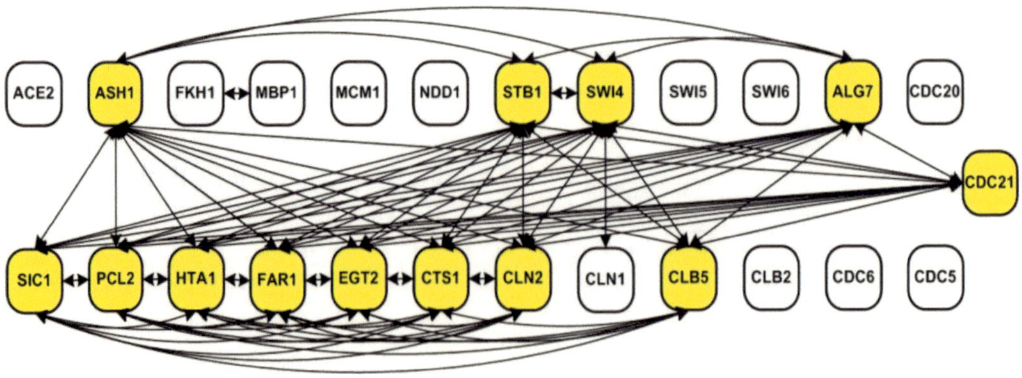

Fig. 14. Influence graph of KGS-based MCC behaviour at t_{17}

Fig. 15. Knowledge acquired by agents at t_{17}

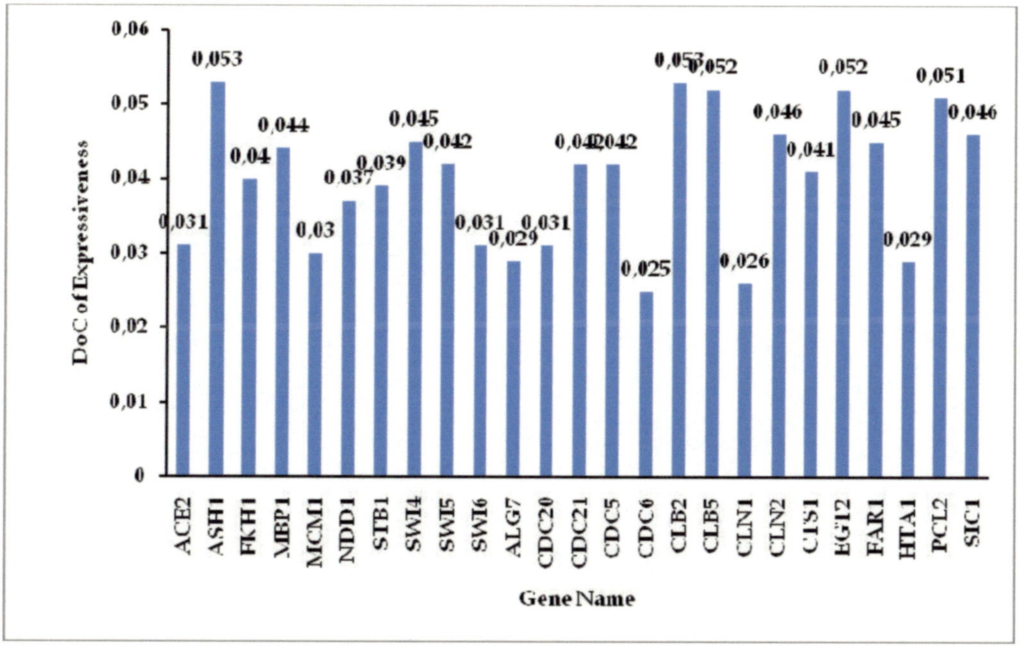

Fig. 16. Knowledge acquired by agents after 17t of interaction time

d. Knowledge Obtained by KGS-based MCC

The computation results in form of the values of DoCs that are produced by KGS-based MCC's fusion agent which are compared with the number of communication paths formed during agents interaction is presented in Fig. 17 and Fig. 18. These DoCs become the ultimate knowledge of the system.

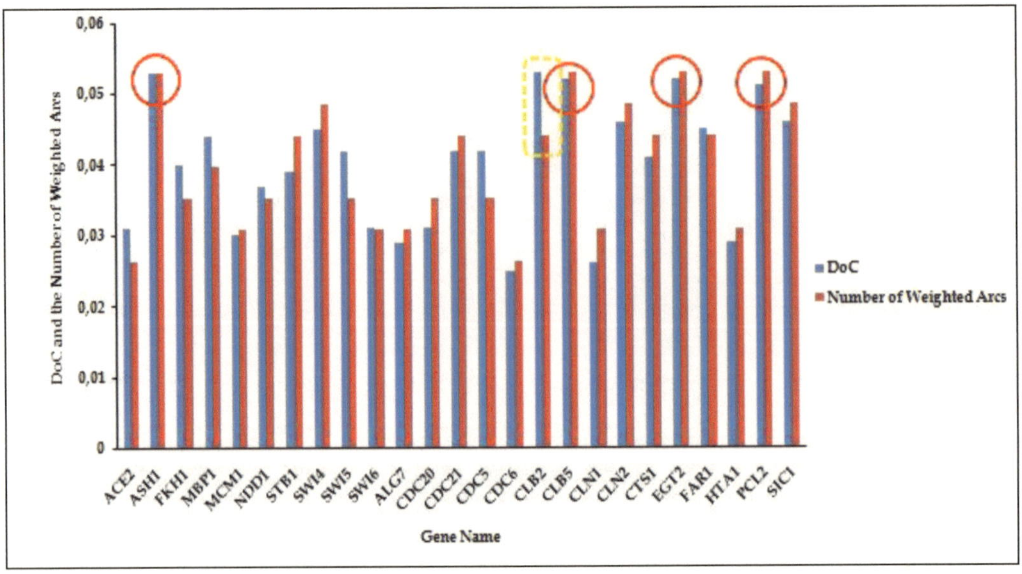

Fig. 17a. The ultimate knowledge acquired by the system regarding individual agents expressiveness after 17t of interaction time. The DoCs of the system's knowledge are compared with the communication paths formed amongst agents

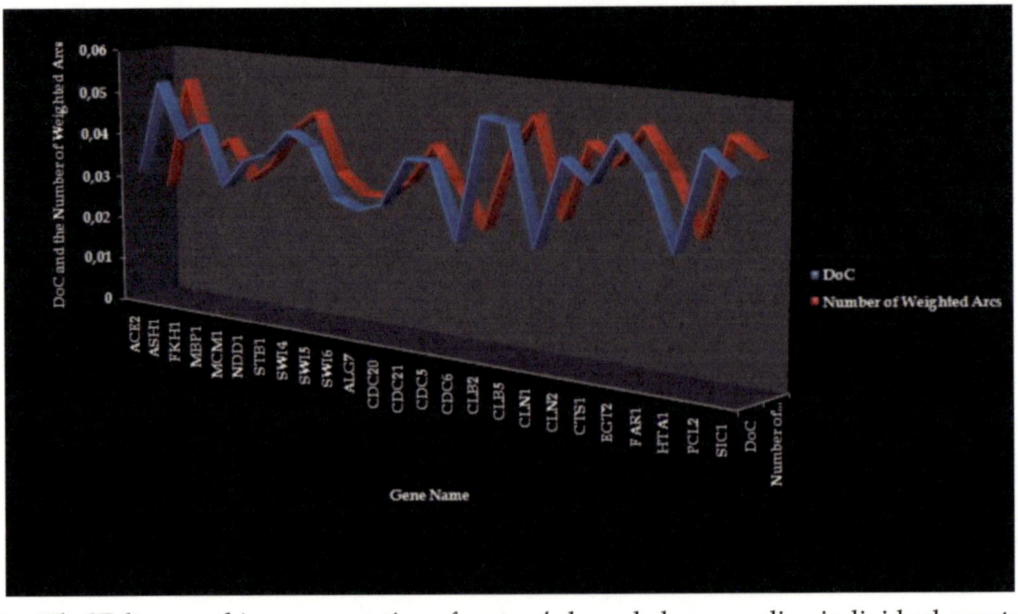

Fig. 17b. 3D line graphic representation of system's knowledge regarding individual agents expressiveness after 17t of interaction time

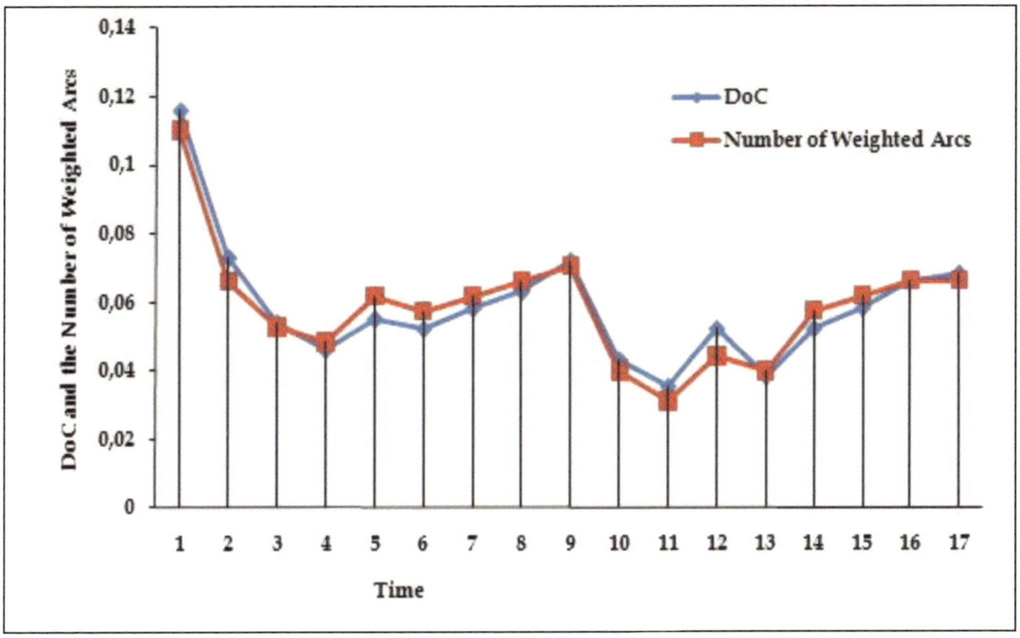

Fig. 18a. The ultimate knowledge acquired by the system regarding all agents behavior during 17t of interaction time

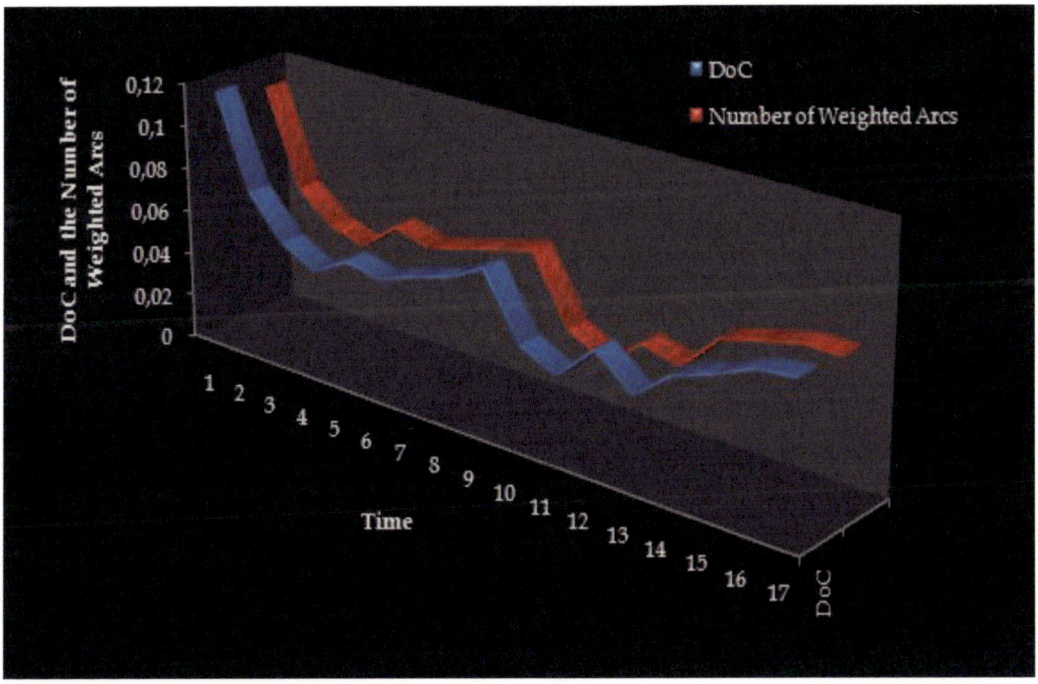

Fig. 18b. 3D line graphic representation of the system's knowledge regarding all agents behavior during 17t of interaction time

After observing Fig. 17 and Fig. 18, we can have knowledge regarding KGS-based MCC agents' behaviour as follows.

1. Viewed from individual agents expressiveness we can obtain knowledge that gene **ASH1** exhibit a dominant role even though there are genes CLB5, EGT2, and PCL2 that also show their expressiveness with **DoC = 0.053**. The certainty that gene ASH1 is the most expressive gene amongst other expressive genes is shown by the difference between DoC and the number of weighted arcs that is very minimum, that is, **0.01%**. Fig. 17 is the comprehensive inferencing of the information given in Fig. 6.
2. The time where the highest interaction is achieved is at t_1 or $t_{high} = t_1$, when 100% of yeast25-cho agents involve in the interaction with **DoC = 0.116**. On the other hand, the time where the lowest interaction is achieved is at t_{11} or $t_{low} = t_{11}$ with **DoC = 0.035**. Fig. 18 is the comprehensive inferencing of the information given in Fig. 7.

4.2 Estimations based on the knowledge obtained by KGS-based MCC

Based on the knowledge obtained by KGS-based MCC regarding the phenomena displayed by all agents, we can make estimations as follow.

a. The most probable gene that will be playing the important role in the interaction time between t_{18} to t_{24}, with the assumption that the interaction cycle will restart every 17t times, is **gene ASH1**. This phenomenon is in line with the information presented in (http://www.yeastgenome.org/) regarding the role of that gene as an inhibitor in transcription process.
b. Estimation of $t_{high} = t_{18}$ and estimation of $t_{low} = t_{28}$

5. Measuring the accurateness of KGS-based MCC results

Validating the results is of importance matter to ensure that the new paradigm we deliver in this paper is valid. For this purpose we have developed some parameters to compare DoC values with the number of arcs which is the representation of the existence of communication paths amongst agents in the influence graphs depicted in previous section. These parameters are:

a. The number of arcs, ξ and weighted arc, Ξ. Arcs are the arcs that connect the active agents in each interaction time and are observed by the help of influence graphs. Weighted arc is normalized value of arc in each interaction time, *t* or for each gene, *g* by the total number of arcs formed in each interaction time, *t*.

$$\Xi = \frac{\xi[i]}{\sum_{i=1}^{n} \xi[i]} \tag{7}$$

with $i = 1,...,n$ and n is the number of genes or one cell cycle, as example 17t.

b. ΔDKJ, $\%\Delta DK$, and $\%\Delta DKJ\_total$. The absolute value of the difference between DoC and the number of arcs formed at each interaction time, *t* or for each gene, *g*. $\%\Delta DK$ is the percentage of ΔDKJ while $\%\Delta DKJ\_total$ is the total number of $\%\Delta DK$.

$$\Delta DKJ[i] = |DoC[i] - \xi[i]| \quad (8)$$

$$\%\Delta DKJ = \Delta DKJ[i] \times 100\% \quad (9)$$

$$\%\Delta DKJ\_total = \sum_{i=1}^{n} \%\Delta DKJ \quad (10)$$

with $i = 1,...,n$ and n is the number of genes or one cell cycle, as example 17t.

c. Behavior match, χ, the total number of match, X, and percentage of the behavior match, %X. Parameter that shows the difference of genes behaviour is viewed from DoC and Ξ with an assumption that the arrangement of genes as given in Table 2 is not changed. Behaviour matching comparison is done by observing the graphic dynamic from gene i^{th} to gene n^{th}.

$$\chi[i] = \begin{cases} 1, & if\ DoC[i] = \Xi[i] \\ 0, & if\ DoC[i] \neq \Xi[i] \end{cases} \quad (11)$$

$$X = \sum_{i=1}^{n} \chi[i]_1 \quad (12)$$

$$\%X = \frac{\sum_{i=1}^{n} \chi[i]_1}{n} \quad (13)$$

with $i = 1,...,n$ and n is the number of genes or one cell cycle, as example 17t. $\chi[i]_1$ is match gene behaviour otherwise it will be $\chi[i]_0$, and $\%X$ is the percentage of behaviour match.

d. Erroneous of behavior match, ε. The percentage of the comparison between the total number of match of gene behavior, X, with the total number of absolute erroneous, $\%\Delta DKJ\_total$.

$$\varepsilon = \frac{\%\Delta DKJ\_total}{X} \quad (13)$$

In this case even though $\%X = 100\%$, ε does not always have value of 0% because of the influence of $\Delta DKJ[i]$ factor.

On the next tables we will see how these parameters are used to measure the accurateness of the application of KGS-based MCC to obtain the knowledge regarding the GRS behaviour. Table 5 contains the system's knowledge taken from Fig. 17 while Table 6 contains the system's knowledge taken from Fig. 18.

g^{th}	$DoC[i]$	$\xi[i]$	$\Xi[i]$	$\Delta DKJ[i]$	$\%\Delta DKJ[i]$	$\chi[i]$
ACE2	0.031	6	0.026	0.005	0.46	1
ASH1	0.053	12	0.053	0.000	0.01	1
FKH1	0.04	8	0.035	0.005	0.48	1
MBP1	0.044	9	0.040	0.004	0.44	1
MCM1	0.03	7	0.031	0.001	0.08	1
NDD1	0.037	8	0.035	0.002	0.18	1
STB1	0.039	10	0,044	0,005	0,51	1
SWI4	0.045	11	0.048	0.003	0.35	1
SWI5	0.042	8	0.035	0.007	0.68	1
SWI6	0.031	7	0.031	0.000	0.02	1
ALG7	0.029	7	0.031	0.002	0.18	1
CDC20	0.031	8	0.035	0.004	0.42	1
CDC21	0.042	10	0.044	0.002	0.21	1
CDC5	0.042	8	0.035	0.007	0.68	1
CDC6	0.025	6	0.026	0.001	0.14	1
CLB2	0.053	10	0.044	0.009	0.89	0
CLB5	0.052	12	0.053	0.001	0.09	1
CLN1	0.026	7	0.031	0.005	0.48	1
CLN2	0.046	11	0.048	0.002	0.25	1
CTS1	0.041	10	0.044	0.003	0.31	1
EGT2	0.052	12	0.053	0.001	0.09	1
FAR1	0.045	10	0.044	0.001	0.09	1
HTA1	0.029	7	0.031	0.002	0.18	1
PCL2	0.051	12	0.053	0.002	0.19	1
SIC1	0.046	11	0.048	0.002	0.25	1
25 gen	**1.002**	**1**	**227**	**0.076**	**7.63**	**24**
X						**24**
%X						**96**
ε						**0.32%**

Legend

- (yellow) The most expressive genes based on the results of $\xi[i]$
- (green) The least expressive genes based on the results of $\xi[i]$
- (blue) Genes with $DoC[i] \neq \Xi[i]$ viewed from $\xi[i]$ perspective

Table 5. The comparison of individual genes expressiveness for yeast25-cho genes based on the similarity between DoCs and the number of arcs after 17t of interaction time

t^{th}	$DoC[i]$	$\xi[i]$	$\Xi[i]$	$\Delta DKJ[i]$	$\%\Delta DKJ[i]$	$\chi[i]$
1	0.116	25	0.110	0.006	0.59	1
2	0.073	15	0.066	0.007	0.69	1
3	0.054	12	0.053	0.001	0.11	1
4	0.046	11	0.048	0.002	0.25	1
5	0.055	14	0.062	0.007	0.67	1
6	0.052	13	0.057	0.005	0.53	1
7	0.058	14	0.062	0.004	0.37	1
8	0.063	15	0.066	0.003	0.31	1
9	0.072	16	0.070	0.002	0.15	1
10	0.043	9	0.040	0.003	0.34	1
11	0.035	7	0.031	0.004	0.42	1
12	0.052	10	0.044	0.008	0.79	1
13	0.038	9	0.040	0.002	0.16	1
14	0.052	13	0.057	0.005	0.53	1
15	0.058	14	0.062	0.004	0.37	1
16	0.066	15	0.066	0.000	0.01	1
17	0.068	15	0.066	0.002	0.19	1
17t	**1.001**	**227**	**1**	**0.06**	**6.46**	**17**
X						**17**
%X						**100**
ε						**0.38**

Legend

t_{high}

t_{low}

Table 6. The behaviour comparison for all yeast25-cho genes based on the similarity between DoCs and the number of arcs after 17t of interaction time

From the comparison results presented in Table 4 and Table 5, we can conclude as follows.

3. Viewed from the individual genes expressiveness in interaction in 17t times, the accurateness of system's result is **24/25 * 100% = 96%**, with the erroneous of behaviour match as much as **0.32%**.
4. Viewed from the behaviour of all genes in 17t times of interaction time, the accurateness of system's result is **17/17 * 100% = 100%**, with the erroneous of behaviour match as much as **0.38%**.

6. The results of the application of KGS-based MCC to other types of yeast25

With the same manner, we apply KGS-based MCC to the other types of yeast25 and the results are presented in Table 7 for individual gene expressiveness and Table 8 for all genes behaviour.

Type	Accurateness	The Most Expressive Genes	Time Interval
Alpha	88%	MBP1, CDC5, FAR1	18t
Cdc15	72%	ASH1, STB1, CLN2, PCL2	24t
Cdc28	92%	CLB5, EGT2	18t
Cho	96%	ASH1	17t
Elu	92%	SWI6, SIC1	18t
Average	**88%**		

Table 7. The accurateness of the application KGS-based MCC to yeast25 database for obtaining knowledge regarding the most expressive genes

Type	Accurateness	Interaction Time	
		t_{high}	t_{low}
Alpha	100%	t_5 , t_6	t_1
Cdc15	100%	t_9 , t_{22}	t_6
Cdc28	100%	t_5	t_{15}
Cho	100%	t_1	t_{11}
Elu	94.4%	t_6	t_{13}
Average	**98.8%**		

Table 8. The accurateness of the application KGS-based MCC to yeast25 database for obtaining knowledge regarding al genes behaviour

Based on the information delivered in the two tables above, we can conclude the accurateness of KGS-based MCC in obtaining knowledge regarding GRS behaviour as follows.

1. The average accurateness of the knowledge regarding the most expressive genes reaches **88%**.
2. The averaged accurateness of the knowledge regarding the behaviour of all genes reaches **98.8%**.

7. Conclusion

GRS is a unique system within all living things which regulates the "core" of living cells called gene, that is, a sequence of DNA. The regulation performed by GRS to the genes displays a interesting phenomena that if we can obtain knowledge about them we can use it to refine the products of the cells in the future. Harmonious with it, in this paper we have presented in concise manner the process in obtaining knowledge regarding GRS behaviour by applying KGS-based MCC paradigm on several types of yeast25 database. The core of KGS-based MCC paradigm is OMA3S information-inferencing fusion method that is developed primarily for KGS, a new perspective in Artificial Intelligence (Sumari, 2010).
From the strategy as well as the research results we have presented in this paper we can conclude that the representation of GRS by means of KGS-based MCC paradigm is a very good approach and very advantegous for obtaining knowledge regarding the behavior of genes in it. The knowldege includes the most expressive genes and all genes behaviour in a

single cell cycle, that is, a certain interval of interaction time. One example, that is yeast25-cho, has already been given and the accurateness of the knowledge acquired by the system is 96% and 100% for having a knowledge of the most expressive genes and all genes behaviour subsequently. By applying the same technique to other types of yeast25, we found that in average the knowledge accurateness of the knowledge acquired by the system is **88%** and **98.8%** for having a knowledge of the most expressive genes and all genes behaviour subsequently. These results show that KGS-based MCC paradigm is one of appropriate means for obtaining knowledge regarding GRS behaviour.
One of our further works will be applying KGS-based MCC paradigm on a larger number of genes from the same database. We have been conducting a research on this matter and in the same time perfecting our method so it can be applied to diverse problems.

8. References

Ahmad, A.S. & Sumari, A.D.W. (2008). *Multi-Agent Information Inferencing Fusion in Integrated Information System*, Institut Teknologi Bandung Publisher, ISBN 978-979-1344-31-9, Bandung.

Ahmad, A.S. & Sumari, A.D.W. (2009a). The modeling of genes' interactions by means of multiagent collaborative computation, *Proceedings of International Conference on Instrumentation, Communication, and Information Technology and Biomedical Engineering 2009* (ICICI-BME2009), *Plenary Speech Paper*, pp. 6-11, ISBN 978-979-1344-67-8, IEEE CFP0987H-CDR, Institut Teknologi Bandung, November 2009, Institut Teknologi Bandung, Bandung.

A Ahmad, A.S. & Sumari, A.D.W. (2009b), A novel perspective on Artificial Intelligence: information-inferencing fusion for knowledge growing, *The 2nd International Conference on Electrical Engineering and Informatics 2009* (ICEEI2009), *Keynote Speech Paper*, Universiti Kebangsaan Malaysia, August 2009, Universiti Kebangsaan Malaysia, Kuala Lumpur.

Ahmad, A.S.; Sumari, A.D.W. & Zubir, H.Y. (2009) Collaborative computation in bioinformatics for better life, *Proceedings of National Seminar on Information Technologi and Its Applications 2009, Keynote Speech Paper*, ISBN 977-208-5234-00-7, Malang State Politechnic, March 2009, Malang State Politechnic, Malang.

Camarinha-Matos, L. M. & Afsarmanesh, H. (eds) (2008). *Collaborative Network: Reference Modeling*, Springer, ISBN 978-0387794259, New York.

Dill, K.; Grodzinski, P. & Liu, R.H. (eds) (2009). *Microarrays: Preparation, Microfluidics, Detection Methods, and Biological Applications*, Springer, ISBN 978-0387727165, New York.

Emmert-Streib, F. & Dehmer, M. (eds) (2008). *Analysis of Microarray Data: A Network-Based Approach*, Wiley-VCH, ISBN 978-3527318223, Weinheim.

Ewens, W. & Grant, G. (2005). *Statisical Methods in Bioinformatics: An Introduction, 2nd Ed*, Springer, ISBN 0-387-40082-6, New York.

Hall, D.L. (1992). *Mathematical Techniques in Multisensor Data Fusion*, Artech House, ISBN 0-890065586, London.

Hall, D.L. & Llinas, J.L. (2001). *Handbook of Multisensor Data Fusion*, CRC Press, ISBN 978-0849323799, New York.

Pasanen, T. dan Vihinen, M. (2005). Gene regulatory networks, In: *DNA Microarray Data Analysis*, Tuimala, J. & Laine, M.M. (Ed.), pp. 135-142, CSC-Scientific Computing Ltd., ISBN 952-5520129, Helsinki.

Reece, R.J. (2004). *Analysis of Genes and Genomes*, John Wiley & Sons, ISBN 978-0470843802, Chichester.

Sumari, A.D.W. & Ahmad, A.S. (2009). Multiagent collaborative computation paradigm for decision-making support system, *Proceedings of International Industrial Informatics Seminar 2009* (IIIS2009), pp. 17-22, ISSN 2085-4854, Sunan Kalijaga Islamic State University, August 2009, Sunan Kalijaga Islamic State University, Yogyakarta.

Sumari, A.D.W.; Ahmad, A.S.; Wuryandari, I. & Sembiring, J. (2009a). A mathematical model of knowledge-growing system: a novel perspective In Artificial Intelligence, *Proceedings* of IndoMS *International Conference on Mathematics and Its Applications 2009* (IICMA2009), pp. 229-240, ISBN 978-6029642605, Gadjah Mada University, October 2009, Gadjah Mada University, Yogyakarta.

Sumari, A.D.W.; Ahmad, A.S.; Wuryandari, I. & Sembiring, J. (2009b), Multiagent-based information fusion system in network-centric warfare paradigm, *Journal of Computer Technology "COMPILE"*, Vol.2, No. 1 (January 2009) pp. 39-55, ISSN 1978-4678.

Sumari, A.D.W.; Ahmad, A.S.; Wuryandari, I. & Sembiring, J. (2009c), The application of knowledge-growing system to multiagent collaborative computation for inferring the behavior of genes interaction, *International Journal of Computer Science & Network Security* (IJCSNS), Vol. 9, No. 11 (November 2009) pp. 82-92, ISSN 1738-7906.

Sumari, A.D.W. (2010). Knowledge-Growing System: a novel perspective in Artificial Intelligence, *Doctor (Dr.) Dissertation*, Institut Teknologi Bandung, July 2010, Institut Teknologi Bandung, Bandung.

Sumari, A.D.W.; Ahmad, A.S.; Wuryandari, I. & Sembiring, J. (2010a). Knowledge sharing in knowledge-growing-based systems, *Proceedings of the First International Conference on Green Computing 2010 and the Second AUN/SEED-Net Regional Conference on ICT* (ICGC-RCICT2010), Gadjah Mada University, pp. 329-333, ISSN 2086-4868, March 2010, Gadjah Mada University, Yogyakarta.

Sumari, A.D.W.; Ahmad, A.S.; Wuryandari, I. & Sembiring, J. (2010b), Constructing brain-inspired knowledge-growing system: a review and a design concept, *The Second International Conference on Distributed Framework and Applications 2010* (DFmA2010), Gadjah Mada University, pp. 95-102, ISBN 978-602974704, August 2010, Gadjah Mada University, Yogyakarta.

Zubir, H.Y. (2008). The modeling of genetic regulatory system using knowledge growing basis, *Doctor (Dr.) Dissertation*, Institut Teknologi Bandung, December 2009, Institut Teknologi Bandung, Bandung.

Willett, E. (2006). *Genetic Demystified*, McGraw-Hill, ISBN 978-0071459303, New York.